DEFENCES IN TORT

This book is the first in a series of essay collections on defences in private law. It addresses defences to liability arising in tort. The essays range from those adopting a primarily doctrinal approach, to others that examine the law from a more theoretical or historical perspective. Some essays focus on individual defences, while some are concerned with the links between defences, or with how defences relate to the structure of tort law as a whole. A number of the essays also draw upon concepts and literature that have been developed mainly in relation to the criminal law, and consider their application to tort law. The essays make several original contributions to this complex, important but neglected field of academic enquiry.

Volume 1 in the series Hart Studies in Private Law: Essays on Defences

Hart Studies in Private Law: Essays on Defences

This series offers a systematic treatment of defences in private law as a connected field. It addresses tort law, unjust enrichment, contract law and equity, in that order. Its aim is to contribute to this theoretically challenging and practically important, yet understudied, area of the law. The essays that constitute each of the collections in this series are written by some of the world's leading judges and scholars. They bring together insights from several jurisdictions, including civilian jurisdictions. The series is of value to academics and practitioners alike.

Defences in Tort

Edited by

Andrew Dyson
James Goudkamp
and
Frederick Wilmot-Smith

·HART·
PUBLISHING
OXFORD AND PORTLAND, OREGON
2017

Hart Publishing
An imprint of Bloomsbury Publishing Plc

Hart Publishing Ltd
Kemp House
Chawley Park
Cumnor Hill
Oxford OX2 9PH
UK

Bloomsbury Publishing Plc
50 Bedford Square
London
WC1B 3DP
UK

www.hartpub.co.uk
www.bloomsbury.com

Published in North America (US and Canada) by
Hart Publishing
c/o International Specialized Book Services
920 NE 58th Avenue, Suite 300
Portland, OR 97213-3786
USA

www.isbs.com

First published in hardback, 2015
Paperback edition, 2017

British Library Cataloguing-in-Publication Data
A catalogue record for this book is available from the British Library.

ISBN: PB: 978-1-50991-416-6
HB: 978-1-84946-526-7

Typeset by Compuscript Ltd, Shannon
Printed and bound in Great Britain by
Lightning Source UK Ltd

Foreword by Lord Hoffmann

This is the first in an ambitious series of essay collections about defences against claims in private law. Defences are a topic to which academic writers have given relatively little attention, compared with, say, the huge literature on the duty of care in negligence or the problems of causation. But in 2013 James Goudkamp published a book on *Tort Law Defences* and he and two other of the younger members of the Oxford Law Faculty organised the conference which has resulted in this book. It shows that the intellectual life of the Faculty is flourishing.

It is unusual for an academic work to have a heroine but this one does: the common law. Flawed in some respects, no doubt, as any plausible heroine must be, but magnificent in her resistance to being confined by systems or taxonomies. The very question of what counts as a defence, as opposed to an element of the cause of action, is disputed ground. Does it depend upon which party bears the burden of proof? Or does the question of the burden of proof depend upon whether, for other reasons, it is regarded as a defence? Even then, Mr Goudkamp is able to produce a Western Australian black swan in the form of the limitation defence, which has to be pleaded by the defendant but, once pleaded, has to be negatived by the claimant. Taxonomy is a subject which, as Lord Macnaughten said of the rule in *Shelley's Case*, can produce 'profound discussions and some very pretty quarrels'; an observation which will be found illustrated in this volume.

Or consider the illegality defence, on which the Chief Justice of Canada has contributed a paper full of good sense and liberal sentiment. English law has no single theory on the subject. It has relied instead, since the time of Lord Mansfield, on a combination of logic and populist penology. This has, it is true, given rise to inconsistencies, caused in some cases, as Lord Sumption recently observed, by 'the distaste of the courts for the consequences of applying their own rule.' On the other hand, the illegality defence is very much a matter of public policy and the courts also have to take into account the likelihood of public distaste for the consequences of not applying it. The efforts of the courts to navigate between these opposing forces without reducing the defence to a rubble of single instances is bound to produce characteristically impure common law solutions.

All the essays in this book contain original and sometimes provocative thoughts and I look forward to the succeeding volumes.

Leonard Hoffmann

Preface

This book is the first part of an investigation into defences in private law. It explores tort law defences. Three further volumes are planned on defences in unjust enrichment, contract and equity. The chapters that constitute the present volume were delivered at a workshop that was held at All Souls College, Oxford, in January 2014. In helping to bring the workshop to fruition, we are grateful, first and foremost, to All Souls College, which provided both the setting for the proceedings and significant financial support. The workshop could not have gone ahead without the further financial assistance of the Oxford Law Faculty and the University of Oxford's Fell Fund. We were also able to call on several members of the Faculty—both academic and administrative—for guidance. Discussions at the workshop were greatly enriched by the contributions of several observers, including Lord Hoffmann, Timothy Endicott and John Gardner and, on behalf of the Law Commission, Sir David Lloyd-Jones and David Hertzell. Finally, Anna Kim, our assistant, helped immeasurably in the lead-up to the workshop.

For their assistance in helping to turn the workshop papers into the chapters that feature in this volume, we are grateful to Jodi Gardner, Elizabeth Houghton, Krishnaprasad Kizhakkevalappil, Niranjan Venkatesan and Binesh Hass. We are indebted to Hart Publishing for their editorial assistance, and in particular to Richard Hart for the characteristic enthusiasm and professionalism with which he embraced the project as a whole. Finally, we are grateful to Lord Hoffmann for generously agreeing to write the Foreword.

Andrew Dyson
James Goudkamp
Frederick Wilmot-Smith

31 August 2014
Oxford

Table of Contents

Contributors

Roderick Bagshaw is a Fellow and Tutor in Law at Magdalen College, Oxford, and an Associate Professor of Law at the University of Oxford.

Andrew Burrows, QC (Hon), FBA, DCL is a Senior Research Fellow of All Souls College, Oxford, and Professor of the Law of England at the University of Oxford.

Paul S Davies is a Fellow and Tutor in Law at St Catherine's College, Oxford, and an Associate Professor of Law at the University of Oxford.

Luís Duarte d'Almeida is a Chancellor's Fellow in Law at the University of Edinburgh.

Esther Dyer is a graduate lawyer at Allens.

Andrew Dyson is an Assistant Professor in Private Law at the London School of Economics and Political Science.

The Hon Justice James Edelman is a Justice of the Supreme Court of Western Australia. He is also an Adjunct Professor at the TC Beirne School of Law, University of Queensland and the Faculty of Law, University of Western Australia and a Conjoint Professor at the Faculty of Law, University of New South Wales.

Richard A Epstein is the Laurence A Tisch Professor of Law at the New York University School of Law, the Peter and Kirsten Bedford Senior Fellow, the Hoover Institution, and the James Parker Hall Distinguished Service Professor of Law Emeritus and Senior Lecturer at the University of Chicago.

John CP Goldberg is the Eli Goldston Professor of Law at Harvard Law School.

James Goudkamp is a Fellow and Tutor in Law at Keble College, Oxford, and an Associate Professor of Law at the University of Oxford. He is also an Honorary Senior Research Fellow at the Faculty of Law, University of Western Australia and an Honorary Fellow at the Faculty of Law, University of Wollongong.

David Ibbetson, FBA, is President of Clare Hall, Cambridge, and Regius Professor of Civil Law at the University of Cambridge.

Lorenz Mayr is a doctoral candidate and a Research Fellow at the Institute of International and Foreign Law at the University of Passau.

Barbara McDonald is a Professor of Law at the University of Sydney. She also a Commissioner at the Australian Law Reform Commission and a Visiting Professor at the New College of Humanities.

The Rt Hon Beverley McLachlin, PC is the Chief Justice of Canada.

Donal Nolan is the Porjes Foundation Fellow and Tutor in Law at Worcester College, University of Oxford.

Stephen A Smith is James McGill Professor at the Faculty of Law, McGill University.

Robert Stevens is a Fellow of Lady Margaret Hall, Oxford, and Herbert Smith Freehills Professor of English Private Law at the University of Oxford.

Graham Virgo is a Fellow in Law at Downing College, Cambridge, and Professor of English Private Law at the University of Cambridge.

Frederick Wilmot-Smith is a Fellow by Examination at All Souls College, Oxford.

Table of Cases

Australia

Canada

European Court of Justice

European Court of Human Rights

Germany

Ireland

New Zealand

Singapore

United Kingdom

United States of America

Table of Legislation

United States of America

Table of Delegated Legislation

United Kingdom

Table of Conventions

Table of Restatements and Model Codes

A. General Issues and Themes

1

Central Issues in the Law of Tort Defences

ANDREW DYSON, JAMES GOUDKAMP AND
FREDERICK WILMOT-SMITH

1. INTRODUCTION

1.1 The Point of the Project

THIS BOOK IS the first in a series of four that is concerned with defences to liability arising in private law. We feel that the topic has not received the attention that it deserves. Engagement with defences is strikingly absent from many theoretical works in private law.[1] Furthermore, whilst specific defences are often well covered in textbooks, there is a lack of understanding as to how the various defences fit together, both within individual branches of private law, and across private law. The purpose of this series is to take steps towards remedying this situation. The present book focuses on tort law. Later books in the series will address unjust enrichment, contract and equity.

1.2 Defences in Tort, Unjust Enrichment, Contract and Equity?

The division of the four volumes in our project reflects an important premise, namely, that there is some value in dividing defences up according to the area of private law to which they pertain. There is surely *some* value in this approach, and the sheer scale of the law concerning defences in private law prevented us from investigating them satisfactorily within a single volume. However, our chosen classificatory scheme itself raises certain difficult issues, and one might legitimately question whether it reflects any divisions of theoretical importance.

One concern with arranging defences in this way is that it might seem to presuppose the stability and coherence of each of the areas of private law that we have identified. Is it right to say that there is a coherent law of tort, unjust enrichment, contract and equity? These issues have long been discussed.[2] We have adopted

[1] See, eg, the almost complete absence of discussion of defences in J Oberdiek (ed), *Philosophical Foundations of the Law of Torts* (Oxford, Oxford University Press, 2014).

[2] See, eg, the essays in P Birks (ed), *The Classification of Obligations* (Oxford, Clarendon Press, 1997).

this classification partly because it is conventional. However, we have also utilised it because we hope that doing so will result in debates about its satisfactoriness being informed by the law on defences. Discussions about the way in which private law should be organised have tended to focus on matters such as the events that generate obligations and the remedies that are available for failure to comply with those obligations. Rarely has thought been given to how defences might be relevant to the organisation of private law. To what extent are tort, unjust enrichment, contract and equity distinct in terms of defences?

A different concern that one might have is not with the coherence of each *area* of private law but with the value of dividing *defences* in this way. How much unity between defences within each area must there be to justify studying them together? How similar are, for instance, *tort* defences to one another? As it happens, several of the defences addressed in this volume—such as illegality and limitation bars—are not exclusive to tort law but are available throughout private law generally.[3] This fact might be thought to count against organising the series in the way that we have. However, it is also the case that many such defences possess features that are unique to, or at least conditioned by, particular branches of private law.

A final general concern that readers might have is with the very concept of a defence. The term might be thought to have so many distinct meanings that it is impossible to discuss defences as a unified subject. We will examine some of the issues raised by the term in this chapter. There is no doubt that many of the contributors to this volume use the word 'defence' in rather different ways from each other. However, we are reassured by the fact that the contributors to this volume engage extensively with each other.

1.3 The Topics of the Book

The chapters in the present book range from treatments of broad theoretical questions to analyses of the minutiae of individual defences. As editors we have tried not to prejudge the disputes or topics of interest that might be raised. Consequently, we have not imposed our own views as to whether, for example, certain rules are appropriately regarded as defences,[4] or whether they are appropriately thought of as part of the 'law of torts'.[5] Of course, not all defences are represented; indeed, some important defences are not discussed at all. One reason for this is that it would be quite impossible to deal satisfactorily with even the most significant tort defences in a single volume. Another reason is that this book is not intended as an encyclopaedia of tort defences. Rather, its aim is to explore themes that run throughout tort defences, especially where those themes might connect with defences in other areas of private law.

[3] This prompted Robert Stevens to contend that illegality should not be studied specifically in relation to tort law: R Stevens, *Torts and Rights* (Oxford, Hart Publishing, 2007) 304–05.

[4] It is, for example, disputed whether contributory negligence is a defence given that it does not prevent liability from arising but merely affects the quantum of recovery. We address this issue below: see Section 2.3.

[5] In relation to the question whether invasion of privacy is a tort, see Barbara McDonald's chapter at pp 289–97.

1.4 The Purpose and Structure of this Chapter

In this chapter, we contextualise some of the debates in the book, in order to bring out some general themes that run through the chapters and also to raise a few questions thrown up by certain specific defences. In selecting general themes, we have tended to focus on issues that generated debate between our contributors, and which featured prominently in discussions at the workshop at which drafts of these chapters were delivered. In selecting for discussion issues that pertain to specific defences, we have attempted to draw out the wider implications of the analyses offered by our contributors and to clarify their relationship with other debates.

We have split this chapter into three principal sections, though the sections are neither exhaustive nor hermetically sealed. We first examine what a defence actually is. In the second principal section we turn to some general questions that the study of defences throws up across private law. Finally, we draw out some themes and defences that are most commonly associated with the criminal law, such as the distinction between justifications and excuses, which may also be of relevance to private law theorists.

2. WHAT IS A DEFENCE?

It quickly became clear at the workshop that there was no consensus as to what the term 'defence' means. There seem to be several disagreements, many of which arise in the chapters that follow. In this section, we begin by considering a conundrum that pervades this field, namely whether it is possible to separate the *definition* of a defence from the *consequences* of something being a defence. We then consider two principal ways in which scholars have tried to understand the concept of a defence. The first attempts to distinguish defences from denials of a cause of action; the second attempts to define defences by reference to their effects.

2.1 Definition or Consequence?[6]

One question that any scholar working on defences faces is: what is a defence? Another question is: what are the implications, if any, of classifying something *as* a defence? These questions might be viewed as distinct: one concerns the *definition* of a defence; the other what the *consequences* are of classifying something *as* a defence.[7] We will, therefore, refer to the distinction as one between definition and consequence. To illustrate the point, consider, first, Tony Weir's assertion that '[c]ontributory negligence is unquestionably a defence … [since] it is for the defendant to plead and prove it'.[8] Implicitly, Weir seems to claim that a defining characteristic

[6] We thank Luís Duarte d'Almeida for his comments on an earlier draft of this section, which saved us from numerous errors.

[7] L Duarte d'Almeida, ch 3 at pp 45–6.

[8] T Weir, *An Introduction to Tort Law*, 2nd edn (Oxford, Clarendon Press, 2006) 129. See also WVH Rogers, *Winfield & Jolowicz on Tort*, 18th edn (London, Sweet and Maxwell, 2010) 120 [4.19] (footnote omitted).

of a defence is that they are rules that the defendant must plead and prove.[9] But now consider Robert Stevens' claim that '[t]he most important practical effect of characterising an issue as being a defence is that it will usually determine who has to prove what as a matter of evidence'.[10] If some doctrine is a defence, Stevens claims, a consequence is that this classification will ('usually') determine which party bears the onus of proof in relation to it.[11]

The interrelation between these questions is important. In particular, it seems that certain answers to the first question cannot be used to infer answers to the second. Consider, for instance, Andrew Burrows' claim that '[t]he very notion of a defence ... carries with it the practical consequence that the legal burden of proving a defence is on the defendant'.[12] This might be understood as a definition, namely, that defences are those doctrines that the defendant must prove. But Burrows also claims: (1) that limitation is a defence; (2) that the burden of disproving limitation is on the claimant and, therefore; (3) that English law should be changed to place the burden of proving limitation on the defendant. This reasoning would be fallacious if Burrows' initial claim indeed were that defences should be defined in terms of their burden of proof: (1) and (2) would then be plainly inconsistent. Whether or not Burrows actually subscribes to this reasoning is debatable, for he also seems to be attracted to defining defences according to the distinction between denials and defences.[13]

2.2 Denials and Defences

If a claimant sues in negligence, the defendant might deny that a duty of care was owed. To many writers, such a claim is not appropriately characterised as a *defence*; instead, it is a contention that, because one of its elements is absent, the cause of action in negligence is not made out. These writers therefore distinguish denials from defences. As Virgo puts it, '[a] denial negates an element of the tort claim, whereas a defence is a rule that relieves the defendant of liability where all the elements of the tort for which the claimant sues are present'.[14]

This distinction raises two important (and closely connected) disputes. The first is whether, as Luís Duarte d'Almeida puts it in his chapter, 'the familiar contrast of denials/defences is substantively warranted'.[15] Several contributors to this volume—including Andrew Burrows,[16] James Goudkamp and Lorenz Mayr,[17]

[9] Our point here is not exegetical: even if we misread Weir's purpose, such a claim is clearly plausible.

[10] See ch 13 at p 250.

[11] Notice that at p 250, Stevens explicitly rejects the suggestion that this proposition is 'a defining feature of what a defence is'. On the relevance of pleadings to defences, see Section 2 of Richard Epstein's chapter: we are unsure whether to read the claim as one of definition or of derivation (or whether he would reject this distinction).

[12] See ch 16 at pp 314–15.

[13] ibid.

[14] See ch 8 at p 139 (footnote omitted).

[15] See ch 3 at p 36. Further disagreements might manifest here over what makes a distinction 'substantively warranted'. Having noted this further important complication, for brevity's sake we set it to one side.

[16] See ch 16 at p 314.

[17] See ch 12 at p 234.

Robert Stevens[18] and Graham Virgo[19]—employ the distinction. But none offers a justification of it. Can a compelling justification be offered? The line between denials and defences can certainly appear razor thin. Most simply, both defences and denials can result in the same substantive outcome, that is, no liability.[20] Further, individual doctrines seem to resist categorisation. This might be for a number of reasons. One reason might be that an individual doctrine can, on some definitions, be *both* a defence *and* a denial. Consider, in this respect, Roderick Bagshaw's claim that defences are 'those doctrines that allow a defendant to resist in whole, or in part, a tort claim, other than by denying an essential element of it'.[21] This appears to endorse the denial/defence distinction. With reference to this definition, Bagshaw claims that the 'intervening acts doctrine' is a defence.[22] But because this doctrine can prevent an action of which damage is the gist, such as negligence, from being constituted,[23] it appears *sometimes* to be a denial. This is not a point Bagshaw contests; his purpose is not to classify the doctrine in terms of defences and denials. But it illustrates a possible hazard of the denial/defence distinction. Perhaps with such concerns in mind, James Edelman and Esther Dyer simply reject the distinction: '[a] defence has always included a plea by way of denial'.[24] In other words, for these writers a defence can include a denial of a cause of action.[25] Most fundamentally, Duarte d'Almeida raises what he calls the 'Incorporationist Challenge'. This argument claims that defences and denials are 'equivalent' because 'both amount to the negation that all the elements required for the claimant to succeed are present'.[26] To answer this challenge, theorists must explain in what the distinction consists.

This raises the second important disagreement enlivened by the distinction between denials and defences: if there *is* a substantially warranted distinction between the two concepts, what, precisely, is it? Duarte d'Almeida suggests a possible answer in his chapter. He suggests that we should understand the distinction in terms of the 'contrasting probatory behaviour' of various facts. He points out that:[27]

> Unless all the elements of a tort (including 'negative' elements like absence of consent) are established, the claimant will fail; but the claimant's success does not similarly depend on the absence of each valid defence being established.

[18] See ch 13 at p 250.

[19] See ch 8 at p 139.

[20] Duarte d'Almeida at p 49 ('from the purely consequentialist perspective there is simply no difference between "denials" and "defences"').

[21] See ch 6 at p 92, cf n 20. Consider also Goudkamp and Mayr's contention that the doctrine of illegality sometimes functions as a denial and sometimes as a defence: see ch 12 at pp 234–38.

[22] Discussed by Bagshaw, ch 6 at p 93.

[23] See, eg, *Modbury Triangle Shopping Centre Pty Ltd v Anzil* [2000] HCA 61; (2000) 205 CLR 254.

[24] Ch 9 at p 179. Epstein may also be read as rejecting the distinction. His approach is to favour a minimal prima facie case, supplemented by subsequent pleadings in a theoretically infinite sequence: Epstein, ch 14, Section 2. This may well deny any rigid notion of cause of action and defence. See, further, our discussion at Section 3.2.

[25] See, for instance, *Chakravarti v Advertiser Newspapers Ltd* [1998] HCA 37; (1998) 193 CLR 519, 527 [8] (Brennan CJ and McHugh J): 'defences are either by way of denial or confession and avoidance'.

[26] See ch 3 at p 37.

[27] ibid 44. For a fuller account, see L Duarte d'Almeida, 'A Proof-Based Account of Legal Exceptions' (2013) 33 *OJLS* 133 and L Duarte d'Almeida, *Allowing for Exceptions: A Theory of Defences and Defeasibility in Law* (Oxford, Oxford University Press, 2015).

Does this suggestion adequately capture the distinction that commentators seek to draw by employing the vocabulary of denials and defences? The account will prove controversial. But we hope that it will also prompt others to explain in depth how *they* understand the distinction.

2.3 What do Defences do?

Legal concepts might be defined wholly or partly in terms of their legal effects.[28] For instance, a cause of action has been defined as 'a factual situation the existence of which entitles one person to obtain from the court a remedy against another person'.[29] Likewise, Peter Birks once argued that unjust enrichment and restitution 'quadrate', such that all restitutionary responses are instances of unjust enrichment.[30] Can we, in a similar fashion, define defences in terms of their effects?

Some writers contend that the recognition of something *as* a defence does not determine the legal outcome of the doctrine. For instance, Edelman and Dyer argue that duress ought to be a tort defence but are silent on the question of whether compensation must be paid when it applies: they see this as a question that can be dealt with *once the defence is recognised*.[31] This suggests that, for these writers, not every effect of a defence is crucial to its definition as such. They might claim that *some* effects are constitutive of the concept of a defence. Many would make such a claim. There is, however, disagreement about the precise relationship between definition and effect, a disagreement that we addressed above.[32] Some scholars define defences in terms of their effects (the effect of some doctrine is, in other words, constitutive of that doctrine being a defence);[33] others claim that particular doctrines have (or *should* have) various effects *because they are defences*.[34] In this subsection we do not take sides on these issues, but seek to enumerate some of the various effects that are claimed can constitute, or can be the consequence of, defences.

We should first consider the distinction between substance and procedure. This is often invoked, but in what does it consist? Speaking generally, we suggest that the answer might correspond to the distinction between obligations owed by agents and

[28] By 'effect' we mean, speaking loosely, to denote the consequences that flow from the fact that a defence applies, as distinct from the implications for a given rule of it being classified as a defence.

[29] *Letang v Cooper* [1965] 1 QB 232 (CA) 242–43 (Diplock LJ).

[30] For instance, P Birks, *An Introduction to the Law of Restitution*, rev edn (Oxford, Clarendon Press, 1989) 16–18. Compare his definition of 'wrongs', where any response was thought to be logically possible: P Birks, 'Definition and Division: A Meditation on the *Institutions* 3.13' in P Birks (ed), *The Classification of Obligations* (Oxford, Clarendon Press, 1997) 31. For a general discussion of these issues, see F Wilmot-Smith, '§38 and the Lost Doctrine of Failure of Consideration' in C Mitchell and W Swadling (eds), *The Restatement Third, Restitution and Unjust Enrichment: Critical and Comparative Essays* (Oxford, Hart Publishing, 2013) 64–69.

[31] See ch 9 at p 182. This raises two questions: first, what the defence does, if not relieve the defendant from an obligation to pay damages; and, more generally, how much commentators must explain when they argue that a defence should be recognised.

[32] See Section 2.1 on the distinction between definition and consequence.

[33] This may be the best way to understand Bagshaw's claim that defences are those rules that 'operate to prevent the claimant from being awarded a particular form of remedy which would have been available had the conditions for the applicability of the "defence" not been established': see ch 6 at p 92.

[34] This is one way to read Stevens' claim in ch 13 at p 250.

the ability to have those obligations enforced by a court. By 'substantive' doctrines, theorists seem to denote those doctrines that affect the responsibilities that individuals have. For instance, contributory negligence (which, for some, is a doctrine that counts as a defence) reduces the amount of damages the defendant owes the claimant, and is consequently counted as substantive.[35] Other doctrines—those doctrines that commentators call 'procedural'—do not seem to function in this manner. For instance, Andrew Burrows notes that 'with rare exceptions' a limitation defence does not extinguish the obligation to pay damages;[36] instead, it bars *enforcement* of that duty in court.[37] A practical consequence of this distinction can be demonstrated in the law of unjust enrichment. Suppose that a defendant owes a claimant £100, but the claimant's claim is time barred. If the defendant pays the claimant £100 in the mistaken belief that the claim is not time barred, she cannot recover the money paid.[38] The reason is that, although the expiration of the limitation period barred *enforcement* of the claim, the substance of the claim remained: there is, in the language of *Goff and Jones* a 'justifying ground' for the payment.[39]

Doubtless, the import of this distinction between substance and procedure remains a topic worthy of further consideration. For our purposes, however, the crucial question is whether the distinction furthers our understanding of what a defence is. Duarte d'Almeida claims that it is vital.[40] He distinguishes elements which bear 'on the merits' of the case from '[b]ackground presuppositions and conditions … that are often called "procedural"'.[41] The procedural rules are not, he claims, the proper subject of a theory of defences: hence he excludes challenges to jurisdiction and limitation as defences.[42] Bagshaw disagrees. He includes within his definition of defences those rules that 'will prevent a claimant from being awarded an injunction if he or she has waited too long before seeking such a remedy'.[43] As these rules concern the enforcement of an obligation, Bagshaw implicitly rejects Duarte d'Almeida's claim.

This provides us with an illuminating lens through which to consider the famous case of *Vincent v Lake Erie Transportation Co.*[44] A captain secured his ship to the claimant's dock to prevent it from being destroyed by a storm. The storm repeatedly threw the ship against the dock, damaging the dock in the process. The defendant ship owner was found liable to the claimant in trespass even though (the court held) the captain had acted reasonably in securing the ship to the dock. The conventional

[35] We do not think that it matters in this connection whether one believes the defendant to be under a duty to pay these damages, or merely a liability: see also n 36.

[36] There is some controversy over whether the defendant is under a *duty* to pay damages: eg, S Smith, 'Why Courts Make Orders (And What This Tells us About Damages)' (2011) 64 *Current Legal Problems* 51. However, whatever term is used, we suggest that it is important to distinguish between the defendant's responsibility to pay damages and his liability to a court order enforcing that responsibility.

[37] Burrows, ch 16 at p 314, n 12.

[38] *Moses v Macferlan* (1760) 2 Burr 1005; 97 ER 676.

[39] C Mitchell, P Mitchell and S Watterson, *Goff and Jones: The Law of Unjust Enrichment*, 8th edn (London, Sweet and Maxwell, 2011) para 1–12.

[40] We believe that his distinctions at ch 3 pp 48–49 roughly track ours.

[41] Duarte d'Almeida, ch 3 at p 48.

[42] ibid 48, 50.

[43] See ch 6 at p 92.

[44] 109 Minn 456; 124 NW 221 (1910).

way of explaining this case, which is embraced by Graham Virgo in his chapter,[45] is to say that it recognises a privilege to act out of private necessity.[46] This privilege is said to be evident from the fact that, were it possible to obtain injunctions instantly, and had the claimant sought one to restrain the captain from tethering the ship to his dock, a judge would have refused one.[47] But the privilege is incomplete. It is incomplete because the defendant was still liable to pay damages to the dock owner. How we should understand the case remains a hotly disputed matter.[48] That is not a question we consider; instead, our concern is with the possible implications for the concept of a defence. Let us suppose that the suggested privilege simply recognises that an injunction will not be granted to restrain a trespass committed in circumstances of private necessity. Assuming that it is right to understand these rules as procedural, that is, as concerning when a court will specifically enforce an obligation an individual has, whether so-called incomplete privileges are an appropriate topic for scholars of defences then turns on whether it is correct to define defences as *substantive* doctrines.

Plainly, not every substantive doctrine is a defence. Assuming that defences are substantive doctrines, then, *which* substantive doctrines are they? Can we, in particular, use the different substantive effects that doctrines can have to delineate the concept of defences yet further? (Or are defences delineated by reference to some other criteria?) For instance, some doctrines defeat entirely a defendant's responsibility, while others merely reduce the extent of the defendant's obligations. By way of example, a successful plea of illegality might result in no liability;[49] whereas a successful plea of contributory negligence might merely reduce the damages owed from (say) £100 to £50. Does this distinction have any value when it comes to defining defences? Bagshaw[50] and Stevens[51] deny that it does: both claim that contributory negligence is a defence. However, other scholars, such as Francis Trindade, Peter Cane and Mark Lunney, have claimed that the fact that contributory negligence only reduces the extent of damages means that it is not a defence.[52]

To sum up, one popular way of understanding defences is to distinguish them from denials. Another way (and the way that we have addressed here) is to hive off procedural rules and to exclude them from the concept of a defence. Of course,

[45] See ch 8, Section 3.2.

[46] See, eg, WP Keeton, DB Dobbs, RE Keeton and DG Owen, *Prosser and Keeton on Torts*, 5th edn (St Paul MN, West Publishing Co, 1984) 147–48.

[47] The privilege is also thought to be revealed from the fact that had the claimant cut the ship loose, the claimant would have been liable to the ship owner: *Ploof v Putnam* 81 Vt 471; 71 A 188 (1908).

[48] This reading of the case is controversial amongst our contributors. As well as Virgo, see Goldberg, ch 4 at p 62 and Smith, ch 5 at pp 75–76.

[49] *Joyce v O'Brien* [2013] EWCA Civ 546; [2014] 1 WLR 70. Illegality can in some cases merely reduce the extent of the primary obligation: *Hewison v Meridian Shipping Services Pte Ltd* [2002] EWCA Civ 1821; [2003] ICR 766 (the illegality prevented the recovery of lost illegal earnings, but not the recovery of damages for other losses suffered as a result of injury caused to the claimant).

[50] See ch 6 at p 93.

[51] See ch 13 at p 250 ('it … is better described as a remedial defence' (footnote omitted)). See also Barbara McDonald's chapter where she refers to contributory negligence as 'a key defence to a negligence action': ch 15 at p 298.

[52] '[C]ontributory negligence is strictly a plea in mitigation of damages rather than a defence': F Trindade, P Cane and M Lunney, *The Law of Torts in Australia*, 4th edn (Oxford, Oxford University Press, 2007) 685.

neither way of trying to get to grips with the idea of a defence suggests a comprehensive definition of a defence. They are both just ways of saying what defences are not. It is clear, for instance, that even if procedural rules are not defences, not all substantive rules qualify as defences. These two ways of conceiving of defences do not exhaust the possible bases by which the concept of a defence might be isolated. We have focused on these ways of determining what a defence is because they have featured prominently in the chapters that constitute this volume.

3. THEMES ACROSS PRIVATE LAW

3.1 The Interplay of Causes of Action and Defences

It is trite that the elements of a cause of action must have a bearing on the defences that are available to liability arising in that action. This point applies across private law's causes of action. For example, if the absence of justification is part of the definition of a cause of action, it is impossible for there to be a justificatory defence to liability arising in that action.[53] If the defendant was justified, the action will not be constituted; it follows that no question of defences can arise. But commentators have not explored this type of interrelation in any depth.

In her contribution to this volume, McDonald makes some general claims on the topic. She suggests that the 'fault element in the tort can influence the available defences'.[54] For instance, she claims that 'negligence is essentially about a defendant's failure to take reasonable precautions against a *foreseeable* risk of injury to the claimant'.[55] It follows, she claims, that it is 'morally justifiable' for the law 'to consider also the claimant's behaviour in relation to that risk'.[56] This leads McDonald to the conclusion that the doctrine of contributory negligence is justifiably applicable in the context of negligence-based torts.[57] Other scholars, including Ernest Weinrib[58] and Kenneth Simons,[59] have made broadly similar claims regarding the doctrine of contributory negligence. In contrast to the tort of negligence, McDonald says that:[60]

> intentional torts generally involve a prima facie wrong and a more culpable level of fault, and thus will be more difficult to defend, requiring a higher level of culpability or responsibility

[53] This point is made, albeit in slightly different terms, by Steve Smith in his contribution to this volume: see ch 5 at pp 65–66.
[54] See ch 15 at p 298.
[55] ibid (emphasis in original).
[56] ibid.
[57] Cf Robert Stevens' chapter in this volume.
[58] 'The defense [of contributory negligence] expresses an idea of transaction equality: the plaintiff cannot demand that the defendant should observe a greater care than the plaintiff with respect to the plaintiff's safety. ... Because contributory negligence looks at the fault of the plaintiff relative to the fault of the defendant in their interaction, it is entirely a transaction notion': EJ Weinrib, *The Idea of Private Law* (Cambridge MA, Harvard University Press, 1995) 169 n 53.
[59] '[W]hat victims can legitimately expect of injurers, injurers can legitimately expect of victims': K Simons, 'The Puzzling Doctrine of Contributory Negligence' (1995) 16 *Cardozo Law Review* 1693, 1722 (footnote omitted).
[60] See ch 15 at p 298 (footnote omitted).

> on the claimant's part to excuse the defendant's conduct. Thus while contributory negligence is powerful in a negligence claim, it is irrelevant to an intentional tort.

McDonald applies these claims to the defence of public interest to a privacy tort.[61] She argues that breach of privacy is an intentional wrong and claims that we should therefore 'immediately ignore defences to negligence actions. Contributory negligence, for example, should be no more a defence to an invasion of privacy than it is to any other intentional tort'.[62] Depending on how McDonald defines the term 'defence', we suspect that this claim is too strong, since it is doubtful that *all* defences to negligence should be inapplicable to actions for breach of privacy. Does McDonald mean to say that limitation bars, for example, should have no application to actions for breach of privacy?[63] Regardless, the general claim that the presence or lack of a fault element may influence, or should influence, the availability of defences is worthy of further investigation.

Richard Epstein, in his chapter on voluntary assumption of risk, also engages with the interaction between causes of action and defences. He argues: 'As a matter of basic normative theory, the proper role of defences is heavily dependent on the content of the prima facie case, which in turn depends heavily on whether the starting point for liability is strict liability, negligence, or intention'.[64] If one incorporates a fault rule into what he calls the 'prima facie case', many pleas that could otherwise be introduced as defences are dealt with by the fault rule and cannot therefore operate as defences. Conversely, if the cause of action is based on strict liability, a much larger number of pleas are available to function as defences. Epstein believes this to be an advantage of strict liability. His reason for so thinking is that putting the minimum amount of information in the 'prima facie case' necessary to put the defendant under an onus of explanation sharpens the enquiry. This is primarily because it allows the pleas to be introduced in a clear and logical sequence.

3.2 The Generality and Specificity of Defences

Although some scholars have argued to the contrary,[65] the prevailing view today is that we have a law of torts rather than a law of tort, in the sense that there is no single principle of liability that unites this entire branch of private law.[66] We have many different *actions* in tort, rather than a single action in tort, and similar observations can be made about other areas of private law, such as unjust enrichment, where it is conventional to speak of *an* action in unjust enrichment rather than *the* action in unjust enrichment. It is interesting to observe a parallel here between

[61] McDonald has in mind the action in cases such as *Campbell v MGN Ltd* [2004] UKHL 22; [2004] 2 AC 457.

[62] See ch 15 at p 302.

[63] McDonald might, instead, deny that limitation is a defence: for a possible route to this conclusion, see Section 2.3 and Duarte d'Almeida, ch 3 at pp 50–51.

[64] See ch 4 at p 267.

[65] Eg, PH Winfield, *The Province of Tort Law* (Cambridge, Cambridge University Press, 1931) ch 3.

[66] Eg, WVH Rogers writes: 'There is ... no doubt that we have a collection of torts rather than a single principle of liability': WVH Rogers, *Winfield & Jolowicz on Tort*, 18th edn (London, Sweet and Maxwell, 2010) 63. The contribution that has come to epitomise the 'law of torts' view is B Rudden, 'Torticles' (1991–1992) 6/7 *Tulane Civil Law Forum* 105, which seeks to list all torts.

causes of action and defences. It would be perfectly possible to have, for example, a single justificatory defence operating across all of tort law. However, what we find (at least according to the way in which defences tend to be presented in tort textbooks) is a large number of justificatory defences that each operate within their own spheres of influence.[67] These justificatory defences include rules such as necessity, self-defence, defence of property, publication of a defamatory statement in the public interest, and so on.

Why have tort defences (and, perhaps, defences in some other branches of private law) developed in this way? Furthermore, is this state of affairs satisfactory? Several of the chapters in the present volume offer thoughts in this connection. Barbara McDonald, for example, queries how defences should be developed in relation to an action for breach of privacy. The law could opt for a very broad defence of public interest, or it could fashion several more precise defences that are sensitive to public interest considerations. McDonald (without expressing a firm conclusion) seems to be sympathetic to the latter approach, on the basis that defendants will be able to predict more easily whether they will benefit from a defence than would be possible if there were a single broad, generalised defence. A broad defence, she claims, will 'leav[e] it to the judgment of an individual judge as to whether the balance justifies the defendant's behaviour in the particular case'.[68]

Paul Davies, in his chapter on defences and third parties, also touches upon this theme. His major concern is with the defence of justification in the context of secondary participation in a breach of contract. Davies asks whether the defence should be cast broadly or instead confined to specific situations, which is very closely related to the point addressed by McDonald.[69] Davies enunciates some arguments for and against making the defence available to the entire ocean of factual situations in which accessories might incur liability in tort, versus what might be called an 'island' approach. He sees a broad approach as having the advantage of flexibility but at the cost of reduced certainty, and notes that the criminal law in the context of the statutory offence of assisting or encouraging crime[70] has taken this route.[71]

3.3 Theories of Tort Law and Defences

Several scholars have offered general theoretical accounts of the law of torts. These include economic accounts[72] and explanations of torts as a law of interpersonal

[67] Of course, some of these defences have a larger sphere of influence than others and there is an extensive amount of overlap. For example, the defence of necessity (which is addressed by Graham Virgo in his chapter in this volume) is not limited by much of the fencing that confines the defence of self-defence, although both defences cover some of the same terrain. If the two defences might be envisaged in terms of intersecting circles, we suggest that the circle representing necessity would be considerably larger.

[68] See ch 15 at p 309.

[69] See ch 15 at pp 110–13.

[70] Serious Crime Act 2007 (UK), ss 44–49.

[71] ibid s 50.

[72] Richard Posner was responsible more than anyone else for what might be called the first wave of the law-and-economics movement, mainly as a result of his RA Posner, 'A Theory of Negligence' (1972) 1 *Journal of Legal Studies* 29 and WM Landes and RA Posner, *The Economic Structure of Tort Law* (Cambridge MA, Harvard University Press, 1987).

wrongs.[73] Some of these theorists contend that their account can explain not just tort law but private law generally.[74] The chapters by Chief Justice McLachlin, John Goldberg and Robert Stevens raise an issue as to the significance of defences for such theories. Two questions are presented. The first is how we should understand particular defences within general theories of tort law. The second is what should be done if we find that a particular defence does not seem to cohere with the theory in particular. What are the implications of a lack of concordance between a defence and a theory?

3.3.1 Corrective Justice

Several theorists, such as Ernest Weinrib[75] and Allan Beever,[76] claim that tort law is explained by a theory of corrective justice. Very simply, these theorists argue that torts are injustices committed by a single defendant against a single claimant, and that tort remedies aim to reverse that injustice. The Chief Justice, in her contribution to this volume, posits that these theories provide a 'principled basis for the law of tort'.[77] However, her inquiry is not into the theory as a whole; instead, she aims to explain how the law on illegality can be squared with the corrective justice theory.[78]

Two key claims are made in the Chief Justice's chapter. The first is that invoking the doctrine of illegality to deny claims simply because the claimant happened to be injured while acting illegally, even if the criminal act is causally implicated in the claimant's damage, is inconsistent with corrective justice. This is because it 'asks the court to consider the claimant independently of the defendant. In doing so it disrupts the correlative and integrated structure of a corrective justice model'.[79] The fact that the claimant acted illegally has nothing, the Chief Justice writes, to do with the relationship between the parties. The second claim is that in very limited circumstances denying recovery on the ground of illegality is consistent with corrective justice. The main situation that the Chief Justice has in mind is where the claimant seeks damages in respect of the imposition of a criminal law sanction. The Chief Justice considers that rejecting such claims via the illegality defence is consistent with corrective justice on the basis that the claimant has suffered no loss, and without a loss, there is not correctible injustice.[80]

The Chief Justice considers that the law on illegality in Canada complies with corrective justice,[81] while the very different rules that govern the defence elsewhere in the common law world do not.[82] She does not state whether she believes that the

[73] We have in mind here writings such as Weinrib (n 58), Stevens (n 3) and JCP Goldberg and BC Zipursky, 'Torts as Wrongs' (2010) 88 *Texas Law Review* 917.

[74] See, eg, Weinrib (n 58).

[75] ibid.

[76] A Beever, *Rediscovering the Law of Negligence* (Oxford, Hart Publishing, 2007).

[77] See ch 11 at p 208.

[78] ibid 209.

[79] ibid 220–21.

[80] ibid 221–22.

[81] See, especially, *Hall v Hebert* [1993] 2 SCR 159 (SCC).

[82] See, eg, *Miller v Miller* [2011] HCA 9; (2011) 242 CLR 446 and *Gray v Thames Trains Ltd* [2009] UKHL 33; [2009] 1 AC 1339.

law elsewhere, which she asserts does not comply, at least not fully, with corrective justice, ought to be changed *on account of* the lack of compliance with corrective justice. However, significantly, she criticises the law on illegality in tort in other jurisdictions on the basis that it is unsupported by policy considerations, such as whether the doctrine deters offending.[83] Given that the centrality of corrective justice theory to her chapter, this suggests that she regards policy considerations as relevant to corrective justice accounts of tort law, contrary to the views of several prominent corrective justice theorists.[84]

3.3.2 Rights Theory

In *Torts and Rights*, Stevens contended that a rights-based theory provides the best explanation of the whole of the law of torts.[85] Expressed very simply, the central idea is that torts are violations of primary rights and that, inter alia, tort law provides victims of such violations with a remedy that is substitutive of that primary right. Stevens' analysis in *Torts and Rights* only addressed the doctrine of contributory negligence in passing.[86] It did not consider the relationship between the doctrine and his theory of tort; instead, Stevens confined himself to criticising the drafting of the British apportionment legislation, namely, the Law Reform (Contributory Negligence) Act 1945 (UK).[87]

In his contribution to this volume, Stevens specifically addresses the law on contributory negligence. He argues that the entire law on contributory negligence (and not just the scheme of apportionment adopted by the 1945 Act) should be abolished, with the result being that fault on the part of the claimant would ordinarily have no bearing on either liability or the quantification of damages. Contributory negligence should, in his view, cease to be a free-standing rule, and fault on the part of the claimant should be relevant only insofar as other rules, such as the principle of intervening causation, are sensitive to it.

Stevens regards the defence of contributory negligence as incompatible with his rights theory. He begins by suggesting that the issue of 'whether contributory fault should be a defence [should be] determined by why it is thought that damages are payable for the commission of torts'.[88] Stevens then claims: (1) that tort law is about rights; and (2) that the doctrine of contributory negligence is not explicable in terms of rights because the claimant's rights are unaffected by carelessness on his part that risks only his own interests.[89] As a further step, Stevens also implies (3) that the law

[83] See ch 11 at pp 212–13.

[84] See, eg, Beever (n 76) 52–54; Weinrib (n 58) 220–21.

[85] Stevens (n 3).

[86] ibid 125–27. Other theorists who are committed to explaining tort law in terms of rights have similarly not engaged with the doctrine. John Goldberg and Benjamin Zipursky, for example, have not, so far as we can tell, tried to accompany the doctrine (which is generally known as the doctrine of comparative responsibility in the United States) with their theory of tort law. The defence is not treated in the recent collection of essays on rights theory edited by Donal Nolan and Andrew Robertson: see D Nolan and A Robertson, *Rights and Private Law* (Oxford, Hart Publishing, 2012).

[87] Stevens (n 3) 124–26.

[88] See ch 13 at p 252.

[89] '[T]he risks I run in relation to my own interests are nobody's concern but mine' (at p 253).

should be changed to bring it into conformity with the rights-based understanding of tort law, by abolishing apportionment for contributory negligence.[90]

3.3.3 Civil Recourse Theory

John Goldberg has promoted a theoretical account of tort law that is based on civil recourse for wrongs.[91] This theory shares much in common with both corrective justice theory (it has been argued that the theories are effectively the same[92]) and with rights theory. The gist of civil recourse theory is that tort law is not a system for providing compensation for losses caused by accidents, or for deterring inefficient behaviour (although it has those effects), but is a mechanism by which victims of interpersonal wrongs can hold the wrongdoer to account. Goldberg's chapter in this volume addresses the role of excuses in tort law through the lens of civil recourse theory.[93] We discuss excuses directly later,[94] and engage more fully with Goldberg's chapter there. For present purposes, we confine our remarks to the implications of Goldberg's analysis for civil recourse theory. Goldberg considers that tort law is largely insensitive to excuses although he believes that excuses occasionally intrude into tort law. What are the implications of this claim (if it is correct) for his theory? One might think that the general lack of excuses is a challenge to the theory: if excused defendants are not released from liability does that mean that tort is affixing liability to conduct that is not really wrong?[95] Goldberg's response is that it is possible coherently to say that an excused defendant commits a wrong. This leads him to the conclusion that tort law 'can cogently refuse to recognise excuses'.[96] As this expression suggests, Goldberg does not appear to regard excuses as anathema to tort law. However, he does seem to regard a tort law without excuses as more principled than one without them. He suggests that the exclusion of excuses 'grants to victims' of wrongs 'the power to excuse'. This 'directs wrongdoers to make their excuses to the victim'. For this reason, tort law might be seen as implementing the principle of civil recourse more fully when it excludes excuses.

[90] It is worth noting that, although a radical reform, Stevens is not alone in making this recommendation. Patrick Atiyah famously suggested that the doctrine should be abandoned, at least in the context of personal injuries: P Cane, *Atiyah's Accidents, Compensation and the Law*, 8th edn, (Cambridge, Cambridge University Press, 2013) 52–7. Given that Atiyah had very different theoretical allegiances from Stevens, it is not surprising that Atiyah's argument is distinct from that of Stevens.

[91] Probably the fullest statement of this thesis is Goldberg and Zipursky (n 73).

[92] EJ Weinrib, 'Civil Recourse and Corrective Justice' (2011) 39 *Florida State University Law Review* 273, 297 arguing that 'differences between civil recourse and corrective justice, if they exist at all, are gossamer thin'. Cf BC Zipursky, 'Civil Recourse, Not Corrective Justice' (2003) 91 *Georgetown Law Journal* 695.

[93] The contribution to this volume is part of a wider project on excuses in tort law: see, further, JCP Goldberg, 'Inexcusable Wrongs' (2015) 103 *California Law Review* (forthcoming).

[94] See Section 4.2.3.

[95] This does seem to be a concern of Goldberg: see the discussion ch 4 at p 56.

[96] ibid. We suggest, below, that Goldberg might in parts of his chapter go rather further than this and claim that tort law is properly insensitive to excuses: see Section 4.2.3.

3.4 Statute Law and Defences

Several chapters in this volume engage with defences that are at least partially statute-based. For instance, Andrew Burrows tackles issues in the law of limitation of actions, much of which is legislative in origin. There are several important points to make in this respect. First, the present law on limitation is a warning to those considering piecemeal statutory reform. As Burrows highlights, many seemingly arbitrary differences exist as one moves from one cause of action to another in relation to both the duration of the limitation period[97] and the point at which time begins to run.[98] Secondly, limitation is also an excellent illustration of the fact that, generally speaking, legislation has infiltrated the law on tort defences to a much greater extent than in relation to that part of the law of torts that specifies the elements of causes of action. The fact that the legislature's attention has been skewed in this way is a notable feature of tort law. One possible explanation for this focus is that when the legislature wants to provide a particular group of stakeholders with protection from liability in tort, it finds it easier to do this by way of tweaking the law on defences rather than the elements of torts. It is relatively simple to single out specific groups of persons for heightened protection by changing the law on defences, whereas if the elements of torts are altered there is (or might be thought to be) an increased risk that the change will be broader than necessary.[99]

In his contribution, Donal Nolan is also concerned with statutory tort defences. Nolan's principal interest is the law regarding the effect of planning permission and its relationship with the defence of statutory authority. Judges regularly observe, as Nolan notes, that the fact a defendant has been granted planning permission to carry out a given activity is not the same as statutory authorisation of that activity. However, Nolan argues that 'in amenity nuisance cases where the implementation of planning permission is deemed to have changed the nature of the locality, the planning consent has the same effect as the statutory authorisation of the defendant's activity'.[100] Nolan claims that this rule concerning planning permission is, therefore, a de facto extension of the statutory authority defence. Nolan criticises this situation on the ground that allowing planning permission to mimic the defence of statutory authority is unsupported by the rationale for recognising the defence of statutory authority, namely, that it gives expression to the will of Parliament. As Nolan puts it: 'the justification for allowing direct expression of legislative will to abrogate private rights [via the defence of statutory authority] does not extend to administrative decisions of the kind involved in the planning process'.[101] This argument illustrates another cautionary tale of statutes and the common law: the need to examine carefully a particular statutory defence (including its rationale) before relying on it for a common law analogy. Although Nolan is concerned only with the law of nuisance,

[97] Burrows, ch 16.

[98] ibid.

[99] This suggestion is discussed further in J Goudkamp 'Statutes and Tort Defences' in J Steele and TT Arvind (eds), *Tort Law and the Legislature: Common Law, Statute and the Dynamics of Legal Change* (Oxford, Hart Publishing, 2013).

[100] See ch 10 at p 191. Locality is irrelevant in physical nuisance cases pursuant to *St Helen's Smelting Co v Tipping* (1865) 11 HL Cas 642, 650–51; 11 ER 1483, 1486.

[101] See ch 10 at p 193.

his analysis is of wider significance. One area of the law on which it might throw light is the defence of illegality, where judges have, at least in some jurisdictions, often developed the common law on this point by reference to the criminal law legislation that the claimant contravened.[102]

4. THEMES FROM THE CRIMINAL LAW

4.1 Is Criminal Law Scholarship and Doctrine Relevant?

In contrast with the scant learning that exists regarding tort defences, the scholarship on defences in the criminal law is voluminous and highly sophisticated.[103] It is tempting, therefore, for tort scholars to look to this work for inspiration and arguments, especially given the apparent parallels that exist between many tort law defences and criminal law defences. One might also be inclined to argue that tort law should adopt certain criminal law principles. Virgo does both of these things in his chapter, as do Edelman and Dyer. For instance, in thinking about the defence of necessity, Virgo makes 'extensive reference ... to criminal law theory and doctrine'.[104] He does this 'in part because much more work has been done by criminal law theorists in analysing the nature of defences generally and necessity in particular'.[105] Edelman and Dyer claim that the definitional elements of the tort of intimidation were developed by reference to criminal liability for unlawful pressure (menaces). They then suggest that '[t]he same process of parallel development, applied to defences, would see the well-recognised defence of duress in criminal law extended to torts'.[106] But whether it is legitimate to draw upon criminal law scholarship and principles is contentious. As Chief Justice McLachlin observes in her chapter:[107]

> The traditional approach is to think of tort law and criminal law as non-overlapping magisteria, or separate bodies of law. While the norms of tort law and criminal law can sometimes be applied to the same event, neither body of law is relevant to the other because their objectives are different.

A question that arises, therefore, is the extent to which these scholars can make use of criminal law theory and doctrine. Is it permissible to incorporate directly large amounts of criminal theory and doctrine? Should they, instead, proceed more cautiously and selectively? Or should torts scholars refrain completely from looking to

102 See, eg, *Revill v Newbery* [1996] QB 567 (CA); *Miller v Miller* [2011] HCA 9; (2011) 242 CLR 446.

103 For a taste of the criminal law writing, see HLA Hart, *Punishment and Responsibility: Essays in the Philosophy of Law* (Oxford, Clarendon Press, 1968); G Williams, 'Offences and Defences' (1982) 2 *Legal Studies* 233; GP Fletcher, *Rethinking Criminal Law* (Boston, Little, Brown & Co, 1978) chs 7, 9–10; PH Robinson, *Criminal Law Defences* (St Paul MN, West Publishing Co, 1984) (two volumes); J Gardner, *Offences and Defences: Essays in the Philosophy of Criminal Law* (Oxford, Oxford University Press, 2007) chs 4–9; J Horder, *Excusing Crime* (Oxford, Oxford University Press, 2004); Victor Tadros, *Criminal Responsibility* (Oxford, Oxford University Press, 2005) chs 4, 10–12; RA Duff, *Answering for Crime* (Oxford, Hart Publishing, 2007) chs 9, 11.

104 See ch 8 at p 135.

105 ibid.

106 See ch 9 at p 159.

107 See ch 11 at p 218 (footnote omitted).

the criminal law for guidance? At this last extreme, Jules Coleman claims that '[t]he differences between torts and the criminal law are so fundamental that the net result of applying one's understanding of the criminal law to torts is bad philosophy and total confusion'.[108]

A slightly different question from that of whether criminal law theory and doctrine should ever be applied in the tort law context is whether tort law's rules ought to be fashioned in the light of the criminal law's principles. Chief Justice McLachlin contends that it is imperative that tort law (and, as we read her, private law generally) ought to be so developed, on the ground that the law as a whole must be coherent for rule-of-law reasons.[109]

Regardless of where one stands on the broader methodological issues, scholarship in tort law is increasingly dealing with several themes most commonly associated with criminal law defences. In the remainder of this section we examine two of these themes which were pertinent at the workshop and in the chapters in this book.

4.2 Justifications and Excuses

4.2.1 Is the Division Useful?

Criminal lawyers conventionally distinguish between justificatory and excusatory defences, and a vast literature exists in this regard.[110] Should tort lawyers think in these terms? This question proved to be highly controversial at the workshop. Some participants were concerned only with the substantive outcomes of a successful plea and, considering that both justificatory and excusatory defences (assuming that the latter already exist in tort law or are introduced into tort law[111]) yield a verdict for the defendant, doubted whether we should care about such a classification. In their chapter on duress, James Edelman and Esther Dyer reject the usefulness of employing the labels 'justification' and 'excuse' in tort law for different reasons. Their main claim in this regard is that these terms are unhelpful because there is no consensus as to their meaning.[112] In particular, they point out that criminal lawyers are deeply divided as to whether the defence of duress is a justification or an excuse (or both, as some have argued[113]). This leads them to argue that, if a defence of duress is introduced into tort law, it should be known as a 'privilege'.[114]

Nevertheless, several contributors to this volume insist on retaining the distinction between justifications and excuses both for theoretical and practical reasons. John Goldberg, for example, sees at least theoretical value in separating justifications from

[108] JL Coleman, *Risks and Wrongs* (Oxford, Oxford University Press, 1992) 222.

[109] See ch 11 at pp 218–20.

[110] Douglas Husak observes that '[p]erhaps the most significant and controversial research program among contemporary criminal theorists is the investigation of the advantages and limitations of applications of the distinction between justification and excuse': DN Husak, 'Justifications and the Criminal Liability of Accessories' (1989) 80 *Journal of Criminal Law & Criminology* 491, 491.

[111] See, in this connection, Section 4.2.3.

[112] See ch 9 at p 178.

[113] See, eg, K Greenawalt, 'The Perplexing Borders of Justification and Excuse' (1984) 84 *Columbia Law Review* 1897, 1912.

[114] See ch 9 at p 181.

excuses. As we will discuss below, he believes that tort law properly admits justifications to its repertoire of defences but for the most part refuses to recognise excuses.[115] In his chapter, Paul Davies points to one way in which the distinction might be significant in practical terms. He contends that if a principal wrongdoer has a defence, the issue of whether it is a justification or an excuse may affect whether an accessory is entitled to the same defence.[116] Consider the following two situations (our examples, not Davies'). In the first situation, D1 uses reasonable force against C, who was about to attack her. D2 assists D1. If D1 is justified (as she plainly is), D2 might be able to invoke that justification. In the second situation, D1 strikes C because C provoked her. D2 (who was not provoked) assists D1. Many theorists believe that in this situation D1 merely has an excuse,[117] and it might be asserted that any defence that the law gives to D1 should not, because D1 is excused, be enjoyed by D2.[118]

We note that, if the distinction between justifications and excuses is brought to bear on tort law defences, it would plainly not capture all tort defences. For example, limitation bars (which are addressed by Andrew Burrows in his chapter) are neither in the nature of a justification nor an excuse.[119] The same is true of the doctrine of illegality, which is treated by Chief Justice McLachlin, and by Goudkamp and Mayr in their chapters. The non-exhaustive nature of the distinction between justifications and excuses is specifically adverted to by Edelman and Dyer in their chapter, and they seem to see that as a reason for tort lawyers to avoid using the distinction.[120] We have reservations about whether that is a good reason to shun the distinction as an organising device. Justifications and excuses do not exhaust all criminal law defences, and few criminal lawyers contend that the distinction should be abandoned for that reason.[121]

4.2.2 How We Should Understand Justified Acts?

One of the most disputed questions in the philosophy of the criminal law, at least in recent years, is whether justified conduct is wrongful. The conventional view is that justified conduct is not wrong. Endorsing that view, George Fletcher writes: '[c]laims of justification ... challenge whether the act is wrongful'.[122] The rival view, which has lately been gathering support, is that acts that enliven a justification defence remain wrong. John Gardner, for instance, doubts the conventional view.[123] Surely, one might think, if anything calls for a justification, it is a wrong; yet on the conventional view, wrongs cannot be justified (because justified acts on that view are not wrong).[124]

[115] See Section 4.2.3.
[116] See ch 7 at pp 109–10.
[117] See, eg, Gardner (n 103) 109.
[118] See, eg, PH Robinson, 'Criminal Law Defenses: A Systematic Analysis' (1982) 82 *Columbia Law Review* 199, 280.
[119] Of course, it might be disputed whether limitation bars are defences: see Section 2.3.
[120] See ch 9 at p 181.
[121] Antony Duff considers precisely the argument made by Edelman and Dyer in this regard and contends that consigning the justification/excuse distinction to oblivion 'would be an unnecessarily drastic solution': Duff (n 103) 265.
[122] Fletcher (n 103) 759.
[123] Gardner (n 103) especially at 77–82, 96–97.
[124] Consider Gardner's comments, ibid 77.

Three contributors to the present volume appear to endorse the conventional view. John Goldberg writes: 'A *justification* maintains that, even though the defendant's conduct meets the definition of the relevant wrong, it is not wrong when all relevant facts have been considered'.[125] Robert Stevens claims that a justification will entail that 'all things considered, nothing wrongful has been done'.[126] Graham Virgo perhaps embraces the conventional view more strongly than either Goldberg or Stevens, claiming that justified defendants do not even act in a 'morally conflicted fashion'.[127] Paul Davies, by contrast, adheres to the rival view. He asserts that '[a]lthough it has been argued that "justifications deny wrongdoing", the better view seems to be that even where the "primary wrongdoer" is justified, a wrong may might nevertheless have been committed'.[128]

There are several comments that we want to add to the foregoing. First, none of our contributors mounts a full-fledged argument in support of either view. They merely state their position en route to making other arguments. However, that distinct views on the question have arisen shows that the question may deserve closer attention in future work.[129] Secondly, the extent of the practical significance of the distinction between the conventional view and the rival view remains to be seen. Davies suggests one way in which the issue might have real-world consequences. He suggests the rival view means that liability can properly attach to an accessory to a wrong even if the primary wrongdoer is justified.[130] Conversely, he implies, if the conventional view were right, it would not be correct for the law to hold an accessory liable if the principal is justified. Thirdly, we believe that the word 'wrong' may be being used in different ways by different theorists, with the result that supposed differences between theorists may sometimes be illusory.[131] An act might be 'wrong' in the sense of being in infringement of a right. This is how Robert Stevens uses the word in his chapter when he writes: 'If you violate [my] right by punching me, you wrong me'.[132] But an act might not violate any rights, but still be wrong in that there were undefeated, sufficient reasons not to perform it.[133]

A related question to that of whether justified acts are wrong is whether justified acts should be encouraged. Some criminal law theorists, most notably Paul Robinson, have contended that they should be.[134] Graham Virgo, in his contribution to the present volume, subscribes to this view. He writes that where a justification defence applies 'it follows that the defendant's conduct, which would otherwise be

[125] See ch 4 at p 54 (emphasis in original).

[126] See ch 13 at p 250.

[127] See ch 8 at p 140.

[128] See ch 7 at p 109 (footnotes omitted).

[129] The extent to which the criminal law debate can be transplanted depends in part on whether the notion of wrongfulness is shared: on this question, see Goldberg, ch 4 at p 56.

[130] See ch 7 at pp 109–10.

[131] Goldberg alludes to this risk: ch 4 at p 56. See, for the need to specify this term precisely, and multiple meanings, D Parfit, *On What Matters* (Oxford, Oxford University Press, 2011) ch 7.

[132] Stevens, ch 4 at p 253.

[133] We might refer to a driver making a 'wrong turn'. Stephen Smith claims that this refers to a particular breach of a duty: ch 4 at p 69. But we doubt that rights are infringed in such a case.

[134] PH Robinson, 'A Theory of Justification: Societal Harm as a Prerequisite for Criminal Liability' (1975) 23 *University of California Los Angeles Law Review* 266, 274.

unlawful, is lawful and should be encouraged'.[135] The claim that justified conduct ought to be encouraged is controversial. Many criminal law scholars view it with caution.[136] Whether or not this caution is warranted, it seems likely, given the interest that this issue has attracted among criminal law scholars, that it is also an important question for future tort law scholarship.

4.2.3. Do Excuses to Torts Exist? Should They?

It is widely accepted that the criminal law recognises excuses.[137] What do tort lawyers think about their subject in this regard? Tort lawyers sometimes say things like 'A will be liable to B if she does X without "justification or excuse"'.[138] This suggests that some lawyers believe that tort law is sensitive to excuses, although such remarks are often made other than in the course of addressing squarely the issue of whether excuses exist in tort law, and so it is difficult to know how much one can read into them. Many—perhaps most—theorists who have considered directly the question claim that tort law does not recognise excuses.[139] So the prevailing wisdom might fairly be said to be that excuses are alien to tort law. Is that wisdom correct? And, regardless of the answer to that question, should excuses play a role in tort law?[140] Several of the contributors to this volume address these questions in varying degrees of detail. The most extensive engagement is offered by John Goldberg.[141] We have already discussed Goldberg's chapter,[142] focusing on the relevance of excuses to his civil recourse theory of tort law. We return to his chapter here to look directly at what he says about excuses. As we noted earlier, Goldberg claims that tort law is largely insensitive to excuses and that this insensitivity extends not only to the determination of liability, but also to the assessment of damages. However, he accepts that excuses creep in at tort law's margins. For example, he observes that defendants who exercise self-defence on the basis of a reasonable mistake of fact are released from liability,[143] and suggests that at least some of these defendants are excused, while others may be justified. The best way of understanding cases involving a reasonable mistake as to the need for self-defence is a matter of dispute

[135] See ch 8 at p 140 (footnote omitted). Dickson J, in the Supreme Court of Canada, in *Perka v The Queen* [1984] 2 SCR 232 (SCC) 246–47 is quoted at length by Edelman and Dyer (ch 9 at p 180). In this quote his Honour makes similar comments to Virgo.

[136] J Dressler, 'New Thoughts about the Concept of Justification in the Criminal Law: A Critique of Fletcher's Thinking and Rethinking' (1984) 32 *University of California Los Angeles Law Review* 61, 83; J Gardner, 'Justification under Authority' (2010) 23 *Canadian Journal of Law & Jurisprudence* 71, 81.

[137] See, eg, Duff (n 102) ch 11.

[138] See, eg, NJ McBride and R Bagshaw, *Tort Law*, 4th edn (Harlow, Pearson, 2012) 409 (discussing trespass to land).

[139] Gardner (n 135) 92; J Raz, 'Responsibility and the Negligence Standard' (2010) 30 *OJLS* 1, 10.

[140] One of us has discussed whether tort law should recognise excuses: see J Goudkamp, 'Defences in Tort and Crime' in M Dyson (ed), *Unravelling Tort and Crime* (Cambridge, Cambridge University Press, 2014) 217–31.

[141] See, further, the general comments of Stephen Smith (ch 5 at p 65).

[142] See Section 3.3.3.

[143] This is the law in, at least, England and Wales: *Ashley v Chief Constable of Sussex Police* [2008] UKHL 25; [2008] 1 AC 962.

among criminal lawyers.[144] Some criminal theorists believe that defendants who use defensive force as a result of a reasonable mistake are justified while others think that such defendants are excused. The suggestion, however, that there might be both justified and excused defendants in the category of defendants who act on the basis of a reasonable mistake as to the need for defensive force is, we think, a novel one. What does Goldberg say in relation to the issue of whether tort law should recognise excuses? We noted earlier that Goldberg claims that it is justifiable for tort law to deny excuses.[145] However, we wonder whether he is not in fact committed to the proposition that excuses should have no role in tort law. In arguing that tort law can sensibly exclude excuses, Goldberg contrasts tort law (understood in terms of his civil recourse theory) with the criminal law. The criminal law, Goldberg reminds us, provides various protections to defendants, who are 'pitched against the well-resourced state'. These protections include the presumption of innocence, the principle that ambiguous penal statutes should be construed in the defendant's favour, a steeply asymmetrical onus of proof in favour of the defendant, and restrictions on the prosecution leading certain types of evidence, such as evidence of the defendant's bad character. Goldberg claims that these protections include excuses.[146] Conversely, he asserts, in tort law, the parties are equals and the law therefore deals with their interests in a 'more evenhanded way'. Goldberg says: 'because tort law is in the business of empowering those who are wronged [in the inter-personal] sense, the demands placed on claimants are, on the whole, less onerous than those placed on prosecutors'.[147] A key question here is whether withholding excuses actually deals with the parties 'even-handedly'. Why should Goldberg's claim about the general lack of excuses in tort law lead us to think that tort law so deals with the parties? Perhaps the denial of excuses actually gives an undue advantage to claimants. However, if Goldberg is correct, does it follow that the denial of excuses is merely justifi*able*? Given Goldberg's belief that tort law deals with the parties even-handedly, if withholding excuses is necessary in order to treat the parties equally surely the absence of excuses in tort law is justifi*ed*?

Graham Virgo considers that tort law recognises an excuse in the form of private necessity. Since (at least in some jurisdictions[148]) the defendant remains liable to pay damages in private necessity cases, he reasons that the defendant cannot be

[144] Compare, eg, GP Fletcher, 'Domination in the Theory of Justification and Excuse' (1996) 57 *University of Pittsburgh Law Review* 553, 63–67 (contending that a person who reasonably but mistakenly thinks that they are justified is excused) and, eg, Tadros (n 103) 280–90 (contending that a person who proceeds on the basis of a reasonable mistake is justified).

[145] See Section 3.3.3.

[146] Goldberg writes:

> Because criminal prosecutions are brought by a powerful state that operates the system through which accountability occurs, and because the point of such prosecutions is to inflict punishment, criminal law provides certain protections for defendants. These include ... the recognition of excuses both with respect to liability and punishment (ch 4 at p 57).

Associating excuses with the procedural protections that the criminal law affords to defendants is a highly controversial move, to which few, if any, criminal lawyers have subscribed. There is little consensus among criminal lawyers as to the precise reason why excuses exist. But the accounts offered (several are addressed in Fletcher (n 103) 798–817; see also HLA Hart's analysis: Hart (n 103) 17–24) differ radically from Goldberg's.

[147] See ch 4 at p 57.

[148] Eg, Minnesota: *Vincent v Lake Erie Transportation Co* 109 Minn 456; 124 NW 221 (1910).

justified. This suggests, Virgo says, that the defendant must instead be excused.[149] It is unclear to us precisely what Virgo thinks defendants in private necessity cases are excused *from* if they remain liable to pay damages.

Edelman and Dyer's chapter is also relevant to the issue of whether excuses should exist in tort law. They contend that a defence of duress should be ushered into tort law. We have already noted that Edelman and Dyer prefer to avoid using the label 'excuse', at least in relation to duress.[150] However, duress is often thought to be in the nature of an excuse. If, contrary to what Edelman and Dyer contend, the label 'excuse' is rightly applied to duress, it is interesting to consider what implications their analysis may entail. One question is whether their analysis also supports welcoming certain other defences that are generally thought to be excuses into tort law, such as provocation (or loss of control, as it is now called in English criminal law[151]). Some might argue that consistency demands this: if duress, which is often considered to be one of the criminal law's core excuses, is ushered into tort law, it might be thought strange to exclude other excusatory defences found in the criminal law. Edelman and Dyer are silent on this issue.

5. THE STRUCTURE OF THE BOOK

We have divided this book into two parts. Part A is concerned, roughly speaking, with issues of general interest to tort law defences as a whole. Part B is concerned with specific tort law defences. The distinction we have sought to draw is a rough one. Some of the chapters on general issues engage with some specific defences in detail; some of the chapters on specific defences raise questions of general interest. Indeed, some specific defences are of general application (for instance, limitation bars and illegality are defences to all torts) and some are not (contributory negligence, for example, probably applies only to the tort of negligence).

149 See ch 8 at pp 149–50.
150 See above the text accompanying n 111.
151 Coroners and Justice Act 2009 (UK), ss 54, 56(1).

2

Pleading Defences in Tort: The Historical Perspective

DAVID IBBETSON

THE PURPOSE OF the present chapter is to bring a historical perspective to the role of defences in English tort law, between the thirteenth century and the pleading reforms of the second half of the nineteenth century. Its principal focus is the area covered by the action of trespass and the core of the action on the case, where compensation was claimed for personal injury or damage to property. Its argument is, first, that for most of its history prima facie liability in trespass was grounded simply on the causation of damage or loss, subject to a range of defences which could be pleaded by the defendant; the scope of liability was therefore largely defined by the range of defences that was permitted. Secondly, in the core of the action on the case, liability was dependent on some form of fault on the part of the defendant, and there was little scope for defences to be pleaded except purely formal defences such as limitation or *res judicata*; here, therefore, defences played no significant part in the fixing of the scope of liability. Thirdly, changes in legal process in the eighteenth century, in particular the reservation of cases for discussion by the court *in banc* after facts had been found by the jury, allowed the recognition as defences of certain features which were not pleaded as such. The dissociation between rules of special pleading and defences was locked in place by the Rules of Court put in place by the Judicature Acts of 1873 and 1875.

Although in its origins 'trespass' meant no more than 'wrong', by the latter part of the thirteenth century the action of trespass had crystallised into something like its classical form, subdivided into three species: trespass to land, trespass to goods, and trespass to the person.[1] In all three of these liability was strict, in the sense that the defendant was prima facie liable once it was shown that he or she had done the act complained of. The claimant did not allege any fault on the defendant's part, and except in very rare circumstances it was not open to the defendant simply to deny fault.[2] Hence, in *Hulle v Orynge (The Case of Thorns)*,[3] the question arose whether

[1] SFC Milsom, *Historical Foundations of the Common Law*, 2nd edn (Oxford, Oxford University Press, 1981) 285–89; D Ibbetson, *Historical Introduction to the Law of Obligations* (Oxford, Oxford University Press, 1999) 39–43.

[2] MS Arnold, 'Accident, Mistake, and Rules of Liability in the Fourteenth-Century Law of Torts' (1979) 128 *University of Pennsylvania Law Review* 361.

[3] (1460) YB Mich 6 Edw IV, fo 7v, pl 18; JH Baker, *Baker and Milsom: Sources of English History: Private Law to 1750*, 2nd edn (Oxford, Oxford University Press, 2010) (hereafter 'B&M') 369.

a wrong would have been committed where a man had clipped his thorn hedge and the thorns had fallen onto the claimant's land; it was held by Littleton and Choke JJ that prima facie this did constitute a trespass. The civil wrong was distinguished from the criminal felony. In the latter there would be no liability if the injury had been done without the defendant's will, whereas in the civil claim that was irrelevant: '[i]f a man suffers damage it is right that he be recompensed'.[4]

A related issue had arisen a few years earlier, where an action of trespass to the person was brought against a four-year-old child who had, it appears, put out the claimant's eye with an arrow.[5] While it was accepted that a child of such an age could not commit a felony and would therefore have to be acquitted even if a jury had found him guilty, it was said that trespass was different. However, the reason for the difference was important: it was not that the child should necessarily be liable in trespass (which was not decided), but that in trespass unlike felony it was possible to plead defences and so there was no need to give discretion to the judges:[6]

> [T]here is no remedy in felony but to plead Not guilty, because felony may not be justified; and therefore the justices at their discretion may dismiss him if it appears that he is of such an age that he has no discretion. But it is otherwise in trespass, for in a writ of trespass the party may justify the trespass and is not compelled to plead Not guilty; and therefore the justices do not have the like power.

It might have been the same in *The Case of Thorns*: though prima facie the claim lay, it might have been open to the defendant to plead that he could not have acted in any other way, or that he had done all he could to keep them out.[7]

These cases reveal very clearly the crucial function of defences in the writ of trespass. Practically all the definition of the law was the result of the defences which were pleaded rather than the way in which the claimant's claim was formulated.

A whole range of justificatory defences to actions for trespass to land can be seen, for example: that the defendant had entered the claimant's land pursuant to a right to hunt game (perhaps even if his dogs had entered beyond his alleged right while they were in pursuit of their quarry and he had entered to fetch his dogs); that he was exercising a right of self-help to destroy a nuisance or something that had been wrongfully erected in breach of a franchise which he claimed; that he was a legal officer acting under a valid warrant; that he was entering the land under an express or implied licence; that he had a right to enter the claimant's land to dig turf or the like; that he was exercising a right of way, and so on.[8] It would be a great mistake to see this as a closed list of defences—at least we do not find any such closed list being explicitly formulated. Rather, a defendant who wished to claim that he had had a right to enter the land in question could do so by raising an appropriate plea asserting that right. Clearly we can think of these as justificatory defences where they are expressly pleaded as such in answer to the claimant's claim. But it is conceivable that sometimes a defendant who could have pleaded such a defence chose

[4] ibid 373 (Littleton J).
[5] *Anon* (1456) YB Mich 35 Hen VI, fo 11v, pl 18; B&M 368.
[6] *Anon* (1456) B&M 368, 369 (Moyle J).
[7] ibid 373 (Choke J).
[8] MS Arnold (ed), *Select Cases of Trespass from the King's Courts 1307–1399*, vol 100 (London, Selden Society, 1984) lxx–lxxxiii.

simply to plead not guilty and rely on the jury to find in his or her favour: all we can say for certain is that these justifications might be pleaded as defences. Sometimes we find matters pleaded by way of defence which would surely arise more normally as questions of fact behind a general plea of not guilty and which were in no sense justifications of an apparently wrongful act, as where a defendant in an action for entering the claimant's land simply alleged that the land was his.[9] We might choose to call this a defence in so far as it was pleaded as such, but that is our choice and not something that is inherent in the structure of liability. In other words, we cannot draw an absolutely clear line between matters which were central to the claim and matters which constituted defences: the lawyers on each side were doing no more than trying to get certain matters onto the record or to keep them off the record, without being concerned about any sophisticated classification.

A similar ambiguity is visible in cases of trespass to goods.[10] A defendant might justify an apparently wrongful taking by pleading that he had lawfully arrested the goods or distrained them as a legitimate part of legal process; or he might say that he had properly taken animals *damage feasant*, ie, when they were injuring his crops. If the action was based on injuring or killing an animal, he might say that the animal had been entrusted to him for some purpose (typically shoeing by a farrier or veterinary treatment by a marshal), and that the death or injury had occurred while he was properly and carefully doing what he had been asked to do. We might say here too that the killing or injuring was prima facie wrongful and therefore required justification: but it is very probable that in these situations the defendant would simply have pleaded the general issue of not guilty and left the matter in the hands of the jury—it is very striking that we find only a tiny number of pleas in this form, all dating from within a few years of each other. We do, however, find defendants sued for taking goods pleading that the goods were in fact theirs, not the claimant's, frequently explaining the basis of their own title (gift, sale, legacy etc) or possessory right; they might even say that they belonged to a third party rather than to the claimant. Although pleaded by the defendant, it is hard to see this as a defence rather than an element of the claimant's claim that was being denied. As was the case with trespass to land, the fact that something was pleaded explicitly by the defendant indicates no more than that he or she wanted to get it onto the record of the case.

So too with trespass to the person. First, there was a more or less indeterminate range of justificatory defences:[11] self-defence, defence of others (but probably not defence of one's property), arrest or imprisonment pursuant to some valid authority, reasonable chastisement (as where a feudal lord punished his villein, a mistress slapped her maid, or a schoolmaster caned his pupil in the customary way), or consensual fighting. Secondly, though, there were pleas which effectively denied the defendant's causal responsibility, in particular where it was said that the claimant was to blame for his own misfortune, as where he had walked across the line of fire between a bowman and his target. We might, of course, see this as indicating

[9] ibid lxxix, fn 628.
[10] Arnold (n 8) l–lxx.
[11] Arnold (n 8) xxxiv–xliii.

that there was a 'defence' of contributory negligence,[12] though it is probably better to see it as a denial by the defendant that he had done the harm, something that could have been raised under the general issue if the defendant had chosen to do this rather than plead specially.

In a sense, we can say that anything that was pleaded by the defendant in bar of the claimant's claim must by definition be a defence to that claim, even if it appears to have been in truth nothing more than a denial of a central element of the claim itself. However, in formal pleading terms, we might usefully distinguish between those pleas which took effect as confessions and avoidance and those which took effect as special traverses. In the former, the defendant admitted the allegations made by the claimant but then alleged additional matter which he asserted exonerated him from legal liability, whereas in the latter he denied some relevant fact alleged by the claimant and asserted something contrary to it. A good example of a confession and avoidance is provided by *de Okeover v de Okeover*, where the defendant lord justified imprisoning the claimant on the grounds that he was his villein who was behaving wrongfully:[13]

> And the aforesaid [defendant] says as before that the aforesaid [claimant] was his villein on the day and year aforesaid of his manor of Okeover and he took the same [claimant] there and not at Ashbourne and detained him because he was rebellious etc. until he would submit himself to justice, as well he might. And he offers to prove this by the country etc.; and [the claimant] does likewise.

This can be contrasted with the special traverse in *Goodson v Walkin*, where the defendant in a standard-form action for battery, involving a trampling under the hooves of the defendant's horse, explained that her horse had run away and that the claimant was helping her to recapture it:[14]

> And the aforesaid [claimant] being in the way there attempted to stop the same horse in aid of the same [defendant], whereupon the horse in running knocked the same [claimant] to the ground with his breast and his feet. And thus they say that if any harm came to the same [claimant] there it was due to the foolishness and fault of the said [claimant] in form aforesaid and not to any malice or wrong of the same [defendant].

However, although we might always want to characterise pleas in the form of confessions and avoidance as raising defences, we cannot say that special traverses did no more than negative some element in the claimant's case. So, in *Kirby v Raven*[15] the defendant Raven specially traversed the claimants' complaint that he had beaten Isot (one of the claimants), claiming that she was a relative who had been living with him at the time of the battery, that she had developed an unhealthy interest in boys (who might perhaps have included the claimant Thomas, who was now her husband), and that as a result of this he had chastised her with small sticks and not beaten her in any other way with force of arms or out of malice. It would surely be perverse—in modern-day terms—to treat this as anything other than a defence of

[12] ibid xli.
[13] (1318) 100 SS 36.
[14] (1376) 100 SS 18.
[15] (1381) 100 SS 26.

reasonable chastisement, but we could not do so if we limited defences to matters which were raised by way of confession and avoidance.

The point of special pleading was purely and simply to narrow down the issue to be determined by the jury, to get some matter onto the record rather than leaving it within the very broad discretion of the jury on how to take it into account. It is this that largely explains the almost complete lack of special pleading by the defendant in the action on the case.

The action on the case emerged in the 1360s as an alternative way of framing writs of trespass. Instead of alleging that the defendant had forcibly interfered with the claimant's land, goods or person, the claimant first set out the background to the claim and then stated that the defendant had somehow acted wrongfully in that context, as a result of which loss had been caused. Perhaps the earliest successful writ in this form was *Broadmeadow v Rushenden*:[16]

> Whereas the left arm and hand of the same Mariot were accidentally injured and the same Roger faithfully promised the aforesaid John and Mariot that he would restore the aforesaid arm and hand to health as well and safely as any surgeon in London, by virtue of which promise the same John and Mariot, trusting in the faithfulness and diligence of the same Roger in this respect, for an appropriate fee committed the cure of the aforesaid arm and hand to the aforesaid Roger, the cure to be effected faithfully in accordance with the aforesaid promise; the same Roger, having undertaken the aforesaid cure and having received part of his aforesaid fee in hand, so carelessly, negligently or maliciously performed the cure at London that the same Mariot completely lost her aforesaid hand by the fault of the same Roger, to the damage of the same John and Mariot of one hundred pounds.

The detailed way in which a claim of this sort was formulated meant that there was very little scope for the defendant to plead specially in response to it: if the jury was not satisfied that the details of the claim were established, then they should give a verdict for the defendant. Moreover, since the claimant had put the defendant's fault in issue it would have been redundant for the defendant to raise an excusatory or justificatory defence such as self-defence which would have served only to deny fault. This is not to say that special pleading was excluded from all sub-types of actions on the case, and it would be relatively common in actions for defamation, which came into the common law courts at the beginning of the sixteenth century; but in this core area, where claims were brought for personal injury or property damage, it was largely unknown.

By the end of the fourteenth century, therefore, we can see two parallel approaches to the role of special pleading, and within that to the role of formal defences. In actions of trespass the claimant made a very broad allegation and there was consequently considerable room for the defendant to plead specially in order to get relevant matters onto the record; in actions on the case, by contrast, the relevant matters were already on the record, so there was practically no room for the defendant to do anything but deny them with a general plea of not guilty.

By the seventeenth century, in the writ of trespass the distinction was being drawn between justifications and excuses. According to Hobart's report of *Weaver v Ward*,[17]

[16] (1364) 103 SS 422.

[17] (1616) Hob 134; 80 ER 284; B&M 375, 376.

justifications were those things pleaded by way of confession and avoidance, concluding *prout ei bene licuit*, while matters falling within special traverses constituted excuses, and 'no man shall be excused of a trespass ... except it may be judged utterly without his fault'. Hence in *Dickinson v Watson*,[18] it was said that an excuse amounting to a plea of accident was formally insufficient without a traverse of the claimant's allegation of a forcible shooting. Similarly, in *Gibbon v Pepper*,[19] a defendant who purported to justify a battery of the claimant by saying that his horse had been frightened in Drury Lane and had run away with him was held to have mispleaded, since this could not have constituted a justification: it was said that he should have pleaded not guilty and raised the circumstances in evidence, or following *Dickinson v Watson*, he might have been able to raise the matter by a special traverse in the nature of an excuse. Similarly, in Charles Viner's massive abridgment published in the middle of the eighteenth century, defences to trespass (taking effect by way of confession and avoidance) are invariably referred to as justifications, leaving only a very small group of cases to be referred to under the heading of excuses.[20] Writing in the early years of the nineteenth century, Serjeant Edward Lawes drew largely the same distinction: a plea in excuse admitted the act complained of but showed special matter which negatived the defendant's culpability, whereas a plea in justification (taking effect by confession and avoidance) admitted that the act had been done deliberately but in the exercise of a legal right.[21] That said, nothing hinged on the terminology, which was fundamentally unstable: in *Knapp v Salsbury*,[22] for example, Lord Ellenborough CJ described a defence of accident in an action of trespass for running against the claimant's post-chaise as a justification which ought to have been pleaded.

In formal terms, matters remained largely unchanged between the late fourteenth century and the end of the eighteenth. The position is graphically revealed in John Wentworth's *A Complete System of Pleading*, published in 1799. A substantial part of volume 8 deals with 'Tort', in essence actions on the case,[23] and while special pleas are found in the precedents of actions on the case for defamation, they are almost completely absent in actions for personal injury or property damage. The section on 'Mixed Nonfeasance and Misfeasance', which included causing injury by careless driving, contains but a single special plea, that judgment had been recovered already;[24] the small section of claims against non-public officers, which included actions against carriers, has no special pleas at all.[25] This contrasts sharply with the position in trespass, which takes up most of volume 9. After giving precedents of claimants' declarations for each of the standard forms of trespass, the author moves onto the defendants' pleas: denials (including both the simple general denial

[18] (1682) T Jones 204; 84 ER 1218; B&M 377.

[19] (1695) 1 Ld Raym 38; 91 ER 922; 4 Mod 405; 87 ER 469; 2 Salk 638; 91 ER 638; B&M 378.

[20] C Viner, *A General Abridgment of Law and Equity: Alphabetically Digested under Proper Titles, with Notes and References to the Whole*, vol 20 (London, Aldershot, 1742–53) 423ff, 476ff, 525f.

[21] E Lawes, *An Elementary Treatise on Pleading in Civil Actions* (London, Brooke and Clarke, Bell Yard and J Butterworth, 1806) 122–26.

[22] (1810) 2 Camp 500; 170 ER 1231.

[23] J Wentworth, *A Complete System of Pleading*, vol 8 (Dublin, J Moore, 1799) 229ff.

[24] ibid 380–438, 388.

[25] Wentworth (n 23) 502–06.

and special traverses), pleas that liability had been discharged, and then 'excuse and justification'.[26] The section on trespass to the person is indicative of the way in which the subject is treated:

1 By Amicable Contest.
2 Authority of Law
  Without Process
    As Individuals
    Officers, and in Aid of Them
  Under Legal Process
    Civil
      Of Courts Superior
        Mesne
        Final
      Of Courts Inferior: Criminal
  Moderate Correction
  Molliter Manus Imposuit (i.e. gently laying hands)
    In Defence of:
      Real Property
      Personal Property
      To Preserve Peace
      To Prevent Mischief
      On Other Lawful Occasions
  Son Assault Demesne
    In Defence of:
      Self
      Third Persons
      Specially, with an *IrâMotus*

To a large extent, transparently, the range of the writ of trespass was determined by the defences available and their detail, not as in the action on the case by the claimant's declaration. Wentworth's explicit contrast is reflected in other pleading books of the latter part of the eighteenth century: the precedents of actions on the case in John Lilly's *Collection of Modern Entries*, for example, contain no special pleading, whereas special pleas are common in the precedents of actions of trespass.[27]

The formal position was summarised by Joseph Chitty in the early part of the nineteenth century. In the action on the case (with the exception of defamation), the defendant was always at liberty to plead the general issue and raise his defence in evidence, and was normally required to do so; but where the defence was purely a matter of law the defendant might choose to plead it specially.[28] This remained the case right up to the abolition of the old rules of pleading by the Judicature Acts of 1873 and 1875.[29] In trespass, on the other hand, it was said that the general issue

[26] Most easily visible in the section titled 'Analysis': see J Wentworth, *A Complete System of Pleading*, vol 9 (Dublin, J Moore, 1799) i–iii (confusingly bound after p 408).

[27] J Lilly, *A Collection of Modern Entries*, 5th edn (London, J Rivington & Sons, 1791).

[28] J Chitty, *Treatise on the Parties to Actions, the Forms of Actions, and on Pleading*, 5th edn, vol 1 (London, Samuel Brooke, 1831) 527–28, 535–36. See, eg, *Bridge v The Grand Junction Rly Co* (1838) 3 M&W 244; 150 ER 1134, sub nom *Armitage v Grand Junction Rly Co* (1838) 6 Dowl PC 340, where the defendant's plea of another's negligence failed because this amounted to the general issue.

[29] E Bullen and SM Leake, *Precedents of Pleadings*, 3rd edn (London, Steven and Sons, 1868) 752–54.

was proper when the defendant was simply controverting the truth of the claimant's claim; but where the defendant was not denying that he had prima facie committed a trespassory act any excuse or justification had to be specially pleaded.[30]

By this time, two crucially important changes in practice had occurred. First, claims for the non-deliberate infliction of personal injury or property damage were increasingly being framed within the action on the case rather than the action of trespass.[31] This had the effect that trespass was used primarily where the defendant had allegedly acted deliberately, and where the issue was whether his act had been justified, leaving case to do practically all of the work where the question was the extent of the defendant's fault or the amount of the claimant's loss. In terms of the structure of liability, it meant that the vast majority of claims for personal injury and property damage were now framed within the action on the case—the action for negligence as it was coming to be called—where there was little room for special pleading. And if there was little special pleading, then any distinction between those elements which formed part of the claimant's cause of action and those elements which formed part of the defendant's defence could not depend on the availability or otherwise of special pleas. The second change in practice played along with this. From the 1760s, if not earlier, it was possible for the trial judge to reserve points of law for the consideration of the court *in banc*.[32] This introduced a measure of judicial control over jury decisions, enabling the judges to discuss openly the scope of liability rather than leaving matters at large before the jury. Moreover, the increasing volume of law reports gave greater publicity to these discussions and decisions. Judicial control could similarly be exercised by rulings on the admissibility of evidence or reaching a judgement of its force: in *Smith v Shepherd*,[33] for example, in an action on the case against a common carrier, Heath J rejected evidence tendered by the defendant to show that he had not been negligent, and directed the jury to find a verdict for the claimant on the grounds that the facts which had been proved in evidence were insufficient to support a conclusion that the injury alleged had resulted from an act of God.

The disconnect between defences and special pleas by the first half of the nineteenth century is completely clear in Edward Lawes' *Treatise on Pleading*. 'Every defence which cannot be specially pleaded may be given in evidence at the trial'.[34] He did not, however, define what was meant by a defence, and it seems clear that what he had in mind was anything that could be alleged by the defendant to exonerate himself. What we might naturally think of as a defence of contributory negligence, for example, was typically raised behind the general plea of not guilty, whereas if the defendant wanted to dispute the claimant's title in a claim that he or she had negligently damaged the claimant's goods, it was essential to plead specially that the goods were not in fact the claimant's property at all.[35]

[30] Chitty (n 28) 538–46, especially 539.

[31] MJ Prichard, 'Trespass, Case and the Rule in *Williams v Holland*' [1964] *CLJ* 234, 239–44; Ibbetson (n 1) 156–57.

[32] MJ Prichard, 'Nonsuit: A Premature Obituary' [1960] *CLJ* 88, 92–95.

[33] (1796) 128 SS 132.

[34] Lawes (n 21) 111.

[35] *Butterfield v Forrester* (1809) 11 East 60; 103 ER 926; Bullen and Leake (n 29) 752, based on Regulae Generales, Trinity Term 1853, rule 16.

The nature of defences, therefore, was problematic. We may even question whether it is right, in the context of the action on the case for negligence, to speak of defences at all. Charles Greenstreet Addison's treatise on the law of torts, first published in 1860, gives no space at all to defences as such. Contributory negligence is dealt with in passing as a rule of causation with roots in Roman law and a well-established pedigree in nineteenth-century common law, and it is recognised that a master owes no duty to his servant in respect of dangers which were or ought to have been known to the servant;[36] but these are treated as no more than atomised rules in the highly fragmented context of liability for negligence rather than as connected doctrines in a broadly principled tort.[37] Case law shows that the maxim *volenti non fit iniuria* was well known—it was found already in Bracton in the thirteenth century and could be traced back to Roman law and canon law—but it was a maxim of general application rather than a defence which had any particular role in the law of tort. It is found far more commonly as a justification for the denial of an adulterous husband's petition for judicial separation on the grounds of his wife's adultery, for example, than it is as an explanation of the unavailability of a remedy in tort; and when it is found in the tortious context it is simply as a Latinised explanation of the narrow rule that a master was not liable to his servants for known dangers[38] or of the 'defence' of contributory negligence.[39]

The end point for this historical treatment of defences has to be the Judicature Acts of 1873 and 1875 and the Rules of Court made under them.[40] Order XIX Rule 20, amplifying Order XIX Rule 17, laid down that the defendant in his defence must deny specifically all allegations made by the claimant that he did not admit, and that that it was no longer sufficient simply to deny generally the elements of the claim. This was the corollary of the basic principle specified in Order XIX Rule 18, that all grounds of defence or reply must be raised by the defendant's pleadings and that the material facts on which reliance was to be placed must be alleged expressly if there was a risk of the opposing party being surprised at trial. It followed from this that the defendant's plea must always state the grounds on which the claimant's claim was being opposed, and that there was no clear distinction which could be drawn formally between the denial of an element in the claimant's case and the raising of a defence to it. It was not possible to rely on the rules of pleading to determine whether something was strictly speaking a defence or not. Hence, writing in 1894, Charles Warren could say that a defendant in an action of negligence had two distinct defences: to deny that his act was the cause of the damage complained of, and

[36] CG Addison, *Wrongs and their Remedies: Being a Treatise on the Law of Torts* (London, V and R Stevens and Sons, 1860) 249.

[37] For the fragmentation of negligence liability in the nineteenth century, see my 'The Tort of Negligence in the Common Law in the Nineteenth and Twentieth Centuries' in EJH Schrage (ed), *Negligence: The Comparative Legal History of the Law of Torts* (Berlin, Duncker & Humblot, 2001) 241–43.

[38] See, eg, *Bird v Holbrook* (1828) 4 Bing 628; 130 ER 911; *Skipp v The Eastern Counties Railway Co* (1853) 9 Ex 223; 156 ER 95; *Potter v Faulkner* (1861) 1 B&S 800; 121 ER 911.

[39] *Senior v Ward* (1859) 1 El & El 385; 120 ER 954; *Clarke v Holmes* (1862) 7 H & N 937; 158 ER 751.

[40] Supreme Court of Judicature Act 1873, Supreme Court of Judicature Amendment Act 1875. References are to the rules contained in the first schedule of the latter Act. See the analysis and discussion in WT Charley, *The New System of Practice and Pleading under the Supreme Court of Judicature Acts 1873, 1875, 1877*, 3rd edn (London, Waterlow and Sons Ltd, 1877).

to deny the duty alleged.[41] Contributory negligence fell within the former, since it was based on the assertion that the claimant was the legal cause of the injury rather than the defendant, while *volenti non fit iniuria* fell within the latter since it effectively denied that the defendant was under any duty. The meaning of 'defence' in a claim of negligence was, therefore, very fuzzy. At the one extreme it could be said that there were no defences, since anything said by the defendant was tantamount to a denial of an element of the claimant's claim, while at the other extreme it could be said that anything that could be pleaded by the defendant was a defence. The scene was set for the lack of coherence and uniformity in the treatment of defences in tort in the twentieth century.[42]

[41] C Warren, '*Volenti Non Fit Injuria* in Actions of Negligence' (1894) 8 *Harvard Law Review* 457, 458.
[42] J Goudkamp, *Tort Law Defences* (Oxford, Hart Publishing, 2013) 1–11.

3

Defining 'Defences'

LUÍS DUARTE D'ALMEIDA*

1. INTRODUCTION

James Goudkamp's very clear and instructive *Tort Law Defences* opens on a methodological note:[1]

> The word 'defence' bears numerous meanings in the tort law context, and a considerable amount of confusion has been spawned by the widespread failure of legal scholars, judges and legislators to indicate what they mean by the word. This situation is a significant impediment to clear thinking in relation to tort law generally. Accordingly, it is essential to begin the analysis by distinguishing the several senses in which the word 'defence' is used in the tort law context and specifying clearly how it will be used in this book.

We should define our terms. But failure to specify what we mean by the word is not the main obstacle to thinking clearly about defences. We also need to avoid confusion about how 'defence' should be defined to begin with. Of course, we are free to choose to use the term in any way we like. But not all choices are equally fit for purpose, and some choices can even defeat the purpose. Theoretical accounts of defences seem to be particularly vulnerable to that risk. The problem is by no means exclusive to tort law defences; but it is here that we now find the best example of how the adoption of an ill-considered working definition of 'defence' can thwart one's efforts to throw light on the topic. The example I have in mind is Goudkamp's own attempt to give an account of defences. It will be my focus in this chapter.

2. 'SENSES' OF 'DEFENCES'

Goudkamp identifies five 'senses' or 'meanings' of the word, and adopts one of them. I will be concerned throughout this chapter with four of these five 'senses'. The crucial sense in which the term should be taken at the outset of a study of defences, however, is absent from Goudkamp's list. He ignores it at his own peril. Or so I will argue.

* I am very grateful to Frederick Wilmot-Smith and James Goudkamp for their helpful comments on an earlier draft.

[1] J Goudkamp, *Tort Law Defences* (Oxford, Hart Publishing, 2013) 1.

Here are Goudkamp's first two senses of the word:[2]

The first sense

First, the word 'defence' is sometimes used to refer to any argument made by the defendant with the aim of persuading the court to hold that he is not liable. So understood, the word 'defence' encompasses denials by the defendant of one or more of the elements of the tort in which the claimant sues.

The second sense

In a second and stricter sense, the word 'defence' refers only to rules that, when enlivened, result in a verdict for the defendant even though all of the ingredients of the tort in which the claimant sues are present … Denials of the elements of the tort in which the claimant sues do not qualify as defences when the word 'defence' is used in this way. Only rules such as limitation bars, public necessity and self-defence qualify. A defendant who relies on any of these rules seeks to avoid liability not by denying the claimant's allegations but by going around them.[3]

Things seem clear enough. In its first sense, 'defence' is an all-encompassing term applying to any circumstance which, if raised and successfully established, will mandate a verdict against the claimant. What holds these circumstances together as a set is their common legal effect. In the second sense, the term applies to only a subset of such circumstances: it does not include 'denials of the elements of the tort in which the claimant sues'. The second sense is the one that Goudkamp adopts in his book.

It is true that these are two senses in which the word is ordinarily used, and 'defences' in the second sense are typically contrasted with 'denials' of 'elements' of torts. But this fact about our linguistic uses does not tell us that there is any important distinction between these two subsets of relevant circumstances. Perhaps there is no deeper difference underlying the terminological partition. Perhaps our best theoretical account of defences will show that there is no relevant line to draw between 'denials' and 'defences'. Indeed, a central goal of a theory of defences is to investigate whether the familiar denials/defences contrast is substantively warranted. If there is a difference, a theory of defences should explain what the difference is.

Could it plausibly be suggested that 'defences' in the second sense really do boil down to 'denials'? Of course it could. Consider another of Goudkamp's 'senses' of the word—this is the fifth on his list:[4]

The fifth sense

It is sometimes asserted that the absence of defences is the final element of certain torts or of all torts. John Fleming used the word 'defence' in this way. He asserted that the action in negligence consists in five elements, the fifth of which was the absence of any defences. In a similar vein, the Restatement (Second) of Torts organises the action in negligence into four elements, the last of which is the inapplicability of any defences. Perhaps the most striking usage of the term 'defence' in this sense is found in the writings of John Wigmore. Wigmore argued that all torts have three elements: a damage element, a responsibility element and a defences or 'excuse or justification' element.

[2] ibid 2 (footnote omitted).
[3] ibid.
[4] ibid 5 (footnotes omitted).

Goudkamp has some odd remarks to make about this fifth 'sense' of 'defences'. Before I get to those, however, several points need clarification. *What*, exactly, does the word refer to in this fifth 'sense'? Goudkamp's syntactically equivocal description does not help us with this question. Indeed the question is misplaced. Despite what Goudkamp says, the view he reports here does not bring out a different usage or 'sense' of the word 'defence'. It is not as if there is something that can be identified as 'the final element' of an action in tort, and those authors happen to be using the word 'defence' to refer to *that*. Rather, what those authors hold is that defences are *best understood as* denials of an essential element of an action in tort. This is a theoretical claim about defences. The word 'defence' is obviously being used in some sense. But it is not *ipso facto* being used in any new, *sui generis* way.[5]

In fact the opposite is true. What the authors mentioned by Goudkamp maintain is that those circumstances commonly referred to as 'defences' *in a sense much like Goudkamp's second sense* are logically equivalent to those circumstances commonly referred to as 'denials'. Why are denials and defences equivalent? Because—think these authors—both amount to the negation that all the elements required for the claimant to succeed are present. Call this the 'incorporationist' view of defences.[6] It is a theoretical view about the relation between denials and defences. It will be discussed in the next section; but the point now is that whoever wishes to take issue with the incorporationist view must use the relevant terms in the same sense.

Goudkamp misses this point. He writes that 'unlike the second meaning', this fifth 'usage ... does not regard defences as rules that stand outside of the elements of the tort in which the claimant sues'.[7] But if 'regard[ing] defences as rules that stand outside of the elements of the tort in which the claimant sues' means rejecting the incorporationist view of defences, then the 'second meaning' entails no such thing. We can use 'defence' in the second sense—to refer to a particular subset of the circumstances on whose presence or absence the claimant's success depends—while remaining perfectly neutral with regard to the question whether denials and defences are logically equivalent (as the incorporationist maintains). Indeed we can use 'defence' in the second sense—we can use the words 'denials' and 'defences' to refer to the two subsets of relevant circumstances—and *endorse* incorporationism, maintaining that the two labels fail to track any deeper distinction of kinds of circumstances. Or we may think the incorporationist view is mistaken. But then it is our task to refute it. We can't simply define it away.

[5] An example may help to clarify the difference between using a term '*x*' in a specific sense and making a theoretical claim about some object called '*x*' (in some sense of the term). Suppose I say that 'a right is an entitlement to an action or omission by someone else' and you say that 'a right is the mere absence of a duty'. We are using the term 'right' in different senses. I am using the term 'right' to refer to a Hohfeldian claim-right, whereas you are using it to refer to a Hohfeldian liberty. We are not disagreeing. Each of us could accept the other's claim. But now suppose I say that 'a right is the correlative of a duty'. By saying this I am not using the term 'right' in a *third* sense, to refer to something which is neither a Hohfeldian claim-right nor a Hohfeldian liberty. Rather, I am making a point about what a right *in the sense of a Hohfeldian claim-right* involves. So I am using the term 'right' in the *same* sense in which I used it in my assertion that 'a right is an entitlement to an action or omission by someone else'.

[6] See my paper 'A Proof-Based Account of Legal Exceptions' (2012) 33 *OJLS* 133.

[7] Goudkamp (n 1) 5.

3. THE INCORPORATIONIST CHALLENGE

Part of the problem is that Goudkamp seems to think that incorporationism is a view so extraordinarily absurd that it dispenses refutation:[8]

> The fifth meaning of the word 'defence' is downright bizarre. It is doubtful whether those who use the word in this way really intended to do so. The idea that the absence of defences constitutes the final *element* of actions in tort (as opposed to the final *question* to be asked in deciding whether liability should be imposed) simply does not enjoy support in the case law. It is notable that those who claim that the absence of defences is the final element of torts do not cite any authorities that endorse this position. The fifth meaning of the word 'defence' should be assiduously avoided.

On the contrary, there is nothing bizarre about 'the idea that the absence of defences constitutes the final *element* of actions in tort'; nor is it in the least notable that those who adopt that idea 'do not cite any authorities that endorse this position'. Take Goudkamp's main exemplar of this supposedly unfounded view of defences: Wigmore's analysis of 'tort-relations'.[9] Wigmore offers what he terms a 'tripartite division of the tort relation', distinguishing:[10]

> *first*, the Damage element, *i.e.* the various kinds of harm, corporal, social, proprietary, and other, which the law recognizes as the subject of a recovery; *secondly*, the Responsibility element, *i.e.* the principles which determine whether, under given circumstances, a particular person is to be held responsible for the infliction of one of these kinds of legal harm; and *thirdly*, the Excuse or Justification element, *i.e.* the conditions in which no legal liability is recognized, even though there may exist a conceded or assumed responsibility for a conceded or assumed harm.

Wigmore's tripartite arrangement is evidently being put forth as a means of promoting our understanding of this branch of law:[11]

> [A]s to method, the fundamental idea [underlying the tripartite division] is, not to follow fancy not to force a symmetrical grouping, but, neglecting accidents of appearance and surface differences, to examine reasons and causes, to ascertain the intrinsic meaning of principles and the considerations actually treated as controlling decisions, and thus at once to reach a scientific and natural basis of grouping, as well as to indicate the true lines of argument and discussion on which the development of principles must proceed.

It is relative to these purposes that Wigmore's systematisation stands to be assessed. It may hinder more than it helps. It may fail adequately to represent all relevant aspects of the 'tort relation'. It may be fruitless or otherwise unserviceable as a theo-

[8] ibid 6 (emphases in the original; footnote omitted).

[9] Goudkamp asserts, as we saw, that 'perhaps the most striking usage of the term "defence" in this sense is found in the writings of John Wigmore': cf the passage accompanying n 4 above. In the two essays by Wigmore that Goudkamp cites, however, the term 'defence' is actually *never* used (except to refer to varieties of self-defence and self-redress, which of course is an entirely different matter.) See JH Wigmore, 'The Tripartite Division of Torts' (1894) 8 *Harvard Law Review* 200; JH Wigmore, 'A General Analysis of Tort-Relations' (1895) 8 *Harvard Law Review* 377.

[10] Wigmore, 'A General Analysis of Tort-Relations' (n 9) 377.

[11] ibid.

retical model.[12] But what is the point of asking for *authority* supporting the use of a novel scheme of classification and analysis?

Nor should we be puzzled by Wigmore's qualification of the absence of justificatory or exculpatory circumstances as 'elements' of torts. First, it is abundantly clear that Wigmore is using 'tort'—or 'tort-relation'—to refer to the conjunction of all the circumstances that have to be in place if the claimant is to succeed on the merits.[13] But more importantly—labels aside—that basic aspect of Wigmore's analysis does look quite plausible; and it seems to me that despite his protests, Goudkamp is rationally committed to endorsing it.

I can illustrate these claims by a simple example. Consider the tort of battery. Let us agree for the sake of argument that (as Goudkamp explicitly holds)[14] 'battery' is to be defined without reference to defences. In other words, let us agree that absence of defences is *not* an 'element' of the tort of battery. And let us moreover say that 'battery' can be analysed into a number of 'elements' *a*, *b*, *c*. (As in criminal law, where offences are often broken down into 'elements', this is common terminology.) Now is it sufficient that *a*, *b*, and *c*, the elements of the tort of battery, be established for the claim to succeed on the merits? The answer is obviously negative. If any one of the admissible defences happens also to be established—for example, if it is shown that the defendant acted in self-defence—the claimant will fail. If we use '*x*', '*y*' and '*z*' to stand for the admissible defences, we can articulate the following representation of the conditions on which a verdict for the claimant ('*VC*') depends:

If *a* **and** *b* **and** *c* **and** *not x* **and** *not y* **and** *not z*, **then** *VC*

This is a simple descriptive model of the circumstances that have to be in place for the claimant to succeed on the merits. Under this model, as we can see, (a) each one of the elements of the tort—*a*, *b*, *c*—has to be present; and (b) each one of the admissible defences—*x*, *y*, *z*—has to be absent. That is meant to replicate the way in which the two kinds of circumstances operate in law. It certainly matches Goudkamp's view of the role of defences as circumstances that 'result in a verdict for the defendant even though all of the ingredients [ie the 'elements'] of the tort in which the claimant sue are present'.[15] Goudkamp should agree, given what he tells us, that this is a satisfactory model. Under this model, however, the absence or negation of each admissible defence—'*not x*', '*not y*', '*not z*'—is shown to play *precisely* the same role as the presence or assertion of each element—'*a*', '*b*', '*c*'—of the tort. There is no difference in function between the two subsets of relevant circumstances. The members of the subset {*not x*, *not y*, *not z*} are—just like the members of the subset {*a*, *b*, *c*}—'elements' proper *of the condition* of *VC*.

[12] Goudkamp does discuss a few aspects of Wigmore's taxonomy: see Goudkamp (n 1) 155–57.

[13] That Wigmore is using 'tort' in this partly stipulated sense—a sense which does not coincide with Goudkamp's narrower use of the word to refer to only *some* of Wigmore's 'elements'—is made clear in many passages. For example: 'the failure of the reader to accept the analysis thus briefly set forth need not prejudice the validity of what is now to be said, for it has been given only that the scope of the relations *included by the writer under Torts* may not be misunderstood': Wigmore, 'The Tripartite Division of Torts' (n 9) 201. See also n 28 below: Glanville Williams's point about the 'ambiguity and question-begging tendency of the word "offence"' could also have been made by Wigmore with regard to the word 'tort'.

[14] See Goudkamp (n 1) 106–07.

[15] ibid 2.

Yet this view—a view that Goudkamp cannot but endorse—is exactly what proponents of incorporationism, as I proposed to call it, characteristically promote. And if, following Wigmore, one chooses to coin and use the label 'Tort-relation' to designate the conjunction of all those 'elements', the claim that the absence of a defence is an 'element' of that relation—on a par with the ingredients of the tort itself—is anything but bizarre. Goudkamp may dislike the label, but that is really what his supposed disagreement with Wigmore boils down to. *De nominibus non est disputandum.*

This is not the last of Goudkamp's worries. His implicit commitment to the simple incorporationist model casts a dark shadow over his own view of tort law defences. Perhaps sensing trouble, Goudkamp claims that Wigmore's analysis 'would require claimants to disprove defences'.[16] This is untrue as well as uncharitable, given Wigmore's explicit remark that his tripartite systematisation does not neatly map onto any particular distribution of probatory burdens:[17]

> As a rule certain principles of pleading are based on the distinction between [the third 'element', ie absence of 'excuse or justification'] and the first and the second [elements, namely 'damage' and 'responsibility'], throwing on the defendant the business of making out the existence and the application of these limitations. For example, justifications for a battery and privileges for defamation are left to the defendant to urge. Sometimes, however, the principles of pleading cannot be relied upon to show in this way the line of distinction. For instance, in actions for malicious prosecution, these tertiary limitations vindicate or exempt the defendant, if he brought the suit upon reasonable or probable ground and without malice; nevertheless, it is the plaintiff who is required to show that this reasonable or probable ground did not exist,—a sensible requirement which we must not allow to obscure the true nature of this element.

Why then does Goudkamp's commitment to the incorporationist model clash with his explicitly held views on defences? Goudkamp is convinced that there *is* a 'fundamental difference'[18] between the ingredients of torts—elements '*a*', '*b*', and '*c*'—in the simple incorporationist model described above—and the absence of valid defences—elements '*not x*', '*not y*', and '*not z*'. He thinks that to deny an element of the tort in which the claimant is suing is something significantly distinct from invoking a defence—and that this difference 'is one of the most basic organising devices in tort law'.[19] But then he owes us an explanation of what, precisely, that difference is. For what the simple incorporationist model seems to show is precisely that there is *no* difference—no formal or structural or logical difference at any rate. A defendant who denies an element of the tort in which the claimant sues—arguing, for example, that element *a* is *not the case*—seems to be doing exactly the same as a defendant who invokes a defence—arguing, for example, that element *not x* is *not the case*. Both are seeking to establish the *absence* of an element on which the claimant's success depends. So—asks the incorporationist—where is the difference?

[16] ibid 5.

[17] Wigmore 'The Tripartite Division of Torts' (n 9) 207–08. The fact that elsewhere Goudkamp quotes part of this very passage makes his criticism even harder to understand; see Goudkamp (n 1) 47–48.

[18] Goudkamp (n 1) 6.

[19] ibid 5.

(Can it be that the ingredients of torts are 'positive' elements, described in terms of what has to *be the case* ('*a*', '*b*', '*c*'), whereas absence-of-defence elements are 'negative' elements, described in terms of what has *not* to be the case ('*not x*', '*not y*', '*not z*')? That cannot be the difference: there is nothing conceptually suspicious to the idea that torts can have positive as well as negative elements.)[20]

To see just how deep this worry runs, let us briefly turn our attention to the criminal law, where an analogue distinction between offence elements and defences is commonly taken to be, as Goudkamp puts it, a 'central feature'.[21] Yet here, too, the incorporationist view has prominent proponents. Glanville Williams is perhaps the best known. Williams argued that there is 'no intrinsic difference between the elements of an offence and an exception (or defence) to that offence':[22]

> [A] rule that is subject to an exception is only partly true if it is stated without the exception ... The exception is, rationally regarded, part and parcel of the rule. Hence looking for the line between a rule and an exception is, to use the proverbial simile, like looking in a dark room for a black cat that isn't there. There are no characteristic features of exceptions: 'exceptions' are merely linguistic constructs. Since they lack any specific definition, the negative of an element of an offence can be regarded as an exception, and the negative of an exception can be regarded as an element of the offence.[23]

Given that 'all the exceptions (or defences) can be stated in negative form as part of the offence, instead of as something outside the offences', the 'offence package' consisting of 'the offence elements and the negative of defences' is, says Williams, an 'indivisible whole'.[24]

Goudkamp mentions and briefly discusses this claim.[25] He thinks that Williams's incorporationism is falsified by Kenneth Campbell's influential view—Goudkamp calls it the 'practical conflicts thesis'—that offence definitions 'describe acts that [according to law] one has a *prima facie* reason not to perform' and defences 'specify circumstances in which [according to law] the *prima facie* reasons against engaging in the behaviour described in the offence definition are outweighed by opposing reasons'.[26]

[20] Goudkamp agrees: see, for example, his discussion of consent as a *denial* rather than a defence in the context of the tort of battery (which means 'that non-consent is an element of the tort of battery'): Goudkamp (n 1) 65ff.

[21] ibid 5. Goudkamp draws attention to 'the many fundamental similarities between tort law and the criminal law in so far as their defence regimes are concerned', and notes that his own account of tort law defences draws on 'criminal law writing': cf ibid 25–26. I discuss criminal law defences in L Duarte d'Almeida, '"O Call Me Not to Justify the Wrong": Criminal Answerability and the Offence/Defence Distinction' (2012) 6 *Criminal Law and Philosophy* 227.

[22] G Williams, 'The Logic of Exceptions' (1988) 47 *CLJ* 261, 277.

[23] ibid 278.

[24] ibid 280.

[25] Goudkamp (n 1) 42–43. Since Williams's view is effectively the same as Wigmore's, it is puzzling that Goudkamp should agree that the former has some standing as a view worth debating, but think that the latter can be dismissed as 'utterly bizarre'.

[26] ibid 43. See K Campbell, 'Offence and Defence' in IH Dennis (ed), *Criminal Law and Justice* (London, Sweet and Maxwell, 1987) 73–86; and cf also J Gardner, *Offences and Defences: Selected Essays in the Philosophy of Criminal Law* (Oxford, Oxford University Press, 2007) 77–79, 96, 144–45; and RA Duff, *Answering for Crime: Responsibility and Liability in the Criminal Law* (Oxford, Hart Publishing 2007) 35, 216–19.

But Goudkamp is mistaken about this as well. Campbell's 'practical conflicts thesis' is consistent with Williams's incorporationism. Williams is making the 'logical' point, as he calls it, that 'there are no exceptions as self-subsisting concepts': 'an exception distinct from a rule is inconceivable'.[27] The absence of defences is therefore just as much an 'element' of the rule setting out the substantive conditions of criminal liability as are the elements of what is strictly called the 'offence'. Both subsets of circumstances are elements of the broader 'offence package'.[28] Self-defence, for example, is 'impliedly incorporated' in 'negative form' into each of the crimes in which it is a valid defence; in other words, the absence of self-defence is 'a negative element of the crime, just as the woman's non-consent is a negative element of rape'.[29] How is this 'logical' view in any way contradicted by the claim that some of the elements of a crime—namely, the ingredients of offences in the strict sense—describe actions which according to law we have prima facie reason not to perform, and that some other elements of a crime—namely, the elements whose denial we call a 'defence'—negate that those prima facie reasons are outweighed by opposing reasons?

Note, moreover, that there is no reason why a 'practical conflicts' account of differences among elements of a crime should necessarily map onto the ordinary partition of those elements into 'defences' and 'offences' *stricto sensu*. Consider, for example, the role of consent in rape. Goudkamp believes that the 'practical conflicts' view:[30]

> explain[s] why the criminal law counts the absence of consent as an element of the offence of rape as opposed to treating it as a defence. Were consent a defence to rape, that would imply that there is [according to the law] a *prima facie* reason to refrain from sexual intercourse *tout court*. Because there is no such reason, at least according to our sexual morality, this is why criminal law builds non-consent into the definition of rape.

But this is a *non sequitur*. It is perfectly possible to hold the view that *there is* a prima facie reason to refrain from sexual intercourse *tout court*, but simultaneously and consistently maintain that absence of consent should be an element of the criminal offence (*stricto sensu*) of rape (as opposed to consent being a defence); and vice versa.[31]

Goudkamp refers to incorporationism as a 'minority view', proposed by Williams and defended only by a 'small number of theorists'.[32] This misrepresents the field. The claim 'the absence of a valid defence' is 'the third basic element of every crime'—alongside the 'external' and the 'mental' elements—is pretty

[27] Williams (n 22) 279.

[28] Williams' 'offence package'—a term he introduces 'to avoid the ambiguity and question-begging tendency of the word "offence"—is analogous to Wigmore's 'Tort-relation'. It encompasses *both* the elements of offences *stricto sensu* and the absence of defences. See ibid 280.

[29] ibid 278–79. See also G Williams, 'Offences and Defences' (1982) 2 *Legal Studies* 233, 237–39 and 247–49.

[30] Goudkamp (n 1) 43 (footnote omitted).

[31] On this very point, see MM Dempsey and J Herring, 'Why Sexual Penetration Requires Justification' (2007) 27 *OJLS* 467, 470f.

[32] Goudkamp (n 1) 42.

mainstream textbook stuff.[33] In the context of jurisprudential discussions, likewise, incorporationism has lost none of its appeal, and is perhaps *the* dominant account of so-called 'explicit' defences.[34]

In any event—whether or not many people support it—the worry remains: if incorporationism is right, it calls into question the view that there is a 'fundamental' or 'basic' distinction between torts and defences (to use Goudkamp's adjectives) upon which the law of torts is 'built'.[35]

4. A WORKING DEFINITION OF 'DEFENCES'

It is important not to misunderstand the nature of the challenge set out in the previous section. No doubt there is something unsatisfactory about the incorporationist account of defences. It may be difficult to put our finger on it (and I say more on the topic below); but we do seem to have reason to hypothesise—pre-theoretically—that the distinction between elements of torts and defences does track some basic structural feature of tort law. We do, as lawyers, ordinarily speak as if there is a distinction between 'denials' and 'defences'; we seem to think that there is such a distinction; some might say we support this hypothesis 'intuitively'. Still, it is but a pre-theoretical hypothesis: one that stands to be either confirmed or refuted—and which can only be confirmed or refuted by a theoretical account of defences. But although we should remain open to the possibility that a fully worked-out theory of defences will reveal that there is really no significant difference between 'denials' and 'defences' after all, we certainly have reason to adopt as our starting point an ostensive working definition of 'defence' that tracks that common linguistic usage, reserving the word to refer only to circumstances whose absence cannot be construed as a 'denial' of the elements of a tort *stricto sensu*. That does not mean, as we shall see, that our working definition should coincide with Goudkamp's 'second sense' of the word. It shouldn't. But for now the point is that the adoption of a working definition is merely a way of identifying the object of a theoretical account yet to be developed.

[33] See, eg, AP Simester, JR Spencer, GR Sullivan and GJ Virgo, *Simester and Sullivan's Criminal Law: Theory and Doctrine*, 5th edn (Oxford, Hart Publishing, 2013) 18–20.

[34] For endorsements of the incorporationist strategy, see, for example, JL Mackie, 'Responsibility and Language' (1955) 33 *Australasian Journal of Philosophy* 143, 146–47; G Nakhnikian, 'Contemporary Ethical Theories and Jurisprudence' (1957) 2 *Natural Law Forum* 4, 26; MS Moore, 'The Semantics of Judging' (1981) 54 *Southern California Law Review* 151, 238; M Martin, *The Legal Philosophy of H.L.A. Hart: A Critical Appraisal* (Philadelphia, Temple University Press, 1987) 119–20; RE Susskind, *Expert Systems in Law* (Oxford, Clarendon Press, 1987) 196; MD Bayles, *Hart's Legal Philosophy* (London, Kluwer, 1992) 12; RHS Tur, 'Subjectivism and Objectivism: Towards Synthesis' in S Shute, J Gardner and J Horder (eds), *Action and Value in Criminal Law* (Oxford, Clarendon Press, 1993) 214f; N MacCormick, 'Defeasibility in Law and Logic' in Z Bańkowski, I White and U Hahn (eds), *Informatics and the Foundations of Legal Reasoning* (London, Kluwer, 1995) 100; F Atria, *On Law and Legal Reasoning* (Oxford, Hart Publishing, 2001) 124f, 137f; RHS Tur, 'Defeasibilism' (2001) 21 *OJLS* 355, 359f, 367; or W Waluchow, 'Defeasibility and Legal Positivism' in J Ferrer Beltrán and GB Ratti (eds), *The Logic of Legal Requirements: Essays on Defeasibility* (Oxford, Oxford University Press, 2012) 260. Even Hart—who earlier in his career had firmly rejected incorporationism—maintained in *The Concept of Law* that if some overriding factor can be identified as an exception, it can then be 'reduced to [the general] rule': see HLA Hart, *The Concept of Law*, 3rd edn (Oxford, Oxford University Press, 2012 [1961]) 134, 139.

[35] Goudkamp (n 1) 29.

Now as we saw in the previous sections, what incorporationism offers is precisely a theoretical account of defences *in the same sense of the term*. Far from postulating or in any way involving a new sense of the word 'defence', incorporationism starts from the very same working definitions of 'denials' and 'defences': but it offers an argument for the conclusion that there is ultimately no deeper difference between those two subsets of relevant circumstances. So whoever finds incorporationism unsatisfactory—as Goudkamp claims he does—and wishes to insist that our terminological distinction between 'denials' of elements of torts and 'defences' does map on some deeper, basic structure of tort law, faces the challenge of coming up with a *better* theoretical account: an account that displaces incorporationism and vindicates our pre-theoretical judgment that the 'denials'/'defences' distinction is actually something more than a mere matter of convenient labelling. That is why, as noted above, the burden is on Goudkamp for explaining what, precisely, that distinction is, in a way that shows that his account does not collapse into incorporationism.[36]

One might think that there is a natural route that Goudkamp (or anyone else) could explore in order to begin to meet this challenge. Does the difference between denials and defences not become apparent if one considers their contrasting probatory behaviour? Unless all the elements of a tort (including 'negative' elements like absence of consent) are established, the claimant will fail; but the claimant's success does not similarly depend on the absence of each valid defence being established. Does this not bring out an important structural disanalogy between the elements of torts and the absence of defences? And is this not a basic difference which the simple incorporationist model simply fails to capture, given that it treats negative elements of torts as structurally equivalent to the absence of valid defences?

But Goudkamp pointedly refuses to take this route. Consider the following passage, describing what he thinks is yet another possible 'sense'—the fourth in his catalogue—of the word 'defence':[37]

> *The fourth sense*
>
> [A] defence is sometimes said to be a rule the applicability of which is for the defendant to prove. Tony Weir used the word 'defence' in this way when he wrote: 'Contributory negligence is unquestionably a defence … [since] it is for the defendant to plead and prove it.' So did the current editor of *Winfield & Jolowicz* when he said that arrest and certain other pleas that may be raised in the context of false imprisonment 'are defences in the true sense, that is to say, it is for the defendant to raise and to establish them'.

Once again it seems to me mistaken—or at least misleading—to isolate this as a distinct 'sense' or 'meaning' of the term. One could of course decide to use the word 'defence' to refer to any circumstance (a) the establishment of which mandates a verdict for the defendant, but (b) the non-establishment of which is not required as

[36] To be perfectly clear, the burden is not to make a *normative* case for the distinction. The burden is to explain—at a purely descriptive level—what the difference actually *is*. Incorporationism is not a normative thesis about the absence of good reasons for law to draw the distinction. Rather, it is a descriptive thesis stating that *there is* no such distinction drawn in law. The incorporationist model is meant to be a descriptively accurate representation of law. That is why the burden on anyone who disagrees is to give an account of what, precisely, the difference between 'denials' and 'defences' is. It is not sufficient to assert baldly that the difference exists, and that it is of great importance.

[37] Goudkamp (n 1) 3.

a condition of the claimant's success. But there is a far more plausible reading of the claim that Goudkamp reports in the passage just quoted. It can be read as a candidate *account* of those circumstances we refer to as 'defences' under our working definition of the term. It can be read, that is, as an alternative to incorporationism. We can call it the burden-of-proof account of defences. It says that defences are circumstances, the establishment of which burdens the defendant, rather than circumstances, the establishment of the negation of which 'burdens' the claimant. It is an alternative to incorporationism because, first, it is concerned with the same explanatory task (the task of providing an account of defences *in the same sense of the word*); but, second, it offers an explanation of the 'denial'/'defence' divide that—differently from incorporationism—vindicates our pre-theoretical hypothesis that the two classes of circumstances are importantly different.

But consider some of Goudkamp's comments on his fourth supposed 'sense' of 'defences' and on how it differs from the second sense (which, as noted above, he adopts):[38]

> It is possible to illuminate the difference between the second and fourth senses in which the word 'defence' is used by considering limitation bars. A limitation bar is a defence in the second identified sense (it is a rule that defeats liability that is external to the elements of the claimant's action) but it is not (at least in England) a defence on the fourth meaning of the word. It is not a defence in the fourth sense of the word because, rightly or wrongly, once a limitation bar is put in issue by the defendant, the claimant bears the onus of showing that the action was brought in time. In the words of the English Law Commission, 'the claimant has the burden of disproving a limitation defence where the defendant has pleaded one'. This reveals the difference between the second and fourth definitions of the word 'defence'. The difference exists because rules that are defences in the second sense of the word do not always need to be established by the defendant.

And further ahead, explaining why he doesn't favour using the term in the fourth 'sense':[39]

> It is difficult to support using the word 'defence' in the fourth identified way. A major problem with saying that defences are rules in respect of which the defendant carries the burden of proof is that it draws within its net many rules that no one would intentionally count as defences. Foreign matter that is identified as defences on this meaning of the word includes the very many procedural rules the applicability of which must be established by the defendant. Such rules encompass the provisions that enable defendants to obtain security for their costs, to obtain accelerated service of a claim form and to amend their pleadings after service. To apply the term 'defence' to any of these rules would be a gross distortion of language.

The objection in this second passage seems to me to miss its mark. To claim that 'defences are rules in respect of which the defendant carries the burden of proof' is to say that if something is a defence, then it is for the defendant to establish it. That is evidently the idea underlying the remarks of those authors Goudkamp quotes as adopters of the 'fourth meaning' of 'defences'. In this passage, however, Goudkamp fallaciously converts that conditional, attacking the very different claim that if something is for the defendant to establish, then it is a defence.

[38] ibid 4 (footnote omitted).
[39] ibid 6.

But of course in the first excerpt Goudkamp argues, giving the example of limitation bars, that not all defences are for the defendant to establish. Is that a good point against the burden-of-proof account of defences? Before we answer this question, consider Goudkamp's claim, in the second excerpt, that there are many procedural rules which are clearly not to be counted as defences. That is true. But *why* are such procedural rules 'foreign matter' if our concern is with the topic of defences? Some procedural rules simply have no bearing on whether the verdict in a tort action should be for the claimant or for the defendant; 'provisions that enable defendants to obtain security for their costs' are an example. But that is not true of all rules we would classify as 'procedural'. Think of the rules that enable defendants to challenge a court's jurisdiction. Do we want to say that a defendant who disputes the court's jurisdiction is thereby offering a defence? This is a normative question regarding the domain of circumstances that constitute the subject of a theory of defences. Another way of asking it is this: should our working definition of a 'defence' encompass such rules as those that enable defendants to challenge a court's jurisdiction? Or more broadly: should our working definition of a 'defence' encompass each and every conceivable liability-preventing rule which does not amount to a denial of the 'elements' of a tort? My suggestion will be that the answer must be negative. To see why, we must first learn a bit more about the shortcomings of incorporationism.

We saw in Section 3 that Glanville Williams refers to defences as 'exceptions'. But exceptions to what? To *rules*: his view was that 'a rule that is subject to an exception is only partly true if it is stated without the exception'.[40] What then would a rule look like 'if stated without the exception'? Williams was concerned with the criminal law, and the relevant rules would be those linking a description of some criminal offence with a verdict against the defendant. To use one of his examples, we could say that *as a rule* 'applying force to another is a crime';[41] and self-defence would be an exception *to* this rule. Williams's claim—the incorporationist claim—is that the rule could and should be restated to mention the absence of self-defence (and any other valid exception).

Still, it seems something is lost in the incorporationist move. Let me illustrate the point by another of William's own examples: an 'old squib, written by some English classicist against his German counterparts':[42]

The Germans in Greek
Are badly to seek.
All, save only Hermann—
And Hermann's a German!

[40] See passage quoted above to n 23.

[41] Williams (n 22) 279.

[42] ibid 277–78. This is a corrupted version of an epigram attributed to Richard Porson, who was Regius Professor of Greek at the University of Cambridge between 1792 and 1808. The original (vastly superior) is given with some context in *Facetiae Cantabrigienses*, 3rd edn (London, Charles Mason, 1836) 85 as follows:

The Germans, in Greek,
Are sadly to seek;
Not five in five-score,
But ninety-five more,—
All, save only Herman,
And Herman's a German.

Williams points out that this seems to give rise to a 'paradox':[43]

> Does Hermann lack proficiency in Greek or not? All Germans lack it (premise 1), and we know Hermann is a German, so he does lack it. But he is an exception (premise 2); therefore he does not lack it. Which is true? If we are daft enough, we may begin to think that we have two premises, closely related yet yielding contrary conclusions.

We know what Williams's way out—the incorporationist way out—is:[44]

> The paradox, a puerile one of course, disappears as soon as one realises that an exception modifies the rule. Premise 1 is modified by premise 2, and should be rewritten 'All Germans except Hermann are poor at Greek.' One can no longer argue from premise 1 in its original unqualified form. Hermann does not belong to the class 'Germans except Hermann'.

Williams is right that if Hermann is both a German and not poor at Greek, then the statement 'Germans are poor at Greek' cannot be true if construed as a universal statement (as '*All* Germans are poor at Greek'). But he is wrong to conclude that the only way out of the paradox is to embed the exception into the universal statement (as 'All Germans except Hermann are poor at Greek'). Another way out would be to insist that the statement 'Germans are poor at Greek' and 'Hermann is not poor at Greek' are *both* true as originally phrased—but that the former is to be understood not as a universal statement but as a statement of what is *generally* the case, of what is true *as a rule*. Such a statement could be used as a premise to license the 'defeasible' inference that this person, *a*, is poor at Greek, whenever we know that *a* is a German *and we have no information about a's identity*. And if we came to learn that *a* is actually Hermann, we would then retract our original conclusion (since Hermann is an exception to our general rule).

That is a popular way of thinking about exceptions and their relation to rules, and it does seem to capture an important feature of our common notion of an exception. As some authors put it, exceptions are in some sense 'external' to the rules *to which* they are exceptions.[45] This is a thought which the simple incorporationist account not only ignores, but is unable to accommodate. Under this alternative account exceptions *cannot* be embedded in finer restatements of the relevant rules. Properly understood and stated, the rule would still read simply as 'Germans are poor at Greek'.

Now it is not by accident that Williams speaks of defences as 'exceptions'. It seems plausible to think of self-defence, say, as an exception to the rule that whoever intentionally assaults another person is guilty of a crime. By contrast, it seems clear that absence of consent is to be embedded as a negative 'element' into the rule regarding rape. This way of seeing things allows us to bring out not only how exceptions differ from denials, but also what both kinds of circumstances have in common. To claim that sexual intercourse is consensual is to *deny* the charge or claim that rape was committed. It is to offer an answer of the plain 'No' variety: 'No, I didn't do it'. To invoke self-defence in a case of assault, on the other hand, is to offer an answer of the 'Yes, but …' variety. But there is an important feature that these two kinds of answers

[43] Williams (n 22) 278.
[44] ibid.
[45] See, eg, CO Finkelstein, 'When the Rule Swallows the Exception' in L Meyer (ed), *Rules and Reasoning: Essays in Honour of Fred Schauer* (Oxford, Hart Publishing, 1999) 507–08.

have in common. It is not merely that answers of both kinds, if successful, will lead to the same consequence of preventing the claimant or prosecutor from succeeding; the point is that answers of both kinds, if successful, will prevent the claimant or prosecutor from succeeding *on the merits*. That is because a rule and its exceptions must both speak to the same issue. If something is to count as an exception to a rule, it must be concerned with the same substantive issue addressed by the rule.

Why is this point important? Because not every circumstance that prevents a claimant from succeeding is a circumstance that prevents him from succeeding on the merits. Above I gave the example of a successful challenge to a court's jurisdiction. The claimant will fail—but not on the merits. Jurisdiction is in no sense an 'element' of the substantive rule on which the claimant grounds his action; nor is lack of jurisdiction *in any sense* an 'exception' to that rule. Rather, jurisdiction is more like a background presupposition that has to be in place before the court can even consider the relative merits of the claimant's case and the defendant's answers.

Background presuppositions and conditions like that are often called 'procedural'. They are not a proper part of the 'substantive' rules and exceptions that govern the merits of an action in tort or crime.[46] That is precisely why they are often not discussed—sometimes they are not even *mentioned*—by authors concerned with providing an account of the 'denial'/'defence' distinction. Take once again Wigmore's tripartite analysis of 'tort-relations'. It is exclusively concerned, as one would expect, with circumstances that bear on the merits of an action in tort. Wigmore's 'Excuse or Justification element',[47] his general category for what we would call 'defences', includes no mention of such procedural circumstances as, say, procedural immunities, lack of jurisdiction, or limitation bars. Again, such factors may still determine that the claimant's action will not succeed. But they remain squarely outwith the universe of circumstances that prevent the claimant from succeeding on the merits even though the elements proper of a tort have been unquestionably established.

So now note that the challenge of providing a theoretical account of the 'denial'/'defence' distinction only arises with regard to those circumstances which do bear on the merits of the action before the court. There is no difficulty in explaining why a lack of procedural requisites will prevent a claimant from succeeding. The real puzzle of defences lies in making sense of the idea that there can be circumstances whose presence will prevent the claimant from succeeding *on the merits*, but the absence of which is not satisfactorily thought of as an 'element' on a par with other circumstances—namely, the elements proper of torts—that similarly bear on the merits of the case. The relevant contrast picked up by the 'denial'/'defence' pair of terms is a contrast between two kinds of substantive (or merits-relative) circumstances. After all, what makes defences stand out as a distinct subset of relevant circumstances can be neither (a) the fact that they mandate a verdict against the claimant

[46] I do not mean to suggest that it is easy to give a precise jurisprudential account of this distinction between 'procedural' conditions and 'substantive' elements that bear on the 'merits' of the action. It is a stock distinction of legal discourse, though, and one I trust I can leave undefined without risking confusing my readers as to what I mean in the context of this chapter. (Goudkamp does the same. He speaks of limitation bars as 'procedural defences', contrasting this notion with that of a rule which is 'concerned with the merits of the claimant's action and is hence a substantive rule': see Goudkamp (n 1) 210.) I say more about this topic in 'Substantive Norms and Substantive Questions' [2014] *Analisi e Diritto* 11.

[47] Wigmore, 'A General Analysis of Tort-Relations' (n 9) 377; see the passage accompanying n 10 above.

(since from the purely consequentialist perspective there is simply no difference between 'denials' and 'defences'); nor (b) the mere 'negative' fact that defences seem not to be reducible to (or explainable in terms of) 'denials' of elements of torts. What makes defences stand out as a distinct subset of relevant circumstances is also (c) the fact that they are *related* to denials in a distinctive way. *That*, then, is the class of circumstances we tend pre-theoretically to think of as importantly different from the class of 'denials': a class of circumstances reducible neither to 'denials' nor to the absence of merely procedural requisites of a claimant's success. That is the class whose distinctiveness it is the task of a theory of defences to clarify. It is therefore the class that a working definition of 'defence' should track.

That is why the answer to the question 'Should our working definition of a "defence" encompass each and every conceivable liability-preventing rule which does not amount to a denial of the "elements" of a tort?' must be—as I said above—'No'. And yet that is precisely the sense in which Goudkamp proposes to use 'defences' himself. He adopts, as we saw, what he calls the 'second sense' of the term. This leaves out denials, of course. But it includes virtually any other factor or argument, substantive or procedural, whose presence will prevent a claimant from succeeding.

Goudkamp thinks that his definition has the merit of not suppressing 'the difference between the claimant's cause of action and liability-defeating rules that are external to the elements of the claimant's action'.[48] He is right about that. But he is wrong that *that* is the distinction that constitutes 'one of the basic organising devices in tort law'.[49] The distinction that is indeed uniformly 'recognised ... throughout the law of obligations', and comparable to the 'corresponding distinction [the offence/defence distinction, which] is also a central feature of the criminal law',[50] is a different one. It is a distinction drawn within the universe of the circumstances that bear on the merits of an action in tort.

It is puzzling that Goudkamp chooses to adopt this widely heterogeneous working definition of 'defence'. His definition is at odds with several general comments he has to make about tort law defences. He claims, for example, that 'defences are second-tier questions':[51]

> The first major question that a court trying a tort action needs to consider is whether all of the elements of the tort in which the claimant sues are present. A court should ask whether a defence applies only if it decides that all of the elements of the relevant tort exist.

This sounds plausible but only if one rejects Goudkamp's 'second sense' and takes the relevant class of 'defences' to range only over substantive, merits-relative considerations. Indeed when expanding on what he calls the 'temporal logic' of tort law Goudkamp writes that:[52]

> [t]ort law is structured so that trial judges should deal with certain issues in a prescribed sequence. It is necessary to grasp this logic in order to understand how defences fit into

48 Goudkamp (n 1) 5.
49 ibid.
50 ibid.
51 ibid 10.
52 ibid 13 (emphases added). Here Goudkamp makes the common mistake of conflating logical and chronological priority; see Duarte d'Almeida (n 21) at 230ff.

> tort law's framework. The first matter with which a trial court should deal is whether a tort has been committed. If no tort has been committed, judgment should be entered for the defendant. *No other substantive issues* arise for consideration. If however, all of the elements of a tort are in place, the court should ask whether a defence is applicable. If a defence is engaged, the court should rule in favour of the defendant. *All other substantive issues* fall away.

Yes; and yet Goudkamp's 'defences', in the 'second sense', encompass such non-substantive issues as whether limitation bars have expired: issues that are obviously not 'second-tier'. In fact they are not even 'first-tier'. They are conditions without which a court will not be able to even begin to address—at any rate to address in a consequential way—the 'first-tier' issue of whether 'all of the elements of the relevant tort exist'.

My suggestion is, not simply that as a matter of sound methodology, a working definition of 'defence' should track only merits-relative liability-defeating considerations that are not 'denials'. My suggestion is also that that is the best way of either reading or reconstructing much of the existing theoretical literature on defences. That brings me back to my conjecture that a burden-of-proof account of the 'denials'/'defences' distinction may well be on the right track. It also brings me back to the related discussion of Goudkamp's fourth sense of 'defences'. At one point Goudkamp bemoans Goldberg and Zipursky for 'confusingly' using the word 'defence' in two 'different ways' in the narrow space of two sentences:[53]

> The distinction between the second and the fourth meanings of the word 'defence' is harder to spot [than the distinction between the fourth and the first meanings] and many tort scholars have failed to notice it. Consider the following passage in John Goldberg and Benjamin Zipursky's *The Oxford Introductions to US Law: Torts*:
>
> 'Affirmative defences are legally recognized grounds for defeating liability even when a legal wrong has been committed. To treat these grounds as affirmative defences is to say that it is the defendant's burden, rather than the plaintiff's, to raise them in court pleadings and to prove them.'
>
> Confusingly, Goldberg and Zipursky use the word 'defence' in different ways in this passage. The first sentence adopts the second meaning of the word 'defence', while the second sentence embraces the fourth meaning.

And then, in a passage I already quoted:[54]

> It is possible to illuminate the difference between the second and fourth senses in which the word 'defence' is used by considering limitation bars. A limitation bar is a defence in the second identified sense (it is a rule that defeats liability that is external to the element's of the claimant's action) but it is not (at least in England) a defence in the fourth meaning of the word.

It seems to me that there is no equivocation in the excerpt by Goldberg and Zipursky. It is much more natural to read their claim—that affirmative defences are liability-defeating grounds which it is the defendant's burden to establish—as

[53] Goudkamp (n 1) 4 (footnote omitted); Goudkamp is quoting from JCP Goldberg and BC Zipursky, *Torts* (Oxford, Oxford University Press, 2010) 110.

[54] Goudkamp (n 1) 4; this passage was quoted at greater length at the text accompanying n 38.

an endorsement of the burden-of-proof account of defences. Goudkamp makes the perfectly fair point that in English law it is for claimants to disprove any limitation 'defence' pleaded by the defendant.[55] But this point, though it works as a counter-example to Goldberg and Zipursky's claim, does not undermine the soundness of the burden-of-proof account. The reason Goudkamp's point works as a counterexample to Goldberg and Zipursky's claim is that they do list limitation bars as part of the class of 'affirmative defences'.[56] But that is precisely where they go wrong. Their explanandum, their working definition of an 'affirmative defence', is just too widely carved out. The adoption of a more carefully considered working definition of 'defence' would have left out (for the reasons explained above) such procedural liability-defeating rules as limitations.[57] Goudkamp's counterexample would lose its strength—and the burden-of-proof account would remain at play as an at least prima facie plausible explanation of the 'denial'/'defence' divide.[58]

The irony is that Goudkamp's explanandum is just as widely carved out as Goldberg's and Zipursky's. And while these two authors at least endorse a particular account of defences—the burden-of-proof account—Goudkamp seems in the end to have given us *no* explanation of the 'denials'/'defences' distinction. He often claims that there *is* a significant, 'fundamental' difference between these two subsets of relevant circumstances. He calls it 'one of the oldest and most basic' distinctions upon which tort law is built,[59] and 'one of the most recognisable features of the law of torts'.[60] He insists that the difference should not be 'obscured'. And yet he fails to clarify it himself. He does not offer a positive account of the difference.[61] He has

[55] ibid.

[56] Here is what they write immediately after the passage that Goudkamp quotes: 'Some tort affirmative defences, such as *statute of limitations* defences that bar claims simply for being brought too late, are procedural. Others amount to justifications for conduct that would otherwise be tortious ... Still others take the form of status-based *immunities*'. See Goldberg and Zipursky (n 53) 110.

[57] In a recent piece Eric Descheemaeker makes (if I read him correctly) this same point. Descheemaeker endorses the burden of proof account (although he seems also to endorse incorporationism) and specifies that he is 'only concerned with liability-defining rules': see 'Tort Law Defences: A Defence of Conventionalism' (2014) 77 *MLR* 493, 499 n 19.

[58] In his contribution to this volume, Andrew Burrows faces a similar difficulty. In the face of authority for the proposition that the 'burden of proving limitation is on the claimant', Burrows asks 'What should one make of this'? He considers two possibilities. 'One approach is to conclude that the burden of proof is not a conclusive indicator of whether the law in question is a defence or not'. The alternative and 'preferable' approach 'is to say that the law has here taken a [conceptually] wrong turn'. Neither approach is fully satisfactory; but because Burrows is working with a loosely defined notion of 'defence' there is no other immediately apparent way out. A more carefully defined working definition of 'defence' enables us to be clear that the burden-of-proof account does not apply to limitation or any other procedural liability-defeating rule; a theory of defences is therefore perfectly compatible with the burden of proving limitation being on either claimant or defendant. See A Burrows, 'Some Recurring Issues in Relation to Limitation of Actions', at p 314 in this volume.

[59] Goudkamp (n 1) 28.

[60] ibid 45.

[61] He is prevented from endorsing the burden-of-proof account, since it clearly does not fit with his wide notion; he wants to 'rigorously separate defences from rules the applicability of which it falls to the defendant to prove': cf ibid 35. And yet at several points Goudkamp comments on the close links between the 'denials'/'defences' contrast and the criteria for the allocation of the onus of proof. He writes that 'it is a general and well-established rule that the claimant bears the onus of proving facts that satisfy the elements of the tort in which he sues, while it is for the defendant to establish facts that enliven any defences' (ibid 12); he notes that 'the distinction between torts and defences is the mechanism between by which the onus of proof is distributed between the parties' (ibid 38), that 'the onus of proof is allocated by reference to the division between torts and defences' (ibid 41); and again that 'the general

no answer to the very simple question 'What *is* the difference between denials and defences?' He wants to resist incorporationism, but his broad and ill-considered working definition of a defence prevents him from offering any alternative view.

Indeed it seems that for Goudkamp 'denials' and 'defences' are after all just different *names* for two subsets of circumstances whose function is precisely the same. Both 'denials' and 'defences' seem in his view to amount to the negation of an 'element' required for the claimant to succeed. He can therefore be accused of embracing incorporationism. And against this charge I don't see that he has a good defence.

rule concerning the allocation of the onus of proof in the tort context is clear and uncontroversial: the claimant bears the onus of proof … in relation to the elements of the tort in which he sues, whereas the defendant carries the onus of proof with regard to defences' (ibid 138). What explains these conspicuous links? We are never told.

4

Tort Law's Missing Excuses

JOHN CP GOLDBERG*

IN A FORTHCOMING article, I discuss Anglo-American courts' longstanding disinclination to allow tort defendants to invoke excuses as a basis for limiting or avoiding liability. Their having done so, I argue, is consistent with tort law's aspiration to define injurious wrongs and to provide victims with redress against those who have wrongfully injured them.[1] In this chapter, I briefly rehearse the argument of the article, respond to contrary claims offered by fellow contributors to this volume, and conclude with some thoughts about the larger significance of tort law's indifference to excuses.

1. TORTS AS 'INEXCUSABLE' WRONGS

As other scholars have emphasised, to appreciate what it means for tort law not to allow excuses, one must distinguish excuses from other kinds of response to allegations of wrongdoing.[2] These include denials, claims of general incapacity, and justifications.

A *denial* maintains that an alleged perpetrator's conduct fails to meet the definition of the wrong he is alleged to have perpetrated. A person who responds to an accusation of criminal assault by asserting that he unintentionally came into contact with the victim denies having committed assault. Likewise, a person sued for negligence who asserts that he acted with ordinary care, or that his carelessness did not cause the injury, denies having committed negligence.

An assertion of *incapacity* is a claim by, or on behalf of, a person that he is unfit to be held legally accountable or answerable for her actions. Claims of incapacity do not concern the character or circumstances of particular actions, but rather go to the question of who can be deemed a responsible agent. In criminal law, infancy and insanity are perhaps the most familiar examples of incapacities.

Justifications and excuses come into play only when a person with the requisite capacities has acted in a manner that fits the definition of an alleged wrong.

* Eli Goldston Professor, Harvard Law School. My thanks to Andrew Dyson, James Goudkamp, and Frederick Wilmot-Smith for organising the workshop that gave rise to this volume, and for providing me with excellent feedback on the topic of excuses in tort. Thanks also to fellow conferees for their many insights. Remaining errors are mine.

[1] JCP Goldberg, 'Inexcusable Wrongs' (2015) 103 *California Law Review* (forthcoming).

[2] J Goudkamp, *Tort Law Defences* (Oxford, Hart Publishing, 2013).

A *justification* maintains that, even though the defendant's conduct meets the definition of the relevant wrong, it is not wrong when all relevant facts are considered. For example, an intentional striking of an assailant meets the definition of a criminal assault or tortious battery, and in that sense is a prima facie wrong. Yet if it was a proportionate act of self-defence, it is justified. In this and other exceptional cases, conduct that ordinarily amounts to a wrong is not a wrong when done for certain reasons.

An actor who offers an *excuse*, like one who offers a justification, acknowledges that his conduct meets the definition of the alleged wrong. However, unlike a justified actor, an excused actor does not claim to have acted in a permissible manner—he concedes that his action was wrong even after all things are considered. He nonetheless claims that, because it was particularly difficult for him to avoid committing the wrong, he should not be held answerable, or should be held answerable on more favourable terms. To excuse a wrong is to identify circumstances that render the commission of the wrong more forgivable, such that the wrongdoer has a claim to leniency in the terms on which he is held to account. A person who attacks another under duress, or who steals out of private necessity, will cite those trying circumstances as grounds for giving him a 'break' when it comes to answering for the wrong.

To make excuses is, if only implicitly, to invoke norms as to the resilience one is expected to display in the face of obstacles to acting rightly. Criminal law's nominate excuses in effect codify such norms, though for various reasons it tends to specify them in relatively demanding ways. Thus, one cannot claim duress as a ground for exculpation unless one is exposed to a threat of imminent harm sufficient to induce a person of ordinary fortitude to commit such a crime. And if the crime is particularly serious, the law may refuse to acknowledge even a seemingly compelling excuse, in effect asking more of the defendant than can reasonably be expected of any person. Such is the case, for example, with murder, for which excuses such as duress generally are not recognised.

Armed with a more precise understanding of what counts an excuse, we can now turn to the question of whether tort law recognises them. Here the answer seems abundantly clear, as a comparison with criminal law establishes. Criminal law contains certain nominate excuses that, when applicable, exonerate the defendant or reduce his punishment, including duress, necessity, and provocation. Tort law does not. A trespass committed out of private necessity is neither justified nor excused, which is why damages are owed for harm caused by such a trespass. Likewise, negligence liability is famously insensitive to excuses. An instance of careless driving might be entirely understandable: the product, say, of enormous and unexpected stress, or a simple lack of experience. That it is understandable does not count in favour of the defendant avoiding liability or facing reduced liability.

Finally—and perhaps of greatest practical importance—there is nothing in the determination of compensatory tort damages that corresponds to the role that excuses often play in reducing a criminal defendant's punishment. At the punishment phase of a criminal proceeding, a judge or jurors can consider a broad array of excuses in exercising whatever discretion he or they enjoy to set the defendant's punishment. The question of excuses barely figures, if it figures at all, in the assessment of compensatory damages, which focuses on the claimant's injury rather than the defendant's conduct. A criminal defendant, for example, can argue for a lesser punishment by pointing to the fact that his crime resulted in part from his drug addiction, or his difficult personal circumstances. Such considerations have no obvious relevance to the question of the compensatory damages a tort defendant will be required to pay to the claimant.

Like any broad claim about a body of doctrine, the claim that tort law does not recognise excuses requires certain qualifications. I will briefly mention three. First, in practice, defence lawyers no doubt find ways to introduce evidence supporting an excuse that, strictly speaking, is not relevant to liability or damages. In courts in the United States, at least, there are few if any procedural devices that would prevent a jury from taking such evidence into account in their deliberations over liability and damages.

Second, even at the level of doctrine, there are perhaps a handful of scenarios—including certain cases of reasonably mistaken self-defence and certain instances of carelessness in response to sudden emergencies—in which courts may sometimes excuse tort defendants from liability. Still, any such scenarios are truly marginal—the result of courts bending over backwards to make sure that they are giving full effect to valid denials and justifications.

Third, excuses, or excuse-like considerations, sometimes do play a role in setting punitive damages and in apportioning liability. That they do so is not surprising. When a person is being held accountable in the particular manner of being punished, he is ordinarily entitled to special protections, including the opportunity to offer excuses to legal decision-makers. Apportionment of liability, meanwhile, takes account of excuse-like considerations yet does not in fact recognise excuses. For example, if Tom and Terrence, acting independently, each tortiously cause an indivisible injury to the claimant, the fact-finder would be entitled to assign a lesser percentage of liability to Tom on the ground that he acted under duress, or in response to a provocation. But this lower percentage would not reflect a judgment that Tom deserves leniency in the terms on which he is held accountable to the claimant. Rather, it would merely reflect a comparative judgment of responsibility as between Tom and Terrence. As to the claimant, Tom has no excuse. Hence, under the traditional common law scheme of joint and several liability, the claimant would be entitled to collect the entirety of her damages from Tom, irrespective of whether Tom could obtain contribution from Terrence.

The foregoing qualifications do little to undermine the core claim that tort law imposes liability for compensatory damages without regard to excuses. In this important respect, the rules of tort law really are unforgiving, more so even than the rules of criminal law:[3]

> [Tort law] directs us to refrain from attacking others even when we are provoked or under duress. It requires us to avoid trespassing on or converting others' property even out of necessity. It insists that we be careful even in the face of pressures that would induce carelessness in a cautious and resilient person.

To note the absence of excuses in tort law naturally invites the question of whether that absence is defensible. One can envision two distinct lines of argument in support of an affirmative answer to this question.

[3] Goldberg (n 1).

First, one might argue that tort law's indifference to excuses is defensible because: (1) excuses belong within institutions and practices whose point is to hold persons responsible for their wrongs, and (2) tort law, despite appearances, is *not* such an institution or practice. If one supposes that the 'real' point of imposing tort liability is to incentivise actors to take cost-efficient precautions, one could argue that courts' refusal to recognise excuses better enables tort law to do what it is supposed to do—the question of whether to recognise excuses would be instrumental and empirical. Likewise, tort law's lack of excuses might be explicable if tort is understood as law that aims to distribute losses fairly among persons who are eligible to bear them. After all, as between an innocent victim and a wrongful injurer who has a valid excuse, fairness might well call for the wrongful injurer to bear the loss.

In contrast to this kind of 'yes' answer to the question of the defensibility of tort law's failure to recognise excuses, a second and more satisfactory version takes the bull by the horns. It grants that tort law *is* primarily about wrongdoing and responsibility. Yet it insists that tort law nonetheless can cogently refuse to recognise excuses. To grasp this response, one must appreciate that, within the genus of wrongs, there are different species that correspond to different notions of responsibility and accountability. To label conduct as 'wrongful' for purposes of criminal law means one thing, and comes with certain conditions. To label conduct as 'wrongful' for purposes of tort law means another, and comes with different conditions. This is why tort law, unlike criminal law, can justifiably leave no place for excuses.

Within the category of legal wrongs, torts form a distinctive sub-category. Torts are injurious wrongs. There are inchoate crimes, but no inchoate torts—until there is a victim, there is no tort.[4] Torts are also relational wrongs. Misconduct that causes injury is not a tort unless it amounts to conduct that is wrongful *as to the victim*. Conduct that is merely anti-social, or wrongful toward someone other than the person who happens to get hurt, is not tortious.

It is hardly coincidental that the nominate torts—negligence, battery, fraud, strict products liability et al—are defined as relational, injurious wrongs, and that the commission of a tort generates a private right of action in the victim.[5] Torts are defined so as to be victimisations, and tort law empowers victims to respond to their victimisation. Accordingly, the state, in providing tort law, plays a particular role. Rather than prosecuting on behalf of the public, it makes courts available to adjudicate claims made by putative victims. Tort suits typically result in an award of compensatory damages (or injunctive relief) because the whole point is to enable victims to demand something tangible from tortfeasors as redress for the wrongs done to them. This is also why the measure of tort compensation is keyed to the victim's loss, and in turn why many defendants' complaints of being made to pay compensation 'out of proportion' to the gravity of their wrong fall on deaf ears. In tort, defendants are not held accountable in proportion to culpability. They are held answerable to the victim for what they have done to him.

[4] JCP Goldberg and B Zipursky, 'Unrealized Torts' (2002) 88 *Virginia Law Review* 1625, 1636–40.
[5] JCP Goldberg and B Zipursky, 'Torts as Wrongs' (2010) 88 *Texas Law Review* 917, 945–47.

Because criminal prosecutions are brought by a powerful state that operates the system through which accountability occurs, and because the point of such prosecutions is to inflict punishment, criminal law provides certain protections for defendants. These include heightened evidentiary burdens for the prosecution, efforts to ensure that fair warning is given to potential defendants as to when criminal liability will be triggered, and a norm of construing legal ambiguities against the state. They also include the recognition of excuses both with respect to liability and punishment.

In tort law, by contrast, the interests of the putative injurer and the putative victim are delineated in a more evenhanded way. Once the rights and duties of each have been set through the definition of particular torts, a victim who establishes that his right has been violated by the defendant establishes his entitlement to redress. And because tort law is in the business of empowering those who are wronged in this sense, the demands placed on claimants are, on the whole, less onerous than those placed on prosecutors. Likewise, liability can be keyed to outcomes even granted that tortfeasors lack a substantial degree of control over them.[6] And conduct can count as tortious that is neither criminal nor blameworthy in a strong sense.

Just as tort law can cogently require clumsy persons to live up to the standard of a person capable of ordinary prudence, it can cogently define wrongs in a manner that is insensitive to excuses. The innocent victim of an attack perpetrated by an attacker acting under duress has still been victimised. So too has the victim of a trespass undertaken out of private necessity or of an act of negligence committed under circumstances in which one could not have expected even a resilient person to act carefully.

This last observation points to a related dimension of tort that further explains its indifference to excuses. Excuses in criminal law allow defendants to make arguments against liability that are directed to a judge or jury. A criminal defendant's duress defence, for example, is an argument that asks a judge or a jury to relieve him of liability because of the pressures he faced at the time he committed the crime. By not recognising excuses, tort law in effect directs wrongdoers to make their excuses to the victim himself. In other words, tort law provides a framework of accountability for wrongs that grants to victims of those wrongs—rather than chief executives, prosecutors, judges, or jurors—the power to excuse.

2. TORT DOCTRINE REVISITED

2.1 Edelman and Dyer on Duress

In their contribution to this volume, James Edelman and Esther Dyer argue for the recognition of a duress defence in tort.[7] Their argument rests primarily on the following claims: (1) the decisional authority against the recognition of a duress

[6] JCP Goldberg and B Zipursky, 'Torts Law and Moral Luck' (2007) 92 *Cornell Law Review* 1123, 1143–64.

[7] J Edelman and E Dyer, 'A Defence of Duress in the Law of Torts?' in this volume: ch 9. They do not specify whether they are envisioning the tort defence of duress as an excuse or justification.

defence is thin; (2) duress is a well-defined feature of criminal law that, as such, can readily be adapted to the tort setting; (3) duress bears a close resemblance to the established tort defence of private necessity; (4) compensation is not such an overriding goal of tort that its pursuit warrants imposing liability on persons who injure others while acting under duress; and (5) recognition of duress as a defence would not threaten the notion of voluntary action that tort law presupposes.[8]

Working backwards through these arguments, I agree with the claim of (5). However, it merely responds to a possible objection to a duress defence, rather than giving a reason for it. Argument (4) assumes without argument that victim compensation is potentially the most compelling policy justification for not allowing a duress defence. The burden of my article,[9] however, is to show that there are other, more compelling reasons for tort law not to allow for this defence, at least insofar as it constitutes an excuse, to wit: the formal recognition of excuses is out of keeping with the notions of wrongdoing and responsibility that are at work in tort.

I will have more to say about (3) below. In essence, I contest that private necessity is a valid tort defence. As to (2), the fact that criminal law has perhaps worked out an adequate duress defence tells us little about whether that defence is appropriately incorporated into tort law. If, as I maintain, tort and criminal law involve distinctive notions of wrongdoing and responsibility, there is no more reason to incorporate criminal law's duress defence into tort than there is to incorporate tort notions of fault into the law of contract.

Argument (1) raises some basic questions about common law reasoning. It is in one sense correct to observe that there is little doctrinal authority specifically on the question of whether duress is a tort defence. Indeed, the matter seems to have first been decided in English law by the terse 1647 King's Bench decision in *Gilbert v Stone*.[10] Moreover, at least one other high court decision, *Waller v Parker*, an 1868 decision of the Tennessee Supreme Court, seems to allow for a duress defence.[11]

On the basis of these seemingly meagre and conflicting authorities, how can one justifiably assert that duress is not a defence in Anglo-American tort law? In fact, there is nothing particularly odd about tracing settled common law rules to a single decision. *Weaver v Ward*,[12] for example, plays a role comparable to *Gilbert* in establishing the unavailability of an insanity defence to tort liability. The same might be said for *Vaughan v Menlove*[13] with respect to the objectivity of the standard of care in negligence.

In any event, it is artificial to look at *Gilbert* on its own, divorced from the larger doctrinal patterns in which it figures. *Gilbert*, *Weaver*, *Vaughan*, and other leading decisions are all of a piece in suggesting that culpability matters less for tort liability than for criminal liability. This distinction between tort and crime was

[8] ibid 159–60, 175–77.

[9] Goldberg (n 1).

[10] (1647) Style 72; 82 ER 539.

[11] 45 Tenn 476; 5 Cold 476 (1868).

[12] (1616) Hob 134; 80 ER 284.

[13] (1837) 3 Bing NC 468; 132 ER 490. As Edelman and Dyer note, *Gilbert*'s 'standing' as a significant precedent was later bolstered when given an approving nod from Blackstone J in his dissenting judgment in *Scott v Shepherd* (1773) 2 Blackstone W 892, 896; 96 ER 525, 527: see Edelman and Dyer (n 4) at p 161.

already well-established by the eighteenth century, as a glance at Books III and IV of Blackstone's *Commentaries* would suggest. Book IV devotes an entire chapter to questions about a criminal defendant's 'capacity' to commit a crime. Included under this heading are discussions of the significance of insanity, necessity, duress and other conditions for criminal liability and punishment.[14] There is no comparable chapter in Book III's discussion of 'private wrongs', and indeed no discussion of any of these as grounds for avoiding or mitigating civil liability. Another treatise from the turn of the nineteenth century, which is quoted in *Inexcusable Wrongs*, expresses the same thought even more explicitly in its discussion of infancy, dementia, ignorance, necessity and duress:[15]

> Ordinarily none of these do excuse those persons, that are under them, from civil actions to have a pecuniary recompense for injuries done, as *trespasses*, *batteries*, *woundings*; because such a recompense is not by way of penalty, but a satisfaction for damage done to the party: but in cases of crimes and misdemeanors, where the proceedings against them is *ad poenam*, the law in some cases, and under certain temperaments takes notice of these defects, and in respect of them relaxeth or abateth the severity of their punishments.

Gilbert cannot be treated as an isolated datum. It was and is part and parcel of an understanding of the distinctive notions of wrongdoing and responsibility at work in tort. *Gilbert*'s force as a precedent owes less to the fact that later courts have cited it mechanically and more to the fact that its holding meshes with an overall understanding of tort law as concerned to identify, and allow the redress of, a special category of wrongs that is less concerned with culpability and more concerned with the question of whether the alleged wrongdoer failed, for whatever reason, to live up to an applicable standard of conduct and thereby injured another.

The reasons marshalled by Edelman and Dyer thus fail to make a compelling case for the inclusion in tort law of a duress defence.

2.2 Virgo on Necessity

In his chapter, Graham Virgo argues for the recognition of a private necessity defence in tort.[16] As he notes, 'private necessity' can refer either to a justification or an excuse. Understood as a justification, necessity is sometimes referred to as the 'choice of evils' defence. In criminal law, for example, a prisoner who escapes from a prison to avoid being assaulted may be able to avoid conviction for the escape crime on the ground that it was the lesser evil. Understood as an excuse, a plea of necessity points toward the defendant's urgent need as a ground for leniency in the terms on which he is held accountable for his wrong.

Virgo further suggests that this difference is not merely conceptual but doctrinal. English cases, he argues, tend to treat necessity as a justification that defeats liability,

[14] W Blackstone, *Commentaries on the Laws of England*, 1st edn, vol 4 (Chicago, University of Chicago Press, 1769).

[15] Goldberg (n 1), quoting M Hale, *The History of the Pleas of the Crown*, vol 1 (S Emlyn (ed), London, E and R Nutt and R Gosling, 1736) 15–16.

[16] I will focus here on claims of private necessity. Clams of public necessity can justify, rather than excuse, certain conduct that is otherwise tortious.

whereas American cases, especially *Vincent v Lake Erie Transportation Co*,[17] treat it as an excuse.[18] He further suggests the American approach is preferable because it is more consistent with what he takes to be tort law's focus on victim compensation over punishment of wrongdoers.[19]

I am doubtful that this purported doctrinal distinction between American and English law holds up. We can start with the English cases. It is by no means clear that they treat necessity as a justification. Here it is important to attend to the distinctions, noted above, between denials, on the one hand, and justifications and excuses, on the other.

Virgo cites *The Lords Bailiff-Jurats of Romney Marsh v The Corporation of the Trinity House*.[20] In heavy winds and a rising tide, the crew of the defendants' vessel carelessly allowed her to become grounded about 1000 yards from the claimants' sea wall. The wind and the tide eventually pushed the vessel into the wall, damaging the wall and wrecking the ship (although the crew could have avoided grounding the vessel in the first place, once it was grounded, the crew had no ability to prevent the vessel from reaching the wall). For the next five days, each time the tide came in, the ship further battered the wall. Yet, by the second day, it was within the power of the crew to break up the ship and thereby spare the wall from further damage. The crew declined to do so because there was valuable property on the ship that would be lost if it were broken up. Instead the crew and the owners arranged for the salvage of the property while the vessel continued to damage the wall. After the property was removed, the ship was broken up.

The owners of the damaged sea wall sued the shipowners for negligence, claiming carelessness in the initial grounding of the vessel, and carelessness in delaying before breaking up the vessel. I read the Court of Exchequer to have reasoned as follows:

(1) there was no carelessness by the defendants in failing to break up the vessel once it was upon the wall, because it was reasonable to incur the delay in order to salvage the valuable property that would be lost if the vessel were immediately broken up;
(2) thus, had there been no negligence on the part of the defendants in allowing the vessel to reach the wall in the first place, there would be no liability;
(3) however, there was prior carelessness on the part of the crew in allowing the ship to be grounded, and the damage caused to the wall was proximately caused by *that* carelessness, ergo there was liability for the damage to the wall, including damage suffered beyond the second day after the grounding of the ship.

On this reading, the court's treatment of 'necessity' is dictum. More importantly, the dictum in question does not treat necessity as a defence. Rather, necessity is raised in connection with the application of negligence law's reasonable care standard. On that issue, the court concluded as follows: when, through no one's fault, the property of a person ends up in a position such that it is causing modest damage to the

[17] 109 Minn 456; 124 NW 221 (1910).
[18] G Virgo, 'Justifying Necessity as a Defence in Tort Law' at pp 153–54 in this volume.
[19] ibid 154–55.
[20] (1869–1870) LR 5 Ex 204 (Exch).

property of another, and when such damage can be avoided only by destroying the property and thereby causing a significant loss to the property's owner, the owner does not act carelessly by delaying its destruction for a reasonable period so as to reduce his loss. Rather than recognising an excuse, the 'necessity' discussion in *The Lords Bailiff-Jurat* credits the defendants with a cogent *denial* of the claim that they had acted carelessly by declining to break up the ship immediately.

In *Cope v Sharpe (No 2)*, the claimant obtained a two-year lease from the defendant to hunt game on the defendant's land.[21] During the lease period, a fire broke out on the land. The defendant's servant set a separate fire in an effort to prevent the first fire from killing pheasants that were nesting in a 'cover' on the land. The Court of Appeal held the defendant not liable for the damage to the claimant's property caused by the intentionally set fire because it was reasonable for the servant to conclude that setting the fire was necessary to save the pheasants.

Unlike in *The Lords Bailiff-Jurats*, liability in *Cope* turns on a claim of trespass rather than negligence. And the judges who decided the case admittedly framed the question before them as the question of whether the defendant's trespassory conduct was justified. Nonetheless, *Cope* is hardly clear authority for the recognition of private necessity as a justification to an otherwise actionable trespass.

As noted, the defendant was not a stranger to the land in question. He was a 'tenant' who 'had property and rights which might have been injuriously affected by the fire'.[22] The defendant's lease rights may well have included a right to take reasonable measures to protect the game on the property.[23] So thought Kennedy LJ:[24]

> the [servant] was, as against the plaintiff, entitled to stand in the same position as his master as lessee of the sporting rights who had, as tenant, the right to maintain the game by all means which did not involve unreasonable interference with, or damage to, the property of the lessor.

In short, the absence of liability in *Cope* arguably rests on the ground that the defendant was exercising rights that had been conferred on him by the lease, rather than on a claim of necessity.

Finally, in *Esso Petroleum Co Ltd v Southport Corp*, the House of Lords held that the owner of a tanker was not liable for despoiling the claimant's property by intentionally releasing oil from the vessel in order to prevent it from breaking open, with possible risk to life and limb.[25] *Southport* turned largely on the pleadings, which their Lordships interpreted as pressing a claim of negligence. Specifically, they ruled that the trial court was correct to have rejected the claim as pleaded because there was insufficient proof of carelessness.[26] Lord Tucker additionally opined that, when a possessor of property located adjacent to a public way suffers property damage because of the defendant's involvement in an accident on that public way,

[21] [1912] 1 KB 496 (CA).

[22] *Cope v Sharpe (No 2)* [1912] 1 KB 496 (CA) 503 (Buckley LJ).

[23] 'The test, I think, is whether, having regard to the *rights of the sporting lessee*, there was such a real and imminent danger to *his property* as that he was entitled to act and whether his acts were reasonably necessary in the sense of acts which a reasonable many would properly do to meet a real danger': ibid 504 (Buckley LJ) (emphasis added).

[24] ibid 509 (Kennedy LJ).

[25] [1956] AC 218 (HL).

[26] ibid 238 (Lord Normand) 241 (Lord Morton) 244 (Lord Radcliffe).

the possessor, unlike other possessors suing for trespass and nuisance, must prove carelessness on the part of the defendant.[27]

What about the American side of the ledger? The key decisions, as Virgo notes, are *Vincent v Lake Erie Transportation Co*[28] and its predecessor, *Ploof v Putnam*.[29] Read in the light of *Ploof*, *Vincent* is often said to have recognised an 'incomplete privilege of private necessity', according to which a person is privileged to enter or remain on another's land to avoid imminent, serious harm, but must pay compensation for any damage caused.[30] In doing so, *Vincent* (according to Virgo), treats necessity as a partial excuse. That is, it treats the defendant's trespass as a wrong, but nonetheless bars the landowner from responding to the wrong by ejecting the trespassing defendant, instead requiring the defendant merely to compensate for damage done.

It is awkward to read *Vincent* and *Ploof* as recognising excuses. When one makes an excuse, one admits to having done wrong, but pleads for leniency on the ground that the commission of the wrong was understandable, given the circumstances. Excuses are invoked to mitigate the harshness of the terms on which one is held answerable for having wronged another. Yet neither *Vincent* nor *Ploof* invokes necessity as a basis for leniency in the terms on which a trespasser is held accountable to the victim. At least on the 'incomplete privilege' reading of these cases, necessity has little or nothing to do with answerability. Instead, it operates to deny property owners a right to take certain actions to prevent a trespass from happening.

Indeed, as is argued in *Inexcusable Wrongs*, the focus of *Vincent* and *Ploof* on necessity as a ground for partially 'disarming' landowners provides an important clue as to the proper interpretation of those decisions. Together, they stand for two points. First, a trespass undertaken out of private necessity is neither justified nor excused. This is why the defendant is liable for any damage caused by the trespass. The fancy machinery of incomplete privilege is not required to explain this result. A trespass done out of necessity is just that—a trespass. And as with any other trespass, compensation is owed for damage resulting from it.[31]

So what is the significance of 'necessity' in these cases? Here we arrive at their second point. Just as the law allows a person to take measures to protect himself against imminent attack, a possessor of land is permitted to take measures to prevent a trespass. In both cases, however, the right is constrained by a requirement of reasonableness.

Suppose that, in the midst of an argument, Jones realises that Smith is about to spit in his (Jones's) face. In ordinary circumstances, Jones might be permitted to preempt Smith's 'attack' by pushing Smith away from him—were Smith to sue Jones for battery on the basis of the push, Jones could claim self-defence as a justification

[27] ibid 244–45 (Lord Tucker).

[28] 109 Minn 456; 124 NW 221 (1910).

[29] 81 Vt 471; 71 A 188 (1908).

[30] FH Bohlen, 'Incomplete Privilege to Inflict Intentional Invasions of Interests of Property and Personality' (1926) 39 *Harvard Law Review* 307, 313.

[31] The fact that it was done for a good reason, and that we might even commend the trespasser for having done the right thing, all things considered, does not render the conduct justified or excused in the eyes of the law. It does, however, constitute a denial of any claim by the claimant that the defendant committed the sort of wanton or wilful trespass that permits an award of punitive damages.

that defeats Smith's claim. However, if Smith happens to be standing on a ledge, such that Jones was aware that a push would cause Smith to fall in a manner likely to cause death or serious injury, Jones's pushing of Smith would not be deemed reasonable, and Jones would have no justification for his battery.

Cases of trespass out of necessity, like the Smith-on-a-ledge case, are cases that mark the limit of what can count as a reasonable effort to prevent a trespass. It is not reasonable for a possessor to use force if doing so creates a significant risk that the trespasser will suffer imminent and serious bodily harm (*Ploof*), or if it threatens the destruction of property of a much greater value than any loss the possessor can be expected to suffer (*Vincent*). Necessity here has nothing to do with an assessment of the defendant-trespasser's conduct. Rather, it sets a limit on the claimant-possessor's conduct.

It would seem, then, that neither English nor American tort doctrine recognises, or is pointing toward the recognition of, a private necessity defence.

3. RETHINKING WRONGS

In her book *Breaking the Cycles of Violence*, Martha Minow addressed the question of how government and law should respond to grave injustices.[32] Her particular concern was atrocities on a mass scale. Abominable wrongs have been perpetrated. Now what?

Minow first considered a familiar possibility—vengeance upon the perpetrators on behalf of victims. She counselled against this response as destined only to engender further wrongdoing.[33]Another option is forgiveness, but she rejected this as well. To require forgiveness of victims of atrocities is inhuman—'it requires a kind of transcendence that cannot be achieved on command'.[34] The trick instead is to forge a middle path. Candidates for this middle path include prosecutions, reparations, and truth commissions. With her usual acumen, Minow identified promises and pitfalls associated with each.[35]

Though atrocities involve tortious conduct, torts are not atrocities. Atrocities are 'inexcusable' in the particular sense of being beyond the pale, unimaginable, perhaps unforgivable. Garden-variety torts are prosaic and predictable and thus *not* inexcusable in the sense just described. Quite the opposite, instances of negligence and trespass tend to be perfectly understandable—the sort of thing that each of us can imagine doing, even if we try and hope not to.

Yet torts are in their own way inexcusable, and for reasons that ultimately connect to Minow's claim about the need for law and legal institutions to locate a 'space' between vengeance and forgiveness. Tort duties are often unforgiving. That which must be done to avoid breaching them is not as much in our control as we might like. Best efforts are not enough to avoid liability for negligence. Reasonable

[32] M Minow, *Breaking the Cycles of Hatred: Memory, Law, and Repair* (Princeton, Princeton University Press, 2002).
[33] ibid 17.
[34] ibid 18.
[35] ibid 19–27.

care is not enough to avoid liability for trespass. And tort law requires us to live up to its standards even when we act in circumstances that make it very difficult to meet them. It is in this very different sense that torts are 'inexcusable'.

But to appreciate the demandingness of tort duties is at the same time to appreciate that a tort is not ordinarily the sort of wrong that warrants harsh condemnation or punishment. Indeed, it is partly because tort law identifies wrongs on unforgiving terms that the commission of a tort, in and of itself, does not warrant a punitive or strongly blameworthy response. Rather, torts generate a different kind of accountability—accountability in the form of being subject to a victim's demand for a compensatory payment, or a victim's demand that one cease engaging in tortious activity.

It is in some respects difficult to avoid committing torts. On the basis of this observation, many scholars have concluded that torts are not 'really' wrongs. In so reasoning, they tend to rely on an over-inflated version of the ought-implies-can principle.[36] It is in the nature of a wrong, they suppose, that it must be defined so as to give individuals a high degree of control over whether it is committed. This line of reasoning is fallacious. A wrong is simply a violation of a conduct-guiding directive grounded in certain important interests of others (such as the interest in bodily integrity). Wrongs come in different shapes and sizes, with different degrees of avoidability. Torts tend to be easier to commit than *mala in se* crimes. This is why torts—unless they are committed in some special, aggravated manner—are not punished. And it is why the courts have had, and continue to have, good reason to decline to recognise excuses to tort liability.

[36] See, eg, Goldberg and Zipursky (n 6); J Gardner, 'Obligations and Outcomes in the Law of Torts' in P Cane and J Gardner (eds), *Relating to Responsibility: Essays in Honour of Tony Honoré on His 80th Birthday* (Oxford, Hart Publishing, 2001) 111, 127–29, 141–43.

5

Duties to Try and Duties to Succeed

STEPHEN A SMITH

LAW STUDENTS IN common law jurisdictions are typically introduced to defences as part of their study of criminal law. A major theme of most such introductions is the importance of distinguishing defences that operate as 'justifications' from those that operate as 'excuses'. According to the conventional view of this distinction, a successful justificatory defence—for example, a successful plea of self-defence—demonstrates that the defendant's apparently wrongful act was not, in the circumstances, a wrong at all.[1] It is permissible—and so not a wrong—to use reasonable force to defend ourselves from others. In contrast, a successful excusatory defence—for example, a successful plea of reasonable mistake—demonstrates that notwithstanding that the defendant committed a wrong, it would not be fair to punish or otherwise hold the defendant legally liable for the wrong. An excuse, in the conventional view, relieves defendants of liability for wrongful acts on the ground that, in the circumstances, they were not at fault for what they did, that is, that their mistake was a reasonable mistake.

For anyone introduced to legal defences in this fashion, perhaps the most striking feature of the law of tort defences is that it does not recognise excuses. Unlike a defendant in a criminal trial, a defendant in a tort case cannot avoid liability for a tortious act on the ground that the act 'was not my fault'. The full story, however, is more complex. Many torts, including the tort of negligence, have a fault requirement built-in to their cause of action. It is not possible to commit the tort of negligence except through faulty (or 'inexcusable') behaviour. The question raised by the absence of excusatory defences in tort law is therefore not 'why is fault unimportant in tort law', but rather 'why is fault important only with respect to certain torts and, further, why, in those torts where fault is important, is proof of fault a part of the cause of action rather than proof of no-fault a defence?'

The question of whether and when fault should matter in tort law is the subject of a voluminous literature. For the most part, this literature focuses on the substantive issue of whether and when it is appropriate to require defendants who were not at fault to pay damages. The literature asks whether it is fair, efficient, or otherwise appropriate to hold defendants who have neither intended to cause harm nor acted

[1] 'Conventional' should perhaps be inside quotation marks in view of the long-standing definitional disputes in this area: see, eg, J Dressler, 'Justifications and Excuses: A Brief Review of the Concepts and the Literature' (1987) 33 *Wayne Law Review* 1155; J Goudkamp, *Tort Law Defences* (Oxford, Hart Publishing, 2013) 76–88.

carelessly legally responsible for harms that they have caused. I touch upon this issue in this chapter, but prompted by the invitation to discuss tort law defences, my primary concern is the analytic (or 'structural') question of how and at what stage in their reasoning courts should take account of fault when assessing a claim for tort damages. Thus, I will join the law in assuming that there are good reasons for courts to care about fault when assessing at least certain kinds of tort claims, but then ask what precisely is the legal significance of the defendant's fault or absence of fault. In particular, should fault be taken into account when specifying a defendant's duty, that is, when determining if a defendant committed a wrong? Or should fault be taken into account only when specifying a defendant wrongdoer's liability, that is, when determining whether a defendant who has committed a wrong ought to pay damages? And in the latter case, is fault a condition of liability or is no-fault an excuse that avoids liability?

My discussion of these questions is preliminary and speculative. Although I will say something about how fault is understood in the positive law, my primary aim is to develop a framework for thinking about the different ways in which fault might be legally significant. Specifically, the proposed framework is organised around two ways that we might imagine lawmakers formulating private law duties. The first way, which I call the 'outcome model', supposes that legal duties are requirements to bring about particular states of affairs or 'outcomes'. An example would be a duty 'not to trespass': this duty requires its subjects to achieve the outcome of 'not trespassing'.[2] The second way of drawing up legal duties, the conduct model, supposes that legal duties stipulate requirements to try to bring about outcomes. An example would be a legal duty 'to try to avoid harming others'.[3] As we will see, each of these models allows for the possibility that the faultiness (or 'reasonableness') of a defendant's behaviour may be relevant to the defendant's liability to a judicial ruling to pay damages (hereafter 'liability to pay damages'[4]). But the way in which fault may matter under these models differs. In the outcome model, fault, or more strictly the absence of fault, is relevant only as a potential excusatory defence: absence of fault, in this model, is a possible reason to deny liability for an admitted breach of duty. In contrast, in the conduct model fault is always relevant as part of the cause of action: there is no breach without fault. After setting up these models in Sections 2 and 3 (and querying the coherence of 'mixed' models in Section 4), I turn, in Section 5, to the law, and suggest that while both models can account, at least in broad outline, for the rulings handed down in tort cases, neither can account for the ways in

[2] As this example illustrates, 'outcomes', as I use the term, include 'negative' outcomes.

[3] Throughout this chapter, the concept of 'harm' is understood broadly. In particular, references to harmful outcomes are intended to include the possibility that a non-consensual interference with another's person, property, or liberty may be harmful notwithstanding that it does not make the person worse off in any meaningful sense. So a 'mere' trespass to land, that is, a trespass that does not affect the value or use of the property or in any other way make the owner worse off, can qualify as a wrong.

[4] There is a debate among tort scholars as to whether tort liabilities are liabilities to falling under a substantive duty, arising at the moment of injury, to pay damages or are instead merely liabilities to being ordered by a court to pay damages. I touch upon this issue briefly in Section 5, but nothing in my general argument turns on its resolution. To avoid constant qualification, 'liabilities to pay damages' will be understood as referring to liabilities to being ordered to pay damages (whether or not that liability confirms a prior duty to pay damages). For similar reasons, 'duties' will be understood as referring to what are sometimes called 'primary duties', that is, to duties that arise from non-wrongful events, such as forming a contract, or from being in the jurisdiction ('secondary duties', for scholars who use this terminology, are duties to pay damages).

which those rulings are explained. I conclude, in Part 6, with a historical explanation (not a justification) of the contemporary understanding of fault's role in tort law, together with a plea to think more seriously about the nature of private law duties.

1. LEGAL DUTIES

Tort damages, as conventionally understood, are damages for a tort, that is, for a legal wrong.[5] A legal wrong is the breach of a legal duty. To understand what kinds of actions might lead to a liability to pay damages, the first question we need to ask therefore is what kinds of actions might appropriately be the object of a legal duty.

Or is it? According to one way of understanding legal duties, the question 'what kinds of actions are appropriate objects of legal duties?' is just another way of asking 'what kinds of actions are appropriate conditions of legal liabilities?' What is sometimes called the 'sanction' theory of legal duties supposes that statements of private law duties merely describe the circumstances in which citizens may become liable to pay damages.[6] According to this theory, to say that D has a duty to φ is equivalent to saying that in the event that D does not φ, D is liable to pay damages.[7] The sanction theory is vulnerable to a number of well-known objections.[8] I will just mention two as they are closely related to this chapter's concerns. First, the sanction theory cannot explain why courts regularly hold that defendants who, according to the courts themselves, have committed legal wrongs, are not liable to pay damages. Examples include cases in which a limitation period has expired, the parties have signed a contract of settlement, or the defendant is a foreign diplomat.[9] These examples make clear that it is not part of the common law's understanding of 'legal duty' that the actions required by legal duties mirror the conditions in which the law imposes liability. A second, more fundamental, objection to the view that duty-statements are mere reflections of liability statements is that this view does not explain why legal duties are 'duties'. If lawmakers want to make clear that anyone who φ's is liable to pay damages, the obvious way to do this is not to say 'Everyone has a duty not to φ', but to say 'Anyone who φ's is liable to pay damages'.

The straightforward and indeed unavoidable meaning of a statement to the effect that 'everyone has a duty to φ' is simply that everyone ought to φ. Legal duty

[5] Some so-called damage awards arguably do not satisfy this definition: see the discussion of 'free-standing liabilities' in Section 3.

[6] Examples, with qualifications, include: WE Rumble (ed), *Austin: The Province of Jurisprudence Determined* (Cambridge, Cambridge University Press, 1995) 18; H Kelsen, *Pure Theory of Law* (M Knight tr, Berkeley, University of California Press, 1967) 55.

[7] Being ordered to pay damages is not strictly a sanction, but defendants who fail to comply with orders to pay damages are liable, more or less automatically, to sanctions, typically in the form of execution against their property. Prior to the introduction of the Civil Procedure Rules 1998, the English courts did not order defendants to pay damages, but instead 'adjudged' that claimants 'shall recover' a sum of money from the defendant. In this system, it was possible for an award of damages to be 'executed' immediately. Defendants may also be sanctioned if they fail to comply with an injunction, though, again, it is failure to comply with the injunction, not failure to comply with the anterior duty that attracts the sanction.

[8] See in particular HLA Hart, *The Concept of Law* (Oxford, Clarendon Press, 1961) 27–42.

[9] For a discussion of these and 20 other examples of what the author describes as 'public policy defences', see Goudkamp (n 1) 105–13.

statements tell citizens how the law expects them to behave. This observation does not presume that private law is a regulatory tool, much less that duty statements should be assessed by their effectiveness in influencing behaviour. It is simply an acknowledgment that to say that citizens have a duty to φ is to say that, from the law's perspective, citizens ought to φ.

The question, then, is what sorts of actions might we imagine as the objects of legal ought statements, that is, as objects of duty-imposing rules? More specifically (since my concern is with private law, in particular tort law), what sorts of actions might be the proper objects of rules that impose private law duties? There appear to be two possibilities.

2. THE OUTCOME MODEL: DUTIES TO SUCCEED

The first way in which lawmakers might frame legal duties is by specifying particular states of affairs, or 'outcomes', that citizens are required to bring about. For example, lawmakers might enact a rule stating that 'everyone has a duty not to trespass' or that 'everyone has a duty not to take others' property'. The duty created by this kind of rule may be described, adopting John Gardner's language,[10] as a 'duty to succeed' because its fulfilment turns exclusively on whether the subject succeeds in bringing about the stipulated outcome. It is irrelevant when determining whether defendants fulfilled such duties how much or how little effort they expended: all that matters is whether the outcome was achieved. Of course, the full specification of a duty to succeed would normally be more elaborate than simply saying 'do not trespass' or 'do not convert others' property'. In the case of trespass or conversion, while it may be reasonable for the law to suppose that such actions are generally undesirable, there are obvious exceptions: in an emergency, a trespass or conversion may be permissible if not positively desirable. To account for such exceptions, the definitions of trespass and conversion, or the description of the circumstances in which they ought not to happen, must be qualified in the formulation of the duty.

Properly qualified, however, a duty to succeed is perfectly coherent. True, it is possible to breach a duty to succeed notwithstanding that one acted perfectly reasonably. If I walk onto your land without permission, I will be in breach of a duty 'not to trespass' even if the explanation for my entry is that city employees mistakenly erected 'public park' signs on your land. Yet the fact that my mistake was reasonable—something for which I should not be blamed—does not change the fact that it would have been better had I not entered your land. And if it would have been better for me to have not entered your land, then it is perfectly coherent for the law to say that I ought not to have entered your land. Another way of

[10] J Gardner, 'The Wrongdoing That Gets Results' (2004) 18 *Philosophical Perspectives* 53. This chapter owes a large debt to Gardner's pioneering work. In addition to the above essay, see, J Gardner, 'The Gist of Excuses' (1998) 1 *Buffalo Criminal Law Review* 575; J Gardner, 'Obligations and Outcomes in the Law of Torts' in P Cane and J Gardner (eds), *Relating to Responsibility: Essays for Tony Honoré* (Oxford, Hart Publishing, 2001) 111; J Gardner, 'In Defence of Defences' and 'Justifications and Reasons' in J Gardner, *Offences and Defences: Selected Essays in the Philosophy of Criminal Law* (Oxford, Oxford University Press, 2007) 77, 91; J Gardner, 'What is Tort Law For? Part 1: The Place of Corrective Justice' (2011) 30 *Law and Philosophy* 1; J Gardner, 'Reasons and Abilities: Some Preliminaries' (2013) 58 American Journal of Jurisprudence 63.

making this point is that there is a straightforward sense in which the breach of a duty to succeed is a 'wrong'. This sense is that which is intended when I say that I took a 'wrong turn' when driving or that I grabbed the 'wrong' umbrella from a checkroom—notwithstanding that in each case my actions were perfectly reasonable in the circumstances (say because, respectively, a road sign was mislabelled and someone had taken my umbrella). Such actions are wrongs because they bring about the wrong outcome. This observation does not deny that we often use the term 'wrong' to refer to undesirable conduct, regardless of the conduct's outcome. So I tell my children that it is wrong to drive carelessly on the highway, and I do not qualify this statement by saying that it is only wrong if someone gets hurt. The 'right' way to drive, I say, is to drive carefully. As I discuss in Section three, this second way of understanding wrongdoing is the one that is presumed by duties to try. For the moment, it is sufficient to observe that we regularly attach the label 'wrong' to actions for which the actor cannot be faulted, that is to say, actions that were, in the circumstances, perfectly reasonable ways of behaving.

Even if duties to succeed are coherent in principle, it might still be asked whether they are a plausible model for *legal* duties. As we have seen, duties to succeed are strict in the sense that they may be breached notwithstanding that one took reasonable care to try to comply with them, or even that one took extreme care. The only way to be certain never to breach a duty 'not to trespass' is never to move your body (and even this method guarantees success only if you are not already trespassing). Given that we ought to comply with our legal duties, it might be objected that strict duties indirectly counsel citizens to take extreme care, even to the point of not moving. The law clearly cannot want citizens to take such care. Taking more than reasonable care is by definition not reasonable.

The short response to this objection is that it could be directed at any duty statement, however formulated. A duty statement describes what must happen in the future. Unless the duty simply instructs its subjects to do what they would do anyway (in which case it is no duty at all), there is always a risk of failure. For example, the only way to be certain not to breach a duty to try, for example, a duty to take reasonable care to try to avoid harming others, is, again, never to move your body (and even this method guarantees success only if you are not already under a positive duty to act). Duties to take reasonable care are strict in the sense that there is no excuse for failing to take reasonable care: the strong and the weak are held to the same standard.[11] And even if a duty to try is framed subjectively, so that reasonable care is defined as the care that the subject of the duty can reasonably be expected to take, the risk of failure remains.

The longer response to the 'extreme care' objection is that a duty to succeed does not even indirectly counsel or promote extreme care. A rule imposing a duty 'not to trespass' says nothing about how much care citizens should take to avoid trespassing. Like other duty-imposing rules, what such a rule provides is two kinds of reasons.[12] First, the rule provides a first order or 'ordinary' reason not to trespass, that is to say, a reason not to trespass that in the usual case must be taken into

[11] This proposition is defended in more detail in Gardner 'Obligations and Outcomes' (n 10), building on Tony Honoré's landmark essay, 'Responsibility and Luck' (1988) 104 *LQR* 530.

[12] J Raz, *Practical Reasons and Norms* (Oxford, Oxford University Press, 1999) 39. Raz describes the combination of these two kinds of reason as providing a 'protected' reason for action (because the second reason protects the first).

account along with all the other reasons that we have to act in one way or another. Second, the rule provides a second order or 'exclusionary' reason to ignore any other reasons that we may have to trespass or not trespass. This second, exclusionary reason explains why a legal duty not to trespass provides a sufficient ground (from the law's perspective) never to choose to trespass. In deciding whether to trespass or not, the exclusionary reason tells us that, unlike in the usual case, the only reason we should take into account is the first order ordinary reason to not trespass. But the exclusionary reason drops out of the picture when we are making decisions about how much care we should take to not trespass because it is meant only to exclude reasons to *choose* to trespass. A decision to take less or more care to avoid trespassing is not a choice to trespass or to not trespass. The only reason that a duty not to trespass provides to someone deciding how much care to take not to trespass, is the ordinary reason not to trespass. Without the exclusionary reason to protect it, this ordinary reason stands alongside all the other ordinary reasons that citizens have to take more or less care (for example, that taking more care is costly, that taking less care saves time, and so on). Further, a duty not to trespass does not tell citizens how much weight they should accord to the ordinary reason not to trespass, that is, it does not tell them the magnitude of the undesirability of trespassing. Citizens must answer this question themselves. If citizens reason correctly, however, they will by definition take a reasonable amount of care, where reasonable means an appropriate amount given, on the one hand, the likelihood and magnitude of the harm caused by trespassing and, on the other, the legitimate reasons they have to bring about or avoid other outcomes. They will reach this result because reasoning correctly means giving reasons the weight that is due to them.

The conclusion to draw from these remarks, then, is that while a legal duty not to trespass does not make it a legal wrong to fail to take reasonable care not to trespass, it provides citizens with a reason to take just such care (and does not provide a reason to take more than reasonable care). Not coincidentally, a similar observation can be made with respect to duties to try. The existence of a legal duty to drive with reasonable care does not give me a reason to take extreme steps to try to achieve this standard (for example, never driving if I slept badly the night before, never driving if I am upset or in a hurry, never driving with passengers, and so on). The duty merely gives me a reason to take reasonable steps to try to achieve the standard.

The conclusion that duties to succeed do not counsel their subjects to take extreme care should not come as a surprise. The common law includes many duties that are conventionally expressed as duties to succeed, including the duty 'not to trespass'. Yet not even the most cautious lawyers would advise their clients that the law expects them to do everything in their power to make sure they never commit an accidental trespass. What the law expects, any lawyer would say, is that they never choose to trespass and that they take reasonable steps to avoid accidentally trespassing. The same observation applies to non-legal duties to succeed. When I tell my son 'do not throw balls into the neighbour's yard', my expectation is not that he will stop playing ball games altogether (notwithstanding that this is the best way to ensure that he never throws a ball into the neighbour's yard). What I expect is that he will never intentionally throw a ball into the neighbour's yard and that he will take reasonable steps to avoid accidentally throwing a ball into the yard (which steps will take into account, inter alia, the hardness of the balls, the proximity of large windows, etc).

2.1 The Strict Liability Objection

A different objection to duties to succeed is that they give rise to strict liabilities—and strict liabilities, according to this objection, are unfair, inefficient, or otherwise undesirable. In this view, only citizens who act unreasonably should run the risk of having to pay damages. As I mentioned earlier, this chapter takes no position on the substantive merits of strict versus fault-based liabilities. However, it is not necessary to enter this debate to point out that the strict liability objection is not an objection to duties to succeed, but rather an objection to a particular liability regime (specifically a strict regime). It does not follow from the fact that I have breached a legal duty that I should be held legally liable for the consequences of that breach. How we should act, and whether (and in what way) we should be held responsible for the consequences of our actions, are different questions. Of course, the law might well decide that anyone who breaches a duty should be liable to pay damages. But that decision is a choice, not a logical necessity (and the law clearly recognises that it is a choice, as illustrated by the earlier-mentioned tort defences of delay, settlement, and diplomatic immunity, not to mention the excusatory defences recognised by the criminal law).

The observation that a liability to pay damages need not automatically attach to the breach of a legal duty does not mean that liability and duty are unrelated. If the conventional definition of damages as a monetary award made in response to a wrong is accepted, then the only defendants who can be liable to pay damages are those who have breached a duty (though non-breaching defendants may be liable on other grounds). It might also be the case that it is part of the meaning of 'legal duty' that the breach of such a duty *normally* or prima facie gives rise to a liability to pay damages (again, this appears to be the conventional understanding). The point is simply that the breach of a legal duty need not always give rise to a liability to pay damages. It is perfectly coherent for a court to say to a defendant 'you acted wrongly, but given the circumstances we will not hold you liable to pay damages'. In short, it is perfectly coherent for the private law to recognise duties to succeed but then to allow defendants to plead, by way of an excusatory defence, that 'it was not my fault'.[13]

[13] Alternatively, the law could recognise duties to succeed, but then hold that liability for breach of such duties is subject to an additional condition, namely proof that the wrongdoer was at fault. Nothing in my argument turns directly on whether fault operates as a condition of liability or an excuse to liability. However, the latter option fits better with the role of damages when they are awarded for breach of a duty to succeed. As I explain in the following sub-section, damages for breach of a duty to succeed are most naturally interpreted as a second-best means of fulfilling the defendant's original duty. It makes sense to suppose, then, that a prima facie duty to pay damages arises automatically on failure to comply with the original duty. Another way of making this point, is that while it makes sense to suppose that absence of fault is a reason for excusing defendants from the necessity of fulfilling, in the best way now possible, their original duty, it sounds odd to suppose that defendants are under no obligation at all to fulfil, in the best way now possible, their original duty unless they are at fault.

2.2 The Nature of a Liability for the Breach of a Duty to Succeed

Notwithstanding that the 'breach-question' is different than the 'liability-question', when common law courts award damages, they award them for a wrong, that is to say a breach of a duty. The question thus arises as to whether anything can be said about the form, or perhaps more strictly the purpose, of paying damages in cases where the wrong to which they respond is the breach of a duty to succeed. In what way, if any, might paying one's victim a sum of money be an appropriate response to the wrong of failing to succeed in bringing about an outcome?

The short answer (a complete answer would require another essay) is that the natural role of damages in a system where duties specify outcomes is to make the world, so far as money can, as close as it can be to the world that would have existed had the required outcomes been achieved. Damages, in this view, are a second-best way of bringing about the very outcome that the defendant had a duty to achieve. As we have seen, breaching a duty to succeed carries no implication of blame or moral culpability or disrespect to the right-holder: the only implication that follows from breaching a duty to succeed is that the wrongdoer has caused an outcome that is, in broad terms, undesirable. It would be inappropriate, then, for a court to award damages with the intent of denouncing or condemning or in any other way responding to the defendant's behaviour. The only wrong in such a case is the failure to bring about a stipulated outcome. It follows that the only way that paying damages can redress this kind of wrongdoing is if they are an attempt, so far as this is possible, to make the world as it would have been had the desired outcome been achieved in the first place. The wrong of failing to succeed is corrected by succeeding in the best way now possible. In cases where it remains possible to bring about directly the specific outcome contemplated by the duty (for example, an unperformed contractual duty to deliver goods), the best way to make the world as if the stipulated outcome had been realised is of course for the wrongdoer to bring about that outcome as soon as possible. So the best way for a vendor who has failed to deliver promised goods to make the world as if the goods had been delivered is normally to deliver them as soon as possible. But where it is too late to perform the original duty or where late performance is not identical to timely performance (or where, if the matter goes to court, there are institutional objections to specific relief), then it seems reasonable to assume that the best way to make the world as if the wrong had never happened is for the defendant to provide a sum of money sufficient for the claimant to repair the harm or to purchase an alternative, or to provide a sum of money in addition to late performance. If I make a 'wrong' turn when driving, I will try to cure this wrong by turning around and going the right way. Similarly, if I take the 'wrong' umbrella when leaving a restaurant, I can cure the wrong by returning the umbrella or, if returning it is no longer possible (say because I lost it), then by giving the owner money to buy a replacement.

What I will call the 'second-best performance' model of damages is one way of understanding the familiar idea that damage awards should aim to put claimants in the positions that they would have been in had the wrong not occurred. This model of damages has also been defended in recent years on philosophical grounds by writers such as John Gardner and Ernest Weinrib. According to what Gardner calls the 'continuity thesis', the explanation for why tortfeasors have to pay damages is that the reasons underlying legal duties persist or 'continue' after a duty has been breached, giving rise to a new, closely related, duty to do the next best thing—which in practice is to pay damages (or to perform late and pay damages).[14] For Weinrib, the explanation of damages is that the duty itself lives on after its breach, albeit the duty changes in form to a duty to pay damages.[15] Both Gardner and Weinrib assume, then, that paying damages is the best method (or at least an appropriate method), post-breach, of fulfilling the tortfeasor's original duty or the reasons underlying that duty. Both analogise paying damages to the late performance of a contractual promise, for example, the late delivery of goods. To be sure, neither writer presents his theory of damages as a theory specifically of damages for breaching duties to succeed. However, their theories are naturally interpreted as providing just such an explanation.

3. THE CONDUCT MODEL: DUTIES TO TRY

A second way that lawmakers might frame legal duties is by specifying the efforts that citizens must make to try to bring about outcomes. So, for example, a lawmaker might stipulate that there is a duty 'to take reasonable care to try not to harm others'. Because such duties require that citizens try to bring about outcomes rather than that they actually bring about those outcomes, they may be called (again following John Gardner) 'duties to try'.[16]

Duties to try are related to duties to succeed because the efforts they prescribe are efforts to bring about specified outcomes, for example, not harming others. An abstract or 'undirected' duty to take reasonable care is meaningless. In common with duties to succeed, therefore, duties to try presume that it is possible to identify outcomes that are desirable regardless of how they are brought about. There is no reason to impose a duty to try not to harm others unless harming others is itself undesirable, regardless of how it happens. Similarly, the existence of a duty to succeed in not harming others presumes that we have reasons to try not to harm others.[17] There is a sense, then, in which duties to try assume the intelligibility of duties to succeed, and vice versa. Duties to try are nonetheless distinct from duties to succeed because they can be fulfilled—or broken—regardless of whether the desired

[14] Gardner, 'What is Tort Law For?' (n 10), building on J Raz, 'Personal Practical Conflicts' in P Baumann and M Betzler (eds), *Practical Conflicts: New Philosophical Essays* (Cambridge, Cambridge University Press, 2004) 172, 191.

[15] E Weinrib, *The Idea of Private Law* (Cambridge, Harvard University Press, 1995) 135; E Weinrib, 'Two Conceptions of Remedies' in C Rickett (ed), *Justifying Private Law Remedies* (Oxford, Hart Publishing, 2008) 3. See also A Ripstein, 'As if it had Never Happened' (2007) 48 *William and Mary Law Review* 1957.

[16] Gardner, 'Wrongdoing' (n 10).

[17] Gardner argues that while a reason to succeed is normally also a reason to try, and vice versa, there are exceptions. For example, Gardner says that although I have a reason to save someone who is drowning in the ocean, I would have no reason to attempt a rescue if the attempt would be futile (say because I cannot swim): see Gardner, 'Wrongdoing' (n 10) 55–57. It does not strike me as self-evident that I have no reason to try at all in such a case. If I have a reason to succeed in a rescue then success must be possible (even if unlikely) so it would seem that I have a duty to try to do something (though not to try to swim if I cannot swim). In any event, possible exceptions of this kind do not appear relevant to understanding private law duties.

outcome is achieved. A duty to try is not a duty to try and succeed, nor even a duty not to fail to succeed through want of trying: it is simply a duty to try to succeed.

It might be asked why lawmakers framing private law rules would care whether citizens *try* to bring about outcomes, other than in cases where their failure to try leads to the outcome not being achieved. Whatever the criminal law's concerns, the private law, it might be thought, has no reason to care about citizens' actions except insofar as those actions actually harm others. If my failure to try does not lead to harm, why should the law get involved? This is indeed a valid question if by 'getting involved' we mean that a mere failure to try may lead to a liability to pay damages. As I explain in more detail in a moment, it would be reasonable for the law to hold that the breach of a duty to try is actionable only on proof that the breach led to the outcome that the duty was directed towards avoiding. But the reasons underlying such a requirement are reasons for making *liability* conditional on proof of harm; they are not reasons for making duties similarly conditional.

Of course, it might still be asked why the law should care about trying, even if only at the stage of formulating duties. Why does it matter that someone fails to try except insofar as that failure causes the outcome that trying was meant to avoid? The answer is that trying matters because there is a straightforward sense in which failing to try may be a wrong.[18] If I carelessly or intentionally (and without justification) put you in danger, then I fail to treat you with proper, that is to say equal, concern and respect.[19] Treating you with equal concern and respect means treating your interests (or at least those the law merits worthy of concern) as equally important as my own. Carelessly firing a gun in your general direction places my interest in firing guns above your interest in bodily safety. If it were permissible for me to carelessly put you in danger, then it would be permissible for me to treat your interests as less important than mine. Indeed, what makes firing a gun in your general direction careless or 'unreasonable' is precisely that it is the kind of action that might be taken by someone who does not consider your interests worthy of concern. Further, the action remains unreasonable, and so carries this message, regardless of whether it leads to harm. Of course, if my actions harm you, then my failure to do anything subsequent to the harm by way of apology or repair may show a further failure of respect. But my failure to try, regardless of its outcome, is itself a distinct failure to show you proper respect and concern. This failure explains why we get angry when others attempt to harm us or expose us to unreasonable risks, even if we are not in fact harmed, and why we expect apologies from those who commit such actions.[20]

[18] This view is conventionally associated with Kant and his followers. John Gardner queries the conventional view, though primarily in order to show that Kant's position allows room for the significance of outcomes: Gardner, 'Wrongdoing' (n 10).

[19] Note that it not necessary that one's failure to take reasonable care be an intentional failure in order for it to qualify as a failure to treat others with equal concern and respect. Insofar as our focus is on how individuals should treat one another (rather than, say, on personal virtue), then conduct, like communications, is normally assessed objectively. Whether my actions treat your interests with proper concern turns not on my intentions but on whether my efforts show proper concern. As I noted earlier, duties to try are not 'duties to try to try', but simply 'duties to try'; in other words, they are 'duties to succeed at trying'.

[20] It also explains why attempts may qualify as criminal wrongs. Just as there would be no reason for the criminal law to hold me to a duty not to intentionally damage your property unless intentionally damaging your property was a wrong to you, there would be no reason for the criminal law to hold me to a duty not to attempt to steal your property unless such attempt was also a wrong to you. The fact

3.1 Duties to Try, Liabilities to Pay Damages, and Outcomes

We saw in Section 2 that breaching a duty to succeed need not lead automatically to a liability to pay damages. The law might reasonably allow defendants to plead a defence of excuse to avoid liability in some or all cases where a duty to succeed has been breached. A parallel observation applies to duties to try. Although it is possible in theory that a liability to pay damages might arise merely from the breach of a duty to try, in practice it is likely that such a liability would be conditional on the breach actually leading to harm. This requirement might derive from a substantive theory of liability. For example, if it is thought that the aim of damages is to provide redress for the tangible consequences of rights infringements, then insofar as there are no such consequences, no liability should arise. Similarly, if it is thought that the aim of damages is to give potential wrongdoers incentives to act properly, then it might be thought that sufficient incentives are provided by holding wrongdoers liable only for the actual harm they have caused. And irrespective of whatever substantive theory of liability is adopted, it might also reasonably be thought that it is simply not practical to allow private legal actions to be brought in cases where no tangible harm has occurred. Leaving aside the difficulty of determining on what basis damages would be assessed, it might reasonably be thought that state-sponsored judicial redress should be reserved for wrongdoing that has tangible consequences.

It would be coherent, then, for a legal system to frame private law duties as duties to try, but then to add that it is not possible to bring an action for damages except where the breach of a duty has caused the outcome that the duty was directed to prevent, for example, harm to another.[21] Further—and this addition is critical—such a legal system might also provide that liabilities to compensate can arise merely on proof that the defendant caused an undesirable outcome, regardless of whether the defendant breached a duty to try. That is, the system might recognise what I will call 'free-standing' liabilities to compensate—liabilities that arise without wrongdoing of any kind. Thus, a legal system in which the only duties are duties to try might hold that defendants who cause harm while engaged in dangerous activities must compensate their victim regardless of whether they breached a duty to try to avoid the harm. The recognition of such liabilities is not required by the conduct model of legal duties, but it is perfectly consistent with that model.

Although the label may be unfamiliar, the idea of free-standing liabilities is well known to lawyers. While it is not strictly a liability to compensate, a mistaken payee's liability to return a payment may arise without wrongdoing of any kind. Indeed, most liabilities to make restitution are similarly free-standing. Closer to present concerns, the liability recognised in the American case of *Vincent v Lake*

that the criminal law allows you to waive these duties shows that in each case they are fundamentally duties owed to you.

[21] An alternative way to reach the same result would be to hold that liability for breach of a duty to try may be avoided by an excuse of 'no harm'. Nothing in my argument turns on whether harm is a condition of liability or no-harm an excuse to liability, but the first option fits better with the idea, noted above, that the law should in principle not get involved unless a defendant's wrongdoing has led to harm. If no harm functions as an excuse, then it must be supposed that in principle harmless wrongdoers should pay damages.

Erie Transportation Co[22] to compensate for what might loosely be called 'necessitous trespasses' is free-standing. In *Vincent*, the defendant shipowner refused to untie his ship from the claimant's dock because a storm was impending that would likely cause severe damage to the ship if it was on the open sea. The court held that the defendant's refusal to untie was reasonable. This finding is clearly correct: whether we think of the defendant's duty in terms of outcomes or efforts, it would be absurd if the law held that the defendant should have put his ship to sea in the storm. Notwithstanding this finding, the court went on to hold the defendant liable to compensate the claimant for damage caused as a consequence of the ship hitting against the dock during the storm. Short of suggesting that this holding is wrong on the merits (which suggestion, so far as I am aware, has never been advanced), the obvious interpretation of the result in *Vincent* is that the defendant was liable notwithstanding that he committed no wrong.[23] The natural interpretation of *Vincent*, in other words, is that the court recognised a free-standing liability to compensate.

The idea of free-standing liabilities to compensate raises a number of questions. Are they liabilities to fall under a duty to compensate (which duty would be, in the system now under consideration, a duty to try to compensate that could then be backed up by orders to pay) or are they only liabilities to being ordered by a court to pay compensation? A second question (or group of questions) concerns the potential scope of such liabilities. Is the free-standing liability for necessitous trespasses recognised in *Vincent* one example of a broader category of liability for faultless trespasses? And might a free-standing liability for harms arising from dangerous activities be defended on a similar basis? Finally, but perhaps most importantly, what is the justification for free-standing liabilities? These questions cannot be answered without first developing a substantive theory of free-standing liabilities. However, for present purposes it is sufficient to acknowledge the legal possibility of free-standing liabilities to compensate.

3.2 The Nature of a Liability for the Breach of a Duty to Try

As we have seen, the wrong committed by breaching a duty to try is different than the wrong committed by breaching a duty to succeed. The wrong of failing to try is basically the wrong of failing to treat others with proper respect. Further, the wrong retains this character even if the legal system conditions liability to pay damages on proof that the wrong led to harm. It should be no surprise, then, that the justification for requiring defendants to pay damages where they have breached a duty to try is different from the justification for requiring defendants to pay damages where they have breached a duty to succeed. Rather than being awarded to erase or

[22] 109 Minn 456; 124 NW 221 (1910).

[23] Some writers have suggested that the payment in *Vincent* is restitution to reverse an unjust enrichment (eg, Weinrib, *Idea of Private Law* (n 15) 196–203), but this theory cannot explain why the payment was set at the amount of damage suffered by the claimant. Other writers have maintained that the defendant in *Vincent* did indeed commit a wrong: see, eg, Gardner, 'Corrective Justice' (n 10); J Goldberg, 'Tort Law's Missing Excuses' ch 4 in this volume, at p 62. The difficulty with this view is that it presumes the existence of legal duties to do things that the law cannot plausibly want done (such as to put to sea in a storm).

undo the wrong outcome, the natural role of damages for breach of a duty to try is to erase or undo the defendant's failure of respect.[24] Broadly speaking, damages must aim to restore the parties' formal equality: the award must make clear that, notwithstanding the defendant's actions, the parties are equally deserving of each other's respect. Another way of making this point is to observe that insofar as damages are intended to redress the breach of a duty to try, they are structurally similar to criminal punishment. No one supposes that criminal punishment is intended to force defendants to comply, in the best way now possible, with their original duty or the reasons underlying that duty. Going to jail is not a second-best way of not killing. Criminal punishment is not a response to an unfulfilled duty, but rather a response to an outstanding wrong. The nature of that response is described differently in different theories of punishment, but in theories that view the wrong as failing to respect one's victim, the general aim of punishment is to restore a moral balance between society and the wrongdoer that the latter's action has upset.[25] From this perspective, the main difference between damages (in the model now under consideration) and criminal punishment is that rather than restoring a moral balance between society and the wrongdoer, damages aim to restore a moral balance between wrongdoers and their victims.

It might be asked how paying a sum of money could restore a moral balance between claimant and defendant. I have addressed this question elsewhere (as have others),[26] so I will limit my response to two observations. First, the availability of nominal and punitive damages (and arguably also damages for mental suffering) shows that the common law assumes that damages are, at least sometimes, an appropriate response to what might be called purely intangible harms. Second, the same general question is asked of the theories of punishment described above. How can paying a fine or spending time in jail restore the moral balance upset by an assault or a murder? While not everyone is convinced by the answers that such theories provide, they cannot be rejected out of hand. In any event, regardless of whether one believes that paying money can restore the parties' equality, the point I wish to make is that such restoration, broadly understood, is the natural role of liability for wrongdoing in a legal system that adopts the conduct model of duties.

[24] I defend an account of damages roughly along these lines in S Smith, 'Duties, Liabilities, and Damages' (2012) 125 *Harvard Law Review* 1727 and S Smith, 'Remedies for Breach of Contract: One Principle or Two?' in G Klass, G Letsas and P Saprai (eds), *Philosophical Foundations of Contract Law* (Oxford, Oxford University Press, 2014). The understanding of damages found in civil recourse theories, though not described in exactly these terms, is also roughly along the above lines: see J Goldberg and B Zipursky, 'Rights and Responsibility in the Law of Torts' in D Nolan and A Robertson (eds), *Rights and Private Law* (Oxford, Hart Publishing, 2012) 251; BC Zipursky, 'Civil Recourse, Not Corrective Justice' (2003) 91 *Georgetown Law Journal* 695.

[25] I refer here to what are generally described as retributivist theories of punishment. A structurally similar account of damages could be told from the perspective of instrumental (or 'deterrence') theories. Thus in the same way that deterrence theories of criminal punishment suppose that the aim of punishment is to provide incentives for citizens to devote appropriate effort to trying not to commit undesirable acts, a deterrence theory of tort damages for failing to try will explain such damages as incentives for future citizens to try not to commit undesirable acts. Insofar as the aim of damages is to influence future behaviour their availability should in principle be triggered (merely) by failures to try appropriately (though in practice there may be instrumental reasons to limit damage awards to cases where that failure leads to harm).

[26] Smith 'Duties' (n 24) 1753–56; Smith 'Remedies' (n 24).

In such a legal system, damages are fundamentally symbolic: rather than being awarded to make the tangible world as close as it can be to the world that would have existed had the wrong not occurred, they aim to make the 'moral' world, or perhaps the moral register, as close as it can be to the world that would have existed had the wrong not occurred.

4. MIXTURES

The previous sections describe two starkly different ways in which a legal system might frame private law duties. The question arises whether there are other ways in which a legal system might approach this task. In this section, I explore briefly what might be thought the most obvious alternative (and one that the common law appears to have at least partly adopted), namely to mix duties to try and duties to succeed. Specifically, I will examine three mixtures: (1) combination duties to try and to succeed; (2) overlapping duties to try and duties to succeed; and (3) non-overlapping duties to try and duties to succeed. The conclusion will be that only the third of these possibilities is even prima facie stable.

4.1 Combination Duties

'Combination duties' involve a combination of requirements to try and requirements to succeed. Two such combinations seem possible. First, a legal system might hold that some or all of its legal duties are 'conjunctive' in the sense that that they require citizens both to try to achieve a particular outcome and, as well, to actually achieve the outcome. For example, a legal system might hold that citizens have a duty to try not to trespass and, as well, a duty not to trespass. The duty is conjunctive because it can be breached either by failing to try not to trespass or by trespassing or by both failing to try and by trespassing. The second possibility is that the combination duty is 'disjunctive' in the sense that it is a duty not to bring about a specified outcome by failing to try. This second combination is how the tort of negligence is usually described: a defendant is said to commit the tort of negligence if she fails to take reasonable care not to harm the claimant *and* that failure leads to the claimant suffering harm. The duty is disjunctive because it can be satisfied either by taking reasonable care not to harm the claimant or by not harming the claimant.

The objection to both conjunctive and disjunctive combination duties is that they are ad hoc mixtures of qualitatively different and independently complete concepts. As we have seen, the wrong of failing to achieve a particular outcome is not affected by whether the wrongdoer also did, or did not, try to achieve that outcome. Similarly, the wrong of failing to try to achieve an outcome remains the same whether or not the wrongdoer actually achieved the outcome. To be sure, a legal system that consisted exclusively of duties to succeed might decide that liability for breaching such duties should be subject to an excusatory defence of reasonable behaviour; similarly, a legal system that consisted exclusively of duties to try might decide that liability for breaching such duties should be conditional on the breach causing harm. It is also theoretically possible (though in practice unlikely) that a legal system might make liability to pay damages conditional on proof that two wrongs were committed. But at the stage of articulating *duties*, there appears to be no reason to combine duties to try and duties to succeed. Two wrongs are worse than one, but a single wrong remains a wrong. Duties to try and duties to succeed are complete in themselves.

4.2 Overlapping Duties to Try and to Succeed

The observation that combination duties to try and to succeed are really just pairs of separate duties suggests a second way in which a legal system might mix duties to try and duties to succeed: by enacting separate, but overlapping, duties to try and to succeed. For example, a legal system might enact a rule imposing a duty to take reasonable care to try to avoid trespassing and, at the same time, enact a separate rule that imposes a duty not to trespass.

In theory, overlapping duties are prima facie coherent. The wrong of failing to try is distinct from the wrong of failing to succeed, so it might seem perfectly sensible to suppose that the law would give citizens reasons to avoid both kinds of wrongs. In ordinary life, both kinds of wrongs are recognised; we apologise when we fail to try and when we fail to succeed, and we apologise doubly when we both fail to try and fail to succeed. In practice, however, overlapping legal duties raise two problems. The first is that the overlap may lead to confusion over what actions are required by the law. I noted earlier that a duty to succeed—for example, a duty not to trespass—does not direct or indirectly counsel citizens to take extreme care not to trespass. Yet if the law enacts a duty 'not to trespass' alongside a duty to 'take reasonable care to try not to trespass', citizens might reasonably be forgiven for assuming that the first duty is counselling them to take more than reasonable care. More broadly, citizens might reasonably wonder what kind of guidance the duty to try is meant to provide that the duty to succeed does not already provide—and vice versa. Why have two duties if they support the same actions?

The potential for confusion is increased when we turn to consider the second problem associated with overlapping legal duties: overlap provides conflicting grounds for liability. It is true, as I have stressed, that the question of what duties a legal system should enact is different from the question of what liabilities to pay damages it should impose. Nonetheless, it would be odd if a legal duty could be breached generally without risk of liability. Liabilities to pay damages, as well as the enforcement mechanisms by which they are backed up, are part of the quid pro quo for the law's demand that citizens comply with their duties. It seems reasonable to assume, then, that a legal system which recognises overlapping duties will also recognise overlapping liabilities. For example, if lawmakers enact a duty to try to avoid trespassing as well as a duty to avoid trespassing, a defendant who has committed an intentional or careless trespass will presumably have breached both duties and, in principle, be liable to pay damages on both grounds. The question, then, is how these different liabilities would fit together. There is no clear answer because, as have seen, the justification for, and the nature of, damages differ depending on whether they are awarded in response to breaching a duty to try or a duty to succeed. It is no solution to say that the defendant's liability in such a case is simply to pay the sum of the amounts justified on each basis. For one thing, damages for breach of a duty to succeed should in principle be paid immediately following the breach because, as we have seen, the payment is a continuation of the original duty (or the reasons underlying it). In contrast, damages for breach of a duty to try should presumably be due only following a court ruling because, like criminal punishment, they can only serve their restorative purpose if ordered by a court (as is true of a fine).[27] More importantly, the issue of over-determination that we saw with respect to overlapping duties arises again with respect to overlapping liabilities. The payment of a single sum of money by the defendant cannot at the same time be a second-best way of fulfilling the defendant's original duty and a means of affirming the parties' equality. The latter aim, in particular, can only be achieved insofar as it is understood that it is the reason for the payment. Treating the liabilities as completely separate avoids this problem, but then leads to the risk of double recovery. In short, the liability scheme in a system of overlapping duties seems impossibly complicated.

4.3 Non-overlapping Duties to Try and to Succeed

A third way that a legal system might mix duties to try and duties to succeed is by directing duties to try and duties to succeed towards different outcomes. For example, the system might hold that with respect to, say, harm to property, citizens have duties to succeed, while with respect to harm to persons, citizens have duties to try. If legal duties were arranged in this way, then the previous objections are avoided. Nor is there any obvious objection to any particular duty to try or to succeed in such a system because, as we have seen, both duties to try and duties to succeed are prima facie coherent. A duty not to damage property is coherent and a duty to try to avoid harming others is also coherent.

However, the obvious question raised by such a system is on what basis are some duties framed as requirements to try and others as requirements to succeed. The answer is again not clear. It might well be that there are reasons to prefer duties to try generally over duties to succeed, but it is not clear why there would be reasons to prefer duties to try in some areas of life and duties to succeed in others. It is no answer to say that duties to succeed are appropriate when and only when strict liability is appropriate (for example, when the defendant was engaged in an abnormally dangerous activity or when the defendant caused a certain kind of harm, such as a trespass). Strict liabilities do not require strict duties. As we have seen, a legal system could confine itself to enacting duties to try to avoid causing harms, but then add that citizens who cause harm through their dangerous activities or by trespassing incur a free-standing liability (not based on the breach of any duty) to compensate for that harm.

It is worth mentioning that the practical objections to overlapping duties also apply, albeit not as strongly, to non-overlapping duties. Insofar as a legal system enacts both duties to try and duties to succeed, citizens may reasonably wonder if the guidance provided by these duties is meant to be the same. Further confusion

[27] I defend this suggestion in more detail in Smith 'Duties' (n 24).

may arise when courts (or citizens) attempt to work out the appropriate liabilities for breaching duties. If it is not apparent why certain duties are duties to try and others duties to succeed, the risk of misunderstanding the nature of the duty and its associated liability is increased. It is, of course, possible that there is a reason to prefer duties to try in certain areas of life and duties to succeed in others. But so far as I am aware this reason has never been articulated, nor is it obvious what it might be.

5. THE LAW

The conclusion suggested by the preceding discussion is that while both duties to try and duties to succeed are prima facie coherent, mixing such duties is prima facie incoherent, impractical, or at least (in the case of a non-overlapping mixture) in need of a yet-to-be provided explanation. How does the positive law compare to this picture? One observation is that the kinds of situations in which damage awards are available in the common law are consistent, at least in rough outline, with both the outcome and conduct models of legal duties. Broadly speaking, damages are available in two kinds of situations. The first is where the defendant has directly interfered with the claimant's person, property or liberty (the so-called 'intentional torts').[28] The second situation is where the claimant's person, property or liberty was indirectly harmed as a consequence of the defendant's failure to take reasonable care or of the defendant's engagement in a particular type of activity, for example, storing water on his property (ie, liability under *Rylands v Fletcher*[29]). Both the outcome and conduct models of duties can account for such liabilities, although they do so differently. On the outcome model, all the liabilities just described can be understood as liabilities for the breach of duties to succeed, in particular duties not to directly or indirectly harm the claimant's person, property, or liberty. From this perspective, the difference between the two groups of liabilities is that liability for indirect harm is in most circumstances only a prima facie liability because it may be avoided by a defence—an excusatory defence—of reasonable behaviour. According to the outcome model, then, liability for negligence must be understood as liability for the breach of a strict duty to succeed, which is then subject to a possible defence of reasonable care. In contrast, the conduct model of duties explains liability for negligence as liability for the breach of a duty to try, specifically a duty to try to take reasonable care not to interfere with another's person, property, or liberty, albeit the liability is conditional on proof that the failure to try led to harm. The conduct model's explanation of damages that are awarded without proof of fault, that is, without proof of a failure to try, is that such awards are not strictly awards of damages. According to the conduct model, rather than being responses to wrongdoing, awards for so-called intentional torts or *Rylands v Fletcher* awards

[28] Interference is direct if the interfering action was intentional, for example, intentionally walking onto the claimant's land, intentionally touching the claimant, or intentionally confining the claimant. It is sufficient that the defendant intended the act: the defendant need not have been aware that the act constituted a trespass, battery, etc.

[29] (1868) LR 3 HL 330.

must be understood as instances of what I described earlier as free-standing liabilities to compensate.

If we were to pursue this line of inquiry further, the next question would be whether the actual amounts of damages that the courts award are consistent with the outcome and conduct models. As we have seen, the models justify awards of damages on different grounds, and so it would not be surprising to find differences in how they quantify awards. For example, it might be expected that their approach to punitive damages, nominal damages and damages for emotional distress would differ. A further question is whether the rules governing *when* a duty to pay damages arises are consistent with both models. As I mentioned, the outcome model suggests that the duty should in principle arise at the moment of breach, while the conduct model appears more consistent with the duty arising only once a damages award is made. These questions are important and interesting, but as I have discussed them elsewhere,[30] the question on which I will focus in the remainder of this chapter is whether either model can account for the way that the law presents and explains the above liabilities. Does the law explain them in the same way as either of the above models?

The short answer is that neither model fully accounts for how the law explains the above liabilities. The closest fit is between the outcome model and liabilities that are not dependent on proof of fault. An award of damages that may be made merely on proof that the defendant interfered directly with the claimant's person, property or liberty, or on proof that water that escaped from the defendant's property harmed the claimant, is prima facie consistent with the outcome model of duties. The courts say that damages in such cases are awarded for a tort, that is, a wrong, and the only wrong that could arise from an innocent trespass or a faultless escape of water is the breach of an outcome duty. It is worth noting, however, that even in such cases the conventional language in which the law is described is not consistent with the outcome model. Rather than describing defendants in such cases as being liable for the breach of a 'strict' duty (that is, a duty to succeed), what courts and commentators typically say is simply that the defendant is 'strictly liable'. The rules laid down in *Rylands v Fletcher,* in particular, are classified in textbooks under the heading 'strict liabilities' (not 'strict duties'), and lawyers talk of a strict liability for harm caused by escaping water rather than a strict duty to prevent water from escaping. Such language is less evident in discussions of intentional torts (though it is common when focussing on the relatively rare cases in which the defendant's actions were entirely innocent), and it could be argued generally that lawyers refer to strict liability merely to make clear that defendants cannot plead, by way of an excuse to liability, that their behaviour was reasonable. Still, if the law recognised duties to, say, not allow water to escape from one's property, we would expect that the analysis of the law governing such escapes would begin by identifying the duty rather than, as is the usual case, focussing immediately on the liability. The focus on the liability is, however, consistent with the conduct model's explanation of such liabilities as free-standing.

[30] Smith 'Duties' (n 24); Smith 'Remedies' (n 24).

Neither model is even prima facie consistent with the conventional understanding of fault-based liabilities, such as liability for negligence. In the outcome model, fault may be relevant to liability, but only in the form of an excusatory defence of 'reasonable care'. In the conduct model, legal duties are duties to take reasonable care, but harm is relevant in this model as a condition of liability. Neither explanation, then, fits the conventional view that liability for negligence and other fault-based torts arises from the breach of a mixed duty not to cause harm through failing to take reasonable care. Admittedly, the common description of negligence duties as duties 'to take care not to cause harm' is arguably ambiguous as to whether not causing harm is an element of the duty or a condition of liability.[31] However, it is orthodox law that the tort—that is, the wrong—of negligence is not committed unless the defendant has harmed the claimant. On the conventional account, then, the tort of negligence can only be committed by a combination of failing to try *and* failing to succeed. As we have seen, neither model of duties explains this combination: on the contrary, what the models suggest is that this combination is inexplicable.

6. AN HISTORICAL EXPLANATION

One conclusion that might be drawn from the previous section is that my explanation of the different ways in which we might imagine a legal system framing legal duties is flawed or incomplete. If neither the conduct nor the outcome model can explain the law, so much the worse for the models. The other conclusion that might be drawn is that the law is confused. Much more needs to be said about framing legal duties before either conclusion is adopted, but rather than pursue that task here I will change track. In this last section, I try to lend some indirect support to the second conclusion by suggesting that, in light of the common law's history, it would not be surprising to find that its understanding of duties is problematic.

For most of the common law's history, the very idea of substantive law, in the sense of rules stating how citizens ought to treat one another, is largely absent. Until recently, 'law' meant rules about how to get into court, how to present a case in court, and what kinds of relief are available from courts.[32] The law, and in particular the antecedents of what we would now call private law, was essentially law about the availability and content of judicial remedies: it was about the rules governing liabilities to judicial rulings. The 'forms of action' that aspiring lawyers had to learn were forms for getting into court. Judges no doubt thought it was wrong to injure others, that debts should be paid, and so on, but they did not think it was the law's business to tell citizens how to go about their day-to-day lives.[33] The law's

[31] The second view is defended in N McBride, 'Duties of Care—Do They Really Exist?' (2004) 24 *OJLS* 417.

[32] John Baker describes the twelfth century text on the 'laws and customs of England', traditionally attributed to Glanville, as 'primarily about how to gain access to those courts [the Royal Courts] and what to do when there', adding later that '[t]he forms of action were the first object of legal study. The two earliest treatises on the common law, *Glanville* and *Bracton*, were essentially books about writs and the procedures generated by them': see J Baker, *An Introduction to English Legal History*, 4th edn (London, Butterworths, 2002) 14, 56.

[33] 'In the fourteenth century there was no law of England, no body of rules complete in itself ... There were justice and right, absolute values; but it was not yet the lawyer's business to comprehend them in

business was to resolve disputes, and so the law consisted of rules governing how this should happen.

Blackstone's *Commentaries*, published in 1765–69, were the first attempt to provide a reasonably comprehensive account of private law organised around rights and duties that citizens held against one another. It is not clear exactly how it first came to be thought that the law might be described in this way, though the influence of continental natural law theorists and civil law thinking more generally in this transformation is evident. When Blackstone and others started to think seriously about the structure of the common law (spurred in part by the pedagogic demands of teaching law for the first time in universities), they naturally turned to consider how the civil law—which had long reflected on such questions—organised itself. What they found in the civil law (and in the work of the philosophers who influenced that tradition) was a law of 'obligations', that is, a law organised around different kinds of legal obligations or duties. What happened, though it took many centuries, is that Blackstone and the other writers responsible for the modern understanding of the common law developed an organisational scheme that resembled in broad outline the scheme adopted in civilian codes. Following the civil law, the common law came to recognise a law of 'contract', a law of 'tort', and, more recently, a law of 'unjust enrichment'. However, one problem was that the legal materials on which this organisational scheme was first imposed consisted mostly of rules about procedure and remedies. Not surprisingly, what appears to have happened is that writers and judges worked backwards from remedial rules to substantive rules. Substantive duties were derived from the rules governing remedies.[34] Thus, if a claimant could obtain damages on proof that the defendant had trespassed (regardless of fault), the lesson to draw was that the common law recognises a strict duty not to trespass. Similarly, if a claimant could obtain damages on proof that the defendant's lack of care had caused him harm, the common law must contain a duty not to cause harm through failing to take care.

This way of thinking about substantive legal duties remains common today. The reason this chapter began by considering the prima facie implausible view that duty statements are the mirror-image of liability statements is that it is often assumed by common law lawyers. Oliver Wendell Holmes' statement that 'the duty to keep a contract at common law is merely a prediction that you must pay damages if you do not keep it'[35] is often criticised, but it is also the best-known description of a common law duty. The continuing popularity of Holmes' description among common law lawyers helps to explain their relative enthusiasm (in comparison to civilian lawyers) for the idea of 'efficient breach' and for other efforts to explain the law in terms of the material incentives that it creates. More broadly, the habit of

the sense of knowing what was the just and right result upon these facts and those. His business was procedural, to see that disputes were properly submitted to the appropriate deciding mechanism': SFC Milsom, *Historical Foundations of the Common Law*, 2nd edn (London, Butterworths, 1981) 83.

[34] Hence Lord Dunedin's classic statement '... the common law (though there is no harder lesson for the stranger jurist to learn) began with the remedy and ended with the right': see *Nocton v Lord Ashburton* [1914] AC 932 (HL) 964. Sir Henry Maine made essentially the same point when he famously observed that, in the common law's early days, substance was 'secreted' in the 'interstices' of procedural law: see H Maine, *Dissertation on Early Law and Custom* (London, John Murray, 1883) 389.

[35] OW Holmes, 'The Path of the Law' (1881) 10 *Harvard Law Review* 457, 462.

understanding duties as reflections of liabilities is seen in the still common practice of starting common law contracts courses by discussing remedies for breach and, more generally, in the importance placed in all courses on remedial issues. Arguably the most significant doctrinal development in private law over the past hundred years in common law jurisdictions is the recognition of a legal subject-matter that was first described, and is often still today described, in terms of a remedial response: restitution. Even writers who have dropped this title in favour of 'unjust enrichment' continue to discuss the law in terms of the liabilities that it imposes. Throughout the common law world, it is more common to speak of a 'liability to reverse an unjust enrichment' than of a duty to do this.[36] More broadly, writers continue to describe substantive areas of the law partly or exclusively in terms of judicial remedies: 'A contract is an agreement ... enforced by law...';[37] '[T]ort law is a collection of causes of action, each made up of three main components: an interest protected by the law, conduct affecting that interest which the law sanctions, and a remedy by which the interest is protected and the conduct sanctioned'.[38]

The conclusion suggested by this brief overview is that the common law's understanding of private law duties has been heavily influenced by, and in many cases directly lifted from, the rules governing liability. Duty requirements have been derived from liability conditions. The question of whether this is an appropriate way of determining duties and, further, whether the duties so identified make sense when placed alongside one another, has rarely been asked. But it must be asked. As I have stressed throughout this chapter, duties and liabilities may be related in different ways. It is important not to confuse liability conditions with duty requirements. Just such confusion appears to have influenced the common law's understanding of duties and liabilities.

The lesson to draw from these historical observations is that contemporary common law lawyers need to think seriously about legal duties as duties. And the lesson to draw from my earlier arguments is that part of thinking seriously about legal duties is thinking about the kinds of actions that they demand of their subjects. Does the law require us to try or to succeed? Is there a third option? And regardless of what the law requires, what should it require? None of these questions admit of easy answers (though I have argued against the coherence of a 'third option'). But if we want to understand legal duties—and the law's response to their breach—they must be asked.

[36] An example of the common law's tendency to define duties in terms of liabilities is the view that the duty to make restitution in cases where the defendant's enrichment is in the form of property received is a duty to hand over the monetary value of the property rather than the property itself. The explanation for this prima facie odd understanding, it appears, is that courts are typically unwilling to order specific restitution.

[37] G Treitel, 'Contract' in P Birks (ed) *English Private Law*, 1st edn, vol 2 (Oxford, Oxford University Press, 2000) 4.

[38] J Davies, 'Tort' in P Birks (ed) *English Private Law*, 1st edn, vol 2 (Oxford, Oxford University Press, 2000) 408.

6

Balancing Defences

RODERICK BAGSHAW

1. INTRODUCTION

1.1 Distinguishing some Types of General Proposition about Tort Defences

IN THIS CHAPTER I seek to illuminate some of the issues that a lawmaker ought to consider when deciding in a particular context whether to design a tort law defence so that it requires the balancing of something on a defendant's side against something on a claimant's side, or balancing some public interest against something on the claimant's side, with that balancing being conducted on the facts of the instant case. This goal is premised on my belief that torts are designed by lawmakers, rather than emerging through revelation or pure deduction from moral fundamentals,[1] and that their choices between different possible designs often require context-focused trade-offs between different desiderata. Thus in one context a lawmaker may choose a design that incorporates some factor that is relatively more costly to verify through adversarial litigation but which better tracks a common idea of moral culpability, such as a subjective mental state, whilst in another context a lawmaker may choose a design that incorporates a standard which is less perfectly aligned with culpability but easier for a court to apply, such as 'what a reasonable man in the defendant's position ought to have known'. Clearly there might be advantages if similar designs were used across the whole law of torts: the law might be easier to master, there would be fewer mystifying inconsistencies of the sort that trigger costly disputes, and any necessary judicial clarifications of the law would take effect across a broader range of situations. Such uniformity might also facilitate the task of theorists eager to demonstrate that the law of torts can be interpreted in a way that makes it coherent and comprehensible. But because different parts of the law of torts are used to perform very different socially useful tasks, and we can expect those who use it in different contexts to be placed very differently with regard to such matters as the importance they attach to predictability and the resources they can reasonably be expected to expend in obtaining reliable legal advice, I do not believe that any single schema of trade-offs is likely to be

[1] I do not intend to suggest that anybody actually believes that the rules of tort law *are* simply a product of revelation or pure deduction from moral fundamentals. It is simply easier to triangulate my position by reference to artificial poles rather than by relating it to the complex and nuanced positions of named scholars.

optimal across all torts and with regard to all defences. For example, in a field where tort law is primarily used to determine which of two insurance companies ought to absorb a particular instance of a regularly recurring loss, and subsequently pass it on to a particular pool of customers, a schema that facilitates the efficient settlement of disputes may be more attractive, but in a field where tort law is regularly used to achieve public condemnation, and delivers stigma, a design that attaches significance to finer moral distinctions may be more appropriate. Moreover, the advantages and disadvantages of expressing the law using particular concepts vary across contexts: for example, the advantages of incorporating reference to the standard of 'reasonable skill and care in accordance with a responsible body of professional opinion' vary depending on the extent to which the profession concerned has mechanisms for establishing and promulgating its standards.

For the avoidance of doubt, I should emphasise that my belief that torts are designed by lawmakers is distinguishable from the extravagant delusion that every aspect of every rule in the encyclopaedia of tort law is a product of a conscious and fully-informed design process. Clearly in England choices have sometimes been made by lawmakers who were apparently unaware of the significance of their selection between options, and may even have been unaware of the range of options that were available (in the sense that they made no mention of the fact that other options were utilised elsewhere in the English law of torts). Equally, choices have often been made through the use of opaque and indirect methods of reasoning, such as appeal to analogy, rather than a fully transparent contest which addresses all defensible design norms. I also do not intend to suggest that I believe that English constitutional law grants all lawmakers full and equal freedom to adopt any design that appeals to their individual preferences. Clearly Parliamentary legislators and judges (at various levels in the precedential hierarchy) may be subject to constraints with regard to the design options open to them, and the content and status of these constraints may differ. But, my claim that lawmakers often make context-specific choices between designs rejects, at least tacitly, the notion that law-making in private law is in practice simply a matter of identifying moral rights or performing some heroic feat of logical processing. Perhaps judges could reason their way to 'one right answer' in a world where all facts were known, all future behaviour could be reliably predicted, and disputes as to the fair distribution of wealth and power could be properly understood as being between the enlightened and the mistaken. But that is not the world in which current lawmakers must resolve disputes about tort law, and those making the necessary choices gain no assistance by asking themselves 'would I make the same choice if I knew everything?'

As might be anticipated, my general belief that torts are often a product of context-dependent design includes a more specific belief that tort defences are (and were) frequently designed by lawmakers who appreciate that the rules that they fashion will be used by different types of users for a variety of purposes in a variety of contexts.[2] Indeed, it seems to me to be almost beyond serious dispute that when lawmakers

[2] Perhaps the vast majority of human beings share an interest in the scope of the defence of self-defence, but some tort defences are likely to benefit only limited classes of people, eg, the defence of 'act of God' to a claim under *Rylands v Fletcher* (1868) LR 3 HL 330, the defence under s 9 of the Animals Act 1971 (UK) where a dog is killed or injured to protect livestock, and sovereign immunity.

are designing defences their choices are often influenced by features of the context in which they expect those defences to operate. A plain example is provided by sections 4 and 5 of the Animals Act 1971 (UK), the statutory successor to the tort of cattle trespass, where the limited range of defences reflects the expressed preference of farmers for a straightforward liability regime that would enable low-value disputes between neighbours to be quickly and amicably settled, as opposed to a regime that would require more contentious and laborious investigations of a defendant's culpability.[3] But I think it is also clear that features of the specific practical contexts were influential when choices were being made by the judicial lawmakers in such cases as *Ashley* v *Chief Constable of Sussex Police*,[4] *Lumba* v *Secretary of State for the Home Department*,[5] and *Hayes* v *Willoughby*.[6]

If it is so obvious that tort defences are designed by lawmakers in the way that I have suggested then why is it valuable to highlight the point at the outset? I do so because the sorts of general propositions about 'balancing defences' that I set out later in this chapter, relating to the potential advantages and disadvantages of choosing to use a 'balancing' structure in contexts with particular features, may at first seem rather unambitious when contrasted with the three types of general proposition exemplified by the claims that: all tort defences currently recognised as part of English law either conform to model A or model B, the best interpretation of English law as a coherent unity involves all tort defences conforming to either model A or model B, and English lawmakers *can only legitimately* design tort defences that conform to model A or model B.[7] How might I defend not striving to formulate general propositions of these different types about 'balancing defences'? Whilst I will provide a brief descriptive account of several 'balancing defences' later in this

[3] See R Bagshaw, 'The Animals Act 1971' in TT Arvind and J Steele (eds), *Tort Law and the Legislature* (Oxford, Hart Publishing, 2013) 213. Another plain example might be the Road Traffic Act 1988 (UK), s 149(3), which prevents the defence of 'willing acceptance of the risk' being raised against a passenger injured in a road accident.

[4] [2008] UKHL 25; [2008] 1 AC 962. The immediate choice related to whether a defendant's honest but unreasonable belief as to the existence of a threat could give rise to a defence of self-defence in a claim for trespass to the person. The House of Lords decided that it could not, but left open the question whether a belief as to the existence of a threat could provide a defence where it was a belief that was reasonable in the light of what the defendant had been told but unreasonable from the perspective of how the claimant had actually behaved. That question clearly raised difficulties in the context of police officers acting following a briefing.

[5] [2011] UKSC 12; [2012] 1 AC 245. The choice related to whether exercise by a public defendant of a statutory power to detain could give rise to a defence in a claim for false imprisonment where the exercise of power had involved a breach of public law principles but the claimant could have been legitimately detained through an exercise of the power without such a breach.

[6] [2013] UKSC 17; [2013] 1 WLR 935. The choice related to the interpretation of the defence in s 1(3) of the Protection from Harassment Act 1997 (UK) for a course of conduct 'pursued for the purpose of preventing or detecting crime', and in particular whether a defendant could establish such a 'purpose' if his or her decision to act was not reached through a 'rational' process. Clearly one difficulty with the interpretation of the 1997 Act is that it will often have to be applied to defendants who reason in unusual ways.

[7] The variety of general propositions that are commonly made means that one must be careful when contemplating James Goudkamp's claim that all the defences currently recognised by English tort law can be classified in accordance with a taxonomy that divides them between those that are based on public policy and those that rely on a reasons-based justification: J Goudkamp, *Tort Law Defences* (Oxford, Hart Publishing, 2013) ch 4. Even if this is a solely *descriptive* claim its accuracy depends on several doctrines within tort law that are frequently referred to as defences, such as 'truth' in relation to a defamation claim, being understood as denials of elements that must be present in order to establish a wrong.

chapter, it is certainly true that I will not provide an exhaustive bestiary, nor will I seek to promulgate the most economical scheme for classifying its contents. One reason, however, for not undertaking these tasks is that it would be exceptionally difficult to provide a reliable description of all the 'balancing defences' recognised by English law when so many points are unsettled: in such circumstances there might be considerable utility in illuminating some of the issues that a lawmaker ought to consider when deciding what the structure of a tort law defence ought to be in any particular context.

My explanation for not seeking to *interpret* existing 'balancing defences' so as to expose a coherent unity is not that I believe that this would be impossible, but I harbour doubts about whether it is necessary, or particularly useful, to prioritise 'coherence'.[8] Of course, I do not seek to defend any radical heresy such as that tort law should strive to be incoherent. Rather, by not treating identification of 'coherence' as a primary goal it becomes easier to explore why different designs for tort defences might appeal to lawmakers whose focus is on the particular practical contexts where the rules that they formulate will operate.

With regard to the third type of general proposition, that English lawmakers *can only legitimately* design tort defences that conform to some model, my excuse for not seeking to formulate this type of general proposition is that such a project would require an extended account of English constitutional law, and given the doctrine of Parliamentary sovereignty it is not easy to see how any proposition of this type could ever be valid with regard to all lawmakers. Moreover, any proposition about the scope of legitimate judicial law-making would be unlikely to be specific to the field of 'judicial law-making relating to tort defences', still less 'balancing defences'.

1.2 What are 'Balancing Defences'?

What I mean by 'balancing defences' are those defences that have a structure based around balancing something on a defendant's side against something on a claimant's side, or balancing some public interest against something on the claimant's side, with that balancing being conducted on the particular facts of the instant case rather than at the stage of 'rule design'. Thus, on my definition, the defence of 'consent'[9] in tort law is clearly *not* a 'balancing defence'. If 'consent' is a potential defence to the relevant tort then its availability will turn solely on whether the claimant can be held to have 'consented' to the conduct that would otherwise have been wrongful, and not on the 'weighing' of the claimant's state of mind or actions or the consequences of those actions against anything on the defendant's side.[10] Similarly, instances of

[8] Eg, A Beever and C Rickett, 'Interpretive Legal Theory and the Academic Lawyer' (2005) 68 *MLR* 320; R Stevens, 'The Conflict of Rights' in A Robertson and HW Tang (eds), *The Goals of Private Law* (Oxford, Hart Publishing, 2009) 141: 'Coherence alone cannot make law valuable, but it is rather a necessary condition that both the law and theories about it must satisfy in order to qualify as such'.

[9] Goudkamp (n 7) 65–68, tentatively concludes that when consent is relied on in answer to a claim for trespass to the person, it operates as a denial of an element that is essential for liability rather than as a defence.

[10] Of course, the answer to the question whether the claimant consented may very well turn on an assessment of what the defendant did—in the sense that what we might look for by way of evidence of a claimant's consent might be influenced by an assessment of how potentially egregious the defendant's

absolute privilege in defamation and some process defences such as *res judicata* involve no balancing: the applicability of the relevant defence depends solely on particular facts being established. By contrast, the defence of 'lawful exercise of free expression' to a claim for breach of confidence by the wrongful publication of private information is one which (currently in English Law) manifestly demands a 'balancing' on the facts of the instant case of the claimant's interests in preventing the disclosure of private information against the defendant's interest in remaining free to publish such information.[11] Similarly, balancing on the facts of the instant case would clearly have been demanded by the Law Commission's provisionally recommended version of the illegality defence[12] to a claim in tort.[13] This would have required the court 'in each individual case' to assess the strength of five listed policies 'against the objective of achieving a just result, taking into account the relative merits of the parties and the proportionality of denying the claim'.[14] Many other defences involve a degree of balancing through a condition that makes them applicable only if the force used by the defendant, or other steps taken, was 'proportionate' or 'reasonable in the circumstances'.

Some defences that do not require balancing on the facts of the instant case no doubt reflect a balancing of general claimant and defendant interests (or the public interest) conducted at the time when the rule which defines the defence was fashioned. For example, 'long-stop' limitation periods, such as those in the Limitation Act 1980 (UK), s 11A(3) (10 years for a claim based on injury or damage caused by a defective product) and s 14B (15 years for a negligence claim not involving personal injuries) are probably a product of such a general balancing.[15] But it is not

particular violation of the claimant's rights would be in the absence of consent. But any such doctrine, if it can claim to be a 'doctrine' at all, is probably only a specific instance of the general truism within evidential practice that it takes 'more' concrete and unshakeable evidence to convince a court that something rare and unexpected (such as, that a claimant consented to the defendant exposing him or her to a substantial risk that the defendant could have easily acted to obviate) was the case than that something commonplace was the case.

[11] Eg, *McKennitt v Ash* [2006] EWCA Civ 1714; [2008] QB 73, where the Court of Appeal considered that the trial judge had been correct to assess, on the facts of the case, the significance of the private information from the perspective of the claimant and the weight of the defendant's claim that it should nonetheless be publishable so that she could 'tell her own story', or because the claimant was a 'public figure', or in order to expose the claimant's hypocrisy. This defence is discussed in more detail in Barbara McDonald's chapter in this volume, at pp 304–09.

[12] Goudkamp (n 7) 61–62, argues that as a result of *Gray v Thames Trains Ltd* [2009] UKHL 33; [2009] AC 1339 the doctrine of illegality operates as a denial of causation rather than as a defence. The alternative view, that I prefer, is that the doctrine still ought to be recognised as a defence even if it formally resorts to a fictitious denial of causation. The conclusion that, eg, in *Pitts v Hunt* [1991] 1 QB 24 (CA), the defendant's negligent driving *did not cause* the claimant's injuries relies, in my opinion, on an obfuscatory fiction.

[13] Law Commission, *The Illegality Defence: A Consultative Report* (CP No 189, 2009).

[14] ibid para 7.69. The Law Commission subsequently decided that it was not appropriate to recommend legislative reform to the illegality defence in the field of tort because the case law was already moving incrementally in the direction that it had provisionally recommended: Law Commission, *The Illegality Defence* (Law Com No 320, 2010). It may be reasonable to doubt, however, the Law Commission's rather bold assertion, at para 1.13, that the cases had adopted 'exactly the approach we suggested would be most helpful'; the cases certainly refer to the policies underlying the defence, but do not appear to assess the proportionality of denying a remedy to the claimant on the facts of the case.

[15] A further example of a rule where balancing took place at the time of design of the rule, and may be revisited whenever the rule is revised, might be the defence of 'act of God' to a claim under the rule in *Rylands v Fletcher*.

my intention to discuss issues relating to the design of such defences, in particular the issue of 'class delimitation'[16] and the difficult *distributional* questions that this can raise. Clearly any rule that applies across a class of non-identical cases may do injustice in cases at the edges of the class—for example, a 10-year long-stop limitation period in product liability claims *may* represent a fair balance in the mean, median and modal cases, but be unduly generous to defendants in some exceptional cases.[17] But, equally, there may be considerable efficiency advantages in defining classes relatively broadly and avoiding a proliferation of exceptions. By excluding defences based on rule-balancing from my ambit I can avoid discussing the legitimacy of trade-offs between unfairness in exceptional cases and efficiency, though clearly the availability of relatively homogeneous classes may play a significant role in the decision whether to choose a 'rule-balanced' design rather than a design which incorporates case-by-case balancing.

1.3 Some Disputed Cases

James Goudkamp's monograph has exposed the uncertainty that surrounds the concept of 'defences' in tort law and this uncertainty means there is scope to dispute which doctrines are properly classified as 'balancing defences'. My view is that there are advantages in treating (at least) two groups of doctrines as 'balancing defences' even though they fall outside the definition of 'defences' that Goudkamp advocates. The first group of doctrines is those that operate to prevent the claimant from being awarded a particular form of remedy which would have been available had the conditions for the applicability of the 'defence' not been established. An example of such a doctrine would be that which will prevent a claimant from being awarded an injunction if he or she has waited too long before seeking such a remedy. Goudkamp's monograph would not classify these as defences because it relies on a typology of rules in terms of the formal effect of their application: some rules prevent a defendant being held liable (and are thus properly called 'defences') whilst others merely restrict the remedy that a claimant may be able to obtain. But typologies are merely tools,[18] and my alternative groups together as 'defences' those doctrines that allow a defendant to resist in whole, or in part, a tort claim, other than by denying an essential element of it. This rival typology has the advantage of collecting together claim-resisting rules that reflect similar substantive values weighing against

[16] What I mean by 'class delimitation' is the process of defining a 'class' all members of which will be held subject to, or benefit from, the rule. For example, in jurisdictions which have enacted a special defence for 'good Samaritans' a contentious issue has been how to define the class entitled to benefit from the defence? Should it, for example, exclude those with particular qualifications (for example, medical practitioners) or those who had been employed by third parties to provide assistance? See M McInnes, 'Good Samaritan Laws: A Summary and Analysis' (1992) 26 *University of British Columbia Law Review* 239.

[17] I do not seek to defend the opinion that some particular 'long-stop' limit was chosen because it was fair in mean, median and modal cases. Other design desiderata are, naturally, always likely to be influential, eg, the ease of calculating '10 years' would give such a 'round-number' limit a particular attractiveness, such that we would be highly surprised if a lawmaker decided to select, for instance, 'nine years and forty-one weeks' as the appropriate limit.

[18] Like other tools they can be evaluated in terms of how well they perform their intended function.

allowing a claim to succeed, thus highlighting the *similarity* between, for example, the defences under the Limitation Act 1980 (UK), ss 11, 11A and 12, particularly in light of the discretion under section 33 to exclude these provisions,[19] and the rule that laches may provide a basis for refusing to grant an injunction.

The second group of doctrines that I treat as 'defences' against Goudkamp's recommendation, which includes some doctrines which utilise 'balancing' designs, is those doctrines which allow a defendant to resist a tort claim in whole, or in part, in response to co-responsibility for the wrongs concerned. These doctrines do not involve a claim of justification, or a transparent appeal to some goal of good public policy, but cover cases where a defendant seeks to resist a tort claim, in whole or in part, by identifying the claimant as himself or herself co-responsible, or a third party as co-responsible. Thus I treat contributory negligence as a defence, even in jurisdictions where it can merely reduce the amount of damages that a claimant will be awarded. And, likewise I treat some parts of the 'intervening acts' doctrine as involving a defence; particularly the rule that relieves a defendant from liability (despite the fact that his or her wrongdoing caused the claimant's loss) because of the claimant's or a third party's co-responsibility (eg, where a third party chose to exploit the opportunity presented by the defendant's wrongdoing[20]). The use of a form of balancing on the facts of the case within these doctrines is often masked by the use of other metaphors, such as that a defence is provided where the co-responsibility 'eclipses' the defendant's responsibility,[21] but there are advantages in treating the doctrines alongside other defences which are similarly founded on co-responsibility.[22]

2. THE DISADVANTAGES OF 'BALANCING DEFENCES'

The obvious reason why a lawmaker might choose to incorporate a 'balancing element' into a design for a tort defence must be that he or she believes that such an element will provide a degree of flexibility in accommodating competing values. But clearly a price may have to be paid for this flexibility. From a design perspective, one disadvantage of including an element of balancing on the facts of the instant case is that such a design is likely to require a higher investment in dispute resolution

[19] Section 33 of the Limitation Act 1980 (UK) grants to the courts a power to disapply the statutory provisions which set time limits on the bringing of actions with respect to personal injuries '[i]f it appears to the court that it would be equitable to allow an action to proceed'. This power is expressly to be exercised only after taking account of the degree to which the ordinary limits prejudice the claimant and the degree to which a decision to disapply them would prejudice the defendant, and the judge must have regard to the reasons for the delay and the effect that it is likely to have on the cogency of the evidence.

[20] HLA Hart and T Honoré, *Causation in the Law*, 2nd edn (Oxford, Clarendon Press, 1985) 136; *Reeves v Commissioner of Police of the Metropolis* [2000] 1 AC 360 (HL) 367.

[21] *Webb v Barclays Bank* [2001] EWCA Civ 1141; [2002] PIQR P8. The term 'eclipse' is also used several times in the relevant passages in MA Jones and AM Dugdale (eds), *Clerk & Lindsell on Torts*, 20th edn (London, Sweet and Maxwell, 2010), eg, para 2–102.

[22] Eg, several defences to forms of strict liability, such as under the rule in *Rylands v Fletcher* and under the Animals Act 1971 (UK), appear to be founded on co-responsibility, but do not incorporate balancing on the facts of the particular case. It seems plausible that balancing designs are less frequently used in defences to *strict* liability because the basic liability rule will not have required an evaluation of the defendant's conduct.

than a design that only incorporates issues of fact which are reasonably discernible. Relatedly, balancing defences *may* tend to be less effective at influencing behaviour: if a defendant cannot know, or at least predict with some confidence, whether his or her behaviour will be covered by a defence *at the time of deciding how to behave* then clearly *the defence* will struggle to influence his or her decision, and information about claimant-sided factors may be less accessible to defendants than information about, for example, their own acts and states of mind.

2.1 Investment in Dispute Resolution

In general terms a defence which requires an assessment of something on a claimant's side, and then an assessment of either something on the defendant's side or some aspect of the public interest, and a balancing of those matters that were assessed, all conducted on the facts of the instant case, is likely to require a higher investment in dispute resolution than a defence which requires an assessment of fewer elements, perhaps merely the finding of particular facts, or less complex computations with the assessed elements. For example, a version of the defence of self-defence that asked solely whether the defendant's application of force to the claimant was caused by the defendant's perception of a threat to his or her physical safety would be likely to require a lower investment than a version of the defence which asked the further question whether the defendant's response was *proportionate* to the perceived threat.[23] Similarly, a version of the limitation defence that sets a simple, fixed, time limit requires less investment by way of dispute resolution than a version that requires the court to make the assessments required under section 33 of the Limitation Act 1980 (UK).[24]

Is it possible to make any general propositions about the circumstances in which the English law of torts has shown itself willing to incur the extra costs that come with selection of a design that incorporates such balancing? I am inclined to make three general propositions.

First, it seems that there is some degree of correlation between the value attached to the type of interest of the claimant that will have to be surrendered in the event of the successful invocation of a defence and the likelihood that the defence will be made conditional on the outcome of a balancing process. Thus balancing defences are more likely to be employed where a claimant's interest in life or bodily security

[23] Clearly the cost of operating the first version of the defence might vary in accordance with the complexity of the notion of 'causation' encoded in the defence: a bare 'material contribution' notion of 'causation' would be cheaper to apply than a notion which sought to assess whether the cause was, for example, 'predominant', or a notion which sought to exclude certain 'causal chains', such as where the defendant had 'consciously decided to take advantage of the opportunity offered by the threat'. (The hypothetical versions of the defence that are discussed are not intended to reflect English tort law, which appears to incorporate an additional question about the claimant's 'responsibility' for the defendant's perception.)

[24] Law Commission, *Limitation of Actions* (Report 270, 2001), noted the uncertainty and inconsistency associated with s 33, and was informed by some consultees that 'claimants are encouraged to make applications to the court where the prospects of success, if not completely hopeless, fall well below fifty per cent' (para 3.158), but was eventually persuaded to recommend the retention of a discretion to disapply the basic limitation period in personal injury actions.

is at stake than where the issue is about the security of a claimant's property or, so far as they are protected at all, purely economic interests. This proposition can be supported by drawing attention to the proportion of defences that apply to personal injury claims that employ balancing, for example, self-defence (where a balancing test is used when assessing the proportionality of the force used), the proportion of defences that apply to property and reputation claims when non-balancing models are employed,[25] and the proportion of defences that apply to purely economic claims where a non-balancing model is employed (such as the trade disputes immunity and the defence of justification to the tort of procuring of a breach of contract[26]). Of course, such a correlation should not be surprising: where the effect of allowing a defence to be operative will be more severe for the would-be claimant there is an easy explanation for a willingness to make a greater investment in investigating the force of the case for such a defence on the particular facts. But it is clear that even in cases involving personal injuries the courts attach significance to the cost of operating 'balancing defences'. Thus in *Stanton v Collinson*[27] the Court of Appeal emphasised that in applying the defence of contributory negligence in cases where a claimant injured in a road accident had not been wearing a seatbelt there was 'a powerful public interest' in there not being an 'enquiry into fine degrees of contributory negligence, so that the vast majority of cases can be settled according to a well-understood formula and those few which entail trial do not mushroom out of control'.[28] Further, the court suggested that it might only be appropriate to rely on expert evidence as to the precise extent to which the claimant might have been protected by a seatbelt where the claim involved grave injury and large sums at stake.[29]

Secondly, where the interest that underpins a potential defence is acknowledged to be of varying significance this increases the likelihood of a balancing defence being adopted. A clear example of such an interest is 'freedom of expression': clearly restrictions on some types of expression would be far more concerning than restrictions on other types of expression, and whilst it may be possible to isolate particular kinds of expressive acts so as to apply non-balancing defences to them (for example,

[25] My claim is only that a *greater proportion* of defences to property torts do not incorporate a balancing element (for example, several of the defences to claims under the rule in *Rylands v Fletcher*) and not, of course, that *no* defences to any torts protecting property incorporate a balancing element. The latter claim would clearly be false, and blatantly inconsistent with my insistence that it is helpful to treat as 'balancing defences' both contributory negligence and various grounds for refusing to grant injunctions. In reaching its decision to recommend a discretion to disapply the standard limitation period *only in personal injury claims*, the Law Commission expressly relied on the argument that 'The claimant who has suffered a personal injury can justifiably be said to have suffered a more extreme form of harm than the claimant with a claim relating to property damage or economic loss' (ibid para 3.160).

[26] The defence of justification to the tort of procuring a breach of contract appears to protect the defendant when he or she relies on 'an equal or superior' right, and the claimant cannot succeed by showing that the damage that the defendant avoided was far less than the damage that his or her actions inflicted.

[27] [2010] EWCA Civ 81; [2010] RTR 26.

[28] ibid [26]. Confirming the authority of *Froom v Butcher* [1976] QB 286 (CA). The 'well-understood formula' recommends a deduction of 25 per cent when a claimant would have probably avoided injury by wearing a seat belt and a deduction of 15 per cent if his or her injuries would probably have been less severe if a seat belt had been worn.

[29] ibid [25].

expressive acts of non-expert witnesses in court[30] or participants in Parliamentary proceedings) balancing defences seem to have been selected as an appropriate way of covering residual cases. Thus the *Reynolds* defence of 'responsible journalism'[31] clearly adopted a broad view of 'journalism'[32] and incorporated a balancing element, in that what was expected of a 'reasonable journalist' varied in accordance with the nature of the allegation being made against the potential defendant and the significance of the sort of information being published.[33] A further example of an interest that underpins a defence and varies in significance, thus encouraging the adoption of a balancing defence, may be a defendant's interest in claims being brought promptly.[34]

The flipside of the second proposition is that a defence is less likely to incorporate a balancing element when the significance of the interest that underpins the defence is more constant, such as the interests that underpin absolute defences such as judicial immunity and the immunity of lay witnesses. Moreover, in some circumstances balancing on the instant facts is likely to be rejected as a design option because of the monolithic and fragile nature of the particular public interest that underpins the defence. For example, if the particular public interest is such that it will be wholly destroyed by any intrusion, like a child's balloon, then this will obviously weigh heavily against the adoption of a balancing design which would prevent the public interest from underpinning a defence whenever the claimant's interest was sufficiently weighty. This may help to explain the form of defences such as sovereign immunity, and also why, for example, non-professional witnesses are entitled to an absolute privilege against claims in defamation (and probably other torts as well), and there is no clamour to consider instead allowing claims to proceed where the claimant's interest is sufficiently strong.

My third general proposition is that in some circumstances one of the reasons why it seems acceptable to incur the extra costs (by way of dispute resolution) of a 'balancing' design may be because such a design will allow a court to deal with some *different* issue, such as preventing 'abuse of privilege' or 'abuse of rights' by defendants. Here I stray into controversy about the form of various doctrines of English law. I am prepared, however, to claim that one of the reasons why the English doctrine of proportionate self-defence may be attractive is because it provides a mechanism for withdrawing the defence in situations where the person who invokes it was using the opportunity provided by a perceived attack as a subterfuge for an

[30] This rule is supported by *Watson v M'Ewan* [1905] AC 480 (HL), which extended its application to statements made by potential witnesses in preparation for litigation. The limitation to *non-expert* witnesses reflects the effect of *Jones v Kaney* [2011] UKSC 13; [2011] 2 AC 398.

[31] The defence's name reflected its origin in the case of *Reynolds v Times Newspapers Ltd* [2001] 2 AC 127 (HL). It has now been abolished by s 4(6) of the Defamation Act 2013 (UK), and replaced with a new statutory defence of 'publication on matter of public interest'.

[32] *Seaga v Harper* [2008] UKPC 9; [2009] 1 AC 1 [11]: 'any person who publishes material of public interest in any medium ...'.

[33] In *Reynolds* (n 31) Lord Nicholls identified 10 factors to be taken into account: *Reynolds* (n 31) 205. Subsequent case law sought to address the concern that some judges treated the 10 factors as individual 'hurdles' that a defendant had to surmount in order to succeed: *Jameel (Mohammed) v Wall Street Europe SPRL* [2006] UKHL 44; [2007] 1 AC 359.

[34] This interest may be taken into account within a 'balancing defence' when an application is made to exclude the ordinary limitation period under Limitation Act 1980 (UK), ss 32A or 33.

act of punishment, vengeance or sadism.[35] Indeed, the desirability of a mechanism to respond to such abuse may even be the primary reason for the adoption of a 'balancing' design: In cases of simple 'imbalance', where the person who is alleged to have behaved 'disproportionately' has merely miscalculated the degree of force necessary to achieve self-protection, he or she will often be protected from liability as a result of the sub-doctrine that insists that a court will not use a 'jeweller's scales' in gauging the proportionality of the response.[36] Clearly an alternative design could have allowed the defence to be explicitly withdrawn whenever the defendant was found to have been motivated by a goal other than self-protection. But it might be cheaper, in terms of the overall cost of dispute resolution, to measure the degree of force used in the light of the threat posed by the claimant rather than seeking to interrogate the defendant's mental processes directly.

2.2 Balancing and Influencing Behaviour

My second claim about the disadvantages of balancing defences from a design perspective was that such defences may tend to be less effective at influencing behaviour: if a defendant cannot know, or at least predict with some confidence, whether his or her behaviour will be covered by a defence *at the time of deciding how to behave* then clearly *the defence* will struggle to influence his or her decision, and it is often harder for a defendant to be able to predict the outcome of a balancing process than to know that some relevant fact exists. Similarly, if a claimant cannot know, or predict with some confidence, whether a defendant's behaviour is covered by a defence then he or she may be unsure whether he or she would be justified in resisting that behaviour.[37]

Concerns about the effect that a balancing design can have on the capacity of the law to influence defendants' behaviour may help to explain why a significant proportion of the balancing defences that currently exist in English law reflect public policies that are *not* aimed at influencing the behaviour of potential defendants at the time of possible torts.[38] Some such defences are focused on behaviour *after* a tort was committed. For example, clearly the limitation defence, which may sometimes require a balancing of the claimant's interest in such a claim being allowed to proceed despite the passage of time against the reasons why it might be unfair and undesirable for a court to resolve such a stale dispute, is not a defence which seeks to influence the behaviour of the alleged *tortfeasor* at the time of the alleged tort.

[35] *Lane v Holloway* [1968] 1 QB 379 (CA).

[36] *Cross v Kirkby* The Times, 5 April 2000 (CA).

[37] Of course, the fact that a defence will insulate the defendant's behaviour from giving rise to tort liability *does not* mean that a defendant will necessarily be unable to justify resisting it.

[38] The defence of illegality, so far as it exists to maintain the integrity of the legal system, appears to provide a good example of a defence that does not focus on influencing the potential defendant's behaviour at the time of the tort. Thus on this understanding of the defence it would not have been an objection to the Law Commission's proposed reformulation of the defence (see text to nn 13–14, above) that inclusion of a balancing element would *impede* the capacity of the defence to influence defendants' behaviour. The Law Commission, however, was of the opinion that 'deterrence is an important policy behind the illegality doctrine': Law Commission (n 13) para 2.23.

Similarly, doctrines such as the 'prohibition on collateral attack'[39] and the 'rule in *Henderson v Henderson*'[40] do not seek to regulate how the defendant ought to have behaved on the day in question. In other cases the defence may be underpinned by a public policy that is concerned with justifying a court in refusing to resolve a particular claim rather than being aimed at influencing a potential defendant's behaviour at the time that the alleged tort was committed. This might help to explain the extension of the 'abuse of process' defence to defamation claims where 'the game is not worth the candle': it seems improbable that the purpose of such a defence is to encourage defendants to behave in a different way.[41]

Equally, it seems clear that one of the prominent reasons why a non-balancing design may be chosen is that the context is one where *certainty* of potential defendants at the time that they act, or the *certainty* of potential claimants at the time that they must decide whether to resist action, is thought to be particularly important. Thus the contextual significance of defendant certainty may help to explain the non-balancing model used in the absolute privilege defences for witnesses and Parliamentarians[42] and the contextual significance of claimant certainty may help to explain the severe limits put on the availability of 'necessity' as a defence available to public defendants.[43]

Of course, the fact that a balancing design may reduce the capacity of the law to influence a defendant's behaviour if that defendant will find it difficult to predict whether his or her behaviour will be covered by the defence *at the time of deciding how to behave* means that such designs may be more attractive where they turn on matters that defendants *will* be able to assess, and that the law would like to encourage them to assess. An obvious example might be the availability of the defence of

[39] This doctrine is best exemplified by the decision in *Hunter v Chief Constable of the West Midlands* [1982] AC 529 (HL). Whilst there is little evidence of 'balancing' in that case, though reference was made to the intending claimant having had 'a full opportunity of contesting' the previous decision (at 541) and the possibility of an exception where new evidence has emerged that 'entirely changes the aspect of the case' (at 545), subsequent cases such as *Walpole v Partridge & Wilson* [1994] QB 106 (CA) and *Secretary of State for Trade and Industry v Bairstow* [2003] EWCA Civ 321; [2004] Ch 1 have evinced an approach that can more plausibly be described as requiring 'balancing'. Cf *Amin v The Director General of the Security Service (Mi5)* [2013] EWHC 1579 (QB).

[40] *Henderson v Henderson* (1843) 3 Hare 100; 67 ER 313 has supplied the label for a species of 'abuse of process' defence that will apply where a party 'could and should' have raised a matter so that it could be litigated in previous proceedings. See *Johnson v Gore Wood (No 1)* [2002] 2 AC 1 (HL).

[41] This defence is associated with the case of *Jameel (Yousef) v Dow Jones & Co Inc* [2005] EWCA Civ 75; [2005] QB 946. Its common law formulation clearly involves a greater degree of balancing than the new statutory rule that a 'statement is not defamatory unless its publication has caused or is likely to cause serious harm to the reputation of the claimant': Defamation Act 2013 (UK), s 1. See also the Offences Against the Person Act 1861 (UK), ss 44 and 45.

[42] With regard to the privilege of those speaking in Parliament, Lord Browne-Wilkinson emphasised the importance of certainty for the speaker in *Prebble v Television New Zealand* [1995] 1 AC 321 (PC) 334: 'The important public interest protected by such privilege is to ensure that the member or witness *at the time he speaks* is not inhibited from stating fully and freely what he has to say' (emphasis added).

[43] Famously, in *Entick v Carrington* (1765) 19 St Tr 1029; 95 ER 807 Lord Camden condemned an attempt to rely on 'state necessity' as a defence in tort. This line of authority was not apparently cited to the Court of Appeal in *Austin v Commissioner of Police of the Metropolis* [2007] EWCA Civ 989; [2008] QB 660, which must cast doubt on the weight that should be attached to that Court's acceptance, at [49], that 'necessity' unassociated with what might be in a claimant's best interests (cf *R v Bournewood Community and Mental Health NHS Trust, Ex p L* [1999] 1 AC 458 (HL)) can be raised as a general defence by a public defendant to a claim for false imprisonment. (The Court of Appeal's conclusion on the common law was not appealed to the House of Lords: see [2009] UKHL 5; [2009] 1 AC 564 [11].)

self-defence turning on the degree of threat that the claimant posed to the defendant: a defendant might be reasonably well placed to assess this,[44] and there might clearly be good reasons for encouraging a defendant to consider the matter.[45] Similarly, the adoption of a balancing test in cases where a defendant invokes the importance of free expression to try to justify publishing private information seems to have been partly based on a belief that the defendants would often be professional journalists who could be expected to recognise when the material that they were proposing to publish was 'private'.[46]

3. THE STRUCTURE OF 'BALANCING DEFENCES'

I have noted that the obvious reason to choose to incorporate a 'balancing element' into a design for a tort defence is that it will provide a degree of flexibility in addressing competing values. Where a 'non-balancing' design is used then it is likely to treat the value to be attached to the claimant's interest as a constant, and make the defence available where the defendant's behaviour meets a particular description or particular circumstances exist sufficient to trigger a public interest defence. By contrast, a 'balancing' design will allow for the possibility of the defendant's behaviour having to meet different conditions in accordance with different weights being attached to the claimant's interest.

Whilst 'non-balancing' designs treat the value to be attached to the claimant's interest as a constant, most 'balancing defences' do not go to the other extreme and leave the question of how to value the claimant's interest and how it relates to competing values as matters for each trial judge to decide as a matter of first impression. The way in which a particular 'balancing element' is structured will often reflect the lawmaker's opinion about the relationship between the particular values. For example, the doctrine that allows a defendant to avoid responsibility where the co-responsibility of another's wrongdoing 'eclipses' his own contribution to the causal mixture reveals a particular view about how far the law is willing to sacrifice the primary defendant's interest in only being held liable to an extent proportionate to his own responsibility in order to protect the claimant's interest in securing full redress,

[44] As noted above, text to n 36, the law is willing to tolerate a degree of misjudgement by defendants in this context.

[45] I suggested above, text to nn 35 and 36, that the *primary* reason for this doctrine—proportionality in self-defence—might be deterring abuse of the privilege. But this suggestion is not inconsistent with the claim that the degree of threat posed by a claimant can often be assessed by a defendant. Moreover, this claim should not be read as implying that I believe that the defence should be unavailable when the defendant did not appreciate that the claimant was threatening him or her: it may be appropriate for a lawmaker to choose to extend the defence to such cases even without claiming that the defendant's behavior was *justified* in the circumstances.

[46] The Court of Appeal in *Campbell v MGN Ltd* [2002] EWCA Civ 1373; [2003] QB 633 [63]–[71], rejected the 'ambitious submission' that 'a defendant will only be liable for breach of confidence if (a) he knows that the information that he publishes is confidential and (b) he knows that publication cannot be justified on the ground that it is in the public interest'. The Court stated: 'We consider that the media can fairly be expected to identify confidential information about an individual's private life which, absent good reason, it will be offensive to publish'. By contrast, when the case reached the House of Lords, both Lord Hoffmann and Lord Hope stated that to be liable the defendant would have to have 'notice' that the information was 'confidential': [2004] UKHL 22; [2004] 2 AC 457 [47]–[48] and [85] respectively.

and at what point this interest of the claimant's must give way to concerns about the symbolism of the law and the risk of it being brought into disrepute.[47] Similarly, Parliament's provision of a defence for all but 'grossly disproportionate' acts where a claim for trespass to the person is brought by someone who committed an imprisonable offence and there was a defined sort of connection between the tort and that offence clearly demonstrates a ranking of the competing interests.[48] Moreover, over time case law tends to produce relatively reliable 'benchmarks' for assessing how competing interests are to be valued within an established structure. Thus it may already be the case that a lawyer specialising in the protection of private information could give fairly reliable guidance on how a claimant's interest in controlling the publication of different types of private information would be balanced against various forms of free expression such as contribution to political debate, contribution to a generally educative documentary, artistic expression, autobiography, and contribution to general public entertainment.

Under the previous heading (Section 2.2) I sought to identify some of the potential costs of adopting a 'balancing' design. Below I seek to identify some further questions that a lawmaker will have to confront if he or she is inclined to adopt such a design. These questions reflect the fact that there is more than one way of structuring a 'balancing defence'.

3.1 What is there to Balance on the Claimant's Side?

My description of 'balancing defences' is that they are built around a balancing of something on a claimant's side against something on a defendant's side, or against some public interest, with that balancing being conducted on the facts of the instant case rather than at the stage of 'rule design'. But it is important to note that what is weighed on the claimant's side is not the same in all designs. One variable is whether the 'balancing' process assesses the significance of the *right* of the claimant that was invaded or jeopardised by the defendant's behaviour or the significance of the *consequences* for the claimant of being deprived of the opportunity to pursue a claim. For example, when the question is the proportionality of action taken in self-defence, or in defence of another, or in defence of property, it seems that the relevant matter from the claimant's side is the importance of the right being infringed and the magnitude of the *risk* to the interest underlying that right. The scale of the

[47] If the reasoning behind this sentence is opaque then it may be illuminated by considering a situation where the claimant's non-divisible injuries are caused by two torts, one committed by D1 and the other by D2, where only D1 has resources which will enable him to pay compensation. English tort law's rule is that D1 must compensate C in full, and will be granted only a worthless claim for contribution against D2, unless D2's responsibility is such as to 'eclipse' D1's (a conclusion often expressed using the peculiar metaphor that D2's wrong 'broke the chain of causation' between D1's tort and C's injury). My claim is that this rule reflects a preference for C's interest in receiving full compensation, even at the expense of making D1 pay a far greater proportion of the cost of doing so than would be fair if D2 had resources, until a point is reached where D2's responsibility seems so dominant that to hold D1 responsible for C's injuries would send an inappropriate message to the public about responsibility ('symbolism') and bring the law into disrepute.

[48] Criminal Justice Act 2003 (UK), s 329. The required connection between the imprisonable offence and the tort is defined in s 329(5).

consequential loss that a claimant suffered, and will be unable to recover for if the defence is successfully invoked, seems less relevant: there is no sign that a defendant is required to use less force when defending himself or herself against an assailant with very high earnings (who might consequently suffer a greater loss if injured) than against an assailant with very low earnings.[49] A second issue is whether the 'balancing' should rely on what was *actually* at stake for the claimant or on what the defendant (reasonably) believed was at stake. For example, a lawmaker must choose whether the 'proportionality' for the purposes of self-defence will be assessed in accordance with the claimant's actual position, as a person with brittle bones, or in accordance with the defendant's belief as to the claimant's physical state. A third variable is whether the claimant's responsibility for the events that give rise to the claim, or for the events that give rise to the potential defence, should be brought into the balance, and if so whether responsibility should reflect relative culpability, relative causal influence, or some combination of both. In cases of contributory negligence it seems that very little attention is paid to the significance of the consequences for the claimant if the defence is successfully invoked: thus it is rare to see any discussion of what will happen in practice if a claimant is deprived of, say, 25 per cent of the amount that was calculated to be necessary to provide future medical care and support for independent living. Instead, the primary question from the claimant's side appears to be the claimant's relative responsibility for both the incident giving rise to the claim and the degree of loss suffered, judged in terms of both culpability and 'causal potency'.[50] By contrast, where the question is whether it would be proportionate to disapply the standard limitation period in a personal injury case it seems clear that the practical consequences for the claimant of applying the defence are taken into account through reference to the size of the claim (qualified by its likelihood of success),[51] whether the claimant will be left with a cast-iron claim against his or her solicitors, and the ways in which having to pursue such a claim may be thought to be less attractive than retaining a right to sue the primary defendant.[52] These matters are considered alongside the issue of how far the claimant (or his or her advisers) can be held responsible for the delay. Whilst the magnitude of the claim can be relevant on the claimant's side there may also be circumstances where it becomes relevant on the defendant's side as well, for instance where delay has increased the likelihood of an erroneous decision in favour of the claimant as a consequence of reduction in the availability of reliable evidence.

[49] Similarly, there is no sign in the cases that in justifying the amount of force that I used to protect my near valueless pet cat against an attack by a dog it is relevant that the dog was very valuable.

[50] *Froom v Butcher* [1976] QB 286 (CA). See also *The Miraflores and the Abadesa* [1967] 1 AC 826 (HL) (Lord Pearce). A strong indication of the lack of attention to *practical consequences* can be found in the fact that in road accidents courts regularly make similar standard reductions in damages regardless of whether the claim before them is mainly for pain, suffering and loss of amenity or mainly for pecuniary losses.

[51] *Adams v Bracknell Forest BC* [2004] UKHL 29; [2005] 1 AC 76 [54]–[55], endorsing the opinion of Sir Murray Stuart-Smith in *Robinson v St Helens Metropolitan Borough Council* [2002] EWCA Civ 1099; [2003] PIQR P128.

[52] It seems to be accepted that a claimant may suffer some 'prejudice' in having to make a professional negligence claim against his or her solicitors instead of being permitted to continue a claim against the primary tortfeasor: *Thompson v Brown* [1981] 1 WLR 744 (HL) 750; cited on this point with apparent approval in *Horton v Sadler* [2006] UKHL 27; [2007] AC 307 [32] (Lord Bingham), [48] (Lord Hoffmann) and [53] (Lord Carswell).

Is it possible to make any general propositions about when designs for defences will incorporate these different claimant-sided elements? I would suggest that when the 'balancing' in a defence is focused on evaluation of the defendant's behaviour at the time of the alleged wrongdoing (for example, can the defendant justify his or her behaviour?), the relevant factor on the claimant's side is likely to be the immediate intrusion on the claimant's rights and reasonably foreseeable *risk* to the claimant's interest, whilst when the 'balancing' is focused on the furtherance of a public interest independent of the defendant's tortious behaviour, such as the need to ensure that cases are litigated within a reasonable time, the relevant factor is likely to be the actual consequences for the claimant if he or she is prevented from pursuing a claim. In all cases the extent to which the claimant can be held responsible for the circumstances that are said to support the defence may be incorporated into the design.[53] In some circumstances, however, a claimant's responsibility may be treated as an issue which precludes the availability of a 'balancing defence' altogether rather than a factor which is taken into account in the 'balancing'.[54]

3.2 Balancing and 'Self-Sacrifice'

I have suggested that 'balancing defences' can be structured in different ways so as to reflect different rankings between the competing interests, and here I want to focus on a particular example of such structuring. Where a defendant raises a defence to the effect that he or she acted so as to harm the claimant's interests *in order to protect* his or her own interests, or the private interests of some other, it would clearly be theoretically possible to make the validity of the defence depend on the defendant showing that he or she acted so as to cause less harm to the claimant than what he or she would have otherwise suffered—in other words, that his or her actions resulted in a net reduction in harm. It seems, however, that lawmakers frequently choose to incorporate a form of 'balancing' that does not involve such an inquiry. For example, I have already noted that a defendant may still be able to establish that his or her behaviour constituted 'proportionate' self-defence even if it resulted in the claimant suffering much greater harm than the defendant was seeking to protect himself or herself against provided that the *risk* of the claimant suffering such harm as a result of the acts of self-defence was proportionate to the threat. For example, if the defendant pushed away a claimant who was trying to kiss him without consent, and the claimant stumbled, fell and fractured her skull, the fact that the

[53] It is not always clear what role, if any, a claimant's responsibility has played in determining the proportionality of a defence. Eg, in 'necessity' cases reference is sometimes made to the general expectations in the circumstances of those in the same position as the claimants, but it is unclear whether willingly attending a protest where others are expected to be disorderly *extends* the range of behaviour which will be ruled to be 'necessary'.

[54] Thus it is commonly thought that a defendant cannot rely on the defence of 'necessity' if he or she was at fault in bringing about the circumstances that made his or her subsequent behaviour necessary: *Rigby v Chief Constable of Northamptonshire* [1985] 1 WLR 1242 (QBD) 1253, where Taylor J stated that this proposition was 'clearly right'. See also Devlin J in *Esso Petroleum Co Ltd v Southport Corp* [1953] 2 All ER 1204 (QB) 1210, whose judgment was subsequently restored by the House of Lords: [1956] AC 218 (HL). For similar reasons it seems that someone who initially acted as the aggressor will only be able to rely on the defence of self-defence in very limited circumstances.

harm from a fractured skull is greatly in excess of any harm that could conceivably result from an unwanted kiss would not, in itself, establish that the force used was disproportionate. Some support for this proposition can be found in the case of *Revill v Newbery*,[55] where an elderly man was held liable for wounding a burglar by firing a gun through a hole in a door without checking where it was pointing, but Neill LJ suggested that the case might have been different if the gun had been fired in the air to frighten the burglar and he had unexpectedly been on the roof.[56]

A more important exception to the 'net reduction' idea is provided by the fact that many 'balancing' defences do not appear to require 'proportionate self-sacrifice'. Thus, if a claimant threatens to pluck a single hair from the defendant's head then it seems that the defendant is entitled to use *at least the minimum force necessary to prevent the hair being plucked*, and is not required to tolerate the plucking simply because the minimum force will be far greater than what he or she is likely to experience through the plucking of a hair.[57] This is most apparent from the cases concerning the lawfulness of using force to resist an *unlawful* arrest, where clearly the amount of force used often involves a greater immediate physical impact and carries a risk of far greater consequential harm than would usually be inflicted by an arrest.[58] Similarly, 'balancing' does not appear to require 'proportionate self-sacrifice' in cases where a defendant acts so as to prevent the flooding of his or her land,[59] or its invasion by a swarm of locusts,[60] and thereby diverts the threat onto the claimant's land. In such cases it does not seem that the defendant must demonstrate that the claimant's land was less valuable or the diversion led to a net reduction in total harm.

In such cases 'balancing' does not involve a determination of whether more harm was done by or avoided by the defendant's actions. Instead the calculation may be whether the defendant did greater harm to the claimant's interests than was necessary in order to defend the interest that he or she was entitled to defend. Thus in *Gerrard v Crowe* Viscount Cave suggested that the law might insist that 'a landowner in protecting his land from the common enemy must use reasonable care and skill and must not do more than is reasonably necessary for that purpose'.[61] The absence of a general obligation of 'proportionate self-sacrifice' also appears coherent with the common law's well-recognised refusal to impose general duties

[55] *Revill v Newbery* [1996] QB 567 (CA).

[56] ibid 578. Neill LJ did not expressly discuss the case in terms of self-defence, but the other two members of the Court of Appeal understood their discussion to be premised on the view that the defendant had used more force than was reasonable.

[57] ibid 580 (Millett LJ): 'Violence may be returned with necessary violence'.

[58] See also the rule relied on in *R v Hussey* (1925) 18 Cr App R 160 (CCA) 161, where the defendant fired a gun and wounded two people who were trying to evict him without having given him a valid notice to quit, and Lord Hewart CJ reiterated that 'In defence of a man's house, the owner or his family may kill a trespasser who would forcibly dispossess him of it'.

[59] *Gerrard v Crowe* [1921] AC 395 (PC). There are exceptions to this rule covering, in particular, obstruction of an established flood channel (*Menzies v Breadalbane* (1828) 3 Bligh (NS) 414; 4 ER 1387) and active discharge onto the claimant's land of flood water which had accumulated on the defendant's land (*Whalley v Lancashire and Yorkshire Railway* (1884) 13 QBD 131 (CA)).

[60] *Greyvensteyn v Hattingh* [1911] AC 355 (PC). The locusts in this case were juveniles, and consequently walked rather than flew.

[61] *Gerrard v Crowe* [1921] AC 395 (PC) 400.

to confer benefits on strangers, even in situations of extreme and immediate peril.[62] It may, however, be difficult to reconcile it with the claim that the defence of private necessity in English tort law automatically gives rise to a parallel obligation to tolerate the intrusions that are said to be necessary.[63] The cases of defence against a common enemy appear to contemplate that one landowner's liberty to divert the threat to the disadvantage of his neighbour is counter-balanced by an equal, reciprocal liberty.

3.3 The Procedural Problem with Forms of 'Balancing' that Require Private Litigants to Make Submissions about the Weight of a Public Interest

Where a lawmaker is inclined to incorporate a balancing element that will require the balancing of some element on the claimant's side against some aspect of the public interest it may be important to structure the element so as to take account of the procedural difficulties that private parties may face in making submissions about the public interest, particularly where they lack expertise with regard to the public interest concerned. Suppose, for instance, that a defendant who is accused of driving negligently or making an incompetent valuation must establish the weight that should be properly given to the importance of finality in litigation, or the desirability of preventing any one case from consuming a disproportionate share of overall judicial resources, or the need to avoid the suggestion that the civil law will relieve criminals of some of the consequences of their choices to offend. In such cases the defendant may be poorly placed to assist with weighing the public interest on the facts of the particular case in order to proceed with 'balancing' it against some claimant-sided interest; indeed the fact that the defendant may 'gain' from the public interest defence being established may lead to his or her submissions being treated with scepticism. There is no easy solution to the problem of 'balancing defences' being used in contexts where the defendant may be ill-equipped to assist the court in assessing the significance, on the facts of the instant case, of the public interest concerned. But the problem may be one that weighs in favour of rejecting a 'balancing defence' in favour of a design forged through 'rule balancing', or at least in favour of a 'balancing' structure which incorporates a provisional ranking of the competing interests.

A related procedural problem may arise where a balancing process is structured so as to require computations that the parties are ill-equipped to conduct. Elsewhere I have written at length about the difficulties that can be caused by a tort design which incorporates a 'balancing process' that requires a litigant to establish that a goal cannot be achieved by a less intrusive method.[64] A simple example may be the journalist's defence to a claim for the wrongful publication of private information that the intrusion into the claimant's privacy went no further than necessary in order

[62] *Smith v Littlewoods Organisation Ltd* [1987] AC 241 (HL).

[63] *Ploof v Putnam* 81 Vt 471; 71 A 188 (1908). This issue receives more detailed discussion in Graham Virgo's chapter in this volume, at pp 150–52.

[64] R Bagshaw, 'Privacy and Tort Design' in KS Ziegler (ed), *Human Right and Private Law: Privacy as Autonomy* (Oxford, Hart Publishing, 2007) 82–85.

to properly respect the human right to free expression, in other words, that the goal of proper respect for free expression could not have been achieved in any way which did less harm to privacy interests. Suppose that the claimant responds that the journalist is incorrect, and the right to free expression would in fact have been sufficiently respected by allowing him or her greater control over private information, for instance, by having given him some period of time to make his or her own disclosure, with journalistic publication following only if he or she did not do so, or the voluntary disclosure was misleading. If a legislator proposed to formulate a general rule limiting freedom to publish private information in this way—by creating a general requirement to give notice and an opportunity to make a voluntary disclosure—then clearly we would expect certain sorts of evidence and argumentation to be generated in order to defend the proposal, and a court reviewing such legislation would, in all likelihood, assess the evidence and argumentation in the light of its opinions as to the legislator's expertise on the matter and the legitimacy of its choices with regard to the accommodation of the competing values. But can a private litigant be fairly expected to make submissions with regard to *the same sort of* balancing of competing interests *on the facts of a particular case* in order to negate a defence? To put the point in more practical terms, what sort of evidence would it be reasonable to demand from a private litigant in support of a submission that the same goal could have been achieved in the instant case by less intrusive methods? There are clearly dangers in transplanting a form of 'balancing test' developed for the review of legislative initiatives into the design for a tort to be applied through case-by-case argumentation by private parties.

4. CONCLUSIONS

The analysis above has not sought to support a general prohibition on the use of 'balancing defences' in the law of torts. It has, however, sought to caution lawmakers against incorporating 'balancing elements' into designs for defences too readily or indiscriminately.[65] In some circumstances, such as where a defence is being designed to protect a public interest which will be severely jeopardised by any intrusion, no matter how minor, a 'balancing defence' may be wholly unsuitable. In other circumstances suitability may instead require consideration of the costs and advantages of a 'balancing defence' in the context, the relative merits of the different ways in which 'balancing' might be structured, and the possibility, or otherwise, of accommodating the competing values in a satisfactory way through 'rule design'. Such issues rarely appear in judicial reasoning, and it may be that they are easy to overlook if a lawmaker is led towards relying heavily on less transparent methods such as analogy, and appeals to consistency or symmetry. But it is not only judges who neglect such issues, or at least fail to defend their choices openly. They are frequently ignored by those legal academics who prioritise coherence, and consequently tend to over-emphasise general moral reasoning at the expense of more context-specific practical issues.

[65] This problem has been easier to observe in fields of law that tend to attract a greater degree of legislative and appellate attention: see, eg, C Tapper 'The Law of Evidence and the Rule of Law' (2009) 68 *CLJ* 67, 71.

7

Defences and Third Parties: Justifying Participation

PAUL S DAVIES*

MORE THAN ONE person may be involved in the commission of a wrong. For example, a defendant who induces a primary wrongdoer to commit a tort or breach of contract can be held liable as an accessory.[1] Such liability is generally considered to be tortious.[2] But what defences are available to accessories? This important question has not received the attention it deserves.[3] The language of 'secondary liability' may have led some to conclude that defences against the primary wrongdoer will necessarily also benefit an accessory,[4] and even that an accessory ought not to be able to exploit any defence that is not equally available to the primary wrongdoer.[5] As will be seen, both conclusions are misconceived. A better appreciation of the existence and nature of defences to accessory liability should help to demarcate the distinctiveness of accessory liability, albeit that such liability must be parasitic to a primary wrong. Well-recognised and stable defences may also ensure that just results can be reached in a more transparent and coherent manner, rather than by unpredictably twisting the conduct elements of accessory liability to inculpate or exculpate a defendant.[6]

This chapter will first consider when a defence successfully relied upon by a primary wrongdoer will also benefit an accessory, before analysing the range of

* I am particularly grateful to James Goudkamp for his comments and advice on this chapter. This chapter derives from a slightly broader consideration of accessory liability in the private law: PS Davies, *Accessory Liability* (Oxford, Hart Publishing, 2015) 250–51.

[1] The language of 'accessories' is used both where the wrong induced is a breach of contract (eg, *OBG Ltd v Allan* [2007] UKHL 21; [2008] 1 AC 1 [8]) and a tort (eg, *Dramatico Entertainment Ltd v British Sky Broadcasting Ltd [2012] EWHC 268 (Ch);* [2012] 3 CMLR 14 [72]).

[2] Indeed, even where the defendant is liable as an accessory for inducing a breach of an equitable obligation, this has been described as an 'equitable tort': *Abou-Rahmah v Abacha* [2006] EWCA Civ 1492; [2007] 1 All ER (Comm) 827 [2]. For reasons of space, the focus here will be upon common law wrongs.

[3] See similarly S Deakin and J Randall, 'Rethinking the Economic Torts' (2009) 72 *MLR* 519, 550.

[4] Cooper has written that '[w]ithout primary liability there can be no secondary liability, and so any defence to the liability of the primary wrongdoer will also be a defence to the liability of the secondary party': D Cooper, 'Secondary Liability for Civil Wrongs' (PhD thesis, University of Cambridge 1996) 160.

[5] Cf *Football Dataco Ltd v Stan James plc* [2013] EWCA Civ 27; [2013] 2 CMLR 36 [100] (Sir Robin Jacob).

[6] PS Davies, 'Aid, Abet, Counsel or Procure?' in S Pitel, J Neyers and E Chamberlain (eds), *Tort Law: Challenging Orthodoxy* (Oxford, Hart Publishing, 2013).

possible defences that are particular to accessories. The tortious liability of third parties who participate in a breach of contract or a tort will generally be considered together, although the applicability and success of a defence may well depend upon whether the claim is based upon a breach of contract or tort. However, more attention has been paid to possible defences where the primary wrong is a breach of contract than a tort, and it may be that lessons learned from the more contractual context can be applied in the purely tortious sphere. This is particularly important as regards the defence of justification, which is the most significant defence available to an accessory.

It is helpful at the outset to determine the scope of the wrongs considered in this chapter. The tort of 'inducing a breach of contract'—also known as the 'tort in *Lumley v Gye*'[7]—is the focus of accessory liability to a breach of contract. The other so-called 'economic torts' will not be considered: liability for intentionally inflicting harm by unlawful means, for instance, is a form of primary liability that is not parasitic upon a wrong committed by another.[8] Accessory liability to a tort is more difficult. The label of 'joint tortfeasance' is incredibly broad and covers a wide range of defendants, including accessories. The focus will be on defendants who incur liability as a result of their participation in a tort; in England and Wales, it appears that such liability might arise where the defendant induces or authorises a tort, or participates in a 'common design' to commit a tort.[9] Vicarious liability, which is based upon a 'relationship link' rather than a 'participation link',[10] is beyond the scope of the present chapter.[11]

1. DEFENCES AVAILABLE TO A PRIMARY WRONGDOER

Even though it will generally be the case that a claim against an accessory will fail if the claim against the primary wrongdoer is thwarted by a defence, some claims against accessories may nevertheless succeed. The claimant may still have suffered a wrong, and it is to that wrong that accessory liability can attach.[12] The defence a primary wrongdoer has may be personal to him or herself, and not assist an accessory, who could still have to compensate the victim of the wrong.

[7] After the leading case: (1853) 2 E&B 216; 118 ER 749.

[8] *OBG Ltd v Allan* (n 1) (Lord Hoffmann). Nor is conspiracy parasitic upon the commission of a wrong committed by another: see, eg, *Revenue and Customs Commissioners v Total Network SL* [2008] UKHL 19; [2008] 1 AC 1174 [100]–[104] (Lord Walker), [116]–[124] (Lord Mance), [225]–[230] (Lord Neuberger). Indeed, it is suggested that the grouping of 'economic torts' lacks any inherent unity and serves to confuse: R Stevens, *Torts and Rights* (Oxford, Oxford University Press, 2007) 297; *Revenue and Customs Commissioners v Total Network SL* (ibid) [224] (Lord Neuberger).

[9] See generally H Carty, 'Joint Tortfeasance and Assistance Liability' (1999) 10 *Legal Studies* 489.

[10] For the language of 'relationship link' and 'participation link', see ibid.

[11] Vicarious liability arises as a matter of policy due to the defendant's employment of the primary tortfeasor; once the employee commits a tort during the course of his or her employment, the employer will be liable and cannot rely upon any particular defences. See generally P Giliker, *Vicarious Liability in Tort* (Cambridge, Cambridge University Press, 2010).

[12] This mirrors the position in the criminal law: see, eg, *R v Bourne* (1951) 36 Cr App R 125 (CCA); *R v Cogan*; *R v Leak* [1976] QB 217 (CA).

Although it has been argued that 'justifications deny wrongdoing',[13] the better view seems to be that even where the 'primary wrongdoer' is justified, a wrong might nevertheless have been committed[14] and that an accessory will not invariably escape liability even where a primary wrongdoer has a justificatory defence. For instance, a 'primary wrongdoer' may escape liability in battery on the basis of self-defence. But whether or not a defendant who encourages such force can also benefit from the defence of justification might depend upon whether or not that defendant realised that defensive force was justified.[15] In the rare situation where the defendant knew that the aggressor did not in fact represent any real threat—despite objective appearances to the contrary—and nevertheless encouraged the use of force in order to harm the aggressor, accessory liability may still be appropriate. If the defendant knew that the gun the aggressor was brandishing was unloaded, it may be reasonable for the 'primary wrongdoer' to use force to protect himself against an apparent threat, but the defendant would not be similarly justified in throwing a weapon to the 'primary wrongdoer' to be used upon the aggressor.

This same divergence between defences available to the primary wrongdoer and accessory may occur where the 'primary wrongdoer' has an absolute privilege or immunity from liability;[16] for example, if the primary wrongdoer has a defence of diplomatic immunity, there is no reason why an accessory should automatically also be able to benefit from that defence.[17] The same logic underpins the imposition of accessory liability in circumstances where the 'primary wrongdoer' avoids liability because he or she can deny a subjective element of the wrong.[18] If a defendant encourages a person to lock a door, thereby falsely imprisoning the claimant, the defendant might be liable as an accessory even though the person who locked the door may not have known that somebody was inside and therefore lacked the fault element of the tort; a wrong of false imprisonment was nevertheless committed, and the accessory may be liable for that infringement of the claimant's right to freedom. This mirrors the approach adopted in the criminal law: in *Cogan and Leak*,[19] the principal had sexual intercourse with the defendant's wife, but was acquitted of rape because he believed, on the basis of what the defendant told him, that the wife was consenting. The defendant was nevertheless guilty as an accessory; the wife had clearly been raped,[20] and the defendant's liability was parasitic to the conduct

[13] P Cane, *Responsibility in Law and Morality* (Oxford, Hart Publishing, 2002) 90; see too A Ripstein, *Equality, Responsibility and the Law* (Cambridge, Cambridge University Press, 1999) 138: 'justifications exculpate by showing that an apparently wrongful act was not wrongful'.

[14] J Goudkamp, *Tort Law Defences* (Oxford, Hart Publishing, 2013) ch 4; J Gardner, *Offences and Defences: Selected Essays in Philosophy of Criminal Law* (Oxford, Oxford University Press, 2007) ch 4.

[15] See, eg, Goudkamp (n 14) 143.

[16] 'If two persons would otherwise be liable for a harm, one of them is not relieved from liability by the fact that the other has an absolute privilege to act or an immunity from liability to the person harmed': *Restatement (Second) of the Law of Torts* § 880.

[17] Although, of course, the defendant might also be personally covered by a similar defence.

[18] Goudkamp (n 14) 143. However, if an objective element of the wrong is denied by the 'primary wrongdoer' then no claim will succeed against either the primary wrongdoer or the accessory. For example, if defamatory remarks cause no damage to the claimant, then the objective element of damage can be denied by all defendants: Goudkamp (n 14) 143.

[19] *R v Cogan; R v Leak* (n 12).

[20] ibid at 223 (Lawton LJ): 'If we are right in our opinion that the wife had been raped (and no one outside a court of law would say that she had not been)'. See too S Kadish, 'Complicity, Cause and Blame: A Study in the Interpretation of Doctrine' (1985) 73 *California Law Review* 323, 374.

element of that offence,[21] even though the primary wrongdoer lacked the necessary *mens rea* to be convicted himself.

A defendant can even be liable under the *Lumley* tort in situations where the primary wrongdoer does not have to compensate the claimant. For example, a defendant could incur liability for inducing the breach of an unenforceable contract.[22] And it may well be that an accessory could not rely upon a limitation clause in the contract in the same manner as the contract-breaker.[23] This further emphasises that it is too quick generally to assume that a defence available to a primary wrongdoer will necessarily also benefit the accessory; the defence available to a primary wrongdoer will not invariably eliminate the primary wrong, and accessory liability can be parasitic to that wrong. In some situations, the relevant defence will also defeat a claim against the defendant, but this depends upon the facts of the case and defence presented. Where the focus is upon the claimant's conduct, any claim is likely to fail against both primary wrongdoer and accessory. For instance, if the claimant has provided fully informed consent to the primary wrong and violation of his or her rights,[24] then that consent should ordinarily prevent the claimant from suing either the primary wrongdoer or any accessory.[25]

2. JUSTIFICATION

The most significant potential defence to accessory liability is that of justification. This defence has been best recognised in the context of the *Lumley* tort.[26] Participation in a breach of contract may be easier to justify than participation in other private law wrongs: contractual rights may often appear to be of 'lesser' importance than other rights protected by the law of tort, such as freedom and

[21] The court seemed to think that the defendant could be viewed to have acted through the primary offender as an 'innocent agent', but this is surely misconceived because rape cannot be committed through an innocent agent: see now Sexual Offences Act 2003 (UK), s 1; A Simester et al, *Simester and Sullivan's Criminal Law: Theory and Doctrine*, 5th edn (Oxford, Hart Publishing, 2013) 465.

[22] *Smith v Morrison* [1974] 1 WLR 659 (Ch) (Plowman J). See too *Restatement (Second) of the Law of Torts* § 766, cmt f; J Danforth, 'Tortious Interference with Contract: A Reassertion of Society's Interest in Commercial Stability and Contractual Integrity' (1981) *Columbia Law Review* 1491, 1517–19. Cf T Weir, *Economic Torts* (Oxford, Clarendon Press, 1997) 36.

[23] This seems to be the position in the equitable context of dishonestly inducing a breach of trust: see, eg, J Mowbray, *Lewin on Trusts*, 18th edn (London, Sweet and Maxwell, 2008) [40.20]; S Gardner, 'Knowing Assistance and Knowing Receipt: Taking Stock' (1996) 112 *LQR* 56; however, this issue is not free from doubt: cf Deakin and Randall (n 3) 538.

[24] Indeed, it is unclear whether any wrong is committed if the claimant consents: see, eg, WVH Rogers, *Winfield & Jolowicz on Tort*, 18th edn (London, Sweet and Maxwell, 2010) 108.

[25] A similar analysis can be applied in other situations; for example, if the claimant's loss arises as a result of his or her own illegal conduct, then his or her claim may not be allowed to succeed against any defendant: see, eg, *Gray v Thames Trains Ltd* [2009] UKHL 33; [2009] 1 AC 1339.

[26] For example, in *OBG Ltd v Allan* (n 2) Lord Nicholls said: 'In *Quinn v Leathem* [1901] AC 495 the House upheld the decision in *Lumley v Gye*. In doing so their Lordships expressed the principle underlying that decision in broad terms. Lord Macnaghten, at 510, said that *Lumley v Gye* was rightly decided, not on the ground of malicious intention, but: '... on the ground that a violation of legal right committed knowingly is a cause of action, and that it is a violation of legal right to interfere with contractual relations recognised by law if there be no sufficient justification for the interference'. It has also received some recognition in the equitable context: see, eg, *Royal Brunei Airlines v Tan* [1995] 2 AC 378 (PC) 389 (Lord Nicholls).

bodily integrity.[27] But this does not mean that an entirely different approach should be taken as regards justification: fundamentally, it must be established that the defendant was acting reasonably, and only to the extent necessary,[28] to protect something that trumps the claimant's rights. Various factors will be important in this balancing exercise; the nature of the claimant's rights might affect the weight to be given to particular factors, but different rights do not necessitate different tests of justification.[29]

However, the contours of the defence of justification have not been clearly defined, and it is perhaps easiest to begin by considering what is not sufficient for the defence of justification.[30] It is clearly inadequate for the defendant simply to assert an absence of malice; indeed, the defendant will not be able to exploit this defence even if 'he acted as an altruist, seeking only the good of another and careless of his own advantage'.[31] Nor can a defendant escape liability by explaining that he or she was motivated by a similar wrong committed by the claimant;[32] revenge does not justify participation in a wrong when recourse to the courts for the original wrong should be sought.[33] Significantly, the fact that the defendant was motivated by 'the mere protection of the defendants' own interests' is insufficient for justification, even where the defendant acted in order to stave off its own insolvency[34] or for a common interest.[35] The fact that the defendant acted to further his or her own best interests does not, without more, justify accessoryship.[36] Although one reason motivating the defendant's conduct may well be self-interest, the defence of justification requires further factors to counterbalance the infringement of the claimant's rights, and will only cover acts which were reasonably necessary for the justifying purpose.[37]

[27] Cf *Southport Corp v Esso Petroleum Co Ltd* [1953] 3 WLR 773 (QBD) 779 (Devlin J): 'The safety of human lives belongs to a different scale of values from the safety of property. The two are beyond comparison'. See generally N McBride, 'Tort Law and Human Flourishing' in Pitel et al, *Tort Law* (n 6); P Cane, *The Anatomy of Tort Law* (Oxford, Hart Publishing, 1997) ch 3.

[28] *Zhu v Treasurer of New South Wales* [2004] HCA 56; (2004) 218 CLR 530 [170]–[171].

[29] Any contrary approach would introduce unnecessary complexity and unclear distinctions; Howarth has noted that defences to accessory liability might 'provide a bulwark against the possibility of divergence between contractual and non-contractual confidentiality doctrines' by operating in a similar manner in both: D Howarth, 'Against *Lumley v Gye*' (2005) 68 *MLR* 195, 230.

[30] *Edwin Hill and Partners v First National Finance Corp plc* [1989] 1 WLR 225 (CA) 230.

[31] *Read v Friendly Society of Operative Stonemasons of England, Ireland and Wales* [1902] 2 KB 88 (KBD) 97 (Darling J); see too the decision of the Court of Appeal: [1902] 2 KB 732 (CA) 737 (Collins MR); *Smithies v National Association of Operative Plasterers* [1909] 1 KB 310 (CA); *Glamorgan Coal Co Ltd v South Wales Miners' Federation* [1905] AC 239 (HL); *Pratt v British Medical Association* [1919] 1 KB 244 (KBD) 266 (McCardie J).

[32] *Smithies v National Association of Operative Plasterers* (ibid) (Buckley LJ).

[33] This is a feature of all justificatory defences: see, eg, Goudkamp (n 14) 107. See too *Camden Nominees v Forcey* [1940] Ch 352 (Ch) 366 (Simonds J): 'It is a dangerous proposition that inequality in wealth or position justifies a course otherwise actionable'.

[34] *De Jetley Marks v Lord Greenwood* [1936] 1 All ER 863 (KBD) 873 (Porter J).

[35] Cf *Camden Nominees v Forcey* [1940] Ch 352 (Ch D) 365 (Simonds J). This reasoning is often problematic for trade unions, but statute has now intervened: Trade Union and Labour Relations (Consolidation) Act 1992 (UK), s 219(1)(a); see Section 7.

[36] *Read v Friendly Society of Operative Stonemasons of England, Ireland and Wales* (n 31) at 97 (Darling J) and at 737 (Collins MR); *Glamorgan Coal Co Ltd v South Wales Miners' Federation* (n 31) at 252 (Lord James); *Pratt v British Medical Association* (n 31); *De Jetley Marks v Lord Greenwood* (n 34).

[37] *Zhu v Treasurer of New South Wales* (n 28).

It is therefore possible to identify some common factors which will be insufficient to establish a defence of justification. However, a positive formulation of what does constitute justification is more difficult. Broad formulations of the defence are often relied upon. For instance, in *Glamorgan Coal Co Ltd v South Wales Miners' Federation* Romer LJ said:[38]

> I think it would be extremely difficult, even if it were possible, to give a complete and satisfactory definition of what is 'sufficient justification,' and most attempts to do so would probably be mischievous… I respectfully agree with what Bowen L.J. said in the *Mogul Case*[39] when considering the difficulty that might arise whether there was sufficient justification or not: 'The good sense of the tribunal which had to decide would have to analyze the circumstances and to discover on which side of the line each case fell.' I will only add that, in analyzing or considering the circumstances, I think that regard might be had to the nature of the contract broken; the position of the parties to the contract; the grounds for the breach; the means employed to procure the breach; the relation of the person procuring the breach to the person who breaks the contract; and I think also to the object of the person in procuring the breach. But, though I deprecate the attempt to define justification, I think it right to express my opinion on certain points in connection with breaches of contract procured where the contract is one of master and servant. In my opinion, a defendant sued for knowingly procuring such a breach is not justified of necessity merely by his shewing that he had no personal animus against the employer, or that it was to the advantage or interest of both the defendant and the workman that the contract should be broken.

This was described as a 'broad brush' approach by counsel in *Edwin Hill and Partners v First National Finance Corp plc.*[40] Essentially, it only requires the courts to consider all the circumstances, providing little guidance concerning the principles or application of justification.

A broad defence of justification maintains the flexibility to deal with novel situations and the myriad of ways by which a defendant might participate in a primary wrong. Justification could be defined widely; a defence of 'acting reasonably' has been adopted in the criminal sphere for the inchoate statutory offence of assisting or encouraging crime,[41] and Howarth has strongly argued that a justificatory defence based upon the criteria of 'fair, just and reasonable' is not too uncertain, particularly given the familiarity of these terms in the context of negligence claims.[42] Howarth labelled this a 'maximalist' approach, and preferred it to a 'minimalist' approach which meant that justification would only provide a defence in situations where it has been decided that a defence should be available; although the latter might seem to lead to greater certainty for litigants, 'that certainty might turn out to be illusory if the process of establishing a new extension of the justification defence merely suggested other extensions'.[43]

A wide defence might be criticised as leading to an unacceptable degree of uncertainty, but some lack of precision in the context of defences may be tolerated in

[38] [1903] 2 KB 545 (CA) 573–574.
[39] *Mogul Steamship Co Ltd v McGregor, Gow & Co* (1889) 23 QBD 598 (CA) 618.
[40] [1989] 1 WLR 225 (CA) 229.
[41] Serious Crime Act 2007 (UK), s 50. See too the US Model Penal Code § 3.02.
[42] Howarth (n 29) 225–31. See similarly the defence contained in Trustee Act 1925 (UK), s 61.
[43] Howarth (n 29) 225.

this context.[44] Heydon has even argued that '[i]t seems better to accept the risk of greater uncertainty in the hope of greater justice when the court comes to balance the interests, values, and aspirations underlying each party's conduct';[45] Howarth has claimed that the defence of justification 'allow[s] in substantive normative judgments ... [and] makes the court announce its assessment openly, rather than rely silently on an assumption that all persuasion to breach a contract is immoral'.[46] But predicting the content of the factors to be assessed remains unclear. In *Edwin Hill and Partners v First National Finance Corp plc*,[47] Stuart-Smith LJ expressed the view that the courts 'have over the years worked on this principle', but in *Stocznia Gdanska SA v Latvian Shipping Co (No 2)*, Rix LJ noted the 'significance of [justification], an area which has not been clearly worked out in the cases'.[48] Any work undertaken by the courts to develop this defence is little appreciated and the outline of justification remains largely murky. Nevertheless, the suggestion in *Clerk & Lindsell* that 'it is impossible to lay down any general rule about the nature of this defence'[49] seems overly pessimistic and defeatist. The law in this area is not easy,[50] but some further guidance is both possible and helpful, even if the broad shape of justification remains flexible and any list of factors to be considered cannot purport to be exhaustive. The following discussion will focus on some of the key considerations.

3. EQUAL OR SUPERIOR RIGHT

In *Read*, Darling J said that 'sufficient justification for interference with plaintiff's right must be an equal or superior right'.[51] It is commonly thought that property rights are superior to personal, contractual rights, for example.[52] However, such superior rights can only ground a defence of justification if they were acquired without knowledge of any inconsistent contract.[53] The leading decision on this

[44] Goudkamp (n 14) 139 has written that 'Because justifications are not supposed to guide people in their behaviour in the same way as the duties created by the causes of action in tort, it might be less objectionable, for the purposes of the rule of law, if their ambits are uncertain'. See too J Gardner (n 14) ch 5.

[45] JD Heydon, 'The Defence of Justification in Cases of Intentionally Caused Economic Loss' (1970) 20 *University of Toronto Law Journal* 139, 180. The tension between goals of 'certainty' and 'justice' will be discussed further below.

[46] Howarth (n 29) 225.

[47] Above n 30.

[48] [2002] EWCA Civ 889; [2002] 2 All ER (Comm) 768 [130].

[49] A Dugdale (ed), *Clerk & Lindsell on Torts*, 20th edn (London, Sweet and Maxwell, 2010) 24–55.

[50] Eg, *Glamorgan Coal Co Ltd v South Wales Miners' Federation* (n 38) at 573 (Romer LJ): 'But although, in my judgment, there is no doubt as to the law, yet I fully recognise that considerable difficulties may arise in applying it to the circumstances of any particular case. When a person has knowingly procured another to break his contract, it may be difficult under the circumstances to say whether or not there was "sufficient justification or just cause" for his act'.

[51] *Read v Friendly Society of Operative Stonemasons of England, Ireland and Wales* (n 31) 96–97.

[52] C Carpenter, 'Interference with Contract Relations' (1928) 41 *Harvard Law Review* 728, 747–48. See too JD Heydon, *Economic Torts*, 2nd edn (London, Sweet and Maxwell, 1978) 40.

[53] *De Mattos v Gibson* (1858) 4 De G&J 276; 45 ER 108; *Swiss Bank Corp v Lloyds Bank Ltd* [1979] 1 Ch 548 (Ch D). It would seem to be the case that a defendant who later acquires knowledge of a prior inconsistent contract can justify inducing a breach of that contract in order to protect his or her proprietary interests provided that the defendant had no such knowledge at the time the proprietary right was acquired: see, eg, *Edwin Hill and Partners v First National Finance Corp plc* (n 30) at 226, in which

issue is *Edwin Hill and Partners v First National Finance Corp plc.*[54] The defendant lent money to Leakcliff Properties Ltd, a property development company. The loan was secured by a legal charge over the property planned for development. Unfortunately, there were significant delays, a collapse in the property market, and Leakcliff was unable to afford the repayments of the mortgage. The defendant was owed £9 million, and had the right to exercise its power of sale under the charge. However, it instead reached a settlement with Leakcliff under which the defendant would finance the redevelopment of the property itself. By so doing, the defendant hoped to stave off greater losses and eventually recover the money it was owed. As part of the agreement, the defendant insisted that Leakcliff replace the architects it had been using with a more established firm, in the belief that this would make the development more attractive. Leakcliff reluctantly agreed and terminated the architects' contract. The architects then sued the defendants for inducing a breach of contract, but this claim failed. Stuart-Smith LJ said: [55]

> Why, it may be asked, should the defendants be justified in interfering with the plaintiffs' contract if they exercise their power of sale as mortgagee in possession, but not if by agreement they permit the mortgagor to conduct the sale in the hope of achieving a better deal for both? Why should they be justified if they appoint a receiver, who has power to build-out the development and appoint architects, but not if they agree to finance the mortgagor to perform this task? I cannot find any logical answer to these questions.
>
> Moreover, I think it would be undesirable if the law were to insist that a mortgagee in such a position should exercise his strict legal rights if he is to be justified in interference with contracts between the mortgagor and third parties; and could not be justified if he reached some sensible and reasonable accommodation which may be to the benefit of both himself and the mortgagor, but which has the same effect on the third parties' contract. The accommodation is designed to protect or defend the mortgagees' equal or superior right as a secured creditor, who had in this case financed the entire purchase and development of the site so far. And the accommodation was reached against the background of the remedy of sale or the appointment of a receiver. There can be no doubt that these rights existed once a formal demand for payment was made, a demand which could not have been met.

This result must be right: the claimants could not have complained if the defendant had exercised its power of sale, and thereby deprived the claimants of their job, so it would be very odd if the defendant were to be liable for producing the same result through a more sensible commercial arrangement with Leakcliff.

In *Edwin Hill*, the right under the legal charge was a proprietary right. Yet the thrust of the reasoning in the Court of Appeal seems to focus on the contractual nature of the rights at issue. Stuart-Smith LJ said that:[56] 'Justification for interference with the plaintiff's contractual right based upon an equal or superior right in the defendant must clearly be a legal right. Such right may derive from property, real or personal, or from contractual rights'.

Stuart-Smith LJ was quite relaxed about the timescale of events, provided the right was acquired without knowledge of the inconsistent contract. See too *Granby Marketing Services Ltd v Interlego* [1984] RPC 209 (Ch D) 215. See too *James v Commonwealth of Australia* [1936] AC 578 (PC).

[54] Above n 30.
[55] ibid 232–33.
[56] ibid 233.

It may not be unreasonable for a defendant to seek to defend his or her agreed contractual rights; why should the defendant allow his or her contract to be breached, rather than act in a way which would protect that contract but lead to the claimant's inconsistent contract being breached?

One relevant consideration concerns which contract was concluded first; in *Smithies v National Association of Operative Plasterers*, Buckley LJ said that 'if the contract between B. and C. is one which B. could not make consistently with his preceding contractual obligations towards A., A. may not only induce him to break it, but may invoke the assistance of a Court of Justice to make him break it'.[57] This approach to competing contracts is similar to that of competing equitable rights:[58] as a general rule, the right created first in time has priority.[59] However, there is some suggestion that even if a defendant enters into a contract with the primary wrongdoer *after* the latter had already concluded a contract with the claimant, the defendant may be justified in acting to protect his or her contractual rights, provided the defendant had no knowledge of the claimant's agreement when he or she contracted.[60] This can be explained on the basis that the defendant's contractual right is equal to the claimant's similar right, and there is no reason for the defendant not to defend such a right acquired in good faith. The situation is different, however, if the defendant knew of the claimant's contract when he or she concluded an agreement with the primary wrongdoer; in such situations, the defendant will not be able to justify participation in the primary breach of contract by relying upon his or her subsequently acquired rights.[61]

This appears to represent the law in England. Yet in Australia it seems that only a superior, and not merely an equal, right may be relied upon as a justification for participating in a primary breach of contract. For example, in *Independent Oil Industries Ltd v The Shell Co of Australia Ltd*, Jordan CJ said that 'it does not appear to have yet been authoritatively decided that anything short of the protection of an actually existing superior legal right will justify the wilful procuring of a breach of contract'.[62] This was approved by the High Court of Australia in *Zhu v Treasurer of New South Wales*, which explained that:[63]

> Jordan CJ meant a right in real or personal property, not merely a right to contractual performance. The former type of right may be seen as superior to the latter because the

[57] Above n 31, 337. Cf *Pritchard v Briggs* [1980] Ch 338 (CA) 415 (Goff LJ).

[58] See J McGhee (ed), *Snell's Equity*, 32nd edn (London, Sweet and Maxwell, 2010) ch 4.

[59] See, eg, *Hendler v Cuneo Eastern Press Inc* 279 F 2d 181, 185 (2d Cir 1960) (Learned Hand J): 'If A has promised one performance to B and has later promised the same performance to C, A cannot satisfy both promises. If he chooses to perform his contract with C he remains liable to *B* and that liability is measured by the value of what *B* has lost, though, as we have said, the remedy is not the same thing as performance. There is no justification for allowing *A* the liberty to choose which of the two obligees he will grant the advantage: he is the wrongdoer. While it is true that *B* and C are equally innocent, there must be a choice between them, and if *A* is eliminated as chooser the basis for choice can only be he who has the earlier claim. He may justly insist on preference; it cannot be a wrong against *A* that he seeks to induce C not to enforce that performance to which as between them *B* himself has the preferred claim'.

[60] *Read v Friendly Society of Operative Stonemasons of England, Ireland and Wales* (n 31) 95; *Smithies v National Association of Operative Plasterers* (n 57); *Pratt v British Medical Association* (n 31) 265.

[61] *British Homophone Ltd v Kunz* [1935] All ER 627 (KBD) 633–634 (Du Parcq J).

[62] (1937) 37 SR (NSW) 394 (Full Ct) 416.

[63] Above n 28, [139]. See generally [108]–[171].

> former is proprietary, while the latter is at most quasi-proprietary ... Two competing rights to contractual performance involving no proprietary interest would be equal rights, neither being superior to the other; but Jordan CJ did not mention the protection of an equal right as a form of justification. The conclusion that by 'superior legal right' Jordan CJ meant a right to real or personal property is also indicated by the fact that he limited his examples of persons justified in interfering with contracts to the owners of rights in real or personal property that were inconsistent with rights created by contracts between other persons.

This approach greatly limits the protection and freedom afforded to defendants who do not 'directly' breach the claimant's contract. It is suggested that the English approach is preferable; defendants should be able to defend their contractual rights acquired in good faith by participating in breaches of inconsistent contracts, unless the claimant enjoys a superior right. Simple contractual rights enjoyed by the claimant should not, without more, prevail over the defendant's contractual rights and require the defendant to forego attempts to protect his or her legal interests.

It will generally be more difficult to justify participating in a tort on the basis of a 'superior right'. But there does seem to be a hierarchy of rights protected by tort law,[64] such that participating in some torts might be justifiable on the basis of furthering a higher, inconsistent right. For instance, participating in a private nuisance committed by a primary wrongdoer might be defensible if the defendant was threatened with physical harm if he refused to do so and therefore only acted in order to protect his right to bodily integrity.[65] And if the defendant reasonably acts in self-defence in encouraging a primary tortfeasor to attack a perceived aggressor, the defendant may be justified in participating in the primary tort of battery, even if the primary tortfeasor was not similarly justified and attacked the claimant unaware that the claimant posed a threat to the defendant.

A defendant may also seek to rely upon rights protected by the European Convention on Human Rights (ECHR) in order to justify knowing participation in a primary wrong. However, such rights are often subject to qualifications, and will not inevitably outweigh the primary right violated: a balancing exercise is required. Nevertheless, some illustrative instances where fundamental rights have come to the aid of a defendant are instructive. The disclosure of confidential information concerning the perpetration of fraud or a crime is generally justified, and this conclusion is supported by the right to free speech protected in Article 10 of the ECHR.[66] Freedom of expression is particularly significant when defendants are sued for participating in the infringement of intellectual property rights,[67] and also supports other justificatory defences such as innocent dissemination in the context of defamation.[68] Freedom of assembly might be relied upon by protestors who trespass

[64] See n 27 above.

[65] For further consideration of the existence and nature of a defence of duress in tort law, see Edelman and Dyer's contribution to this volume: ch 9.

[66] *Initial Services v Putterill* [1968] 1 QB 396 (CA); *Cream Holdings Ltd v Banerjee* [2004] UKHL 44; [2005] 1 AC 253. See J Ulph, *Commercial Fraud: Civil Liability, Human Rights, and Money Laundering* (Oxford, Oxford University Press, 2006) [7.28].

[67] See, in the criminal context, *R v Rock and Overton* T20097013 (Gloucester Crown Court, 6 February 2010) [10].

[68] See Defamation Act 1996 (UK), s 1.

and members of unions who picket. Such rights could be especially important when assessing justification in the context of accessory liability.

4. PERFORMANCE OF A DUTY

A defendant's duty to a third party might trump the obligation not knowingly to participate in a primary wrong. This depends upon the nature of the primary wrong and, again, requires a balancing exercise. For example, a doctor who, in the performance of his or her duty as a doctor, orders a patient to go home and thereby breach a contract with a claimant, should not be liable under the *Lumley* tort: the fact that the doctor was performing his or her professional duty in good faith is sufficient to justify his or her actions.[69] The same reasoning might enable police officers to escape liability in situations where they encourage a primary wrongdoer to breach obligations of confidence, for example, in order to prevent the commission of crime.[70]

In practice, the most important aspect of this element of the defence of justification concerns the performance of a duty in the course of employment. It has posed particular problems as regards the relationship between a company and company director. In *Said v Butt*,[71] a theatre critic bought a ticket, through a friend, for the first night of a theatre performance. He was then denied entry to the theatre, and consequently sued the managing director of the theatre company for inducing a breach of contract between the claimant and the theatre company. On the facts, it was held that there was no contract and therefore the issue of accessory liability was moot, but McCardie J nevertheless expressed the view that even if there had been a breach, the agent should not be liable for the wrong of his principal. His Lordship said:[72]

> But the servant who causes a breach of his master's contract with a third person seems to stand in a wholly different position. He is not a stranger. He is the alter ego of his master. His acts are in law the acts of his employer. In such a case it is the master himself, by his agent, breaking the contract he has made, and in my view an action against the agent under the *Lumley v Gye* principle must therefore fail, just as it would fail if brought against the master himself for wrongfully procuring a breach of his own contract.

McCardie J was concerned to ensure both that directors of a company not be liable every time a company breached a contract, and that the doctrine of corporate limited liability be maintained.

This approach of McCardie J, based upon the agent being the alter ego of the principal, has often been followed,[73] and even applied to a situation where council committee members induced the council to breach a contract.[74] But despite the

[69] Cf *Gillick v West Norfolk and Wisbech Area Health Authority* [1986] AC 112 (HL).

[70] *Hellewell v Chief Constable of Derbyshire* [1995] 1 WLR 804 (QBD); *Malone v Metropolitan Police Commissioner* [1979] Ch 344 (Div Ct); *R v Chief Constable for the North Wales Police, ex p AB* [1999] QB 396 (CA).

[71] [1920] 3 KB 497 (KBD).

[72] ibid 505–06.

[73] Eg, *Ridgeway Maritime Inc v Beulah Wings Ltd (The Leon)* [1991] 2 Lloyd's Rep 611 (QBD) 624.

[74] *Scammell & Nephew Ltd v Hurley* [1929] 1 KB 419 (CA).

apparent acceptance of this rule, it has also been criticised. In *Welsh Development Agency v Export Finance Co Ltd*,[75] the defendants were receivers of a company, and procured the breach of the company's contract with the claimants by encouraging the company's customers to pay debts directly to the company, rather than—as was required by a contract between the company and the claimant—to an account controlled by the claimant. The Court of Appeal held that the principle enunciated in *Said v Butt* applied, since the receivers were effectively agents for the company and therefore could be regarded as the alter ego of the company. However, the Court of Appeal also expressed some dissatisfaction with this reasoning. Dillon LJ said:[76]

> Personally, I have grave reservations over the reasoning of McCardie J in *Said v Butt*. Since the agent or employee is normally personally liable for any tortious acts he does to third parties in the course of his agency or employment, I would not find any conceptual difficulty in holding that an employee or agent who, in the course of his employment or agency, wrongfully causes a breach of a contract between his employer or principal and a third party is liable in tort to the third party for his tortious act of wrongfully causing a breach of contract, notwithstanding that the liability of his employer or principal for the agent's wrongful acts lies in breach of contract rather than in tort.

Nevertheless, his Lordship thought that because the law had 'stood for so long and been so widely accepted'[77] it was inappropriate for the Court to depart from *Said v Butt*. In a similar vein, Staughton LJ opined that 'the rule, if such it be, seems anomalous to me and must be justified on policy grounds'.[78]

It is suggested that the 'alter ego' aspect of the reasoning of McCardie J is flawed.[79] If it were correct, it might be expected to apply equally to other torts as well, but it does not.[80] Indeed, the alter ego principle is generally invoked to impose liability upon companies, and it seems odd that it is used to relieve company directors of accessory liability. In *Said v Butt*, McCardie J also said that:[81]

> Nothing that I have said today is, I hope, inconsistent with the rule that a director or a servant who actually takes part in or actually authorizes such torts as assault, trespass to property, nuisance, or the like may be liable in damages as a joint participant in one of such recognized heads of tortious wrong.

But the alter ego rule would necessarily preclude accessory liability to torts and equitable wrongs just as to breaches of contract.[82] As McCardie J recognised, this is inappropriate. The reasoning in *Said v Butt* should be jettisoned.[83]

[75] [1992] BCC 270 (CA).
[76] ibid 289.
[77] ibid 290.
[78] ibid 305.
[79] See too Cooper (n 4) 169–72.
[80] R Stevens, 'Why do Agents "Drop Out"?' [2005] *Lloyd's Maritime and Commercial Law Quarterly* 101, especially 107.
[81] *Said v Butt* (n 71) 506.
[82] See, eg, *Welsh Development Agency v Export Finance Co Ltd* (n 75) 289 (Dillon LJ).
[83] It cannot be saved by reference to other justifications raised in the case either. For example, although it is sometimes said that any contrary approach might lead to the company being liable twice over—once for the breach of contract, and again vicariously for a director's participation in that breach of contract (see *Said v Butt* (n 71) 506)—this is patently inappropriate since a primary wrongdoer cannot be an accessory to its own wrong.

The result in *Said v Butt* is best explained on the basis of justification. Company directors owe a fiduciary duty to act in the company's best interests. This duty trumps the contractual rights of the victim of the breach of contract. Heydon has expressed this as 'the agent ... performing an independent and prior contractual duty to his principal which prevails over the plaintiff's rights'.[84] It should be recognised that the agent is still prima facie liable for knowingly participating in a breach of contract, but this can be justified because it is reasonable for the agent not to breach the 'more important' fiduciary duties owed to the company.[85] However, sometimes a director *should* be liable for knowingly participating in the company's breach of contract. This will be the case where the director acted beyond his or her powers, for example;[86] yet under the alter ego analysis favoured in *Said v Butt*, this result might not be achieved. Stevens has written that, '[p]erhaps the rule in *Said v Butt* should today be seen as an example of the defence of justification which applies generally to claims for inducing breach of contract ... Perhaps it is significant that at the time of *Said v Butt* the defence of justification was underdeveloped'.[87] It is suggested that the existence of a defence of justification does indeed help to explain the result in *Said v Butt*.

It is important to appreciate that this defence rests upon a duty owed by the defendant to a third party. Directors of a company have a positive duty to act in the best interests of that company, and are not merely acting in their own interests. It is therefore surprising that in *De Jetley Marks v Greenwood*, Porter J expressed the view that a defendant would not be justified in participating in the company's wrong on the basis that he was acting to protect the company's interests since '[t]he justification must, I think, involve an action taken as a duty, not the mere protection of the defendants' own interests'.[88] Such reasoning seems unsatisfactory. The defence of justification should have been available, since the defendant was acting in accordance with a duty owed to the company.

This analysis is perhaps strengthened by the judgment of David Richards J in *Lictor Anstalt v Mir Steel UK Ltd*.[89] On an application for summary judgment, the judge thought it arguable that administrators[90] could claim that their acts were justified when, in pursuit of their statutory functions and purposes, they sold assets of the company in breach of contracts made by the company. This approach seems sensible; the duty to administer the company satisfactorily outweighs any competing duty to ensure the fulfilment of the company's contracts, even if the contractual

[84] Heydon (n 45) 164–65. See too *Imperial Oil Ltd v C&G Holdings Ltd* [1990] 62 DLR (4th) 261 (Newfoundland CA) [11]: 'A company's directors are agents of it and, consequently, owe to it certain duties flowing from that fiduciary relationship. The general duty to abstain from knowingly violating the legal rights of others must be weighed against the concomitant obligations of a director to the company and his or her functions relative to its operations'.

[85] Cf *Phillips v Montana Education Association* 187 Mont 419; 610 P 2d 154 (1980).

[86] *Thomson v Deakin* [1952] 1 Ch 646 (CA) 681 (Evershed MR); *Ridgeway Maritime Inc v Beulah Wings Ltd (The Leon)* (n 73).

[87] Stevens (n 80) 108.

[88] Above n 34.

[89] [2011] EWHC 3310 (Ch); [2012] 1 All ER (Comm) 592. This issue was not considered on appeal: [2012] EWCA Civ 1397; [2013] 2 All ER (Comm) 54.

[90] The judge thought that the principle of *Said v Butt* was equally applicable to administrators as to receivers, as decided in *Lictor Anstalt v Mir Steel UK Ltd* (ibid) [52].

provision purports to restrict the company's power of sale.[91] It is important to appreciate that proprietary rights and restrictions are expressly respected by statute in the administration process, although administrators have the power to apply to the court to deal with the company assets free from such proprietary rights.[92] But in *Lictor Anstalt*, only personal, contractual rights were at issue. These might be considered not to require such extensive protection, and as a result participation in their infringement might be more readily justifiable.[93]

Although the judge in *Lictor Anstalt* did not need to engage in the reasoning underpinning *Said v Butt* as regards the administrators themselves, he did need to consider the position of the company that purchased the assets sold by the administrators in breach of contract. David Richards J held that such purchasers would be entitled to a defence of justification.[94] His Lordship drew an analogy with *Edwin Hill* and said:[95]

> If an administrator is unable to sell assets without exposing purchasers to a liability in tort for inducing a breach of contract, it is likely to have a damaging effect on the ability of the administrator to obtain the best price for the assets. If the company were to go into liquidation, the liquidator would be able to disclaim the contract containing the third party restriction, a procedure not available to an administrator, and thereby be in a position to sell the relevant assets without any concern on the part of the purchasers that they may expose themselves to a liability in tort.

Since a purchaser would be able to acquire assets from a liquidator without fear of accessory liability, it seems sensible to allow a purchaser also to have a defence against accessory liability if it buys assets from an administrator. However, the judge recognised that this was 'an entirely new point on which there is no authority'[96] and did not have to decide the issue conclusively as he was content that the argument based on justification could not be dismissed on the application for summary judgment. But, tellingly, his Lordship overtly recognised that a defence of justification in the context of accessory liability calls for a balancing exercise to be carried out:[97]

> The proper balancing of competing interests involved in administration as an insolvency process may well be achieved by providing a defence of justification to a claim in tort in respect of a sale by an administrator in circumstances where there is a purely contractual restriction on sale.

This approach to providing a defence of justification is of more general import. The fact that a defendant owes a duty to a third party may be a significant factor to consider when deciding whether a defence to accessory liability is appropriate.

[91] ibid [57].

[92] Insolvency Act 1986 (UK), Sch B1.

[93] 'Given the lesser status of such restrictions as against proprietary interests, it would seem altogether more likely that the legislative assumption was that the administrator had such entitlement without the need for court sanction rather than that such sales free of such restrictions should not be permissible without the consent of the relevant contracting party': *Lictor Anstalt v Mir Steel UK Ltd* (n 89) [57].

[94] See too I Fletcher, J Higham and W Trower, *Corporate Administrators and Rescue Procedures*, 2nd edn (London, Bloomsbury, 2004) [5.29]–[5.30].

[95] *Lictor Anstalt v Mir Steel UK Ltd* (n 89) [58].

[96] ibid [60].

[97] ibid [59]

Can a defendant rely upon a duty owed to an employer to justify his or her participation in a tort? In the criminal context, it has been suggested that a shopkeeper might have a defence if prosecuted as an accessory where the shopkeeper, in the ordinary course of business, sold an item later used to commit a crime.[98] This defence has been rejected by the criminal law,[99] but it may seem more acceptable in the civil law. For example, a checkout assistant at a supermarket might sell a primary tortfeasor a knife later used to commit an assault, or a can of spray paint used to graffiti on a neighbour's wall. Should the defendant be able to point to a contractual duty owed to his or her employer to escape liability as an accessory? One advantage of such a defence is that it would help to protect freedom to trade in situations where the defendant has, in practice, very little discretion about to whom lawful goods can be sold.[100]

However, although situations in which a claim against a shop assistant as an accessory are plausible, they are inevitably uncommon: only rarely will a claimant be able to prove that the defendant knew that the primary wrongdoer would commit an offence.[101] The very strong presumption when dealing with lawful goods is that the purchaser will use those goods in a lawful manner; it will be very difficult to establish that the defendant knew the contrary to be the case. But where the defendant did actually know that a tort would be committed—for example, because the primary tortfeasor openly bragged about his or her plans—does the defendant really deserve a defence to his or her knowing participation in the primary wrong? It may well seem more reasonable for the defendant to refuse to serve that customer. The claimant's rights might outweigh the duties owed by the defendant to his or her employer.

Admittedly, though, this issue is finely balanced. Selling a knife used to commit an assault seems intuitively worse than selling spray paint used to commit a trespass to property. Whilst the former seems very difficult to justify, views might legitimately differ about whether or not a shop assistant acts reasonably in selling spray paint, especially given the ease with which spray paint may be acquired elsewhere. But even in these unusual situations where the defendant does possess the required mental element for accessory liability, it does not seem unduly onerous to rank the claimant's rights higher than the contractual duty owed by an employee to his or her employer.

[98] See, eg, G Williams, *Criminal Law: The General Part* (London, Stevens & Sons, 1961) 373.

[99] *National Coal Board v Gamble* [1959] 1 QB 11 (Div Ct) 23 (Devlin J); A Simester and A von Hirsch, *Crimes, Harms and Wrongs: On the Principles of Criminalisation* (Oxford, Hart Publishing, 2011) 83–85.

[100] Although such a defence might be restricted by the particular terms of employment: if a supermarket instructed its employees not to sell knives or spray paint to those whom they suspect will use such products to commit unlawful acts, the duty owed by the employees to the employer would be governed by the express contractual terms.

[101] The need to establish actual knowledge of the primary wrong is clear under the *Lumley* tort (see, eg, *OBG Ltd v Allan* (n 1) [39] (Lord Hoffmann) and [202] (Lord Nicholls) and seems also to be necessary where the primary wrong is a tort (eg, *Roadshow Films Pty Ltd v iiNet Ltd* [2012] HCA 16; (2012) 86 ALJR 494 [110]; cf *Grimme Maschinenfabrik GmbH v Derek Scott (t/a Scotts Potato Machinery)* [2010] EWCA Civ 1110; [2011] FSR 7 [106]; see generally J Dietrich, 'Accessorial Liability in the Law of Torts' [2011] *Legal Studies* 231, 244–47).

5. STAPLE ARTICLE OF COMMERCE

In the context of intellectual property rights, there is some recognition that accessory liability will generally be inappropriate where the defendant has simply provided a staple article of commerce which is later used to infringe a claimant's rights. The roots of this doctrine can be found in the law of patents. Section 60 of the Patents Act 1977 (UK) provides that:

> (2) Subject to the following provisions of this section, a person (other than the proprietor of the patent) also infringes a patent for an invention if, while the patent is in force and without the consent of the proprietor, he supplies or offers to supply in the United Kingdom a person other than a licensee or other person entitled to work the invention with any of the means, relating to an essential element of the invention, for putting the invention into effect when he knows, or it is obvious to a reasonable person in the circumstances, that those means are suitable for putting, and are intended to put, the invention into effect in the United Kingdom.
>
> (3) Subsection (2) above shall not apply to the supply or offer of a staple commercial product unless the supply or the offer is made for the purpose of inducing the person supplied or, as the case may be, the person to whom the offer is made to do an act which constitutes an infringement of the patent…

Section 60(2) enables liability to be imposed upon a person who supplies, or offers to supply, the primary wrongdoer with the means necessary to infringe the patent. Admittedly, this provision also covers inchoate liability, but where the primary infringement actually occurs this very closely resembles common law accessory liability for assistance or facilitation.[102]

Significantly, section 60(3) provides a defence where a defendant supplies a staple commercial product which might be used to commit an infringement and the defendant did not have an unlawful purpose. Such a structured approach might be mimicked in the common law; this has evolved in America in the context of copyright, inspired by the statutory example set in patent law.[103] The leading decision is *Sony Corp of America v Universal City Studios Inc.*[104] The case concerned Sony Betamax, which was a machine which enabled individuals to record on to VCR. This facilitated the copying of copyright materials, and the copyright holders consequently brought a claim against Sony. The Supreme Court recognised that a party which takes steps to assist the commission of a wrong, knowing that that primary wrong will be committed, runs the risk of 'contributory liability'.[105]

[102] On the differences between the statutory provision and common law, see, eg, *Grimme Maschinenfabrik GmbH v Derek Scott (t/a Scotts Potato Machinery)* (ibid) [88]. Moreover, despite the existence of s 60, the common law remains of crucial importance in the context of patent disputes. This is for two reasons. First, the statute adds to the common law, but does not alter the fact that the general principles of joint tortfeasance remain applicable in the context of patents. Secondly, and increasingly significantly, s 60(2) only applies if a 'double territorial requirement' is satisfied: the supply, or offer of supply must take place in England, and the means supplied must be suitable for putting, and intended to put, the invention into effect in the UK: *Virgin Atlantic Airways Ltd v Delta Air Lines Inc* [2010] EWHC 3094 (Pat); [2011] RPC 8 [89] (not disturbed on appeal: [2011] EWCA Civ 162; [2011] RPC 18).

[103] Eg, *Sony Corp of America v Universal City Studios Inc* 464 US 417 (1984).

[104] ibid 442.

[105] Synonymous, for these purposes, with secondary, or accessory, liability. See too *Re Aimster Copyright Litigation* 334 F 3d 643 (7th Cir 2003).

But the defendants in *Sony* were, ultimately, not held liable, since the Supreme Court found that the product supplied by Sony was capable of 'substantial non-infringing use', and that the defendants should therefore have a defence to accessory liability. Such use consisted largely of recording programmes in order to watch them at a later date—so-called 'time-shifting'. The Court explicitly drew upon the analogous statutory defence in the context of patents in saying:[106]

> We recognize there are substantial differences between the patent and copyright laws. But in both areas the contributory infringement doctrine is grounded on the recognition that adequate protection of a monopoly may require the courts to look beyond actual duplication of a device or publication to the products or activities that make such duplication possible. The staple article of commerce doctrine must strike a balance between a copyright holder's legitimate demand for effective—not merely symbolic—protection of the statutory monopoly, and the rights of others freely to engage in substantially unrelated areas of commerce. Accordingly, the sale of copying equipment, like the sale of other articles of commerce, does not constitute contributory infringement if the product is widely used for legitimate, unobjectionable purposes. Indeed, it need merely be capable of substantial noninfringing uses.
>
> The question is thus whether the Betamax is capable of commercially significant noninfringing uses. In order to resolve that question, we need not explore *all* the different potential uses of the machine and determine whether or not they would constitute infringement. Rather, we need only consider whether on the basis of the facts as found by the District Court a significant number of them would be non-infringing. Moreover, in order to resolve this case we need not give precise content to the question of how much use is commercially significant. For one potential use of the Betamax plainly satisfies this standard, however it is understood: private, noncommercial time-shifting in the home. It does so both (A) because respondents have no right to prevent other copyright holders from authorizing it for their programs, and (B) because the District Court's factual findings reveal that even the unauthorized home time-shifting of respondents' programs is legitimate fair use.

This defence of 'substantial non-infringing use' is an important bulwark to prevent a 'chilling effect'[107] upon the advancement of new technologies. The defendant clearly provided a machine that was capable of being exploited to commit infringements of copyright. However, although causal participation in such primary wrongs may feasibly have been established, it is worth emphasising that it is far from clear that the defendant possessed the requisite mental element for accessory liability: after all, the defendant did not know whether any particular individual would commit a tort. But if a broader approach to the mental element of accessory liability is preferred,[108] then the defendant would be required to rely upon a justificatory defence: despite knowing that the product would be used to commit primary wrongs, it was reasonable for the defendant nevertheless to provide the product given the substantial lawful uses to which that product could be put.

[106] *Sony Corp of America v Universal City Studios Inc* (n 103).

[107] See the concurring opinion of Justice Breyer in *Metro-Goldwyn-Mayer Studios Inc v Grokster Ltd* 545 US 913 (2005).

[108] Sony must have known that a large number of people would have used the machine for an illegal purpose; this issue is discussed further in PS Davies, 'Accessory Liability: Protecting Intellectual Property Rights' [2011] *Intellectual Property Quarterly* 390.

This obviously raises the difficult question of deciding upon the scope of 'substantial lawful use'. In *Sony,* this requirement was fulfilled once it was accepted that time-shifting was itself a legitimate use of the recorders, and this conclusion was compounded by the fact that not all copyright holders had any problem with the devices anyway.[109] However, different views were expressed by members of the US Supreme Court in *Metro-Goldwyn-Mayer Studios Inc v Grokster Ltd.*[110] The defendant, Grokster,[111] distributed software that allowed individual computer users to share electronic files through peer-to-peer networks. The vast majority of these files were shared in breach of the claimants' copyright, and a claim was brought against Grokster. However, Grokster did not *directly* infringe the claimants' copyright; Grokster did not host the infringing material on any server, and the infringing material was passed directly between users' computers. Grokster was nevertheless sued on the basis that 'they knowingly and intentionally distributed their software to enable users to reproduce and distribute the copyrighted works'. On the facts of the case, the United States Supreme Court held that Grokster had actually taken 'active steps to encourage infringement',[112] since it promoted unlawful uses of the website and relied upon them to generate profit, and this was sufficient to constitute 'active inducement', to which the *Sony* defence could not apply. But absent such 'active inducement', the ambit of the *Sony* defence would have been of paramount importance, and the discussion would have focused upon the important question of when a defendant who knowingly assisted a wrong deserves to escape accessory liability. Although not required for the decision in *Grokster*, some members of the Supreme Court did consider the potential application of the *Sony* defence. The two concurring opinions of Justice Ginsburg and Justice Breyer each gained the support of two other Supreme Court Justices, but each provides a very different perspective.[113]

Justice Ginsburg thought that the defence would not assist the defendants, since the website was almost exclusively used for infringing purposes, and there was no 'substantially non-infringing use' at issue. She said:[114]

> [T]here was evidence that Grokster's and StreamCast's products were ... overwhelmingly used to infringe ..., and that this infringement was the overwhelming source of revenue

[109] There was in fact evidence to suggest that the devices helped to improve viewer numbers. Although compare the dissent of Justice Blackmun at 464 US 417, 498–99 (1984):

> Such a definition essentially eviscerates the concept of contributory infringement. Only the most unimaginative manufacturer would be unable to demonstrate that a image-duplicating product is 'capable' of substantial noninfringing uses. Surely Congress desired to prevent the sale of products that are used almost exclusively to infringe copyrights; the fact that noninfringing uses exist presumably would have little bearing on that desire. More importantly, the rationale for the Court's narrow standard of contributory infringement reveals that, once again, the Court has confused the issue of liability with that of remedy. The Court finds that a narrow definition of contributory infringement is necessary in order to protect 'the rights of others freely to engage in substantially unrelated areas of commerce.' *Ante* at 788. But application of the contributory infringement doctrine implicates such rights only if the remedy attendant upon a finding of liability were an injunction against the manufacture of the product in question. The issue of an appropriate remedy is not before the Court at this time, but it seems likely that a broad injunction is not the remedy that would be ordered. It is unfortunate that the Court has allowed its concern over a remedy to infect its analysis of liability.

[110] Above n 107.

[111] Along with StreamCast.

[112] *Metro-Goldwyn-Mayer Studios Inc v Grokster* (n 107) 924.

[113] Justice Ginsburg was joined by Chief Justice Rehnquist and Justice Kennedy, whereas Justice Breyer was joined by Justices Stevens and O'Connor.

[114] *Metro-Goldwyn-Mayer Studios Inc. v Grokster* (n 107) 948 (2005).

from the products…Fairly appraised, the evidence was insufficient to demonstrate, beyond genuine debate, a reasonable prospect that substantial or commercially significant noninfringing uses were likely to develop over time.

In particular, Justice Ginsburg was keen to differentiate between the use of the software products at issue in the case, rather than the use of peer-to-peer technology generally. She was able to distinguish *Sony* because, in *Grokster*, there was no finding of fair use, and little beyond anecdotal evidence of non-infringing uses.[115] Moreover, Justice Ginsburg thought that even if the total number of non-infringing files shared over the Grokster software was large, that would not necessarily mean that the *Sony* defence would apply: the number of 'legitimate' files could still be dwarfed by the total volume of files shared, such that 'substantial' lawful use may not be established.[116] The requirement of 'substantiality' involves a balancing exercise that must take into account the scale of lawful and unlawful uses on either side.[117]

By contrast, Justice Breyer considered that the restrictive approach to the *Sony* defence evinced by Justice Ginsburg would cast a long shadow over the development of technology generally.[118] Justice Breyer insisted that the *Sony* defence should be interpreted in a broad manner, such that the court should be relatively generous in deciding whether or not the product could be used for non-infringing uses. He noted that '*Sony's* word "capable" refers to a plausible, not simply a theoretical, likelihood that such uses will come to pass, and that fact anchors *Sony* in practical reality'.[119] Future uses should be taken into account, and Justice Breyer accepted the evidence that around 10 per cent of the number of files available on Grokster were likely not to be infringing. In contrast to Justice Ginsburg, Justice Breyer thought this sufficient to constitute substantial lawful use.[120] Justice Breyer was concerned not to narrow the *Sony* defence and said:[121]

Sony's rule is clear. That clarity allows those who develop new products that are capable of substantial noninfringing uses to know, *ex ante*, that distribution of their product will not yield massive monetary liability. At the same time, it helps deter them from distributing products that have no other real function than—or that are specifically intended for—copyright infringement.

115 ibid 946.

116 ibid 948.

117 Cf J Ginsburg and S Ricketson, 'Inducers and Authorisers: A Comparison of the US Supreme Court's Grokster Decision and the Australian Federal Court's KaZaa Ruling' (2006) 11 *Media & Arts Law Review* 1, 7: 'Speculation is hazardous, but one might predict that, where a device facilitates infringement on a massive scale, its distributor will likely be found to have intended that result. Where the infringement the device enables is relatively modest in scale, inducement will not be found, but neither will the *Sony* threshold for liability be held to have been crossed, whatever its height'.

118 'Justice Ginsburg's approach would require defendants to produce considerably more concrete evidence—more than was presented here—to earn *Sony's* shelter. That heavier evidentiary demand, and especially the more dramatic (case-by-case balancing) modifications that MGM and the Government seek, would, I believe, undercut the protection that *Sony* now offers': *Metro-Goldwyn-Mayer Studios Inc v Grokster* (n 107) 959.

119 ibid 958; cf *Re Aimster Copyright Litigation* 334 F 3d 643 (7th Cir 2003).

120 Justice Breyer thought a similar figure appeared to suffice in *Sony*; however, in *Sony* it was also held that time-shifting uses were legitimate.

121 *Metro-Goldwyn-Mayer Studios Inc v Grokster* (n 107) 957.

Justice Breyer was particularly keen to emphasise the need to prevent any 'additional chill of technological development'.[122] But even though he was much more willing to offer protection to Grokster under the substantial lawful use doctrine, the approach of the two concurring opinions seems to be fundamentally similar: both require a difficult balancing exercise to be undertaken between the rights at issue on both sides. This was explicitly recognised by Breyer J:[123]

> The third question—whether a positive copyright impact would outweigh any technology-related loss—I find the most difficult of the three. I do not doubt that a more intrusive *Sony* test would generally provide greater revenue security for copyright holders. But it is harder to conclude that the gains on the copyright swings would exceed the losses on the technology roundabouts.

This raises central issues concerning the balancing process required to establish a defence of justification. The problem is perhaps particularly acute in the context of intellectual property rights, given the very real concern not to impede the development of original technologies.[124] This is a significant factor when weighing various considerations within a justificatory defence. Inevitably, difficult decisions will need to be made. On balance, the opinion of Justice Ginsburg seems preferable. Where there are only minimal non-infringing uses of a product, the inherent culpability in furthering unlawful activity on a large scale might outweigh any fears about hindering technological advancement. Yet the issue of scale may well be important; where the infringements will only be minor or rare, then a different conclusion might be reached.[125]

This approach means that such a defence will depend heavily upon the particular facts of a case. However, relevant considerations can be elucidated by decided cases, and the test of justification is assessed objectively. This should enable defendants to have a reasonable idea about whether or not they are able to rely upon a defence. Defendants who intentionally or knowingly participate in primary wrongs should be required to question whether or not their conduct is reasonable, and should not be allowed to exploit their own particular, and perhaps idiosyncratic, moral compass to escape liability.[126] It will be important to factor in the social good that may come about from developing lawful new technologies, but weigh that against the harm caused by wrongful acts. If the potential for technological advancement is very high, and little harm inflicted by the primary wrongdoer, the court may sensibly be more inclined to apply a defence of justification than if the converse were true. A transparent recognition of the nature of this defence might at least force courts to explain their reasoning clearly.

Are there any lessons that can be learned from the *Sony* defence outside the context of intellectual property rights? Some of the relevant factors might be

[122] ibid 960.

[123] ibid 960.

[124] Lord Templeman's concerns in *CBS Songs Ltd v Amstrad Consumer Electronics plc* [1988] AC 1013 (HL) not to stultify the legitimate business of Amstrad may have been best considered under a defence similar to that in *Sony*.

[125] Ginsburg and Ricketson (n 117) 7–10.

[126] This is in keeping with the fact that it is the courts that are the arbiters of what is reasonable, not the defendant or any group of private persons.

applied more widely. For example, the scale of wrongdoing and potential for future developments are important considerations more generally. The sale of a lawful, innocuous product by a shopkeeper which is used to commit criminal damage may be more readily justifiable than the sale of a gun used to commit murder. But the shopkeeper's personal interest in making a profit is not enough, purely by itself, to constitute justification.[127] It must be coupled with broader factors relating to the public interest in protecting the free trade of lawful goods.

In any event, it is clear that any defence will not apply where the defendant acted for the purpose of contributing to primary wrongs.[128] As Giblin-Chen has noted, '[t]here is no justification for giving a bad acting business with a new technology a "get out of jail free card" simply because it can also be used for non-infringing uses'.[129] This raises an issue of general importance: defendants will only be able to rely upon a defence of justification if their motives were also justified.[130] As Collins MR said in *Read*, 'justification to be of any avail must cover their whole conduct, the means they used as well as the end they had in view'.[131] It seems similarly principled to suggest that specific knowledge should also be able to trump the *Sony* defence. For example, if a particular customer were to email Grokster to ask how he or she could access infringing material, and Grokster were to assist the customer to do so, then it would seem inappropriate to allow Grokster to rely upon any justification-based defence. There is no danger of liability expanding too greatly and 'chilling' technological development if it is kept within bounds by a stringent requirement of culpability; any lawful advantages the technology may have appear to be of subsidiary importance if actual knowledge of a specific wrong is possessed by a defendant.

6. PUBLIC MORALS

A defendant may justify participation in a primary wrong on the basis that he or she was acting to protect public morals. This requires the court explicitly to balance the social evil which has been prevented against the violation of the claimant's rights. The defendant does not seek to justify his or her actions by reference to his or her own private interests, but rather to the public good. As Carpenter has observed, '[w]hether a privilege of invasion exists depends upon whether it is of greater moment to society to protect the defendant in the invading activities than it is to protect and guard the plaintiff's interest from such invasions. An evaluation and

[127] See n 36 above.

[128] *Metro-Goldwyn-Mayer Studios Inc v Grokster* (n 107); see too Patents Act 1977 (UK), s 60(3): 'unless the supply or the offer is made for the purpose of inducing the person supplied'.

[129] Cf R Giblin-Chen, 'Rewinding *Sony*: An Inducement Theory of Secondary Liability' (2005) 27 *European Intellectual Property Review* 428, 436.

[130] Goudkamp has written that 'it is doubtful that the label of justification should be applied to defectively motivated defendants': Goudkamp (n 14) 98. Where the defendant's motives are mixed, the better view is that the defence is not necessarily lost: see similarly Heydon (n 52) 45.

[131] *Read v The Friendly Society of Operative Stonemasons of England, Ireland and Wales* (n 31).

balancing of the social import of the conflicting interests of the respective parties and of the social interests *per se* are involved.'[132]

This aspect of the defence of justification is well recognised in the contractual sphere. Indeed, in *Mir Steel*, David Richards J said that '[i]n many of the cases in which the defence has succeeded it has involved what may be described as a higher moral purpose, justifying as a matter of public policy what would otherwise be a tortious interference with contractual relations'.[133] However, few cases have hinged upon justification due to moral rights. The leading example is *Brimelow v Casson*:[134] the defendants who induced theatre proprietors to break contracts with a theatre manager were justified in so doing, since the theatre manager was paying his chorus girls so little that the women had to turn to 'immoral earnings'. As Russell J put it, '[t]hey have found by experience that the payment of less than a living wage to chorus girls frequently drives them to supplement their insufficient earnings by indulging in misconduct for the purpose of gain, thus ruining themselves in morals and bringing discredit on the theatrical calling'.[135]

The decision in *Brimelow v Casson* has not escaped criticism. It has been described as 'isolated',[136] and Heydon has written that 'the decision has been often attacked and never followed'.[137] Scepticism surrounding the decision is perhaps founded upon a notion that courts ought not to sanction private attempts at social reform.[138] Nevertheless, such criticisms are ultimately unconvincing.[139] The better view is that some moral evils are sufficiently grave to justify a person's participating in a primary wrong to prevent more obnoxious outcomes. Clearly, the more serious the evil at issue, the more likely a court will be to accept that a defendant's conduct was justified. This seems particularly apt since '[i]nducing a person to breach a contract may not be wrong if the contract is itself a vehicle of wrongdoing'.[140] Although it has been argued that '[t]he facts of *Brimelow v Casson* were so striking and almost unique that the case has little value as a precedent',[141] it is suggested that, in principle, a defendant should be able to resort to public morality as a basis for justifying his or her participation in any primary wrong. The courts will need to be convinced that a real danger to a serious public interest is posed and can reasonably be deterred or prevented through participation in the

[132] Carpenter (n 52) 745.

[133] *Lictor Anstalt v Mir Steel UK Ltd* (n 89) [55]. Although Dugdale (n 49) [24]–[55] contends that '[t]he defence [of justification] appears to be limited to fulfilment of a "moral duty" which appeals to the "good sense of the tribunal"' this seems too narrow.

[134] [1924] 1 Ch 302 (Ch D).

[135] ibid 312.

[136] Dugdale (n 49) 24–55.

[137] Heydon (n 52) 42, citing *Independent Oil Industries Ltd v The Shell Co of Australia Ltd* (1937) 37 SR (NSW) 394 (Full Ct) 416; *Camden Nominees v Forcey* [1940] Ch 352 (Ch D) 366; *Crofter Hand Woven Harris Tweed Co Ltd v Veitch* [1942] AC 435 (HL) 495–496.

[138] (1924–1925) 38 *Harvard Law Review* 115, 116.

[139] Cf Lord Halsbury: 'Some cases may be suggested when higher and deeper considerations may, in a moral point of view, justify the refusal to do [or interference with] what has been agreed to be done. Such cases may give rise to the consideration whether, in a moral or religious point of view, you are not bound to indemnify the person whom your refusal injures ...', *Glamorgan Coal Co Ltd v South Wales Miners' Federation* (n 31) 245, described by Heydon as 'cynical': Heydon (n 52) 43.

[140] P Cane, '*Mens Rea* in Tort Law' (2000) 20 *OJLS* 533, 554.

[141] Heydon (n 52) 43.

primary wrong; in the balancing exercise that must be undertaken, the 'severity' of the primary wrong itself will be relevant,[142] as will the nature of the concerns of public morality at issue.

7. STATUTORY JUSTIFICATION

Whereas justification based upon general concerns of public morality is sometimes questioned on the basis of judges and private parties not being capable of deciding complicated issues of public morals, the same fears do not apply where Parliament has declared certain actions justifiable. The most important example of statutory justification protects trade unions and the right to strike. At common law, it has been decided by the House of Lords that unions which induce industrial strike action by their members can be liable for inducing breaches of contract, since self-interest alone is insufficient to justify the infringement of a claimant's rights.[143] This is one of the principal reasons why accessory liability in contract law 'touches a nerve'.[144] However, in 1906 Parliament passed the Trade Disputes Act 1906 (UK) to protect trade unions from liability. In effect, defendants who knowingly participate in primary breaches of contract can justify their actions through relying upon statute. This provides clear guidance as to whether or not a defendant's conduct should be characterised as reasonable such that accessory liability is not warranted, and is now encapsulated in section 219(1)(a) of the Trade Union and Labour Relations (Consolidation) Act 1992 (UK), which provides that:

> (1) An act done by a person in contemplation or furtherance of a trade dispute is not actionable in tort on the ground only—
>
> (a) that it induces another person to break a contract …

This legislation maintains the freedom of defendants to act in order to further socially important industrial objectives,[145] although it should not be abused nor used for political purposes.[146]

[142] Thus it may be easier to justify a breach of contract—as in *Brimelow* itself—rather than a tort, for example.

[143] *Glamorgan Coal Co Ltd v South Wales Miners' Federation* (n 31); see n 36 above.

[144] Howarth (n 29) 196.

[145] 'The common law confers no right to strike in this country. Workers who take strike action will usually be acting in breach of their contracts of employment. Those who organise the strike will typically be liable for inducing a breach of contract, and sometimes other economic torts are committed during the course of a strike. Without some protection from these potential liabilities, virtually all industrial action would be unlawful. Accordingly, ever since the Trade Disputes Act 1906 (UK) legislation has been in place to confer immunities on the organisers of strikes from certain tort liabilities provided, to put it broadly, that the purpose of the action is to advance an industrial rather than a political objective. This is achieved by a requirement that the industrial action must be "in contemplation or furtherance of a trade dispute". The current protection is afforded by section 219 of the 1992 Act. The legislation therefore secures a freedom rather than conferring a right as such': *National Union of Rail, Maritime and Transport Workers v Serco Ltd (t/a Serco Docklands)* [2011] EWCA Civ 226; [2011] ICR 848 [2] (Elias LJ).

[146] For some restrictions on the application of s 219, see ss 222–225.

Statutory justifications can be found beyond the confines of the law on industrial relations. For example, in *Scammell and Nephew Ltd v Hurley*,[147] the Court of Appeal held that the chairman of a council committee[148] was not liable as an accessory to a breach of contract, despite knowingly participating in the deprivation of the claimant's electricity supply: the committee was covered by a statutory immunity provided by the Public Authorities Protection Act[149] since the committee was acting in the execution of its public powers. In a similar vein, in *Stott v Gamble*,[150] licensing magistrates were held to be justified in banning a film, even though that induced a breach of the claimant's contract, because they were acting under statutory authority.[151] Such statutory authorisation could equally alleviate liability for other private law wrongs.[152]

8. CONCLUSIONS

Accessories may be considered to lie at the limit of tort liability, but defences still have an important role to play in this area. Although it might be possible largely to obviate the need for defences by further restricting the conduct and mental elements of accessory liability,[153] this could have the consequence of narrowing the net of liability such that defendants who ought to be liable would escape the scope of the law of accessories.[154] It is therefore important overtly to appreciate the scope and significance of appropriate defences. This might help accessory liability to adopt a more coherent structure.[155] Moreover, explicit recognition that the defences available to a primary wrongdoer and accessory are not always the same[156] might bolster the contention that the nature of liability imposed upon the primary wrongdoer and accessory are different.[157]

Insufficient attention has been paid to the importance of defences in the context of accessory liability. Indeed, defences appear often to have been mixed up within

[147] Above n 74.

[148] The future Prime Minister, Clement Atlee.

[149] Public Authorities Protection Act 1893 (UK), s 1.

[150] [1916] 2 KB 504 (KBD).

[151] Cinematograph Act 1909 (UK), ss 5–6.

[152] See, eg, *Whittaker v Child Support Registrar* [2010] FCA 43; (2010) 264 ALR 473, in which it was held that where the defendant customs officers acted under statutory authority, this provided a 'short answer' to a claim of accessory liability. In the context of intellectual property, see, eg, E-Commerce Directive (European Parliament and Council Directive 2000/31/EC of 9 June 2000), arts 12–15.

[153] See generally Goudkamp (n 14) ch 2.

[154] See generally PS Davies, 'Accessory Liability for Assisting Torts' (2011) 70 *CLJ* 353; Dietrich (n 101) 231.

[155] Cf the impact of the change of position defence upon the elements of a claim in unjust enrichment after *Lipkin Gorman v Karpnale Ltd* [1991] 1 AC 548 (HL). See further J Goudkamp and C Mitchell, 'Denials and Defences in the Law of Unjust Enrichment' in C Mitchell and W Swadling (eds), *The Restatement Third, Restitution and Unjust Enrichment: Comparative and Critical Essays* (Oxford, Hart Publishing, 2013).

[156] Space precludes further consideration of other defences which might avail an accessory but not the primary wrongdoer, such as withdrawal: cf *Lemons v Kelly* 239 Or 354, 359–60; 397 P 2d 784, 787 (1964); Cooper (n 4) 173; PS Davies, *Accessory Liability* (Oxford, Hart Publishing, 2015) 250–51.

[157] Similarly, the remedy awarded against an accessory may differ from that available against the primary wrongdoer, for instance: see, eg, *Lumley v Gye* (n 7) (1853) 2 E&B 216, 233–234; 118 ER 749, 756; *Said v Butt* (n 74) 504–05.

the conduct and mental elements of accessory liability.[158] The effect of this has been to distort at times the concepts of 'inducement' and 'common design' according to whether or not judges thought liability to be appropriate.[159] This has already led to a degree of uncertainty; it would be better for judges to be open about their reasoning, and to rely upon clear but flexible defences. Defences such as justification clearly afford judges a degree of discretion. But this does not seem unreasonable,[160] nor lead to any greater uncertainty than currently exists in the grappling of the conduct and mental elements demanded for accessory liability.[161] Indeed, since it will only be in relatively few instances that a claimant will be able to establish that a defendant fulfils both the conduct and mental elements required, it might be expected that the issue of defences will rarely be enlivened. Nevertheless, it is important that it is open to defendants to justify their actions, and the principles underpinning justification deserve fuller consideration.

158 For example, Carty has observed that 'at times the [*Lumley*] tort and its justification are mixed together to provide an unsatisfactory analysis': H Carty, *An Analysis of the Economic Torts* (Oxford, Oxford University Press, 2001) 73.

159 See further PS Davies, 'Aid, Abet, Counsel or Procure?' in S Pitel et al (eds), *Tort Law* (n 6).

160 Indeed, all justificatory defences follow the same structure, and some uncertainty is inherent in the judicial role. As Oliphant has argued, 'To be preferred is an approach based on the identification of relevant factors and their flexible assessment on the facts of individual cases. The exercise of judgment by the court—and the uncertainty that this necessarily entails—should be recognised as inherent in the judicial role, and as desirable rather than something to be distrusted and constrained. The role of the appellate courts should be conceived as setting the parameters within which this balancing exercise is conducted, and establishing the weight that is to be attached to the factors considered, rather than trying to lay down rules that lower courts are constrained to apply mechanically': K Oliphant, 'Against Certainty' in S Pitel et al (eds), *Tort Law* (n 6).

161 For some discussion about the boundaries of the elements of accessory liability in tort, see recently *Fish & Fish Ltd v Sea Shepherd UK and others* [2013] EWCA Civ 544; [2013] 1 WLR 3700, noted PS Davies, 'Joint Tortfeasance and Common Design' (2013) 129 *LQR* 495. See generally Davies (n 156) ch 6.

B. Specific Defences

8

Justifying Necessity as a Defence in Tort Law

GRAHAM VIRGO

> [W]hat justification can necessity afford for the breach of any rule laid down by reason? (Bentham)[1]

Despite Bentham's rejection of necessity, it is acknowledged as a defence to tort claims in various jurisdictions. An explanation for its recognition was identified by Bacon:

> The law chargeth no man with default where the act is compulsory and not voluntary, and where there is not a consent and election; and, therefore, if either there be an impossibility for a man to do otherwise, or so great a perturbation of the judgement and reason as in presumption of law man's nature cannot overcome, such necessity carrieth a privilege in itself.[2]

But the legitimacy of the necessity defence has long been a matter of controversy. Milton called it 'the tyrant's plea',[3] but also poetically endorsed its recognition:[4]

> [A]t length that grounded maxim,
> So rife and celebrated in the mouths
> Of wisest men; that to the public good
> Private respects must yield; with grave authority
> Took full possession of me, and prevailed;
> Virtue, as I thought, truth, duty, so enjoining.

The legitimacy, ambit and function of necessity within tort law remain uncertain. This chapter seeks to resolve that uncertainty by examining the role and relevance of necessity in contemporary tort law. In doing so extensive reference is made to criminal law theory and doctrine, in part because much more work has been done by criminal law theorists in analysing the nature of defences generally and necessity in particular. Criminal law is considered for another reason. This chapter forms one

[1] J Bentham, 'Rationale of Judicial Evidence' in J Bowring (ed), *Works* (Edinburgh, William Tait, 1843), vol VII, 167.

[2] F Bacon, 'The Elements of the Common Laws of England' in B Montague (ed), *Works* (London, William Pickering, 1831), vol XIII, 160.

[3] J Milton, *Paradise Lost*, Bk 4, line 393: 'So spake the Fiend, and with necessity, the tyrant's plea, excused his devilish deeds'. Cited by Lord Coleridge LCJ in *Dudley and Stephens* (1884) 14 QBD 273 (Div Ct) 288, who considered the defence 'might be made the legal cloak for unbridled passion and atrocious crime'.

[4] J Milton, *Samson Agonistes*, lines 865–70.

part of a larger project to investigate the relationship between the criminal law and the law of tort, to identify differences of approach and, if they cannot be justified, to seek appropriate assimilation of the law by virtue of the need to ensure consistency.[5] This principle of consistency is especially significant as regards the operation of necessity in both criminal and tort law.

1. THREE FUNDAMENTAL QUESTIONS

At the outset it is important to consider three questions about the role of necessity in tort law.

1.1 What is Necessity?

A useful definition of necessity was suggested by Sussmann as a doctrine which 'negatives tort liability for an intentional invasion of the interests of another, where the defendant has inflicted the damage under the stress of circumstances for the purpose of preventing a threatened substantially equal or greater harm'.[6] Focusing on this definition enables necessity to be distinguished formally from other doctrines, notably the 'common enemy' rule and defence of oneself or another, even though they are undoubtedly closely related to necessity.

1.1.1 The 'Common Enemy' Rule

The 'common enemy' rule is a defence of particular relevance to the tort of nuisance, which applies where an owner or occupier of land takes reasonable steps to defend the land against an external threat, even though the effect of the action is to divert the threat onto a neighbour's land. This rule can be distinguished from the defence of necessity because the defendant does not set out to invade the neighbour's interests, but acts simply to protect his own property, even though this has the consequence of incidentally interfering with the claimant's right to enjoy his land.[7] Usually the rule operates where the 'common enemy' is riparian floodwater,[8] and it was in that context that it was considered and applied in the leading case of

[5] See G Virgo, 'We do this in the Criminal Law and that in the Law of Tort: a New Fusion Debate' in SGA Pitel, JW Neyers and E Chamberlain (eds), *Tort Law: Challenging Orthodoxy* (Oxford, Hart Publishing, 2013) ch 4.

[6] F Sussmann 'The Defence of Private Necessity and the Problem of Compensation' (1967) 2 *Ottawa Law Review* 184, 184.

[7] *Whalley v Lancashire and Yorkshire Railway* (1884) 13 QBD 131 (CA) 135 (Brett MR), 140 (Lindley LJ).

[8] See, eg, *Maxey Drainage Board v Great Northern Railway Co* (1912) 106 LT 429 (Div Ct); *Gerrard v Crowe* [1921] 1 AC 395 (PC) and *Home Brewery plc v William Davis and Co (Leicester)* [1987] QB 339 (QBD). The rule was extended to protection from seawater: *R v Pagham, Sussex Sewers Comrs* (1828) 8 B & C 355; 108 ER 1075. The rule was also applied by the Privy Council in *Greyvensteyn v Hattingh* [1911] AC 355 (PC), where a farmer had driven locusts away from his land to that of his neighbour.

Arscott v The Coal Authority.[9] The defendant landowner had deposited colliery waste in a field bordering a river to protect its land from floodwater, but this had the effect of diverting floodwater to the claimants' houses. The defendant was held to have acted reasonably to protect its land from the common enemy of floodwater and so was not liable in a claim for nuisance.

That the 'common enemy' rule is distinct from necessity, being founded on defence of property rather than intentional invasion of another's interest, is reflected in a significant limitation[10] on the operation of the rule, namely that it is inapplicable where the defendant has taken measures which cause something which had come onto the defendant's land, or will inevitably come onto the land, to pass from it onto the neighbour's land.[11] In these circumstances the defendant can be considered to have intentionally invaded the neighbour's land in order to protect his own, through the transfer of the common enemy. Whilst the common enemy rule will not apply in such circumstances, it might still be possible for the defendant to plead the specific defence of necessity, but only to allow the defendant to act and not to negate the defendant's liability to compensate the claimant for harm suffered.[12]

1.1.2 Defence of the Person

The defence of 'self-defence'[13] is distinct from necessity, because self-defence is engaged where the defendant is protecting himself from the claimant, who is the source of the danger and so responsible for it, whereas necessity need not be provoked by any actual or threatened danger by the claimant.[14] The nature of this distinction is illustrated by *Lewis v Arnold*,[15] where a group of men unlawfully entered a private box in a theatre when there was no room for them in the pit. The proprietor, who removed them from the theatre using reasonable force, was held to have acted in self-defence (or perhaps more appropriately private defence, because he was protecting a property right rather than his personal autonomy), since the threat to the defendant came directly from the claimants' actions in trespassing in the private box and this justified the defendant's use of reasonable force.

It is unclear, however, where the dividing line between self-defence and necessity should be drawn. In particular, which defence is engaged where the threat to the defendant's right derives from the claimant's property rather than from his actions? For example, in *Cresswell v Sirl*[16] the defendant shot the claimant's dog, which had

[9] [2004] EWCA Civ 892; [2005] Env LR 6. The Court traced the rule back to *Farquharson v Farquharson*, Deans of Court of Session, William Maxwell Morison (1811) vol XXIX–XXX, 12779.

[10] A further limitation is that the rule will not apply where an established watercourse is diverted to protect the defendant's land: *R v Trafford* (1831) 1 B & Ad 874; 109 ER 1011.

[11] *Arscott v The Coal Authority* (n 9) [37] (Laws LJ). See, eg, *Hurdman v NE Ry Co* (1878) 3 CPD 168 (CA); *Whalley v Lancashire and Yorkshire Railway* (n 7).

[12] See further Section 3.2.

[13] In a strict sense, self-defence involves defence of the defendant from attack by the claimant. There is a related defence of private defence which encompasses the use of force to protect property from harm by the claimant. There is a further defence of public defence which is engaged where the defendant uses reasonable force to protect a third person from harm from the claimant.

[14] P Glazebrook, 'The Necessity Plea in English Criminal Law' (1972A) 30 *CLJ* 87, 90.

[15] *Lewis v Arnold* (1830) 4 C & P 354; 172 ER 737.

[16] [1948] 1 KB 241 (CA).

been worrying the defendant's father's sheep, which were in lamb. The claimant sued for trespass, but it was held that the defendant was justified in shooting the dog. This might be considered to be self-defence, particularly because the dog was running towards the defendant when it was shot, or private defence, because the defendant was found to have been acting reasonably to protect property. However, in *Cresswell v Sirl* itself the court specifically relied on earlier cases which had recognised the defence of necessity,[17] and the case has been treated subsequently as recognising this defence.[18] If *Cresswell* involved necessity rather than self-defence, it follows that the latter defence should only be considered to be engaged where the threat to the defendant derives directly from the claimant's actions rather than from the claimant's property.

1.2 Why Should Necessity be Recognised in Tort Law?

The author of *Winfield and Jolowicz*[19] considers the doctrine of necessity to be founded on 'charity, the maintenance of the public good and self-protection'. Despite Bacon's assertion to the contrary, it is not founded on the involuntariness of the defendant's conduct because, as Hobbes recognised, '[t]here [is] nothing there involuntary, but the hardness of the choice'.[20] Necessity is certainly not founded on physical involuntariness, because the defendant has a choice whether or not to act, but the nature of that choice might be considered to involve moral, or normative, involuntariness.[21] This is because the circumstances of necessity mean that the defendant interferes with the claimant's rights in order to avoid greater harm, such that the exercise of the choice to act cannot be considered to be freely made.

An important explanation for the recognition of defences was provided by Serjeant Pollard in *Reniger v Fogossa*:[22]

> [I]n every law there are some things which when they happen a man may break the words of the law, and yet not break the law itself ... for breaking the words of the law is not breaking the law, so as the intent of the law is not broken ... and that is, where the words of them are broken to avoid greater inconveniences ... And this manner of expounding and construing laws is not a mistaking them or a wrong judgment of them, but it is a tempering [of] the rigour of the law.

This explanation was subsequently relied on by Williams to explain why necessity should be recognised, because it involves conduct which 'promotes some value higher than the value of literal compliance with the law'.[23]

[17] Including *Cope v Sharpe (No 2)* [1912] 1 KB 496 (CA). See at p 152.
[18] *Monsanto plc v Tilly* [2000] Env LR 313 (CA) [33] (Stuart-Smith LJ).
[19] WVH Rogers, *Winfield & Jolowicz on Tort*, 18th edn (London, Sweet and Maxwell, 2010) 1169.
[20] T Hobbes, *Elements of Law* (first published 1640), ch 12.3.
[21] G Fletcher, *Rethinking Criminal Law* (Boston, Little, Brown and Co, 1978) 804.
[22] (1551) 1 Plowden 1, 18; 75 ER 1, 29. See also *Moore v Hussey* (1609) Hob 93, 96; 80 ER 243, 246.
[23] G Williams, *Criminal Law: The General Part*, 2nd edn (London, Stevens, 1961) 722.

1.3 Is Necessity a Defence?

Goudkamp has drawn a vital distinction between denials and defences. A denial negates an element of the tort claim, whereas a defence is a rule that relieves the defendant of liability where all the elements of the tort for which the claimant sues are present.[24] He considered that defences identify situations where the duties created by torts can be disregarded.[25] Consequently, they can be characterised as privileges which the defendant is allowed to do, but is not obliged to do. Whether necessity is properly characterised as a defence will therefore depend on whether it operates by denying an element of the particular tort or is only applicable once the elements of the claim have been established by the claimant.

In determining whether necessity should be characterised as a defence or a denial, it is first necessary to consider the relevance of a vital component of defence theory, the distinction between justifications and excuses.

2. JUSTIFICATIONS AND EXCUSES

The nature of the distinction between justification and excuse has been considered at great length by criminal law theorists, and is increasingly being considered by tort theorists. In criminal law, the nature of the distinction has proved to be particularly significant when analysing the true function of necessity.

2.1 Criminal Law Theory

2.1.1 Justification

Classical writers considered that necessitous acts are lawful and so justified.[26] This has been endorsed by modern writers, many of whom conclude that justification negates an assertion of wrongful conduct such that there is nothing wrong with acting in that way.[27] Glazebrook in particular recognised that the effect of justificatory necessity is that the defendant cannot be considered to have committed the *actus reus* of the crime;[28] thus necessity would constitute a denial in Goudkamp's scheme. Robinson, however, considered that, although the justified actor engages in conduct which is not culpable because its benefits outweigh the harm of the offence,[29] such

[24] J Goudkamp, *Tort Law Defences* (Oxford, Hart Publishing, 2013) 7.
[25] ibid 39.
[26] Eg, M Hale: '*Necessitas est lex temporis et loci; Quod necessitas cogit, defendant*' (Hale 1 PC 54).
[27] Fletcher (n 21) 759; JC Smith, *Justification and Excuse in the Criminal Law* (London, Stevens & Sons Ltd, 1989); P Cane, *Responsibility in Law and Morality* (Oxford, Hart Publishing, 2002) 90; A Ripstein, *Equality, Responsibility and the Law* (Cambridge, Cambridge University Press, 1999) 138; J Coleman *Risks and Wrongs* (Oxford, Oxford University Press, 1992) 217; M Berman, 'Justification and Excuse, Law and Morality' (2003) *Duke Law Journal* 1, 5; A Simester, 'On Justification and Excuse' in L Zedner and J Roberts (eds), *Principles and Values in Criminal Law and Criminal Justice: Essays in Honour of Andrew Ashworth* (Oxford, Oxford University Press, 2012) 99.
[28] Glazebrook (n 14) 93.
[29] P Robinson, 'Criminal Law Defenses: A Systematic Analysis' (1982) 82 *Columbia Law Review* 199, 203.

justified conduct 'causes a legally recognised harm or evil. The conduct remains generally condemned and prohibited. It is tolerated only when, by the infliction of the intermediate harm or evil, a greater societal harm is avoided or benefit gained.'[30] Similarly, Fletcher distinguished between definitions and defences, asserting that an element is definitional where its 'inclusion is necessary to formulate a coherent moral imperative in the core cases of the offense'.[31] He considered that justifications do not form part of the definition of a crime, because justified conduct is harmful in the sense that the harm typically associated with the definition of an offence will have occurred, such as the death of a human being where the defendant is charged with homicide and pleads self-defence, but the justification is engaged because there are good reasons for the defendant inflicting that harm in the circumstances.[32] It follows that justifications are properly characterised as defences. This is the preferable view.

If necessity does operate as a justificatory defence, arising where there is no net harm to society or its members,[33] it follows that the defendant's conduct, which would otherwise be unlawful, is lawful and should be encouraged.[34] This has a number of practical implications, including that it is not possible to use force against a person whose acts are justified and that a third party cannot be liable as an accessory to a justified act.

Even though many theorists consider justified acts to be morally permitted responses,[35] some others consider justified conduct to be permissible but morally conflicted. So, for example, Fletcher recognised that when we violate a prohibition and invade another's rights, 'even if the right is trumped or overridden [by a justification], we should retain a certain sense of loss in witnessing the overriding of the right'.[36] But can it really be the case that a defendant whose act is justified, and so lawful, should necessarily be considered to have acted in a morally conflicted fashion? If the requirements for necessitous intervention are met, the defendant's conduct should surely be considered to be morally appropriate.

2.1.2 *Excuse*

A defence which operates as an excuse does not negate the wrongfulness of the defendant's act. As Berman recognised,[37] whereas a justification qualifies a norm of behaviour by providing that one who is justified does not violate the governing norm, an excuse serves to release one who has violated a norm from some or all of the consequences that ordinarily attach to its violation. Simester defines an excuse

[30] ibid 220.

[31] G Fletcher, 'The Right Deed for the Wrong Reason: A Reply to Mr Robinson' (1975) 23 *University of California at Los Angeles Law Review* 293, 319.

[32] ibid 320.

[33] P Robinson, 'A Theory of Justification: Societal Harm as a Prerequisite for Criminal Liability' (1975) 23 *University of California at Los Angeles Law Review* 266, 291.

[34] ibid 274. Fletcher famously disagreed with Robinson's analysis, not as regards the recognition of justifications, but instead as to whether the defendant's intent had to be meritorious in order to rely on the defence (n 31).

[35] See, eg, Simester (n 27) 99.

[36] G Fletcher, 'The Right and the Reasonable' (1985) 98 *Harvard Law Review* 949, 978.

[37] Berman (n 27) 5.

to mean that the defendant was not culpable (or was less culpable) for acting, but the act is still not permissible.[38] He considers that with excuses we do not consider whether the defendant acted wrongly, but instead we consider why they acted.[39] For Fletcher,[40] excuses avoid attribution of the act to the actor and for Robinson they negate personal culpability through lack of responsibility for the deed.[41]

The differential effects of justifications and excuses reflect the origin of the distinction between the two categories of defence in the criminal law. For, whereas a defendant who was justified in acting was acquitted of any crime, a defendant who was excused would still be convicted but might be pardoned by the Crown, although their goods would still be forfeited.[42]

2.1.3 *Role of Necessity in the Criminal Law*

In the English criminal law different interpretations of necessity are recognised,[43] such that the defence may operate either as an excuse or as a justification.

2.1.3.1 Excusatory Necessity Necessity operates as an excuse in the form of the defence of duress of circumstances.[44] This is available as a defence to any crime other than murder where the defendant commits the crime to save himself or another from a threat of death or serious injury. The recognition of necessity conceptualised as an excuse was defended by Dickson J in *Perka v The Queen*[45] on the ground that, even though the normal human instincts of self-preservation or altruism compel disobedience to the law, the conduct remains wrongful. As he said, 'praise is not bestowed, but pardon is'.

2.1.3.2 Best Interests Intervention The defendant will have a justificatory defence where he has intervened in the victim's best interests in circumstances where the victim lacks the capacity to give or refuse consent. This will typically arise in a medical context, where the life or health of the victim is endangered and medical intervention is required.[46]

2.1.3.3 Justificatory Necessity Exceptionally, it has been recognised that the defendant will have a defence of justificatory necessity where he has acted for the greater public interest. This was recognised in *Re A (children) (conjoined twins: surgical separation)*,[47] where doctors were authorised to separate conjoined twins, even though this would inevitably lead to the death of the weaker twin, but in order to save the life of the stronger twin.

[38] Simester (n 27) 100.
[39] ibid 104.
[40] Fletcher (n 21) 759.
[41] Robinson (n 29) 203.
[42] Robinson (n 33) 275.
[43] See F Stark, 'Necessity and *Nicklinson*' [2013] *Criminal Law Review* 947.
[44] *DPP v Bell* [1992] RTR 335 (Div Ct).
[45] [1984] 2 SCR 232 (SCC) 248. See also Aristotle, *Nichomachean Ethics*, Book III, 1101a (translated by D Ross) (Oxford, Oxford University Press, 2009) 38.
[46] *Re F (Mental Patient: Sterilisation)* [1990] 2 AC 1 (HL).
[47] [2001] Fam 147 (CA).

2.2 Tort Theory

2.2.1 Justification

Goudkamp in *Tort Law Defences* has identified two distinct meanings of justification in tort law.

2.2.1.1 The Conventional View According to this view, the effect of the justification is to render the defendant's conduct lawful. This is consequently consistent with the interpretation of justification in the criminal law. As Weinrib recognised,[48] a justification always signifies both that a right has been prima facie infringed (that is, that something occurred that needs to be justified) and that this infringement is not wrongful in the circumstances. But Goudkamp does not consider justifications, in this sense of lawful actions, to constitute a defence because he asserts that the absence of a justification is an element of all torts, such that asserting a justification is a denial of an element of the claim.[49] It follows that, according to this analysis, wrongs can never be justified by means of a defence, but only through denial.

2.2.1.2 The Radical View Consequently, Goudkamp prefers to define a defence as justificatory where the defendant behaved reasonably in committing the tort. Such a defendant does not deny that he has committed a wrong, but offers an explanation for the admitted wrongdoing such that he is not liable.[50] Goudkamp's preference for the radical view is motivated by his desire to ensure a clear taxonomical distinction between denials and defences. The fact that a justified act remains unlawful has, according to Goudkamp, significant normative consequences since the defendant who is justified in committing a tort should still be morally obliged to apologise for committing the wrong and should feel regret that he needed to cause harm to avoid greater harm.[51]

But treating the defendant's act as justified simply because of the reasonableness of the action, such that it remains unlawful, is inconsistent with the predominant view in criminal law theory. That view preserves the distinction between justification and excuse in determining whether the defendant's conduct is rendered lawful, whilst recognising that justifications operate as defences rather than denials.

2.2.2 Excuse

Goudkamp considers that a plea of excuse is qualitatively inferior to a plea of justification, since it does not involve any assertion of reasonableness.[52] Consequently,

[48] E Weinrib, 'Private Law and Public Right' (2011) 61 *University of Toronto Law Journal* 191, 206.

[49] Goudkamp (n 24) 76.

[50] See also J Gardner, *Offences and Defences: Selected Essays in Philosophy of Criminal Law* (Oxford, Oxford University Press, 2007) 77–82, 96–97.

[51] Goudkamp (n 24) 79. Gardner adopts an even more radical approach. In J Gardner 'What is Tort Law For? Part 1. The Place of Corrective Justice' (2011) 30 *Law and Philosophy* 1, 42 he concludes that tort law does not recognise any justificatory defences because all torts are wrongs so that all defendants should remain liable for breaching tortious obligations even if their conduct is lawful.

[52] Goudkamp (n 24) 86.

he concludes that there are no excuse defences in tort law,[53] since unreasonable conduct should not found a defence. This is not the view of Fletcher who, having defined justifications as lawful acts, leaves room for the separate operation of excuses within the law of tort.[54] This reflects the distinction outlined previously, which is vital to the operation of defences within the criminal law.

2.3 Necessity as Justification

Lessons from criminal law theory should inform the law of tort. If the criminal law recognises that conduct may be justified by necessity, and thus lawful, it is appropriate to assume[55] that the defendant's justified conduct should also be lawful for the law of tort, save where a satisfactory explanation for the inconsistency can be identified. No such explanation has yet been identified. Justified acts should therefore be recognised as lawful acts even in the law of tort. If this means that necessity must be treated as a denial rather than a defence, then so be it; one must still identify the boundaries of necessity as a doctrine rather than as a defence. But the preferable view is that necessity is only engaged once the claimant has established the elements of the claim, such that the defendant's actions can be considered to be prima facie unlawful. The burden should then shift to the defendant to establish that the conduct was lawful, by virtue of the defence of necessity.

However, in the same way that the criminal law recognises an excusatory necessity defence, there is no reason in principle why such a formulation should not be available in tort as well, such that the defendant might be permitted to infringe the claimant's rights but is required to compensate the claimant for any loss arising because the conduct will still be considered to be unlawful.

3. THE NATURE OF NECESSITY IN TORT

The true function of necessity in the law of tort is to arbitrate between the clash of legitimate rights. As Weinrib recognised, 'justifications work to adjust the effects of rights so that rights fit within the totality of conditions under which the freedom of all can coexist'.[56] But it appears to be easier to allow the defendant's right to prevail where it benefits others rather than simply himself. Consequently, a vital distinction needs to be drawn between public and private necessity.[57] This is a distinction which is explicitly recognised by the American Law Institute's *Restatement (Second) of the Law of Torts*.[58] Public necessity is invoked as a defence by a defendant who

[53] ibid 101. See also J Gardner, 'Justification Under Authority' (2010) 23 *Canadian Journal of Law and Jurisprudence* 71, 92; J Raz, 'Responsibility and the Negligence Standard' (2010) 30 *OJLS* 1, 10.

[54] G Fletcher 'Fairness and Utility in Tort Theory' (1972) 85 *Harvard Law Review* 537, 551.

[55] Whilst this might be criticised for automatically preferring the criminal law to the law of tort, it is suggested here only as an initial premise and one which is defensible because of the extensive work done by theorists in the criminal law rather than in tort.

[56] Weinrib (n 48) 206.

[57] Goudkamp (n 24) 106.

[58] §§ 196–197, 263.

has acted to prevent 'an imminent public disaster' which will affect many people.[59] Private necessity is recognised as a privilege which enables a defendant to commit an act which would otherwise be a trespass to a chattel, or conversion of it,[60] or trespass to land,[61] where he reasonably believes it to be necessary to protect his person or property or that of another person from serious harm, save where the defendant knows that the person for whose benefit he was acting was unwilling that he should do so. Where, however, the act is for the benefit of the defendant or a third party, he is liable for any harm caused by the exercise of the privilege.[62] So, to use an example from the *Restatement*, if A, a pharmacist, refuses to sell to B a bottle of medicine which is only available from A and which is necessary to save B's life, B is privileged to take the medicine and use it but he is liable to pay A for it.

The existence of this dichotomy between public and private necessity can also be discerned in English law and was explicitly recognised by the House of Lords in *Re F (Mental Patient: Sterilisation)*,[63] although the English jurisprudence is not as developed as that in the United States.

3.1 Public Necessity

There is a complete defence to a claim in tort where the defendant acts for the good of other people or to preserve important public interests from danger: such conduct is justified *pro bono publico*.[64] The fact that the defendant acts for the public good means that this is properly treated as a justificatory defence rendering the defendant's conduct lawful.[65] Goudkamp[66] recognises this defence and concludes that it allows defendants to commit torts against innocent people free from the obligation to pay compensation where it is reasonably necessary to do so to protect an important public interest from an imminent peril. This focus on reasonableness is consistent with Goudkamp's analysis of justifications, although he provides no assistance in determining what is 'reasonable' for these purposes.

Public necessity has been recognised in a variety of contexts. It encompasses a political notion of public need. For example, in *The case of the King's Prerogative in Saltpetre*[67] it was held that the King had a prerogative to dig for saltpetre for the necessary defence of the realm, but he was required to restore the place afterwards. This was held to be a case of State necessity. It was recognised that:

> And therefore by the common law, every man may come upon my land for the defence of the realm ... And in such case on such extremity they may dig for gravel, for the making of bulwarks; for this is for the public, and every one hath benefit by it; but after the danger is over, the trenches and bulwarks ought to be removed, so that the owner shall not have

[59] ibid § 196.
[60] ibid § 263.
[61] ibid § 197.
[62] ibid §§ 197(2), 263(2).
[63] Above n 46, 74 (Lord Goff).
[64] *Southwark London Borough Council v Williams* [1971] Ch 734 (CA) 743 (Lord Denning MR).
[65] *Maleverer v Spinke* (1538) Dyer 35b, 36 (Montague).
[66] Goudkamp (n 24) 115.
[67] (1606) 12 Co Rep 12, 13; 77 ER 1294, 1295.

> prejudice in his inheritance: and for the commonwealth, a man shall suffer damage; as, for saving of a city or town, a house shall be plucked down if the next be on fire: and the suburbs of a city in time of war for the common safety shall be plucked down; and a thing for the commonwealth every man may do without being liable to an action ... And in this case the rule is true, *Princeps et respublica ex justa causa possunt rem meam auferre.*[68]

One of the most important cases on the nature of public necessity is *Mouse's case.*[69] A ferryman from Gravesend took 47 passengers, including Mouse, in his barge on the Thames to London. Whilst on the river, a storm blew up, endangering the passengers. In order to save their lives, property, including Mouse's casket, was thrown out of the barge by some of the passengers. It was held that, because the danger occurred by an act of God, everybody bore their own loss. Since the passengers were acting to protect themselves and their property this might be considered to be a case of private necessity. But the effect of the passengers' conduct benefited each other, including Mouse himself, so this can legitimately be analysed as a case of public necessity,[70] although it remains unclear how many lives need to be endangered before the conduct can be so characterised.

What is particularly significant about *Mouse's case* is that the storm blew up whilst the barge was on a river. Had it been on the sea, the ancient doctrine of general average in maritime law would have been applicable, by virtue of which, where cargo has been jettisoned in a storm at sea to save the ship and other cargo, the owners of the vessel and cargo saved are liable to a rateable contribution towards indemnifying the claimant whose property was lost.[71] But general average does not extend to cargo jettisoned on a river, as was recognised in *Mouse's case.* Whether the recognition of an absolute defence of public necessity in *Mouse's case* can be satisfactorily explained might depend on whether those who threw Mouse's property into the river could be considered to have taken more than they needed. Since Mouse's property would have been lost anyway had the passengers not intervened, he was clearly a beneficiary of their actions, since his life was saved. It follows that, if he had been compensated for his loss, he would have been better off than if his goods had not been thrown overboard.[72] But this analysis assumes that, if the claimant was not better off as a result of the defendant's actions, the defendant should be liable to compensate the claimant for the loss suffered. This contradicts the essentially justificatory nature of public necessity, which renders the defendant's conduct lawful. If the defendant has acted lawfully then he should bear no liability to the claimant for the loss suffered. Of course, whether the defence is established in the first place will depend on the reasonableness of the defendant's actions, but this should not be judged after the event in the light of what actually happened.[73]

[68] 'The king and the commonwealth, for a just cause, can take away my property': 12 Coke 13.

[69] (1608) 12 Co Rep 63; 77 ER 1341.

[70] It was so characterised by the *Restatement (Second) of the Law of Torts* § 196, reporters' notes.

[71] *Strang, Steel and Co v Scott and Co* (1889) 14 App Cas 601 (PC).

[72] D Klimchuk, 'Property and Necessity', in J Penner and H Smith (eds), *Philosophical Foundations of Property Law* (Oxford, Oxford University Press, 2013) 65.

[73] See *Cope v Sharpe (No 2)* (n 17) as regards the operation of the defence of private necessity. See at p 152.

The defence of public necessity can also be identified in *Dewey v White*,[74] involving a stack of chimneys belonging to a house close to a highway which, because they were on fire and were in immediate danger of falling on the highway, were destroyed by some firemen. It was held that the firemen were justified in so doing, and were not liable for damage unavoidably done to an adjoining house as a result of the removal of the chimneys. The firemen's act was specifically justified because of the danger to the lives of people passing along the highway and inhabiting the houses. In *Dwyer v Staunton*,[75] where a storm had rendered a highway impassable, it was held that there was no liability in trespass for anybody who crossed through the claimant's land to continue their journey. Klimchuk has appropriately analysed this case as involving the defence of public necessity, because it involved the assertion of the public right secured by the state to travel through the realm.[76]

But the significance of the defence of public necessity is today much reduced because of the role of the State in responding to emergencies, through agencies such as the fire brigade.[77] This was recognised by Lord Upjohn in *Burmah Oil Co (Burmah Trading) Ltd v Lord Advocate*:[78]

> No doubt in earlier times the individual had some such rights of self-help or destruction in immediate emergency, whether caused by enemy action or by fire, and the legal answer was that he could not in such circumstances be sued for trespass on or for destruction of his neighbour's property. Those rights of the individual are now at least obsolescent. No man now, without risking some action against him in the courts, could pull down his neighbour's house to prevent the fire spreading to his own; he would be told that he ought to have dialled 999 and summoned the local fire brigade. No man now could conceivably erect a bulwark to prevent enemy invasion.

He went on to describe the public rights of necessitous intervention as 'ancient, trivial and individual'. But there will still be some cases where the defendant needs to infringe the claimant's interest in order to protect the rights of others, where the action is urgent and State agencies cannot be expected to intervene in time. So, for example, in the American case of *People v Scott*,[79] Kaufman J recognised that, if the life of the President was in danger so that the defendant, a government agent, commandeered vehicles to save his life, the defendant's actions would have been legally justified under the doctrine of necessity. In *Burmah Oil* itself the Crown, in the exercise of the royal prerogative, was held to be able to confiscate and destroy property in the dire emergency of war to prevent it from falling into enemy hands, although it was recognised that the Crown had to pay compensation, perhaps because it was the Crown rather than an individual citizen who had acted.[80] Where a private citizen relies on the defence there should be no liability to pay.[81]

[74] (1827) M & M 56; 173 ER 1079.
[75] (1947) 4 DLR 393 (Alb Div Ct).
[76] Klimchuk (n 72) 64.
[77] *Carter v Thomas* [1893] 1 QB 673 (QBD).
[78] [1965] AC 75 (HL) 164. See also *Monsanto plc v Tilly* (n 18) [30] (Stuart-Smith LJ).
[79] 146 Cal App 3d 82 (Ct App 1983).
[80] Similar to the operation of the private necessity defence.
[81] F Bohlen, 'Incomplete Privilege to Inflict Intentional Invasions of Interests of Property and Personality' (1926) 39 *Harvard Law Review* 307, 317. See also Klimchuk (n 72) 54.

That there remains a continuing role for public necessity was also recognised in *Monsanto v Tilly*[82] where, exceptionally, it might justify trespass to land or goods where the public was in imminent danger. A further restriction on the operation of the defence was recognised in that case, however, since the defence was held to be unavailable to environmental activists who had destroyed genetically-modified crops and who had pleaded that their action was necessary in the public interest or to protect third parties and their property. Breaking the law to seek publicity for a cause was not considered to be sufficient justification.[83] The defence would only apply where there was an emergency which created serious danger to life or property.

Despite these limitations on the contemporary operation of the public necessity defence, there are certain contexts in which the defence continues to have a significant role.

3.1.1 Police Powers

That the police may be able to rely on the defence of public necessity was recognised in *Rigby v Chief Constable of Northamptonshire*.[84] A psychopath broke into the claimant's gun shop and used guns which he found there to shoot inside and out of the premises. The police fired a CS gas canister into the building, which started a fire and the shop was seriously damaged. The claimant sued for trespass and negligence since the police did not have fire-fighting equipment with them. It was recognised that the defence of necessity was applicable to the trespass, but was unavailable to defeat the claim in negligence because it was unreasonable to have fired the canister in the absence of fire equipment. Here, to the extent it succeeded, the relevant defence was one of public necessity, since the police had intervened to protect the claimant's property, the general public and the psychopath.

The significance of the public necessity defence was also recognised by the Court of Appeal in *Austin v Commissioners of Police of the Metropolis*.[85] The defence was applied where the police had detained several hundred people, some of whom were violent and disorderly, for many hours in Oxford Circus until safe dispersal could be arranged. One claimant was a demonstrator and the other was detained whilst on business. They both sued the police for false imprisonment. It was held that, whilst the test for necessity would only be met in exceptional circumstances where the conduct was reasonable and proportionate, this test was satisfied on the facts. As a result, the curtailment of the claimant's rights was justified and so lawful in order to prevent a breach of the peace.[86]

[82] *Monsanto plc v Tilly* (n 18).

[83] See also *A-G v Leason* [2011] NZHC 1053 (defence not available to military campaigners who symbolically damaged a military installation).

[84] [1985] 1 WLR 1242 (QBD).

[85] [2007] EWCA Civ 989; [2008] QB 660. The defence was not considered on appeal to the House of Lords: [2009] UKHL 5; [2009] 1 AC 566.

[86] ibid [35] (Sir Anthony Clarke MR), relying on *Laporte v Chief Constable of Gloucestershire* [2006] UKHL 55; [2007] 2 AC 105. See also *Connor v Chief Constable of Merseyside Police* [2006] EWCA Civ 1549; [2007] HRLR 6 (necessity available to justify police detention of suspects in a van whilst their

In New Zealand[87] necessity has been recognised as a defence available to the police when sued for trespass, where a police officer reasonably believed in good faith that trespass was necessary to preserve life, to prevent serious physical harm or to render assistance to a victim who had suffered physical harm, such as where the police break into a property having heard an occupant, who is clearly in pain, calling for help.[88] In such circumstances presumably a private individual would also be justified in breaking into the property to assist the occupant if such assistance was reasonably considered to be urgent.

3.1.2 Best Interests Intervention

In the same way that the criminal law recognises a defence of best interests necessity to justify the defendant assisting the victim who is unable to consent, such a defence is also recognised in the law of tort. Indeed, many of the cases which have recognised this defence consider both criminal and tortious liability. Although Lord Goff in *Re F (Mental Patient: Sterilisation)*[89] considered best interests necessity to be a third category of necessity distinct from public and private necessity, the fact that the defendant is acting in the best interests of another person rather than for himself suggests that it involves public necessity.[90] Acting for the best interests of another who is unable to consent justifies the defendant's act and so renders it lawful,[91] in a similar way to the examples of public necessity which have already been considered.

Examples of best interests necessity operating in the law of tort include *Wilson v Pringle*,[92] where Croom-Johnson LJ recognised that a doctor who performs life-saving and urgently-needed surgery on an unconscious patient acts lawfully in doing so. The leading case on best interests necessity is *Re F (Mental Patient: Sterilisation)*,[93] where doctors were held not to be liable for the tort of trespass if they sterilised a mental patient who was sexually active and was incapable of dealing with pregnancy, parturition or maternity, and who was unable to consent to the operation. The medical intervention was considered to be lawful because the doctors were acting in the best interests of the patient. It was recognised that best interests intervention could only be characterised as necessitous if the victim was incapable of

property was searched for firearms). The defence was considered to be compliant with the European Convention on Human Rights: at [68] (Hallett LJ).

[87] *Dehn v A-G* [1988] NZHC 418; [1988] 2 NZLR 564.

[88] The criteria for establishing the defence were considered to be stricter where the police apprehended danger to property rather than the person: ibid 588.

[89] *Re F (Mental Patient: Sterilisation)* (n 46).

[90] Lord Brandon, ibid 55, considered that the defence was engaged because the defendant was acting in the public interest. See also Lord Griffith, 69.

[91] ibid 74 (Lord Goff).

[92] [1987] QB 237 (CA) 252.

[93] Above n 46. A general defence to civil and criminal liability has been created by s 5 of the Mental Capacity Act 2005 where the defendant, having taken reasonable steps to establish that the victim lacked capacity, has done an act in connection with the care or treatment of the victim who did not consent to the act, if the defendant reasonably believed that the victim lacked capacity to consent and that it would be in the victim's best interests for the act to be done. It was recognised in *Aintree University Hospitals NHS Foundation Trust v James* [2013] UKSC 67; [2014] 1 FCR 153 that exceptionally medical treatment might not be in the incapacitated patient's best interests where it would be ineffective and of no benefit, such that the withdrawal of treatment would be lawful.

consenting to it and the act was carried out to save life or to ensure the improvement or to prevent the deterioration of the claimant's physical or mental health.[94] Whilst the typical context for best interests intervention will be medical, this aspect of public necessity will apply whenever the victim is unable to consent, such as where the defendant forcibly drags the victim from the path of an oncoming vehicle.[95] Often best interests intervention will be justified because of an emergency, but this need not be the case where there is a permanent state of affairs which prevents the victim from consenting.[96] Indeed, in *Re F (Mental Patient: Sterilisation)* itself there was no emergency which required the operation to be conducted urgently, but the claimant's mental condition was such that she was incapable of consenting to the operation at any time.

Best interests intervention has also justified the detention of a mental patient in hospital,[97] to preserve the lives of prisoners who were on hunger strike,[98] to perform an abortion on a young rape victim whose life was endangered by the pregnancy,[99] and the separation of conjoined twins even though the operation would inevitably result in the death of one of them.[100] In the latter case the court considered it appropriate to balance the interest of the weaker twin, Mary, in not having the operation performed, against the interest of the stronger twin, Jodie, in having the operation performed, bearing in mind that the operation would give Jodie the prospects of a normal expectation of a relatively normal life, whereas Mary's life was doomed to death.[101] Consequently, the balance was in Jodie's favour. Best interests intervention has not yet been recognised as justifying consensual euthanasia or assisted suicide.[102]

3.2 Private Necessity

Goudkamp does not consider that private necessity should be recognised as a defence.[103] This is presumably because he does not consider that it satisfies the essential test of reasonableness, which is needed to recognise a justification, and he does not recognise excuses. Nevertheless, there is evidence of private necessity being recognised in various jurisdictions, where the defendant has acted in circumstances of necessity to protect his own interests. This defence was recognised by Lord Goff in *Re F (Mental Patient: Sterilisation)*[104] as justifying interference with another person's property where the defendant does so in order to save his own person or

[94] *Re F (Mental Patient: Sterilisation)* (n 46) 55 (Lord Brandon).
[95] ibid 74 (Lord Goff).
[96] ibid.
[97] *R v Bournewood Community and Mental Health NHS Trust, ex p L* [1999] 1 AC 458 (HL), although this was subsequently held to infringe the European Convention on Human Rights on the ground that the common law defence of necessity did not provide sufficient safeguards against abuse: *HL v UK* (App No 45508/99) (2005) 40 EHRR 32.
[98] *Leigh v Gladstone* (1909) 26 TLR 139 (KBD).
[99] *R v Bourne* [1939] 1 KB 687 (CCA).
[100] *Re A (children) (conjoined twins: surgical separation)* (n 47).
[101] ibid 197 (Ward LJ).
[102] *R (Nicklinson and Lamb) v Ministry of Justice* [2013] EWCA Civ 961; [2013] HRLR 36.
[103] Goudkamp (n 24) 114. Neither does John Goldberg, 'Tort Law's Missing Excuses' ch 4 in this volume.
[104] Above n 46.

property from imminent danger. But the defence may operate differently from public necessity, and may not even be a justificatory defence.

Pufendorf justified the recognition of a private necessity defence as follows:[105]

> A necessity that touches our own property apparently allows one the permission to destroy or appropriate the property of another, but with the following restrictions: that the threatened loss to our property…cannot be averted in any more convenient way; that we do not destroy another's article of greater value for one of our own of less value; that we make good the value of the article if it would not have been lost anyway…

It is also recognised in the German Civil Code:[106]

> The owner of a thing is not entitled to prohibit the influence of another person on the thing if the influence is necessary to ward off a present danger and the imminent damage is disproportionately great in relation to the damage suffered by the owner as a result of the influence. The owner may require compensation for the damage incurred by him.

A shared significant feature of both definitions is the emphasis on comparing the nature of the harm done with the nature of the thing saved and that, even where the balance is in favour of the thing saved, the owner of the thing harmed may still receive compensation for their loss. This is consistent with what tort theorists consider to be the leading case on private necessity, *Vincent v Lake Erie Transportation Co.*[107] This case has had a profound influence on the development of the theory and doctrine relating to necessity in the United States; a much more significant influence than the case deserves. Nevertheless, it is important to analyse the impact of that case on the defence. Before doing so, however, a slightly earlier decision needs to be examined.

In *Ploof v Putnam*[108] the defendant owned an island with a dock. The claimant and his family were sailing when a storm forced them to moor at the dock. The defendant's servant unmoored the boat which was later wrecked on land, destroying the boat and injuring the claimant and his family. The claimant sued the defendant for trespass on the ground that the defendant was under a duty to permit the claimant to moor his boat until the storm passed. It was held that the claimant could lawfully trespass on land if it was for reasons of private necessity to preserve human life or to save goods which would otherwise be destroyed. Consequently, the defendant should have tolerated what would otherwise have been a trespass and could not prevent the boat from remaining moored during the storm.

It follows that a defendant is allowed to interfere with another party's property rights in circumstances of necessity. However, if in doing so the defendant causes loss, he will be required to pay compensation. That was recognised in *Vincent v Lake Erie Transportation Co.*[109] The SS Reynolds, a steamship owned by the defendant, was moored at the claimant's dock in order to unload cargo. A violent storm arose and the captain signalled for a tugboat to assist him to leave the dock, but nobody was willing

[105] S von Pufendorf, *On the Law of Nature and Nations* (Oxford, Clarendon Press, 1934) 2.6.8. See also Weinrib (n 48).

[106] BGB, § 904: www.gesetze-im-internet.de/englisch_bgb/englisch_bgb.html#p3644.

[107] 109 Minn 456; 124 NW 221 (1910).

[108] 81 Vt 471; 71 A 188 (1908).

[109] Above n 107.

to do so. The captain decided that the ship should remain docked. It was secured to the dock and the captain replaced the ropes during the storm because they were becoming chafed. The ship was thrown against the dock by the wind and waves causing significant damage to the dock, valued at $500. The claimant sued the defendant in negligence and trespass. The claim in negligence failed, because the defendant was considered to have acted reasonably. But the claim in trespass succeeded since, even though the defendant through the captain had acted for reasons of private necessity, it remained liable to pay damages for the harm caused as a result of the deliberate trespass. It was particularly significant that the defendant had taken positive measures to secure the boat to the dock and had replaced the ropes, rather than simply leaving it where it had been docked; this rendered the case one of necessity rather than accident. O'Brien J stated:[110]

> This is not a case where life or property was menaced by any object or thing belonging to the plaintiffs, the destruction of which became necessary to prevent the threatened disaster. Nor is it a case where because of an act of God, or unavoidable accident, the infliction of the injury was beyond the control of the defendant, but is one where the defendant prudently and advisedly availed itself of the plaintiffs' property for the purpose of preserving his own more valuable property, and the plaintiffs are entitled to compensation for the injury done.

This assists in determining the ambit of the defence of private necessity, which would have been applicable had life or property been endangered by the claimant's property and if the defendant had simply omitted to remove the boat, rather than actively keeping it secured to the dock. *Vincent* was distinguished on this ground in Canada in *Munn and Co v The Sir John Crosbie*,[111] another case involving a ship which damaged the claimant's wharf during a storm. It was emphasised that in *Vincent* the captain had deliberately preserved the ship at the expense of the dock and had consequently taken the risk of damage to the dock, whereas in *Munn* there was no evidence that the defendant had taken any such steps.

Placing *Ploof v Plutnam* together with *Vincent v Lake Erie Transportation Co* reveals the recognition of what has been called an 'incomplete privilege' to perform an act which would otherwise be a tort, such that the defendant has a right to act which the claimant cannot resist or prevent, but liability is still imposed for any material harm caused by the act.[112] This is consistent with Grotius[113] who recognised that: '[T]his Right was not plenary, but limited by the burthen of restoring what was taken, when the necessity was over: for such a Right suffices to preserve the natural equity of the case against the rigour of ownership'. He also said:[114] '[M]ore is not to be taken than it requires; that is, if keeping the thing is sufficient, it is not to be used; if using it is sufficient, it is not be destroyed; if destroying it is requisite, the price is to be repaid'.

The fact that private necessity is treated as an incomplete privilege raises important and difficult questions about the nature of the defence. Since the defendant remains liable to compensate the claimant for harm caused, the defence cannot be

[110] ibid 222.
[111] [1967] 1 Can Exch 94.
[112] Bohlen (n 81) 309; Sussmann (n 6) 188.
[113] 1625, Bk II, ch 2, [9].
[114] 1625, BK III, ch 1 7, [1.1].

considered to be a justification, since, if the defendant's act was lawful, how can he be liable? This suggests that private necessity actually operates as an excuse, giving the defendant a right to act but with an obligation to compensate for consequential harm arising from an unlawful act. But what is the explanation for the defence operating in this apparently contradictory way? Bohlen considered that, as a matter of justice, the defendant should bear the cost of the act because he benefited from it,[115] and that the award of damages satisfies the sense of grievance felt by the claimant at the offence given by the defendant to the claimant's sense of personal dignity.[116] Klimchuk considers liability to compensate to be a consequence of the foundation and scope of rights in property,[117] relying on Pufendorf[118] who recognised that the right of necessity is a right of use rather than exclusion, such that the defendant is only permitted to take what is necessary to extricate himself from the perilous situation, since to take any more would violate natural equity. So, for example, if the defendant needs to consume goods to stave off hunger, he will be required to pay for them, in effect through a forced sale.[119]

Despite the sophisticated analysis of the private necessity defence in the United States as an incomplete privilege, English law appears to interpret the defence very differently, treating it instead as an absolute justification.[120] For example, in *Cope v Sharpe (No 2)*,[121] the gamekeeper of a tenant of sporting rights was held to be entitled to adopt such means as were necessary to extinguish a fire to preserve those rights. A trespass was consequently justified, but without any liability to compensate for damage caused. The claimant landowner let shooting rights to Mr Chase. A heath fire broke out on the land. The claimant's employees sought to beat it out, and the defendant, Chase's head gamekeeper, set fire to a strip of heather between the fire and an area over which Chase had sporting rights where there were some nesting pheasants. The claimant's employees successfully extinguished the earlier heath fire. The claimant sued for trespass to his land. Even though the defendant's action was not, as events turned out, necessary for the protection of Chase's rights, the jury found that it was reasonably necessary in the circumstances since there had been a real and imminent danger to them. Consequently, the defendant was not liable to the claimant despite causing damage.[122]

[115] Bohlen (n 81) 316.
[116] ibid 321.
[117] Klimchuk (n 72) 67.
[118] 1672, Bk II, ch 6.
[119] See also *Vincent v Lake Erie Transportation Co* (n 107) (O'Brien J).
[120] *Milman v Dolwell* (1810) 2 Camp 378, 380; 170 ER 1190, 1190 (Lord Ellenborough).
[121] *Cope v Sharpe (No 2)* (n 17). See also *Cresswell v Sirl* (n 16); *Southport Corp v Esso Petroleum Ltd* [1954] 2 QB 182 (CA).
[122] Since the defendant was acting to protect the rights of his employer this might be analysed as a case of public necessity and so treated as a justification for that reason, although the interests of the defendant were so closely aligned to those of his employer that it is preferably treated as case of private necessity: see [1912] 1 KB 495 (CA) 508 (Kennedy LJ). J Goldberg, 'Tort Law's Missing Excuses' in this volume considers that the defendant was relying on rights which were conferred by the lease, but the judges in the case clearly focused on the defendant's act being justified as reasonably necessary to protect his employer's rights without any reference to the terms of the lease, save as regards the source of the property right which needed protecting.

A similar case to that of *Vincent v Lake Erie Transportation Co* was *The Lords Bailiff-Jurats of Romney Marsh v The Corporation of Trinity House*,[123] where the defendant's vessel was driven against a sea wall and was wrecked. There was valuable property on board which would have been lost if the vessel had been broken up immediately. This property was removed with reasonable speed before the vessel was broken up, but during this time it caused damage to the sea wall. It was held that the defendant was not liable, because it was not subject to any duty to sacrifice the vessel in the interests of the claimant.[124]

Treating the defence of private necessity as a complete justification for the defendant's act has not, however, always been recognised in England. For example, in *Anthony v Haney*[125] Tindal LCJ recognised that, if an occupier of premises refused on request to deliver to its owner a chattel taken by a party and placed on the occupier's premises, 'the owner might in such case enter and take his property, subject to the payment of any damage he might commit'. But this is a rare exception to the general tenor of the English authorities which treats private necessity as an absolute justification. Perhaps English law needs to follow United States law and treat private necessity as a qualified privilege, or perhaps more appropriately a 'qualified license',[126] such that the defendant has permission to act but is required to pay the claimant for loss suffered. But this then raises difficult issues of principle as to whether a qualified privilege operates as a justification or as an excuse.

There is, however, an alternative way of explaining the liability to pay the claimant for harm caused by the defendant's necessitous intervention, which might enable the private necessity defence still to be characterised as a justification. Rather than treating the defendant as being liable to pay the claimant compensatory damages for harm caused, which assumes that the defendant has unlawfully interfered with the claimant's right, the liability might instead be characterised as restitutionary, assessed by reference to the advantage the defendant has gained at the expense of the claimant's disadvantage. This is recognised in the American Law Institute's *Restatement (First) of the Law of Restitution*,[127] under the heading of 'Benefits Derived from the Exercise of Incomplete Privilege':

> A person who is privileged to harm the land or chattels of another while acting to preserve himself or a third person or to preserve his own things or those of a third person is under a duty of restitution for the amount of harm done, except where
>
> (a) The harm which he seeks to avert is threatened by the thing which he destroys or by the tortious conduct or contributory fault of the owner or possessor, or
> (b) His act reasonably appears to be necessary to avert a public catastrophe, or
> (c) He is exercising his privilege as a member of the public to enter land adjacent to a highway which has become impassable.

[123] (1869–1870) LR 5 Exch 204 (Exch). There is no English case which is precisely equivalent to the facts of *Vincent* because, if a ship damages a harbour, dock, pier or quay, the owner of the vessel is absolutely liable to pay compensation: Harbours, Docks and Pier Clauses Act 1847, s 74.

[124] *The Lords Bailiff-Jurats of Romney Marsh v The Corporation of Trinity House* (ibid) 208 (Kelly CB).

[125] (1832) 8 Bing 186, 193; 131 ER 372, 374.

[126] RR Stuart and LH Leigh, 'The Right of Recaption of Chattels' (1955) 1 *Alberta Law Review* 77, 84.

[127] § 122. This does not appear in *Restatement (Third) of the Law of Restitution and Unjust Enrichment*. For arguments in favour of the restitutionary analysis, see Bohlen (n 81); R Keeton, 'Conditional Fault in the Law of Torts' (1959) 72 *Harvard Law Review* 401; Sussmann (n 6) 192; D Friedmann, 'Restitution of Benefits Obtained Through the Appropriation of Property or the Commission of a Wrong' (1980) 80 *Columbia Law Review* 504, 540.

This restitutionary analysis of the defendant's liability might be explained on the ground that the function of the private necessity defence is only to protect the defendant against loss; it should not become a means to enable the defendant to derive a benefit at the expense of the claimant. But resorting to the restitutionary analysis of the defendant's liability is flawed. If it is assumed that the defendant has a justificatory defence of necessity, it follows that the restitutionary claim cannot be grounded on the commission of a wrong, because the necessity defence will defeat the wrong. Consequently, the claim must be founded on unjust enrichment. It will be possible to show that the defendant's gain from interfering with the claimant's proprietary right is an enrichment obtained at the claimant's expense, although this will be highly artificial since the defendant's negative enrichment is likely to be of a very different magnitude to the claimant's loss.[128] For example, if the defendant has saved his ship and cargo by tying it to the claimant's dock, which is consequently damaged, the defendant's gain is likely to be much greater than the claimant's loss, but that loss will cap the restitutionary gain,[129] suggesting that the real focus is on compensation for loss suffered rather than depriving the defendant of gain made. A further difficulty relates to the identification of the ground of restitution which makes the enrichment unjust. This could be necessity.[130] But, assuming that the defendant's act is rendered lawful by virtue of the justificatory necessity defence, it follows that there will be a legal basis for the defendant's enrichment such that any restitutionary claim will be barred.[131] This conclusion can be avoided by characterising the private necessity defence as an excuse. But then, because the defendant will have acted unlawfully albeit subject to a qualified privilege, it is much easier to explain the defendant's liability as one of compensation following the commission of an unlawful act. Therefore nothing can be gained from resorting to a restitutionary analysis of the claim.

English law has a great deal to learn from the American experience as regards the analysis of the private necessity defence as a qualified privilege. The defence should be properly characterised as an excuse such that, although the defendant is allowed to interfere with the claimant's proprietary rights for reasons of necessity, the defendant remains liable to compensate the claimant for any loss suffered. There is, however, one remaining difficulty with this analysis. For, if the defendant is still considered to have acted unlawfully in interfering with the claimant's proprietary right, it follows that the claimant is at liberty to protect his property from the defendant's actions. If the claimant is allowed to do that then it would defeat the purpose of characterising the defence as an excuse, or even a defence at all, and the decision in *Ploof v Putnam* would be incorrect, in that the party acting from necessity should not have any claim against the person who was preventing him from protecting his property. It follows that the claimant should not be allowed to prevent the defendant's interference with the claimant's rights, but the defendant should still compensate the claimant

[128] D Klimchuk, 'Necessity and Restitution' (2001) 7 *Legal Theory* 59.

[129] As occurred in *Vincent v Lake Erie Transportation Co* (n 107).

[130] See G Virgo, *Principles of the Law of Restitution* 2nd edn (Oxford, Oxford University Press, 2006) ch 11.

[131] See G Virgo, 'Demolishing the Pyramid—the Presence of Basis and Risk-Taking in the Law of Unjust Enrichment' in A Robertson and TH Wu (eds), *The Goals of Private Law* (Oxford, Hart Publishing, 2009) 477.

for doing so. The defendant's act appears to be lawful for one purpose, the entitlement to interfere with the claimant's rights, and unlawful for another, resulting in an obligation to compensate for any damage caused. Necessity consequently straddles the line between justification and excuse, involving conduct which is half-right and half-wrong.[132] That is why the language of qualified privilege (or licence) is so useful, to reflect the unusual nature of the defence. Perhaps, more significantly, this is what follows from recognising an excuse in the law of tort: whilst the defendant has a right to defend his person or property in circumstances of necessity, this is still unlawful for the purposes of the law of tort such that an obligation to compensate follows. Further, the private necessity defence functions differently in the law of tort when compared with the criminal law. This inconsistency is defensible, however, because the essential remedial function of tort is not to punish but to compensate another for harm suffered, and this obligation to compensate continues to operate where the defendant's act is excused. There should be no such obligation to compensate where the defendant's act is justified, as occurs where the defence of public necessity applies.

4. THE OPERATION OF NECESSITY

4.1 Application to Particular Torts

The defence of necessity is not applicable to the tort of negligence, since the requisite reasonableness of the defendant's action negates the breach of a duty of care.[133] Or, as Goudkamp recognises[134] as a consequence of his assertion that the absence of justification is a definition element of negligence, it follows that the defendant's assertion of reasonable conduct, which is how he defines the justificatory defence of public necessity, denies the breach of duty.

Necessity is, however, a defence to all other torts. It has proved to be especially significant to trespass to land and goods, but has also been applied, for example, to the torts of false imprisonment[135] and nuisance.[136]

4.2 The Requirements of Necessity

There are numerous examples of cases where the defence of necessity has not been recognised. Whilst this sometimes appears to reflect the complete rejection of the defence, the preferable interpretation typically is that the defence could not be established on the particular facts. This is illustrated by *Southwark London BC v Williams*,[137] which concerned actions for trespass against squatters in council

[132] M Conde, 'Necessity Defined: A New Role in the Criminal Defense System' (1981) 29 *University of California at Los Angeles Law Review* 409, 442.
[133] *Rigby v Chief Constable of Northamptonshire* (n 84); *Vincent v Lake Erie Transportation Co* (n 107). See Gardner (n 51) 42; Goudkamp (n 24) 9.
[134] Goudkamp (n 24) 114.
[135] *R v Bournewood Community and Mental Health NHS Trust, ex p L* (n 97) 490 (Lord Goff).
[136] *Earl of Lonsdale* v *Nelson* (1823) 2 B & C 302; 107 ER 396.
[137] [1971] Ch 734 (CA).

properties who had pleaded necessity through homelessness. Lord Denning MR acknowledged the existence of the doctrine of necessity, but emphasised that it had to be carefully circumscribed. He considered that it was not a defence to theft of food by a starving man,[138] because:[139]

> [I]f hunger were once allowed to be an excuse for stealing, it would open a way through which all kinds of disorder and lawlessness would pass. So here. If homelessness were once admitted as a defence to trespass, no one's house could be safe. Necessity would open a door which no man could shut. It would not only be those in extreme need who would enter. There would be others who would imagine that they were in need, or would invent a need, so as to gain entry. Each man would say his need was greater than the next man's. The plea would be an excuse for all sorts of wrongdoing. So the courts must, for the sake of law and order, take a firm stand. They must refuse to admit the plea of necessity to the hungry and the homeless: and trust that their distress will be relieved by the charitable and the good. Applying these principles, it seems to me the circumstances of these squatters are not such as to afford any justification or excuse in law for their entry into these houses.

Similarly Edmund Davies LJ was concerned that necessity might become simply 'a mask for anarchy'.[140] But the method for avoiding 'anarchy' is to ensure that the defence is interpreted restrictively, by reference to clear conditions, rather than denying the defence in all cases.

Various requirements and restrictions can be identified for the operation of the necessity defence.[141] The burden for establishing the defence is borne by the defendant.[142]

(1) There must be a real and imminent danger.[143] The danger must actually exist and not simply turn on the defendant's belief in the danger, even if that belief is reasonable.[144]
(2) The circumstances for necessitous intervention must not have been created by the defendant's own negligence.[145]
(3) The defendant's conduct must be reasonable. This is determined by considering whether any reasonable person in the circumstances of the case would have concluded that there was no alternative to the commission of the tort.[146] The defendant's response must also be appropriate, such that intervention cannot be justified where there is another more appropriate person who is available and willing to act.[147] The nature of reasonableness was considered in *Cresswell v Sirl*,[148] where the defendant had killed the claimant's dog which was worrying

[138] See also Hale 1 PC 54.
[139] *Southwark London Borough Council v Williams* (n 137) 744.
[140] ibid 745.
[141] See generally N Tamblyn, 'Private Necessity in English and American Tort Law' (2012) *Global Journal of Comparative Law* 38.
[142] *Cope v Sharpe (No 2)* (n 17) 508 (Kennedy LJ); *Cresswell v Sirl* (n 16) 248 (Scott LJ); *Ashley v Chief Constable of Sussex Police* [2006] EWCA Civ 1085; [2007] 1 WLR 398.
[143] *Monsanto plc v Tilly* (n 18) [54] (Pill LJ).
[144] *Cope v Sharpe (No 2)* (n 17) 508 (Kennedy LJ).
[145] *Southport Corp v Esso Petroleum Ltd* (n 121) 194 (Singleton LJ), 198 (Denning LJ); [1956] AC 218 (HL) 242 (Lord Radcliffe); *Rigby v Chief Constable of Northamptonshire* (n 84).
[146] *Cope v Sharpe (No 2)* (n 17) 508 (Kennedy LJ); *Cresswell v Sirl* (n 16) 248 (Scott LJ).
[147] *Re F (Mental Patient: Sterilisation)* (n 46) 74 (Lord Goff).
[148] Above n 16.

sheep. The defendant thought the dog was fierce so that it was not safe to catch hold of it, so he shot it when it had left the sheep and was coming towards him. The claimant sued for trespass to the dog. The claim succeeded at trial because the dog had ceased to attack the sheep when it was shot. The Court of Appeal held that the test was whether the sheep were in real or imminent danger and that any reasonable man in the circumstances of the case would have concluded that there was no alternative to the act of trespass if the property endangered was to be preserved.[149] The defendant's act was considered to be reasonable, so the defence was available. The defence was denied on the ground of unreasonableness in *Kirk v Gregory*,[150] where the sister-in-law of the deceased, who was in his house when he died, removed some jewellery from one room to another in good faith for its preservation, whilst his servants were drinking and feasting. The jewellery was never found. It was held that the defendant was liable for trespass to goods, but she would have had a defence had she established that her conduct was reasonably necessary and carried out in a reasonable manner.

(4) The response must be proportionate such that the harm caused must be less than the harm threatened.[151] This is easier to establish where the necessitous act involves interference with the claimant's property in order to protect the defendant's property, for then the properties can be readily compared with reference to their relative values.[152] Where the defendant damages the claimant's property to avert a threat to the defendant's bodily safety, or that of a third party, it will be easy to establish the defence, because the safety of human lives belongs to a different scale of values than the safety of property.[153] To ensure consistency with the criminal law, bodily endangerment should only encompass the danger of death or serious personal injury. Similarly, where property is endangered the defence should only be triggered where the threat relates to the destruction of the property or substantial damage to it.[154]

5. CONCLUSIONS

Although the nature and function of necessity within the law of tort is a matter of significant confusion amongst the judiciary and commentators, a number of key conclusions can be identified which render the doctrine rational and defensible.

(1) Necessity is properly characterised as a defence to tort claims.
(2) Necessity is appropriately divided into two categories.
    (i) Public necessity, which encompasses best interests intervention, is a justification which renders the defendant's conduct lawful such that the

149 ibid 247 (Scott LJ).
150 (1876) 1 Ex D 55.
151 Sussmann (n 6) 190.
152 *Cope v Sharpe (No 2)* (n 17) 509 (Kennedy LJ). See G Williams. 'The Defence of Necessity' (1953) 6 *Current Legal Problems* 216, 224.
153 *Southport Corp v Esso Petroleum Co Ltd* [1953] 3 WLR 773 (QBD) 779 (Devlin J).
154 See Tamblyn (n 141) 46.

defendant should not be liable to the claimant for any harm caused by his actions, save perhaps where the defendant is a public authority.

(ii) Private necessity is a defence which is properly characterised as a hybrid between justification and excuse. It justifies the defendant in acting, such that the claimant cannot prevent him from doing so, but the defendant should remain liable to compensate the claimant for any harm caused. This appears not to reflect the nature of the defence in English law, which should learn from the more sophisticated and convincing analysis of the defence in the United States. It is appropriate to describe it either as an incomplete privilege or an incomplete licence.

(3) The conditions for recognising the defence of necessity are consistent with it being treated as essentially justificatory, since its application is dependent on proof that the harm caused was less significant than the harm avoided, such that the defendant should be considered to have acted properly when he intervenes for reasons of necessity, albeit that this does not necessarily negate liability to compensate for harm caused where the defendant has acted for reasons of self-interest rather than the greater public good.

Far from being a tool for anarchy or a plea only available to the tyrant, necessity can be justified as a rational and principled defence to tort claims.

9

A Defence of Duress in the Law of Torts?

JAMES EDELMAN AND ESTHER DYER*

1. INTRODUCTION: THE DOMINANT VIEW IN ENGLISH LAW

A VICTIM OF extreme criminal menaces is told that unless she steals goods then she, and her family, will be killed. She complies, steals the goods and provides them to the menacing person. The circumstances provide her with a defence to the crime of theft. But she *will* be liable for the tort of conversion, according to the entrenched view that duress is not a defence to the commission of a tort. The aim of this chapter is to explain why this view, though entrenched, is a dubious one. Our position is preliminary as it has yet to be tested against the concrete reality of a detailed factual scenario. But the following points cast doubt on the view that duress is not a defence to the commission of a tort:

(1) The judicial authority against recognition of a defence of duress is very limited. Although the rejection of duress as a defence is a position adopted by almost every torts textbook, it is a position based on a single English authority (i) which is contrary to United States authority, (ii) which was decided on a demurrer, apparently without argument, and (iii) which was probably decided upon a premise that is today regarded as false.
(2) The operation of pressure in criminal law has developed in tandem with the formation of liability rules in the law of torts. The same process of parallel development, applied to defences, would see the well-recognised defence of duress in criminal law extended to torts.
(3) There is an almost paper-thin distinction between a defence of necessity in criminal law and a defence of necessity in the law of torts (both of which have been recognised) and a defence of duress (which has been recognised in the criminal law but not in the law of torts).
(4) The most common arguments of principle against the recognition of a defence of duress are not compelling. The argument that the central goal of the law of torts is compensation is, at best, questionable. The argument that a tortfeasor who had a choice whether or not to act should not be excused from violating

* Our sincere thanks to Dr James Goudkamp, Dr Fred Wilmot-Smith and Mr Andrew Dyson for their invitation to the extremely stimulating workshop at which this chapter was presented, as well as their insightful comments and criticisms.

the rights of a victim of a tort who had no choice is, at best, question-begging. In contrast, the rationale for the defence, like a tortious defence of necessity, might be that a defendant has a liberty to act, possibly qualified by a liability to pay compensation for any loss caused.

We conclude the chapter with a consideration of matters of nomenclature which have important effects. Is duress properly labelled as a 'defence'? How could it be a defence if it turns out to be a matter which a claimant must disprove? Is it a justification or an excuse? Or is it some other type of defence? The recent monograph by James Goudkamp[1] provides invaluable assistance through this minefield of terminology.

2. THE LIMITED AUTHORITY AGAINST A TORTIOUS DEFENCE OF DURESS

The dominant common law view for nearly four centuries has been that duress does not provide a defence to tortious conduct.[2] Our first point in this chapter is to observe that the judicial authority which supports this view is extremely limited and was based upon what is now a false premise.

The decision usually cited in support of the entrenched view is Style's report of *Gilbert v Stone*.[3] In that case, Gilbert brought a claim against Stone for trespass and the taking of his horse. Stone pleaded that he had so acted because of 12 armed men who were threatening to kill him unless he stole the horse. Gilbert demurred. In Style's report of the proceedings, Roll J (one of only two judges of the King's Bench at the time) is reported by Style as having held that Stone's plea could not justify his actions, 'for I may not do a trespasse to one for fear of threatnings of another, for by this means the part injured shall have no satisfaction, for he cannot have it of the party that threatned'.

Less commonly cited is Aleyn's report of *Gilbert v Stone*.[4] Aleyn focused only upon the claim for trespass on to the property of Gilbert. He reported that there was no argument on the demurrer, and that Roll J rejected the defence on the basis that 'one cannot justifie a trespass upon another for fear, and the defendant hath remedy against those that compelled him'.[5]

The premise of Style's report of the decision is now incorrect and the assertion of Aleyn's is open to doubt. As to Style's report, since the recognition in the twentieth century of the tort of three-party intimidation (described in England as part of a tort of causing loss by unlawful means), a claim could probably be brought by a person in Gilbert's position against the 12 armed men. The armed men committed an unlawful act against Stone, interfering with his freedom to act, and intending to

[1] J Goudkamp, *Tort Law Defences* (Oxford, Hart Publishing, 2013).

[2] See, eg, TM Cooley, *A Treatise on the Law of Torts, or, The Wrongs which Arise Independent of Contract* (Chicago, Callaghan, 1880) 115; C Sappideen and P Vines (eds), *Fleming's The Law of Torts*, 10th edn (Sydney, Thomson Reuters, 2011) 112; MA Jones and AM Dugdale (ed) *Clerk & Lindsell on Torts*, 20th edn (London, Sweet and Maxwell, 2013) 1040. Queried in WE Peel and J Goudkamp, *Winfield & Jolowicz on Tort*, 19th edn (London, Sweet and Maxwell, 2014) 831 [26-107].

[3] (1647) Style 72; 82 ER 539.

[4] (1647) Aleyn 35; 82 ER 902.

[5] ibid.

cause loss to Gilbert. There would also be a possible claim against the armed men on the basis that, through Gilbert, they committed the tort of conversion: 'if A takes the hand of B and with it strikes C, A is the trespasser, and not B'.[6]

As to Aleyn's report, the decision involves mere assertion by Roll J. No reason is given for why a person cannot justify a trespass for reasons of fear. Nor is any authority cited for the proposition that the defendant would have a claim against the armed men. Such a claim would today be regarded as two-party intimidation. It is unclear whether such a claim exists today[7] but even assuming that it does, it amounts merely to an assertion that the existence of such a claim against the armed men by Stone should prevent Stone from defending a claim by Gilbert. The assumption, perhaps reinforced by Style's report, might have been that the best course of ensuring compensation would be to allow Gilbert to sue Stone and to require Stone to sue the armed men. But, as explained below, a focus on compensation cannot justify refusing Stone a defence.

Nevertheless, *Gilbert v Stone* was famously referred to with approval in an obiter dictum in the dissenting judgment of Blackstone J in *Scott v Shepherd*.[8] Blackstone J observed that following *Gilbert v Stone*, '[n]ot even menaces from others are sufficient to justify a trespass against a third person; much less a fear of danger to either his goods of his person;- nothing but inevitable necessity'.[9]

Subsequent endorsement of *Gilbert v Stone* is difficult to find. Contrary authority is also limited.

A United States authority which does, however, explicitly support a defence of duress is the decision of the Supreme Court of Tennessee in *Waller v Parker*.[10] In that case, Parker brought an action for trover against Waller for actions by Waller in scattering Parker's cotton which led to its destruction. Waller alleged that he had done so under the orders of a company of Confederate soldiers. The jury verdict against Waller was quashed, with Henry Smith J, for the Supreme Court of Tennessee, explaining as follows:[11]

> And these threats may be as effective to work up fears to the extent of the duress, which excuses acts done under its power, as well when the threatening or compelling force is not immediately present at the doing of the acts, as where the acts are done in the actual presence of the compelling force.
>
> ...
>
> If the removal and loss were done and suffered by [Waller], under the stress of fears, well grounded, real, sincere, that the armed force could and would return in a short time, and execute their threats if he did not remove and scatter the cotton; and, if, during this time, Waller was without the power or ability to procure power to resist, and to protect himself and property against the execution of the threats, then Waller is not liable to the plaintiff's action.

[6] *Gibbons v Pepper* (1695) 1 Ld Raym 38, 39; 91 ER 922, 922.
[7] *OBG Ltd v Allan* [2007] UKHL 21; [2008] 1 AC 1 [61] (Lord Hoffmann).
[8] (1773) 2 Black W 892, 896; 96 ER 525, 527.
[9] ibid.
[10] 45 Tenn 476 (1868).
[11] ibid 478.

A second authority which is sometimes cited as involving recognition of a tortious defence of duress is *Cordas v Peerless Transportation Co.*[12] On closer examination, however, this decision turns out not to involve such recognition. In *Cordas*, a chauffeur jumped from his moving car in order to escape from a gunman. The driverless car mounted the sidewalk and injured a mother and her two children. Carlin J, in the New York City Court, held that the chauffeur was not liable to the victims of the accident.

George Fletcher has argued that the result in *Cordas* requires recognition of duress as an excuse to liability in the law of torts: although the risk taken by the cab driver in jumping from the vehicle was unreasonable and excessive, the overwhelmingly coercive circumstances excused him from liability.[13] The problem with this argument is that the risk was only unreasonable and excessive if the extraordinary exigencies are ignored. Once the consequences for the chauffeur if the chauffeur were to have remained in the taxi are taken into account, the risk of jumping from the cab is no longer unreasonable. This was, as Fletcher acknowledged, the reasoning of Carlin J, who explained that the chauffeur was not liable because the question of whether he was negligent needed to be assessed in all the circumstances. It could not be said that he was negligent in acting as he did confronted by a gunman: '"who can be wise, amazed, temperate and furious, Loyal and neutral, in a moment"?'[14]

3. A DEFENCE OF DURESS IN THE LAW OF TORTS BY ANALOGY WITH THE CRIMINAL LAW

Moving from the limited state of *direct* authority for or against the existence of a defence of duress in the law of torts, indirect support for the recognition of a defence of duress to tortious liability can be found by extending the application of the defence of duress as it is recognised in the criminal law. There are two strands to this second argument:

(1) The identical ground of *liability* based on duress was developed in the law of torts by extension from criminal law.
(2) The criminal law has developed a sophisticated and concurrent defence of duress and the law of torts could develop coherently by recognition of the same defence.

3.1 Tortious Liability Based on Duress was Developed by Analogy with the Criminal Law

The modern law in relation to the crime of menaces is contained in various criminal statutes that have a lineage at least as far back as Statute 18 Eliz c 5 which created

12 27 NYS 2d 198 (City Ct 1941).
13 G Fletcher, 'Fairness and Utility in Tort Theory' (1972) 85 *Harvard Law Rev* 537, 552–53.
14 Macbeth, Act 2, scene 3.

the crime of compounding of penal actions.[15] But the earliest criminal law in relation to menaces was common law. It is thus in the early common law where we find the matters which influenced the later recognition of the tort of intimidation.

One of the early cases on the common law of menaces was *R v Southerton*.[16] In that case the accused threatened the victim with prosecution for selling an antiseptic called Fryar's Balsam without a stamped label. Money was paid by the victim and a prosecution ensued. The Court held that the defendant had not committed the crime. Lord Ellenborough CJ held that: '[t]o obtain money under a threat of any kind, or to attempt to do it is no doubt an immoral action; but to make it indictable the threat must be of such a nature as is calculated to overcome a firm and prudent man'.[17] The accused was acquitted because his threat was one that the victim ought prudently to have resisted.

This restriction did not last long. In *R v Thomas Smith*,[18] Wilde CJ referred to, and explained, Lord Ellenborough CJ's rule that the threat must be such that it was calculated to overcome a firm and prudent man:[19]

> That rule must be understood to refer rather to the nature of the threat, than to its probable consequences in any particular case. Whether a threat be criminal or no, cannot be taken to depend on the nerves of the individual threatened, but on the general nature of the evil with which he is threatened. Threats attended with duress, or threats of duress, or of other personal violence, or of great injury, such as is imported by this letter will come within the rule.

In other words, there is no requirement that the person threatened have the nerves of a firm and prudent person. The focus is upon whether the threat is of such a serious nature that it would overcome a firm and prudent person.

As the crime of menaces developed, there was no requirement that the threat concern unlawful action. One of the most common examples of menaces was the entirely lawful threat to report an act to the authorities (such as the threat in *Southerton* of reporting the vendor to the prosecuting authorities). A view began to develop in the early twentieth century that a person could not be guilty of the crime of menaces unless the threat was one of unlawful conduct.[20] This new restriction was also short-lived. In *Thorne v Motor Trade Association*,[21] Lord Atkin pointed out with impeccable logic:

> The ordinary blackmailer normally threatens to do what he has a perfect right to do—namely, communicate some compromising conduct to a person whose knowledge is likely to affect the person threatened. Often indeed he has not only the right but also the duty to make the disclosure, as of a felony, to the competent authorities. What he has to justify is not the threat, but the demand of money. The gravamen of the charge is the demand without reasonable or probable cause.

[15] See W Blackstone, *Commentaries on the Laws of England*, vol 4 (Oxford, Clarendon Press, 1765–1769) ch 10, pt 14.

[16] (1805) 6 East 126; 102 ER 1235.

[17] ibid East 140; ER 1241.

[18] (1849) 1 Denison 510, 514; 169 ER 350, 353.

[19] ibid.

[20] *Ware & De Freville v Motor Trade Association* [1921] 3 KB 40 (CA); *Hardie & Lane v Chilton* [1928] 2 KB 306 (CA).

[21] [1937] AC 797 (HL) 806–07.

In contrast with the criminal action for menaces, the tort of intimidation was not truly recognised before the twentieth century. Prior to its emergence, cases of tortious intimidation were dealt with under the forms of action as actions on the case for 'threatening to mayhem'.[22] However, the great case of *Allen v Flood*,[23] and particularly the opinion of Hawkins J, laid the foundation for the recognition of an independent tort of intimidation. It did so by reference to the crime of menaces.

In *Allen v Flood*, the respondents, Flood and Taylor, were woodworkers who were engaged by a company on a day-to-day basis to perform woodwork on a ship. The appellant, Allen, was the union representative for the ironworkers on the ship. The ironworkers, whom Allen represented, discovered that the woodworkers, Flood and Taylor, had previously been ironworkers on another ship. The ironworkers demanded that Allen procure the dismissal of Flood and Taylor. Allen met with the foreman and general manager of the company. Allen told them that unless the woodworkers were dismissed Allen's ironworkers would leave. The woodworkers got the chop. Flood and Taylor sued Allen, alleging that he had maliciously procured their dismissal. The problem faced by Flood and Taylor was that they had no right to be employed by the company. As they were engaged on a day-to-day basis they could be dismissed at will. At the heart of the appeal, therefore, was the question of whether Allen's bad motive could render unlawful an otherwise lawful action.

The trial judge, and the Court of Appeal, unanimously held that bad motive could effectively cause an otherwise lawful action to become an unlawful one. Nine judges heard the case in the House of Lords. After the hearing began, the Lord Chancellor, seeking to persuade his brethren of the correctness of the view below, summoned another eight leading judges to attend and to deliver decisions to assist their Lordships. The case was thus heard before 17 judges in England's final appellate court.

Flood and Taylor's counsel pointed out that a claimant could recover if another maliciously made statements about him with the intention of causing him financial loss; or if another maliciously made statements about him causing him loss of reputation. Counsel argued that it was not clear why the law should treat malicious statements to third parties differently where they cause loss of his liberty to work.

But despite the force of this argument, despite unanimity in the lower courts, and despite majority support from the additional judges called to advise the House of Lords, Flood and Taylor lost in the House, by six judges to three. The effect of the decision of those six judges is still felt a century later as deep suspicion meets any argument that a defendant's motive alone can suffice for a cause of action to recover losses in the law of torts.

One of the judges advising the House of Lords was Mr Justice Hawkins. Hawkins J was firmly of the opinion that Flood and Taylor should have recovered. In a powerful opinion, Hawkins J argued in favour of a tort of intimidation. Importantly, Hawkins J borrowed from the criminal law of menaces and what is now recognised to be an action based on duress in unjust enrichment:[24]

> any menacing action or language, the influence of which no man of ordinary firmness or strength of mind can reasonably be expected to resist if used or employed with the intent to

[22] *Garrett v Taylor* (1619) Cro Jac 567, 568; 79 ER 485, 487.
[23] [1898] AC 1 (HL).
[24] ibid 17–18. Relying on *Williams v Bayley* (1866) LR 1 HL 200.

> destroy the freedom of will in another, and to compel him through fear of such menaces to do that which it is not his will to do, and which being done is calculated to cause injury to him or some other person, amounts to an attempt to intimidate and coerce; and if such attempt is successful, the object attained under such influence is attained by coercion, and the person wrongfully injured by it, whether in his person, property, or rights, may sue the coercer for reparation in damages.

The advice of Hawkins J in *Allen v Flood* was the basis for the recognition of a tort of intimidation by John Salmond in one of the earliest, and leading, English texts on torts. In the first edition, published in 1907, Salmond relied upon the advice of Hawkins J to suggest that there existed a tort of intimidation. Salmond argued that such a tort could arise where the claimant intimidated the defendant into acting in some way which caused the defendant harm (two-party intimidation), or alternatively where a defendant intimidated a third party into acting in some way which caused the claimant harm (three-party intimidation). According to Salmond, 'it is clear that the threat complained of must be a threat to do an act which is itself illegal. No threat to exercise one's legal rights can amount to a cause of action, even if the threat made for the purpose of intimidation or coercion, and even if inspired by malicious motives'.[25] Salmond's approach, in insisting on illegal action, flows logically from the conclusion of the majority of the House of Lords in *Allen v Flood.*

Most noticeably, however, Salmond borrowed from Hawkins J in recognising the tort of intimidation. Following *Allen v Flood*, Salmond imposed a restriction on the recognition of the tort by insisting that the threat concern unlawful conduct. In *OBG Ltd v Allan*,[26] Lord Hoffmann in the leading speech then subsumed three-party intimidation within the tort of causing loss by unlawful means and insisted that the requirement of unlawfulness meant civil wrongdoing.

In summary, despite the differences which emerged between the tort of intimidation and the crime of menaces, the criminal law of menaces provided one of the foundational bases upon which the tort of intimidation was recognised by Hawkins J, then Salmond, then later cases. Tortious *liability* for exerting unlawful pressure upon another (intimidation) thus developed by reference to the criminal liability for such pressure (menaces). The same could be true of a tort *defence* of unlawful pressure, by reference to the criminal defence.

Initially, the defence of duress to a crime was very limited. As Wigmore observed, duress was from the thirteenth century a defence to the penal action of homicide. The 'slayer by misadventure' would have his life spared. Otherwise all liability was absolute, irrespective of any personal blameworthiness for the harm caused.[27]

By the fourteenth century duress as a defence to criminal conduct had been recognised by English law, although there are very few known cases. Sir James Fitzjames Stephen, who knew of only two cases in which the defence had been applied, said that '[c]ompulsion by threats of injury to person or property'[28] was recognised as a defence to a crime in cases where the compulsion was applied by a body of rebels or

[25] J Salmond, *The Law of Torts* (London, Stevens and Haynes, 1907) 440.
[26] Above n 7.
[27] JH Wigmore, 'Responsibility for Tortious Acts: Its History.—III' (1894) 7 *Harvard Law Review* 59, 60.
[28] JF Stephen, *A History of the Criminal Law in England*, vol 2 (London, Macmillan, 1883) 105.

riots and in which the offender took a subordinate part in the offence. Stephen was critical of the defence, arguing that compulsion by threats ought in no case whatsoever to be admitted as an excuse for crime, though it may, and ought, to operate in mitigation of punishment in most cases.[29]

The availability of the defence was historically confined to circumstances in which the accused was facing death for non-compliance with the demands of a third party. Thus Sir Matthew Hale said that:[30]

> if a man be desperately assaulted, and in peril of death, and cannot otherwise escape, unless to satisfy his assailant's fury he will kill an innocent person then present, the fear and actual force will not acquit him of the crime and punishment of murder, if he commit the fact; for he ought rather to die himself, than kill an innocent.

The application of duress was limited to a person faced with 'actual and inevitable danger to his own life'; fear alone would not be enough.[31]

In these early formulations of the defence, the only force that would excuse the criminal act was 'force upon the person, and present fear of death'[32] so that 'an apprehension, though ever so well founded, of having property wasted or destroyed, or of suffering any other mischief not endangering the person of the party, will be no excuse'.[33] In *McGrowther's Case*, Lee CJ directed the jury that 'the fear of having houses burnt, or goods spilled, supposing that to have been the case of the prisoner, is no excuse in the eyes of the law joining and marching with rebels'.[34] To permit one to break the law in order to protect property would mean that it 'would be in the power of any leader of a rebellion to indemnify all his followers'.[35]

Sir William Blackstone took a more expansive view of the defence, describing it as open where one committed a crime due to 'threats or menaces, which induce a fear of death or other bodily harm'.[36] The inclusion of *threats* meant that it was not necessary to show that actual force was exerted: evidence that the defendant was subjected to threats was sufficient.

From these roots emerged the modern defence of duress to a crime in English law. The modern defence involves a two-limb test which comprises both subjective and objective elements. This test was enunciated by Lord Lane CJ in *R v Graham*[37] and subsequently affirmed by the House of Lords in *R v Howe*:[38]

> 1. Was the defendant, or may he have been, impelled to act as he did because, as a result of what he reasonably believe [the person making the threats] had said or done, he had good cause to fear that if he did not so act King [the person] would kill him or (if this is to be added) cause him serious physical injury?

[29] ibid 108.
[30] M Hale, *The History of the Pleas of the Crown* (Philadelphia, RH Small, 1847) 51.
[31] ibid. See also M Foster, *Crown Cases* (Dublin, James Moore, 1791) 217.
[32] *McGrowther's Case* (1746) 18 St Tr 391, 394; 168 ER 8, 8 (Lee CJ).
[33] EH East, *A Treatise of the Pleas of the Crown* (London, A Strahan, 1803) 70–71. See also Foster (n 31) 217.
[34] *McGrowther's Case* (1746) 18 St Tr 391, 393; 168 ER 8, 8.
[35] ibid.
[36] Blackstone (n 15) ch 2, pt 2.
[37] [1982] 1 WLR 294 (CA) 300.
[38] [1987] AC 417 (HL) 459 (Lord Mackay).

2. If so, have the prosecution made the jury sure that a sober person of reasonable firmness, sharing the characteristics of the defendant, would not have responded to whatever he reasonably believed [the person] said or did by [acting as he did]?

The proper scope of, and restrictions upon, the plea of duress as a defence to a crime in English law were considered in the more recent case of *R v Z*.[39] In that case, the defendant had been convicted of aggravated burglary. At trial, the defendant admitted the burglary but pleaded that he had been coerced into acting as he did by threats of harm directed against him and his family. According to the defendant, the person who had threatened him was a drug dealer with a reputation for being violent. The Court of Appeal allowed the defendant's appeal against conviction, finding that the trial judge had misdirected the jury in relation to the defence of duress. However, the House of Lords re-instated the defendant's conviction on the basis that the defendant could not rely on the defence of duress where, as a result of his voluntary association with known criminals, he had foreseen or ought reasonably to have foreseen the risk of being subjected to any compulsion by threats of violence.

Lord Bingham (with whose reasons Lords Rodger and Brown agreed) explained that there are features of the defence which require it to be narrowly confined: in particular, the difficulty for the prosecution in disproving the defence where little detail of it is generally vouchsafed by the defence until the trial is well underway. Lord Bingham also referred to the observations of Lord Simon in *DPP for Northern Ireland v Lynch*[40] (dissenting on the main ruling, which was reversed in *R v Howe*[41]): '[Y]our Lordships should hesitate long lest you may be inscribing a charter for terrorists, gang-leaders and kidnappers ... A sane system of criminal justice does not permit a subject to set up a countervailing system of sanctions or by terrorism to confer criminal immunity on his gang'. Lord Bingham then enumerated the following limits on the operation and scope of the defence of duress in criminal law, which we summarise below:[42]

(1) Duress does not afford a defence to charges of murder, attempted murder and perhaps some forms of treason.
(2) To found a plea of duress the threat relied on must be to cause death or serious injury.
(3) The threat must be directed against the defendant or his immediate family or someone close to him.
(4) The relevant tests pertaining to duress have been largely stated objectively, with reference to the reasonableness of the defendant's perceptions and conduct and not with primary reference to his subjective perceptions.
(5) The defence of duress is available only where the criminal conduct which is sought to be excused has been directly caused by the threats upon which reliance is placed.

[39] [2005] UKHL 22; [2005] 2 AC 467.
[40] [1975] AC 653 (HL) 688–89.
[41] Above n 38.
[42] *R v Z* (n 49) [21].

(6) The defendant may excuse his criminal conduct on grounds of duress only if there was no evasive action that the defendant could reasonably have been expected to take.
(7) The defendant may not rely on duress to which he has voluntarily laid himself open.

It is open for the law of torts to develop the same defence just as the law of torts borrowed from the criminal law in developing an *action* based upon unlawful pressure.

4. OVERLAP BETWEEN A DEFENCE OF NECESSITY AND A DEFENCE OF DURESS

A third aspect of our argument that a tortious defence of duress might be recognised is that the boundary between the recognised defence of necessity and a defence of duress can be paper-thin, whether such a defence arises in criminal law or the law of torts.

4.1 Necessity in Criminal Law

The history of English judicial recognition of the defence of necessity to a crime dates back to the sixteenth century decision of *Reniger v Fogossa*.[43] In that case the Court appeared to accept the argument of Sergeant Pollard which recognised necessity as a defence alongside compulsion or duress:[44]

> in every law there are some things which when they happen a man may break the words of the law, and yet not break the law itself; and such things are exempted out of the penalty of the law ... where the words of them are broken to avoid greater inconveniences, or through necessity, or by compulsion ...

Three years after the decision in the famous case of *R v Dudley and Stephens*,[45] Stephen described the doctrine in the following terms:[46]

> An act which would otherwise be a crime may in some cases be excused if the person accused can show that it was done only in order to avoid consequences which could not otherwise be avoided, and which, if they had followed, would have inflicted upon him or upon others whom he was bound to protect inevitable and irreparable evil, that no more was done than was reasonably necessary for that purpose, and that the evil inflicted by it was not disproportionate to the evil avoided. The extent of this principle is unascertained ... It does not extend to the case of shipwrecked sailors who kill a boy, one of their number, in order to eat his body.

As to more contemporary authority, the defence of necessity to a crime was considered in detail by the Supreme Court of Canada in *Perka v The Queen*.[47] In that

[43] (1551) 1 Plowd 1; 75 ER 1.
[44] ibid Plowd 18; ER 29.
[45] (1884) 14 QBD 273 (Div Ct).
[46] Stephen, *Digest of the Criminal Law*, 4th edn (London, Macmillan, 1877) 24.
[47] [1984] 2 SCR 232 (SCC).

case, the appellants were charged with importing cannabis into Canada. One of their defences was that they were bound for Alaska but that their ship suffered mechanical problems which required them to dock in Canada and offload the cannabis to avoid capsizing. The appellants were acquitted. A Crown appeal was allowed by the Court of Appeal. The Supreme Court of Canada dismissed a further appeal, and in the course of ordering a retrial, affirmed the existence of a defence of necessity as an excuse to criminal liability based on 'a realistic assessment of human weakness ... in emergency situations where normal human instincts ... overwhelmingly impel disobedience'.[48] The defence applied only where the circumstances were such that the person who committed the crime had 'no other viable or reasonable choice available; the act was wrong but it was excused because it was realistically unavoidable'.[49]

4.2 Necessity in the Law of Torts

A defence of necessity was established as a tortious defence by the time of *Mouse's Case*.[50] In that case a barge was in danger of foundering while being used as a ferry across the Thames. A passenger threw the claimant's personal property overboard to lighten the barge. The claimant sued the passenger for trespass. The plea of trespass was refused. The Court held that 'for [the] safety of the lives of passengers ... it is lawful for any passenger to cast the things out of the barge'.[51] The owners could maintain an action against the ferryman for overloading the barge, 'but if no surcharge was, but the danger accrued only by the act of God, as by tempest, no default being in the ferryman, everyone ought to bear his loss for the safeguard and life of a man'.[52]

The decision in *Mouse's Case* is usually regarded as an example of 'public' necessity. A more recent example of the defence is *Southport Corp v Esso Petroleum*.[53] That case concerned a ship which had run aground. The defendant shipowners dumped some oil from their ship into the sea because they feared the ship would break its back and the crew would be endangered if they did not. The oil washed up onto the shore of land belonging to the claimants, who brought an action against the defendants for having committed trespass in dumping the oil. Devlin J held that the defendants could rely on the defence of necessity to justify their actions since 'the necessity for saving life has at all times been considered a proper ground for inflicting such damage as may be necessary upon another's property'.[54]

In contrast with these examples of public necessity, are cases of 'private necessity' as in *Cope v Sharpe (No 2)*.[55] In that case, Mr Chase had shooting rights on the

[48] ibid 248.
[49] ibid 250.
[50] (1609) 12 Co Rep 63; 77 ER 1341.
[51] ibid Co Rep 64; ER 1342.
[52] ibid.
[53] [1953] 3 WLR 733 (QBD). The judgment was reversed by the Court of Appeal but restored by the House of Lords: *Esso Petroleum Co Ltd v Southport Corp* [1956] AC 218 (HL).
[54] See also *Cope v Sharpe (No 2)* [1912] 1 KB 496 (CA).
[55] ibid.

claimant's property. Mr Chase's keeper took various actions which would otherwise have amounted to trespass on the claimant's property to prevent a fire from killing pheasants on the property. The Court of Appeal upheld a decision that the gamekeeper was not liable on the basis of the defence of necessity. There was real and imminent danger to the pheasants at the moment at which he acted, and what he did was reasonably necessary.

A third category of necessity was recognised in *Re F (Mental Patient: Sterilisation)*.[56] That case concerned the lawfulness of a proposed operation of sterilisation upon F, the claimant. F was a 36-year-old woman whose mental incapacity disabled her from giving her consent to a sterilisation operation. Unless a defence applied, the performance of the medical operation would be unlawful, constituting both the crime of battery and tort of trespass to the person. F's mother sought a declaration that the performance of the operation would be lawful. After referring to examples of public necessity and private necessity, Lord Goff explained that there is a third group of cases in which a necessity defence is recognised:[57]

> There is, however, a third group of cases, which is also properly described as founded upon the principle of necessity and which is more pertinent to the resolution of the problem in the present case. These cases are concerned with action taken as a matter of necessity to assist another person without his consent. To give a simple example, a man who seizes another and forcibly drags him from the path of an oncoming vehicle, thereby saving him from injury or even death, commits no wrong. But there are many emanations of this principle, to be found scattered through the books. These are concerned not only with the preservation of the life or health of the assisted person, but also with the preservation of his property (sometimes an animal, sometimes an ordinary chattel) and even to certain conduct on his behalf in the administration of his affairs. Where there is a pre-existing relationship between the parties, the intervenor is usually said to act as an agent of necessity on behalf of the principal in whose interests he acts, and his action can often, with not too much artificiality, be referred to the pre-existing relationship between them. Whether the intervenor may be entitled either to reimbursement or to remuneration raises separate questions which are not relevant in the present case.

Although these three categories of necessity as a defence to a tort appear to have the potential for broad application, courts have insisted that they be applied with circumspection. For example, in *London Borough of Southwark v Williams*,[58] the English Court of Appeal denied that extreme hunger could excuse a theft or that homelessness could excuse a trespass. The reason according to Lord Denning MR was that 'if hunger were once allowed to be an excuse for stealing, it would open a door through which all kinds of disorder and lawlessness would pass'.[59] Similarly, Edmund Davies LJ said:[60]

> But when and how far is the plea of necessity made available to one who is prima facie guilty of tort? Well, one thing emerges with clarity from the decisions, and that is that the law regards with the deepest suspicion any remedies of self-help, and permits those remedies

[56] [1990] 2 AC 1 (HL).
[57] ibid 74.
[58] [1971] 1 Ch 734 (CA).
[59] ibid 744.
[60] ibid 745–46.

to be resorted to only in very special circumstances. The reason for such circumspection is clear—necessity can very easily become simply a mask for anarchy. As far as my reading goes, it appears that all the cases where a plea of necessity has succeeded are cases which deal with an urgent situation of imminent peril.

4.3 The Lack of a Clear Distinction between Necessity and Duress

The following three observations illustrate that there is, at least, a conceptual oddity in recognising a tortious defence of necessity but not a tortious defence of duress.

First, as we have already explained, in the earliest cases where the defences were first recognised in criminal law, the judges spoke interchangeably of the defence of necessity and compulsion.

Secondly, in criminal law the defence of duress has been developed, in part, by reference to the defence of necessity. In the leading English decision on the criminal defence of duress, *R v Z*,[61] Lord Bingham drew support for the restrictions on the defence of duress from the 'analogous defence of necessity' held by the Court in *Perka* to apply in 'urgent situations of clear and imminent peril' where 'compliance with the law [would be] demonstrably impossible'. Similarly, in *R v Ruzic*,[62] the Supreme Court of Canada recognised that the defences 'share the same juristic principles'; their differences were sought to be explained by their different contexts. In *Taiapa v The Queen*,[63] the High Court of Australia considered that the common law criminal defence of necessity shares features in common with the defence of duress.

Thirdly, it is extremely difficult to maintain a conceptual distinction between the defence of duress and the defence of necessity. Indeed, the defence of necessity is sometimes expanded to include, or provide an analogy with, cases involving a species of duress that is described as 'duress of circumstances'.[64] And the defence of duress is sometimes described as 'force of circumstance'[65] and commonly treated as a species of necessity.[66] As Bacon explained in his commentary on *necessitas inducit privilegium quoad jura privata*, '[n]ecessity carrieth a privilege in itself. Necessity is of three sorts—necessity of conservation of life, necessity of obedience, and necessity of the act of God or of a stranger'.[67] And as Lord Simon said in his dissenting speech in *Lynch*,[68] '[d]uress is, thus considered, merely a particular application of the doctrine of "necessity"'.

An illuminating case of duress and necessity being treated as part of the same principle is the Scottish decision of *Moss v Howdle*.[69] Mr Moss was driving his car when his passenger suddenly cried out in great pain. Believing his passenger to be

[61] Above n 49, [25].
[62] [2001] 1 SCR 687 (SCC) [64].
[63] [2009] HCA 53; (2009) 240 CLR 95 [36].
[64] *R v Conway* [1989] QB 290 (CA); *R v Martin* [1989] 1 All ER 652 (CA); *R v Graham* (n 37); *State of Queensland v Nolan* (2002) 1 Qd R 454 (SC).
[65] *R v Willer* (1986) 83 Cr App Rep 225 (CA).
[66] See *R v Howe* (n 38) 429; *R v Goldman (No 4)* [2004] VSC 291; (2004) 147 A Crim R 472; *Southwark London Borough Council v Williams* (n 58).
[67] F Bacon, *Works of Francis Bacon*, vol 4 (London, Longmans, Green, Reader and Dyer, 1824) 34.
[68] *DPP for Northern Ireland v Lynch* (n 40) 692.
[69] 1997 SLT 782 (HCJ).

seriously ill, Mr Moss drove to the nearest service station at more than 100 miles per hour. Mr Moss was charged with speeding. He relied upon a statutory defence of necessity. He was convicted. He appealed to the High Court of Justiciary. The appeal was dismissed, although the Court considered the defence of necessity in careful detail.

The Court's decision was delivered by Lord Justice-General Rodger who, it bears noting, was to make an extraordinary contribution to English law as a Lord of the House of Lords and later in the Supreme Court of the United Kingdom. The Court explained that the defence was one of 'necessity or duress'. In the course of discussing the defence it was said that there was no difference in principle between necessity and duress:[70]

> [An] accused may drive dangerously in order to avoid an immediate threat of death from an incipient heart attack, or to avoid an immediate threat of death by drowning in a flood or to avoid an immediate threat of death by drowning due to the deliberate actings of a third party. For the purposes of deciding whether they afford a defence to a charge of dangerous driving, the law should regard all of these threats in the same way.

In *Moss*, the Court also quoted from a famous passage of the Lord Chief Justice in *R v Dudley and Stephens*,[71] who delivered the decision of five judges of the Queen's Bench to whom a question of law had been referred after a special verdict from the jury. It was in that case recognised that there existed a defence of necessity, although such a defence did not exempt the prisoners from being culpable for the murder of the cabin boy.

That the treatment of the defences of necessity and duress as part of the same principle is well-established in English law, is evidenced by the approach taken in more contemporary cases. As Lord Hailsham said in *R v Howe*:[72]

> There is, of course, an obvious distinction between duress and necessity as potential defences; duress arises from the wrongful threats or violence of another human being and necessity arises from any other objective dangers threatening the accused. This, however, is, in my view a distinction without a relevant difference, since on this view duress is only that species of the genus of necessity which is caused by wrongful threats. I cannot see that there is any way in which a person of ordinary fortitude can be excused from the one type of pressure on his will rather than the other.

Rupert Cross argued that it would be 'the apotheosis of absurdity' to allow a defence of duress by threats while disallowing it for duress of circumstances where the compulsion on the defendant is exactly the same.[73] A strong argument can be made that the reverse should also apply in the law of torts. That is, it can be argued that there is no principled reason to recognise a defence of necessity in the law of torts but to refuse a defence of duress.

[70] ibid 785–86.
[71] Above n 45.
[72] Above n 38, 429.
[73] R Cross, 'Murder Under Duress' (1978) 28 *University of Toronto Law Journal* 369, 377.

5. THE THEORETICAL BASIS FOR RECOGNITION OF A DEFENCE OF DURESS

5.1 The Objection that a Defence of Duress is Inconsistent with the Goal of the Law of Torts

The first objection to the availability of a defence of duress in the law of torts is premised upon a perceived inconsistency between the recognition of such a defence and what is said to be the fundamental goal of the law of torts. This objection argues that to recognise the defence represents an attempt by the defendant to shift the costs of his or her own problems on to the claimant. As we have seen, this was essentially the objection which, according to Style's report and perhaps implicitly in Aleyn's report, led to the rejection of the defence 350 years ago in *Gilbert v Stone*.[74]

The argument is perhaps put most eloquently in Richard Epstein's words: '[t]he only proper question for tort law is whether the plaintiff or the defendant will be required to bear the loss ... it is fairer to require the defendant to bear the loss because he had the hard choice of harming or being harmed when, given what is alleged, the plaintiff had no choice at all'.[75] According to Epstein, the defence of compulsion imposed upon the defendant by the acts or threats of a third party should not be recognised because it constitutes an attempt by the defendant to shift the costs of his own problems to the plaintiff:[76] 'one man should not be able to solve his own problems at the expense of physical harm to another ... [so that] a man who injures another will be treated, to the extent possible, as though he had injured himself'.[77]

The notion that compensation is the fundamental goal of the law of torts also casts doubt upon all of the arguments above concerning extensions and analogies with the criminal law. As JC Smith explained in his consideration of the interaction between criminal law defences and civil liability:[78]

> The object of the civil law is to provide compensation for some injury which has occurred and to decide on which of two persons the loss should properly fall. The damage has been done, it has been done by the defendant and—we will assume—to a perfectly innocent person; and, as between that person and the defendant, certainly if he has been negligent, the defendant ought to bear the loss. But in the criminal court we are concerned not with compensation (except incidentally), but with punishment. The question is not how to allocate the burden of some existing loss but whether a new loss should be inflicted on the defendant—loss of his liberty or loss of his money by the imposition of a fine which goes to the state, not the victim. The question is whether the defendant deserves to be punished.

There are three answers to this objection concerning compensation as the fundamental goal of the law of torts: one partial answer and two complete answers.

[74] Above n 3.
[75] RA Epstein, 'Defenses and Subsequent Pleas in a System of Strict Liability' (1974) 3 *Journal of Legal Studies* 165, 169.
[76] ibid.
[77] ibid.
[78] JC Smith, *Justification and Excuse in the Criminal Law* (London, Hamlyn Trust, 1989) 10.

The partial answer is that, unlike as at the time of *Gilbert v Stone,* the common law now recognises a tort of intimidation. A third party who, with the requisite intention to cause loss to the claimant, induces the defendant by unlawful threats to commit a tort which causes loss to the claimant will be liable to the claimant for the tort of intimidation. The claimant will potentially have a source to recover compensation even if the third party might not have the means to pay. The reason that the answer is only partial is that the third party might not be a source of complete compensation. The answer is also, in some respects, unsatisfactory. It would suggest that a defence should be allowed for duress where compensation might be recovered from a third party, but that the very closely related defence of necessity should not be permitted because compensation could not be recovered from the third party. This point reveals the problems associated with developing legal doctrine by reference to consequential concerns about compensation.

The second answer is more satisfactory. It is that the basic goal of the law of torts is not to compensate for loss but is instead a concern with a person's rights. This is the basic thesis of Robert Stevens' influential and powerful monograph *Torts and Rights.*[79] Many arguments could be made in favour of the thesis concerning rights over the thesis that the fundamental goal of the law of torts is compensation. If the latter is correct, why are many torts actionable without any loss being suffered? Why are injunctions awarded to prevent tortious conduct? Why do gain-based damages, or exemplary damages, exist for torts? Indeed, should the fundamental goal of the law of torts be compensation, it would become increasingly difficult to justify the entire system of torts in light of empirical evidence which, if accepted, indicates that compensation might be delivered far more cheaply, and considerably more effectively, by state systems of compensation.

Nevertheless, this complete answer is controversial because of the dogma, insisted upon by many commentators and courts, that compensation is, in the famous words of one of Australia's greatest judges, the 'one principle that is absolutely firm, and which must control all else'.[80] But, at the least, the second answer could be that any compensation goal cannot explain *all* of the law of torts, and hence it begs the question to assert that, in the instance of the defence of duress, a lack of compensation for the wrongdoer should prevent the defence. This is particularly the case since it does not defeat the defence of necessity.

The third answer is that even if compensation were thought to be a fundamental goal of the law of torts, and even if compensation from the defendant were thus thought to be essential (including in cases in which the defendant were subjected to extreme duress), duress could still exist as a defence in the form of a privilege while at the same time being made subject to a liability to pay compensation for any loss caused. In other words, the defendant could lawfully act in the manner in which he or she did as a result of the duress, and could not be injuncted from doing so, but would remain liable to pay compensation. To put it another way, duress would be a privilege which would be qualified by a liability to pay compensation.

[79] R Stevens, *Torts and Rights* (Oxford, Oxford University Press, 2007).

[80] *Skelton v Collins* (1966) 115 CLR 94 (HCA) 128 (Windeyer J).

5.2 The Objection that Duress Involves Unwarranted Erosion of the Claimant's Right

5.2.1 The Argument: Duress as a Defence Operates to Negate Intention and this is Unjustifiable

A second objection to the recognition of duress as a defence to a tort focuses upon the nature of the claimant's rights. The objection is that the recognition of duress is an unwarranted erosion of the scope of the claimant's right in that a violation of that right should be recognised even if the otherwise voluntary conduct of the defendant has been affected by some mental impairment.

The answer to this objection, and the reason why the argument should therefore be rejected, is that duress does not operate as a denial of the voluntariness element of an intentional tort. The basis for the objection is thus misconceived.

In criminal law, the defence of duress has sometimes erroneously been said to be based upon the will of the accused having been overborne by the wrongful threats imposed by another to inflict harm on the accused or the accused's family.[81] Hence, Lord Parker in *R v Hudson*[82] spoke of the commission of the alleged offence no longer being the voluntary act of the accused.

The same erroneous assumption concerning the operation of the defence of duress has led to the assertion that the rationale for the defence is, in the words of Murnaghan J, that '[a]ll the elements producing culpability concur in this conviction except the free exercise of will, and the point is accordingly narrowed down to the consideration whether there was such an absence of will as to absolve from guilt'.[83] Even Blackstone apparently placed the defence of duress on the footing that it negatived the voluntariness required by the intention element of the offence: '[a]s punishments are ... only inflicted for the abuse of ... free-will ... it is highly just and equitable that a man should be excused for those acts, which are done through unavoidable force and compulsion'.[84] In Australia, duress has also been differentiated from necessity on the basis that duress, unlike necessity, is said to involve a situation in which 'the person's mind is not irresistibly overcome by external pressures'.[85]

The notion that duress operates to negate the voluntariness element of an offence or tort should be rejected, both as a matter of principle and as a matter of authority.

5.2.2 Rejecting the Argument as a Matter of Principle

As a matter of principle, the argument should be rejected for the following reasons.

In intentional torts the violation of a claimant's right requires voluntary conduct by the defendant. A defendant commits conversion, false imprisonment,

[81] *R v Ortiz* (1986) 83 Cr App R 173 (CA); *R v Hurley and Murray* [1967] VR 526 (SC); *R v Conway* (n 64); *R v Martin* (n 64).

[82] [1971] 2 QB 202 (CA) 206.

[83] *A-G v Whelan* [1934] IR 518 (CCA).

[84] Blackstone (n 15) ch 2, pt IV. See P Rosenthal 'Duress in the Criminal Law' (1989) 32 *Criminal Law Quarterly* 199, 200–01.

[85] *State of Queensland v Nolan* (n 64) [19] (Chesterman J).

defamation, or battery if he or she chooses to assert control over the claimant's chattels, assert control over the claimant's liberty, make a statement which impairs the claimant's reputation or assert force, however minimal, over the plaintiff's body. In each case, it is the voluntary choice of the defendant that is an essential ingredient of the tort. This was the reason why the claim failed in *Smith v Stone*.[86] Stone pleaded justification to Smith's claim of trespass. Stone said that he had been carried across the boundary onto Smith's land by the force and violence of others. Smith demurred. Roll J accepted the plea of justification. Stone's conduct was not voluntary. Voluntary choice is now well-established as a requirement of trespass.[87] But in contrast with the requirement of voluntary conduct in each case, it does not matter whether or not the defendant's voluntary conduct is a result of some impairment of his or her decision, such as a mistake. Mistake is not a defence. It is hard to see why other factors which vitiate intention, such as duress or undue influence, should have the effect that the requirement of voluntary conduct is not satisfied. As Peter Cane has explained, the law of torts is not concerned with the quality or extent of a voluntary act:[88]

> When we move to the civil law paradigm of liability, the inadequacies of the choice theory of responsibility [become] obvious. In the civil law paradigm, the interests [rights] of victims are given at least as much weight as those of agents. This is reflected in the fact that the basic measure of civil law remedies is the impact of the proscribed conduct on the victim, not the nature of the agent's conduct or the quality of the agent's will.

The reason why duress does not 'destroy' or 'overcome' the will was explained by James Fitzjames Stephen:[89]

> A criminal walking to execution is under compulsion if any man can be said to be so, but his motions are just as much voluntary actions as if he was going to leave his place of confinement and regain his liberty. He walks to his death because he prefers it to being carried. This is choice, though it is a choice between extreme evils.

The notion of choice is also central to Holmes' conception of liability in the law of torts: 'the philosophical analysis of every wrong begins by determining what the defendant has actually chosen, that is to say, what his voluntary act or conduct has been ... and then goes on to determine what dangers attended ... the conduct under the known circumstances'.[90]

A further reason of principle why duress cannot be understood as negating an intention element of an offence or tort is because if it were, then it is hard to see why a recognised situation of duress would not apply to all intentional torts and to all crimes where intention is a necessary element of the offence. In contrast, as a privilege, duress applies in the limited circumstances in which the privilege is recognised. It derives its force from the scope of the privilege, which is a separate question of principle from the question of the scope of the elements of the offence. So,

86 (1647) Style 65; 82 ER 533.

87 *Network Rail Infrastructure Ltd v Conarken Group Ltd* [2010] EWHC 1852 (TCC); *Public Transport Commission (NSW) v Perry* (1977) 137 CLR 107 (HCA) 126 (Barwick CJ), 133 (Gibbs J).

88 P Cane, *Responsibility in Law and Morality* (Oxford, Hart Publishing, 2002) 99.

89 Stephen (n 28) 102.

90 OW Holmes, *The Common Law* (Boston, Little Brown, 1881) 161.

in *R v Howe*[91] Lord Griffiths held that duress is not a defence to charges of murder 'based on the special sanctity that the law attaches to human life and which denies to a man the right to take an innocent life even at the price of his own or another's life'. Article 8 of the Nuremberg Statute was based on the same idea.

5.2.3 Rejecting the Argument as a Matter of Authority

As a matter of authority, the view that the effect of duress is to negate the element of voluntariness was rejected by Lord Wilberforce in *Lynch*.[92] Lord Wilberforce explained that:

> whatever the ultimate analysis in jurisprudence may be, the best opinion, as reflected in decisions of judges and in writers, seems to be that duress per minas is something which is superimposed upon the other ingredients which by themselves would make up an offence, i.e., upon act and intention ... One may note—and the comparison is satisfactory—that an analogous result is achieved in a civil law context: duress does not destroy the will, for example, to enter into a contract, but prevents the law from accepting what has happened as a contract valid in law ...

Lord Wilberforce's view is also consistent with the foundation upon which the criminal defence was initially recognised. The focus was upon the boundaries of the wrong once the elements were proved. It was not a focus on the boundaries of voluntariness or intention required for proof of the offence. By the mid-seventeenth century Hobbes said that:[93]

> If a man by the terrour of present death, be compelled to doe a fact against the Law, he is totally Excused; because no Law can oblige a man to abandon his own preservation. And supposing such a Law were obligatory; yet a man would reason thus, *If I doe it not, I die presently*; if I doe it, I die afterwards; therefore by doing it, there is time of life gained; Nature therefore compells him to the fact.

More recently, the suggestion that duress operates to negative the element of intention was rejected by the Supreme Court of Canada.[94]

5.3 A Different Basis for Recognition of a Defence of Duress: a Privilege

The answer to this second objection is therefore as follows: if duress is to be recognised as a defence in the law of torts, as a matter of principle and authority it should not be based on any notion that it negates the intention required for an intentional tort. It must instead take the form of a privilege which is external to the elements of the offence. Although duress shares with every privilege the difficulty of principle

[91] Above n 38, 439.
[92] Above n 40, 679–80.
[93] T Hobbes, *Leviathan*, vol 2 (N Malcolm (ed), Oxford, Clarendon Press, 2012) 468 (emphasis in original) (footnotes omitted).
[94] *R v Ruzic* (n 62).

involved in determining its boundaries, Lord Bridge was correct in his speech in *R v Howe*[95] to reject the conception of the defence of duress as negating voluntariness:

> [T]he defence of duress, as a general defence available at common law which is sufficient to negative the criminal liability of a defendant against whom every ingredient of an offence has otherwise been proved, is difficult to rationalise or explain by reference to any coherent principle of jurisprudence. The theory that the party acting under duress is so far deprived of volition as to lack the necessary criminal intent has been clearly shown to be fallacious.

On the other hand, Lord Bridge's suggestion that the defence is otherwise difficult to explain or rationalise by reference to coherent principle need not be accepted. The defence of duress operates as a privilege. It does not negate intention but rather involves the recognition that when certain criteria are satisfied no duty will exist.

The conception of duress as a privilege is also consistent with the approach taken to the defence of necessity which, on any view, is at least closely related. In relation to necessity this can be seen from the decision in *Re F (Mental Patient: Sterilisation)*.[96] In the Court of Appeal, Neill LJ held that the performance of the operation would be lawful because it was in the public interest.[97] In the House of Lords it was held that the operation was lawful because of the defence of necessity. But Lord Griffiths suggested that there was no difference between these two formulations:[98]

> Whether one arrives at this conclusion by applying a principle of 'necessity' as do Lord Goff of Chieveley and Lord Brandon of Oakbrook or by saying that it is in the public interest as did Neill L.J. in the Court of Appeal, appear to me to be inextricably interrelated conceptual justifications for the humane development of the common law. Why is it necessary that the mentally incompetent should be given treatment to which they lack the capacity to consent? The answer must surely be because it is in the public interest that it should be so.

6. LABELLING OF DURESS: A 'DEFENCE', AN 'EXCUSE', A 'JUSTIFICATION' OR A 'PRIVILEGE'?

In criminal law, it is unclear how the defence of duress should properly be labelled. In *Lynch*, Lord Simon observed that a 'principal difficulty in this branch of the law is the chaotic terminology, whether in judgments, academic writings or statutes'.[99] This uncertainty would undoubtedly flow into the law of torts if duress were recognised as a tortious defence.

The uncertainty can be illustrated by Lord Bingham's remarks in *R v Z* that where the defence of duress is made out it does not ordinarily operate to negate any legal ingredient of the crime which the defendant has committed nor to justify the accused's conduct.[100] Rather, duress is properly regarded as a defence which, if

95 Above n 38, 436.
96 Above n 56.
97 (1989) 86 (10) LSG 42 (CA).
98 Above n 56, 69.
99 *DPP for Northern Ireland v Lynch* (n 40) 688.
100 Above n 39, 489.

raised and not disproved, excuses what would otherwise be criminal conduct.[101] Several issues flow from this analysis.

First, in what sense is duress a 'defence' if the onus of negating the 'defence' lies on the claimant? In particular, as James Goudkamp has observed, it is well recognised that the onus of proof is on a defendant to establish the facts which enliven a defence.[102]

There are two answers to this apparent conundrum. The first, in criminal law, lies in the difference between what are sometimes described as an 'evidentiary onus' and a 'substantive onus'. An evidentiary onus requires a defendant to show that, on the evidence in the case, there is an issue as to the matter in question which is fit for consideration by the tribunal of fact.[103] Once this is done, the substantive onus is sometimes placed upon the claimant to disprove the defence. In this sense, duress can be understood as a defence in precisely the terms in which it is identified by Goudkamp, that is, a 'liability defeating rule that is external to the elements of the claimant's cause of action'.[104] Of course, the concept of a 'defence' was never limited to this sense of 'confession and avoidance'. A defence has always included a plea by way of denial which, in most pleadings today, involves denial of some or all factual elements necessary for proof of a claim. Goudkamp would prefer to use the word 'denial' to describe this manner of responding to a claim in a defence plea.

The second answer is that a defence of duress in the civil law of torts need not involve the same onus as the defence in the criminal law. Indeed, this assertion is fortified by observing that the defence of self-defence in criminal law imposes an onus upon the prosecution but the onus in civil law lies upon the defendant.[105]

Second is the difficulty of describing duress as an excuse. Why should duress be said to operate as an 'excuse' rather than as a 'justification'? There are three difficulties with answering this question.

One difficulty is that as a matter of authority, cases use the two terms in different senses. Early uses of the terms contrasted 'justification' as an act which is 'permitted' and 'excuse' as an act which is 'without fault'. Examples of the latter in trespass were situations which are now almost universally regarded as involving a lack of the volitional requirement of the cause of action such as 'if a man takes my hand and strikes you'.[106]

As we explained above, in *R v Z* the language of excuse was used by Lord Bingham to describe the defence of duress. On other occasions duress was described as a justification. For instance, Stephen considered that '[i]t is just possible to imagine cases in which the expediency of breaking the law is so overwhelmingly great that people may be justified in breaking it'.[107] In the closely analogous cases of the necessity defence, the language of justification has also commonly been employed,

101 ibid; *DPP for Northern Ireland v Lynch* (n 40) 671, 680, 710–711.
102 Goudkamp (n 1) 12.
103 *Sheldrake v DPP* [2004] UKHL 43; [2005] 1 AC 264 [1] (Lord Bingham).
104 Goudkamp (n 1) 2.
105 *Ashley v Chief Constable of Sussex* [2008] UKHL 25; [2008] 1 AC 962 [24] (Lord Slynn).
106 *Weaver v Ward* (1616) Hob 134; 80 ER 284.
107 Stephen (n 28) 109.

as in *Re L*,[108] where Lord Goff held that the detention and treatment of a mentally disabled patient who posed a danger to himself was not a false imprisonment because it was justified by necessity. Lord Goff said that 'in so far as they might otherwise have constituted an invasion of his civil rights, [the actions] were justified on the basis of the common law doctrine of necessity'.[109]

It may be that the confusion in authority can be resolved through the approach taken in *Perka v The Queen*[110] by Dickson J who provided definitions of excuse and justification. There remains considerable controversy about the definition, but his Honour's approach probably represents the dominant usage in criminal law:

> Criminal theory recognizes a distinction between 'justifications' and 'excuses'. A 'justification' challenges the wrongfulness of an action which technically constitutes a crime. The police officer who shoots the hostage-taker, the innocent object of an assault who uses force to defend himself against his assailant, the Good Samaritan who commandeers a car and breaks the speed laws to rush an accident victim to the hospital, these are all actors whose actions we consider rightful, not wrongful. For such actions people are often praised, as motivated by some great or noble object. The concept of punishment often seems incompatible with the social approval bestowed on the doer.
>
> In contrast, an 'excuse' concedes the wrongfulness of the action but asserts that the circumstances under which it was done are such that it ought not to be attributed to the actor. The perpetrator who is incapable, owing to a disease of the mind, of appreciating the nature and consequences of his acts, the person who labours under a mistake of fact, the drunkard, the sleepwalker: these are all actors of whose 'criminal' actions we disapprove intensely, but whom, in appropriate circumstances, our law will not punish.

In *Perka*, Dickson J (with whom Ritchie, Chouinard and Lamer JJ concurred) concluded that the defence of necessity was an excuse, not a justification. Necessity was said to involve a utilitarian choice of one evil ahead of the greater evil that would result in complying with the law. In the words of Blackstone it involves a 'choice of two evils'. Dickson J explained that the reason why the defence did not involve a justification is because to do so would invite a court, contrary to the judicial function, to second-guess the legislature and to assess the relative merits of social policies underlying criminal prohibitions.[111] On the other hand, where an excuse is recognised, praise is not bestowed, only pardoned.

However, it is strongly arguable that defining necessity as an excuse, in the manner as did Dickson J, involves trespassing beyond the limits of judicial power. One might question how, in the context of a criminal law sentencing regime which generally permits a wide range of possible sentences (from spent convictions with no punishment to lengthy terms of imprisonment) is it legitimate for a judge, without statutory authority, to confer a 'judicial pardon' and conclude that although the offence has been committed the offender is not liable to be sentenced and will be deemed to be not guilty?

[108] [1999] 1 AC 458 (HL). Compare the case in the European Court of Human Rights: *HL v UK* (2005) 40 EHRR 32.

[109] [1999] 1 AC 458 (HL) 488–89.

[110] Above n 47, 246–47.

[111] ibid 248.

A further difficulty with the approach of Dickson J is that justification and excuse are differentiated on the basis that justified actions are those considered by the judge to be 'rightful' or subject to 'social approval'. In jurisdictions in which the relevant offence is a common law offence, there is an incongruity between, on the one hand, saying that the conduct amounts to an offence but, on the other hand, concluding that the offender is not guilty because the conduct would be approved socially. This difficulty is exacerbated in circumstances in which the offence is statutory. Further, how is 'social approval' to be assessed? One suggestion made by Goudkamp directs focus to the concept of 'reasonableness'.[112] But, as the High Court of Australia explained in *Taiapa v The Queen*,[113] quoting from Gleeson CJ,[114] '[r]easonableness is not designed to allow people to choose for themselves whether to obey the law'.

Finally, even if a consistent and coherent scheme for the definitions of excuse and justification could be established, it is likely that, as Goudkamp recognises, these concepts would not exhaust all defences in the law of torts.

In the case of duress, an alternative approach emerges, independent of the terminology of excuse and justification and yet still coherent. This approach is to understand the defence by reference to the jural relations recognised almost a century ago by Wesley Hohfeld.[115] In Hohfeld's well-accepted and understood terminology we could comprehend duress as a privilege or liberty. The defence of duress would involve releasing a defendant from a duty which would otherwise exist by reference to the same considerations of principle employed by the common law in determining the scope or extent of any duty.

The recognition of a privilege would mean that the conduct of the accused or defendant would not be treated as criminal or tortious. And the privilege would still be a defence in the sense in which Goudkamp defines a defence in that it would be external to the elements of the duty even if (as in the criminal law) the onus were upon the defendant to show that there is evidence to support the raising of the defence before the substantive onus is imposed.

We consider that if the defence of duress were to be recognised as a tortious defence then it ought to be regarded as a privilege. The language of justification and excuse, even if it is to be preserved in the criminal law, should be eschewed in the law of torts.

7. CONCLUSION

In *Re L*,[116] Lord Goff observed that '[i]t is perhaps surprising … that the significant role [the defence of necessity] has to play in the law of torts has come to be recognised at so late a stage in the development of our law'. This applies a fortiori to duress in the law of torts.

[112] Goudkamp (n 1) 86.
[113] Above n 63, [37].
[114] *R v Rogers* (1996) 86 A Crim R 542 (NSWCA) 547.
[115] WN Hohfeld, *Fundamental Legal Conceptions as Applied in Judicial Reasoning* (WW Cook (ed), New Haven, Yale University Press, 1964) 23–64.
[116] [1999] AC 458 (HL) 490. Compare the case when it reached the European Court of Human Rights: *HL v UK* (2005) 40 EHRR 32.

The purpose of this chapter has been to challenge the nearly unanimous approach in commentary over close to four centuries, which has denied the existence of duress as a defence to a tort. There were four strands to our argument: (1) the limited and questionable authority upon which the denial is based involving a single English case, contrary to United States authority, and decided on a demurred apparently without the benefit of argument; (2) analogy with the criminal law; (3) analogy and overlap with the recognised defence of necessity; and (4) a coherent theoretical foundation. Although we have sketched a possible theoretical foundation for the defence of duress, if it were to be recognised there would remain significant questions. Two of the larger are as follows: (1) should the conditions of the privilege be the same as the defence of duress in criminal law? (2) should the defence of duress be a privilege which is qualified upon payment of compensation by the defendant to the party against whom the tort is committed and if so, in what circumstances? This chapter has focused only on the question of recognition. The first necessary step would be to assess whether the arguments in favour of recognising the defence are sufficient for judges to change the direction of the course of the limited law and near unanimous commentary in this area over the last four centuries.

10

Nuisance, Planning and Regulation: The Limits of Statutory Authority

DONAL NOLAN*

1. INTRODUCTION

IN AN ARTICLE published in 1966, Allen Linden claimed that the importance of statutory authority as a defence to a nuisance action was 'on the wane', and that its future might be 'short-lived'.[1] But far from having withered away in the face of judicial opposition (as Linden predicted), the defence looks to be in good health. In Linden's native Canada, a period of uncertainty following the decision of a divided Supreme Court in *Tock v St John's Metropolitan Area Board*[2] was brought to a close by a reassertion of orthodoxy in *Ryan v Victoria (City)*,[3] and although the courts adopt a relatively restrictive approach to the defence, its future seems secure. As for the United Kingdom, in the leading case of *Allen v Gulf Oil Refining Ltd*,[4] the House of Lords rebuffed an attempt to limit the defence's operation by a narrow reading of the relevant private Act, and more recently Parliament has effected an unprecedented expansion of the scope of the defence by extending its protection to all 'nationally significant infrastructure projects' granted planning permission under the special procedures laid down in the Planning Act 2008 (UK).[5]

Indeed, far from statutory authority withering away, it will be argued in this chapter that if we let our guard down the de facto extension of the defence could threaten the continued vitality of private nuisance as a cause of action. I say 'de facto extension' because the danger comes not from the defence itself—which remains subject to tight restraints—but from potential developments in other areas of nuisance law which have in common the fact that they effectively mimic the operation of statutory authority, even though the justification for the operation of that defence is missing. These potential developments concern the relevance to a private nuisance claim

* I am grateful to Andrew Dyson for his helpful comments on an earlier draft. The usual caveat applies.

[1] AM Linden, 'Strict Liability, Nuisance and Legislative Authorization' (1966) 4 *Osgoode Hall Law Journal* 196, 220–21.

[2] [1989] 2 SCR 1181 (SCC).

[3] [1999] 1 SCR 201 (SCC).

[4] [1981] AC 1001 (HL).

[5] Planning Act 2008 (UK), s 158. This provision is innovative in that the scope of the defence is determined not by reference to the nature of the defendant's activity, but by reference to the procedure through which permission for the development in question is given.

of a grant of planning permission for the defendant's activity, and whether the law of private nuisance should recognise a defence of regulatory compliance.

Two preliminary points should be made. The first is that, as my formulation of these issues suggests, my concern is with private nuisance, not public nuisance. And while it is true that some of the relevant cases were litigated in public nuisance, generally the circumstances were such that private nuisance actions would also have lain. The second preliminary point is that we need to distinguish from the outset between two possible ways in which planning permission and regulatory compliance might affect the liability issue in a private nuisance case.[6] The first is that they are *dispositive*, meaning that they amount to self-contained reasons for rejecting a claim. This first possibility can be expressed in ordinary legal parlance by saying that the permission or compliance is operating as a 'defence' to the claim. The other possibility is that they are merely factors to be taken into account in determining whether the defendant's activity is substantially interfering with the claimant's use and enjoyment of his or her land. And the gist of this chapter is that, while there is nothing objectionable about factoring these considerations into the substantial interference inquiry, making them dispositive amounts in effect to an unjustified extension of the statutory authority idea. In order to substantiate that claim, I must begin by identifying the essential characteristics of the statutory authority defence itself.

2. THE ESSENCE OF STATUTORY AUTHORITY

Although it is frequently claimed that the statutory authority defence first developed in a series of nineteenth-century 'railway cases', beginning with *R v Pease*,[7] its origins can be traced back much further. As Kostal points out, '[f]or centuries before steam railways, common law protection of estates in land existed only at the sufferance of the sovereignty of Parliament',[8] and in Georgian England the promoters of toll bridges, turnpikes, docks and canals had frequently used private bill legislation to compel the sales of land necessary to bring their projects to fruition.[9] And if the 'coerced alienation of land ... was an indisputable feature of English law and public policy',[10] then it naturally followed that any common law land right, including the right to be free from substantial interference with the use and enjoyment of one's property, could be swept aside by Parliament if it so desired. For eighteenth-century judicial acknowledgement of this, one need look no further than *British Cast Plate Manufacturers v Meredith*,[11] where the defendants had partially obstructed the entrance to the claimant's property by raising the height of the street in front of

[6] For the possibility that these considerations might be taken into account at the remedial stage, see below, text following n 129.

[7] (1832) 4 B & Ad 30; 110 ER 366.

[8] RW Kostal, *Law and English Railway Capitalism 1825–1875* (Oxford, Clarendon Press 1994) 176.

[9] In the words of AWB Simpson, private Acts of Parliament were 'the typical enabling legal instrument of the agricultural and industrial revolution', and the mechanism through which 'the common law's enthusiasm for property rights' was reconciled with social and economic progress: AWB Simpson, *Victorian Law and the Industrial Spirit* (London, Selden Society, 1995) 22–23.

[10] Kostal (n 8) 176.

[11] (1792) 4 TR 794; 100 ER 1306.

it. The Court of King's Bench dismissed the claimant's action in nuisance on the grounds that the defendants had acted under the authority of a private Act for the paving of various streets in the area. According to Lord Kenyon CJ:[12]

> If this action could be maintained, every Turnpike Act, Paving Act, and Navigation Act, would give rise to an infinity of actions. If the legislature think it necessary, as they do in many cases, they enable the commissioners to award satisfaction to the individuals who happen to suffer; but if there be no such power, the parties are without remedy, provided the commissioners do not exceed their jurisdiction.

At the end of his short judgment, Lord Kenyon summed things up by saying that the legislation had given express power to the defendants to raise the pavement, and that no action could therefore lie for anything which they did within the scope of that power. Therein lies the essence of the statutory authority defence: that a nuisance claim will fail if the action which caused the interference with the claimant's use and enjoyment of their land was authorised by the legislature. The case law on the defence over the last two centuries should be seen as (for the most part) no more than the clarification of various ambiguities in this central notion of legislative authorisation, such as whether the authorisation of the defendant's action must be express, or can be implied;[13] whether the defendant's conduct is authorised where a nuisance arises out of the exercise of a statutory discretion;[14] and the extent to which authorisation extends to cases where the defendant is alleged to have interfered with the claimant's use and enjoyment more than was necessary in order to fulfil the objects of the legislation.[15] The current state of play on the reach of the defence was summarised by Lord Wilberforce in his opinion in *Allen v Gulf Oil*:[16]

> It is now well settled that where Parliament by express direction or by necessary implication has authorised the construction and use of an undertaking or works, that carries with it an authority to do what is authorised with immunity from any action based on nuisance … To this there is made the qualification, or condition, that the statutory powers are exercised without 'negligence', that word here being used in a special sense so as to require the undertaker, as a condition of obtaining immunity from action, to carry out the work and conduct the operation with all reasonable regard and care for the interests of other persons …

For present purposes, there are four particular features or aspects of the defence which we should note. The first is that the rationale of the defence is quite simply the sovereignty of Parliament. In the words of Lord Halsbury LC, '[t]he legislature is supreme, and if it has enacted that a thing is lawful, such a thing cannot be a fault or an actionable wrong'.[17] Of course, when Parliament legislates, we can presume that it does so in accordance with its perception of where the public interest

[12] ibid TR 796; ER 1307.
[13] See, eg, *Allen v Gulf Oil Refining Ltd* (n 4).
[14] See, eg, *Metropolitan Asylum District Managers v Hill* (1881) 6 App Cas 193 (HL).
[15] *Tate & Lyle v Greater London Council* [1983] 2 AC 509 (HL).
[16] Above n 4.
[17] *Canadian Pacific Rly Co v Roy* [1902] AC 220 (PC) 231. See also *Wheeler v JJ Saunders Ltd* [1996] Ch 19 (CA) 28 (Staughton LJ); A Beever, *The Law of Private Nuisance* (Oxford, Hart Publishing, 2013) 137.

lies, but it does not follow that statutory authority is a 'public interest' defence,[18] and characterising it as such obscures the point that the defence is grounded on the sovereignty of Parliament, *and nothing else*.[19] This is shown by the fact that even if we could be certain that a particular private Act was contrary to the public interest, actions authorised by that Act would still attract the protection of the defence. This explication of the rationale of the defence has clear implications for attempts to extend it de facto to administrative decisions which purport to be taken in the public interest but which lack the authority our legal system accords to a direct expression of legislative will.

The second point is that statutory authority is a judicial, as opposed to a statutory defence, since the authority for the proposition that statutory authorisation immunises the defendant from liability in nuisance comes from case law rather than legislation. Statutory authority should therefore be distinguished from instances whereby the legislature itself expressly bars actions in nuisance in certain types of case, as in the Ontario legislation which lays down that municipalities cannot be sued in nuisance in connection with escaping water or sewage.[20] Statutory immunities of the latter kind are generally distinguishable from the statutory authority defence not only by virtue of their legislative origin, but also because they provide the defendant with a complete immunity, and are not hedged about with the restrictions applicable to the common law defence.[21] Having said that, the legislature is of course free to incorporate similar restrictions if it so wishes, and this technique has been employed by various Canadian provincial legislatures, which have, for example, immunised farms from nuisance liability provided they operate in accordance with generally accepted agricultural practices, and do not threaten public health and safety, and protected businesses more generally from liability for odour nuisances unless they fail to comply with zoning legislation or regulatory norms.[22] Another noteworthy technique used in Canada is legislation which forbids the court from issuing an injunction in certain types of nuisance cases, while not impinging on the right to recover damages.[23] Again, the availability of these legislative techniques must be borne in mind when evaluating de facto judicial extensions of the statutory authority defence.

[18] Cf *Allen v Gulf Oil Refining Ltd* (n 4) 1023 (Lord Roskill) ('[t]he underlying philosophy' of the defence is that 'the lesser private right must yield to the greater public interest'); K Barker et al, *The Law of Torts in Australia*, 5th edn (Melbourne, Oxford University Press, 2012) 203 ('A plea of statutory authorisation is in substance a plea of public interest').

[19] For a similar argument, see Beever (n 17) 138.

[20] Municipal Act 2001, SO 2001, c 25. In the United Kingdom, immunities of this kind are usually found in statutes establishing regimes of strict liability for damage caused by a particular activity: see, eg, Civil Aviation Act 1982 (UK), ss 76(1), 77(2); Merchant Shipping Act 1995 (UK), s 156.

[21] That this is a significant difference is shown by the controversy surrounding the passage of s 158 of the Planning Act 2008 (UK). The provision as originally drafted would have conferred complete immunity from suit in nuisance on the developers and operators of nationally significant infrastructure projects, but following a vociferous campaign by various interest groups the clause was redrafted so as merely to confer on their activities the more limited protection afforded by the common law statutory authority defence. See further, F Moor, 'Planning for Nuisance?' (2011) 3 *International Journal of Law in the Built Environment* 65, 69–71.

[22] AM Linden and B Feldthusen, *Canadian Tort Law*, 9th edn (Toronto, LexisNexis, 2011) 600–01.

[23] For examples, see E Brubaker, *Property Rights in the Defence of Nature* (London, Earthscan, 1995) 103–04.

The third point worth highlighting about statutory authority is that the courts have generally taken a restrictive approach to the defence. As Major J said (speaking for the Supreme Court of Canada) in *Ryan v Victoria (City)*, '[s]tatutory authority provides, at best, a narrow defence to nuisance'.[24] This restrictive approach is an application of the principle that legislation limiting common law rights is subject to strict construction, so that the presumption that the legislature does not intend to interfere with individual rights is rebutted only by the manifestation of a clear intention to the contrary.[25] Linden showed in his 1966 article that a range of judicial techniques have been employed to limit the scope of the defence,[26] and even if we might now question his claim that the use of these techniques reflects judicial antipathy to the statutory authorisation concept, there is no denying that the tenor of the case law is that the courts will not lightly hold common law rights to have been abrogated by legislative action. This is obviously a significant consideration when evaluating de facto extensions of the defence.

And the final point which should be made is that the application of the statutory authority defence is often, though not invariably, accompanied by legislative provision of compensation for those worst affected by the authorised activity. Hence, for example, under the Land Compensation Act 1973 (UK) there is a general right to compensation for a depreciation of the value of land caused by 'physical factors' (including noise, smell, vibration, fumes and smoke) incident upon the operation of public works where common law rights of action have been removed by statutory authorisation.[27] Furthermore, the wide range of major infrastructure projects on which statutory authority is conferred by the Planning Act 2008 (UK) are to be treated as 'public works' for the purposes of the 1973 Act,[28] while the 2008 Act itself lays down that compensation must be paid to anyone whose land is 'injuriously affected' by the construction of the infrastructure projects in question.[29] The widespread availability of compensation in genuine cases of legislative authorisation must be borne in mind when considering de facto extensions of the defence which are inevitably unaccompanied by such provision.

3. THE RELEVANCE OF PLANNING PERMISSION

3.1 The Case Law on Nuisance and Planning Permission

Although it is sometimes now said to be surprising that the relationship between planning permission and the law of nuisance was not the subject of judicial consideration until the early 1990s, it seems that this was because before then it was

[24] *Ryan v Victoria (City)* (n 3) [54].

[25] See *Benning v Wong* (1969) 122 CLR 249 (HCA) 256 (Barwick CJ); *Allen v Gulf Oil Refining Ltd* (n 4) 1020 (Lord Keith); *Tock v St John's Metropolitan Area Board* (n 2) 1226 (Sopinka J); *British Waterways Board v Severn Trent Water Ltd* [2001] EWCA Civ 276; [2002] Ch 25 [36] (Peter Gibson LJ); PW Hogg et al, *Liability of the Crown*, 4th edn (Toronto, Carswell, 2011) 193–94.

[26] Linden (n 1) 202–07.

[27] See further K Davies, *Law of Compulsory Purchase and Compensation*, 5th edn (Croydon, Tolley, 1994) ch 9.

[28] Planning Act 2008 (UK), s 152(7).

[29] ibid s 152(3).

simply assumed that 'private rights to claim in nuisance were unaffected by the permissive grant of planning permission',[30] so that it was not really thought that there was any relationship between the two at all.[31] In *Tetley v Chitty*,[32] for example, where liability was imposed for noise generated by a go-kart track situated close to a residential neighbourhood, the fact that planning permission had been granted for the track was only mentioned in passing, in the course of the description of the factual background, and there was no suggestion that it had any bearing on the action. Similarly, in the Court of Appeal in *Allen v Gulf Oil Refining Ltd*, Lord Denning MR said that although planning permission had been obtained for the defendant's oil refinery, that could not exempt it from liability in nuisance,[33] and no mention was made of the planning permission in the House of Lords, where the opinions dealt only with the question of whether the private Act authorising the construction of the refinery implicitly authorised its operation as well. Likewise, in a planning case decided in 1990, Simon Brown J made it clear that planning permissions obtained by two companies engaged in noxious trades conferred on them 'no right to commit nuisances against their neighbours either now or in the future'.[34]

Everything changed three years later, with a first instance decision in a public nuisance case, *Gillingham BC v Medway (Chatham) Dock Co*.[35] Following the closure of the Chatham Royal Naval dockyard in 1982, the claimant council—anxious to create alternative employment for local residents—had granted the defendants planning permission to operate part of the site as a commercial port complex, in the full knowledge that this would result in round-the-clock heavy goods traffic through a residential area close to the port. Five years later, the council's priorities having changed, it brought proceedings against the defendants in public nuisance, seeking a declaration that the traffic amounted to a public nuisance and an injunction limiting it to daytime hours. The defendants argued (inter alia) that in the light of the grant of planning permission, the court should refuse the relief sought. In response to this argument, Buckley J said that while planning permission was not 'a licence to commit nuisance',[36] nevertheless 'where planning consent is given for a development or change of use, the question of nuisance will thereafter fall to be decided by reference to a neighbourhood with that development or use and not as it was previously'.[37] And since he took the view that the noise from the lorries was not excessive in an area containing a commercial port complex which operated round-the-clock, the action failed.

[30] *Wheeler v JJ Saunders Ltd* (n 17) 35 (Peter Gibson LJ).

[31] There are early North American authorities denying that compliance with planning or regulatory laws entitled a defendant to rely on the defence of statutory authority, or was otherwise conclusive against liability in nuisance. See, eg, *Beamish v Glenn* (1916) 28 DLR 702 (Ont SC) (permission of a municipal authority to build a blacksmith's shop did not authorise the owner to commit a nuisance); *Price v Grose* 133 NE 30 (Ind App Ct, 1921) (license from state veterinarian to build and operate a fertiliser plant conferred no immunity in nuisance); and *Rockenbach v Apostle* 47 NE 2d 636 (Mich, 1951) (city zoning ordinance permitting funeral home in residential district 'permissive only', and not a defence to a nuisance claim).

[32] [1986] 1 All ER 663 (QB).

[33] *Allen v Gulf Oil Refining Ltd* [1980] QB 156 (CA) 168.

[34] *R v Exeter CC, ex p JL Thomas & Co* [1991] 1 QB 471 (QB) 481 (Simon Brown J).

[35] [1993] QB 343 (QB).

[36] ibid 359.

[37] ibid 361

We should immediately note that the claim in *Gillingham* was weak on the merits, since it appears that the council brought public nuisance proceedings in order to avoid having to pay the compensation the defendants would have been entitled to if the council had instead revoked the planning permission or altered it so as effectively to limit the operating hours of the port.[38] Furthermore, since the council still had this option if the public nuisance proceedings were dismissed, Buckley J's ruling simply put the ball back in the council's court, as it would have to decide whether the interests of the local residents in the quiet enjoyment of their properties justified the cost of compensating the defendants for the commercial consequences of its change of heart.[39]

Nevertheless, the genie was now out of the bottle, and in *Wheeler v JJ Saunders Ltd*[40] a sceptical Court of Appeal missed the opportunity to put it back in when it chose to distinguish *Gillingham* instead of overruling it. *Wheeler* was a run-of-the-mill private nuisance case concerning the smell generated by two pig housing units situated close to a residential property. The defendants relied on the *Gillingham* decision for the proposition that since they had obtained planning permission for the two units, the smell that emanated from them was incapable of constituting a nuisance. In response to this argument the Court of Appeal did not rule out the possibility that a grant of planning permission could alter the character of an area such that what would previously have amounted to a nuisance no longer did, but held that the planning consent in the instant case had not changed the locality, and hence was irrelevant to the question of whether the odour was actionable. Staughton LJ apparently distinguished the *Gillingham* case on the grounds that it involved a 'strategic planning decision affected by considerations of public interest',[41] while Peter Gibson LJ said that, even if *Gillingham* was rightly decided, it meant only that planning permission might be relevant in the case of a 'major development ... with wide consequential effects such as required a balancing of competing public and private interests before permission was granted', and that even still this might be relevant only to the availability of an injunction rather than liability.[42]

Following *Wheeler*, it seemed generally to be accepted as a matter of authority that while planning consent for the defendant's activity would not necessarily affect the actionability of any interference it caused, it was capable of doing so via the locality principle (according to which the character of the neighbourhood is a relevant consideration when determining whether an interference with amenity interests is actionable in nuisance). In his dissenting opinion in *Hunter v Canary Wharf Ltd*,[43] for example, Lord Cooke endorsed the *Gillingham* principle that a planning consent could alter the character of the area for the purposes of the locality rule, and held that it applied on the facts, with the result that the interference in question was not actionable.[44] At the same time, however, the practical application of the

[38] See ibid 361 (Buckley J).
[39] ibid 364.
[40] *Wheeler v JJ Saunders Ltd* (n 17).
[41] ibid 30.
[42] ibid 35.
[43] [1997] AC 655 (HL).
[44] ibid 722. The issue did not arise for the majority of the House of Lords, although Lord Hoffmann said that in his view it would be 'wrong to allow the private rights of third parties to be taken away by a permission granted by the planning authority to the developer' (ibid 710).

Gillingham principle gave rise to some difficulties, which were illustrated by two conflicting decisions of the Court of Appeal concerning noise generated by motor sports. In the first case, *Watson v Croft Promosport Ltd*,[45] the Court held that the grant of planning permission for the use of land as a motor circuit had not altered the character of an essentially rural area, while in the second, *Lawrence v Fen Tigers Ltd*,[46] it held that the various planning permissions given for the defendant's motor sports complex meant that the noise from the complex was an established part of the character of the locality, so that a nuisance action in respect of it failed. One additional point which emerged from those two decisions was that it was only the *implementation* of the planning permission which was capable of changing the character of the locality.[47] This was a helpful (and logical) clarification of the *Gillingham* principle, which as originally expressed seemed to suggest that the grant of the permission could itself have this effect.

An appeal from the ruling of the Court of Appeal in *Lawrence* was recently heard by the Supreme Court. The judgments in *Coventry v Lawrence*[48] for the most part reject the *Gillingham* principle and the idea that a grant of planning permission is dispositive against liability in a private nuisance case. According to Lord Neuberger:[49]

> [T]he mere fact that the activity which is said to give rise to the nuisance has the benefit of a planning permission is normally of no assistance to the defendant in a claim brought by a neighbour who contends that the activity causes a nuisance to her land in the form of noise or other loss of amenity.

It followed that much of the reasoning in *Gillingham* could not stand.[50] Lord Mance expressed his agreement with Lord Neuberger's analysis of the planning permission issue,[51] and Lord Sumption agreed that the existence of planning permission for a given use was 'of very limited relevance' to the question of whether that use amounted to a private nuisance.[52] Unfortunately, Lord Carnwath muddied the waters somewhat by expressing his support for the approach taken by both Buckley J in *Gillingham* and Lord Cooke in *Hunter*. This was on the basis that:[53]

> [I]n exceptional cases a planning permission may be the result of a considered policy decision by the competent authority leading to a fundamental change in the pattern of uses, which cannot sensibly be ignored in assessing the character of the area against which the acceptability of the defendant's activity is to be judged.

According to Lord Carnwath, the development projects in *Gillingham* and *Hunter* had been exceptional in both their scale and the nature of the planning judgments

45 [2009] EWCA Civ 15; [2009] 3 All ER 249.
46 [2012] EWCA Civ 26; [2012] 1 WLR 2127.
47 See *Watson v Croft Promosport Ltd* [2009] EWCA Civ 15; [2009] 3 All ER 249 [32] (Sir Andrew Morritt C); *Lawrence v Fen Tigers Ltd* (ibid) [65] (Jackson LJ).
48 [2014] UKSC 13; [2014] AC 822.
49 ibid [94].
50 ibid [99].
51 ibid [165].
52 ibid [156].
53 ibid [223].

which led to their approval, whereas in neither *Wheeler* nor *Watson* had the relevant permissions resulted in 'a significant change in the pattern of uses in the area, let alone one which could be regarded as strategic'.[54] While it seems highly probable that Lord Neuberger's approach to the planning permission issue will now be followed, it is noteworthy that the *Gillingham* principle garnered support from a Justice with particular expertise in the field of planning and environmental law.

3.2 Planning Permission, the Locality Principle and Statutory Authority

At this point the reader may be forgiven for asking what any of this has to do with statutory authority. After all, judicial discussions of the relevance of planning permission generally start off with a statement to the effect that planning permission is not equivalent to statutory authorisation, since (unlike Parliament) a planning authority does not have the power to authorise a nuisance, and compliance with planning regulations is not a defence to a nuisance claim.[55] The truth is, however, that in amenity nuisance cases where the implementation of planning permission is deemed to have changed the nature of the locality, the planning consent has the same effect as the statutory authorisation of the defendant's activity, so that the *Gillingham* principle amounted to a de facto extension of the statutory authority defence beyond direct expressions of legislative will, as Peter Gibson LJ recognised in his perceptive judgment in the *Wheeler* case:[56]

> If planning permission cannot license a nuisance, then there is a distinction, in theory, between such permission and direct statutory authority ... But the practical effect of such permission and of direct statutory authority would be the same on Buckley J's approach [in *Gillingham*]. In either case immunity from suit in nuisance is conferred on any activity which is the inevitable result of the authorised development and use.

To understand why this is so, we need to begin with the point that when the courts assess the nature of a particular neighbourhood for the purposes of applying the locality principle, they generally take no account of the activity which is alleged to be causing the nuisance, so that, for example, if an action were brought in respect of the noise and traffic generated by a football stadium situated in an otherwise residential area, the locality would be characterised as residential.[57] What the

[54] ibid.

[55] See *Gillingham BC v Medway (Chatham) Dock Co* (n 35) 359 (Buckley J); *Wheeler v JJ Saunders Ltd* (n 17) 37 (Sir John May); *Hunter v Canary Wharf Ltd* (n 43) 721 (Lord Cooke); *Lawrence v Fen Tigers Ltd* (n 46) [65] (Jackson LJ).

[56] *Wheeler v JJ Saunders Ltd* (n 17) 34–35. See also *Coventry v Lawrence* (n 48) [87] (Lord Neuberger); and C Crawford, 'Public Law Rules Over Private Law as a Standard for Nuisance: OK?' (1992) 4 *Journal of Environmental Law* 264, 271.

[57] Although Lord Neuberger argues in *Coventry v Lawrence* (n 48) that prima facie the defendant's activities *are* to be taken into account when assessing the character of the locality, his reasoning is unpersuasive. The statement which he cites in support of this view from *St Helen's Smelting Co v Tipping* (1865) 11 HL Cas 642; 11 ER 1483 reads as no more than an expression of the locality principle itself. Furthermore, the qualification which he adds (at [65]) that 'to the extent that [the defendant's] activities are a nuisance to the claimant, they should be left out of account when assessing the character of the locality' is difficult to understand, since the character of the neighbourhood is being assessed precisely because it may determine whether or not the defendant's activity *is* a nuisance to the claimant. Lord

Gillingham principle did was to create an exception to this rule in cases where planning permission had been granted for the defendant's activity, so that if the development for which permission had been given was on a large enough scale to change the character of the neighbourhood, then the locality was reclassified accordingly. Hence if planning permission had been granted for the football stadium in our example, the locality would be classified as (in effect) a residential area with a football stadium. And although this might seem fairly innocuous, what it actually meant was that—with the exception of physical damage cases, where the locality is irrelevant[58]—immunity was conferred on the defendant's activity provided that (as with statutory authority) all reasonable care was taken to minimise the interference it caused. After all, in the light of the locality principle, a well-run football stadium can hardly amount to a nuisance in a neighbourhood defined as a residential area containing a football stadium.[59] The end result was that, by redefining the nature of the locality, an activity which would otherwise be tortious had made itself lawful.[60]

The characterisation of the *Gillingham* principle as a de facto extension of the statutory authority defence is borne out by the reasoning in the case itself. According to Buckley J, that defence was based on the presumption that Parliament had decided that any inevitable adverse side effects of the defendant's activity were outweighed by its benefits, and the same principle 'should be utilized in respect of planning permission', since Parliament had 'set up a statutory framework and delegated the task of balancing the interests of the community against those of individuals and of holding the scales between individuals to the local planning authority'.[61] Furthermore, when considering whether the heavy goods traffic into the port amounted to a nuisance in the locality changed by the planning permission for the port, Buckley J drew a direct analogy with the rule in the statutory authority context that immunity attaches only to nuisances which are the inevitable result of the authorised activity.[62] Similarly, in the Court of Appeal in *Lawrence*, where the grant of planning permission also proved decisive, the fact that the motor sports complex had been operated in compliance with the conditions attached to the grant of planning permission effectively doomed the claim to failure.[63] The upshot was that in the amenity nuisance cases where the *Gillingham* principle had purchase,

Neuberger accepts that the circularity involved in his reasoning is problematic, but dismisses the possibility that the defendant's activity should simply be ignored—the proposition argued for here—on the grounds that while it might 'often be the simplest and fairest way of dealing with the issue', in some cases it could be unfair on the defendant (at [72]). Quite why it could be unfair is not, however, made clear. The treatment of this point in Lord Carnwath's judgment is also problematic, and relies on aspects of certain decisions—such as those in *Kennaway v Thompson* [1981] QB 88 (CA) and *Watson v Croft Promosport Ltd* [2009] EWCA Civ 15; [2009] 3 All ER 249—which are readily explicable on other grounds: see K Oliphant (ed), *The Law of Tort*, 2nd edn (London, LexisNexis Butterworths, 2007) [22.101].

58 *St Helen's Smelting Co v Tipping* (ibid).

59 As Lord Neuberger put it in *Coventry v Lawrence* (n 48): '[i]f the matters complained of by the claimant are part of the character of the locality, then it is hard to see how they could be unacceptable by a standard which is to be assessed by reference to that very character' (at [73]).

60 See D McGillivray and J Wightman, 'Private Rights, Public Interests and the Environment' in T Hayward and J O'Neill (eds), *Justice, Property and the Environment* (Aldershot, Ashgate, 1997) 151. See also S Tromans, 'Nuisance and Planning Control' (1995) 54 *CLJ* 494, 495–96 ('the argument tries to pull itself up by its own bootstraps').

61 *Gillingham BC v Medway (Chatham) Dock Co* (n 35) 359.

62 ibid 360.

63 See in particular *Lawrence v Fen Tigers Ltd* (n 46) [79] (Jackson LJ).

planning permission had precisely the same impact as statutory authorisation. As McGillivray and Wightman have pointed out, as long as locality is treated as a matter of fact (which the courts have said that it is):[64]

> [T]he locality rule is not a coherent way of reflecting any special significance attaching to planning permissions short of the established approach to statutory authority. There does not seem to be any half way house: permissions either intrinsically legitimate an interference, or have no special weight at all in the decision on whether the interference is an actionable nuisance.[65]

3.3 Should Planning Permission ever be a Defence to a Nuisance Action?

Turning to the question of whether the de facto extension of statutory authority to at least some grants of planning permission is defensible, we might begin by noting that the fact that the courts have routinely denied that planning permission *is* in fact equivalent to statutory authority suggests that the judiciary themselves are not persuaded of the case for the extension. In any case, the argument for such an extension was perhaps best put by counsel for the defendant in *Watson v Croft Promosport* (as summarised by Sir Andrew Morritt C):[66]

> Counsel for the defendant emphasised the inconvenience which may result if the outcome of a statutory process such as that which governs whether any particular development should be permitted from a public perspective is to be revisited in a private law tort claim. He stressed that in this case [the planning permission] was granted after an exhaustive consideration of the consequences of the noise which would be generated by the developments for which permission was then sought.

The central objections to this argument, and the gist of the case against treating the granting of planning permission as a defence to a private nuisance, relate to the nature and purpose of planning permission, coupled with the argument that the justification for allowing direct expressions of legislative will to abrogate private rights does not extend to administrative decisions of the kind involved in the planning process.

The first relevant point to note about planning permission is that it is merely permissive, so that (as James Penner points out) a grant of planning permission 'should not be regarded in general as a manifestation of the wish of any authority':[67]

> [P]lanning control in England, in respect of the vast majority of grants of permission, is essentially negative. The landowner or occupier submits an application for development permission entirely for private reasons. Planning authorities determine the development of an area not by proposing developments, but by the power to prohibit particular developments.

[64] See, eg, ibid [65] (Jackson LJ); *Coventry v Lawrence* (n 48) [63] (Lord Neuberger).
[65] McGillivray and Wightman (n 60) 152.
[66] Above n 45, [30].
[67] JE Penner, 'Nuisance and the Character of the Neighbourhood' (1993) 5 *Journal of Environmental Law* 1, 24–25.

The essentially negative nature of planning permission is shown by the fact that a planning authority may grant two conflicting permissions for the same land. In such a case, the authority is clearly not *endorsing* the developments, but merely indicating that it *does not object to* them.

The second relevant point about the nature of planning permission is that Buckley J's characterisation of the planning process in *Gillingham* was inaccurate, since it is generally accepted by planning theorists, policymakers and the courts that planning authorities are concerned with what Lord Sumption described in the *Coventry* case as 'the public interest in development and land use, as … defined in the planning legislation and any relevant development plans and policies',[68] and are not expected to balance any competing private interests. In *Buxton v Minister of Housing and Local Government*, for example, Salmon J said that the purpose of planning legislation was 'to restrict development for the benefit of the public at large',[69] and a leading lawyer in the field has argued that 'the planning system, unlike the law of nuisance, is not there to adjudicate between the competing interests of neighbours'.[70] To similar effect is a leading decision on planning law, where the House of Lords characterised planning matters as administrative, rather than judicial or quasi-judicial in nature, in the sense that the decision-maker is determining what the public interest requires, as opposed to 'deciding between the rights or interests of particular persons'.[71] Of course, planners must take account of the interests of individuals who will be affected by a proposed development, but they do so only insofar as their interests bear on the question of where the public interest as a whole lies.[72]

It follows from these two characteristics of planning permission that to allow the grant of such permission to operate as a defence to a nuisance action, is to hold that an administrative decision that a proposed development is not detrimental to the public interest deprives third parties of their right not to have their use and enjoyment of their land substantially interfered with by that development. To see just how surprising and incongruous this conclusion is, recall that it is nuisance law orthodoxy that no matter how great the public interest in the defendant's activity continuing, it does not amount to a defence to a nuisance action, but *at most* provides a justification for refusing an injunction and awarding damages in lieu.[73] Furthermore, this de facto extension of the statutory authority defence is not justified by the underlying rationale of that defence, which we have seen is not the inference that the authorised activity is in the public interest, but the supremacy of

[68] *Coventry v Lawrence* (n 48) [156].

[69] [1961] 1 QB 278 (QB) 283. See also *Wheeler v JJ Saunders Ltd* (n 17) 37 (Sir John May); *R (Alconbury Developments Ltd) v Secretary of State for the Environment, Transport and the Regions* [2001] UKHL 23; [2003] 2 AC 295 [69] (Lord Hoffmann); *Lawrence v Fen Tigers Ltd* (n 46) [53] (Jackson LJ) ('the planning system exists to protect the public interest, not to protect private interests'); *Coventry v Lawrence* (n 48) [89] (Lord Neuberger), [193] (Lord Carnwath).

[70] S Tromans, 'Planning and Environmental Law: Uneasy Bedfellows?' [2012] *Journal of Planning and Environment Law* OP73, OP101.

[71] *R (Alconbury Developments Ltd) v Secretary of State for the Environment, Transport and the Regions* (n 69) [74] (Lord Hoffmann). See also at [139] (Lord Clyde).

[72] *Stringer v Minister of Housing and Local Government* [1970] 1 WLR 1281 (QB) 1295 (Cooke J). See also *Coventry v Lawrence* (n 48) [95] (Lord Neuberger).

[73] See, eg, *Miller v Jackson* [1977] QB 966 (CA); *Kennaway v Thompson* (n 57); *Dennis v Ministry of Defence* [2003] EWHC 793 (QB); [2003] Env LR 34; *Antrim Truck Centre Ltd v Ontario (Transportation)* [2013] SCC 13; [2013] 1 SCR 594. For details, see Oliphant (n 57) [22.51].

Parliament. Needless to say, the decision of a planning authority does not carry the same weight in our legal system as a direct expression of legislative will, even if it could be construed (as a grant of planning permission cannot) as an expression of the authority's wish that the development should proceed.

A further, connected, objection to planning permission operating as a de facto defence to a nuisance action is that third parties have very limited standing in the planning process. They are of course entitled to make representations to the planning authority about a proposed development, but since no appeal lies from a grant of planning permission,[74] the only way for a third party to challenge a decision of a planning authority is by way of judicial review, which does not amount to a full merits review, and is subject to short time limits. By contrast, the Parliamentary procedures governing the private legislation on which the statutory authority defence is usually grounded accord those most likely to be affected by the legislation the right to be informed of it and standing to petition Parliament against it.[75] The central case against extending statutory authority to grants of planning permission was summed up by Peter Gibson LJ in *Wheeler v Saunders*, when he said that the courts should 'be slow to acquiesce in the extinction of private rights without compensation as a result of administrative decisions which cannot be appealed and are difficult to challenge'.[76]

Two further points should be made. The first is that these fundamental objections to the de facto recognition of planning permission as a defence to a nuisance action cannot be overcome by arguing—as both Maria Lee and Allan Beever have done—that whether planning permission should be allowed to mimic statutory authority ought to depend on close scrutiny of the process by which the planning decision was reached. In the light of the analysis here, it is difficult to see any merit in Lee's proposal that 'who and what created the authority of this decision in the planning system will help to work out its authority in private law',[77] while Beever's suggestion that the defence of statutory authority should be extended to grants of planning permission only if the planning authority took into account the claimant's private rights[78] betrays a lack of understanding of the planning process, which we have seen is solely concerned with whether the proposed development is contrary to the public interest as reflected in current planning policy. Quite apart from which, it is questionable how practicable it is for a judge to be required to enquire into matters such as 'the ways in which interests were weighed' in the planning process[79] when determining a private nuisance action.

And the second point is that, in addition to the more fundamental objections to allowing planning permission to operate as a potential defence to a nuisance action,

[74] See the Town and Country Planning Act 1990 (UK), s 78.

[75] House of Commons Information Office Factsheet L4, 'Private Bills' (2010) www.parliament.uk/documents/commons-information-office/l04.pdf, accessed 2 March 2014. It has been said of the passage and implementation of private bill legislation in the Victorian era that it 'was the product of an elaborate process of negotiation and compromise' (Simpson (n 9) 22).

[76] *Wheeler v JJ Saunders Ltd* (n 17) 35.

[77] M Lee, 'Tort Law and Regulation: Planning and Nuisance' [2011] *Journal of Planning and Environment Law* 986, 987.

[78] Beever (n 17) 140–41.

[79] Lee (n 77) 989.

a number of further arguments can be made against such a development. First, the criteria which the courts used to determine whether the grant and subsequent implementation of planning permission had altered the nature of the locality were woolly and incoherent. What made a planning decision 'strategic' or 'major' for these purposes was far from clear,[80] and in any case it was hard to see why the relevance of planning permission for the nuisance analysis should depend on the size of the development for which permission had been given.[81] As for whether the planning decision was made on the basis of 'considerations of public interest', we have seen that in theory this is true of *all* planning decisions. More generally, it was unsatisfactory for some planning permissions to be capable of changing the character of a locality and others not, since it meant that neither claimants nor defendants would know where they stood, and nor would a planning authority know when it granted permission whether it was affecting private rights.[82] Second, as Sir John May pointed out in *Wheeler*, if planning permission could operate as a defence in nuisance, then it could in theory also authorise a trespass, and yet it is a well-established rule that where a development for which planning consent has been given requires, for example, an electricity cable to pass over a neighbouring property, the permission itself is not enough, and the usual procedures for obtaining a way-leave must be followed.[83] Third, any pragmatic argument for allowing planning permission to operate as a defence to a nuisance claim has been undercut by the extension of statutory authority to all nationally significant infrastructure projects in the Planning Act 2008 (UK), not least because developments which have the effect of changing the character of the locality for the purposes of the nuisance analysis are the most likely to benefit from that extension.[84] And finally, making planning decisions determinative in private law proceedings for nuisance may have detrimental consequences for the planning process itself. It might, for example, make it difficult to resist demands for third party appeals in planning cases, while the knowledge that their decisions could cut down private rights may mean that planning authorities can no longer make those decisions on public interest grounds alone, but are required to factor the impact of the proposed development on existing rights into their assessment of the merits of the application.

4. A DEFENCE OF REGULATORY COMPLIANCE?

A not dissimilar issue to the planning permission question is the relevance to nuisance law of the fact that the defendant's activity is subject to regulatory control, and is being carried out in compliance with the applicable regulatory regime. Does and should such compliance amount to a defence to a nuisance action, with the

[80] See *Coventry v Lawrence* (n 48) [91] (Lord Neuberger) ('a recipe for uncertainty').
[81] ibid [87] (Lord Neuberger).
[82] Tromans (n 60) 495.
[83] *Wheeler v JJ Saunders Ltd* (n 17) 38.
[84] The development in the *Gillingham* case, for example, would probably have met the criteria for a nationally significant infrastructure project laid down in the Act: see P Bishop and V Jenkins, 'Planning and Nuisance: Revisiting the Balance of Public and Private Interests in Land-Use Development' (2011) 23 *Journal of Environmental Law* 285, 298.

result that (as the authors of an Australian textbook claim) where 'a statutory scheme allocates power and responsibility to a public body to address environmental risk ... the general rule is that it is these schemes that must be looked to for a possible remedy',[85] and not the common law of nuisance? If the answer is affirmative, then again this would seem to amount in effect to a significant extension of the statutory authority defence.

Common law nuisance and statutory regulation have operated side by side since Parliament first demonstrated a commitment to the latter as a means of environmental protection in the second half of the nineteenth century, and until recently their relationship was essentially one of peaceful co-existence. According to Ben Pontin, in the late Victorian era, '[n]uisance law and regulatory law ... enjoyed an essentially pluralist relationship in which each was equally important in complementary ways'.[86] In particular, common law nuisance was perceived as protecting those with interests in land affected by pollution (and who could afford to go to law), while statutory regulation was seen as the means through which minimum standards of pollution control were enforced for the benefit of the public as a whole.[87] Pontin's analysis is borne out by the events surrounding the passage of one of the cornerstones of Victorian environmental protection legislation, the Rivers Pollution Prevention Act 1876.[88] During the committee stage of the Bill in the House of Commons, pressure from parties with an interest in the discharge of waste effluent into rivers resulted in the adoption of an amendment which would have precluded a court from granting injunctive relief in a nuisance action where the polluter of a river had obtained a certificate under the legislation to the effect that at all material times he was using best practicable means to minimise the pollution and its consequences. This proposed erosion of common law remedies proved highly controversial, however, and the amended clause was replaced with a watered-down provision (section 16 of the Act) which required only that a common law court take into account such a certificate in any nuisance proceedings before it. And when reforms to the regulatory regime governing river pollution were enacted between the 1950s and the 1970s, further attempts to subjugate common law nuisance to statutory regulation consistently foundered on the rocks of Parliamentary opposition, with the result that riparian rights continued to co-exist alongside regulatory law without limitation.[89] As Pontin points out, in this context Parliament could hardly have been more categorical in its rejection of a regulatory compliance defence.[90]

Despite Parliament's forthright defence of common law rights in the river pollution context, the pluralistic conception of the relationship between statutory regulation and common law nuisance has recently come under attack in the courts, and while it seems that the line has just about held, the battle may not yet be over. The first skirmishes in the conflict can be traced to two unreported decisions from

[85] Barker et al (n 18) 185.

[86] B Pontin, 'Nuisance Law and the Industrial Revolution' (2012) 75 *MLR* 1010, 1034.

[87] ibid 1034–35 (citing the annual reports of the first Chief Inspector of the Alkali Inspectorate and the evidence of the draftsman of the Rivers Pollution Prevention Act 1876).

[88] See B Pontin, 'Defending "Fundamental" Common Law Riparian Rights from Proposed Regulatory Law Limitations: Lessons from Parliamentary History' (2006) 17 *Water Law* 3, 7.

[89] ibid 7–12.

[90] ibid 12.

the 1990s in which county court judges took diametrically opposed views on the question. In the first case, *Cook v South West Water plc*,[91] nuisance liability was imposed in respect of an interference with riparian rights caused by pollutants discharged from a nearby sewage works, and the fact that the defendant had at all times complied with the terms of a discharge consent issued under the relevant regulatory regime was considered irrelevant. Conversely, in *Hughes v Welsh Water plc*,[92] which also involved the discharge of effluent by a sewage works, it was held that the defendant's compliance with the terms of its discharge consent meant that it could not be liable in nuisance for damage caused by phosphate in the effluent.

The appellate case law is more recent, and concerns two actions: one about flooding from overburdened sewers, and one about foul odours from a landfill site. The former case is *Marcic v Thames Water Utilities Ltd*, where the claimant lived in a house on the outskirts of London which was regularly subjected to external flooding as a result of overflows from the sewerage system. He brought proceedings against the water company responsible for the upkeep of the sewers in private nuisance and under the Human Rights Act 1998 (UK). Although successful on the second count at first instance,[93] and on both counts in the Court of Appeal,[94] his claims were rejected in their entirety by the House of Lords.[95] The relevance of the case for present purposes lies in the fact that the reason the House gave for dismissing the nuisance action was that to impose liability at common law would be inconsistent with the limitations on the enforcement of sewerage undertakers' drainage obligations laid down in the relevant regulatory legislation, the Water Industry Act 1991. However, it is questionable how significant the decision is for the relationship between regulatory law and nuisance law at a general level, because the case concerned an omission rather than positive conduct, and the reasoning of the House was bound up with the peculiarities of the case law on the liability of sewerage authorities.

Prior to the *Marcic* litigation, it was a well-established rule that a sewerage undertaker could not be held liable in nuisance merely because its sewerage system was rendered inadequate by development in the area it serviced.[96] The Court of Appeal in *Marcic* took the view that this rule could not survive the line of authority associated with the decision in *Leakey v National Trust*,[97] according to which an occupier can be liable for failing to take reasonable steps to prevent a hazard arising on his land from causing a nuisance to his neighbours. However, the House of Lords held that the rule remained good law, and it was in so holding that the House attached significance to the existence of the parallel regulatory regime under the 1991 Act. According to Lord Nicholls, the defendant was 'no ordinary occupier of land',[98] since the sewers in question were vested in it pursuant to the provisions of that

[91] Exeter County Court, 15 April 1992.
[92] Llangefni County Court, 21 June 1995.
[93] *Marcic v Thames Water Utilities Ltd* [2001] 3 All ER 698 (QB).
[94] ibid [2002] EWCA Civ 65; [2002] QB 929.
[95] ibid [2003] UKHL 66; [2004] 2 AC 42.
[96] *Glossop v Heston & Isleworth Local Board* (1879) 12 Ch D 102 (CA); *A-G v Dorking Guardians* (1882) 20 Ch D 595 (CA); *Smeaton v Ilford Corp* [1954] Ch 450 (Ch D).
[97] [1978] QB 849 (CA).
[98] *Marcic v Thames Water Utilities Ltd* (n 95) [33].

Act, and its obligations regarding them could not sensibly be considered without regard to the overall statutory scheme. Under that scheme, the Director General of Water Services (the industry regulator) had the power to issue enforcement orders where he considered it appropriate to do so, and individuals affected by flooding were entitled to bring proceedings under the legislation if an undertaker failed to comply with such an order. In those circumstances, it would not be appropriate to allow them to bring claims in nuisance, since 'the existence of a parallel common law right … would set at nought the statutory scheme', and effectively supplant the Director's regulatory role.[99]

Although there are elements in the reasoning in *Marcic* suggestive of a more complex interplay between regulatory law and common law than that entailed by the 'pluralistic' conception, Maria Lee surely overplays the significance of the decision when she makes it the centrepiece of her argument that the relationship between tort law and statutory regulation cannot be reduced to a simple proposition such as 'pre-empt' or 'don't pre-empt'.[100] Despite Lee's protestation to the contrary,[101] the decision in *Marcic* was clearly premised on the fact that the litigation involved an omission[102]—the claimant was seeking a *mandatory* injunction—and that alone makes it of limited significance where a claim is brought in respect of positive conduct by a defendant engaged in a regulated activity. Furthermore, Lord Hoffmann emphasised that the cases on which the defendant was relying were about sewers and not 'general principles of the law of nuisance'.[103] He pointed out that since sewerage undertakers are under a statutory duty to accept new connections to their sewers, they have no control over the volume of water and sewage entering their sewerage system. And he argued that flooding caused by overburdened sewers fell outside the *Leakey* principle because in such cases the court was being asked to order a statutory undertaking to incur capital expenditure, and the effect of such a ruling would not be limited to the claimant's individual case, but would be extrapolated across the whole country, forcing the water companies to increase their charges, and to adjust their expenditure priorities. The courts were not equipped to make such decisions in ordinary litigation, and that was why for more than a century the question of whether 'more or better sewers should be constructed' had been entrusted by Parliament to administrators,[104] and why in this case the court should defer to the regulator.

[99] ibid [35].

[100] M Lee, 'Occupying the Field: Tort and the Pre-emptive Statute' in TT Arvind and J Steele (eds), *Tort Law and the Legislature: Common Law, Statute and the Dynamics of Legal Change* (Oxford, Hart Publishing, 2013).

[101] ibid 385. In support of this view, Lee claims that Lord Nicholls expressed the belief that the distinction between misfeasance and non-feasance had 'had its day', but the relevant passage of his speech suggests that Lord Nicholls was merely attributing this view to the Court of Appeal in the case, and not adopting it himself: [2003] UKHL 66; [2004] 2 AC 42 [33].

[102] See *Marcic v Thames Water Utilities Ltd* (n 93) [40], where the judge at first instance said that Thames Water had not caused or created the nuisance by any action on its part, so that it had what he called 'non-feasance immunity'.

[103] *Marcic v Thames Water Utilities Ltd* (n 95) [59].

[104] ibid [64].

The other appellate decision on the relevance of regulatory compliance is *Barr v Biffa Waste Services Ltd*,[105] which concerned a nuisance action by residents living in the vicinity of the defendant's landfill site in respect of the smell caused by the waste deposited there. A waste management permit granted to the defendant by the Environment Agency allowed it to deposit controlled waste on the site subject to a number of conditions, one of which was that it prevented or otherwise controlled, minimised and monitored odour at the site by taking measures described in the permit 'or as otherwise agreed in writing' with the Environment Agency. The claimants conceded that the defendant had not been in breach of the permit, nor negligent, and the defendant argued that it followed that the nuisance action must fail, either because compliance with the terms of the permit afforded it a defence of statutory authority, or because in the absence of negligence, or any alleged failure to use the best available techniques, its deposit of waste in accordance with the permit afforded the defendant what it described as a 'defence' of reasonable user of land. At first instance, Coulson J rejected the first of these arguments, saying that the existence of the statutory regime governing waste management did not 'equate or give rise to a complete defence of statutory authority',[106] but in effect accepted the second. On appeal, the Court of Appeal held that he should have rejected them both.

There is little to be gained from going through Coulson J's lengthy judgment in detail, since he did little to justify his view that 'it would be unsatisfactory, to say the least, if the common law did not generally march in step' with the detailed legislation regulating waste management.[107] Two points about his analysis should however be highlighted. The first is that his conclusion that nuisance claims could be made against the defendant only if they arose out of negligent conduct on its part, as opposed to the 'simple performance of the permitted activities',[108] precisely parallels the position where the defendant's activity has been authorised by statute. And the other point is that Coulson J's endorsement of a de facto regulatory compliance defence in the nuisance context turned on a conflation of private law and public law, as was made plain by his reference to the need to balance 'the competing rights and liabilities of *the state*, the operator, and the residents',[109] and by the following central passage of his judgment:[110]

> Why should the situation at common law be any different from the position in criminal law and the position in respect of statutory nuisance? I can see no reason in principle why an operator's common law liability to his neighbours should not be subject to precisely the same limits. In this way, the carrying out of tipping activities outside the conditions of the permit ... would give rise to a common law liability, but the carrying out of

[105] [2012] EWCA Civ 312; [2013] QB 455.

[106] [2011] EWHC 1003 (TCC); [2011] 4 All ER 1065 [319].

[107] ibid [304]. For detailed critiques of Coulson J's judgment, see *Barr v Biffa Waste Services Ltd* (n 105) [51]–[147] (Carnwath LJ); A Mullis and D Nolan, 'Tort' [2011] All ER Rev [25.20]–[25.32]; and M Wilde, 'Nuisance Law in Industrial Wales—Local and National Conflicts (Part Two): Oil Refining, The Common Law and Regulation' in P Bishop and M Stallworthy (eds), *Environmental Law and Policy in Wales* (Cardiff, University of Wales Press, 2013) 52–53.

[108] Above n 106, [359].

[109] ibid [567] (emphasis added).

[110] ibid [346].

activities in accordance with that permit would constitute compliance with all relevant legal obligations, and would therefore afford a complete defence to a claim in nuisance.

By contrast, the decision of the Court of Appeal amounted to a reassertion of the independence of the common law principles governing private nuisance from regulatory norms. Carnwath LJ said that there was no principle that the common law should 'march in step' with a statutory scheme covering similar subject matter,[111] and made it clear that in his view it was simply wrong for the terms of a waste permit issued under regulatory legislation to be treated as 'cutting down the common law rights of local residents', when they had neither agreed to, nor even been consulted on, its terms.[112] His overall conclusion on the relevance of the permit for the common law position was as follows:[113]

> An activity which is conducted in contravention of planning or environmental controls is unlikely to be reasonable. But the converse does not follow. Sticking to the rules is an aspect of good neighbourliness, but it is far from the whole story—in law as in life.

On the other hand, there was a faint suggestion in Carnwath LJ's judgment that the trade-off for the preservation of common law rights in the light of the enactment of parallel systems of regulatory control could be a more flexible approach at the remedies stage, so that in cases of ongoing interference where the defendant is found liable in nuisance despite compliance with the regulatory regime, the courts might be more inclined to award damages in lieu of an injunction.[114]

The objections to the notion that a defendant's compliance with the stipulations of a regulatory regime governing his activity should afford him a defence to a nuisance action parallel those against the de facto extension of statutory authority to grants of planning permission. We can start with the point that it seems strange to argue that the fact that the defendant is *not contravening* a public law norm which (for example) makes it a criminal offence to deposit controlled waste on land without an appropriate permit[115] should immunise him from claims in private law by third parties injuriously affected by his actions. And we can again note that this idea seems especially pernicious when it is borne in mind that those third parties will generally have very limited opportunities to challenge the decisions of the administrative bodies which on this analysis cut down their common law rights. In his judgment in *Barr v Biffa*, Coulson J inadvertently drew attention to precisely this point when he described the claimants' contention that the landfill site should not have been located where it was, and that the Environment Agency had 'got it wrong', as illogical and incoherent, on the grounds that it could not be for the court considering a nuisance claim to put the decision to grant a waste disposal permit under the judicial microscope, since 'that would have been a matter for judicial review, and the time for any such judicial review proceedings has long since passed'.[116] The injustice of recognising a de facto regulatory compliance defence is surely demonstrated by

[111] *Barr v Biffa Waste Services Ltd* (n 105) [46].
[112] ibid [102].
[113] ibid [76]. Lord Neuberger expressed his agreement with this statement in *Coventry v Lawrence* (n 48) [92].
[114] *Barr v Biffa Waste Services Ltd* (n 105) [124].
[115] Environmental Protection Act 1990 (UK), s 33.
[116] Above n 106, [355].

the fact that the administrative decision which (on the judge's view) abrogated the claimants' common law rights could be challenged by them only on narrow grounds in judicial review proceedings subject to strict time limits. Can residents potentially affected by a nuisance caused by a regulated activity such as waste disposal really be expected to commence public law proceedings challenging the terms of a permit issued by the regulatory agency within three months of its issue, even if they are not yet adversely affected by the permitted activity, and even if in any case the terms can (as in *Barr v Biffa*) be varied by agreement between the permit holder and the agency?

More fundamentally, however, the central difficulty with the regulatory compliance defence is that—as Coulson J's judgment demonstrates—it rests on a failure to recognise the importance of the distinction between public law norms as encapsulated in the relevant regulatory regime and private law norms as encapsulated in the common law of nuisance, and between the public interest considerations underlying the former and the private rights underlying the latter. In deciding to issue the waste management permit in *Barr v Biffa*, the Environment Agency doubtless acted in accordance with its perception of the public interest as determined by reference to the relevant statutory framework, but our earlier analysis of the statutory authority defence showed that it is a well-established principle that decisions taken in the public interest curtail private law rights only if they amount to a direct expression of legislative will, and (like a decision of a planning authority) a decision of an administrative agency exercising regulatory powers falls well short of that benchmark.

5. THE REGULATORY FAILURE ARGUMENT

An obvious additional objection to compliance with planning and regulatory law being dispositive against liability in nuisance is the possibility of regulatory failure. This objection is not central to the analysis in this chapter, since in my view such compliance should not operate as a defence to a nuisance claim even where the relevant decision of the planning authority or regulatory agency is unimpeachable. Nevertheless, it provides an additional reason for rejecting the argument that administrative decisions of this kind should effectively cut down private rights, and may convince those unpersuaded by the more fundamental objections to that argument which I have put forward.

The possibility of regulatory failure is of course ever present, and a number of commentators have highlighted the danger in this context, and commended the utility of nuisance law as a back-up or 'long-stop' in such cases. Lee has commented, for example, that we 'do not live in a world of perfect regulation', and that deference to planners and regulators places a great deal of faith in their ability to get things right the first time, and also in the planning and regulatory processes themselves,[117] while McGillivray and Wightman have argued that private law has the 'potential

[117] M Lee, '*Hunter v Canary Wharf Ltd* (1997)' in C Mitchell and P Mitchell (eds), *Landmark Cases in the Law of Tort* (Oxford, Hart Publishing, 2011) 325.

to counteract regulatory failure by providing an institutional means of opening the substance of regulatory decisions to scrutiny'.[118]

As regards planning permission, possible irregularities in the planning process were identified by the courts in *Gillingham*, *Wheeler* and *Watson*.[119] In *Wheeler*, for example, Staughton LJ said that he thought it very likely that the planning committee failed to understand the implications of the additional pig housing units,[120] while Peter Gibson LJ called the decision of the planning authority 'incomprehensible'.[121] And the *Gillingham* example demonstrates that even where the authority which granted the planning permission in the first place has now realised that it made a mistake, it may be reluctant to revoke or modify the permission because of the financial implications of the compensation obligation which will then arise.

Similar points can be made in the regulatory compliance context. According to Pontin, the abrogation of private rights by a regulatory compliance defence 'reflects an idealised, technocratic and ultimately untenable vision of regulation, as free from vested interests and other political distortions'.[122] In the Victorian era, for example, nuisance actions against sewage authorities for river pollution filled a 'vacuum created by ... nascent statutory regulators lacking the will or the means to bring about an adequate official response',[123] while the post-war opposition to a regulatory compliance defence in river pollution cases was in part driven by the fear that river boards would be unduly influenced by 'sectional interests' when exercising their regulatory powers. And in the present day, it is easy to see how a local authority charged with regulatory functions may be inclined to take a lenient approach, for fear of driving away existing sources of local employment and discouraging inward investment.[124]

6. CONCLUSION

I have argued in this chapter that recent developments in the law of private nuisance have threatened in effect to extend the defence of statutory authority to encompass the defendant's compliance with regulatory regimes governing his activity, and at least some instances in which planning permission has been granted for the use of land causing the alleged nuisance. I have also argued that there are fundamental objections to these de facto extensions of statutory authority, and that they are inconsistent with core features or aspects of that defence. The core message of the chapter is summed up by Tony Weir's characteristically pithy remark that 'administrators cannot authorise torts'.[125]

118 McGillivray and Wightman (n 60) 154. See also J Murphy, 'Noxious Emissions and Common Law Liability: Tort in the Shadow of Regulation' in J Lowry and R Edmunds (eds), *Environmental Protection and the Common Law* (Oxford, Hart Publishing, 2000); and Wilde (n 107) 51.

119 Bishop and Jenkins (n 84) 301–02. See also (with respect to *Wheeler* and *Watson*) Lee (n 7) 326.

120 *Wheeler v JJ Saunders Ltd* (n 17) 29.

121 ibid 36.

122 Pontin (n 88) 5.

123 B Pontin, 'The Secret Achievements of Nineteenth Century Nuisance Law: *Attorney-General v Birmingham Corporation* (1858–95) in Context' (2007) 19 *Environmental Law and Management* 271, 289.

124 Murphy (n 118) 58.

125 T Weir, *An Introduction to Tort Law*, 2nd edn (Oxford, Oxford University Press, 2006) 163.

A number of points can be made by way of a conclusion. The first is that we should not lose sight of the fact that the effect of planning permission and regulatory compliance is simply to make lawful what would otherwise be a criminal offence.[126] If compliance with planning and regulatory law operates as a defence to a nuisance action, then this blurs the distinction 'between an instrument that is merely permissive and one that confers an authority',[127] and means that legislation introducing planning controls and regulating potentially noxious activities has had the paradoxical effect of reducing the protection nuisance law gives against the kinds of interference at which the legislation was aimed.

The second point is that perhaps the best way of encapsulating the argument against the determinations of planners and regulators being dispositive in private nuisance law is that private law and planning and regulatory law perform different and complementary functions. Hence the fact that a failure adequately to differentiate between these different bodies of law—and between private law and public law more generally—is characteristic of the case in favour of the de facto extension of statutory authority to determinations of this kind. Furthermore, the common law can properly discharge *its* function of protecting private interests only if it remains free to challenge what planning authorities and regulators have determined is in (or at least not contrary to) the public interest.[128]

The third point is that it is important to remember that while statutory authority proper is frequently accompanied by legislative provision for the compensation of those worst affected by the authorised activity, no compensation will be available where the defence is extended de facto to the decisions of planners and regulators; the entitlement to compensation for a depreciation of the value of land caused by 'physical factors' incident upon the operation of public works, for example, depends on the claimant's common law rights having been removed by statutory authorisation in its strict, or de jure, sense. The absence of compensation in the cases where planning permission operated as a de facto defence to a nuisance claim was highlighted by Lord Neuberger and Lord Mance in *Coventry v Lawrence*.[129]

The fourth, connected, point is that we should note the compromise suggestion that while planning permission or regulatory compliance should not operate as defences to liability in nuisance, they should either be taken into account or be dispositive when a court is considering whether or not to issue an injunction,[130] a suggestion which attracted considerable support (in the planning permission context) from the Supreme Court in the *Coventry* case, albeit with marked differences of emphasis.[131] Against this solution is the fact that it appears to be subject to many of the objections identified in this chapter to making compliance with

[126] Tromans (n 60) 495. See also *Coventry v Lawrence* (n 48) [89] (Lord Neuberger) (all that the grant of planning permission for a development means 'is that a bar to the use imposed by planning law ... has been removed').

[127] Wilde (n 107) 52.

[128] See ibid 53.

[129] *Coventry v Lawrence* (n 48) [90], [165].

[130] See, eg, *Wheeler v JJ Saunders Ltd* (n 17) 35 (Peter Gibson LJ); *Barr v Biffa Waste Services Ltd* (n 105) [124] (Carnwath LJ); Tromans (n 60) 496; M Lunney and K Oliphant, *Tort Law: Text and Materials*, 5th edn (Oxford, Oxford University Press, 2013) 663.

[131] *Coventry v Lawrence* (n 48) [125] (Lord Neuberger), [157], [161] (Lord Sumption), [167]–[168] (Lord Mance), [169] (Lord Clarke), [240], [246] (Lord Carnwath). While Lord Sumption inclined

planning or regulatory law dispositive of the liability question. On the other hand, the suggestion that such compliance be taken into account when deciding which remedy to award is less troublesome than making it dispositive in that regard, and either way relegating the issue to the remedies stage of the nuisance enquiry should at least ensure that those whose private rights are effectively abrogated by administrative decisions receive compensation, since where an injunction is refused for an ongoing nuisance, the court will generally award damages in lieu.

The fifth point is that if in a particular case it is really thought to be wholly impracticable to impose nuisance liability on an activity for which planning permission has been granted, or which is being carried out in accordance with a relevant regulatory regime, then there is always the fallback of statutory authorisation of the traditional kind.[132] After all, the argument of this chapter is not that private rights should never be sacrificed to collective interests, but rather that such sacrifices must be sanctioned by the legislature itself, rather than being inferred from the decisions of administrators exercising delegated powers.

And the sixth point is just to reiterate that I have no objection to the courts taking into account planning decisions and regulatory compliance when determining whether the defendant's activity is substantially interfering with the claimant's use and enjoyment of his land.[133] The substantial interference enquiry central to amenity nuisance cases is flexible enough to accommodate such considerations with ease, and it is appropriate that it should do so.[134] The grant of planning permission for the development which is causing the interference may, for example, provide some evidence of the nature of the relevant neighbourhood for the purposes of applying the locality principle,[135] while it is likely to be more reasonable to expect the occupiers of neighbouring properties to put up with the consequences of an activity which is being carried out in compliance with relevant regulatory norms than with those of an activity which is violating them.[136]

Finally, what are we to make of the protestation that this attempt to insulate private nuisance law from planning and regulatory law is just crying for the moon, since it is inevitable that the rise of collective decision-making will serve to constrain older forms of social ordering centred on private rights adjudication? Is Lee not right to argue that 'private law (and the protections it provides) will find itself increasingly circumscribed in a world dominated by collective determinations of the public interest' unless it engages in what she terms 'a realistic analysis' of those

towards the view that the grant of planning permission for the defendant's activity should be dispositive against an injunction, the other Justices seemed to regard it as at most a factor to be taken into account.

132 See *Barr v Biffa Waste Services Ltd* (n 105) [106] (Carnwath LJ).

133 See, eg, *Hirose Electrical UK Ltd v Peak Ingredients Ltd* [2011] EWCA Civ 987; [2011] Env LR 34 [40], where Mummery LJ said that the fact that the operations of a food additive manufacturer on a light industrial estate were carried on in compliance with planning law and 'without objection or intervention' by the relevant statutory authorities were 'relevant indicators of the levels of discomfort and inconvenience caused by the smell' generated by the operations.

134 For helpful discussion, see Tromans (n 70) OP106–OP107.

135 See *Coventry v Lawrence* (n 48) [96] (Lord Neuberger), [166] (Lord Mance), [224]–[226] (Lord Carnwath). For an example of such reasoning, see *Rockenbach v Apostle* (n 31), where a city zoning ordinance permitting a funeral home was admissible as evidence of the character of the district in question.

136 *Coventry v Lawrence* (n 48) [226] (Lord Carnwath).

determinations?[137] Setting aside the question of quite what such an analysis would entail—Lee's own work suggests at least a degree of subjugation of private law norms to those of public law—the answer to this kind of fashionable fatalism lies in the conclusion to Joshua Getzler's account of the history of common law water rights:[138]

> However quaint and open to demolition by skeptical modern observers, the secular common-law faith in legalism is resilient and valuable. The lesson is that in order to maintain the trust and commitment of participants within any complex system of resource allocation, a strong belief both in individual rights and the consensual justice of adjudication is essential. It is a lesson with purchase across the widest fields of law.

[137] Lee (n 117) 333.
[138] J Getzler, *A History of Water Rights at Common Law* (Oxford, Oxford University Press, 2004) 352.

11

Weaving the Law's Seamless Web: Reflections on the Illegality Defence in Tort Law

BEVERLEY MCLACHLIN*

1. INTRODUCTION

INCREASINGLY, LEGAL SCHOLARS are raising questions regarding the proper foundations of tort law and, as some argue, the theoretical disarray of the subject. They have tackled this problem by building new foundations—or perhaps unearthing old foundations—for tort law, based on the principles of corrective justice.

The doctrine of *ex turpi causa*, or illegality, potentially poses a challenge to the corrective justice model because some versions of the doctrine incorporate policy concerns that are external to and inconsistent with the principles of corrective justice. The solution proposed in this chapter is to adopt a narrow version of the doctrine that seeks to protect the integrity of the legal system. On this view, the doctrine of illegality is rooted in the legal norm of coherence within the legal system. This view of the doctrine of illegality is consistent with a corrective justice model.

The discussion will proceed in the following steps. First, I briefly sketch out concerns regarding the theoretical cogency of torts, particularly negligence, as a branch of the law, and I outline the key elements of corrective justice as one possible theoretical account of tort law. Second, I set out the broad and narrow forms of the illegality doctrine. Third, I consider the principal objection to the notion of coherence in the law that underlies the narrow version of the illegality defence, and discuss possible responses to these objections. Finally, I explain how the narrow version of the defence is consistent with a corrective justice model of tort law.

* This is a revised version of a paper I presented at the workshop 'Defences in Tort' at All Souls College, Oxford on 10 and 11 January, 2014. I am grateful to the participants in the workshop and particularly the editors of this volume for their helpful comments and suggestions.

2. THE EVOLUTION OF NEGLIGENCE LAW: LOSING OUR MOORINGS?[1]

The law of negligence is of relatively recent vintage. It did not find a stable foundation in our law of tort until the early twentieth century when Lord Atkin introduced a general conception of the duty of care based on reasonable foreseeability in *Donoghue v Stevenson*.[2] Lord Atkin described the law of negligence up to that point as containing:[3]

> an elaborate classification of duties as they exist in respect of property whether real or personal, with further divisions as to ownership, occupation or control, and distinctions based on the particular relations of the one side or the other, whether manufacturer, salesman or landlord, customer, tenant, stranger and so on. In this way it can be ascertained at any time whether the law recognises a duty, but only where the case can be referred to some particular species which has been examined and classified.

But judges and academics soon realised that a general duty of care posed a significant problem: it could lead to indeterminate liability. The courts and academics turned to 'policy'—perhaps at some cost to principle—to define the scope of the duty of care. These policy concerns contained, in the words of Allan Beever, 'everything apart from principle. [P]olicy has been held to include issues of distributive justice, social morality, economic efficiency, public opinion and so on.'[4] The invocation of policy in tort law is sometimes inconsistent and downright contradictory.[5] The law of tort is 'awash with conflicting policy arguments that can be utilised to support any conceivable position'.[6]

The task of the jurist is to find a principled basis for the law of tort. A theory of tort based in corrective justice offers such a basis. Although there are a range of corrective justice theories, the essential features of these (on which theorists are largely agreed) can be sketched in brief compass.[7] Corrective justice focuses on whether one party has committed and the other party has suffered a transactional injustice. It seeks to maintain and restore the notional equality of parties who enter into voluntary (contracts) and involuntary transactions (tort). This notional equality 'consists in persons having what lawfully belongs to them'.[8] It is a form of justice that is corrective: it aims at undoing the wrong done by one party to the other. It is therefore bipolar or correlative in nature. It seeks to remedy an injustice only if the injustice is correlative—that is, only if it is the result of a wrong done by the doer

[1] This account of the history of negligence law is based on DJ Ibbetson, *A Historical Introduction to the Law of Obligations* (Oxford, Oxford University Press, 1999) and A Beever, *Rediscovering the Law of Negligence* (Oxford, Hart Publishing, 2007) 3–19.

[2] [1932] AC 562 (HL).

[3] ibid 579–80 (Lord Atkin).

[4] Beever (n 1) 3.

[5] See the list of policy concerns identified in J Stapleton, 'Duty of Care Factors: A Selection from the Judicial Menus' in P Cane and J Stapleton (eds), *The Law of Obligations: Essays in Celebration of John Fleming* (Oxford, Clarendon Press 1998); and see the critique in S Todd, 'Negligence: Breach of Duty' in S Todd (ed), *The Law of Torts in New Zealand*, 6th edn (Wellington, Brookers, 2013) at 418–19.

[6] Beever (n 1) 5.

[7] See EJ Weinrib, 'Corrective Justice in a Nutshell' (2002) 52 *University of Toronto Law Journal* 349 and EJ Weinrib, 'Correlativity, Personality, and the Emerging Consensus on Corrective Justice' (2001) 2 *Theoretical Inquiries in Law* 107.

[8] Weinrib, 'Corrective Justice in a Nutshell' (ibid) 349.

to the sufferer. To put it in legal terminology, it is only concerned with wrongs done by the claimant to the defendant.

This correlative structure is an essential feature of a theory of tort law as corrective justice. Accordingly, any factor that affects liability but which is not correlative—that is, which does not have anything to do with the nature of the relationship between the parties—poses a challenge to corrective justice. Some theories of corrective justice may admit other factors, but the tension is clear. The illegality defence poses such a challenge because it appears to look only at the conduct of the claimant and to provide the defendant a defence based on policy considerations that are external to the relationship between the parties.

My purpose in this chapter is not to defend a theory of tort law based on corrective justice. Tort law based in theories of corrective justice have been given book-length treatment by Ernest Weinrib[9] and, in respect of negligence, Allan Beever.[10] I will assume the legitimacy and utility of a theory of tort based on corrective justice. My aim here is more modest: to consider an answer to the challenge that the illegality defence poses to a law of tort based on corrective justice principles.

3. THE ILLEGALITY DOCTRINE: BROAD AND NARROW VERSIONS

Let me start by defining the subject of our present study. The familiar Latin tag that encapsulates the doctrine of illegality is *ex turpi causa non oritur actio*. The concept has sometimes been expressed in other forms, such as *ex dolo malo non oritur actio* by Lord Mansfield.[11] While I have written elsewhere that I see no harm in using the traditional label provided that the conditions governing the invocation of the doctrine are made clear,[12] for the purpose of this chapter I prefer to use the term 'illegality'.

This immediately raises the question, what forms of illegality justify the application of the doctrine? There are three possible answers. The first is that it is restricted to breaches of the criminal law. The second is that it applies to both breaches of criminal and civil law. And the third is that it could apply to criminal wrongs, civil wrongs, and immoral acts.[13] For the present discussion, I will restrict the definition in our discussion to breaches of the criminal law as I need go no further to develop the argument: the doctrine is primarily, but not exclusively, invoked when the claimant breaches the criminal law and as such criminality serves as a useful focal case for the doctrine.

[9] EJ Weinrib, *The Idea of Private Law* (Oxford, Oxford University Press, 2012); EJ Weinrib, *Corrective Justice* (Oxford, Oxford University Press, 2012).

[10] Beever (n 1).

[11] *Holman v Johnson* (1775) 1 Cowp 341, 343; 98 ER 1120, 1121.

[12] *Hall v Hebert* [1993] 2 SCR 159 (SCC) 169–70 (McLachlin J).

[13] J Goudkamp, 'Ex Turpi Causa and Immoral Behaviour in the Tort Context' (2011) 127 *LQR* 354.

3.1 The Broad Version of the Doctrine: Policy Factors

The doctrine of illegality has a narrow form and a broad form. The broad form is that one cannot recover compensation for loss that one has suffered as a result of one's own criminal act. The broad form of the doctrine is based in policy. The policy 'is not based on a single justification, but on a group of reasons, which vary in different situations'.[14] The Law Commission endorsed this approach in its final report on the illegality defence.[15] The various policy justifications for the broad form of the illegality defence can be summarised as follows:[16] punishment for an illegal act; upholding the dignity of the courts; deterrence; avoiding condonation; and preventing wrongful profit. I will consider each of these rationales in more detail below.

The leading authority in England on the broad form of the defence is the House of Lords' judgment in *Gray v Thames Trains*,[17] where Lord Hoffmann applied the narrow form of the defence to certain claims, while retaining the wider form and applying it to other claims advanced by the claimant. Gray had been injured in an accident caused by the negligence of the employees of Thames Trains. He experienced post-traumatic stress disorder ('PTSD') and depression. While receiving medication and treatment for the condition, Gray had an altercation with a pedestrian who had stepped in front of his car. Gray then tracked the pedestrian down and stabbed him to death. Gray was convicted of manslaughter on the grounds of diminished responsibility caused by PTSD, and was sentenced to be detained in hospital with an indefinite restriction order.

Gray commenced an action for negligence against Thames Trains, claiming, among other damages, loss of earnings until the date of trial and continuing. From the period of his detention after the killing, Gray claimed damages for what he would have earned in his previous occupation and he claimed for future lost wages based on the assumption that he would not be able to find employment after his release from hospital. Finally, Gray also claimed 'general damages for his detention, conviction, feelings of guilt and remorse and damage to reputation and an indemnity against any claims which might be brought by dependants of the dead pedestrian'.[18]

Lord Hoffmann recognised both the wider and narrower form of the defence:[19]

> In its wider form, it is that you cannot recover compensation for loss which you have suffered in consequence of your own criminal act. In its narrower and more specific form, it is that you cannot recover for damage which flows from loss of liberty, a fine or other punishment lawfully imposed upon you in consequence of your own unlawful act. In such a case it is the law which, as a matter of penal policy, causes the damage and it would be inconsistent for the law to require you to be compensated for that damage.

Lord Hoffmann observed that it is necessary to distinguish between the wider and narrower versions of the defence, because there exists a specific justification for

[14] *Gray v Thames Trains Ltd* [2009] UKHL 33; [2009] 1 AC 1339 [30] (Lord Hoffmann).
[15] Law Commission, *The Illegality Defence* (Report 320, 2010).
[16] Law Commission, *Illegality Defence in Tort* (CP 160, 2001) 66–92.
[17] Above n 14.
[18] ibid [23].
[19] ibid [29].

the narrower version of the defence which does not necessarily apply to the wider version—namely the principle of consistency (or what I term coherence).[20] Under the wider version of the defence, Lord Hoffmann held that 'the maxim ex turpi causa expresses not so much a principle as a policy. Furthermore, that policy is not based upon a single justification but on a group of reasons, which vary in different situations.'[21]

The House of Lords, per Lord Hoffmann, denied Gray's claims for loss of earnings after his arrest and for general damages for his detention, conviction and damage to his reputation based on the narrow version of the defence because they were all caused by the criminal sentence imposed on Gray. It denied Gray's other claims—for indemnity and general damages for feelings of guilt and remorse—under the broader version of the defence.[22]

The broader form of the defence was recently reaffirmed in English law in *Les Laboratoires Servier v Apotex Inc* in 2012.[23] The issue on appeal concerned the availability of the defence of illegality to a claim on a cross-undertaking in damages. Servier, the holder of a patent enforceable in the United Kingdom, obtained an interim injunction against the defendant Apotex from selling infringing products in the United Kingdom. The patent was subsequently held to be invalid in the United Kingdom and the injunction was discharged, but the goods that the defendant Apotex would have sold in the United Kingdom, but for the interim injunction, would have been manufactured in Canada in breach of a valid patent granted and enforceable in Canada. The defendant Apotex (who was claiming damages on the cross-undertaking) conceded that there should be deducted from the damages an amount equal to what a Canadian court would have ordered Apotex to pay Servier in Canada for infringement of the Canadian patent in manufacturing and exporting products for sale in the United Kingdom market had there been no interlocutory injunction preventing sales in the United Kingdom.

Etherton LJ, for the majority of the Court of Appeal, held that the policy of comity between national courts applies to this case. Etherton LJ weighed a number of the factors and concluded that, in light of Apotex's concession regarding the deduction, the illegality defence should not defeat Apotex's claim on the cross-undertaking. One of those factors, perhaps the determinative one, was that as a result of its concession, Apotex would be put in precisely the position in which it would have been had there been no interlocutory injunctions in the United Kingdom and without offending comity with Canada. Etherton LJ saw it as a matter of consistency in the law between the two countries:[24]

> There would be consistency in the law by recognising, in the inquiry as to damages, the illegality in Canada in the same way and to the same extent as the Canadian courts would in fact have done in respect of any unlawful manufacture and export in Canada during the relevant period. Expressed in a different way, if Apotex was left with some of the

[20] ibid [32], [37].
[21] ibid [30].
[22] ibid [50].
[23] [2012] EWCA Civ 593; [2013] Bus LR 80. At the time of writing the Supreme Court of the United Kingdom heard the appeal from the Court of Appeal but had not yet rendered judgment.
[24] ibid [69].

> compensation ordered by Norris J even after deduction of an amount reflecting [Apotex's] concession, what would be left is not something that the Canadian courts themselves would regard as properly recoverable under Canadian law for breach of the Canadian Patent. The result, therefore, would neither be offensive to comity with Canada nor any reason for interference on the ground of English public policy.

Etherton LJ's invocation of consistency is about comity between legal systems rather than the internal coherence within a domestic legal system.

In arriving at this conclusion, a number of issues were considered by Etherton LJ. He accepted the rationale of coherence from the Supreme Court of Canada's decision in *Hall v Hebert*[25] (discussed below) and noted that the principle in *Hall v Hebert* has received general recognition in the United Kingdom.[26] But Etherton LJ went on to hold there are other policy rationales that may apply, based on Lord Hoffmann's statement in *Gray*.[27] Relying on the work of the Law Commission on the illegality defence, Etherton LJ identified the following policy bases for the defence: 'furthering the purpose of the rule which the illegal conduct has infringed; consistency; the claimant should not profit from his or her own wrong; deterrence; and maintaining the integrity of the legal system'.[28] He expressed concern that the illegality defence should retain its flexibility. According to Etherton LJ, the foregoing policy rationales can be applied in a way that produces a just and proportionate response to illegality.[29]

In evaluating the policy factors approach from *Gray* and *Laboratoires Servier*, it is necessary to consider each of the policy rationales on their own merits:

(1) **Punishment for an illegal act:** It is argued that it is justifiable to deny a civil claim as a punishment for illegal conduct. However, this policy rationale may be criticised on the ground that punishment is not the purpose of tort law. Tort law aims to undo the harm that the defendant did to the claimant—it seeks to put the claimant back in the position she was in before the harm occurred. Moreover, it is unclear why a claimant needs to be punished beyond the penal sanctions imposed by the criminal law by being denied recovery in tort. Denying recovery in tort may result in a disproportionate punishment. As Goudkamp has observed,[30]

> [e]ven if a plaintiff deserves punishment, the defence is a spectacularly inappropriate mechanism for dispensing it. This is primarily because the penalty that it imposes depends on the extent of the loss suffered by the plaintiff rather than on his or her culpability.

(2) **Upholding the dignity of the courts:** This explanation for the defence maintains that the courts should not 'stoop to the indignity' of adjudicating the merits of

[25] Above n 12.
[26] *Les Laboratoires Servier v Apotex Inc* (n 23) [67].
[27] ibid [73].
[28] ibid [66].
[29] ibid [73], [75].
[30] J Goudkamp, 'The Defence of Joint Illegal Enterprise' (2010) 34 *Melbourne University Law Review* 425, 442.

a claim based on illegal behaviour.[31] The rationale is rooted in the need to preserve the dignity and reputation of the courts and the legal system. However, one answer to this concern is that it is difficult to see how the dignity of the courts is undermined when awarding purely compensatory damages to the claimant for an injury intentionally or negligently caused by the defendant.

(3) **Deterrence**: The courts have frequently invoked the need to deter unlawful or immoral conduct as the basis of the illegality defence.[32] But can we state with any confidence that the application of an obscure doctrine of law would deter wrongdoing, particularly where the criminal law would fail to do so? This may give too much credit to wrongdoers as informed, rational actors, coolly calculating the potential consequences of their actions before engaging in wrongdoing.[33]

(4) **Avoiding condonation**: The courts have sometimes invoked the illegality defence in order to avoid the appearance of condoning the illegal activity or avoiding the appearance of encouraging others.[34] But it cannot fairly be argued, for instance, that the Supreme Court of Canada implicitly condoned drinking and driving in *Hall v Hebert* by allowing the claimant's claim for compensation for the injuries caused by the defendant.

(5) **Preventing wrongful profit**: The courts have often based the rationale for the illegality defence on the need to prevent a claimant profiting from his or her own illegal wrongdoing. It is argued that crime should not pay. To hold otherwise would undermine the punishment that the criminal law imposes.[35] This concern is answered in *Hall v Hebert*. An award of damages in tort compensates the claimant for the injury caused by the defendant; it does not amount to 'profit'.[36] Under the principle of coherence, for example, the claimant could not recover exemplary damages because they are not purely compensatory. Nor could the claimant recover lost wages when his employment income derives from criminal activity.[37]

It appears that none of the foregoing policy factors withstand scrutiny as a sound basis for invoking the illegality doctrine. The final reason for rejecting the broad version of the illegality doctrine is the overarching concern that judicial reliance on policy factors to deny the claimant compensation is inherently arbitrary. This concern is 'heightened by the absence of clear guidance as to when judges could exercise this draconian power and upon what grounds'.[38]

Having considered the broad version of the illegality doctrine, I will turn to the narrow version of the doctrine, which is based on the principle of coherence.

[31] Law Commission, *Illegal Transactions: The Effect of Illegality on Contract and Trusts* (CP 154, 1999) [87]; Law Commission, *Illegality Defence in Tort* (n 16) [4.25].

[32] Law Commission, *Illegality Defence in Tort* (n 16) [4.28]–[4.34]; Law Commission, *Illegal Transactions* (n 31) [6.9]–[6.10].

[33] Goudkamp (n 30) 441.

[34] Law Commission, *Illegality Defence in Tort* (n 16) [4.48]–[4.55].

[35] ibid [4.36].

[36] *Hall v Hebert* (n 12) 172, 174 (McLachlin J).

[37] ibid 175 (McLachlin J).

[38] ibid 169 (McLachlin J).

3.2 Narrow Version of the Doctrine: the Principle of Coherence

The narrow form of the doctrine applies where the claimant seeks to profit from an illegal act or seeks to evade or lessen a penalty imposed by the criminal law, because allowing such a claim would introduce incoherence into the fabric of the law.[39] As I will elaborate below, I characterise this as a *principle*—the principle of coherence implicit in the law—not as a matter of *policy*.

The narrow form of the doctrine first emerged in Canada. In Canadian law, as in English law, illegality was originally a defence in the law of contract. Towards the mid-twentieth century it began to emerge as a defence in Canadian tort law.[40] Over time, defendants increasingly relied on the doctrine in tort actions. Two reasons explain this enthusiasm. First, courts interpreted the *volenti* defence restrictively, mainly because of the introduction of apportionment legislation, whereas illegality had not yet received extensive judicial consideration and was therefore still open-ended.[41] Second, increasing emphasis on tort's fault-based goals encouraged the application of the doctrine. As Lewis Klar explained:[42]

> A move away from the use of tort as a loss distribution device, and a return to its more traditional fault-based goals, will produce an increased emphasis on those aspects of the negligence action which stress the moral basis of fault-based compensation. Illegality is such a defence.

Nevertheless, the illegality defence has had a chequered history. Historically, the treatment of the defence by appellate courts was inconsistent, and not every province accepted that the doctrine could apply in tort law.[43] The doctrine was seen as untidy, with too many 'diverse themes' running through it.[44]

The opportunity for the Supreme Court of Canada to give the defence its sustained consideration arose in *Hall v Hebert* in 1993. The appeal arose out of the tragic combination of youthful exuberance, drink and a 'souped-up muscle car'. Two friends had consumed copious amounts of alcohol. They went out to the local gravel pit and drove out on a spur that ran along the rim of the pit. The owner of the car allowed his friend, who was inebriated, to drive. The car went off the road, down the slope to the pit and flipped upside down. The driver sustained significant head injuries and sued his friend, the owner of the car, for allowing him to drive while intoxicated. The defendant relied on the defence of illegality.

The main doctrinal disagreement among the members of the Court was whether illegality should be retained in tort law as a defence, or whether it should be dealt

[39] ibid 180 (McLachlin J).

[40] D Gibson, 'Illegality of Plaintiff's Conduct as a Defence' (1969) 47 *Canadian Bar Review* 89, 89–90; B MacDougall, '*Ex Turpi Causa*: Should a Defence Arise from a Base Cause?' (1991) 55 *Saskatchewan Law Review* 1, 2–3.

[41] LN Klar, 'Recent Developments in Canadian Law: Tort Law' (1991) 23 *Ottawa Law Review* 177, 237.

[42] ibid 238.

[43] See, eg, *Foster v Morton* (1956) 4 DLR (2d) 269 (Nova Scotia CA) 281 (MacDonald J); *Tallow v Tailfeathers* (1973) 44 DLR (3d) 55 (SC Alta AD) (the reasons of Allen JA); *Tomlinson v Harrison* [1972] 1 OR 670 (Ont HC) 678 (Addy J); *Bond v Loutit* [1979] 2 WWR 154 (Man QB) 166 (Hamilton J); *Mack v Enns* (1983) 44 BCLR 145 (BCCA); *Betts v Sanderson Estate* (1988) 31 BCLR (2d) 1 (BCCA); *Norberg v Wynrib* [1992] 2 SCR 226 (SCC).

[44] Klar (n 41) 238.

with at the stage of finding a duty of care. The majority, for which I wrote, held that the illegality doctrine had a legitimate role to play in tort law as a defence, but only in limited circumstances where it was necessary to invoke it in order to maintain the integrity of the justice system. By contrast, Cory J for the minority held that the illegality doctrine should be eliminated from the law of tort. Instead, the claimant's illegal or immoral conduct should be considered as a policy factor negating the duty of care under the second branch of the *Anns* test. Neither the majority nor Cory J denied the claimant recovery for his injuries.

On behalf of the majority, I narrowed the scope of the illegality defence to occasions where it was necessary in order to preserve the coherence of the legal system:[45]

> I conclude that there is a need in the law of tort for a principle which permits judges to deny recovery to a plaintiff on the ground that to do so would undermine the integrity of the justice system. The power is a limited one. Its use is justified where allowing the plaintiff's claim would introduce inconsistency into the fabric of the law, either by permitting the plaintiff to profit from an illegal or wrongful act, or to evade a penalty prescribed by criminal law. Its use is not justified where the plaintiff's claim is merely for compensation for personal injuries sustained as a consequence of the negligence of the defendant.

The narrow basis for the defence was later unanimously affirmed by the Supreme Court of Canada in *British Columbia v Zastowny*.[46] The decision is notable for being the first time that the Court applied the illegality defence to a claim in tort law, and it confirms the narrow scope of the defence in Canadian law.[47] The claimant was a drug addict who had spent most of his life in prison for various offences. While in prison he was twice sexually assaulted by a prison guard. The sexual assault had exacerbated his drug addiction and the consequent criminal conduct. The claimant sued the provincial government for the sexual assaults, among other things claiming damages for his lost earnings during the years he was imprisoned following the assaults.

The Supreme Court of Canada held that lost earnings were not recoverable because such 'an award would introduce an inconsistency in the fabric of the law'.[48] Rothstein J, writing for the Court, distilled the following principles regarding the illegality defence from *Hall v Hebert*:[49]

> 1. Application of the *ex turpi* doctrine in the tort context invalidates otherwise valid and enforceable actions in tort ...
> 2. Therefore, its application must be based on a firm doctrinal foundation and be made subject to clear limits and should occur 'in very limited circumstances' ...
> 3. The only justification for its application is the preservation of the integrity of the legal system. This concern is only in issue where a damage award in a civil suit would allow a person to profit from illegal or wrongful conduct or would permit evasion or rebate of a penalty prescribed by the criminal law ...

[45] *Hall v Hebert* (n 12) 179–80 (McLachlin J).

[46] [2008] SCC 4; [2008] 1 SCR 27.

[47] It should be noted that the application of the illegality defence may have been at play in obiter comments by Fish J (at [143]) and Bastrache J (at [137]) in *HL v Canada (AG)* [2005] SCC 25; [2005] 1 SCR 401.

[48] *British Columbia v Zastowny* (n 46) [22].

[49] ibid [20].

4. The *ex turpi* doctrine generally does not preclude an award of damages in tort because such awards tend to compensate the claimant rather than amount to 'profit' …
5. The *ex turpi* doctrine is a defence in a tort action. The claimant's illegal conduct does not give rise to a judicial discretion to negate or refuse to consider the duty of care which goes to the relationship between a claimant and a defendant. It is independent of that relationship. The defendant may have caused harm by acting wrongly or negligently, but the 'responsibility for this wrong is suspended only because concern for the integrity of the legal system trumps the concern that the defendant be responsible' …
6. Treating the *ex turpi* doctrine as a defence places the onus on the defendant to prove the illegal or immoral conduct that precludes the claimant's action. And as a defence, it allows for segregation between claims for personal injury and claims that would constitute profit from illegal or immoral conduct or the evasion of or a rebate of a penalty provided by the criminal law.

Canada is not the only jurisdiction to invoke coherence as a basis for the illegality doctrine. Coherence is recognised as one among several bases for the defence in England, as discussed above, and it is the basis of the doctrine in Australia. The coherence principle adopted by the majority of the Supreme Court in *Hall v Hebert* can be traced to English law, where it is recognised as one rationale for the illegality defence. Denning J (as he then was) held, in *Askey v Golden Wine Co Ltd*, that it is a principle of English law 'that the punishment inflicted by a criminal court is personal to the offender, and that the civil courts will not entertain an action by the offender to recover an indemnity against the consequences of that punishment'.[50] Denning J implicitly recognised coherence as a basis for the illegality defence when he wrote that the reasons for the criminal punishment 'would be nullified if the offender could recover the amount of the fine and costs from another person by process of the civil courts'.[51] Although Denning J does not use the label, the principle of coherence was clearly at work as the basis for denying the claimant relief.[52]

Australia, like Canada, has adopted the narrow version of the doctrine based on coherence. The Australian High Court case of *Miller v Miller*[53] is a case of joint illegal enterprise. The claimant had been out drinking at a nightclub. She did not have money for a taxi, so she and her sister decided to steal a car. The defendant saw them leaving the car park and asked to drive. He too had been drinking. He began to speed. The claimant asked to be let out. The defendant refused. Near her home, the claimant again asked to get out. Again, the defendant refused and laughed off her concerns. He sped up and lost control of the car. The claimant was seriously injured and became a quadriplegic. The High Court considered whether the claimant's illegal conduct—her theft of the car, her subsequent use of the car, or a combination of both—defeated her claim for negligence.

[50] [1948] 2 All ER 35 (KB) 38.

[51] ibid. It should be noted, however, that Denning J applied the illegality defence more broadly to include gross negligence.

[52] The narrow rule was also applied in *Clunis v Camden and Islington Health Authority* [1998] QB 978 (CA).

[53] [2011] HCA 9; (2011) 242 CLR 446.

The majority of the High Court applied the narrow version of the doctrine based on 'congruence' or 'coherence'—not only in the way illegality is treated in tort, contract and trusts—but also congruence between the civil and criminal law. It implicitly rejected the broad version of the doctrine.[54] The majority wrote:[55]

> Ultimately, the question is: would it be incongruous for the law to proscribe the plaintiff's conduct and yet allow recovery in negligence for damage sufferance in the course, or as a result, of that unlawful conduct? Other questions, such as whether denial of liability will deter wrongdoers or advantage some at the expense of others, are neither helpful nor relevant. And likewise, resort to notions of moral outrage or judicial indignation serves only to mask the proper identification of what is said to produce the response and why the response could be warranted.

However, unlike in Canada, the illegality doctrine in Australia does not operate as a defence to an action in tort, but negates the duty of care. In this respect, and in the manner in which the test is applied, the Australian approach to coherence differs from the Canadian approach. In Australia, a finding of incongruity requires a close examination of the criminal statute, including its purpose, and a determination that the statute is inconsistent with a duty of care owed by the defendant to the claimant. On this view 'the balance of advantage or disadvantage to criminal participants is a matter for the legislature'.[56] By contrast, in Canada, the illegality doctrine operates as a defence and does not focus on a search for statutory purpose.

The Australian approach can be criticised for turning on a potentially elusive search for a legislative intention to negate the duty of care. The difficulty, identified by Dixon J (as he then was) in *O'Connor v SP Bray Ltd*, is that 'the legislature [may have] in fact expressed no intention upon the subject'.[57] As acknowledged by the High Court, the danger is that a 'legislative intention [will] be "conjured up by judges to give effect to their own ideas of policy and then 'imputed' to the legislature"'.[58]

In addition, difficulties arise from shifting the analysis from illegality as a defence to a doctrine that negates the duty of care. First, the duty approach does not fully capture what is meant when one invokes the principle of illegality. Liability for tort arises out of the relationship between the tortfeasor and the victim, but denying the claimant recovery on the basis that it would undermine the coherence of the legal systems addresses concerns that are external to the relationship between the parties. The principle of illegality in tort is therefore best expressed as a defence rather than a policy for negating the duty of care.[59] Second, it is not clear why the principle should operate to prevent the courts from examining the appropriate standard of care, rather than to simply prevent an otherwise valid claim from succeeding. The principle operates satisfactorily as a defence in contract and trusts, rather than as a basis for negating an element of the cause of action. Practically, this could also raise

[54] ibid [102] (French CJ, Gummow, Hayne, Crennan, Kiefel and Bell JJ).
[55] ibid [16] (French CJ, Gummow, Hayne, Crennan, Kiefel and Bell JJ).
[56] ibid [98] (French CJ, Gummow, Hayne, Crennan, Kiefel and Bell JJ).
[57] (1937) 56 CLR 464 (HCA) 477 (Dixon J).
[58] *Miller v Miller* (n 53) [29] (French CJ, Gummow, Hayne, Crennan, Kiefel and Bell JJ), quoting *Sovar v Henry Lane Pty Ltd* (1967) 116 CLR 397 (HCA) 405.
[59] *Hall v Hebert* (n 12) 172, 181–83 (McLachlin J).

difficulties when the action is pleaded in both contract and tort.[60] Finally, because it is an 'all or nothing' approach, it cannot be applied selectively depending on the heads of damage.[61]

Let me now turn to the main objection to the principle of coherence between different branches of the law,[62] which is that the principles of criminal law and tort law should be kept distinct, lest efforts to import concepts from one domain to the other lead to 'bad philosophy and total confusion'.[63] Lord Scott put it this way:[64]

> [T]his plea for consistency between the criminal law and the civil law lacks cogency for the ends to be served by the two systems are very different. One of the main functions of the criminal law is to identify, and provide punitive sanctions for, behaviour that is categorised as criminal because it is damaging to the good order of society ... The function of the civil law of tort is different. Its main function is to identify and protect the rights that every person is entitled to assert against, and require to be respected by, others. The rights of one person, however, often run counter to the rights of others and the civil law, in particular the law of tort, must then strike a balance between the conflicting rights.

The traditional approach is to think of tort law and criminal law as non-overlapping magisteria,[65] or separate bodies of law. While the norms of tort law and criminal law can sometimes be applied to the same event, neither body of law is relevant to the other because their objectives are different.[66] The goal of tort law is to compensate the claimant for the wrong done to her by the defendant. Tort law is private law, concerned with vindicating and remedying the breaches of personal rights. By contrast, the object of the criminal law is for the state to condemn and punish the wrongdoer for transgressions that disrupt public order. Criminal law is public and aims at maintaining security. This is the way most schools teach the subjects, and it is the approach usually echoed by the courts.

This objection is flawed. It is doubtful that the claim that the criminal and tort law are completely distinct is correct. Consider, for instance, the intentional torts and their cognate crimes. Although the aims of the criminal law and tort law are different, there is overlap in the elements of each. Or, consider modern legislation in environmental law and competition law, which may provide for compensation but which may also attract penal sanctions. Environmental and competition legislation overlap with a number of torts. These are but a few examples of how the boundaries

[60] ibid.

[61] ibid 172, 184–85 (McLachlin J).

[62] This section draws on G Virgo, '"We Do This in the Criminal Law and That in the Law of Tort": A New Fusion Debate' in SGA Pitel, JW Nyers and E Chamberlain (eds), *Tort Law: Challenging Orthodoxy* (Oxford, Hart Publishing, 2013).

[63] J Coleman, *Risks and Wrongs* (Oxford, Oxford University Press, 2002) 222.

[64] *Ashley v Chief Constable of Sussex Police* [2008] UKHL 25, [2008] 1 AC 962 [17]–[18] (Lord Scott), [3] (Lord Bingham).

[65] I borrow this label from the late SJ Gould, 'Non-overlapping Magisteria' in Steven Rose (ed), *The Richness of Life* (New York, Norton and Co, 2007) 590, in which he advances the theory that science and religion each have a domain and that these two domains do not overlap. However, my usage is intentionally different.

[66] Virgo (n 62) 98.

between public law and private law are much more porous than we traditionally conceive them to be.[67]

The critique is also flawed because coherence in the law is necessary for two key reasons. First, if the law is not to be arbitrary, it must justify its normative force to those who are subject to it. Second, the law must be intelligible to those whose actions it guides. Let me consider each of these reasons in turn.

When the courts adjudicate a private dispute, they apply legal rules and principles to a relationship between the claimant and defendant. In arriving at a determination regarding liability and the appropriate remedy, the courts must justify this decision to the parties and to the public. In giving a reasoned judgment, the courts make explicit and thereby give authoritative public recognition to the elements of the relationship between the parties.[68] Justification is therefore essential to any reasoned, non-arbitrary determination regarding the application of legal norms. In this sense, adjudication and thus the common law is a justificatory enterprise.

When courts make determinations regarding the rights and duties of parties, as well as the appropriate remedy for breaches of rights, these determinations are ultimately coercive in nature. The parties are obliged to follow them. For such coercion to be authoritative, legitimate, and ultimately fair, the courts must provide adequate justification for its determinations. As Weinrib rightly observes, '[t]he private law relationship is not merely an emanation of official power; it is a mode of moral association that attaches decisive importance to the justification of the norms that constitute it'.[69]

Coherence is essential to justification. When a justification lacks coherence, the legal relationships it orders become arbitrary. By coherence I mean more than mere consistency.[70] A set of rules are mutually consistent if they do not contradict one another. By contrast, coherence 'is the property of a set of propositions which, taken together, "make sense" in its entirety'.[71] The normative propositions must 'hang together'.[72]

Second, coherence is desirable because incoherence leads to a state of affairs that is intolerable if the law is to provide us with a sound basis for ordering our affairs and reasoning practically about courses of action. To be sound, a legal system must permit those subject to it to reason practically about courses of action. Incoherent laws lose their intelligibility and thereby fail to provide a basis for reasoning practically.

The ideal of coherence does not stop with specific subsets of the legal system: it extends to the law as a whole. In this way, coherence reaches for the essential unity of the law. That is, while a state's domestic law is divided and subdivided

[67] For an extensive discussion of the relationship between public and private law, see K Barker and D Jensen (eds), *Private Law: Key Encounters with Public Law* (Cambridge, Cambridge University Press, 2013).

[68] Weinrib, *The Idea of Private Law* (n 9) 35.

[69] ibid 39.

[70] While I used the term 'consistency' in *Hall v Hebert*, I use the term 'coherence' rather than 'consistency' here because 'coherence' brings out important features of the concept.

[71] N MacCormick, *Rhetoric and the Rule of Law: A Theory of Legal Reasoning* (Oxford, Oxford University Press, 2005) 190.

[72] R Dworkin, *Law's Empire* (Cambridge MA, Harvard University Press, 1986).

into domains such as private law (tort, contract, and unjust enrichment), public law (administrative and constitutional law), and criminal law, these individual branches can only be fully understood within broader values that unite the whole. These broader values are different, but complementary. They are implicit in the branches of the law: 'orderly government and distributive justice; civil peace and retributive justice; private life and market economy, underpinned by remedial measures of corrective justice'.[73] Dworkin expressed a similar idea when he wrote that that the law must 'express a single and comprehensive vision of justice'.[74] In other words, the law is a seamless web.[75] This is the position adopted by the majority of the Supreme Court of Canada in *Hall v Hebert*.

On this view, it is part of a judge's task to seek to develop a coherent system of norms that aims to make sense of different branches of the law. A judge's decision in a particular case should fit with the broader principles in a way that 'makes sense' of the relevant body of law.[76] As McHugh J of the High Court of Australia put it in *Woolcock Street Investments Pty Ltd v CDG Pty Ltd*, '[l]aw is too complex for it to be a seamless web. But, so far as possible, courts should try to make its principles and policies coherent.'[77] This obligation extends to reconciling the subset of norms that make up tort law and the subset of norms that make up criminal law, at least where those two subsets of law intersect. The obligation arises, as we saw above, from the requirements of justification and intelligibility.

This does not mean, however, that the principles of the criminal law necessarily trump those of tort law or even that the principles of the two domains will be relevant to one another in a large number of cases.[78] Criminal and tort law have different objectives and their internal logic often works according to different principles. There are often good reasons for not applying the same principles across these domains, as recognised by Lord Scott. But there are some situations where it may be useful to consider the principles of both domains as a coherent whole, provided this can be done in a way that respects the principles of each domain. The illegality defence is one such situation.

4. RECONCILING THE ILLEGALITY DEFENCE WITH CORRECTIVE JUSTICE

The illegality defence in its broad form presents a challenge to the correlative structure of the corrective justice model.[79] The illegality defence asks the court to consider the claimant independently of the defendant. In doing so, it disrupts

[73] N MacCormick, *Institutions of Law* (Oxford, Oxford University Press, 2007) 304.
[74] Dworkin (n 72) 134.
[75] This is a familiar trope in the law. It is sometimes attributed to FW Maitland, though I am unable to reliably do so. He appears to have expressed the thought in respect to history: 'Such is the unity of all history that anyone who endeavours to tell a piece of it must feel that his first sentence tears a seamless web'. See FW Maitland, 'A Prologue to a History of English Law' (1898) 14 *LQR* 13.
[76] MacCormick (n 71) 189.
[77] [2004] HCA 16; (2004) 216 CLR 515 [102].
[78] Virgo (n 62) 101.
[79] J Goudkamp, *Tort Law Defences* (Oxford, Hart Publishing, 2013) 11–12; Weinrib, *The Idea of Private Law* (n 9) ch 5; Beever (n 1) ch 10.

the correlative and integrated structure of a corrective justice model. As Weinrib observes:[80]

> the treatment of each transaction as a unit implies that its elements are internally integrated. If the harm constitutes an integrated relationship of doing and suffering, the respective parties cannot be considered independently of each other. Normative considerations that are unilaterally applicable either to the doer or to the sufferer are, therefore, out of place.

For example, consider the deterrence rationale for invoking the illegality defence. As we have seen, the courts sometimes claim that denying the claimant recovery on the basis that he has engaged in illegal conduct is necessary in order to deter the claimant and others from illegal conduct. However, deterrence does not sit within a corrective justice model of tort law because deterrence focuses solely on the defendant without reference to the relationship with the claimant. The policy goal of deterrence 'fails to embrace both parties'.[81] The same is true of the other four policy rationales for the broad version of the illegality defence.[82]

The broad version of the illegality defence fits ill with the corrective justice model of tort law. However, the narrow form of the defence maintains the integrity of the correlative relationship between claimant and defendant. On the narrow form, the defence can only be invoked in two situations:[83] 'This concern is in issue where a damage award in a civil suit would, in effect, allow a person to profit from illegal or wrongful conduct, or would permit an evasion or rebate of a penalty prescribed by the criminal law'.

In these two situations, the principles of the criminal law are relevant to the tort law analysis because they tell us that the claimant is asserting a loss of something to which she is not entitled.[84] Since the criminal law holds that she has no legally recognised interest in the profit of her illegal conduct, she cannot therefore establish a loss in tort. Similarly, a claimant has no legally recognised interest in evading or lessening the penalty prescribed by the criminal law and, as such, she cannot establish a loss in tort. As Beever explains:[85]

> The reason the claimant cannot recover is not that she possessed no primary right, nor that the right was not violated by the defendant, but that *in law* the violation of the right had no *value*. In consequence, the defendant need not compensate the claimant because, in the eyes of the law and in the eyes of corrective justice, she suffered no loss.

Therefore, it is not that tort law's objective of providing redress for wrongs is made secondary to the goal of coherence, but rather that by taking a coherent view of the different branches of the law it becomes clear that the law does not accord the

[80] EJ Weinrib, 'The Special Morality of Tort Law' (1989) 34 *McGill Law Journal* 403, 408.

[81] For a variation of this critique, see ibid 408–09.

[82] In the result, the application of the coherence principle overlaps to a certain extent with the application of the policy of 'preventing wrongful profit'. However, this policy rationale has occasionally been applied more broadly than the coherence principle to deny the claimant recovery where the claimant's claim is merely for compensation for personal injuries sustained in the course of illegal conduct as a consequence of the negligence of the defendant. The application of the coherence principle would not deny the claimant recovery in this situation.

[83] *Hall v Hebert* (n 12) 169 (McLachlin J).

[84] Beever (n 1) 381.

[85] ibid 382.

violation of the claimant's right any legal value. In this way, respecting the principle of coherence leads to the interrelation of tort and criminal law, while maintaining the integrity of each. It does not disrupt the correlative relationship between the claimant and the defendant inherent in a corrective justice model of tort law.

5. CONCLUSION

This chapter has sought to provide an account of the illegality defence that fits with a corrective justice model of tort law. The account is based on the principle of maintaining the integrity of the justice system, which is the narrow basis for the defence adopted by the Supreme Court of Canada in *Hall v Hebert*. The notion of coherence within the legal system as a whole may bear fruit, not only at the intersection of tort law and criminal law, but potentially at the intersection between tort law and other domains, such as the law of contract, property and even public law.

12

The Doctrine of Illegality and Interference with Chattels

JAMES GOUDKAMP AND LORENZ MAYR*

1. INTRODUCTION

GIVEN ITS CURRENT prominence, one could almost be forgiven for thinking that the doctrine of illegality, which is often known by way of the maxims *ex turpi causa non oritur actio*[1] and *ex dolo malo non oritur actio*,[2] has a long lineage in tort law. In truth, however, it is a fairly late arrival on the scene. In 1954 in *National Coal Board v England* Lord Porter declared that the doctrine 'is generally applied to a question of contract' and that he was 'by no means prepared to concede where concession is not required that it applies also to the case of a tort'.[3] Glanville Williams, in a note on *England*, concurred. Williams wrote that illegality 'is not one of the general defences recognised in tort'.[4] It was not until well into the second half of the twentieth century that it became firmly established in England[5] and in other parts of the Commonwealth[6] that unlawful conduct by the claimant is an answer to liability in tort.

Considering that the doctrine of illegality was ushered into tort law only relatively recently, the volume of jurisprudence that it has spawned is remarkable. It is now surely one of tort law's most topical rules. It is frequently in issue before the courts, and has lately been addressed by the highest courts in numerous jurisdictions, including Australia,[7] Canada,[8] England[9] and Singapore.[10] Thorough reviews

* We are most grateful to Andy Dyson and Fred Wilmot-Smith for their penetrating comments.

1 'No cause of action may be founded upon an immoral or illegal act': *Revill v Newbery* [1996] QB 567 (CA) 576 (Neill LJ).

2 'No court will lend its aid to a man who founds his cause of action upon an immoral or an illegal act': *Holman v Johnson* (1775) 1 Cowp 341, 343; 98 ER 1120, 1121 (Lord Mansfield).

3 [1954] AC 403 (HL) 419. See also *Betts v Sanderson Estate* (1988) 31 BCLR (2d) 1 (CA) 8.

4 G Williams, 'Contributory Negligence and Vicarious Liability' (1954) 17 *MLR* 365, 365.

5 *Ashton v Turner* [1981] QB 137 (QBD) is generally credited with ushering the doctrine of illegality into English tort law.

6 The foundational decision in Australia is probably *Smith v Jenkins* (1970) 119 CLR 397 (HCA). In Canada the decision that put the doctrine on the juridical map is probably *Tallow v Tailfeathers* (1973) 44 DLR (3d) 55 (SC Alta AD) (the reasons of Clement JA).

7 *Miller v Miller* [2011] HCA 9; (2011) 242 CLR 446.

8 *Hall v Hebert* [1993] 2 SCR 159 (SCC); *HL v Canada (AG)* [2005] SCC 25; [2005] 1 SCR 401; *British Columbia v Zastowny* [2008] 1 SCR 27; [2008] SCC 4.

9 *Gray v Thames Trains Ltd* [2009] UKHL 33; [2009] 1 AC 1339; *Stone and Rolls Ltd v Moore Stephens* [2009] UKHL 39; [2009] 1 AC 1391; *Allen v Hounga* [2014] UKSC 47; [2014] ICR 847; *Les Laboratoires Servier v Apotex Inc* [2014] UKSC 55.

10 *United Project Consultants Pte Ltd v Leong Kwok Onn* [2005] 4 SLR (R) 214.

of the doctrine have been undertaken by the English Law Commission,[11] and there has been an outpouring of analysis by both judges writing extra-curially[12] and academics.[13] However, the attention that has been lavished on the doctrine has largely been confined to the context of actions for negligently inflicted personal injury. The doctrine's role in other situations has been neglected.[14]

This chapter begins the process of redressing this situation. It does so by analysing the doctrine's role in relation to actions for interference with chattels. The chapter unfolds in the following way. In Section 2 we give some hypothetical examples of the types of cases with which we are concerned. These cases will form the basis for the entire analysis. In Section 3 we consider how the hypothetical cases would be decided if they arose. Our focus here is on English law, although we will refer occasionally to the law in other jurisdictions. In Section 4 we seek to identify, with reference to the hypothetical cases, the precise legal route by which the doctrine of illegality can prevent recovery in the context of actions for interference with chattels. In Section 5 we leave the current law behind and consider how the hypothetical cases ought to be decided.

2. THE HYPOTHETICAL CASES

As we have just mentioned, we will use hypothetical cases to explore the doctrine of illegality in the context of interference with chattels. These hypothetical cases, which we will place into four groups, are not exhaustive of the types of situations in which the doctrine can arise in this setting. However, we believe that they cover most of the field.[15]

[11] Law Commission, *The Illegality Defence in Tort: A Consultation Paper* (LCCP No 160, 2001); Law Commission, *The Illegality Defence* (CP 189, 2009); Law Commission, *The Illegality Defence* (No 320, 2010).

[12] See, eg, Chief Justice McLachlin's chapter in this volume: ch 11. See also J Sumption, 'Reflections on the Law of Illegality' (2012) 20 *Restitution Law Review* 1; J Mance, '*Ex Turpi Causa*—When Latin Avoids Liability' (2014) 18 *Edinburgh Law Review* 175.

[13] For a small sample, see EJ Weinrib, 'Illegality as a Tort Defence' (1976) 26 *University of Toronto Law Journal* 28; RA Prentice, 'Of Tort Reform and Millionaire Muggers: Should an Obscure Equitable Doctrine be Revived to Dent the Litigation Crisis?' (1995) 32 *San Diego Law Review* 53; M Fordham, 'The Role of Ex Turpi Causa in Tort Law' [1998] *Singapore Journal of Legal Studies* 238; R Glofcheski, 'Plaintiff's Illegality as a Bar to Recovery of Personal Injury Damages' (1999) 19 *Legal Studies* 6; J Goudkamp, 'A Revival of the Doctrine of Attainder? The Statutory Illegality Defences to Liability in Tort' (2007) 29 *Sydney Law Review* 445; J Goudkamp, 'The Defence of Joint Illegal Enterprise' (2010) 34 *Melbourne University Law Review* 425; JR Spencer, 'Civil Liability for Crimes' in M Dyson (ed), *Unravelling Tort and Crime* (Cambridge, Cambridge University Press, 2014) ch 11; G Virgo, 'Balancing Public Policy and Justice: Illegality's Role in the Law of Tort' in M Dyson (ed), *Unravelling Tort and Crime* (Cambridge, Cambridge University Press, 2014) ch 7.

[14] See, eg, S Deakin, A Johnston and B Markesinis, *Markesinis and Deakin's Tort Law*, 7th edn (Oxford, Oxford University Press, 2013) 776–80; M Lunney and K Oliphant, *Tort Law: Text and Materials*, 5th edn (Oxford, Oxford University Press, 2013) 315–29; J Murphy and C Witting, *Street on Torts*, 13th edn (Oxford, Oxford University Press, 2012) 210–214, 345–347. These authors' discussion of the doctrine of illegality is essentially limited to the domain of negligently inflicted personal injury.

[15] Our hypothetical cases might be criticised on the ground that the claimants in many of them would not in reality bring proceedings. In response to such criticism, we would note that this is an area of the law that often produces unexpected and unusual claims. Some of the more extraordinary cases include *Burns v Edman* [1970] 2 QB 541 (QBD) (claimant dependants sued in respect of loss of financial support from professional criminal); *Meah v McCreamer* [1985] 1 All ER 367 (QBD) (man who was convicted

2.1 The Chattel is Used in the Furtherance of Some Illegal Act

The first group of cases concerns situations where the chattel in question, although lawfully acquired and possessed, is used in the furtherance of some illegal act. We have two cases in this group:

> *Getaway Driver*: C and D rob a bank. They flee from the scene of the crime in C's car. D drives. C and D are chased by the police. D negligently loses control of the vehicle and it collides with a telegraph pole. The car is damaged as a result. C sues D in negligence in respect of the damage done to his car.

> *Meth Cook:* D negligently crashes his car into a van belonging to C. C is a methamphetamine 'cook' and was using his van as a laboratory. C sues D in negligence for the damage caused to the van.

The key difference between these cases concerns causation. In *Getaway Driver* the damage to the car occurred due to C's illegal act. Conversely, in *Meth Cook* the fact that the van was used in the furtherance of an illegal purpose merely gave rise to the occasion on which the collision occurred.

2.2 The Method by which Possession of the Chattel was Acquired is Illegal

In the second group of cases, the issue of unlawful use is not present. Instead, the way in which possession of the chattel was acquired is unlawful. Again, we have two cases in this group:

> *Illegal Sale*: C buys property from X and takes possession of it. A statute stipulates that it is an offence to buy or sell the property in question unless both parties to the transaction have a permit. Neither C nor X had a permit. D converts the property.

> *Television Thief*: D steals a television from C. C had previously stolen it from X. C sues D in conversion.

In both of these cases, the claimant committed an offence in taking possession of the chattel that the defendant then converted. The key difference between them for our purposes concerns the mode of acquisition. In *Television Thief*, the claimant obtained

of rape sued motorist who negligently caused him to suffer brain injury that robbed him of his ability to suppresses sexual desires awarded damages in respect of his imprisonment); *Italiano v Barbaro* (1993) 40 FCR 303 (Fed Ct) (claimant injured while searching for convenient location in which to stage a car accident in order to commit insurance fraud); *Re Commonwealth of Australia v Winter* (1993) Aust Torts Reports 81–212 (Fed Ct) (claimant motorcyclist injured while trying to outrun police); *Vellino v Chief Constable of Greater Manchester* [2001] EWCA Civ 1249; [2002] 1 WLR 218 (man who jumped out of second-floor window in attempt to escape arrest sued the police alleging a negligent failure to stop him from throwing himself out of the window); *Worrall v British Railways Board* [1999] CLY 1413 (CA) (man convicted of sexual offences denied redress in respect of the consequences of his convictions on the ground that he would not have committed the offences but for a negligently inflicted personality change); *Sacco v Chief Constable of South Wales Constabulary* (unreported, Court of Appeal, 15 May 1998) (arrestee who was detained in rear of police vehicle sued police for failing to prevent him from kicking the door of the vehicle open and throwing himself onto the road).

possession of the chattel in question by stealing it, whereas in *Illegal Sale* the claimant came into possession of the chattel under a contract the making of which was illegal.

2.3 Possession of the Chattel is Illegal

The illegality in the previous cases lay in the fact that the chattel was used in the course of some illegal activity (*Getaway Driver* and *Meth Cook*) or in the mode by which possession of the chattel was acquired (*Illegal Sale* and *Television Thief*). In our next group of cases, the claimant committed an offence in possessing the chattel. We have two cases in this group:

> *Heroin Dealer*: C is a heroin dealer. His heroin is negligently destroyed by D. C sues D in negligence in respect of the loss of the heroin.
>
> *Unlicensed Shotgun Owner*: D intentionally destroys a shotgun belonging to C. C did not hold a shotgun certificate and was thus committing an offence in possessing the shotgun.[16] There would have been no offence had C held the necessary certificate. C sues D in trespass to goods.

The difference between *Heroin Dealer* and *Unlicensed Shotgun Owner* that we are hoping to tease out concerns that between incurable illegality (*Heroin Dealer*) and potentially curable illegality (*Unlicensed Shotgun Owner*).

2.4 Chattel Sought by Claimant in Order to Commit an Offence

Our final type of case involves a claimant who is kept out of possession by the defendant of a chattel that he wants to use in order to commit an offence:

> *Assailant*: C lends his baseball bat to D. He later asks for it to be returned to him. C explains to D that he wants to use the bat to murder X. D refuses to return the bat. C sues D in conversion.

3. HOW WOULD THE HYPOTHETICAL CASES BE DECIDED?

The goal of this section is to discover what the outcome in each of the hypothetical cases would be. We will consider the cases *seriatim*.

3.1 The Chattel is Used in the Furtherance of Some Illegal Act

3.1.1 Getaway Driver

It is reasonably clear the claimant in *Getaway Driver* would fail in his action. The principles established in *Gray v Thames Trains Ltd*[17] are determinative here. The

[16] Firearms Act 1968 (UK), s 2.

[17] Above n 9. The decision is noted in J Goudkamp, 'The Defence of Illegality: *Gray v Thames Trains Ltd*' (2009) 17 *Torts Law Journal* 205.

claimant in *Gray* suffered a psychiatric injury in a train accident that had been caused by the defendants' negligence. Approximately two years later, the claimant stabbed to death an intoxicated pedestrian with whom he had become embroiled in an argument. The prosecution accepted a plea of guilty to manslaughter on the basis of diminished responsibility and the claimant received a custodial sentence.[18] The claimant sought damages in respect of various losses that he suffered as a consequence of committing the manslaughter, including his loss of liberty, damage to his reputation caused by the conviction, feelings of guilt and remorse, and the loss of earnings suffered on account of his being detained. The defendants accepted that the claimant would not have killed the pedestrian but for the psychiatric injury that they negligently caused the claimant to suffer but argued that these losses were not compensable by virtue of the doctrine of illegality. The House of Lords agreed. The leading speech was given by Lord Hoffmann.[19] His Lordship said that the doctrine of illegality could be split into two rules: a 'narrow rule' and a 'wide rule'. Pursuant to the 'narrow rule' recovery is not permitted in respect of sanctions imposed by the criminal law.[20] The 'narrow rule', in Lord Hoffmann's words, 'is that you cannot recover for damage which flows from loss of liberty, a fine or other punishment lawfully imposed upon you in consequence of your own unlawful act'.[21] According to the 'wide rule', the law will not allow a claimant to recover in respect of the consequences of his own criminal wrong. The 'wide rule', as Lord Hoffmann put it, 'is that you cannot recover compensation for loss which you have suffered in consequence of your own criminal act'.[22] There is little doubt that the action in *Getaway Driver* would be caught by the 'wide rule'.

In response to the foregoing, it might be contended that *Gray* can be distinguished. In particular, it might be stressed that *Getaway Driver* is a joint illegal enterprise case (C and D were acting in concert) while *Gray* was not (the defendants in *Gray* were obviously not complicit in any way in the claimant's crime). Do the principles adumbrated in *Gray* apply to joint illegal enterprise cases? It is now clear that they do. *Delaney v Pickett*[23] and *Joyce v O'Brien*[24] were decided shortly after *Gray*. Unlike *Gray*, they were both joint illegal enterprise cases. In *Delaney* the claimant passenger was injured in a car accident that was caused by the negligence of the driver of the vehicle in which he was travelling. It was discovered by rescue services when they attended the scene that the claimant and the driver were transporting cannabis. In *Joyce* the parties had stolen a ladder from a residential property. They loaded it onto

[18] The claimant was ordered to be detained in a hospital pursuant to s 37 of the Mental Health Act 1983 (UK), subject to a definite restriction order made under s 41.

[19] Lord Hoffmann's speech and its impact is treated in James Goudkamp, 'A Long, Hard Look at *Gray v Thames Trains Ltd*' in P Davies and J Pila (eds), *The Jurisprudence of Lord Hoffmann* (Oxford, Hart Publishing, 2015) (forthcoming).

[20] Cases that raise the narrow rule are discussed in J Goudkamp, 'Can Tort Law be Used to Deflect the Impact of Criminal Sanctions? The Role of the Illegality Defence' (2006) 14 *Torts Law Journal* 20.

[21] Above n 9, [29].

[22] ibid.

[23] [2011] EWCA Civ 1532; [2012] 1 WLR 2149, noted in J Goudkamp, 'The Defence of Illegality in Tort Law: Wither the Rule in Pitts v Hunt?' (2012) 71 *CLJ* 481. The saga in this case continued in *Delaney v Secretary of State for Transport* [2014] EWHC 1785 (QB).

[24] [2013] EWCA Civ 546; [2014] 1 WLR 70, noted in M Fordham, 'Not So Different After All? A Causation-Based Approach to Joint Illegal Enterprises' [2013] *Singapore Journal of Legal Studies* 202.

a van which the defendant drove. The claimant rode on the back of the van but fell from it as the parties fled from the scene of the crime. The Court of Appeal held that the 'wide rule' was the relevant test in both cases[25] (although in *Delaney* it was found not to be satisfied on the facts[26]). We add, also, that nothing turns on the fact that *Gray* was a personal injury case. The decision is plainly not limited to that context.

3.1.2 Meth Cook

In *Getaway Driver*, the damage to the claimant's car was causally connected to the illegal conduct. In contrast, in *Meth Cook* the fact that the claimant's van contained a methamphetamine laboratory was causally unrelated to the damage done to it. The van would have been damaged just the same had it not contained the laboratory. It is clear, therefore, that the 'wide rule' in *Gray* would not be triggered in *Meth Cook* and, because offending which is causally unrelated to damage suffered will not engage the doctrine of illegality,[27] we believe that the claimant in *Meth Cook* would succeed in his action. A case that is directly on point is *Kelly v Churchill Car Insurance*.[28] The claimant's car in this matter had been damaged by the defendant's negligence.[29] The claimant had stolen a tax disc from his employer and had it on display in his car when the accident occurred. The defendant contended that the claimant's illegal conduct should bar his claim. Unsurprisingly, this submission was rejected. Gibbs J wrote: 'Whilst [the claimant's conduct] was reprehensible, it remains the case that the accident had no sensible causal connection with the use of the tax disc, but arose directly from the negligence of [the defendant]'.[30]

3.2 The Method by which Possession of the Chattel was Acquired is Illegal

3.2.1 Illegal Sale

Neither rule in *Gray* applies to *Illegal Sale*. The 'narrow rule' in *Gray* is obviously irrelevant. The claimant in *Illegal Sale* is not complaining about a criminal sanction that had been imposed on him. The 'wide rule' is also inapplicable. It is untenable to say that the claimant caused the damage that is the subject of his action. But the fact that neither the 'narrow rule' nor the 'wide rule' identified in *Gray* applies to *Illegal Sale* does not mean that *Illegal Sale* and cases like it raise no issues with respect to the

[25] *Delaney v Pickett* [2011] EWCA Civ 1532; [2012] 1 WLR 2149 [37], [64]; *Joyce v O'Brien* (ibid) [25]–[29].

[26] ibid [37], [64].

[27] 'It is not sufficient if the criminal activity merely gives occasion for tortious conduct of the defendant': *Vellino v Chief Constable of the Greater Manchester Police* (n 15) [70]. See also the well-known dictum of Lord Asquith of Bishopstone in *National Coal Board v England* (n 3) 429: 'if A and B are proceeding to the premises which they intend burglariously to enter, and before they enter them, B picks A's pocket and steals his watch, I cannot prevail on myself to believe that A could not sue in tort ... The theft is totally unconnected with the burglary'.

[28] [2006] EWHC 18 (QB); [2007] RTR 26. See also *Delaney v Pickett* (n 25), especially at [37].

[29] The claimant also suffered personal injury.

[30] [2006] EWHC 18 (QB); [2007] RTR 26 [15]. Any claim in respect of any methamphetamine or drug paraphernalia destroyed in the accident would be governed by *Heroin Dealer*, which is discussed in Section 3.3.1.

doctrine of illegality. Rather, the applicability of the doctrine to *Illegal Sale* and cognate cases is governed by other rules. Lord Hoffmann stressed this in *Gray*. His Lordship said that different rules apply to, among other things, 'cases about rights of property'.[31] Lord Hoffmann's language is too broad since *Getaway Driver* and *Meth Cook* are both 'cases about rights of property' (the claimants in both of these cases were complaining about interferences with their property) yet *Gray* dictates how they should be decided, for the reasons that we have given.[32] But Lord Hoffmann's warning about the limited scope of *Gray* nevertheless makes it clear that *Gray* should not to be regarded as laying down some type of comprehensive code on the law of illegality in the tort context.

If, as we have argued, the rules enunciated in *Gray* simply do not govern *Illegal Sale*, which rules do? We believe that four relevant rules can be distilled from other cases. The first rule is that 'property in chattels and land can pass under a contract which is illegal and therefore would have been unenforceable as a contract'.[33] Our legal system does not treat illegal transactions as never having taken place. While it might refuse to enforce those transactions, once a transaction has occurred, title to the property that is the subject of the transaction will have shifted.

The second rule is that relief in respect of interference with chattels will not be withheld on the ground that the mode by which the claimant acquired possession of the property was illegal. This is clear from the well-known decision in *Bowmakers, Ltd v Barnet Instruments, Ltd*.[34] The claimant in this case bought machine tools from a third party. For reasons that are presently irrelevant, the claimant committed an offence in entering into this contract. The claimant then leased the tools to the defendant. The defendant refused to return them and the claimant successfully sued in conversion.[35] Du Parcq LJ, speaking for the Court of Appeal, said:[36]

> In our opinion, a man's right to possess his own chattels will as a general rule be enforced against one who, without any claim of right, is detaining them, or has converted them to his own use, even though it may appear either from the pleadings, or in the course of the trial, that the chattels in question came into the defendant's possession by reason of an illegal contract between himself and the plaintiff, provided that the plaintiff does not seek, and is not forced, either to found his claim on the illegal contract or to plead its illegality in order to support its claim.

It is clear from this passage that the court will not withhold relief in conversion on the ground that the claimant acquired possession pursuant to a contract the entering into which was illegal.

A third rule is also revealed in the passage that has just been quoted, namely, that the claimant's action will fail if the claimant needs to rely on his illegal conduct in

[31] Above n 9 [30].

[32] See Sections 3.1.1 and 3.1.2.

[33] *Tinsley v Milligan* [1994] 1 AC 340 (HL) 370. See also *Singh v Ali* [1960] AC 167 (HL) 176–77.

[34] [1945] 1 KB 65 (CA).

[35] See also *Singh v Ali* (n 33) (action in trespass succeeded against defendant who seized lorry belonging to the claimant although claimant acquired title under an illegal contract); *Belvoir Finance Co v Stapleton* [1971] 1 QB 210 (CA) (action for conversion of cars bought under an illegal contract succeeded against car salesman); *Webb v Chief Constable of Merseyside Police* [2000] QB 427 (CA) (action for conversion of money that constituted the proceeds of drug trafficking succeeded against the police who had lawfully seized the money but refused to return it to the claimant after their statutory power of confiscation expired).

[36] Above n 34, 71.

order to establish any of the elements of the action in which he sues. This 'reliance rule' has been endorsed on many occasions, most notably in *Tinsley v Milligan*.[37] An obvious situation where it would prevent liability from arising is where the claimant complains about interference with property that is illegal to possess in all circumstances. In all tort actions for interference with property, the claimant, in order to establish liability, must identify the property in question. Where the property is necessarily illegal to possess, the claimant cannot plead a cause of action without relying on his illegal possession.

The fourth rule is that the mere fact that the illegal conduct comes to light in the course of the dispute is insufficient to trigger the doctrine of illegality.[38] So, for example, in *Zabihi v Janzemini* it was held that the fact that converted jewellery was (allegedly) smuggled into the United Kingdom by the claimant was not a good answer to liability, since the claimant did not need to rely on the illegal importation in order to establish all of the elements of the action in conversion.[39] To make out that action the claimant needed merely to prove that he was in possession of the property and that the defendant intentionally and directly interfered with that possession. This fourth rule probably reflects a concern to ensure that the issues in proceedings do not mushroom out of control. But for the fourth rule, defendants would have an incentive to drag into the proceedings wrongdoing by the claimant that is only tenuously connected with the dispute.[40]

Since we will return to these rules periodically in this chapter, we enumerate them for ease of reference. They are:

(1) title to property can be acquired under an illegal contract;
(2) an action for interference with chattels can succeed even though the means by which the claimant came into possession of the property were illegal;
(3) a claimant will fail in his action if he needs to rely on his illegal conduct in order to establish it;
(4) illegal conduct by the claimant on which the claimant does not need to rely to establish his action and which merely emerges during the course of the dispute is irrelevant to the determination of the proceedings.

These rules combine to dictate that the claimant in *Illegal Sale* would succeed in his action. The first rule means that the claimant acquired title to the property. This rule is not strictly speaking relevant to *Illegal Sale* since the claimant in that case is complaining about interference with his possession. It follows from the second rule that it is irrelevant for the purposes of the civil proceedings that the claimant committed an offence by the way in which he acquired possession of the property. The third rule is not engaged since the claimant does not need to reveal anything unlawful in order to plead a set of facts that meets all of the elements of the action in conversion.

[37] Above n 33. See also *Clunis v Camden and Islington Health Authority* [1998] QB 978 (CA) 987.
[38] *Tinsley v Milligan* (n 33) 370.
[39] [2008] EWHC 2910 (Ch), [286].
[40] The courts have sometimes warned that the doctrine of illegality should be formulated so as to exclude from consideration offending that is merely collateral to the action: see, eg, *Saunders v Edwards* [1987] 1 WLR 1116 (CA) 1134.

The fourth rule insulates the claimant from the suggestion that his action should be defeated merely because evidence of his offence emerges during the proceedings.

3.2.2 Television Thief

In the discussion of *Illegal Sale* it was noted that the fact that the claimant took possession of property by illegal means will not prevent the claimant from succeeding in an action for interference with that property (rule (2) above[41]). What, however, is the situation where the illegal means by which the claimant came into possession was theft? Does that make a difference? This is the question that *Television Thief* raises. Until relatively recently, it was unclear how *Television Thief* would be decided. However, these doubts were banished by the decision of the Court of Appeal in *Costello v Chief Constable of Derbyshire Constabulary*.[42] This case established that rule (2) applies even if the illegal means by which the claimant came into possession of the property in question was theft. In *Costello* the police seized a car from the claimant. The police did so because they suspected that it had been stolen. The claimant sought the return of the vehicle and damages for its detention. Lightman J, speaking on behalf of the Court of Appeal, held that possessory title vests in a thief or other person who comes into possession of property by unlawful means and that such possession is entitled to protection against interference. As Lightman J put it, such possession 'vests in the possessor a possessory title which is good against the world save as against anyone setting up or claiming under a better title'.[43] *Costello* makes it clear that the claimant in *Television Thief* would succeed in his action.[44]

3.3 Possession of the Chattel is Illegal

3.3.1 Heroin Dealer

The reliance rule dictates that claimants who need to rely on their unlawful conduct in order to establish their cause of action for interference with their chattels will not succeed in their action. The claimant in *Heroin Dealer* would fall foul of this rule. It would be impossible for him to describe in his pleadings a cause of action in negligence without identifying the property that was destroyed. Pleading that one was in possession of heroin *ipso facto* discloses that one committed an offence.[45] That the claimant in *Heroin Dealer* would fail in his action is put beyond doubt by comments

[41] See Section 3.2.1.

[42] [2001] EWCA Civ 381; [2001] 1 WLR 1437, noted in J Getzler, 'Unclean Hands and the Doctrine of Jus Tertii' (2001) 117 *LQR* 565 and D Fox, 'Enforcing a Possessory Title to a Stolen Car' (2002) 61 *CLJ* 27.

[43] [2001] EWCA Civ 381; [2001] 1 WLR 1437 [31].

[44] See also *Ecclestone v Khyami* [2014] EWHC 29 (QB) [125]–[129].

[45] The circumstances in which it is permissible to possess heroin are so unusual that they can be disregarded for present purposes. However, for completeness, it should be noted that the possession of heroin is lawful in exceptional circumstances. For example, it is lawful to take possession of heroin in order to prevent another person from committing a continuing offence in relation to it and with a view to destroying it as soon as was reasonably practicable: Misuse of Drugs Act 1971 (UK), s 5(4)(a).

made in several cases. In *Bowmakers* it was said that a claim could not be brought in respect of interference with a chattel that is 'of such a kind that it is unlawful to deal in [it] at all'.[46] By way of example, the court suggested that it would not be possible to recover damages in respect of interference with obscene books. Another case on point is *Webb v Chief Constable of Merseyside Police*.[47] In this matter the police had seized £36,000 in cash belonging to the claimants that they suspected was the proceeds of drug dealing. The taking was held to be actionable. May LJ, with whom Hale and Pill LJJ agreed, observed that 'money is not something which is unlawful to deal in …'. Conversely, May LJ said that the claimants would have failed if the property that was the subject of their action was controlled drugs.[48]

Would the outcome of *Heroin Dealer* be different if the quantity of heroin was very small, or if the chattel in question was not heroin but a drug the possession of which is regarded as a much less serious offence (such as cannabis)? It is submitted that these variations would probably have no impact on the outcome of the hypothetical case. This is because the claimant would still need to rely on his unlawful conduct (that is, his possession of the drug) in order to establish his cause of action.[49] Would the outcome of *Heroin Dealer* be changed if the heroin, instead of being negligently destroyed, was intentionally destroyed or converted? Again, we think that these additional variations of the facts would not change the result for the same reason.[50]

3.3.2 Unlicensed Shotgun Owner

Unlicensed Shotgun Owner exposes a lacuna in the law. We have not been able to find any case that is analogous to it. However, what we believe would happen is as follows. The crucial issue would be whether the claimant would have been able to obtain a shotgun certificate if he had applied for one (ie, whether the illegality was curable). If the claimant would have been able to obtain a certificate, he would be able to cure the illegality and, we believe, could recover damages. We doubt that a claimant who could cure his illegality would be found to fall foul of the reliance test. Conversely, if on the balance of probabilities the claimant would not have been able to obtain a certificate, the unlawfulness would be incurable and we think that the claimant would fail in his action (the action would be regarded as essentially equivalent to that in *Heroin Dealer*). As we have noted, we have been unable to

[46] Above n 34, 72.

[47] Above n 35.

[48] ibid 444. See also *Costello* (n 42) [34]. Cf *Malone v Commissioner of Police of the Metropolis (No 1)* [1980] QB 49 (CA). In this case the claimant sued the police in respect of foreign currency that they seized from him. The court said that the police were entitled to retain the money because it would be unlawful pursuant to s 2 of the Exchange Control Act 1947 (UK) for the claimant to possess the money (at 64, 70–71).

[49] Although consider the relevance here of the principle that trivial offending does not engage the doctrine of illegality. It has been said repeatedly that venial wrongdoing does not enliven the doctrine: see, eg, *Vellino v Chief Constable of the Greater Manchester Police* (n 15) [70]; *Currie v Clamp* 2002 SLT 196 (OH) [20]–[21].

[50] Consider *R v Smith* [2011] EWCA Crim 66; [2011] 1 Cr App R 30 [9]–[10]. This was an appeal against a conviction for robbery of heroin worth £50. The court was plainly inclined to the view that the possessor of the heroin would not be able to sue for its conversion.

find any cases that are directly on point. However, there are some relevant dicta that support this analysis. The most relevant passage (to which we have already referred[51]) is a comment in *Bowmakers*, where the court made it clear that one cannot recover damages in respect of interference with chattels that are 'of such a kind that it is unlawful to deal in *at all*'.[52] By implication, recovery may be granted where the chattel is one that is lawful to possess in at least *some* situations, such as when one holds a license. We suspect that the court would permit recovery only where the specific claimant is able to cure the illegality, and that it would not be enough that some people, but not the claimant in the instant case, would be able to cure the illegality. Also relevant is a dictum in *Costello* of Lightman J (who spoke for the Court of Appeal) that the court would not order the delivery a gun to a claimant who was not authorised to possess it.[53] This passage strongly suggests that damages would be denied in *Unlicensed Shotgun Owner* if the claimant were unable to obtain a certificate, but it does not exclude the possibility of recovery if a certificate would have been granted had one been sought.

3.4 Chattel Sought by Claimant in Order to Commit an Offence

Assailant is based on a hypothetical situation postulated by Waller LJ in *Guildford Borough Council v Hein*. Waller LJ said that a court would not order a defendant to deliver a gun to a claimant who sought it in order to commit a murder.[54] In formulating this scenario we also had in mind *Chief Constable of Merseyside v Owens*.[55] In this case the police confiscated a CCTV recording belonging to a man whose house had been set deliberately on fire. The recording captured an image of the arsonist, but it proved impossible for the police to identify the offender from the recording, which was of low quality. The police refused to return the recording to the owner of the house because they feared that, if the owner watched it, he would seek revenge against the actual offender or an innocent person whom he mistook for offender. The court held that property will not be ordered to be returned if 'the use of [the court's] process would in fact indirectly assist in or encourage a crime'.[56] The court concluded that this test was not satisfied on the facts of the case, and it consequently ordered the police to return the recording.

Although we have been unable to find a case that is closely analogous to *Assailant* (*Hein* and *Owens* were, relevantly, concerned not with claims for damages, but with the circumstances in which delivery of property would be ordered), the claimant in *Assailant* would clearly be denied damages. The defendant in *Assailant* would likely become an accomplice to murder if he returned the baseball bat to the claimant and the claimant used it to commit murder. Even if the claimant did not commit murder, the defendant, if he gave the claimant the bat, would probably be guilty of aiding

[51] See the text accompanying n 46.
[52] Above n 34, 72 (emphasis added).
[53] Above n 42, [34].
[54] [2005] EWCA Civ 979; [2005] BLGR 797 [65].
[55] [2012] EWHC 1515 (Admin).
[56] ibid [29].

and assisting crime under Part 2 of the Serious Crime Act 2007 (UK). We cannot think that a court would hold the defendant liable in tort for failing to do something that would expose him to liability for these serious criminal offences.[57] The dictum in *Hein* and the decision in *Owens* establish that he would also be unable to obtain an order for delivery.

4. HOW DOES THE DOCTRINE OF ILLEGALITY PREVENT RECOVERY WITHIN THE STRUCTURE OF TORT LIABILITY?

For the reasons given in the previous section, we believe that the claimants in *Getaway Driver*, *Heroin Dealer* and *Assailant* would be unsuccessful in their actions. We also believe that the claimant in *Unlicensed Shotgun Owner* would fail in his action unless he would, on the balance of probabilities, have been granted a shotgun certificate had he applied for one. However, the analysis did not go beyond demonstrating that the claimants in these hypothetical scenarios would fail. We did not isolate the precise way in which the doctrine of illegality would cause the claimants in these cases to fail. For example, we did not explain whether the claimants in these cases would fail because their illegal behaviour would be treated as denying an element of the action in which they sued or would result in their action being met with a defence.[58] Neither, in the event that the doctrine works by denying an element of a cause of action in these cases, did we specify at which element or elements the doctrine strikes. The burden of this section is to identify precisely how the doctrine of illegality would prevent liability from arising in *Getaway Driver*, *Heroin Dealer*, *Unlicensed Shotgun Owner* (if a certificate could not be obtained) and *Assailant*, assuming that we are correct in our conclusion that the claimants in these cases would be unsuccessful and leaving to one side for the moment the question of whether these claimants ought to be unsuccessful.[59] Isolating how the doctrine of illegality operates within the structure of tort law is important in order to achieve a clear conceptual understanding of the doctrine. But it is also significant because, as one of us has endeavoured to show elsewhere, many practical consequences flow from the way in which a rule prevents liability from arising.[60]

[57] The doctrine of illegality is not the only basis on which damages might be denied in a case such as *Assailant*. It is likely that other defences might be triggered, such as the defence of another defence, public necessity, and the defence of prevention of crime in s 3 of the Criminal Law Act 1967 (UK), although we have been unable to locate any cases in which these defences were enlivened in a case with a factual pattern that corresponds to that in *Assailant*.

[58] By the word 'defence' we mean a rule that prevents liability from arising even if the elements of the cause of action in which the claimant sues are present. Regarding the distinction between denials of elements of torts and defences, see J Goudkamp, *Tort Law Defences* (Oxford, Hart Publishing, 2013) chs 1–2.

[59] We consider the latter issue in Section 5.

[60] Goudkamp (n 58) ch 6.

4.1 *Getaway Driver*

We will take *Getaway Driver* first. It has already been explained that the leading case of *Gray* is dispositive of *Getaway Driver*.[61] The 'wide rule' elegantly articulated in *Gray* by Lord Hoffmann is fatal to recovery. But how, specifically, does the 'wide rule' yield this result? Lord Hoffmann explained that the 'wide rule' is engaged when the claimant's illegal conduct severs the causal connection between the defendant's conduct and the claimant's damage. The idea is that when the 'wide rule' applies the claimant rather than the defendant will have caused his own loss. It is trite law that, in order for an action in negligence to be constituted, the defendant's breach of duty must have caused the claimant damage. Thus, the 'wide rule' operates to mark a failure by the claimant to establish all of the ingredients of his action, and not as a defence.

Understanding unlawful conduct on the part of the claimant as negating the causation element (the 'causation approach') of the action in negligence has very important consequences. Because of the general rule that claimants are required to plead and prove the existence of all of the elements of their action, it means that claimants in each and every action in negligence should be required to plead and prove that their loss was not caused by their own unlawful conduct (unless one can show that the general rule does not apply). Such a requirement would be ridiculous (principally because it would result in a waste of time and resources given that there will be countless cases in which the claimant did not engage in any illegal behaviour), and this is a reason for looking askance at the 'causation approach' (and, indeed, any other approach that treats the claimant's unlawful conduct as undermining an element of the action in negligence). However, there are additional problems with treating the claimant's unlawful conduct as striking at the causation element of the action in negligence. It deviates from the general rule that the causation element of the tort of negligence will be established provided that the defendant's conduct is *a* cause of the claimant's damage.[62] The causation element of the action in negligence may be satisfied although the defendant's breach of duty was not the sole cause of the claimant's damage. No reason was given in *Gray* as to why this deviation from the general rule should be tolerated. Finally, what reason is there for treating a claimant's unlawful behaviour as the sole cause of his loss given that the same approach would plainly not apply where there are two defendants and one of them acted illegally? Suppose that D1 and D2 injure C through their negligence and that D1 but not D2's negligent conduct is also illegal conduct. In this scenario, both D1 and D2 are plainly liable to C. D2 would not be released from liability on the ground that D1's conduct in question is unlawful. D1's conduct would not be found to be the sole cause of C's damage. Why, then, should a different rule be applied to claimants?

The 'causation approach' to the doctrine of illegality should be abandoned. Assuming for the moment that the claimant in *Getaway Driver* should fail in his action, what should take its place? We believe that the best approach is for the

[61] See the text accompanying n 17.

[62] For a clear statement of this rule, see *March v E & MH Stramare Pty Ltd* (1991) 171 CLR 506 (HCA) 509.

doctrine of illegality to function as a defence. We prefer this approach primarily because it avoids the difficulties that we have just identified with the 'causation approach' and does not seem to introduce any fresh problems. It avoids the difficulty in relation to the onus of pleading and proof because the general rule in relation to defences is that facts that enliven them must be both pleaded and proved by the defendant. The two other difficulties arose in connection with the causation element of the action in negligence and obviously fall away on a defence approach.

4.2 *Heroin Dealer*

We explained earlier that the claimant in *Heroin Dealer* would fail in his action in negligence for the destruction of his heroin.[63] He would fail because he would need to rely on his illegal conduct in order to establish his cause of action. The courts have, as we have discussed, held that a claimant who needs to rely on his unlawful behaviour in order to make out his action cannot recover. But how, precisely, does this rule achieve this result within the structure of tort law? We believe that the reliance rule probably functions in this case by attacking the damage element of the action in negligence. The idea is that heroin has no value in the eyes of the law, and, therefore, its destruction does not count as damage.[64] Whatever value the black market might place on heroin, the law fixes its value at zero. We will refer to this approach as the 'no damage approach'.

The 'no damage approach' has been endorsed in Germany. The Federal Supreme Court of Justice has held that the loss of a 'factual or legal position to which the claimant is not entitled in law' does not constitute damage.[65] A particularly noteworthy case is one decided by the regional court of Osnabrück.[66] The claimant was a displaced person who had given 13 gold coins to the defendant after he had (allegedly fraudulently) promised to acquire a sewing machine and furniture for the claimant. The defendant converted the gold coins to his own use, whereupon the claimant brought proceedings in the German equivalents of the torts of conversion and deceit.[67] The court dismissed the claimant's action. It did so on the footing that, even if the facts pleaded by the claimant were true, she had not suffered any damage because, owing to a statute that had been passed by the military government, possession of the coins was illegal.[68] The statute also provided that all transactions relating to such coins were void. The court regarded this provision as reinforcing its conclusion that the claimant had not suffered any damage since it deprived the claimant of any legal means of realising the value of the coins.

[63] See Section 3.3.1.

[64] Allan Beever concurs: see A Beever, *Rediscovering the Law of Negligence* (Oxford, Hart Publishing, 2007) 382.

[65] BGH (23.11.2006), NJW-RR 2007, 569, 572; BGH (27.01.1994), NJW 1994, 858, 860; BGH (26.01.1989), NJW-RR 1989, 530, 530.

[66] LG Osnabrück (24.01.1950), NJW 1950, 751, noted by K Larenz, NJW 1950, 752.

[67] The claim was founded on § 823 I, § 823 II BGB in conjunction with § 263 I StGB and § 826 BGB.

[68] Cf *Thomas Brown and Sons v Fazal Deen* (1962) 108 CLR 391 (HCA). In this case, the High Court of Australia held that the claimant, who unlawfully failed to hand over gold to the government could have recovered damages in respect of a failure by the defendant to re-deliver them to the claimant had it not been for the fact that the claimant needed to rely on an illegal contract with the defendant (at 412).

Recall that the claimant in *Heroin Dealer* sued in negligence. Damage is of course an element of that tort, and so the claimant in *Heroin Dealer* would fail because, if the analysis that we have offered is correct, the action in negligence is incomplete. However, the 'no damage approach' is not confined to actions of which damage is the gist. It could also be used in the case of torts that are actionable per se, not to extinguish liability, but to prevent the recovery of substantial damages. Suppose that the defendant in *Heroin Dealer* had intentionally destroyed the claimant's heroin. If the claimant sued in trespass to goods, the action would be constituted but compensatory damages would be unavailable, because the claimant would not have suffered any consequential loss. The claimant would, however, be entitled to nominal damages. Here the doctrine of illegality would not preclude liability. The finding of liability would remain intact; it is only the quantum of recovery that would be affected.

The 'no damage approach' to the doctrine of illegality is not without difficulty. The first and most obvious problem with it concerns the allocation of the burden of pleading and proof. It is a well-established principle that claimants must plead and prove that they suffered damage in the case of torts of which damage is the gist, and even in the case of torts that are actionable per se, the claimants must plead and establish that they sustained damage in order to recover a substantial award. However, on the 'no damage approach' in each and every tort case arising out of the destruction of or damage to property the claimant ought to be called on to plead and prove that their possession of the property was lawful (because it should be for claimants to show that there is no illegality if illegality relates to damage since it is up to claimants to establish that they suffered damage). This would be absurd.[69] This problem would fall away if the illegality doctrine functioned as a defence. If the doctrine operated as a defence, the doctrine would be relevant only if the defendant chose to raise it.

A possible further difficulty with the 'no damage approach' is that where the doctrine of illegality is enlivened it leads, in the case of torts that are actionable per se, to an entitlement to nominal damages (if the doctrine of illegality negates damage it cannot prevent liability from arising in respect of torts that are actionable without proof of damage; the most that it can do is wipe out an entitlement to compensatory damages). This might be thought to be objectionable because the award of nominal damages indicates that the claimant has suffered a wrong.[70] It might be said that the claimant in *Heroin Dealer* has not suffered any wrong because he has no right that other people do not interfere with his heroin. However, it is not clear to us that this is the right way to look at things. The claimant in *Heroin Dealer* was, after all, the owner of the heroin and had possession of it.

[69] The 'causation approach' is afflicted by the same problem, as we have noted: see Section 4.1.

[70] It is interesting to note that treating the doctrine of illegality as a defence may not eliminate this issue. If illegality operates as a defence, nominal damages would not be awarded where the defence applies. But the mere fact that a defendant needs a defence in order to avoid liability might be thought to mean that he is a wrongdoer and that the claimant's rights have been violated.

4.3 *Unlicensed Shotgun Owner*

We believe that if the claimant in *Unlicensed Shotgun Owner* would have been able to obtain a shotgun certificate had he applied for one, he would be able to recover damages in his action in trespass to goods. However, for the reasons that we have given above,[71] we think that the outcome would be different if the claimant would have been unable to obtain a certificate. Assume that a certificate could not be obtained and that we are correct in concluding that the claimant would fail in his action. How, specifically, would this result be produced? Unfortunately, the cases offer little help in relation to this question. It is simply not one with which the courts have dealt. However, we suspect that the courts would adopt the 'no damage approach'. If the claimant in *Unlicensed Shotgun Owner* cannot cure the illegality because he cannot obtain a shotgun certificate, the scenario bears a certain resemblance to *Heroin Dealer* and, as we have shown, it is likely that the court would adopt the 'no damage approach' in *Heroin Dealer*. We have canvassed the difficulties with the 'no damage approach' earlier.

4.4 *Assailant*

We have noted earlier that the claimant in *Assailant* would fail in his action by virtue of the doctrine of illegality.[72] But by what legal route would this outcome be achieved? The situation is murky and no express guidance can be found in the cases. We doubt that the 'no damage approach' would be used. That approach seems to be restricted to actions arising from interference with chattels which are illegal to possess. It is likely, in our view, that the courts would deny recovery in *Assailant* by way of a defence. On this analysis, the claimant's cause of action in conversion in *Assailant* is complete, but he would be unable to recover because of a no-liability rule that is external to the elements of the action. Because defences eliminate liability altogether, not even nominal damages would be recoverable.

5. HOW SHOULD THE HYPOTHETICAL CASES BE DECIDED?

In this section we consider how all of the hypothetical cases ought to be decided. The analysis is in two parts. First, we set out the major arguments that have been offered in favour of rejecting tort actions on the basis that they are tainted with unlawful conduct on the part of the claimant. We contend that most of these justifications are unconvincing. Indeed, many of them are so weak that the regularity with which they are offered by the courts and commentators is surprising. The only argument that has any merit (at least in the context of interference with chattels) is the idea that the doctrine is needed to maintain the integrity of the legal system. Secondly, we argue how the hypothetical cases should be decided in accordance with that justification.

[71] See Section 3.3.2.
[72] See Section 3.4.

5.1 Rationales for Rejecting Actions on the Ground of Illegality

5.1.1 Punishment

It is sometimes suggested that denying actions in tort on account of the claimant's illegality is warranted because it metes out punishment where punishment is deserved. Allen Linden argued that 'tort law is not unwise to reinforce the criminal law by adding the civil sanction of denying recovery to whatever penal sanctions may be imposed for the offence'.[73] Paul Davies has also promoted the punishment rationale.[74] However, this rationale can be quickly discarded. In order for it to be persuasive the following propositions would need to be true: (1) that tort law should be concerned with punishment; (2) that denying recovery in tort law is a form of punishment, at least in some cases; and (3) that denying claimants damages in tort is a justified way of punishing claimants. We leave proposition (1) to one side for the purposes of this chapter. Attending to it would take us too far from the main issues with which this chapter is concerned. We have reservations about whether proposition (2) is correct. However, again, we do not want to engage with this matter in any detail due to limitations of space. We confine ourselves to the observation that when the law denies damages in tort to a claimant we would not ordinarily think that the law is punishing the claimant. Proposition (3) is plainly false. Punishing claimants by denying them damages in tort law does not respect the principle that punishment should be proportionate to the wrongdoing. Compensatory damages in tort law are calculated by reference to the loss that the claimant suffered as a result of the defendant's tort. Accordingly, more seriously injured claimants will be punished to a greater extent than less seriously injured claimants if their actions are denied. It follows that denying a tort action on the ground that the claimant acted illegally cannot be justified on the basis of punishment because there is no guarantee that the punishment handed out will correspond to the gravity of the claimant's illegal behaviour. In fact, it will almost certainly be disproportionate. An illustration may assist to expose the poverty of the punishment rationale. Suppose that the property in issue in *Illegal Sale* is worth £10m, that the claimant was denied damages because of the illegal way in which he acquired the property, and that criminal proceedings were not even brought against the claimant in that scenario on the ground that the offending was so trivial that it did not warrant prosecution. Withholding damages from the claimant because of the illegal way in which he acquired possession of the property cannot be justified on the ground that withholding damages delivers just punishment to the claimant. Assuming that proposition (2) is true, the amount of the punishment dished out is the value of the property converted, namely, £10m. Punishment of this magnitude is plainly unjustified given that it has been stipulated that the claimant's culpability is minimal. It follows that proposition (3) is false. It might be replied that although the doctrine of illegality is prone to inflict

[73] A Linden, *Canadian Tort Law*, 5th edn (Butterworths, Toronto, 1993) 473. This passage does not appear in the latest edition of this book: A Linden and B Feldthusen, *Canadian Tort Law*, 9th edn (Toronto, Butterworths, 2011).

[74] PS Davies, 'The Illegality Defence—Two Steps Forward, One Step Back?' [2009] *Conveyancer and Property Lawyer* 182, 186–87.

disproportionate punishment given that compensatory damages are calibrated to the magnitude of the claimant's loss, the doctrine shows a concern to inflict only proportionate punishment in other ways. However, this reply does not count for much primarily for the simple reason that there is simply minimal evidence that the doctrine is subject to other proportionality constraints.[75]

5.1.2 Deterrence

It is sometimes suggested that it is justifiable to deny tort actions that are contaminated by unlawful conduct of the claimant in order to deter such conduct.[76] In order for this argument to succeed, the following propositions would need to be true: (1) tort law is or should be concerned with deterring unwanted behaviour; (2) denying damages to claimants on account of their illegal behaviour would deter such behaviour; and (3) the deterrent effect of denying recovery would produce a more efficient state of affairs than would be brought about were liability imposed on the defendant. It is not possible to grapple adequately with proposition (1) in the short space available in this chapter, and so we will not say anything about it. We think that proposition (2) is very likely to be false. Consider the facts in *Heroin Dealer*. It cannot be seriously suggested that a person who is considering whether to deal in heroin is likely to be dissuaded from dealing in heroin by the risk that, if his heroin is interfered with, he may be unable to obtain and enforce a remedy in tort against the tortfeasor by virtue of the doctrine of illegality. If all of the much more significant and obvious risks that attend trafficking heroin are insufficient to deter dealing in heroin (such as the risk of being punished by the criminal law, the risk of being injured in drug-related violence, etc), it is far-fetched to think that denying relief in tort law would have any deterrent effect. It is also worth remembering that a would-be heroin dealer is unlikely to even be aware of the doctrine of illegality and, consequently, cannot be deterred by it. Such a person is, as Millett LJ noted in *Tribe v Tribe*, 'unlikely to be a studious reader of the law reports'.[77] Finally, it is unclear whether proposition (3) is true. Recognising the doctrine of illegality in this area of the law would undermine whatever potential it has to deter people from interfering with the property rights of others and it might be that more unwanted behaviour is deterred by imposing liability than by withholding it on the ground of illegality.

[75] See *Les Laboratoires Servier v Apotex Inc* [2014] UKSC 55, [18]–[19]. Although cf the following passages in which it is suggested that the doctrine of illegality will not apply if the damage suffered is disproportionate to the gravity of the claimant's wrongdoing: *Saunders v Edwards* (n 40) 1132, 1134 (Bingham LJ); *Hewison v Meridian Shipping Services Pte Ltd* [2002] EWCA 1821; [2003] ICR 766 [72] (Ward LJ).

[76] Eg, *Thackwell v Barclays Bank plc* [1986] 1 All ER 676 (QBD) 687, 689.

[77] [1996] Ch 107 (CA) 113–114.

5.1.3 Preventing Wrongful Profiting

It is a general principle of law that wrongdoers should not be permitted to profit from their wrong.[78] *Nullus commodum capere potest de injuria sua proprio.*[79] This principle is sometimes offered in support of the doctrine of illegality.[80] However, the doctrine cannot be justified on the ground that it prevents wrongdoers from profiting. Tort actions (including tort actions in respect of interference with chattels) simply do not have the potential to put the claimant into a better position than that in which he stood prior to the tort (which is what we have in mind when we talk of profit). When a claim in tort succeeds, the law merely notionally eliminates the consequences of the defendant's tort. Put differently, tort law puts (or at least strives to put) the claimant in the position in which he would have been but for the tort. Thus, if, for example, the claimant in *Heroin Dealer* was permitted to recover compensation in respect of the destruction of his heroin, he would not be placed in a better economic position than that in which he stood prior to its destruction. He would simply receive such a sum of money as would enable him to purchase replacement heroin. Except in exceptional cases that are irrelevant for present purposes, tort actions simply do not have the potential to facilitate wrongful profiting.[81]

5.1.4 Not Condoning Wrongdoing

It has often been suggested that the doctrine of illegality is justified because it prevents the courts from condoning wrongdoing.[82] This argument can be swiftly dismissed. In the first place, it fundamentally misunderstands what courts do when they enter judgment in favour of the claimant. When a court finds in favour of a claimant, the court does not condone what the claimant did. A finding in favour of a claimant in a tort case indicates merely that the claimant has been the victim of a wrong. One can say that a person has suffered a wrong without committing oneself to the proposition that whatever conduct in which the claimant engaged at the time that he was wronged is desirable and should be repeated. Furthermore, this argument in support of the doctrine of illegality can be turned on its head. Even if a court condoned the claimant's behaviour when it finds in the claimant's favour (which it does not, as we have noted), it would follow that it condoned the defendant's

[78] See, eg, *Beresford v Royal Insurance Co Ltd* [1938] AC 586 (HL) 598–99, 605; *In the Estate of Crippen* [1911] P 108, 112; *Bedford v Bedford* [1935] Ch 89 (Ch D) 92; *Marles v Philip Trant & Sons Ltd* [1954] 1 QB 29 (CA) 39; *Re Callaway* [1956] Ch 559 (Ch D) 562; *Re K* [1985] Ch 85 (Ch D) 87–88; *Kirkham v Chief Constable of Greater Manchester Police* [1990] 2 QB 283 (CA) 295; *Whiston v Whiston* [1995] Fam 198 (CA) 207; *Revill v Newbery* [1996] QB 567 (CA) 579. See also the American cases *Neiman v Hurff* 11 NJ 55, 60; 93 A 2d 345, 347 (1952); *Riggs v Palmer* 115 NY 506, 511; 22 NE 188, 190 (1889).

[79] '[N]o man can take advantage of his own wrong': *Hewison v Meridian Shipping Services Pte Ltd* (n 75) [77] (Ward LJ).

[80] See, eg, ibid.

[81] One such exceptional case is where exemplary damages are awarded. Awards of exemplary damages put the claimant in a better economic position than that which he occupied prior to the defendant's tort, all other things being equal. For a rare case that raised the doctrine of illegality and the issue of exemplary damages, see *Katko v Briney* 183 NW 2d 657 (Iowa 1971).

[82] See, eg, *Gala v Preston* (1991) 172 CLR 243 (HCA) 270–73, 277–79; *Cross v Kirkby* The Times, 5 April 2000 (CA) [76]; *Hall v Woolston Hall Leisure Ltd* [2001] 1 WLR 225 (CA) [42].

conduct (which might be much more turpitudinous than the claimant's) by denying the action. So this argument is as much an argument for excluding the doctrine of illegality as it is an argument for recognising it.

5.1.5 One cannot Rely on One's Own Illegal Act

The reliance rule has been discussed earlier.[83] It holds, recall, that a claimant cannot succeed in an action based on interference with his property if he needs to rely on illegal conduct on his part in order to establish that action. This rule is often touted as a rationale for the doctrine of illegality.[84] However, it offers no support whatsoever to the doctrine. One cannot justify the doctrine simply by referring to a test that is used to determine when it is enlivened. *Why* should claimants be deprived of the right to sue where they need to rely on their own illegal act in order to establish their claim? The mere incantation of the rule that no one may rely on his own unlawful conduct does not justify withholding a remedy.

5.1.6 Maintaining the Coherence of the Legal System

The final rationale for the doctrine of illegality that we will mention concerns the need to maintain coherence in the law. According to this rationale, the doctrine of illegality exists to prevent tort law from coming into conflict with other areas of the law. Influenced by a classic article by Ernest Weinrib,[85] McLachlin J (as her Honour then was) championed this justification for the doctrine in the ground-breaking case of *Hall v Hebert*.[86] In her Honour's words, the doctrine ought to apply where the law would otherwise 'punish conduct with the one hand while rewarding it with the other'.[87] Thus, her Honour envisaged that the doctrine would apply where, for instance, the claimant seeks damages in respect of a criminal law sanction. In *Gray* Lord Hoffmann also endorsed this rationale for the doctrine of illegality. It led him to back the 'narrow rule' that he described,[88] namely, the rule that one cannot recover damages in tort law in respect of criminal penalties. Lord Hoffmann wrote that, in a case that engages the 'narrow rule', it 'is the law which, as a matter of penal policy, causes the damage and it would be inconsistent for the law to require [the claimant] to be compensated for that damage'.[89]

We believe that the coherence rationale, as articulated by McLachlin J and Lord Hoffmann, is a compelling reason for recognising the doctrine of illegality, including in the context of actions for interference with chattels. There are two points that we wish to make in elaboration of this claim. Our first point concerns claims made by

[83] See Section 3.2.1.

[84] See, eg, *Clunis v Camden and Islington Health Authority* (n 37). See also G Schiemann in *Staudingers Kommentar zum Bürgerlichen Gesetzbuch*, (Berlin, Sellier de Gruyter, 2005) § 252 at [10]. For compelling criticism, see F Bydlinski, 'Unerlaubte Vorteile als Schaden' in HJ Ahrens et al (eds), *Festschrift für Erwin Deutsch* (Cologne/Munich, Heymanns, 1999) 71–73.

[85] Weinrib (n 13).

[86] Above n 8.

[87] ibid 176.

[88] See Section 3.1.1.

[89] [2009] UKHL 33; [2009] 1 AC 1339 [29].

Chief Justice McLachlin in her chapter in the present volume.[90] The Chief Justice contends that the coherence rationale of the doctrine of illegality is consistent with Ernest Weinrib's corrective justice theory of tort law.[91] Her Honour endeavours to show that, if the illegality doctrine is formulated with the coherence rationale in mind, it can be rendered compatible with Weinrib's corrective justice account. We think that the coherence rationale is convincing without needing to bring it within the scope of Weinrib's corrective justice theory of private law. It is capable of standing on its own, in our view. For the purpose of this chapter, we remain silent as to the satisfactoriness of Weinrib's theory of tort law.[92]

Secondly, we should say why we think that coherence in the law is important. We believe that coherence is important essentially for the reasons given by Chief Justice McLachlin. Her Honour writes in her chapter:[93]

> coherence is desirable because incoherence leads to a state of affairs that is intolerable if the law is to provide us with a sound basis for ordering our affairs and reasoning practically about courses of action. To be sound, a legal system must permit those subject to it to reason practically about courses of action. Incoherent laws lose their intelligibility and thereby fail to provide a basis for reasoning practically.

In this passage the Chief Justice suggests (as we understand her Honour) that coherence in the law is important because it permits people to make sensible plans for their lives. Expressed differently (although the Chief Justice does not use exactly these words), incoherence in the law violates the idea that the law should be discoverable and that people should be able to predict with a reasonable degree of confidence what the legal consequences will be of taking a particular action. Incoherent laws are, on this view, bad laws for the same reasons why retroactive laws and secret laws are bad. However, there is an important rider that we believe needs to be added to this, namely, that coherence is not something that is of paramount importance. A good legal system has many qualities, and the ruthless pursuit of coherence may result in other important values unjustifiably being sacrificed. There may be situations where it is warranted, all things considered, to tolerate reduced coherence in order to achieve some other end.

5.2 The Hypothetical Cases Revisited

The discussion in the previous section identified the coherence rationale as being capable of justifying the doctrine of illegality. It dismissed the other rationales that have often been put forward. The next task is to determine how, given that the coherence rationale is the only persuasive justification for the doctrine,[94] the hypothetical cases should be decided.

[90] See ch 11.
[91] See EJ Weinrib, *The Idea of Private Law* (Cambridge MA, Harvard University Press, 1995).
[92] Elsewhere, one of us has argued against Weinrib's work: see J Goudkamp and J Murphy, 'Tort Statutes and Tort Theories' (2015) 131 *LQR* 133.
[93] See ch 11 at p 219.
[94] As we have noted earlier, in exceptional cases, the doctrine may be justified in order to prevent wrongful profiting. See n 81.

5.2.1 Getaway Driver

The claimant in *Getaway Driver* would fail in his action.[95] The law in this regard is unsatisfactory. The claimant in *Getaway Driver* should be able to recover damages for the damage done to his vehicle. Denying his action on the ground of illegality serves no useful purpose. In particular, allowing the claimant to recover damages does not threaten the coherence of the law. The claimant is not seeking a remedy that would, if granted, see tort law collide with the criminal law. If the claimant is penalised by the criminal law for his involvement in the bank robbery, the functions served by the imposition of that penalty would not be frustrated by an award of damages for his damaged car.

5.2.2 Meth Cook

The claimant in *Meth Cook* would succeed in his action.[96] The law in this regard produces the correct result. The claimant's action in this scenario does not threaten the coherence of the legal system. The claimant is not, for example, seeking to use tort law to restore to him anything that was taken from him by the criminal law.

5.2.3 Illegal Sale

The claimant in *Illegal Sale* would win.[97] This result is correct, for the same reasons why the law rightly grants relief to the claimant in *Meth Cook*. However, it is necessary to enter a comment here about the reliance rule. This principle, as we have noted earlier, is not enlivened in the case of *Illegal Sale*. The claimant can describe in his pleadings facts that constitute the action in conversion without mentioning the fact that he came into possession of the property that is the subject of his claim by way of an illegal transaction. It is for this reason that the claimant in *Illegal Sale* would succeed. However, the claimant should succeed even if the law required the claimant to plead his illegality. This is because whether or not a given claimant has to rely on his illegal conduct in order to plead a cause of action has nothing to do with the need to maintain a coherent legal system. So, in short, in *Illegal Sale*, the law produces the correct result, but it does so for the wrong reason.

5.2.4 Television Thief

Television Thief is a simple permutation on *Illegal Sale*. As we have shown, the claimant in *Television Thief* would succeed.[98] This result is correct, and it is unnecessary to add anything to what we have just said in relation to *Meth Cook* and *Illegal Sale*.

[95] See Section 3.1.1.
[96] See Section 3.1.2
[97] See Section 3.2.1.
[98] See Section 3.2.2.

5.2.5 Heroin Dealer

The claimant in *Heroin Dealer* would fail in his action.[99] That is the correct result, although the law wrongly produces it by way of the reliance rule. It is the correct result because, in contrast to all of the preceding scenarios, *Heroin Dealer* presents the spectre of incoherence. The law prohibits the possession of heroin. Anyone who possesses heroin is liable to be punished and to have the heroin confiscated and forfeited. A schism would be forged between the criminal law and tort law if the criminal law said that the claimant *Heroin Dealer* should be stripped of his heroin and punished for possessing it and tort law was prepared to compensate the claimant for interference with the heroin.

5.2.6 Unlicensed Shotgun Owner

We have argued that the claimant in *Unlicensed Shotgun Owner* would succeed in his action if he would have been granted a shotgun certificate had he applied for one, but would fail if he would be unable to obtain a certificate.[100] The outcomes produced by the law are satisfactory. Where the claimant in *Unlicensed Shotgun Owner* could cure his illegality the threat of incoherence disappears. Where no certificate could be obtained so that the illegality is incurable, *Unlicensed Shotgun Owner* is not materially different from *Heroin Dealer*, and the law should withhold relief for the reasons that we have given in our discussion of *Heroin Dealer*.

5.2.7 Assailant

Although there is little explicit guidance in the cases as to how the action in *Assailant* would be handled, it is clear that it would fail.[101] *A fortiori* the court would not order the delivery of the bat. This is the correct outcome. It would be inconsistent for the law to say that the defendant is liable in tort for withholding the baseball bat from the claimant given that the defendant would be guilty of serious criminal offences if he returned the bat. Withholding relief is supported by the need to maintain a coherent legal system.

6. CONCLUSION

The satisfactoriness of the doctrine of illegality is a topical issue in tort law. It has generated a literature that is large enough to justify the publication of a bibliography. However, the application of the doctrine in the context of actions for interference with chattels has been largely neglected by theorists. There are also significant lacunae in this area of the law, with no cases that provide definitive guidance as to whether the doctrine applies in particular situations. More fundamentally, what

[99] See Section 3.3.1.
[100] See Section 3.3.2.
[101] See Section 3.4.

little law there is sometimes produces the wrong outcome and, where it delivers the right outcome, it frequently does so for the wrong reasons. Given the foregoing, we, like others,[102] disagree strongly with the Law Commission when it said that the courts have substantially managed to resolve the problems in this area of the law.[103]

[102] See, eg, Sumption (n 12) 8–12; Mance (n 12) 176, 192.

[103] The Law Commission wrote: 'The recent case law shows that the courts have become more open in explaining the policy reasons behind the illegality defence. Therefore, in most areas of law, we think that the illegality defence should be left to developments in the common law': Law Commission (2010) (n 11) vii [1.8].

13

Should Contributory Fault be Analogue or Digital?

ROBERT STEVENS

Law Reform (Contributory Negligence) Act 1945 (UK)

1. Apportionment of liability in cases of contributory negligence

(1) Where any person suffers damage as the result partly of his own fault and partly of the fault of any other person or persons, a claim in respect of that damage shall not be defeated by reason of the fault of the person suffering the damage, but the damages recoverable in respect thereof shall be reduced to such extent as the court thinks just and equitable having regard to the claimant's share in the responsibility for the damage:

Provided that—

(a) this subsection shall not operate to defeat any defence arising under a contract;

(b) where any contract or enactment providing for the limitation of liability is applicable to the claim, the amount of damages recoverable by the claimant by virtue of this subsection shall not exceed the maximum limit so applicable.

...

4. Interpretation

The following expressions have the meanings hereby respectively assigned to them, that is to say—

...

'fault' means negligence, breach of statutory duty or other act or omission which gives rise to a liability in tort or would, apart from this Act, give rise to the defence of contributory negligence.

1. INTRODUCTION

SOUND COMES IN a wave. It varies in both frequency and amplitude. If we are to try and electronically replicate music or speech using radio, it makes sense to modulate a wave to replicate the signal. We do this through either amplitude modulation or frequency modulation to match the radio wave to the changes in the sound wave.

Digital pulses are superficially cruder. They are either off or on, one or zero. However, digital is the future, as digital signals can carry more information, of a higher quality, using less bandwidth.

In private law the move has been away from digital solutions towards an analogue approach of splitting the difference. All or nothing has fallen out of favour,[1] with the judgment of Solomon now delivered seriously. The thesis I shall put forward is that this is much to be regretted with regard to contributory fault, and that it would have been better if the future had been digital.

2. IS IT A DEFENCE?

When asked to write a chapter for a book on defences, I immediately suggested one on contributory fault, only to discover that one of the editors believed it to be no such thing. I am however impenitent; it is a defence, although not all defences are the same. This requires us to understand the difference between being obliged, and being subject to a liability.

The distinction between obligation and liability is frequently confused, just as at the other side of the relation the different senses in which we use the word 'right' can be muddled up. If I have a right against you that you do *X*, you have a duty to me to do *X*. Hohfeld called these rights 'strictly speaking' or claim-rights.[2] Unfortunately this is a misleading label as it implies that for their existence it is a central characteristic that they can be claimed, or enforced. The existence of a duty is a separate question from its enforceability.

A contract that is unenforceable for want of a formal requirement is not a legal nullity. The obligations (and of course the rights) are still there. If performance is rendered, the benefits conferred cannot be recovered, the contract justifying the recipient's enrichment.[3] A third party who procures the breach of an unenforceable contractual obligation may be liable for the quite separate wrong of procuring a breach of contract. If a legal duty is subject to a statutory limitation period that has expired the defendant is no longer liable to the claimant, put identically the claimant no longer has the power to invoke a court's judgement in his favour, but the duty is (usually) still there, and if performed no restitution is possible. It is the liability that is subject to the limitation, not the obligation.

If we abolished the power to bring claims in private law tomorrow, it would not abolish private law. The duties that the positive law states that there are would be untouched, just as public international law exists, and creates valid positive law obligations, despite (frequently) lacking any enforcement procedure. The power of recourse is not a defining feature of private law generally, nor of any particular part of it.[4]

[1] See T Weir, 'All or Nothing' (2004) 78 *Tulane Law Review* 511.

[2] WN Hohfeld, *Fundamental Legal Conceptions as Applied in Judicial Reasoning* (WW Cook (ed), New Haven, Yale University Press, 1919) 45.

[3] See *Moses v Macferlan* (1760) 2 Burr 1005; 97 ER 676 (Lord Mansfield).

[4] Contra the civil recourse theory of the law of torts of Ben Zipursky and John Goldberg. See, eg, JCP Goldberg and BC Zipursky, 'Torts as Wrongs' (2010) 88 *Texas Law Review* 917.

This conclusion is a happy one as if the power to claim were central to having a claim-right there would be no claim-rights outside of the posited law. If, for example, an abhorrent law mandated the torture of a minority, this does not remove, as a matter of justice, the right that those individuals have not to be so treated, regardless of their inability to bring any enforceable claims.

Hohfeld's use of 'claim-right' is understandable as we have no word in English that demarcates that category of rights 'strictly speaking' that are not privileges, immunities and powers, and in law the other variants do not ordinarily carry with them the power to bring a claim. We might refer to them as 'true-rights' in order to emphasise that they are of the correlative duty variety.

Some defences show that the defendant has no duty or obligation, whilst others merely restrict or remove his liability. The defendant's waiver of the duty owed to him, usually travelling under the Latin maxim *volenti non fit iniuria*, is an example of the former. If you punch me with my consent, you commit no battery. I am not a trespasser in the library in which I type these words because an authorised agent of the landowner has given me a licence to enter the premises.

A contractual exclusion or limitation of liability for damages, as its name states, merely excludes or limits the liability, not the duty, although there were those who, following the logic of Oliver Wendell Holmes, claimed that if a court could not be compelled to grant an order no duty existed.[5] If this were so, then surely the reasoning goes, a clause that denied the existence of a (contractual) duty was inconsistent with the contractual duties the agreement purported to create? This 'Bad Man' analysis was rejected by the House of Lords.[6] The exclusion of liability for breach does not impact upon the existence of the underlying duties.

By contrast, the disclaimer by the bank in *Hedley Byrne & Co Ltd v Heller & Partners Ltd*[7] made it clear that they were assuming no responsibility in providing the reference, and were therefore under no duty of care. There was no tort, not merely no liability for its commission. The position of the defence once termed 'justification' (now 'truth'[8]) in the tort of defamation, despite its original name, is obscure in England.

What constitutes a defence, if it can apply to either the underlying duty or the liability to be sued? In private law, the answer is a wholly formal one. Tony Weir stated that '[c]ontributory negligence is unquestionably a defence ... [since] it is for the defendant to plead and prove it'.[9] James Goudkamp, in his new and exemplary work of scholarship, rejects this definition.[10] He does so on the basis that it is over inclusive, as it would include many procedural rules that it is for the defendant to establish, such as security for costs[11] or leave to amend pleadings after service.[12]

[5] Eg, B Coote, *Exception Clauses* (London, Sweet and Maxwell, 1964).

[6] The leading decisions are *Suisse Atlantique Société d'Armement Maritime SA v Rotterdamsche Kolen Centrale NV* [1967] 1 AC 361 (HL) and *Photo Productions Ltd v Securicor Transport Ltd* [1980] AC 827 (HL).

[7] [1964] AC 465 (HL).

[8] Defamation Act 2013 (UK), s 2.

[9] T Weir, *An Introduction to Tort Law*, 2nd edn (Oxford, Clarendon Press, 2006) 129.

[10] J Goudkamp, *Tort Law Defences* (Oxford, Hart Publishing, 2013) 6.

[11] Civil Procedure Rules, r 25.12.

[12] ibid r 17.2.

However, this criticism misses the mark. These procedural rules are not matters of pleading. They may involve the defendant establishing certain facts (such as that the claimant has given an incorrect address in his claim form so that a security for costs order is appropriate), but they would not be asserted in the defendant's pleadings of case, and are not defences.

Clearly, not everything that appears in a defendant's pleadings is a defence. If the claimant pleads 'you negligently ran me over whilst driving your car around Magdalen roundabout in Oxford' the defendant's counter-assertion 'no I didn't' is not a defence, but merely a denial of an essential element of the prima facie claim.[13]

Anything that the defendant pleads which can resist the claimant's action, that does not merely constitute a denial of an element of the claim, is a defence. In the law of torts, some successful defences mean that no tort has been committed. In the tort of battery, for example, the successful invocation of self-defence, when punching someone on the nose who lunged at you with a knife with evil intent, negates the assertion of any tort, just as it means no crime is committed. The defence goes not just to the existence of liability but to the question of whether the defendant breached any duty owed to the defendant. Such a person commits no wrong, although they have acted contrary to the reason of justice why punching people on the nose is a bad thing to do. In the circumstances this reason is outweighed by other reasons so that the conclusion is that, all things considered, nothing wrongful has been done.[14] Contributory fault, as a defence today, does not negate the existence of the wrong in the same way, and so is sometimes referred to as a 'liability rule'. However, it really goes to the quantum of damages recoverable, not to questions of enforceability, and so is better described as a remedial defence.[15] It cuts back the defendant's secondary obligation to pay damages.

This formal approach allows room for further refinements recognised in our positive law, in the form of Replies, counter-Replies, counter-counter Replies and so on. A libel may be resisted by a defence of qualified privilege. This defence may itself be resisted by a plea of malice in a reply. Again, a mere denial of a defence is not a defence to a defence, but anything that the claimant pleads to resist the defence, that does not merely constitute a denial, is.

Weir's definition is however defective if he meant to claim that the onus of proof is a necessary element of what constitutes a defence.[16] The general rule is *ei incumbit probatio qui dicit* (roughly, he who asserts must prove). The most important practical effect of characterising an issue as being a defence is that it will usually determine who has to prove what as a matter of evidence.

This rule is not logically necessary however, and should not be thought of as a defining feature of what a defence is. The law could be that the onus of proof in all matters fell upon the defendant. This would not turn the entire law into a law of defences. In the law as it is, it is not always the case that he who asserts must prove. So, in English criminal law, when the defendant raises self-defence, it is for

[13] Cf Goudkamp (n 10) 2, 6–7.

[14] See further S Smith, 'Duties to Try and Duties to Succeed', ch 5 in this volume.

[15] See further J Goudkamp, 'Rethinking Contributory Negligence' in E Chamberlain, J Neyers and S Pitel (eds), *Tort Law: Challenging Orthodoxy* (Oxford, Hart Publishing, 2013).

[16] See n 10 above.

the prosecution to adduce sufficient evidence to show beyond reasonable doubt that no such defence applies. In private law, it is for the defendant to plead that a claim falls outside the applicable limitation period, but it is for the claimant to prove that he is still within time.[17]

To an extent, we have allowed the cart to come before the horse, practical considerations concerning onus of proof being used to determine whether something should be characterised as a defence. So, in the law of unjustified enrichment, if I mistakenly pay you £500, you have a defence of change of position if, ignorant of my mistake, you give this sum to charity when you otherwise would not have done so. Clearly it makes sense to place the evidential onus upon the defendant; he is in a much better position to show what he did with his wealth subsequent to receipt than is the claimant. It may however be queried, as a matter of justice, whether the claimant's assertion that the defendant was unjustifiably enriched at his expense at some point in the past should be sufficient to show that he ought to make restitution to him today. Whilst we may, for practical reasons, place the onus of proof on the defendant this does not logically entail that what needs to be proven is in fact a defence.

On the boringly formal approach suggested here, illegality is not a defence,[18] nor is any rule that is invoked by a court of its own motion regardless of whether the defendant seeks to rely upon it. If, for example, a hit man seeks to recover the agreed price for a murder he has committed, the defendant will never have to assert any defence for the claim to fail.[19] The rule against illegality prevents a party from relying upon his own illegal conduct in litigation. Even if both parties to a murder contract want a court to resolve an ambiguity in its true interpretation, the court will decline to do so. The rule disabling reliance upon illegal conduct is as true of a defendant as it is of a claimant. If a recipient of a mistaken payment seeks to invoke the defence of change of position by relying upon his expenditure of the money on the funding of world-wide terrorism, he will not succeed.[20]

It is important to notice that this formal answer as to what is or is not a defence given by the private law is unavailable to us in the criminal law. Without any formal system of pleadings, when defendants merely state that they are not guilty, we have no clear positive law answer as to who must assert what. Any division between those ethical reasons which make conduct *pro tanto* criminal, and other countervailing reasons; synonymously between the crime and its defences, is not found in the positive law itself but outside it. We cannot neatly transpose the meaning of 'defence' from one area of law into the other.

Whether an issue that will determine whether a claim will be successful *should* be a defence (that is, who should have to plead what) should be determined by whether the claimant can make out a prima facie claim without addressing it. Consent is illustrative. A punch on the nose is prima facie wrongful, in a way that a kiss is not. In private law, it should therefore be for the claimant to assert that the kiss was not

[17] *Lloyds Bank Plc v Crosse & Crosse* [2001] EWCA Civ 366; [2001] PNLR 34 [41]; *Fiona Trust & Holding Corp v Privalov* [2010] EWHC 3199 (Comm) [135] (Andrew Smith J).

[18] Cf Goudkamp (n 10).

[19] *Cross v Kirby* The Times, 5 April 2000 (CA).

[20] *Barros Mattos Jnr v MacDaniels Ltd* [2004] EWHC 1188 (Ch); [2004] 3 All ER 299.

consensual, but for the punch the assertion 'you hit me' should suffice. Contributory fault follows the same pattern, with the claimant sometimes unable to show, because of his own acts of foolhardy idiocy, that his injuries are the responsibility of another so as to be prima facie wrongful. Usually, however, it is a defence, albeit one that goes to the quantification of damages.

3. SHOULD IT BE A DEFENCE?

The law on contributory fault in England prior to 1945 was such a mess that it is rarely questioned today whether the very brief and superficially straightforward legislative reform that replaced it was the best way forward.

Whether contributory fault should be a defence is determined by why it is thought that damages are payable for the commission of torts. One reason why the wisdom of the Act is so rarely questioned today is that it fits with a particular understanding of the law of torts that has become entrenched in modern thought. Indeed, even those who are critical of the modern conception of torts as expressed in most standard textbooks, do not challenge it. [21]

What is the law of torts about? Some writers place compensation and deterrence at its centre. On one side, loss caused by fault should be compensated, on the other blameworthy conduct should be deterred. On this view the law of torts becomes a system for the allocation of loss caused through fault. If we are to hold a defendant responsible for losses caused by his fault, the *quid pro quo* is that a claimant should bear the responsibility for the losses they are responsible for. On this view a system of law without a contributory fault defence would be doubly defective. First it would mean that defendants were held responsible for losses that were, at least in part, the responsibility of someone else. We would have over-compensation. Second the system would not operate efficiently as a regulator of conduct. In a world without contributory fault, a claimant is not encouraged, as he should be, to take care because the full loss will fall on another. People would be encouraged to take risks in relation to their own wellbeing that would be sub-optimal as they will not have to bear the consequences of their own self harm.

This conception of the law of torts, as a harm allocation mechanism for attributing losses to those responsible for them, is most plausible in relation to the (so-called) tort of negligence, the area that has come to dominate so much of the teaching and writing on the law of torts. This is, I would suggest, reflected in the name of the defence given in the Act, with the negligence principle on both the claimant's and defendant's side appearing to operate symmetrically. This conception of the law is given some plausible theoretical support from some (crude) economic analysis of the negligence principle.[22]

[21] Eg, EJ Weinrib, *The Idea of Private Law* (Cambridge, MA, Harvard University Press, 1995) 169; A Beever, *Rediscovering the Law of Negligence* (Oxford, Hart Publishing, 2007) 342.

[22] Eg, the Learned Hand formula from *United States v Carroll Towling Co* 159 F 2d 169, 173 (1947), a contributory fault case, $B < PL$, where P is the probability of injury, L is its magnitude, and B the cost that would be borne in avoiding the activity including the benefits foregone if it ceased.

If we truly accepted that this is the purpose of the law of torts we could, as others have pointed out, construct a quite different (and possibly more effective and efficient) system for achieving the same ends. We could operate a clearing system, where all those who were guilty of blameworthy conduct were required to pay a sum of money reflecting their culpability into a central fund, whilst all those who had suffered harm through fault (whether another's or their own) could claim upon it. That such a system appears equally plausible on the conception of the law of torts so far presented should alert us to the fact that something is not quite right.

There is a more traditional, and quite different, conception of the law of torts.

At a formal level, the law of torts is a law of interpersonal wrongs. As a matter of both the positive law and justice, I have a right with respect to you that you do not punch me on the nose. If you violate this right by punching me, you wrong me. If that were all the law said, we would still have a law of torts.

The law goes further however, and requires the defendant to pay damages to the person he has injured, and indeed those damages frequently include (but are not limited to) the consequential losses suffered by the claimant as a result of the wrong. The reason for this is that the law seeks to place the claimant, so far as money can do, in the position they would have been in if the wrong had not occurred.[23] The duty not to punch does not just disappear after the blow has been delivered. Rather the underlying reason for the positive duty remains throughout, and the defendant's duty post breach is to do the next best thing now available to him.[24]

It would be possible (if extremely inconvenient) for the law to adopt a principle of general strict liability (or more accurately 'strict responsibility') for all losses that we cause. It is, however, impossible to imagine a law of torts or wrongs that could operate in such a way. All of our actions impose some risk on other people, whether it is sneezing, talking, walking down the street or breathing. All of these things may cause harm to other people, but without more they could not constitute a breach of duty. We cannot all be under duties to do nothing at all, which are then breached whenever harm occurs. To live is to impose risks on others. The negligence standard neither refers to want of virtue (wholly virtuous and competent people of impeccable moral standing can be negligent in the law's sense), nor to economic efficiency, but to the line the law draws, as a matter of interpersonal justice, where your right ends and my liberty begins (and vice versa).

The reason why contributory fault should not be a defence is that the risks I run in relation to my own interests are nobody's concern but mine. If I eat and drink too much, trust people I should not, enjoy high risk sports, don't clean my teeth at night, fail to lock my front door, ignore the warnings on medicine bottles or park my car in East Oxford, no other individual has any standing to complain. It is true that I may owe certain *public* duties that are imposed to safeguard my interests. So,

[23] *Livingstone v Rawyards Coal Co* (1880) 5 App Cas 25 (HL).

[24] For academic support for this idea, see N MacCormick, *Legal Right and Social Democracy* (Oxford, Clarendon Press, 1982) 212; Weinrib (n 21); J Raz, 'Personal Practical Conflicts' in P Baumann and M Betzler (eds), *Practical Conflicts: New Philosophical Essays* (Cambridge, Cambridge University Press, 2004) 172; R Stevens, *Torts and Rights* (Oxford, Oxford University Press, 2007) 59; A Ripstein, 'As if it Had Never Happened' (2007) 48 *William and Mary Law Review* 1957. The best long treatment is J Gardner 'What is Tort Law For? Part 1. The Place of Corrective Justice' (2011) 30 *Law and Philosophy* 1.

paternalistic legislation has been introduced requiring the wearing of safety belts in cars, and crash helmets for motorcyclists. It is one thing for the State, which in the UK will have to pay the bill if I am physically injured, to require its citizens to look after themselves. It is quite another thing for other individuals who have wronged us to say 'you ought to have taken more care of yourself'. It is simply none of their business.

It is sometimes said that symmetry of treatment requires that if the claimant can require the defendant to take care with respect to him, then the defendant can insist that the claimant also care for herself.[25] What is sauce for the defendant goose should be sauce for the claimant gander. There is however no symmetry here. Would we apply the same logic of symmetrical treatment to wrongs of strict liability? If we did, where the claimant and defendant were jointly responsible for the claimant's liability, damages would presumably be reduced to nothing. As we shall see, even within liability for negligence, what negligence means is quite different when applied to the defendant in establishing that there is a tort, from when applied to the claimant and defendant together in applying the defence.[26]

If we contrast the defence of contributory fault with the law of contribution for joint torts the difficulty is illustrated. If two or more people wrongfully inflict the same injury upon a claimant, for example in a car accident involving multiple drivers, each is jointly liable to the tort victim. If the victim sues one alone the payment of damages will to the extent they are coextensive relieve the co-tortfeasor of liability. A defendant may bring a claim for a contribution over against his co-tortfeasor. If no such claim is possible, the co-tortfeasor has his obligation to pay damages relieved at another's expense. One defendant is unjustifiably enriched at another's expense. By contrast, a defendant who is held liable in full for a loss that has been suffered as a result of his wrong does not unjustly enrich the negligent claimant, even if they are both jointly responsible. The claimant was not under any duty to the defendant, or anyone else, to behave in a different way, he is not being relieved[27] of losses he is obliged to anyone to bear. That the defendant can (rightly) show that the loss suffered was not solely his responsibility but also in part that of the claimant does not relieve or reduce his responsibility.

Now this is not to say that contributory fault should *never* be relevant. First, my fault may mean that I am unable to show that I have been wronged. Put in the opaque language of the law, my blameworthy conduct may 'break the chain of causation' or be a *novus actus interveniens*. If my injuries are solely my responsibility, it will not be enough for me to argue that they would not have been suffered but for the negligence of someone else. In order for the defendant to be held liable my injuries must be the result of the instantiation of one of the risks that made his negligence potentially tortious with respect to me.[28] We have no duty to protect other people from all their possible acts of folly. If I deliberately jump off a cliff, I cannot complain that the landowner should have put up a sign warning me of the risks.

[25] Eg, FH Bohlen, 'Contributory Negligence' (1908) 21 *Harvard Law Review* 233, 255; Weinrib (n 21) 169; Beever (n 21) 342.

[26] See the discussion in Goudkamp (n 15).

[27] See generally *Tomlinson v Congleton Borough Council* [2003] UKHL 47; [2004] 1 AC 46.

[28] *South Australia Asset Management Corp v York Montague Ltd* [1997] AC 191 (HL).

Where the claimant's injury is *concurrently* the responsibility of conduct of both the claimant and the defendant, the defendant should not be relieved of liability as he has committed a wrong with respect to the defendant. If I am *jointly* responsible for a wrong with one or more other people I am responsible in full, I am not merely responsible proportionately.

Second, where a claimant has suffered a wrong, he may only recover for those consequential losses suffered that are the wrongdoer's responsibility. If I am summarily dismissed from my job, if I choose to spend my days drinking my cares away, rather than getting another job elsewhere, the sole responsibility for my loss of salary is mine, not my former employer's. These rules of mitigation are simply the rules of causal responsibility playing out post-breach, as exemplified by the Scottish appeal to the House of Lords in *McKew v Holland*.[29] Again, just as they are pre-breach, they are digital. A defendant is either responsible for a loss suffered as a result of his wrong or he is not. There is no question of holding him jointly responsible, and then apportioning some part. This does not mean that the rules of mitigation when applied mean that either all the loss or no loss is recoverable, but rather that only those losses that (1) actually are suffered and (2) are no greater than the loss that would have been suffered if the claimant had acted reasonably, are recoverable.

4. A BRIEF HISTORY OF THE 'CONTRIBUTORY NEGLIGENCE' DEFENCE

The history of the law of 'contributory negligence' prior to the legislature's intervention is not a happy one. On one view the rule that continued to apply up until the Act coming into force was that stated by Lord Blackburn, 'the rule of law is that if there is blame causing the accident on both sides, however small that blame may be on one side, the loss lies where it falls'.[30]

Such a rule is extremely harsh, indeed vicious,[31] and goes far beyond what principles of causal responsibility would require. This supports the view that it was a special rule or defence. The usual illustration is *Butterfield v Forrester*,[32] although the phrase contributory negligence does not appear in the case itself. The defendant set up a pole across the road, the plaintiff did not observe it as he hurtled along the highway at a violent pace. The claimant's want of ordinary care ruled out a claim based upon the defendant's fault.

Unsurprisingly given its harshness, an exception known as the 'last opportunity rule' grew up, usually attributed to *Davies v Mann*.[33] The defendant hobbled his donkey so that it could graze by the side of the highway. The defendant driving his wagon at a 'smartish pace' crashed into it. The donkey owner was held entitled to substantial damages. The rule was said to be that where one party knows of the negligence of the other, he is solely responsible if he fails to exercise reasonable care,[34]

[29] [1969] 3 All ER 1621 (HL).
[30] *Cayzer, Irvine & Co v Carron Co* (1884) 9 App Cas 873 (HL) 881.
[31] T Weir, *An Introduction to the Tort Law*, 2nd edn (Oxford, Clarendon Press, 2006) 123.
[32] (1809) 11 East 60; 103 ER 926.
[33] (1842) 10 M & W 546 (1842); 152 ER 588.
[34] *The Eurymedon* [1938] P 41 (CA) 49 (Green LJ).

although such a rule is difficult to extract from anything said in the judgments in *Davies v Mann*.

This rule was extended by the Privy Council in *British Columbia Electric Railway Co Ltd v Loach*[35] to cases of 'constructive last opportunity'. The defendants were unable to brake in time in order to stop an accident because they had failed to keep their engine in proper repair. Their necessity to brake was however caused by the subsequent negligence of the defendant. Despite not having the actual last opportunity the defendants were held liable. So, the rule became that if the defendant would have had the last opportunity but for his own negligence, he was in the same position as if he had actually had it, and the claimant again recovered in full.

It is possible to imagine a world where the law developed so that the exception swallowed the rule.[36] There were many statements that the rule and its exception were based upon ordinary principles of causation.[37] In an age where the jury trial was dying out, because the pool of male jurors had been dramatically reduced by German machine guns, the need for judges to control jury decisions through special rules of this kind was on the wane. The law could have developed so that there was no special rule for contributory negligence, but rather just an application of ordinary rules of causal responsibility, as there is today with the doctrine of mitigation subsequent to the wrong. It is perfectly possible to imagine a more progressive post-War court building on the various statements that sought to explain contributory fault in terms of causal responsibility, developing the law in this way.

For good or ill, that was not the path the law took. Law reformers do not tend to be dangerous radicals. One option for statutory reform was simply to abolish any special rule applicable to contributory fault. The less dramatic course was to leave the defence in place, but only to allow for an apportionment of liability, as was already done in the Admiralty courts. The position in relation to collisions at sea was governed by the Maritime Conventions Act 1911 (UK), and when the question of reform of the common law was put to the Law Revision Committee they were asked to consider whether that rule should be adopted at common law. The 1911 Act was a product of the Brussels Collision Convention[38] (1910), which had adopted the civilian solution of apportioning liability. However, it should be noted that this civilian model fits into, for example, French law much more comfortably than it does into the common law. The French Civil Code has provisions regarding *responsabilité extra-contractuelle*, for the making good of loss caused by those at fault, but it is not, at least on its face, a law of wrongs in the common law's sense, but rather one of attributing loss for fault.

The British Act was copied, sometimes almost word for word, by other jurisdictions in the Commonwealth in the coming years.[39]

[35] [1916] 1 AC 719 (PC).

[36] But see the disastrous *Swadling v Cooper* [1931] AC 1 (HL). Cf *McLean v Bell* 1932 SC (HL) 21. These cases and the history of the law are illuminatingly discussed by Paul Mitchell in his forthcoming book on the early twentieth century history of the law of torts: P Mitchell, *A History of Tort Law 1900–1950* (Cambridge, Cambridge University Press, 2014).

[37] *Caswell v Powell Duffryn Associated Collieries Ltd* [1940] AC 152 (HL) 165 (Lord Atkin).

[38] Formerly called the Convention for the Unification of Certain Rules of Law with respect to Collisions between Vessels.

[39] Eg, Contributory Negligence Act 1947 (NZ).

5. PROBLEMS

Although extremely brief, the 1911 Act[40] gives rise to a number of knotty problems of interpretation. Such problems are almost inevitable when legislation lacks a clear principled basis.

5.1 Fault Used in Different Senses

The Act's reference to the fault of the defendant and the fault of the claimant gives the impression of symmetry of treatment, with the same standard applicable to both parties. In fact the word 'fault' is employed in two entirely different senses. The definition of fault is given as meaning many (but not all) kinds of breach of duty owed to another. This is however only of relevance when applied to the defendant. Whether or not the claimant is in breach of any duty owed to another is entirely irrelevant. A cyclist who fails to wear a safety helmet is not in breach of any duty owed to anyone else, but may be at 'fault' for the purposes of apportionment. In the Act, fault of the defendant means wrongdoing, fault of the claimant means blameworthiness.

5.2 The Title is Misleading

The conduct of the claimant that may give rise to the defence need not be negligent, despite the title of the Act.[41] The naming of the defence as contributory negligence is therefore inapt. The claimant's conduct may be deliberate or reckless, or even fall short of what would be considered negligent for the purposes of establishing the defendant's wrongdoing. It is for this reason that (where applicable) the defence is sometimes correctly termed comparative fault in the United States.

It may be objected that where liability for negligence is sought to be established, the actual fault of the defendant may go far beyond being negligent. Whilst true, this misses the point. In relation to contributory fault the issue is not whether the conduct of the claimant has crossed a particular boundary of blame. Contributory fault is always a question of degree, and has no necessary relationship to negligence.

5.3 The Standard of Fault Differs in Determining Wrongdoing and Contribution

Labelling the defence as 'contributory negligence' misleadingly implies that the same standard is applied at the stage of determining whether the defendant is a wrongdoer, and in determining the claimant's contributory fault. The standard textbooks simply assume this to be true, the standard being the objective one of the reasonable

[40] The Act is British, applying in England, Wales and Scotland but not (for reasons that are unknown to me) in Northern Ireland.

[41] Eg, *Reeves v Commissioner of Police of the Metropolis* [2000] 1 AC 360 (HL).

man. Again, this gives the impression of a pleasing symmetry of equal treatment for the claimant and defendant. This is incorrect.

First, and most obviously, where the defence is applicable to a wrong where negligence is not the standard, the standard at the stages of establishing liability and apportionment are different. If, for example, the tort to which the defence is applied is, say, breach of statutory duty establishing negligence or blameworthiness on the part of the defendant is (almost always) wholly irrelevant.[42]

Second, even where the claim is based upon the defendant's negligence the standards applied are not the same. When assessing the claimant's contributory fault, the court is concerned with the foreseeable risk to himself that he created, not the foreseeable risk to others,[43] whereas in establishing that there has been a wrong we are concerned with the foreseeable risk the defendant creates in relation to people other than himself. The law (rightly) takes the view at the stage of establishing wrongdoing that we are allowed to be as reckless as we like with regard to our own interests (something inexplicable to the blunt minds of economic theorists). It might be claimed that symmetry is achieved because for both parties what is relevant is the foreseeable risk to the claimant, but when we apply this to the defendant this is inaccurate. In judging the defendant's conduct we look to the degree of risk his behaviour poses to all others, not just the claimant. This is because in, say, driving an ambulance he owes duties to everyone who may be adversely impacted by his conduct. The duties the defendant owes to everyone have to cohere, as a matter of law, coherently. That entails, amongst other things, that drivers of ambulances are allowed to drive faster, and in a quite different manner, in an emergency than drivers of delivery vans, although the risk they may pose to bystanders they might hit by their high speeds may be identical ex ante.

Further, in establishing liability, the negligence standard is digital. You either cross the line of conduct expected of you, or you do not. That the defendant is grossly negligent is irrelevant, his liability does not increase, if his conduct falls just short of negligence he is not held liable in part. At the apportionment stage the approach is analogue. Apportionment is not done solely according to degrees of fault but instead according to the parties' relative 'share of responsibility'. Responsibility is determined partially by degree of fault, but also by degree of causal contribution.[44] The doctor who failed to save the liberal Frederick III from death by disease, so that his illiberal son Wilhelm II became Kaisar, which in turn meant that the Great War occurred when it did, which in turn led to the rise of Hitler, may have been grossly negligent. His causal contribution to the outbreak of World War II was slight as there were by then so many other factors in play. His degree of responsibility for the war was therefore slight.

Responsibility for purposes of apportionment depends upon the *degree* of both fault and causal contribution of *both* parties.[45] It is a completely different, and

[42] Enterprise and Regulatory Reform Act 2013 (UK), s 69 has dramatically cutback claims for breach of statutory duty under the Health and Safety at Work etc. Act 1974 (UK).

[43] *Jones v Livox Quarries Ltd* [1952] 2 QB 608 (CA) 615 (Denning LJ).

[44] ibid.

[45] *Davies v Swan Motor Co (Swansea) Ltd* [1949] 2 KB 291 (CA) 326 (Denning LJ).

more complex exercise, from the simple on/off enquiry at the stage of establishing liability.

5.4 The Piece of String Problem

The analogue nature of the enquiry in determining the degree of contribution means that no demonstrably right answer is capable of being given. This is reflected in appellate statement's that the bar is a high one if a trial judge's decision is to be successfully overturned. Even in a standard car accident case, how can we really say that the degree of responsibility was 75/25, or 46/64? Unsurprisingly, judges seldom select finely tuned figures, 73/27 for example, as their instincts pull them towards more digital solutions.

Some have suggested that the degree of uncertainty can, to an extent, be mitigated by using bright line categories of contribution that the judge is confined to applying (for example, 75/25, 50/50, 25/75).[46] In the context of the failure to wear a safety belt, and flagrantly ignoring the statutory language which permits no such thing, such a rule has been introduced by judicial legislation.[47] The problem however is not so much the difficulty of the exercise, but its impossibility. The court is required to compare two incommensurable things: the claimant's want of regard for his own interests, and the defendant's want of regard for other people. The former is a matter of virtue. Good people do clean their teeth, get out of bed early, wear safety helmets, refrain from drug abuse and so on. The latter is a matter of interpersonal justice. Your want of virtue is no concern of mine, but is gravely concerning to me if you subject me to risk of injury. The judge is being asked to gauge whether three metres or 16 gallons is greater.

This may be contrasted with the recoverability of a contribution from a co-tortfeasor for damage for which they are both liable.[48] Here although again the question is an analogue one, because we are concerned with comparative responsibility, we are at least comparing like with like, one wrong with another.

5.5 Before or After Wrongdoing?

Prior to 1945 it was quite clear that contributory negligence only applied to the claimant's fault before the commission of the wrong. The defence operated as a bar on action (see Lord Blackburn above). It never operated so as to, say, generally rule out a head of loss where the defendant was negligent in subsequently failing to take steps to avoid it. This area was, and is, governed by the law of mitigation.

However, there is nothing on the face of the legislation that necessitates this conclusion today. It makes no distinction between fault going to the wrong, and subsequent fault going to consequential loss. Instead the legislation uses that weasel word

[46] Eg, AS Burrows, *Remedies for Torts and Breach of Contract*, 3rd edn (Oxford, Hart Publishing, 2004) 143–44.

[47] *Froom v Butcher* [1976] QB 286 (CA).

[48] Civil Liability (Contribution) Act 1978 (UK), s 1.

'damage', which can be used in law to cover both *injuria* (the violation of the right, usually to a thing or person) and *damnum* (loss, here consequential). In the simple case of a car accident, the wrong occurs (that is, *injuria* is suffered) when the cars collide. The wrong does not occur, that is, the duty is not breached, through negligent driving alone. The wrong is constituted by negligently injuring, not negligently driving. Loss (that is, *damnum*) is always suffered subsequently, for example costs of repairs or loss of earnings. This distinction is obscured by the modern day tendency to refer to damage as the 'gist' of negligence, which obscures that the former is the essential requirement, not the latter.

Whatever the position intended by the legislature, the courts have assumed without argument that the Act applies to post-wrong contributory negligence. The effect of this in some cases is to treat the claimant *less* favourably than he would have been prior to 1945, when only the principles of mitigation of loss could restrict recoverability post-wrong. So, in *The Calliope*[49] the defendant negligently damaged the claimant's vessel. The damaged vessel proceeded up river to an anchorage to await the ebb-tide. When she was being turned around she suffered further damage because of the claimant's negligence. Brandon J, applying the Maritime Convention Act 1911 (UK) held that it allowed apportionment in such a case. The Court of Appeal in *Spencer v Wincanton Holdings Ltd*[50] assumed without argument that the Law Reform (Contributory Negligence) Act 1945 (UK) applied to cases of post-wrong fault. This approach requires, as pre-wrong, first asking whether the defendant's fault is sufficient to determine causal responsibility, and secondly where the claimant and defendant are concurrently responsible, an apportionment of liability according to degree of responsibility.

5.6 Impact on the Ordinary Rules of Causal Responsibility

As we have seen, it was at least arguable by 1945 that the rules on contributory negligence were an application of the general rules of causal responsibility, and did not, or at least did not any longer, constitute a special rule or defence. Was the impact of the Act to simply replace the old special defence, or was its impact that the ordinary rules of causal responsibility no longer applied to cases of contributory fault by the claimant? Support for the latter broad view can be gained from the wording of the Act: 'a claim in respect of that damage shall not be defeated by reason of the fault of the person suffering the damage'. The better view seems to be that the Act only applies *if* the defendant has committed a tort. If the claimant's contributory fault 'breaks the chain of causation', so that the injury is not the responsibility of the defendant, then there is no tort, and the Act does not apply.[51] If however the rules on contributory negligence prior to the Act were simply a species of the general principles of causal responsibility, then the common law position was left unaltered by the Act. If, for example, the last opportunity rule formed part of the general rules

[49] [1970] P 172 (Probate, Admiralty and Divorce Div).
[50] [2009] EWCA Civ 1404; [2010] PIQR P8.
[51] *Horne v Lec Refrigeration Ltd* [1965] 2 All ER 898 (Assizes); *Stapley v Gypsum Mines Ltd* [1953] AC 663 (HL) 677 (Lord Porter), 681 (Lord Reid), 684 (Lord Tucker), 687 (Lord Asquith).

of causal responsibility (a many judges said it did) then it, and the general rule to which it was an exception, would have survived.

Whatever the truth, the position today is that the rules on contributory fault are now assimilated into the general rules of causal responsibility, with a separate and additional defence of contributory fault now available to the defendant where the parties are jointly responsible. The effect of this is not, as is sometimes said, that the last opportunity rule has been abolished, but rather that it has become the general rule.

5.7 Relationship with Remoteness

In principle the defence of contributory negligence should apply after all other restrictions on the quantum of recovery have been taken into account. So, restrictions such as remoteness and the principles of mitigation apply first, and only then does the defence of contributory negligence apply. If, for example, the defendant negligently damages the claimant's car, causing the claimant to lose an extremely lucrative contract for it to appear in a film production, if the defendant was 50 per cent contributorily negligent, this further reduction should be applied after it has been calculated that the extent of loss that is not too remote. The reason for this order of priority is that we need to ascertain the loss for which the defendant is responsible first, before applying a reduction based upon the claimant's joint responsibility.

Although what the law ought to be is relatively easy to state, what it is is much harder. In *Platform Home Loans v Oyston Shipways Ltd*[52] the House of Lords applied the defence of contributory negligence before making the reduction for remote losses, thereby making a higher award than would be ordinarily justifiable. The justification for this is a mystery.

5.8 Concurrent Liability

Prior to 1945, if contributory negligence was an aspect of causal responsibility, it could only apply to those wrongs that required causal responsibility, such as in the case of negligence in the law of torts. Other wrongs, most obviously breach of contract, do not require the establishment of casual responsibility. A promisor is in breach of contract if the promise he has made is unfulfilled. It is completely irrelevant whether the defendant's conduct caused this promise to be unfulfilled. It therefore never mattered whether one of the reasons why the promisor was in breach was in part, or even primarily, the fault of the promisee. When assessing the loss suffered as a consequence of the breach of contract, causal responsibility does become a necessary condition. Principles of mitigation applied (and apply) at that stage, just as they do in the law of torts. Contributory negligence was a principle

[52] [2000] 2 AC 190 (HL).

going to whether there was a wrong, not to the question of limitation on damages for a wrong, and so never had any application to breach of contract.

That the Act was never intended to apply to claims for breach of contract is made clear by the definition of fault (of the defendant) in section 4 as meaning 'negligence, breach of statutory duty or other act or omission which gives rise to a liability in tort or would, apart from this Act, give rise to the defence of contributory negligence'. The reference to negligence, as the section makes clear, is to negligence that gives rise to liability *in tort*. It is not a reference to negligence in the air as a degree of fault. As a claim for breach of contract was not subject to the defence of contributory negligence prior to 1945, it was not subsequently. The drafting of the Act is unfortunate as it requires it to be understood when and why the defence of contributory negligence applied prior to 1945, an exercise today of investigating ancient legal history that could only appeal to some members of the United States Supreme Court. Are we to take the law as set in aspic at that time, as the law on exemplary damages in England once required,[53] or is the court allowed to speculate as to what the common law would have said if it had continued to develop?

In a case of concurrent liability, where a claimant could make out a claim either in tort for negligence or for breach of contract, the position prior to 1945 was that the claimant's contributory negligence meant that there was no actionable tort, but as a matter of principle had no relevance to the claim for breach of contract.

Post 1945, what is the position as a matter of principle? The general position is that where a defendant has alternative causes of action, he is permitted to assert whichever is more favourable as he sees fit. This principle was reaffirmed by the House of Lords in *Henderson v Merrett Syndicates*.[54] In principle, this should apply where the defendant has a defence of contributory negligence that is only capable of being asserted against one of the claims against him, so that a defendant should be free to assert a claim for breach of contract without being subject to the defence. This was the conclusion of the High Court of Australia in *Astley v Austrust Ltd*[55] in relation to identically worded legislation.

In England the law is quite different. Where the defendant is concurrently liable in contract and for breach of a tortious duty to which the Act applies, the Court of Appeal has held that the defence applies.[56] This gives rise to some bizarre results. Consider:

D contracts with *C* to repair *C's* car. In doing the work *D* without negligence fits components that are defective. *C* is injured partly because of the defect and partly because of his own careless driving.

D contracts with *C* to repair *C's* car. In doing the work *D* negligently fits components that are defective. *C* is injured partly because of the defect and partly because of his own careless driving.

[53] *AB v South West Water Services Ltd* [1993] QB 507 (CA) overturned by *Kuddus v Chief Constable of Leicestershire Constabulary* [2001] UKHL 29; [2002] 2 AC 122.

[54] [1995] 2 AC 145 (HL).

[55] [1999] HCA 6; (1999) 197 CLR 1.

[56] *Forsikringaktieselskapet Vesta v Butcher* [1989] AC 852 (CA), affirming the decision of Hobhouse J in [1986] 2 All ER 488 (QBD), see especially 508; *Barclays Bank plc v Fairclough Building Ltd* [1995] QB 214 (CA).

In the first case D will be liable solely for breach of the strict contractual duty to supply goods of a satisfactory quality and so the defence will have no application. In the latter case because he is negligent the defendant will also be liable in tort. It makes no sense to treat the defendant more favourably in the latter case, by conferring upon him a defence he would not otherwise have. It brings the law into disrepute if defendants are left to argue that they were negligent, whist claimants deny this.

Given where we are, the best solution would be for the Supreme Court to overturn the Court of Appeal, and to deny the application of contributory negligence to all claims for breach of contract. Even applying the defence to all claims for breach of contract would be better than the law's current irrational condition.

5.9 Which Torts does the Act Apply to?

Going back to the old common law, contributory negligence was, and therefore continues, to be inapplicable to torts such as deceit and other claims based upon dishonesty,[57] and (after some judicial hesitation) trespass to the person,[58] and cannot be applied in a claim for conversion under the Torts (Interference with Goods) Act 1977 (UK)[59] even where the conversion is unintentional.[60] It never seems to have been thought applicable to equitable wrongs such as breach of confidence. Where the source of the defendant's duty of care is that he has voluntarily assumed the duty to the claimant, as is the case in most instances of professional negligence, it is inappropriate to apply the defence. If, say, a financial adviser carelessly advises a client on the investments to make, if the client acts on the advice and suffers a terrible loss, it should not be open to the adviser to argue that the client should not have been such a fool as to make the reckless investments in any event. The client's own ignorance in the ways of money was the very thing the adviser was supposed to protect him from. It seems probable, as the Law Revision Committee assumed, that it is impossible to commit in relation to trespass to land and defamation.[61]

The reason, again, is that no question of causal responsibility for injury arises in these cases. If the defendant walks on his neighbour's land without permission, or publishes a libel about him, or discloses confidential information, he has committed a tort or wrong and that is the end of the matter. That the defence only applies to certain torts also supports the view that where it applies it is only relevant to acts of fault by the defendant that contribute to his initial injury, and not subsequent actions that contribute to his consequential loss. If the defence applied to the latter, it should apply to all wrongs.

[57] *Standard Chartered Bank v Pakistan National Shipping Corp* (Nos 2 and 4) [2002] UKHL 43; [2003] 1 AC 959.

[58] *Co-Operative Group (CWS) Ltd v Pritchard* [2011] EWCA Civ 329; [2012] QB 320.

[59] Torts (Interference with Goods) Act 1977 (UK), s 11.

[60] For criticism of this restriction, see Burrows (n 46) 135.

[61] Law Revision Committee, *Eighth Report*, *Contributory Negligence* (Cmd No 6032, 1939) 18.

6. CONCLUSION

The law is in a better condition than it was in 1945. The harsh special rule of the nineteenth century, to the extent that it persisted into the modern era, had little to support it. The apportionment of responsibility by judges, whilst a bit rough and ready, is not a disgrace. Some judges tend like analogue rules that allow for a variety of possible answers to be legitimately given, rather than digital rules that are either right or wrong. It is always nice to be incapable of being wrong. It is one of the jobs of the academic to deprecate these discretionary rules as contrary to the predictability of the rule of law.

The law could, however, have been better still. The Law Revision Committee proposals that led to the Act are remarkably brief by modern standards, and amount to little more than a statement that the apportionment rule seems to work well enough in the Admiralty Courts (and in Ontario where it had been introduced in 1922). The Act itself is remarkably sloppily drafted, reflecting the lack of any underlying normative justification for the rule. Perhaps in 1945 the members of the legislature had more important things on their minds.

Twenty years ago the English Law Commission recommended the extension of the Act to some (but not all) claims for breach of contract.[62] There seems little enthusiasm for such a reform. Why not? The problems of uncertainty created that are sometimes invoked as an objection are no different in kind than in those areas where the rule is already in operation.

The law of contract is not, and is not perceived as being, a mechanism for the allocation of loss to those who are blameworthy. The same thought underlies the exclusion of the defence in cases of conversion or battery. It is the law of negligence, and related areas such as workers' compensation for breach of statutory duty, where the view that the law is in the business of allocating losses to responsible persons holds sway, and where the defence of contributory negligence (sic) seems most plausible. This is a false division, however. The law of negligence concerns interpersonal wrongdoing just as much as breach of contract or conversion of goods. We should feel no more comfortable with this historically anomalous defence, which is a compromise reform of an old unjustifiable rule, in the negligence context than anywhere else.

The best solution would not be a return to the harsh rule that existed pre-1945. We should continue to rule out a claim for a tort where the claimant's conduct means that he, and not the defendant, is causally responsible for his injuries. We should go no further, and no apportionment rule should be retained.

If this solution is rejected the next best thing would be to reform the Act and limit its scope of operation. We should try to reduce uncertainty by introducing fixed rules of apportionment, clarify that the rule does not apply to post-tort fault, stipulate that it only applies after the application of all other rules restricting the attribution of loss to the defendant, and restrict the class of wrongs to which the Act applies, specifically excluding actions for breach of contract.

It would be better still to go digital.

[62] Law Commission, *Contributory Negligence as a Defence in Contract* (Report 219, 1993).

14

Assumption of Risk in a System of Strict Liability: Conceptual Tangles and Social Consequences

RICHARD A EPSTEIN

1. INTRODUCTION: TORT AND PLEADING IN CONCERT

THE PURPOSE OF this volume is to examine the role of defences in determining tort liability. To focus my contribution to this issue, I shall concentrate on one defence—assumption of risk. Preliminarily, it is a mistake to think about assumption of risk, or indeed any affirmative defence in tort law, as though it is a stand-alone enterprise. That approach is likely to get the analysis off on the wrong foot, unless care is taken to place this inquiry into its proper doctrinal context, a task that raises profound procedural issues. In particular, two caveats have to be introduced for any systematic treatment of defences to be tractable. The first deals with the articulation of the prima facie case. The second deals with the use of replications and other subsequent pleas to flesh out a complete system of liability rules. Both topics have been something of a minor obsession throughout my legal career.[1]

In working through the role of assumption of risk, it should be evident that the defence has many different roles to play, some large and some small. In some instances, one version of the defence is used to convert a system of strict liability into one of negligence, without any proof of a given claimant's mental state in any given case. In other instances it requires specific demonstration that a given claimant had assumed the risk of the defendant's conduct, not only because he knew of the risk but also because he waived any cause of action that might have otherwise been available. In tackling this issue I will discuss three categories of assumption of risk. The first category is the *global form*. These cases involve a generalised claim of assumption of risk that rests on larger social considerations. The rules apply with varying force to actions between strangers; most notably, blasting, vibration and private nuisance cases of all size and dimension. At the root, the cases that invoke the notion of assumption of risk put too much weight on the term. In all these cases,

[1] See RA Epstein, 'Pleadings and Presumptions' (1973) 40 *University of Chicago Law Review* 556; RA Epstein, 'The Not So Minimum Content of Natural Law' (2005) 25 *OJLS* 219; RA Epstein, 'Moral Incrementalism' in *Skepticism and Freedom: A Modern Case for Classical Liberalism* (Chicago, University of Chicago Press, 2003).

the mental state of the claimant plays no part in the overall analysis, which in fact turns on the way in which rules of 'implicit-in-kind compensation' do, or do not require a deviation from a baseline rule of strict liability.

This *global form* set of cases stands in contrast to the *individualised form* of assumption of risk cases that are specific to certain personal interactions. The second and third categories of cases to be discussed both fall within the *individualised form*. The second category concerns the interaction of assumption of risk when there is *parity* between the type of roles that the claimant and defendant each occupy in any given setting. In these cases, I show how the pleading system, rigorously applied, removes conceptual underbrush that has added an unneeded layer of conceptual confusion to the law of tort, but has had little effect on the larger operation of social systems. The difference in outcome dictated by the choice of general rule reflects only a small number of cases, and is thus too small to drive the transformation of any major social issue dealing with personal injury or property damage.[2]

The third category of cases deals with those situations where individual actions or agreements are said to underlay the defence in a particular case. There are no global arguments in these cases. The key cases involve some willingness to take on a risk by waiving, either explicitly or implicitly, by actions or by words, the right to sue. In these highly individuated contexts, I hope to show that the defence of assumption of risk has, and ought to have, real bite, and that the necessary qualification of implied assumption of risk does not open the way for a judicial removal of a right of action, as is the case when assumption of risk is used in its global sense. I shall conduct this inquiry by looking at a number of great English and American cases that have examined the choice between negligence and strict liability, by showing how, rightly understood, that cases that have previously been analysed under a negligence theory framework are better explained by adopting a theory of strict liability coupled with assumption of risk, subject to further exceptions that in most instances invoke matters of either negligence or intention. The cases that I choose are all well known, indeed canonical within the literature. Many of them involve situations where strict liability is rejected in favour of a negligence standard even though the *outcome* turns out to be the same when an assumption of risk defence is added onto the prima facie case of strict liability.

I am not insisting that in all contexts the choice of outcome will transform how the tort system, taken as a whole, influences the rate of accidents on the one hand, or of overall productive activity on the other. The distinction made between the two sets of cases (negligence and strict liability) is often overblown in light of the high concurrence in outcomes across any large sample of randomly selected accident cases when the parties stand in rough parity to each other. Nonetheless, one point of the exercise is to show how clarification of the relevant concept leads to a more coherent and easily administrable system of tort liability within a sound theory of corrective justice. In my view, liability has previously, and wrongly, been thought to require proof of either intention or negligence in the prima facie case.[3]

[2] A point I stressed years ago in RA Epstein, 'The Social Consequences of Common Law Rules' (1982) 95 *Harvard Law Review* 1717.

[3] For discussion, see RA Epstein, 'The Contextualization of Tort Law' (2010) 88 *Texas Law Review* See Also 105 in response to JCP Goldberg and BC Zipursky, 'Torts as Wrongs' (2010) 88 *Texas Law Review* 917.

The focal point of the analysis is reversed in the third category of assumption of risk cases in a variety of *institutional* contexts where the parties are not in rough parity with each other. The relevant settings include medical malpractice, workers' compensation and product liability that deal with asymmetrical arrangements; for example, doctor/patient, employer/employee, manufacturer/consumer relationships where it is more difficult to converge on the optimal form of rules, such that both custom and contract are routinely subject to greater scrutiny.[4] The doctrinal complexities are often less, but the social consequences can be, and in the American context, are far greater. Given the more or less permanent set of arrangements, the scope of the assumption of risk doctrine is not shaped as much by social interactions as by two other processes. The first of these is explicit contracts intended to govern the relationships, usually driven by firms but subject to market constraints. The second are the public policy arguments introduced to invalidate these contracts, and thus turn risk allocation into a matter of direct judicial and legislative control, where the consequences have proved very dramatic, especially in the United States.

So the progression of this chapter runs as follows. The first section addresses the relationship between pleading and substance. The second part turns to the three categories of assumption of risk. The global arguments come first; individuated cases of parity come second; and asymmetrical institutional forms of assumption of risk come third. A short discussion of the relationship of these issues to the notion of corrective justice concludes.

2. PLEADING: THE PRIMA FACIE CASE AND BEYOND

As a matter of basic normative theory, the proper role of defences is heavily dependent on the content of the prima facie case, which in turn depends heavily on whether the starting point for liability is strict liability, negligence, or intention. Under the conventional account, strict liability establishes the prima facie case without any showing of either specific intention to harm (broadly construed to cover reckless and perhaps a simple intention to touch, without harm), the failure to exercise reasonable care under the circumstances, or indeed, even without any specific objective whatsoever. That theory stands in opposition to the two other theories, both of which reject strict liability for its failure to articulate a valid prima facie case. One of these theories is the law of negligence. It stresses the role that a failure to take reasonable precautions, whether defined by custom or cost/benefit analysis, plays in the overall system. The second is the class of intentional harms that deal with actions performed with the intention of causing harm to the claimant. This theory is often modified in ways that do not require the intention to harm, but only the intention to bring about the actions that in fact cause harm,[5] the intention to touch the individual or his property without causing harm,[6] or even under the

[4] On the asymmetry see, RA Epstein, 'The Path of the T.J. Hooper: Of Custom and Due Care' (1992) 21 *Journal of Legal Studies* 1.

[5] See, eg, *Garratt v Dailey* 46 Wash 2d 197; 279 P 2d 1091 (1955), as modified, 49 Wash 2d 499; 304 P 2d 681 (1956); *Cleveland Park Club v Perry* 165 A 2d 485 (DC 1960).

[6] See, eg, *Vosburg v Putney* 80 Wis 523; 50 NW 403 (1891).

doctrine of 'transferred intention' to cause harm to third parties.[7] These variations tend to narrow the gap between intentional harms and the strict liability position, without closing it altogether. All of them become largely irrelevant under a consistent theory of strict liability that allows for multiple stages, for at the third stage, the intent to harm has its ordinary strong meaning.

It should be evident that no theory of tort law can be adequate to the task if it banishes any one of these three bases of liability from consideration. All three theories have played a central role in the development of tort law, so that it becomes necessary to fashion a comprehensive theory that takes them all into account. In discharging this task, it will not do to lay all three theories side by side, as if the claimant had the option to choose one over the other. If that were the case, why should any claimant choose any path other than the easiest to hoe? Strict liability would become the only game in town.

The challenge here, therefore, is to find an alternative approach that allows for the peaceful integration of the three theories of liability. The method that I have long urged to achieve this particular result is the method of presumptions that builds on the classical pleading systems articulated with great clarity as early as Gaius's *Institutes*.[8] The Institutes articulated at the earliest time what later became the rules of common law pleadings, all of which were clearly influenced by the general, if erratic, importation of Roman into English common law.[9]

The point of this system is to impose the following constraint on how cases are pleaded: start with that complaint which says the *least* that is needed to shift the onus over to the other side. Under this approach, information that is omitted at the outset can be added in at some later time as the system of pleading progresses. Indeed, the less that is said at the outset, the greater the number of potential elements that can be introduced in subsequent stages. The possibility for the delayed introduction of new matter means that there is no reason to include complete information at the first stage, or indeed any other subsequent stage. A claimant is safe in the knowledge that each particular element can be introduced in its proper place in due course. In some cases this process can run with commendable clarity through six, or even more, stages.[10] In principle, revisions could go on indefinitely so long as the parties have something they wish to add. The system for deciding how these pleas are layered involves the interaction of the demurrer and the plea in confession and avoidance, which allows new matter to be introduced at any stage in an extended argument.

Analytically, that two-stages-and-out approach is fatally inconsistent with the basic notion of 'defeasibility' which underlies the basic effort to fill out the complete contours of the system. If the prima facie case can be rebutted by a new matter, the same is true in principle of any affirmative defence or subsequent plea. Defeasibility, or the ability of a pleading to be defeated, has nothing to do with the meaning of

[7] See, eg *Talmage v Smith* 101 Mich 370; 59 NW 656 (1894).

[8] Gaius, *Institutes*, Book IV G§§ 116–29.

[9] See, eg, R Sutton, *Personal Actions at Common Law* (London, Butterworths, 1929).

[10] For this position in connection with the Roman sources, see RA Epstein, *One Step at a Time in Roman Law: How Roman Pleading Rules Shape the Substantive Structure of Roman Private law* (forthcoming).

particular legal terms like contract or property (as HLA Hart wrongly supposed in his essay on 'The Ascription of Responsibility and Rights'[11]). It has everything to do with the substantive allegations that a given fact is sufficient to tip the balance of responsibility away from the party who has made it. That position makes no sense if we take the same view on minimum sufficiency with respect to defences that we take with respect to the prima facie case. It follows therefore that we can introduce a third, fourth, indeed an infinite number of pleas so long as it is understood that each has to be able to withstand the demurrer and that each is in principle subject to defeasance by further pleas in confession and avoidance. In practice this pleading system may appear to be a bit clumsy, but sooner or later this exercise has to be carried out for the overall conceptual structure of the law to make sense. By getting the sequences correct, it becomes possible to integrate all three elements—causation, assumption of risk and the intention to harm—into a single case. In practice, of course, most new cases give rise to a denial, at which point the case turns on a disputed question of fact which will be of no further relevance to developing the overall law.

The soundness of this approach is evident through its ability to work through and resolve hard cases in a superior way to that found when the detailed pleading stages are systematically ignored. In principle I have no doubt that the methods that I develop here can be applied to the full range of tort defences, which include the variations on them of causation and self-defence, necessity and consent. But for these purposes, it is helpful to focus the argument by two limitations. The first is concentrating on global forms of assumption of risk (category one) as they work in relation to theories both of negligence and strict liability, and explaining how that clean resolution sets up the situation for dealing with consent to, of course, a deliberate harm. The second is the way in which the assumption of risk defence is used in those individual cases (categories two and three) where the presumptions applicable to the global form do not apply.

3. GLOBAL ASSUMPTION OF RISK

The first variation of the defence of assumption of risk in no way depends on the mental attitude of a particular person toward a given type of risk. Rather, it turns on the view that the overall social situation is improved if the defence is introduced on a universal basis. The term 'universal' is critical to this phase of the argument because it highlights the claim that strict liability should be rejected as a matter of first principle, often for the somewhat grandiose reason that it reduces the overall level of economic development. Perhaps the best judicial statement of this point is

[11] HLA Hart, 'The Ascription of Responsibility and Rights' (1949) 49 *Proceedings of the Aristotelian Society* 171. For early criticisms, see P Geach, 'Ascriptivism' (1960) 69 *Philosophical Review* 221, 224; G Pitcher, 'Hart on Action and Responsibility' (1960) 69 *Philosophical Review* 226. On how this relates to the issue of presumptions, see Epstein, 'The Not So Minimum Content of Natural Law' (n 1). To his credit Hart abandoned his earlier position and declined to have the essay reprinted in his *Punishment and Responsibility*: see HLA Hart, Punishment and Responsibility, 2nd edn (Oxford, Oxford University Press, 2008) v.

found in *Losee v Buchanan*,[12] which rejected the strict liability rule established in *Rylands v Fletcher*[13] in England five years earlier. *Losee* involved a suit brought by the claimant for damage sustained when the defendant's boiler exploded causing injury. The Court denied recovery for this loss on the ground that it was not shown that the boiler was a nuisance while in ordinary operation and it had not been operated with either intentional fault or negligence. The specific reason for denying the liability was that there was a manufacturing defect that was neither known nor discoverable to the defendant. It is worth noting that in the companion case of *Losee v Clute*,[14] liability by the manufacturer was rejected because there was no evidence of negligence where a boiler had been inspected by the buyer before being put into service, and which worked well for three months after the initial sale. Thus neither the party who manufactured the boiler, nor those who operated it, were held liable for the harm to an innocent third party. Relevant to this discussion is the assumption of risk type argument articulated by Earl J:[15]

> By becoming a member of civilized society, I am compelled to give up many of my natural rights, but I receive more than a compensation from the surrender by every other man of the same rights, and the security, advantage and protection which the laws give me. So, too, the general rules that I may have the exclusive and undisturbed use and possession of my real estate, and that I must so use my real estate as not to injure my neighbor, are much modified by the exigencies of the social state. We must have factories, machinery, dams, canals and railroads. They are demanded by the manifold wants of mankind, and lay at the basis of all our civilization. If I have any of these upon my lands, and they are not a nuisance and are not so managed as to become such, I am not responsible for any damage they accidentally and unavoidably do my neighbor. He receives his compensation for such damage by the general good, in which he shares, and the right which he has to place the same things upon his lands. I may not place or keep a nuisance upon my land to the damage of my neighbor, and I have my compensation for the surrender of this right to use my own as I will by the similar restriction imposed upon my neighbor for my benefit. I hold my property subject to the risk that it may be unavoidably or accidentally injured by those who live near me; and as I move about upon the public highways and in all places where other persons may lawfully be, I take the risk of being accidentally injured in my person by them without fault on their part. Most of the rights of property, as well as of

[12] 51 NY 476 (1873).

[13] *Fletcher v Rylands* (1865) 3 H & C 774; (1865) 159 ER 737, reviewed *Fletcher v Rylands* (1865–66) LR 1 Ex 265, affirmed *Rylands v Fletcher* (1868) LR 3 HL 330. In the House of Lords, both Lord Chancellor Cairns and Lord Cranworth adopt a general strict liability principle. They do not, however, make any explicit reference to implicit-in-kind compensation. Hints to Earl's argument are found in Blackburn J's earlier argument in the Exchequer, at 286:

> Traffic on the highways, whether by land or sea, cannot be conducted without exposing those whose persons or property are near it to some inevitable risk; and that being so, those who go on the highway, or have their property adjacent to it, may well be held to do so subject to their taking upon themselves the risk of injury from that inevitable danger; and persons who by the licence of the owner pass near the warehouses where goods are being raised or lowered, certainly do so subject to the inevitable risk of accident.

Note the progression from 'inevitable risk' which people 'may beheld to' accept to licensees who 'certainly do' accept the inevitable risk of accident. Note too, the word 'inevitable' does not do much work here. So long as the risk is above zero, it is inevitable. This is a far cry from the 'inevitable accident' in *Weaver v Ward* (1616) Hob 134; 80 ER 284, discussed below at p 278.

[14] Above n 12, 494.

[15] Above n 12, 484–85.

person, in the social state, are not absolute but relative, and they must be so arranged and modified, not unnecessarily infringing upon natural rights, as upon the whole to promote the general welfare.

There is little doubt that the themes of assumption of risk and economic development are alive and well in the last two sentences of this argument. Accordingly it is necessary to explain why this formulation is incorrect, because of the incomplete way in which it integrates the various elements into a single theory. The initial point to note is that the rejection of the strict liability approach is confined to the *Losee's* case of the accidental explosion, but the accepted negligence approach was not followed in the earlier case of *Hay v The Cohoes Co*,[16] which adopted the strict liability approach for deliberate blasting, even when done with all possible care to avoid harm to others. Negligence was also rejected in cases where the vibrations from one person's factory caused damage to his neighbour, in the instance of ordinary nuisances[17] and in the diversion of a running stream.[18] So the question remains, why is it that the strict liability rule somehow dampens productivity less than in those cases of indirect harms remediable under the action on the case. There is nothing about the length of the causation chain that governs the case, for by virtue of the fact that liability exists for negligence, it has to be conceded that causation in this case was not too remote. The argument that Holmes made in *The Common Law*, namely that the length of the causal chain should have nothing to do with liability, is correct.[19] The question therefore is whether the uniform negligence or strict liability rule is correct.

In dealing with these questions, the assumption of risk argument is used to tilt the balance in favour of the negligence rule. But what is lacking from that argument in this context is showing that proof of negligence is needed to advance overall social welfare. Earl J seeks to remedy that gap by referring to a notion of implicit-in-kind compensation that is surely correct in form, even if it may prove in the context wrong in fact. Thus the sound instinct behind this determination is that one has to revert back to the ex ante state of the world to make estimations about the impact of a change in rules on overall levels of investment and growth. The initial point is that as the rate of explosions and similar risks declines, the importance of the choice of liability rule is reduced. The second point is that within that reduced class it is important to look at both sides of the equation. The rule that protects individuals who operate boilers is one that impacts negatively on the activities of others whose own industrial establishments are damaged, possibly without recompense. If there is any systematic skew therefore, the negligence rule favours those firms that enter into risky business relative to those that do not, and by insulating them for liability, it reduces their incentive to relocate their operations to places that minimise harmful interactions. Netting out the two effects therefore makes the impact on investment indeterminate at best. The situation is further clouded when the administrative costs of running the system are factored in. It seems clear that under a negligence system parties will, on average, be subject to fewer suits for damage than under a

[16] 2 NY 159 (1849).
[17] *McKeon v Lee* 4 Rob Superior Court R 449.
[18] *Bellinger v The New York Central RR* 23 NY 42 (1861).
[19] OW Holmes, *The Common Law* (first published 1881) 90–94.

strict liability system. But that effect is likely to be small given that most courts in these cases apply *res ipsa loquitur* because the dangerous instrumentality is in the exclusive possession of the defendant and the claimant has done nothing to contribute to the harm. So the cases that remain are subject to higher expenses and greater error in dealing with a negligence standard, which in this context ultimately boils down to a question of degree. In these cases I see nothing wrong with sticking with the minimalist strict liability case that puts the loss on the party who invaded the space of another, not on the party whose space was forcibly, if indirectly, invaded. Indeed, that result is even stronger given that there was a defect in the equipment in question, which will not be brought to account by any direct action against the manufacturer in *Losee v Clute* because of the want of privity of contract.

In making this particular claim, it does not follow that the implicit-in-kind compensation argument should always be rejected, for in some contexts the benefit received to both sides exceeds the cost. That is surely true with the live-and-let-live arguments that were advanced so ably by Baron Bramwell in *Bamford v Turnley.*[20] On the facts of that case, Bramwell LJ held the defendant liable for the noxious fumes from baking bricks in a kiln that made his neighbours ill. But it is worth noting that Bramwell LJ's logic would have imposed a strict liability rule in *Losee,* where the isolated mishaps from using defective equipment are hard to calculate. In such cases, there is no reason to think that the two losses will balance out just because the risks as stated are reciprocal, given the wide variation in how different firms operate their equipment in their respective businesses.

A no liability conclusion is, however, much more defensible in the live-and-let-live cases set out in *Bamford* for low-level intrusions that commonly occur, when the damage associated with each intrusion is low. While saving all administrative costs is a huge advantage, that result is only possible if the defence *cannot* be overridden by proof of negligence in cases of this sort, which if allowed would otherwise swamp the system. So the Bramwell rule admits exceptions for low-level harm, but draws the line at harm either 'done wantonly or maliciously'. The best way to think of this substantive move is as an exception to the live-and-let-live defence, which comes in at the third stage of the argument. Note the explicit relationship between malice and an intention to harm. The latter may create a prima facie case of the former, but that is negated by the presence of some excuse or justification, the possibility of which has to be negated before malice can be established. In normal cases the intent to harm is justified not just by the gains to the party who acts, but also by the systematic social gains that are obtained when everyone follows the same course of action. The notion of malice here involves actions that are meant solely to harm the other party without providing any benefit to the party who takes them, which is consistent with the basic Bramwell position with respect to low-level reciprocal harms.

The efficiency rationale for this position, moreover, is rather easy to see, because the frequency of suits for malice covers only a tiny fraction of the low-level nuisances,

[20] (1860) 3 B & S 62; 122 ER 25. I have discussed these points at greater length in RA Epstein, 'Nuisance Law: Corrective Justice and Its Utilitarian Constraints' (1979) 8 *Journal of Legal Studies* 49, which operates for the backdrop of this section, and RA Epstein, 'For a Bramwell Revival' (1994) 38 *American Journal of Legal History* 246.

and with that motivation the severity is likely to increase so as to take the case out of the rule. All tolled, therefore, the administrative costs, which are overwhelming in routine low-level nuisances are now far lower, and they are in any event justified by the deterrence of antisocial behaviour that they create. The bottom line here is that the contrast between the two situations of intent to harm and malice shows why the global assumption of risk argument cannot be either rejected or accepted in its entirety. The ability to identify the circumstances that flip the switch is essential to making the argument. But by the same token, the invocation of assumption of risk language does nothing to advance the argument which turns, as the initial sentences in *Losee v Buchanan* suggest, on the proper use of the implicit-in-kind compensation arguments that have to stand or fall on their own.

The same approach applies to the issue of lateral support in construction cases, where again the obligations are largely reciprocal (with complications for properties built on grade). In the 1855 decision in *Farrand v Marshall* it was held that: 'A man may dig on his own land, but not so near that of his neighbor as to cause the land of the latter to fall into his pit, thus transferring a portion of another man's land to his own'.[21] Here we see a deviation from the usual nuisance rules because this case does not involve efforts to restrict liability for invasive nuisance, but rather to create liability in non-invasive situations. Here too, the support obligation is always mutual so that a strict duty not to carve out land to the margins is likely to increase the value of both parcels of land at little or no administrative costs, by blocking people from engaging in excavation, typically for construction, that will upset the balance between neighbours.

It is critical to note that the rule stated in *Farrand* is consciously limited to land in its natural state and that different rules apply to 'land in non-natural state'.[22] That qualification is necessary to one person's building up to the boundary in order to further restrict the level of construction that can be done by the other. The proper response in these cases is to prevent one landowner's strategic effort to expand the support obligation, which is done by allowing an action for the loss of the building if in fact the land would have remained in place if no construction had occurred.[23] In these cases, the proper response is to require any landowner, before he starts excavation, to give the other party notice so that he can relocate the construction away from the boundary line. Knowing that this is a costly option, the sensible response is to situate the structure away from the boundary line in the first instance. At this

[21] 21 Barb 409, 409 (SC NY 1855).

[22] See *Birmingham v Allen* (1877) 6 Ch D 284 (CA) 287 (Jessel MR). Courtesy of Google books, I found RF MacSwinney *The Law of Mines, Quarries, and Minerals*, 3rd edn (1890) which organises its discussion of support rights around 'the distinction between "land in natural state" and "land in non-natural state"' (271ff). There are no functional explanations offered anywhere I read, but the rules as announced are unerring in maximising the joint value of the relevant landowners. Accordingly in the pleadings the claimant 'has never been obliged to allege or prove, that he was entitled to support; the burden, both in pleading and in proof, being upon him who asserts that the position is different from that existing as of common right'. In Coasean terms, the law starts with the best initial position from which variation is allowed by contract. The division of land always carries with it implied obligation of support both ways (at 272). Liability is also strict. 'A mine owner cannot avoid liability by merely showing that his workings have been proper, and in the usual method. And the mere fact that he cannot work, or cannot work at a profit, if he has to leave support, does not entitle him to remove the support' (at 273–74) (footnote omitted).

[23] MacSwinney (n 22) 414.

point, the early construction gives no additional advantage to the party engaged in it, so that neither party has an incentive to hasten construction in order to impose a restrictive covenant against his neighbour. Building decisions are thus based solely on ordinary calculations of whether the benefits of the expected construction exceed its cost. Certainly, there may be some cases where the model does not quite hold. Thus if the plot is so narrow that this retreat is not possible, the preferable solution is to acquire an easement of support explicitly before construction, or to engage in some combined activity that avoids the boundary-line risk. There is nothing about the global 'assumption of risk' defence that precludes additional voluntary transactions in those cases where the topography works against the one-size-fits-all solution. Overall, however, the implicit compensation arguments dominate. Any reference to risks assumed have nothing to do with the subjective state of mind cases to which I now turn.

4. INDIVIDUALISED ASSUMPTION OF RISK: CASES OF PARITY

The second set of assumption of risk cases do involve the mental state of the claimant. Within a system of negligence, there is of course no need to show that the claimant assumed the risk of purely accidental harm on a case-by-case basis. That form of assumption of risk is built into the negligence law as a categorical matter, because a claimant will never be able to show that a defendant has breached the duty of care. At this point, assumption of risk does not arise as a separate affirmative defence, because in the absence of a breach of duty, the claimant cannot make out a prima facie case. Within this conceptual framework, therefore, it follows that the question of assumption of risk never arises as a question of fact.[24]

The situation under strict liability is quite different. Here the prima facie case of minimum sufficiency takes the position that there is a huge moral gap between those cases in which the defendant kills the claimant and those in which the claimant dies because the claimant was shot or poisoned by someone else, by his own hand, or a natural event. At this point, the prima facie case is established, such that the assumption of risk defence *only* applies to the bare-bones allegation found in the complaint. All the defendant has to show is that the claimant accepted the particular risk of accidental harm. There is no need to establish any other element of the case. Since this is a very broad claim of responsibility, it is far easier to show, on the facts of any particular case, an assumption of risk of accidental harm than an assumption of risk of harm brought about by the defendant's negligence. Once the assumption of risk defence is upheld against a complaint that sounds only in strict liability, it remains a separate question whether the claimant assumed the risk of harm that could have been obviated by taking reasonable care.

The first step in this inquiry is to ask whether there is any assumption of risk at all. The point often arises in connection with the related question of whether a claimant *knew* of a risk or had *assumed* it. This is the traditional distinction

[24] On this no breach of duty position, see F James, 'Assumption of Risk' (1952) 61 *Yale Law Journal* 141. For a modern restatement of the position, see S Sugarman, 'Assumption of Risk' (1997) 31 *Valparaiso University Law Review* 833.

between *volenti non fit iniuria* and *scienti non fit iniuria*, where the first of these propositions is true and the second is not. For example, suppose that a potential defendant announces to the rest of the world that all people who enter a public highway do so at their own peril because he is determined to shoot them if they appear. Someone hears the threat and ignores it. The case is somewhat different from the situation where a defendant announces that he will kill whatever persons he finds, no questions asked. In this second situation, the potential victim has undertaken no action at all, and may well cower at the thought of an attack, the knowledge of which in no way represents a waiver of the cause of action in response to a threat which itself should be a prime candidate for civil and criminal assault.[25] The same principle applies when one person's threat is meant to force everyone else to surrender their lawful options (of which walking down a public street is one) in order to avoid some greater harm.[26] In the law of contract a threat to constrain choice goes under the name of duress of goods, whereby one person puts another to a choice between two entitlements.[27] For example, if you were entitled to the return of goods upon payment of an agreed price, suppose that the holder of the goods now gives you the choice to pay an excess fee or forfeit the return of the goods. It is one thing to say that a person always has to make a choice between his money and the goods that he wishes to purchase from another individual, which is competition at its best. It is quite another to force one person to choose between two of his own entitlements. Forcing (and allowing) someone to make a 'money or your life' choice is the surest way to undermine a free society. The same argument applies in tort. An individual has both the right to use public highways and to preserve bodily integrity. So either the assumption of risk defence must be rejected or, if accepted, is subject to the reply that that assumption was vitiated by duress. The line between these two scenarios is very thin. Moreover, that point is illuminated by the different forms in which the pleadings are stated. The first route denies that the defence applies. The second introduces a reply to show that the application of the defence is vitiated by the reply of fraud. Either way the threat must never be allowed to work.

The next question is what, if anything, should be done when one person encounters an obstacle that is left by another on, say, a public street. These cases need not presage any form of criminal intent because the blockage may well be unintentional, and there is no evidence that the defendant had any intent to pursue or execute a threat against the claimant. In these situations, however, it is still the case that a person is confronted with a choice: either abandon or curtail the entitlement to use the public road or take the risk of injury. In these situations, the right course of action for the claimant is always to back off a known hazard. One does not run into a barricade, and if he does the assumption of risk defence applies to someone who, by his by actions, was just 'asking for trouble'. But by the same token, it must be understood that mitigation of harm is not the same as return to the status quo ante. Therefore, in these cases the correct measure of damages, if any, depends on the size and nature of the interference. In those cases where they are trivial and frequent, the

[25] Recall the basic (libertarian) norm covers both the use and threat of force, and for very good reason.
[26] See, eg, *Marshall v Ranne* 511 SW 2d 255 (Tex 1974).
[27] For discussion, see RA Epstein, *Bargaining with the State* (Princeton, Princeton University Press, 1993) 42–44.

correct response involves yet another application of the live-and-let-rule whereby everyone is better off if they suffer the *de minimis* harms inflicted by others, leaving it to public officials to deal with the blockage by direct administrative action: clear the road and fine the offender is one common combination. This solution has long been in place in connection with the law of public nuisance, which has always allowed private rights of action for special damages, but no remedy for (low-level) harm experienced by a broad segment of the population.[28]

In many cases, however, the argument that the claimant assumed the risk is far more potent than in those cases where it is thrust upon him. One indicator that has had real staying power is where the claimant moves towards, rather than away from, a known risk. Another is whether the claimant and defendant are engaged in some collaborative enterprise so that the notion of reciprocal risks, both of which may be assumed, is a central part of the overall scheme. These elements are present in the decided cases and analytically it is important to unpack them from notions of intention, voluntarism, fault, and inevitable accident that make their way into the case law. The question arises: should assumption of risk be a rule of negligence (so that the risk of injury is always conclusively presumed) or should it be a strict liability system where the defence of assumption of risk remains, subject to further qualifications, at the third and subsequent stages in the argument? What is remarkable about the key cases that I shall consider is that *none* of them advances a systematic argument in favour of one rule or the other. Far from independent justifications, what is commonly done is to rephrase the basic rule without offering a reason why it should be adopted.

One reason for this impasse is that it is difficult to draw any strong consequentialist lessons from the cases about the optimal rule from an ex ante perspective that is intended in some fashion to minimise, to use Guido Calabresi's useful formulation, the sum of accident costs, avoidance costs, and administrative costs, when these three elements vary independently and often in contradictory ways.[29] The efforts to impose this system are made much more difficult when the parties do not stand in rough parity in relation to each other, raising genuine questions of role differences.[30] It is therefore useful to work out how the system plays out in cases of parallel interests before addressing those cases where the different social positions of the parties complicate the analysis.

4.1 Positions of Parity

The most influential decision opting for the negligence rule (and contributory negligence as an absolute bar to recovery) is *Brown v Kendall*,[31] a Massachusetts decision of Shaw CJ. In that case, the defendant was separating two dogs that were fighting with each other, one owned by each party. As he was beating them with

[28] *Anonymous* YB Mich 27 Hen 8 f 27, pl 10 (1535).

[29] G Calabresi, *The Costs of Accidents* (New Haven, Yale University Press, 1970).

[30] For example, between occupiers and various types of entrants, employers against workers, manufacturers against consumers and patients against physicians.

[31] 60 Mass 292 (1850).

a stick, he proceeded backward. At the same time the claimant proceeded 'a step or two toward the dogs' when the defendant's stick struck the claimant in the eye severely injuring him. The defendant had requested instructions that the claimant could recover only if he had exercised reasonable care when the defendant had not. The trial judge gave a more complex set of instructions, in two parts: first, if the defendant was acting under a duty to separate the dogs, the standard of ordinary care would apply. But if the defendant was under no duty to separate the dogs, the claimant could recover unless the defendant could show that his conduct had met the higher standard of 'extraordinary care, so that the accident was inevitable, using the word not in a strict but a popular sense'.[32] The jury returned a verdict for the claimant, and the judgment was set aside because of the inclusion of the 'extraordinary care' instruction.

My view is that the decision of Shaw CJ set the law off in the wrong direction. Start by asking the simple intuitive question: which party should bear the loss? On this question it surely should be the claimant who had both more information and greater freedom of action. Ironically, on this version of the facts, it is hard to see why the claimant was entitled to receive even the new trial which Shaw CJ ordered on the entire case. Rather, as in most cases decided in a strict liability regime, it seems proper to order a directed verdict for the defendant on the facts stated by Shaw CJ. To see why this is so, it is important to put the legal issues in proper order. On this point, start with an older assertion by Brian (before he was a judge) in *Hulle v Orynge (The Case of Thorns)*: 'in my own defence I raise my stick to strike him, and a man is behind me and in raising my stick I wound him, in this case he shall have an action against me, and yet the raising of my stick to defend myself was lawful and I wounded him me invito'.[33] In essence Brian was saying that if B hits A, he is subject to a prima facie case of strict liability to which his efforts to defend himself against an attack of C is not a valid affirmative defence, but which (although he did not say it) gives rise to an action of indemnity to the party subject to the attack. In effect, what this does is align causal responsibility in this hierarchical order: aggressor (C), middle man (B), innocent claimant (A), so that the task of the legal system is to figure out efficient procedural ways to try all three of these relations, including the possibility of a direct action of A against C, even if C is (not literally) the proximate cause of A's injury. Authority on the point is divided but I think that Brian has the better of the position.[34]

In any event, his hypothetical case is distinguishable from *Brown*, where the assumption of risk defence takes on powerful proportions given the claimant's decision to move closer to the risk when he had full information about the peril. In addition, the negligence defence seems appropriate for a second reason: the action of the defendant under conditions of necessity was not only undertaken for the defendant's own benefit but for the claimant's as well. In those cases of joint benefit, the standard of ordinary care seems to be appropriate, which was the decision of

[32] ibid 297.
[33] (1460) YB Mich 6 Edw IV, fo 7v, pl 18.
[34] See Digest 9.2, 45.4 (disallowing the defence); *Morris v Platt* 32 Conn 75 (1864).

Baron Bramwell in *Carstairs v Taylor*,[35] who was also a strong defender of the strict liability position in stranger cases.[36]

The great vice of *Brown* was that it looked solely at the conduct of the defendant, ignoring the actions of the claimant. In this regard, any finding of negligence must be impossibly weak at a time when the case for recovery was indefensible on the record. The reader who instinctively inserts the claimant's conduct back into the case can be forgiven for thinking negligence is the right rule. But if the identical blow had struck against an innocent passerby, that intuition becomes far weaker. In addressing this question, Shaw is at pains to reject the view of the trial judge that the defendant had to use extraordinary care if his actions were not necessary, but otherwise was only required to use ordinary care under the circumstances if he were duty bound to separate them. The difficulty with both sets of instructions is that they ignore the role of the claimant in bringing about his own harm.

Shaw's opinion also plays fast and loose with the term 'inevitable' which derives from the phrase 'inevitable accident' in *Weaver v Ward*.[37] In that case, the trial judge construed inevitable as referring to the need for the defendant to use extraordinary care in the case, which Shaw, as already noted, was using 'using the word inevitable not in a strict but a popular sense'.[38] But there are no two meanings to the term inevitable, which means that 'it had to happen', and does not refer to any level of care, high or low. Indeed in *Weaver* the operative passage reads as follows:[39]

> [Y]et in trespass, which tends only to give damages according to hurt or loss, it is not so; and therefore if a lunatick hurt a man, he shall be answerable in trespass: and therefore no man shall be excused of a trespass (for this is the nature of an excuse, and not of a justification, prout ei bene licuit) [as it well appeared to him] except it may be judged utterly without his fault.
>
> As if a man by force take my hand and strike you, or if here the defendant had said, that the claimant ran cross his piece when it was discharging, or had set forth the case with the circumstances, so as it had appeared to the Court that it had been inevitable, and that the defendant had committed no negligence to give occasion to the hurt.

The most striking feature of this short passage is how it organises the various pleas. Lunacy is not a defence because the obligation to compensate cannot be defeated by the defendant seeking to export his personal woes upon a stranger. The Court is right to note that this could, if accepted, only count as at most as an excuse, because by no stretch of the imagination could insanity make the act proper, that is, one that should be repeated if the opportunity presented itself. The Court then uses the phrase 'utterly without fault,' to paint in broad strokes the three disparate illustrations that follow. No fair reading of this phrase equates it with Shaw's rendition of responsibility 'for failure to exercise reasonable care'. The first case in *Weaver* is a general denial: the defendant did not do it because some third party took his hand. In the second, the defendant is not responsible, because the claimant violated

[35] (1871) LR 6 Ex 217.
[36] *Powell v Fall* (1880) 5 QBD 597 (CA).
[37] Above n 13.
[38] *Brown v Kendall* (n 31) 293.
[39] Above n 13, 284.

the norms of the business by running into the line of fire. This is, in effect, a causal defence of the type that says a defendant who hits a claimant may be prima facie liable in tort, but has a defence if the claimant had blocked his way. It should be noted as well that, prima facie, the defendant, if injured, would have a cause of action for blocking the road, subject to exceptions, as if he had seen the obstacle and had failed to stop, which harks back to last clear chance.[40]

The third strand involves the elusive notion of inevitable accident, which refers to situations where the defendant is put into a position (say being left on someone else's land), where he had to commit a trespass no matter what he did, at which point he is excused unless his own antecedent negligence got him into the position from which he caused the harm. To this list should be added assumption of risk, which may be buried in the middle category, but is applicable here since claimant and defendant were members of the same company, which makes it plausible for all parties to release each other in advance for simple accidents, which is the norm in modern times, where a compensation system is installed to displace all tort remedies.[41] But what is clear is that the effort to construe 'inevitable' to mean 'without negligence or intention' misreads the text, and misstates the pleading rules as well. The defendant's negligence comes in at stage three (negligence that occasioned the harm) and cannot therefore be introduced as a denial at stage two.[42]

The confusion is then compounded when Shaw explains the variable level of care that is needed when he writes: 'A man, who should have occasion to discharge a gun, on an open and extensive marsh, or in a forest, would be required to use less circumspection and care, than if he were to do the same thing in an inhabited town, village, or city'.[43] This statement appears to be the soul of common sense, in so far as it suggests a rule of prudence that links the level of care to the proportionate risk. But, unfortunately, does not answer the question of whether those *inputs* should determine whether the defendant is liable, which can require extensive information about levels of care usually not available after the fact.

In contrast, under a strict liability standard, the court need only look at the negative *output* to reach its decision. But knowing the likely consequences of its action, the defendant will surely calibrate his action to the circumstances, taking the requisite level of care. But what needs to be explained is, as between him and the claimant, why the defendant who exercises greater care should be excused when he shoots an innocent stranger in either setting.[44] The probability of harm should not come into

[40] *Davies v Mann* (1842) 10 M & W 546; 152 ER 588.

[41] Just that result happens when explicit regulations take over, at which point, compensation is generally provided under an explicit compensation scheme for military. See, for discussion, *Feres v United States* 340 US 135 (1950), denying tort action when compensation was available under an explicit military system of compensation run on the model of state workers' compensation systems (144–45). Jackson J wrote 'claimants cite us no state, and we know of none, which has permitted members of its militia to maintain tort actions for injuries suffered in the service, and, in at least one state, the contrary has been held to be the case' (142). Jackson J also cited *Weaver v Ward* (n 13).

[42] For the incongruity on the pleading side, see M Arnold, *Select Cases of Trespass from the King's Courts—1307-1399* (Selden Society, vol 100, 1984) ix.

[43] *Brown v Kendall* (n 31) 296.

[44] The phrase 'as between claimant and defendant' when used in the decided cases is always a prelude to a strict liability norm. See Holmes (n 19) 84: 'In the cases put [variations on *Weaver v Ward*], the plaintiff has done nothing; the defendant, on the other hand, has chosen to act. As between the two, the party whose voluntary conduct has caused the damage should suffer, rather than one who has had no

play with a completed accident. It only comes into play to determine whether some private injunction or public law should stop the using of weapons, where the case for that is surely stronger in the city than in the country, and only because we know that tort damages can never supply perfect relief in the event of death or serious injury. In the end there is not a single passage in *Brown* that addresses the relative merits of the two systems, or explains why the probabilities of harm ex ante should determine liability ex post. The better rule by far is one of uniform strict liability, where the level of precautions determines only the likelihood of harm, not the likelihood of recovery, which is constant in all cases of an adverse event. Small gradations in probability should never generate an on/off liability switch.[45]

A similar analysis applies to the important 1891 English decision of *Stanley v Powell*[46] which arose out of a hunting accident. The claimant was employed by Greenwood to carry cartridges for shooting and to haul back the game that was shot. The defendant was shooting quail, and his second shot glanced off an oak tree, striking the claimant in the eye. The question was whether the claimant could recover for that loss. Denman J, inexplicably, did not deal with the issue of assumption of risk,[47] instead he launched into an arcane discussion of the relative merits of negligence and strict liability. His extensive argument consisted solely of reviewing all the relevant authorities (and citing *Brown v Kendall)* after which he dismissed all historical passages in favour of strict liability. During the course of that opinion, similarly to Shaw CJ, Denman J misread the key passage in *Weaver v Ward* by wrongly treating inevitability as 'a defence under the general issue', when it was clearly conceived as an affirmative defence.

Reinserting assumption of risk back into the case, the issue becomes: should the claimant, who was part of the shooting party, be subject to that defence. A credible answer to that question could be yes. If the defence is allowed, there is no way to override it by proving either negligence, let alone intent, given the fluke nature of the ricochet. This analysis leaves open the question of the separate employment relationship between the claimant and Greenwood. At this point, the question becomes: what term should be implied into a contract of employment when the worker is injured on the job without the complicity of the employer. My own sense is that the employer should, in the manner of the workers' compensation cases, pick up the medical expenses for the event, subject of course to some agreement to the contrary, at which point the overall outcome of the case would start to make sense. But since those collateral arrangements are not in evidence here, it is hard to render a final judgment on the point.

share in producing it'. For the record, Holmes's refutation of this position strikes me as wrong on every point, most notably the way in which he caricatures causation so that there is no stopping point to the theory, when clear lines exist between the indirect harms covered by the action on the case and those which are too remote. Thus in *Rylands v Fletcher* the harm is not too remote when the water leaks out of the reservoir. It is when it is carted away by a stranger and poured somewhere else.

[45] For the same point in the context of eminent domain, see RA Epstein, 'The Takings Clause and Partial Interests in Land: On Sharp Boundaries and Continuous Distributions' (2013) 78 *Brooklyn Law Review* 589.

[46] [1891] 1 QB 86 (QBD).

[47] ibid 86, n 7.

Next on the list of cases to discuss is *Vosburg v Putney*,[48] which involved an incident in a schoolroom where the defendant gently tapped the claimant on the shin of his right leg with his own foot, without any intention to harm him. He did so under the table in order to attract the claimant's attention. The kick was apparently consistent with the general practice of students in the room. Indeed the touch was so light that the claimant did not feel it. But a few moments later the claimant screamed out in pain. The questions of causation were murky because the claimant had suffered a skiing accident shortly before and the wound had not yet healed. Indeed a medical examination revealed dead bone near the site of the kick, which probably related to the earlier accident. Procedurally, the case is notable for its special verdicts in which the jury concluded first that the kick was the 'exciting' cause of the harm, and second that there was no intention to harm.[49] The underlying cause of the harm was brittle bones caused by a prior sledding accident that had not healed. The court found liability in this case as an intentional tort, even without the specific intention to harm. In holding the defendant liable Lyon J wrote:[50]

> [A]s applied to this case, if the kicking of the plaintiff by the defendant was an unlawful act, the intention of [the] defendant to kick him was also unlawful. Had the parties been upon the play-grounds of the school, engaged in the usual boyish sports, the defendant being free from malice, wantonness, or negligence, and intending no harm to plaintiff in what he did, we should hesitate to hold the act of the defendant unlawful, or that he could be held liable in this action.

No one is confident what the first sentence means, but it appears to refer to the fact that the classroom had been called to order before the kick had taken place so to that extent the action was branded as 'unlawful'. What is lacking is any explanation as to why an infraction of a minor school rule should lead to the imposition of major tort liability. Yet by the same token there seems to be no ground to hold the claimant liable for negligence, given his ignorance of the condition. So the claimant's case is shaky at best, both as an intentional and a negligent tort. Nonetheless, a strict liability analysis would impose liability given that the defendant kicked, however softly, the claimant. The question of the antecedent condition raises a difficult causal question of whether this accident was sure to happen in any event given the fragile condition of the leg, at which point a substantial reduction in damages in needed to account for the vast fraction that was likely to occur shortly in any event.

Yet what of assumption of risk? Lyons J acknowledged that this defence applies to the playground, where it is surely implied and not express. In good pleading style he notes that the defence can be overridden by malice, wantonness, or negligence. He is surely right about the first of these three, malice, and surely wrong about the third, negligence. The status of the second, wantonness, is a bit ambiguous, but is generally and correctly grouped with malice, as a rough equivalent to reckless disregard of the safety of others.[51] As with the live-and-let-live cases the invocation of

[48] 80 Wis 523; 50 NW 403 (1891).

[49] ibid NW 403.

[50] ibid NW 403–04.

[51] That equation is found in many other contexts, such as defamation law, where the United States Supreme Court equates the two in defamation cases. See *New York Times v Sullivan* 376 US 254, 280 (1964): 'The constitutional guarantees require, we think, a federal rule that prohibits a public official

malice connotes more than an intention to harm, but covers those cases where the harm in question is beyond the scope of the implied licence, which does not include the right to maim another person. By the same token, the negligence exception is far too wide, both in informal settings[52] and in cases of organised sports as well.[53] The risk of playground accidents is reciprocal, and the frequency of negligence is doubtless very high. Let this exception work and virtually every case has to go to the jury. All parties are better off if no one can sue anyone else for the harms of this sort, where the release in advance gives implicit-in-kind compensation to everyone else. Wantonness is hard to define and police, and thus adds little to the account of malice. The strict liability system thus covers these cases well once the replies are accurately sorted out.

The harder question is whether assumption of risk should apply to actions that take place inside the classroom. The answer should be in the affirmative. One striking feature about the law of tort generally is that it contains two kinds of rules that operate side by side. The rules on causation under strict liability involve push/pull types of causal arrangements, in which it is never appropriate to ask whether the defendant took reasonable care to avoid or prevent the harm in question. But the rules of assumption of risk are deeply contextual and (as with *Stanley v Powell*) depend therefore on a close reading of the social situation. In the classroom setting, it is clear that no one can use the level of force that is appropriate for a game on the playground, so that the risks assumed are narrower than they are on the playground. But in this instance, it appears as though there was a common practice of lightly tapping classmates below the table in order to achieve two results: first, to avoid the angry stares of the teacher; second, to satisfy the youthful urge to communicate about all matters great and small. These are all two-way communications so that the conditions of reciprocity that are found on the playground hold equally well here. Once that defence is accepted, the burden is now placed on the claimant to show in reply a factor that takes the case out of the basic mould. That could be done on grounds of recklessness or specific intent to harm if the defendant knew at the time of the kicking that the fragile condition of the claimant's shin meant that even a gentle tap could result in a major injury. But as nothing of the sort appears here, *Vosburg* is wrongly decided. Note too, if the kick had been done to a total stranger on a public street, the outcome would likely be the same, given that both parties are entitled to equal use of the same space. But the liability might well be reversed if the claimant while at home were hit by a ball that flew into the window, given the general (and difficult) rule that says, at least in stranger cases, the defendant takes his victim as he finds him. Yet here the result is not clear because

from recovering damages for a defamatory falsehood relating to his official conduct unless he proves that the statement was made with 'actual malice'—that is, with knowledge that it was false or with reckless disregard of whether it was false or not'.

[52] *Marchetti v Kalish* 53 Ohio St 3d 95; 559 NE 2d 699 (1990) (informal game of kick the can).

[53] See, eg, *Nabozny v Barnhill* 31 Ill App 3d 212; 334 NE 2d 258 (App Ct 1975) (amateur soccer match); *Turcotte v Fell* 68 NY 2d 432; 502 NE 2d 964 (1986) (professional racing): 'As a general rule, participants properly may be held to have consented, by their participation, to those injury-causing events which are known, apparent or reasonably foreseeable consequences of the participation. [But] the rule is qualified to the extent that participants do not consent to acts which are reckless or intentional' (NY 2d 439; NE 2d 968).

in many extra-sensitive situations a credible argument could be made on the global assumption of risk grounds above; that persons of extraordinary sensitivity have to take care to locate themselves out of harm's way.[54]

The assumption of risk issue also arose in the great American case of *McGuire v Almy*,[55] where the claimant nurse was employed full time to take care of the defendant, an insane person. On the day of the incident, '[the] plaintiff heard a crashing of furniture and then knew that the defendant was ugly, violent and dangerous'.[56] The claimant then called Mr Emerton, the defendant's brother-in-law to assist. At this time the defendant was holding up the leg of a 'low-boy' as if she were going to strike. The claimant inched toward the defendant while Emerton, and Miss Maroney (the maid), stayed in the doorway. The claimant tried to disarm the defendant, at which point the defendant struck the claimant's head. Justice Qua never bothers to identify the claimant's employer, even though he might, as in *Stanley v Powell*, have a contractual duty to compensate for those injuries. In allowing the tort action against the insane defendant, Justice Qua's discursive opinion starts with an extended discussion of mental states of the insane, but it is clear that a prima facie case exists in a strict liability system. It is equally clear in this case that the claimant had taken the risk of harm by walking into the room when she was knew the likelihood that the defendant would cause her damage.

In the end Justice Qua held that the jury verdict in favour of the claimant should be sustained under the rule that provides 'where an insane person by his act does intentional damage to the person or property of another he is liable for that damage in the same circumstances in which a normal person would be liable'.[57] The rule is all too favourable for the defendant because it excuses liability in those cases where the madness is so strong that the defendant is not aware that he or she is hitting another person. But for these purposes, the difficulties in Justice Qua's opinion lie in his forced reading of the assumption of the risk defence, on the contrived ground that the risk became 'plain and obvious'[58] only after she entered the room, moments before the assault, such that a sudden emergency undercuts the claim that the risk had been voluntarily assumed. At this point, Qua J refers to the unexamined employment relationship: 'The plaintiff had assumed the duty of caring for the defendant. We think that a reasonable attempt on her part to perform that duty under the peculiar circumstances brought about by the defendant's own act did not necessarily indicate a voluntary consent to be injured'.[59] The employment relationship clearly colours the tort action, and again points to a possible solution akin to workers' compensation. The claimant was entering the room not for her own benefit, but for that of the defendant and her employer. It is not too difficult to imagine an implied term of an employment contract, a workers' compensation type solution to cover this instance, at which point some recovery, perhaps only for lost income and medical expenses, is appropriate.

[54] See, on this point, *Rogers v Elliott* 146 Mass 349; 15 NE 768 (1888) (denying recovery to a claimant recovering from serious sunstroke for the standard ringing of a nearby church bell).
[55] 297 Mass 323; 8 NE 2d 760 (1937).
[56] ibid Mass 324; NE 2d 761.
[57] ibid Mass 328; NE 2d 763.
[58] ibid.
[59] ibid.

4.2 Asymmetrical Positions

The arguments for assumption of risk are always more difficult to resolve, other things being equal, in those cases where the parties are not in reciprocal positions to each other. To be sure, the same pattern of argument applies: start with the strict liability case, and then introduce assumption of risk as a defence, subject to defeasance. The hard question is what situation is needed to overcome that defence in a wide set of circumstances. It is useful to set out briefly some of the common circumstances in which this issue arises.

First on the list are actions for medical malpractice. Within a strict liability universe the invariant prima facie case is that the defendant hurts the claimant, say by creating a surgical wound. Yet it takes little reflection to realise that medicine and surgery are bygone professions if surgical wounds are made actionable by a strict liability rule. No physician could afford to practice unless he set a fee that exceeds the cost of the expected tort liability that would inevitably follow, which is why the standard rule has even viewed with suspicion those supposed contracts whereby the physician guarantees an outcome in particular cases.[60] At this point, the question of liability shifts to the issue of whether ordinary negligence should be sufficient to overcome the initial assumption of risk defence, to which the standard answer is in principle yes, given that the case thus far has only raised a strict liability prima facie case.[61] It is of course possible that the claimant could assume the risk of the negligent infliction of harm as well, at which point the ante has to be raised so that the claimant is required to prove either gross negligence or recklessness to recover for poor treatment. Yet it is at just this point that tort law loses all its power. The assumption of risk defence is a crude yes/no filter that seeks to control the question of liability by manipulating the standard of liability without making any adjustments to the level of damages that should be awarded in the particular case. At this point, the market will implode unless and until it can be shown that the fees generated for the services are sufficient to cover the liability for future harms along with all the other necessary expenses of undertaking the surgery in question. As damages awards are allowed to increase, the likelihood of the system working is reduced, which in turn leads to efforts that I have long endorsed, to introduce an explicit contractual scheme that defines both the standard of care and the remedy for breach.[62] The standard response to this position is that the inequality of bargaining power is such that the various disclaimers imposed should be invalidated on grounds of public policy,[63] which in turn is met by the objection that competitive markets are able to handle that position.[64] The situation, at least in the United States, remains guarded because of the difficulties of finding a no-fault solution for

[60] See, eg, *Hawkins v McGee* 84 NH 114; 146 A 641 (1929) (where the powerful basic norm was only overcome because the defendant wished to engage in an experimental treatment that flopped); *Sullivan v O'Connor* 363 Mass 579; 296 NE 2d 183 (1973).

[61] RA Epstein, *Torts* (New York, Aspen Law & Business, 1999).

[62] RA Epstein, 'Medical Malpractice: The Case for Contract' (1976) 1 *American Bar Foundation Research Journal* 87, 108–13.

[63] *Tunkl v Regents of University of California* 60 Cal 2d 92; 383 P 2d 441 (1963).

[64] See G Robinson, 'Rethinking the Allocation of Medical Malpractice Risks Between Patients and Provider' (1986) 49 *Law and Contemporary Problems* 173.

medical injuries,[65] and the unwillingness of courts to allow parties to contract out of an (inefficient) tort rule.

The same dynamic, with a somewhat different end has been applied to industrial accidents, which cut a far deeper path in English and American law during the late nineteenth and early twentieth century.[66] The initial determination in this area was that the common employment doctrine categorically barred actions by one employee against the employer for the wrongful act of another employee. The two earliest statements of the rule were the 1837 English decision in *Priestly v Fowler*[67] and *Farwell v Boston & Worcester RR Corp*[68] both of which provoked massive protests and eventually resulted in the overturning of common employment by statute in both England[69] and the United States.[70] The passage of that statute then brought to the fore the question of how assumption of risk, as opposed to knowledge of the risk, should be made out in common law cases. The basic solution was that the claimant did assume the risk of a known peril if he continued to work in that setting, subject to an exception whereby the worker did not assume the risk during the short period needed to lodge a complaint with the employer.[71] Under that rule the employer remained liable for latent hazards. But again, the crude tools of the common law cannot generate a sensible allocation of risk if they are unable to control both damages and coverage. That point became clear to all concerned, so that even before 1880, many businesses had elaborate contractual arrangements that adopted the key features of the workmen's compensation statutes of the late nineteenth and early twentieth statutes. These featured broad coverage for injuries caused during the course of employment (as with *Stanley v Powell* and *McGuire v Almy),* included explicit compensation schedules, and made liability subject to an exception for wilful injuries that resulted either from the reckless disregard of the employer of safety issues, or the reckless disregard of employees for their own welfare.[72] These contracts then formed the prototypes of the workers compensation statutes that followed. Once again, the institutionalised arrangement pushed the pleading issues to the back, and the economic and structural ones to the fore.

The third area that has undergone this type of transformation is products liability law. In its earliest stages, there was a categorical ban on these actions in the absence of privity between the parties.[73] Thereafter a number of inspections developed such that the manufacturer, even in the absence of privity, was responsible for those latent

[65] For discussion, see, eg, P Danzon, *Medical Malpractice: Theory Evidence and Public Policy* (Cambridge MA, Harvard University Press, 1985) 214–20; R Keeton, 'Compensation for Medical Accidents' (1973) 121 *University of Pennsylvania Law Review* 590.

[66] For a longer account of these developments, see RA Epstein, 'The Historical Origins and Economic Structure of Workers' Compensation' (1982) 16 *Georgia Law Review* 775.

[67] (1837) 3 M & W 1; 150 ER 1030.

[68] 45 Mass 49 (1842).

[69] Employers' Liability Act 1880 (43 & 44 Vict c 23).

[70] Federal Employer's Liability Act, 45 USC § 51 et seq (1908).

[71] *Lamson v American Axe & Tool Co* 177 Mass 144; 58 NE 585 (1900). In England the *Lamson* rule was rejected in *Smith v Baker & Sons* [1891] AC 325 (HL), over the dissent of Baron Bramwell: 'It is a rule of good sense that if a man voluntarily undertakes a risk for a reward which is adequate to induce him, he shall not, if he suffers from the risk, have a compensation for which he did not stipulate' (at 344).

[72] For accounts of these statutes, see *Ives v South Buffalo Ry* 201 NY 271; 94 NE 431 (1911); *New York Central Railway v White* 243 US 188 (1917), for descriptions.

[73] *Winterbottom v Wright* (1842) 10 M & W 109; 152 ER 402.

defects in products that could not be detected by ordinary inspection, so long as the claimant had engaged in normal and proper use[74]. So formulated, the difference between the negligence and strict liability standards were very small, in part because *res ipsa loquitur* could be used to help the claimant and in part because the tight restrictions on downstream use cut out virtually all cases of systematic risk. As the system evolved over time, the courts began to expand liability for product sellers and manufacturers, so that, as with medical malpractice, manufactures introduced limited warranties (usually for repair or replacement only and excluding personal injuries). In both product liability and medical malpractice cases, suppliers of goods and services began to insert clauses limiting their tort liability, and in the early 1960s, the oft-indignant judicial response was to render these contractual limitations inoperative.[75] Now that tort law governed the full range of issues, contractual correction of judicial error was no longer possible. Over time, the normal and proper limitation found in *Escola* was rejected, in consequence of which too little weight was placed on downstream misconduct. That error in turn created serious distortions that hearken back to some of the disputes over industrial accidents in the late nineteenth century. Once assumption of risk was off the table as an effective defence, the rejection of the open and obvious defence created vast scope for liability even when the claimant had knowingly encountered a risk, especially in machine tool cases.[76] Indeed, since the parties are interacting at a distance, the cases of deliberate concealment of known risks should be relatively infrequent. The consequence was, at least in the United States, a vast expansion of tort liability on the American side that has resulted in serious market dislocations. This has extended beyond machine tools to pharmaceutical products where, under the current law, it is hard to imagine any warning that would be adequate, no matter how detailed and specific.[77] In these cases, the conceptual confusion found in the classical debates over negligence and strict liability have little or no relevance. The question is here is the extent to which the tort rules that are imposed, when contractual solutions are blocked, deviate from the set of efficient contracts that would emerge in a voluntary market. On this score American adventurism again has proved much more dangerous than English prudence.

[74] *Escola v Coca-Cola Bottling Co* 24 Cal 2d 453, 468; 150 P2d 436, 444 (1944): 'The manufacturer's liability should, of course, be defined in terms of the safety of the product in normal and proper use, and should not extend to injuries that cannot be traced to the product as it reached the market'. The key earlier precedents, both carefully guarded were *MacPherson v Buick* 217 NY 382; 111 NE 1050 (1916); *Donoghue v Stevenson* [1932] AC 562 (HL). For an earlier discussion, see RA Epstein, *Modern Products Liability Law* (Westport, Greenwood Press, 1980) ch 2.

[75] *Greenman v Yuba Power Products* 59 Cal 2d 57; 377 P 2d 897 (1963) (rejecting contractual limitations in product liability cases); *Tunkl v Regents of University of California* 6 (n 63). The two cases were decided six months apart, but *Tunkl* did not cite *Greenman*, let alone discuss any product liability case.

[76] Contrast two cases. *Campo v Scofield* 301 NY 468, 473–4; 95 NE 2d 802, 804 (1950): 'in cases dealing with a manufacturer's liability for injuries to remote users, the stress has always been upon the duty of guarding against *hidden* defects and of giving notice of *concealed* dangers' (italics used in New York, but not Northeast reporter); *Micallef v Miehle Co* 39 NY 2d 376, 379; 348 NE 2d 571, 573 (1976): 'The time has come to depart from the patent danger rule enunciated in *Campo v Scofield*'.

[77] See, eg, *Wyeth v Levine* 555 US 555 (2009), which I condemn in the harshest terms in RA Epstein, 'What Tort Theory Tells Us About Federal Preemption: The Tragic Saga of *Wyeth v. Levine*' (2010) 65 *New York University Annual Survey of American Law* 485, addressing both the tort issues and the federal preemption questions.

5. CONCLUSION

It should be very clear in this chapter that the role of defences takes on different colouration depending on the context. In the early history of tort law, the key battles were over the choice between negligence and strict liability in a wide range of random interactions.[78] In these cases, the correct approach in my view is the method of presumptions that relies on the minimally sufficient, that is, strict, prima facie case. In dealing with these issues if is often said that a theory of corrective justice cannot accommodate a regime of strict liability because that theory offers no definitional account of what conduct is 'wrongful'.[79] But that is in fact one of the strengths of the theory because it explains why that term cannot be reduced to the semantic equivalent of the defendant's negligence or intention. Instead this incremental pleading method invites a systematic expansion of legal discourse through an orderly method of acquisition by staged pleadings that have none of the conceptual tangles found in many of the leading common law decisions, a small fraction of which have been examined here.

The very fact that that these ambiguities survive in the law is, ironically, testimony to the proposition that small errors in system design do not generate major social dislocations, which is one reason why the legislature tends to stay its hand on these matters. But the modern application of assumption of risk notions in the asymmetrical cases of medical malpractice, workers' compensation and product liability really do matter in terms of the size and the frequency of various legal actions. In these areas, legislative intervention becomes the norm and not the exception, resulting in strong squabbles between those who want to curtail the scope of the law and those want to expand. These issues loom far larger in the American system than in the English system, from which I draw this sober lesson. Judicial innovation is a dangerous activity unless it is tethered to the correct common law theories. The rejection of assumption of risk in the modern legal construct is a rejection of the fundamental precepts of a market economy, with large resource implications that reverberate through the legal and social system every day.

[78] For a longer discussion, see David Ibbetson, ch 2 in this volume.

[79] For just this point, see G Williams 'The Aims of the Law of Tort' (1951) 4 *Current Legal Problems* 137, 151.

15

Privacy Claims: Transformation, Fault, and the Public Interest Defence

BARBARA MCDONALD

1. INTRODUCTION

GIVEN THE JURIDICAL basis of the key protections of privacy that have been forged in the United Kingdom—that is, rights in equity and rights under the Human Rights Act 1998 (UK)—and the longstanding absence of a freestanding tort of invasion of privacy in the United Kingdom and the author's own jurisdiction,[1] it may seem a little precocious at this stage in the development of the law to discuss actions of invasion of privacy in a book entitled *Defences in Tort*. But it is clear that, despite legal history, privacy claims sit slightly uncertainly on the traditional boundaries of tort, equity, and even, sometimes, contract law, so that the discussion is not totally out of place.

Although defences become relevant only once a wrong has been made out, defences are of course an intrinsic and critical part of any cause of action, in a broad sense.[2] It is, in fact, difficult to think of a legal obligation or wrong to which there are no defences whatsoever. This suggests that it is only by acknowledging the existence of defences that the cause of action becomes settled. Absolute liability is usually unacceptable—simply because it is too absolute a consequence for the vagaries of human conduct.

Some foundational issues have turned out to be the major focus of this chapter. It begins with a discussion of why, despite history, modern privacy law arguably fits best in the province of tort law. Then, because the availability of defences in tort law tends to depend on whether the facts give rise to an intentional tort, a tort of negligence, or a tort of strict liability, further foundational analysis and classification is required.[3] The chapter therefore analyses the fault element in claims for breach of

[1] *Wainwright v Home Office* [2003] UKHL 53; [2004] 2 AC 406. The High Court of Australia in *Australian Broadcasting Corp v Lenah Game Meats Pty Ltd* [2001] HCA 63; (2001) 208 CLR 199 held that a previous High Court decision *Victorian Park Racing and Recreation Grounds Co Ltd v Taylor* (1937) 58 CLR 479 (HCA), in which it was said, for example, at 517, that English law does not recognise any general right to privacy, did not stand in the way of the development of such a cause of action. Despite the High Court's encouragement, there is as yet no appellate authority in Australia recognising such a tort. See further the Australian Law Reform Commission, *Serious Invasions of Privacy in the Digital Era* (Law Com Rep No 123, 2014).

[2] See J Goudkamp, *Tort Law Defences* (Oxford, Hart Publishing, 2013) 5.

[3] This is not of course the only way to classify defences as Goudkamp discusses; see ibid 1–5.

privacy, deriving as they do in the United Kingdom from the action for breach of confidence.[4] In particular, is liability in that latter action strict or is it fault based? If it is fault based, what type of fault is required for liability? The answer to this fundamental question will often determine the appropriateness of some of the defences that may be raised as possible defences to a breach of privacy action. The chapter concludes with a discussion of a common but contentious defence in an action for the misuse or disclosure of private information, that of public interest, and finds that even such a seemingly objective concept does not ignore the defendant's state of mind or motives. It concludes that the issue of classification of privacy claims is one issue that needs to be settled, so that other issues, such as the range of defences, can in turn be settled more easily.

2. ARE INVASIONS OF PRIVACY BEST TREATED AS TORTS?

There is a growing body of judicial and scholarly commentary classifying a privacy action as an action in tort.[5] This classification is contentious; legal purists may rightly object, and it is certainly difficult to pinpoint precisely when the legal transformation from equitable action for breach of confidence to tort of invasion of privacy occurred.[6] However, there are a number of reasons why the time may have come to accept that actions for invasions of privacy should be classified as actions in tort, regardless of the fact that only 10 years ago the House of Lords confirmed that no general tort action for invasion or breach of privacy was recognised in the English common law.[7]

First, in the absence of human rights legislation or a bill of rights or similar legislative or constitutional protection, it is generally to tort law that a person will turn for protection against the activities of other members of the community which arise not out of a pre-existing consensual obligation but out of an obligation imposed by law.[8] The torts of trespass to the person, comprising assault, battery and false imprisonment, malicious prosecution, defamation and injurious falsehood, and the tort of trespass to land all protect fundamental rights by civil redress. If privacy is such a right, and that right is at least partly located in the private or civil sphere (in addition to the criminal and public spheres), then tort law is the logical home for an action for invasion of privacy. This is not merely a matter of educational or scholarly convenience, of deciding where we as academics should situate actions for

[4] *Campbell v MGN Ltd* [2004] UKHL 22; [2004] 2 AC 457.

[5] See below (n 45).

[6] In *Vidal-Hall v Google Inc* [2014] EWHC 13 (QB) [54], [57] before determining that a claim for misuse of private information was to be considered a tort claim for the purpose of a practice direction, even though a claim for breach of confidence is not, Tugendhat J said: 'Judges commonly adopt one or both of two approaches to resolving issues as to the meaning of a legal term, in this case the word "tort". One approach is to look back to the history or evolution of the disputed term. The other is to look forward to the legislative purpose of the rule in which the disputed word appears. … [H]istory does not determine identity. The fact that dogs evolved from wolves does not mean that dogs are wolves'. This begs the question of when the evolution occurred. It is understood that an appeal from that decision will be heard by the Court of Appeal: *Weller v Associated Newspapers Ltd* [2014] EWHC 1163 (QB) [24] (Dingemans J).

[7] *Wainwright v Home Office* (n 1).

[8] C Sappideen and P Vines (eds), *Fleming's The Law of Torts*, 10th edn (Sydney, Lawbook Co, 2011) 4.

invasion of privacy when teaching the law or writing about it. It is also a matter of logical classification of laws within a legal system, relevant to the application of ancillary rules and helpful to those who have to navigate their way through the complex web of judge-made and statute law that is found in a common law jurisdiction.

Defining what is a tort precisely, exhaustively, and exclusively is a surprisingly difficult task.[9] Leading texts tend to answer the question in relatively general terms. *Fleming's The Law of Torts*, for example, defines a tort as 'an injury other than a breach of contract, which the law will redress with damages', but then goes on that 'this definition is far from informative'.[10] Whether created by common law or statute,[11] 'torts' tend to be defined by reference to two key elements. First, a tort is defined as a civil (as opposed to a criminal) wrong, which the law redresses by an award of damages. Secondly, the wrong consists of a breach of an obligation, often in negative terms such as not to harm or interfere with the claimant, imposed by law (rather than by agreement).[12]

Liability for conduct invading the privacy of another is analogous to, and will often co-exist with, other torts protecting people from interferences with fundamental rights. Situating the cause of action within tort law would allow the application of common law principles settled in analogous tort claims, particularly in relation to fault, defences, vicarious liability, the award of damages, other remedies, and choice of relevant law.[13] It may also clarify the applicability of statutory provisions on both substantive and procedural matters. Distinguishing *Douglas v Hello! Ltd (No 3)*,[14] in which the Court of Appeal held that the Douglases' action for breach of confidence 'does not fall to be treated as a tort under English law', Tugendhat J recently classified the action for misuse of private information as a tort for the purposes of the applicable Civil Procedure Rules and Practice Direction about service of a claim outside the jurisdiction.[15]

Secondly, while the legal protection of private information properly reflects equity's objective to protect confidences as much as it reflects tort law's objective to redress wrongs, it is clear that invasions of privacy comprise more than just the misuse and dissemination of private information. They are often constituted by invasions into or interferences with someone's personal space or personal affairs. While

[9] And one that among scholars at least is contentious: J Gardner, 'Torts and Other Wrongs' (2011) 39 *Florida State University Law Review* 43 reviews recent scholarly and judicial analysis of how torts can be distinguished from other private wrongs, particularly equitable wrongs. Cf J Edelman, 'Equitable Torts' (2002) 10 *Torts Law Journal* 64, arguing for a broader concept of civil wrong.

[10] Sappideen and Vines (n 8) 3.

[11] KM Stanton et al, *Statutory Torts* (London, Sweet and Maxwell, 2003) 6: 'Indeed, the only answer [to the question "What is a Tort?"] may be to say that a compensation right is of a tortious character if it is generally regarded as tortious … the phrasing of the statute is likely to play a large part in the classification of rights'.

[12] Neither of those elements is exclusive to tort law and neither is always borne out, as most texts go on to discuss.

[13] Claims for violations of privacy, like defamation claims, are expressly excluded from the Rome II Regulation, Regulation (EC) no 864/2007 OJ L 199/40. Gardner (n 9): 'Legally, designating some wrong as a tort is a way of taking quite a significant body of doctrine off the shelf and applying it to that wrong. Not only do we import the right to reparative damages, with all of its implications, we also import … various standard common law doctrines about causation, remoteness, quantification, mitigation of damage, exclusion and limitation of liability, and so on'.

[14] [2005] EWCA Civ 595; [2006] QB 125 [96].

[15] *Vidal-Hall v Google Inc* (n 6). See also the text at n 6.

the majority of 'privacy' cases in the United Kingdom have been concerned with disclosure of private information, recent case law has also now dealt with intrusions or invasions of personal space.[16] This latter focus—on 'invasion' or 'interference' or 'intrusion'—is much more clearly associated with tort law than with equity.

Thirdly, the nature of the remedy which courts of the United Kingdom have often granted in cases involving disclosure of private information since the Human Rights Act 1998 (UK)—damages for emotional distress—indicates that tort law is a more logical home for action for invasions of privacy in the broad field of obligations law than is equity.[17] Toulson and Phipps comment: 'it is more realistic to regard such damages as based in tort than on a strained concept of an equitable obligation.'[18] The concern of equity has primarily been with the protection of property in all its forms. We can only say 'primarily' because clearly notions of confidence, conscience, good faith, and loyalty are at the heart of equity's intervention generally,[19] especially in the law relating to fiduciary relationships and confidential information. This law owes more to notions deriving from human expectation than to the inanimate qualities of property in all of its forms.[20] Nevertheless, the awarding of damages for emotional distress was a sudden and significant development in equity jurisprudence. Searches have not turned up one example of compensation for emotional distress or the like in any case based on the equitable action for breach of confidence prior to *Campbell v MGN Ltd*.[21] It is true that equity had intervened to protect personal information and secrets through the breach of confidence action as much as it had protected trade secrets or commercial information. *Prince Albert v Strange*,[22] in which Prince Albert was granted an injunction to restrain the publication of a catalogue describing the Queen's etchings, was really a privacy case in today's terms as much as one of information protected by a pre-existing duty of confidence. Many other prominent cases involving personal confidences, including *Argyll v Argyll*[23] and *Lennon v News Group Newspapers Ltd*[24] followed. However, all of the reported cases dealing with personal confidences, and relying on the equitable principles alone, were cases where the remedy obtained or refused was an

[16] *Tsinguiz v Imerman* [2010] EWCA Civ 908; [2011] Fam 116 [66]; *Goodwin v News Group Newspapers Ltd* [2011] EWHC 1437 (QB), [2011] NLJR 850; see further NA Moreham, 'Beyond Information: The Protection of Physical Privacy in English Law' (2014) 73 *CLJ* 350.

[17] *Campbell v MGN Ltd* (n 4); *Mosley v News Group Newspapers Ltd* [2008] EWHC 1777 (QB); *Spelman v Express Newspapers* [2012] EWHC 355 (QB) [109]–[114].

[18] RG Toulson and CM Phipps, *Confidentiality*, 3rd edn (London, Sweet & Maxwell, 2012) 40. The argument would be even stronger if exemplary damages were to be given: See *Mosley v New Group Newspapers Ltd* [2008] EWHC 1777 (QB); [2008] NLJR 1112 [181]–[184] (Eady J).

[19] Gardner (n 9) 51: 'So the emphasis in equity is on the diversion of advantage—in the form of assets or profits—as opposed to the causation of loss, which is tort law's first concern'.

[20] It is well settled that confidential information is not to be characterised as property: *Douglas v Hello! Ltd (No 3)* (n 14) [119], [126]–[127]; see also *Moorgate Tobacco Co Ltd v Phillip Morris Ltd (No 2)* [1984] HCA 73; (1984) 156 CLR 414, 437.

[21] Above n 4.

[22] (1849) 2 De G & Sm 652; 64 ER 293. The same point was made by SD Warren and LD Brandeis in their influential article 'The Right to Privacy' (1890) 4 *Harvard Law Review* 193.

[23] [1967] Ch 302 (Ch D).

[24] [1978] FSR 573 (CA). This case and *Cornelius v de Taranto* [2001] EWCA Civ 1511; [2002] EMLR 112 were both claims based on a breach not of a mere equitable duty but of contract.

injunction.[25] It was in commercial cases that the claimant would seek an account of profits or compensation for losses,[26] and these were assessed purely in financial terms.

There *were* cases where the remedy of compensation or damages for disclosure of *private* information was either sought or discussed but a closer examination of those cases reveals that none was authority for the award of compensation for mere emotional distress in a claim in equity. Cases such as *Cornelius v de Taranto*,[27] *Archer v Williams*,[28] *Stephens v Avery*,[29] and *Woodward v Hutchins*[30] are all sometimes cited as authority for an award of damages for emotional distress resulting from a breach of confidence. However, the first two cases were based in contract, where damages for emotional distress may be awarded in limited circumstances,[31] while an analysis of the last two cases shows that they provide no or scant authority for an award of compensation for emotional distress in equity.

In *Woodward v Hutchins*, singer Tom Jones and others sought an injunction to restrain publication of what their former agent had told the Daily Mirror, on the basis of defamation, breach of contract and breach of confidence. The Court of Appeal discharged the injunction obtained in the court below, as the paper said it could justify the story. The only statements by the court, which would support the notion that there might be damages payable if the breach of confidence were made out, were, first, a statement by (an unsympathetic) Master of the Rolls (Lord Denning MR):[32]

> Suppose that this case were tried out and the plaintiffs failed in their claim for libel on the ground that all that was said was true. It would seem *unlikely that there would be much damages awarded for breach of confidentiality*, I cannot help feeling that the plaintiffs' real complaint here is that the words are defamatory …

And another by an equally unsympathetic Bridge LJ:[33]

> If the defendants cannot in due course make good that claim, it is quite clear that the plaintiffs will recover very considerable damages for libel, to say nothing of any damages they may recover for breach of confidentiality. But, if the defendants substantiate the claim, it

[25] Lord Cairns' Act (21 & 22 Vict c 27) passed in 1858 allowed a court of equity to grant damages in addition to or in lieu of an injunction. However, this Act was concerned with equity's auxiliary jurisdiction in respect of common law claims rather than equitable claims such as breach of confidence. See further RP Meagher, JD Heydon and M Leeming, *Meagher, Gummow and Lehane's Equity: Doctrines and Remedies*, 4th edn (London, Butterworths LexisNexis, 2002) ch 23.

[26] After *Seager v Copydex Ltd (No 2)* [1969] 2 All ER 718 (CA); *Douglas v Hello! Ltd (No 3)* [2007] UKHL 21; [2008] 1 AC 1.

[27] Above n 24.

[28] [2003] EWHC 1670 (QB); [2003] EMLR 869.

[29] [1988] Ch 449 (Ch D).

[30] [1977] 2 All ER 751 (CA).

[31] In *Cornelius v de Taranto* (n 24) [69] Morland J talks of the novelty of his award for injury to feelings caused by breach of confidence but it is clear that the claim is one based in contract: 'The duty of confidence was an essential indeed fundamental ingredient of contractual relationship … which [the defendant] breached'. Although Morland J does note that equity is yet to award damages for injury to feelings, the novelty he was referring to about his own judgment was in adding this type of claim to the categories of where *contract law* would support damages for mental distress, not in opening up a new remedy for an equitable wrong.

[32] Above n 30, 755 (emphasis added).

[33] ibid 756 (emphasis added).

is clear that the plaintiffs will recover no damages in libel; and I think that *they could only recover nominal damages for the breach of confidentiality,* if there was one.

Stephens v Avery[34] is another case often cited as an example of a claim for protection of *private* information. There the claimant sought damages for the breach by her former lover of an obligation of confidence in relation to information about the claimant's sexual conduct, which the first defendant had told to The Mail on Sunday, the second defendant newspaper. The defendants sought to have the claim struck out on the basis either that the type of information would not attract a duty of confidence or that the particular information was not imparted under an obligation of confidence. Both arguments were rejected and the application refused. This then was a case where an injunction was too late and the only remedy sought was damages. But damages for what? The report states that the 'statement of claim sought, inter alia, damages for *personal injury*, loss and damage suffered by the plaintiff as a result of the disclosure'.[35] It looks therefore as if the claimant was at least alleging some form of psychiatric or physical injury, and not mere emotional distress.[36]

Thus, until the impact of the Human Rights Act 1998 (UK), the equitable action had not resulted in an award of compensation for emotional distress. In 2002, Morland J decided the case of *Campbell v MGN Ltd*,[37] awarding Naomi Campbell a small sum, damages of £2,500 plus £1,000 as aggravated damages for injured feelings. When a majority of the House of Lords restored his judgment in Campbell's favour, holding that an extended or transformed equitable action for breach of confidence protected the claimant's Article 8 rights of privacy, the emphasis was on the liability rather than the remedy.[38]

The novelty of a claimant being awarded compensation for emotional distress in a claim derived from equity in *Campbell v MGN Ltd* has barely been remarked upon. This is perhaps explained by the ready acceptance of the Human Rights Act 1998 (UK) as the underlying basis of the court's jurisdiction to intervene in such cases, [39] or alternatively, by a lack of concern with rigid historical legal classifications. There is much to be said for the view that the change in the underlying values that the action protects must bring with it a change in the injury which the claimant

[34] Above n 29.

[35] ibid 450 (emphasis added).

[36] The judge also offered a caution that the case raised some fundamental questions such as where the line between aggressive intrusion of sectors of the press into the private lives of individual and public interest ('as opposed to general public titillation') should be drawn. His question at [1988] Ch 449 (Ch D) 457: 'Moreover, is the press to be liable in damages for printing what is true?' shows that the question of liability for publications tended still to be approached with a mindset informed by defamation law.

[37] [2002] EWHC 499 (QB); [2002] IP & T 612.

[38] Above n 4. The following year in *Archer v Williams* [2003] EWHC 1670 (QB); [2003] EMLR 869 a case concerning the *contractual* obligation of a former employee to keep her former employer's confidences, Jackson J referred to Morland J's decisions in *Cornelius v de Taranto* (n 24) and *Campbell v MGN Ltd* (n 4), and held at [76]: 'On the basis of these two authorities I accept that where a breach of confidence causes injury to feelings, this court has power to award general damages. General damages for injury to feelings should be kept to a modest level and should be proportionate to the injury suffered. Such awards should be well below the level of general damages for serious physical or psychiatric injury'.

[39] As explained in *Campbell v MGN Ltd* (n 4) [51]: 'As Sedley LJ observed in a perceptive passage in his judgment in *Douglas v Hello! Ltd* [2001] QB 967 (CA) 1001, the new approach takes a different view of the underlying value which the law protects. Instead of the cause of action being based upon the duty of good faith applicable to confidential personal information and trade secrets alike, it focuses upon the protection of human autonomy and dignity'.

will be assumed to suffer from the wrong: if the action of breach of confidence has morphed into an action for breach of privacy, and privacy is a matter of human dignity, then it is to be expected that injury to dignity, to feelings, with emotional consequences, will follow.[40] To then limit compensation to financial losses would be to deny the very protection which the law is seeking to provide.

A fourth and by no means subsidiary reason for situating the action for invasions of privacy within tort law is that this classification supports the coherence of legal obligations and remedies. It allows meaningful and logical comparisons to be drawn between the law's redress for breaches of some fundamental rights with redress for breaches of others, and between restrictions on recovery in various circumstances. Why, for example, should intentional invasions of privacy be actionable for mere emotional distress when malicious practical jokes or harassment or bullying are not?[41] If the breach of privacy was negligently caused, as may be the case in many unintended disclosures, should actionability be subject to the same restrictions as negligence actions generally, particularly that of requiring actual damage in the form of a recognised psychiatric illness?[42] These are questions that will inevitably arise as the case law develops.

There is a growing body of judicial and scholarly classification of a privacy action as a tort. The classification of the action as a 'tort of misuse of private information' was first suggested by Lord Nicholls in *Campbell*:[43]

> The common law or, more precisely, courts of equity have long afforded protection to the wrongful use of private information by means of the cause of action which became known as breach of confidence. A breach of confidence was restrained as a form of unconscionable conduct, akin to a breach of trust. Today this nomenclature is misleading. The breach of confidence label harks back to the time when the cause of action was based on improper use of information disclosed by one person to another in confidence.
>
> ...
>
> This cause of action has now firmly shaken off the limiting constraint of the need for an initial confidential relationship. In doing so it has changed its nature. ... The continuing use of the phrase 'duty of confidence' and the description of the information as 'confidential' is not altogether comfortable. Information about an individual's private life would not, in ordinary usage, be called 'confidential'. The more natural description today is that such information is private. *The essence of the tort* is better encapsulated now as misuse of private information.

[40] Professor Cornish, as quoted by Toulson and Phipps (n 18) 126, quoted in turn by Morland J in *Cornelius v de Taranto* (n 24) [73].

[41] *Wilkinson v Downton* [1897] 2 QB 57 (QBD); *Wainwright v Home Office* (n 1); *Nationwide News Pty Ltd v Naidu* [2007] NSWCA 337; [2007] 71 NSWLR 471. The Anglo-Australian approach, in contrast to the position in the United States is to deny liability for mere emotional distress, even intentionally caused. In *Wilkinson v Downton*, the plaintiff claimed for her psychiatric illness, not mere emotional distress. Wright J at 58: 'the effect ... on the plaintiff was a violent shock to her nervous system, producing vomiting and other more serious and permanent physical consequences at one time threatening her reason, and entailing weeks of suffering and incapacity to her as well as expense to her husband for medical attendance'.

[42] S Deakin, A Johnson and B Markesinis, *Markesinis and Deakin's Tort Law*, 7th edn (Oxford, Oxford University Press, 2012) 124. In Australia, this common law requirement has generally been entrenched in tort reform statutes such as the Civil Liability Act 2002 (NSW), pt 3. For the common law, see *Mt Isa Mines v Pusey* [1970] 125 CLR 383 (HCA) 394 (Windeyer J).

[43] Above n 4, [13]–[14] (emphasis added). See also Lord Nicholls in *Douglas v Hello! Ltd* (n 26) [255]: 'As the law has developed breach of confidence, or misuse of confidential information, now covers two distinct causes of action, protecting different interests: privacy, and secret ("confidential") information'.

Lord Nicholls' classification does not appear to have been shared by the other members of the House of Lords at the time,[44] and has not been widely accepted, yet it is gaining increasing, possibly indirect, acceptance.[45] Eady J has commented about Lord Nicholls' description: 'It is reasonable to suppose that he used the word ['tort'] advisedly and that he *may* have intended to convey that infringements of privacy should now be regarded as an independent tort uncluttered by any limitations deriving from its equitable origins'.[46]

Leading texts on tort law, even those without a North American connection,[47] now include 'Privacy' as a separate chapter, although some, such as *Clerk & Lindsell on Torts*,[48] take an expansive approach, referring to 'Breach of Confidence' too. Texts on breach of confidence draw a very clear line between the traditional action for breach of confidence and the 'post-*Human Rights Act*' action. Toulson and Phipps argue that the latter should be regarded as a separate cause of action in tort for infringement of privacy, even though it may sometimes overlap with the causes of action in contract or equity for breach of confidentiality.[49] The authors of *Gurry on Breach of Confidence* refer to post-Human Rights Act 1998 (UK) developments as the '"extended" breach of confidence' and restrict its reach to misuse or unauthorised disclosure of private information. They add:[50]

> [I]f English courts seek to protect against 'intrusions' into private life as well as disclosure of private information then the connection to breach of confidence will become increasingly tenuous and the case for recognizing a separate tort of privacy much stronger.

However recognition of the tortious character of the action does not necessarily entail recognition of a *general* tort of 'invasion of privacy', with both 'invasion' and 'privacy' undefined. For a start, that would be contrary to the explicit holding in *Wainwright v Home Office*,[51] and would seem a giant leap. Secondly, there

[44] Eg, Baroness Hale noted in *Campbell v MGN Ltd* (n 4) [132] that 'The 1998 Act does not create any new cause of action'.

[45] Many commentators now use this nomenclature: eg, R Clayton and H Tomlinson, 'The Human Rights Act and its Impact on the Law of Tort' in TT Arvind and J Steele (eds), *Tort Law and the Legislature: Common Law, Statute, and the Dynamics of Change* (Oxford, Hart Publishing, 2012) 466–67. Lord Neuberger MR in *Imerman v Tchenguiz (Rev 4)* [2010] EWCA Civ 908, [2011] 1 All ER 555 [65] said, in a passage which does not clarify the issue: '[F]ollowing ... *Campbell* ..., there is now a tort of misuse of private information: as Lord Phillips of Worth Matravers MR put it in *Douglas v Hello! Ltd (No 3)* ... a claim based on misuse of private information has been "shoehorned" into the law of confidence'. Compare *Coogan v News Group Newspapers Ltd* [2012] EWCA Civ 48; [2012] 2 All ER 74 [48] where Lord Neuberger MR, said: 'it is probably fair to say that the extent to which privacy is to be accommodated within the law of confidence as opposed to the law of tort is still in the process of being worked out'. In Australia, a stricter approach to the classification of legal wrongs is evident: *Farah Constructions Pty Ltd v Say-Dee Pty Ltd* [2007] HCA 22; [2007] 230 CLR 89; *Bofinger v Kingsway Group Ltd* [2009] HCA 44; (2009) 239 CLR 269; *Harris v Digital Pulse Pty Ltd* [2003] NSWCA 10; [2003] 56 NSWLR 298; cf *Giller v Procopets* [2008] VSCA 236; (2008) 24 VR 1.

[46] *Mosley v News Group Newspapers Ltd* (n 17) [182].

[47] Such as Sappideen and Vines (n 8), now in its 10th edition, which long had a separate chapter on privacy.

[48] A Dugdale and M Jones, *Clerk & Lindsell on Torts*, 20th edn (London, Sweet and Maxwell, 2010) with Third Supplement (2013). See also NJ McBride and R Bagshaw, *Tort Law*, 4th edn (Harlow, Pearson Education, 2012) ch 21: 'Invasion of Privacy'. M Lunney and K Oliphant, *Tort Law Text and Materials*, 5th edn (Oxford, Oxford University Press, 2013) ch 14: 'Privacy'.

[49] Toulson and Phipps (n 18) 24.

[50] T Aplin, L Bentley, P Johnson and S Malynicz, *Gurry on Breach of Confidence: The Protection of Confidential Information*, 2nd edn (Oxford, Oxford University Press, 2012) 286 [7.102].

[51] Above n 1.

are justifiable misgivings about converting a value that underlies the law into a cause of action in itself. It is unnecessary to do so: in recent years, tort law has increasingly recognised the value of individual autonomy as underlying many actions in both battery and negligence,[52] yet there is no suggestion of a tort action for 'breach of autonomy'. So with privacy. What Lord Nicholls suggested was a much more specific tort of 'misuse of private information', restricted in similar fashion to the common law action developed by the New Zealand courts. This is the 'tort' to which Tugendhat J recently referred.[53] Whether or not a tort action for intrusion per se should be recognised in English law may depend on whether it is judged that the Protection from Harassment Act 1997 (UK) provides sufficient protection.[54] In New Zealand the absence of a civil right of compensation in its Harassment Act 1997 (NZ) is the background to the courts developing a common law intrusion tort.[55]

There would be many legal ramifications of classifying the action for breach of privacy as a tort action, not least the issue of whether compensation to a successful claimant becomes as of right rather than discretionary, and this chapter will not go into them.[56] It is enough to use this suggestion of classification as a tort merely as a justification for analysing actions of invasion of privacy in this volume. The fact that the law of other jurisdictions, such as that of the United States,[57] New Zealand,[58] and Canada[59] tend to cite civil privacy actions in tort law, whether in common law or under statute, lends further justification.

3. DEFENCES TO WHAT? CLASSIFYING THE FAULT ELEMENT IN PRIVACY CLAIMS

Merely moving privacy actions into tort law does not end all classification problems. Most descriptions[60] of defences in tort law tend to draw a distinction between defences to intentional torts and defences to negligence (and perhaps, rarely,

[52] *Re F (Mental Patient Sterilisation)* [1990] 2 AC 1 (HL); *Rogers v Whitaker* (1992) 175 CLR 479 (HCA).

[53] *Vidal-Hall v Google Inc* [2014] EWHC 13 (QB); [2014] FSR 30.

[54] *Hayes v Willoughby* [2013] UKSC 17; [2013] 1 WLR 935; *Howlett v Holding* [2006] EWHC 41 (QB); *Thomas v News Group Newspapers Ltd* [2001] EWCA Civ 1233. See also Moreham (n 16).

[55] *C v Holland* [2012] NZHC 2155; [2012] 3 NZLR 67.

[56] Eady J was dealing with one issue which would arise more clearly if the action were tortious than if equitable: the availability or appropriateness of exemplary damages. He declined to award them in *Mosley v News Group Newspapers Ltd* (n 17). Note that the New South Wales Law Reform Commission recommended against calling its proposed statutory cause of action a 'tort' action: New South Wales Law Reform Commission, *Report 120: Invasion of Privacy* (2010) [5.54]–[5.57], because it wanted to free the action from the confines of tort remedies.

[57] WL Prosser, 'Privacy' (1960) 48 *California Law Review* 383; *Restatement (Second) of the Law of Torts* § 652A.

[58] *Hosking v Runting* [2004] NZCA 34; [2005] 1 NZLR 1.

[59] British Columbia: Privacy Act RSBC 1996 c 373 s 1(1); Manitoba: Privacy Act RSM 1987 P125 s 2(2); Newfoundland and Labrador: Privacy Act RSN 1990 c P-22 s 3(1); Saskatchewan: Privacy Act RSS 1978 c P-24 s 2; see also *Jones v Tsige* [2012] ONCA 32; [2012] 108 OR (3rd) 241.

[60] Eg, Sappideen and Vines (n 8) chs 5 and 12; Deakin, Johnson and Markesinis (n 42) deals with the defences to intentional torts when discussing each tort and with defences more generally in a separate chapter. Goudkamp (n 2) is a notable and recent exception, arguing, and leaving to one side defences such as limitation bars that arise after the tort, that all tort law defences can be separated into justification defences and public policy defences. He also distinguishes mere denials (at 5).

defences to torts of strict liability), because the defences usually depend on the fault that underlies the tort itself.[61] It may thus be important, in order to determine what defences are relevant or appropriate in privacy cases, to establish what type of fault, if any, underlies a cause of action for invasion of privacy. This section begins with showing how the fault element in the tort can influence the available defences. It then discusses whether fault is an element of the equitable action from which the modern privacy actions springs, in order to identify any fault element in the new 'tort' action.

A defence which clearly shows the relevance of the underlying fault element in the tort is contributory negligence. A claimant's contributory negligence in relation to a risk is a key defence to a negligence action, albeit only partially since the introduction of apportionment legislation.[62] This is because, if negligence is essentially about a defendant's failure to take reasonable precautions against a *foreseeable* risk of injury to the claimant, it is morally justifiable to consider also the claimant's behaviour in relation to that risk. The claimant's voluntary assumption of the actual risk that eventuated may also be relevant.[63] Perhaps it is relevant that conduct involved in negligence cases is not usually prima facie wrongful:[64] it only becomes negligent in law once the circumstances are assessed, and it only becomes actionable where damage is suffered and a pre-existing duty owed. It may not even be very culpable behaviour from a moral standpoint: primary negligence liability, as opposed to apportionment of liability, is not concerned with degrees of conduct.[65] A small degree of negligence will do. In contrast, intentional torts generally involve a prima facie wrong and a more culpable level of fault, and thus will be more difficult to defend, requiring a higher level of culpability or responsibility on the claimant's part to excuse the defendant's conduct. Thus while contributory negligence is powerful in a negligence claim, it is irrelevant to an intentional tort.[66] Mere provocation by the claimant will not excuse the defendant's tort;[67] only conduct that goes beyond provocation and becomes so threatening that self-defence is justified. While assumption of risk may be enough to defend an action in negligence and may be inferred from conduct showing knowledge of and appreciation of a risk,[68] *actual* consent to the particular conduct, either express or implied, is required for defending an intentional tort.

[61] What may be described as procedural defences such as time limitation bars do not vary in nature depending on the fault element.

[62] Law Reform (Contributory Negligence) Act 1945 (UK).

[63] Although this defence is now only rarely successful: Deakin, Johnson and Markesinis (n 42) 762–69.

[64] Cf the concept of 'negligence per se' better known to North American tort lawyers, see, for example, in *Martin v Herzog* 228 NY 164, 168; 126 NE 814, 815 (1920) (Cardozo J).

[65] Sappideen and Vines (n 8) [7.180].

[66] *Co-Operative Group Ltd v Pritchard* [2011] EWCA Civ 329; [2012] QB 320; *Standard Chartered Bank v Pakistan National Shipping* (Nos 2 and 4) [2002] UKHL 43; [2003] 1 AC 959; *Horkin v North Melbourne Football Club Social Club* [1983] 1 VR 153 (SC); *State of New South Wales v Riley* [2003] NSWCA 208; (2003) 57 NSWLR 496 (although in the last case the New South Wales Court of Appeal reduced the claimant's damages for the unintended consequences of the false imprisonment on the grounds of his contributory negligence).

[67] *Lane v Holloway* [1968] 1 QB 379 (CA); it may negate or reduce exemplary damages only: *Fontin v Katapodis* (1962) 108 CLR 177 (HCA).

[68] See Sappideen and Vines (n 8) [12.310]; particularly now under tort reform statutes in Australia, eg, Civil Liability Act 2002 (NSW), pt 1A div 4 'Assumption of Risk'.

What this analysis shows is that, outside the procedural defences such as limitation bars, the range of defences to a claim will be influenced by the fault element of the cause of action. *Deliberate* conduct which invades another's rights will require strong grounds establishing a weightier competing interest or some other high level of justification to excuse it. Careless conduct on the other hand may be more easily tempered by the carelessness of others or by the force of circumstances. Strict liability may be very difficult to avoid by way of defence, although some strict liability, favouring the claimant on a prima facie level, still lends itself to a defence of no-fault, the onus being on the defendant to prove reasonable care or lack of intent, for example, the defence of innocent dissemination in a defamation action.[69] What ramifications do these distinctions have where the cause of action at issue has its origin in the equitable wrong of breach of confidence?

If we contrast the role of fault in tort law with its role in equity, we find that 'fault' is rarely discussed in that express term in equity. Rather, equity is concerned with conscience. While it is of course concerned to prevent and redress dishonesty or fraud in the common law sense of deliberate deceit where that occurs, the concept of equitable fraud is much broader than its common law counterpart,[70] and probably therefore easier to prove. Equitable fraud will cover a wide range of conduct which is against good conscience, or 'unconscionable', but which may fall short of any intent to injure. Fiduciary duties are said to be strict, in the sense that good faith on the part of the defaulting fiduciary is no defence,[71] but, leaving constructive trusts to one side, fiduciary duties generally arise because of a prior *voluntary* undertaking by the fiduciary to prefer the interests of the principal or beneficiary.

Breach of confidence actions might be regarded also as involving strict liability for unauthorised disclosure, much like a breach of fiduciary duty, but in fact we find that there are underlying elements of the action, the fulfilment of which would bind the conscience of the actor. As Lord Neuberger said recently in *Vestergaard Frandsen A/S v Bestnet Europe Ltd*,[72] 'an action in breach of confidence is based ultimately in conscience.'[73]

Traditionally, the element that bound the actor's conscience was the pre-existing obligation arising out of an express agreement, or an implied term of an express agreement,[74] such as between employer and employee or partners in a joint venture

[69] Defamation Act 1996 (UK), s 1. A defendant to a claim based on *Rylands v Fletcher* may deny causation. See Goudkamp (n 2) 58–60.

[70] See generally Meagher, Heydon and Leeming (n 25) [12-040]: 'One must never lose sight of the evolution of all these [equitable] principles and doctrines from a general concept of fraud as abhorrent to good conscience'.

[71] *Boardman v Phipps* [1967] 2 AC 46 (HL). Meagher, Heydon and Leeming (n 25) [5-110] note that while the role of intention may be contentious in respect of conflicts of duty and duty, 'on no view is intention required where the conflict is between duty and interest and a profit is made'.

[72] [2013] UKSC 31; [2013] ICR 981.

[73] ibid [22].

[74] Eg, *Archer v Williams* (n 28) [47] (Jackson J): '[I]t was an express term of the defendant's contract of employment that she would keep confidential all personal or business information which she acquired during the course of her employment relating to the claimant or any member of her family. If I am wrong that this was an express term of the contract, then it must have been implied. Both parties conducted themselves on the basis that the defendant had such an obligation. Such an obligation was necessary to give efficacy to the contract of employment. If there was not such an obligation, it would not have been possible for the defendant to fulfil her role as PA, as that role had evolved over the years'.

or partnership, or a relationship of confidence which gave rise to an implied duty of confidence.[75] Once that obligation was proved, the conscience was bound and any unauthorised disclosure was a breach. (Lord Neuberger noted that the state of mind of the person under the obligation *at the time of breach* is irrelevant.[76] Only to that extent may it be accurate to say the liability for breach of confidence is 'strict' in the sense of not requiring proof of intention or negligence at that time as to the interference or infringement of the claimant's rights.)[77] The cases tended to turn on elements of the action other than the actor's state of mind, such as whether the information (still) had the quality of confidence or whether detriment was required and what was the appropriate remedy.[78]

The absence of a pre-existing obligation means that facts engaging the defendant's conscience must be a key issue in the claim. There has to be some factor that would trigger or alert the conscience of the defendant. In many contexts where liability does not rest on a pre-existing obligation, it is accepted that the actor must have a sufficient level of actual knowledge of the circumstances to bind his or her conscience. Once a person is *told* that information she or she has received is confidential, the conscience becomes bound.[79] Mere negligence, in the form of failing to appreciate a problem or failing to enquire, is not sufficient for liability. However, knowledge is not treated purely as a subjective matter because it would be too easy for a fraudster simply to give a blanket denial. So the equity courts have long been embroiled in a discussion of what amounts to actual knowledge. The discussion has become so bedevilled by fine distinctions that the Privy Council was moved to say in *Royal Brunei* that:[80]

> Framing the question [of liability, in terms of knowledge] all too often leads one into tortuous convolutions about the 'sort' of knowledge required, when the truth is that 'knowingly' is inapt as a criterion when applied to the gradually darkening spectrum where the differences are of degree and not kind.

Nevertheless, knowledge continues to be a key factor for engaging the conscience of the defendant and it is clear from the extensive case law on accessorial liability for breach of fiduciary duties in the United Kingdom, Australia, and elsewhere that in some cases, knowledge of the facts that would tell of a problem to a reasonable person is enough to fix the defendant with knowledge of the problem itself.[81] A defendant cannot hide behind his or her own moral obtuseness.[82] A defendant

[75] *Argyll v Argyll* (n 23).

[76] *Seager v Copydex Ltd* [1967] 2 All ER 415 (CA), cited on this point in *Vestergaard Frandsen A/S v Bestnet Europe Ltd* (n 72) [24] (Lord Neuberger SCJ): 'once it was found that they had received the information in confidence, their state of mind when using the information was irrelevant to the question of whether they had abused the confidence'.

[77] Thus defamation is a tort of strict liability as it does not require proof of intent to defame or negligence as to the defaming of the claimant: *Hulton v Jones* [1910] AC 20 (HL).

[78] *Coco v AN Clark (Engineers) Ltd* [1968] FSR 415 (Ch D).

[79] *Vestergaard Frandsen A/S v Bestnet Europe Ltd* (n 72) [25].

[80] *Royal Brunei Airlines Sdn Bhd v Tan* [1995] 2 AC 378 (PC) 391.

[81] *Consul Developments Pty Ltd v DPC Estates Pty Ltd* (1975) 132 CLR 373 (HCA); *Barlow Clowes International Ltd & Anor v Eurotrust International Ltd* [2005] UKPC 37, [2006] 1 WLR 1476.

[82] *Consul Developments Pty Ltd v DPC Estates Pty Ltd* (ibid) 398 (Gibbs J): 'It would not be just that a person who had full knowledge of all the facts could escape liability because his own moral obtuseness prevented him from recognizing an impropriety that would have been apparent to an ordinary man'.

may be fixed with what might be described as an *objective* knowledge of the problem. His or her conscience will be engaged.

In the context of a breach of confidence action, an unauthorised disclosure of the information becomes actionable only when the discloser is fixed with knowledge that the information is confidential. Thus, in *Vestergaard Frandsen A/S v Bestnet Europe Ltd*,[83] the Supreme Court of the United Kingdom held that a person who was involved in the development of a new product by an associate was not liable for a breach of the contractual duty of confidence owed to her former employers, because she was unaware that the new product had been developed by her associate using the former employer's trade secrets, and she had been unaware of the trade secrets herself. 'The absence of such knowledge would appear to preclude liability, at least without the existence of special facts. After all, an action in breach of confidence is based ultimately on conscience.'[84] Lord Neuberger, with whom the other judges agreed, went on to argue that a person who assists a recipient of confidential information to misuse it may be secondarily liable but she would normally have to know that the recipient was abusing confidential information. However, he recognised that knowledge in equity extends beyond actual subjective knowledge and may include what is sometimes called 'blind-eye knowledge'[85] and, quoting Lord Nicholls from *Royal Brunei Airlines Sdn Bhd v Tan*,[86] that dishonesty can sometimes be indicated where a person has acted in reckless disregard.

A similar analysis has been applied to actions involving the tort of inducing a breach of contract, where it has been recognised that knowledge and *intention* are inextricably linked. Indeed knowledge becomes the basis for inferring an intention on the part of the actor. Lord Hoffmann in *OBG Ltd v Allan*:[87]

> To be liable for inducing breach of contract, you must know that you are inducing a breach of contract. It is not enough that you know that you are procuring an act which, as a matter of law or construction of the contract, is a breach. You must actually realize that it will have this effect. Nor does it matter that you ought reasonably to have done so.

In the *Spycatcher* case,[88] the House of Lords famously extended the action for breach of confidence beyond pre-existing relationships or obligations of confidence (or against recipients to whom the known confidential information had been passed) to situations where the obligation of confidence was found to exist because of the

[83] Above n 72.

[84] ibid [22].

[85] ibid [27]: 'Knowledge in this context would of course not be limited to her actual knowledge, and it would include what is sometimes called "blind-eye knowledge"', citing *Royal Brunei Airlines Sdn Bhd v Tan* (n 80). See also Lord Goff in *A-G v Guardian Newspapers Ltd (No 2)* [1990] 1 AC 109 (HL) 281: 'I of course understand knowledge to include circumstances when the confidant has deliberately closed his eyes to the obvious'.

[86] Above n 80.

[87] [2007] UKHL 21; [2008] 1 AC 1 [39]. See also *Hospitality Group Pty Ltd v Australian Rugby Union Ltd* [2001] FCA 1040; [2001] 110 FCR 157 [127] (Finkelstein and Hill JJ): 'The gravamen of the tort of inducing breach of contract is intention. Although the requirement of knowledge of the contract is sometimes discussed as if it were a separate ingredient of the tort, it is in fact no more than an aspect of intention. The requirement that the alleged tortfeasor have sufficient knowledge of the contract is a requirement that he have sufficient knowledge to ground an intention to interfere with contractual rights. Both the intention to interfere with contractual rights and the necessary supporting knowledge of the contract refer to the state of mind of the alleged tortfeasor'.

[88] *A-G v Guardian Newspapers Ltd (No 2)* (n 85).

very *nature* of the information which had come passively, accidentally or innocently, into the hands of the defendant.[89] Lord Goff referred to hypothetical instances of 'obviously confidential' documents wafting from an office into a crowded street or a private diary dropped in the street. This extension was undoubtedly a key step in the transformation of the breach of confidence action into a breach of privacy action, but we should note that the extension was, so far, confined to '*obviously*' confidential information. The element of obviousness was essential to bind the conscience of the possessor of the information. If and when they disclosed it, they would be acting, in equity's terms, *unconscionably*.

Now openly in the context of 'privacy' rather than 'confidence', the courts have had to grapple with *how* and when certain information or activity is to be recognised as private, where it is not stamped 'private' or 'confidential'. This is critical for the defendant. A person in the position of the defendant needs to be able to recognise that the nature of the information he or she has obtained or received about another is 'private'. It *may* be that it is 'obviously private', like health information. However, the courts have held that even if not obviously private, it may still be information as to which a person of ordinary susceptibilities in the position of the claimant would have a reasonable expectation of privacy. Do they still, with an eye to the origins of the action in equity, require the conscience of the defendant to be bound? Presumably, the defendant is *expected* to recognise this private quality about the information or activity that is the subject of the claim. Presumably, it is again a situation where the defendant will be fixed with knowledge of the circumstances and, therefore, by analogy with the treatment of knowledge in other civil wrongs, the defendant will be taken to have intended the breach.

Does it follow then that we should treat a disclosure in breach of confidence, and now, a disclosure in breach of privacy, as essentially an *intentional* wrong, rather than one of strict liability? There are some grounds for answering 'yes' to this question or 'yes, at least in the vast majority of cases'. If a defendant cannot be liable unless his or her conscience is bound, if his or her conscience is bound by knowledge, and if knowledge is to be equated with intention, there is implicit recognition that in the vast majority of cases the defendant will have acted intentionally.

The consequence of such a conclusion for a discussion of the defences to actions for breach of privacy is important: it *should* mean that we can concentrate on deciding which defences to intentional torts should be applicable in a privacy action and immediately ignore defences to negligence actions. Contributory negligence, for example, should be no more a defence to an invasion of privacy than it is to any other intentional tort. If we are not dealing with strict liability, then innocent disclosure should not be necessary as a defence.

The position on fault in privacy claims may not, however, be so simple. It might be said, for example, that, by basing the actionability of the wrong on whether the claimant had a *reasonable* expectation of privacy, the law has introduced the language of negligence—that is, the defendant will be liable where he or she *ought* to have realised the information was private even if it was not obviously so.[90]

[89] ibid 281 (Lord Goff).

[90] The Protection from Harassment Act 1997 (UK), s 1(2) provides that 'the person whose course of conduct is in question ought to know that it amounts to harassment of another if a reasonable person

The issue of 'whether the matters relied on to show the circumstances giving rise to the reasonable expectation of privacy of the plaintiff need to be "known or ought to be known" by the publishers of the information' was recently considered by Dingemans J in *Weller & Ors v Associated Newspapers Ltd*[91] in a claim for invasion of privacy arising from the publication of photographs of the three claimants, children of a well-known musician, while on a family outing shopping and at a cafe. After considering the origins of the modern action, the requirement in breach of confidence cases that the defendant knew or ought to have known of the confidentiality of the information, and the case law since the action extended into one protecting private information, Dingemans J concluded that the publisher's knowledge or what they ought to have known was relevant to the question of whether the claimant had a reasonable expectation of privacy:[92]

> In my judgment the law as it has now been developed is as stated in the broad objective test for the '*reasonable expectation of privacy*' set out in paras 35 and 36 of *Murray v Express Newspapers*. ... [which] takes account of all the circumstances of the case. However, and relevantly, this specifically includes '*the absence of consent, and whether this was known or could be inferred*' by the publisher, '*and the circumstances in which and the purposes for which the information came into the hands of the publisher*'. This broad test allows the Court to assess what the publishers knew, and what they ought to have known. It also allows publishers to take account of matters which they did not know, and could not have known about, at the time of publication to show that there was no reasonable expectation of privacy. This may be important to ensure proper respect for freedom of speech. The broad nature of the test also allows individuals to be shown the respect that is properly due for their private life.[93]

4. DEFENCES TO PRIVACY ACTION

As recent cases show, many fundamentals of the modern cause of action for 'misuse of private information', whether it is a tort or not, are still being worked out by the courts. More work and thought needs to go into the fault element of the cause of action. Only then can the full range and the elements of appropriate defences be identified. This chapter does not attempt a comprehensive analysis of defences to privacy claims, and it is certainly the case that the boundaries of defences to privacy actions are still being settled.[94] One key matter that was important in breach of confidence cases—public interest—is discussed in some detail below in the context of the new action.

in possession of the same information would think the course of conduct amounted to harassment of the other'.

[91] Above n 6.

[92] ibid [37].

[93] Dingeman J at ibid [36] appeared to accept the defendant's argument that the word '*respect*' [for 'private and family life'] in Art 8(1) was significant in calling attention to the defendant's state of knowledge.

[94] See M Warby, 'Justification and Defences' in M Warby, N Moreham, and I Christie (eds), *The Law of Privacy and the Media* 2nd edn (Oxford, Oxford University Press, 2011).

Most privacy actions appear to proceed on the basis of conduct by the defendant that was intentional, involving a deliberate decision to publish information about the claimant: certainly that has been the case with media defendants, although it is possible to imagine situations of unintended exposure of private information about someone, for example, a family member of the main subject of a story. Defences to intentional torts typically include defences such as self-defence, defence of others, necessity, and consent. All of these, or defences by analogy with these, may have a role in claims for invasion of privacy, depending on the circumstances.

An important defence in privacy claims will be that the claimant consented, expressly or impliedly, to the disclosure.[95] This is a matter of fact. It is also closely related to the question of whether the claimant still has any reasonable expectation of privacy when he or she has already exposed private details to publicity.[96] Solove and others have challenged the notion of meaningful consent in the internet age, where users of online sites and services may have little actual awareness or capacity to comprehend what they have apparently agreed to, and where changes to privacy policies and settings may be made with little warning.[97]

5. PUBLIC INTEREST

Open most books or chapters on breach of confidence and you will find only one 'defence' discussed (and sometimes not so-described):[98] that of public interest.[99] Whether it is a matter of true defence in the sense of a confession and avoidance or justification,[100] or whether it is rather a denial of an element of the cause of action, in particular, that the claimant had a reasonable expectation of privacy in the circumstances,[101] or that the invasion of privacy was unjustified, it is appropriate to note that public interest is a key defence in many privacy claims.

Undoubtedly the use of a defence of public interest assumes that the disclosure or relevant conduct was intentional: the actor is justifying his or her positive conduct by reference to a positive, competing value, and by reference, it can generally be assumed, to a deliberate judgment on the part of the defendant that this competing value trumps the claimant's interests in privacy. There is an interesting question, which parallels the use of public interest in defamation, of whether a defendant who was actually disclosing the information for a different purpose than the public interest should be able to rely on the defence. For example, should the defence be

[95] ibid [12.05]–[12.23].

[96] See *Theakston v MGN Ltd* [2002] EWHC 137 (QB); *A v B* [2005] EWHC 1651 (QB); [2005] EMLR 851; *X v Persons Unknown* [2006] EWHC 2783 (QB); [2007] 3 FCR 223; and *Murray v Express Newspapers plc* [2008] EWCA Civ 446; [2009] Ch 481 [36].

[97] DJ Solove, 'Privacy Self-management and the Consent Dilemma' (2013) 126 *Harvard Law Review* 1880.

[98] Eg, Meagher, Heydon and Leeming (n 25) describe public interest under the heading of 'Justification'.

[99] Eg, Aplin, Bentley, Johnson and Malynicz (n 50); Toulson and Phipps (n 18).

[100] See Goudkamp (n 2) 1–5 on the different usages of the term 'defence'.

[101] It should be noted that a very important issue that arises in privacy claims is whether the claimant still has a reasonable expectation of privacy in view of publicity already given to the relevant facts. A 'defence' that the claimant has no reasonable expectation of privacy at the relevant time is arguably a denial of the element of the cause of action.

defeasible either by motives as serious as 'malice' or merely an improper motive, as is the case with qualified privilege at common law? The High Court of Australia, dealing with qualified privilege in a defamation case, noted:[102]

> Communications made on such occasions are privileged because their making promotes the welfare of society. But the privilege is qualified ... by the condition that the occasion must not be used for some purpose or motive foreign to the duty or interest that protects the making of the statement.

It might be argued that this qualification reflects the narrow context in which qualified privilege operates as a defence, being concerned with limited, personal, reciprocal duties or interests,[103] even though the welfare of society underlies the defence. However, arguably the same qualifying principle should apply to disclosures of private information to which a public interest defence is claimed. An analogous principle can be found in the new public interest defence to defamation, which replaces the '*Reynolds* responsible journalism defence',[104] in section 4 of the Defamation Act 2013 (UK); the defendant must show that he or she 'reasonably believed that publishing the statement complained of was in the public interest'.[105]

Turning to what is encompassed within the public interest defence, we find that 'public interest' is a compendious variable and nebulous term,[106] and it often covers a range of values and interests which compete for legal protection. Referring to public interest as a *defence* to breach of confidence or breach of privacy also tends to hide the public interest value in privacy itself. The courts have long recognised that the equitable principles on breach of confidence are founded not so much on notions of *property* in the confidential information, but more on the *value* of upholding confidences for their own sake. Unless people can feel safe in imparting confidential information, they will not do it. There is a social value in the exchange of confidential information between interested parties, not just for commercial and economic development but also in other important social contexts such as health care or care for the young or the vulnerable, and more generally in the development of worthwhile and strong personal relationships. Just as there is a public interest in protecting confidences, so there is a public interest in protecting privacy.[107] People can develop as individuals and make autonomous decisions if they have the 'space' to do so. Protecting privacy protects freedom of speech, of movement, of association, even perhaps indirectly, of thought.[108]

A distinction can be drawn between the role of public interest in traditional claims for breach of confidence and its role in the new landscape of breach of

[102] *Roberts v Bass* [2002] HCA 57; (2002) 212 CLR 1 [62] (Gaudron, McHugh and Gummow JJ).

[103] *Adam v Ward* [1917] AC 309 (HL) 334.

[104] Developed in *Reynolds v Times Newspapers Ltd* [2001] 2 AC 127 (HL) and *Jameel (Mohammed) v Wall Street Journal Europe Sprl* [2006] UKHL 44; [2007] 1 AC 359.

[105] For discussion of this new defence, see J Price and F McMahon (eds), *Blackstone's Guide to The Defamation Act 2013* (Oxford, Oxford University Press, 2013) ch 5.

[106] French CJ noted in *Hogan v Hinch* [2011] HCA 4; (2011) 243 CLR 506 [31] that when used in statute, the term 'public interest' derives its content from the subject matter and the scope and purpose of the enactment in which it appears.

[107] *Prince of Wales v Associated Newspapers Ltd* [2006] EWHC 11 (Ch); [2006] IP & T 583 [67].

[108] See NM Richards, 'Intellectual Privacy' (2008) 87 *Texas Law Review* 387 and NM Richards, 'The Perils of Social Reading' (2013) 101 *Georgetown Law Journal* 689.

privacy claims in the United Kingdom since the Human Rights Act 1998 (UK). In the cause of action for breach of privacy, public interest is undoubtedly a balancing factor which goes to the very heart of the question of whether there has been an actionable invasion of privacy at all.[109] In the breach of confidence action, there was some judicial disagreement as to whether it was a defence or rather whether it operated to deny the obligation of confidence in the first place. The favoured view seems to be that public interest is a factor that may qualify the content of any obligation. Thus Gummow J said in 1987:[110]

> That principle, in my view, is no wider than one that information will lack the necessary attribute of confidence if the subject-matter is the existence or real likelihood of the existence of an iniquity in the sense of a crime, civil wrong or serious misdeed of public importance, and the confidence is relied upon to prevent disclosure to a third party with a real and direct interest in redressing such crime, wrong or misdeed.

In *A-G v The Observer* (the *Spycatcher* case) in 1990,[111] Lord Goff referred to a 'balancing operation, weighing the public interest in maintaining confidence against a countervailing public interest favouring disclosure.'

Traditionally, because, as we have seen above, the claim for breach of confidence was based on a pre-existing obligation of confidence, often contractual, it would take a very strong public interest to override the explicit conferral and acceptance of the obligation and to justify the breaking of the confidence. Generally, the concept of 'iniquity',[112] derived from the judgment of Sir William Page Wood V-C in *Gartside v Outram,* was a restricted one, but it has been given a wider interpretation by some judges.[113] In Australia it has been taken as extending 'at most ... to disclosure of actual or threatened breaches of security of the law or misdeeds of similar gravity relating to such things as public health'.[114]

In the United Kingdom, a more extensive notion of a public interest defence was briefly propounded by Lord Denning MR in *Woodward v Hutchins*,[115] where it was held that Tom Jones and others could not complain of his manager's breach of the contractual undertaking of confidence because the latter had acted to correct publicly the false image the pop star had promoted about himself: Lord Denning called this maxim 'truth in publicity'. However, other courts rejected this notion.[116]

[109] In New Zealand, the new common law tort of invasion of privacy by wrongful disclosure, there is a defence that the matter was of legitimate public concern: *Hosking v Runting* (n 58) [129] and see *C v Holland* (n 55) [96].

[110] *Corrs Pavey Whiting & Byrne v Collector of Customs (Vic)* [1987] 14 FCR 434, 456. See also *A-G v The Observer* [1990] 1 AC 109 (Ch D) 159–160 (Scott J).

[111] Above n 85, 282.

[112] *Gartside v Outram* (1856) 26 LJ Ch 113; 3 Jur NS 39.

[113] *Belloff v Pressdram Ltd* [1973] 1 All ER 241 (Ch D) 260 (Ungoed-Thomas J); *Lion Laboratories Ltd v Evans* [1985] QB 526 (CA) 550 (Griffiths LJ). See generally, Aplin, Bentley, Johnson and Malynicz (n 50).

[114] Meagher, Heydon and Leeming (n 25) [41]–[115].

[115] Above n 30. (His approach reflected the same lack of sympathy for pop stars that he had shown in *Lennon v News Group Newspapers Ltd* (n 24), where he rejected the claim for an injunction on other grounds, namely that the couple had already been very public about their relationship and could not expect to close the door when things went bad.)

[116] In *Castrol Australia Pty Ltd v Emtech Associates Pty Ltd* (1980) 33 ALR 31 (NSWSC), Rath J held that a just cause for the breaking for confidence must be more weighty and precise that a public interest

Previously, Lord Denning had stated a more acceptable and narrower principle, that the 'just cause' defence—that is, the just cause for breaking a confidence—extended to 'crimes, frauds and misdeeds', whether committed or in contemplation, 'provided always—and this is essential—that the disclosure was justified in the public interest.'[117] It is implicit in this formulation that the mere fact that the confidential information is *about* a crime, fraud, or misdeed is not enough on its own to justify its disclosure in breach of the undertaking or obligation of confidence. The public interest in the *disclosure* has to be sufficiently strong to outweigh the public interest in the protection of confidences. The relevant point in time is the time of the disclosure. A legal 'right to be forgotten' is still inchoate. The need for such a right in the internet era has been keenly debated in Europe, and it was a key component of a proposal for a General Data Protection Regulation for the European Union.[118] However, the recent decision of the European Court of Justice has found in existing directives and Articles 7 and 8 of the Charter of Fundamental Rights of the European Union a qualified right to have data removed from internet search engines if its inclusion in search results is no longer in the public interest.[119] The long-term impact of the decision is hard to predict, given the practical, political and legal difficulties of enforcing any such right internationally. In general terms, disclosures about past misdeeds will only have relevance to the public interest if they bear on a current or future matter of public interest, such as the subject presenting some danger to other relevant persons[120] or such as the suitability of the subject for public office.

Turning from the traditional action for breach of confidence to the action in its new form of one for breach of privacy in the United Kingdom, public interest is usually a prime factor for consideration by the courts. Privacy as a 'human right', protected by Article 8 of the European Convention on Human Rights, is one of many rights, and foremost as a counterweight to privacy is the human right in the freedom of expression, protected by Article 10. Neither has priority over the other. The balancing process was described by Lord Steyn in *Re S* as involving an intense focus on the comparative importance of the rights claimed in the individual case, considering the justifications for interfering with the other rights, and a proportionality test being applied to each.[121]

It is well recognised that within the public interest in freedom of expression lie many ancillary interests. Most importantly, the freedom of the press or the media is seen as a vital component of freedom of expression in a democratic society. There is an interesting issue, in relation to defences, as to whether including freedom of the media under the overall umbrella of the freedom of expression that everyone should

in the truth being told, as cited by Gummow J in *Corrs Pavey Whiting & Byrne v Collector of Customs (Vic)* (n 110) 451 where Gummow J reviews the authorities.

[117] *Initial Services Ltd v Putterill* [1968] 1 QB 396 (CA).

[118] J Rosen, 'The Right to be Forgotten' 64 *Stanford Law Review Online* 88; D Lindsay, 'The "Right to be Forgotten' in European Data Protection Law' in N Witzleb, D Lindsay, M Paterson, S Rodrick (eds) *Emerging Challenges in Privacy Law: Comparative Perspectives,* (Cambridge, Cambridge University Press, 2014).

[119] C-131/12 *Google Spain SL and Google Inc v Agencia Espanola de Proteccion de Datos and Mario Costja Gonzales*, European Court of Justice (Grand Chamber), 14 May 2014.

[120] *W v Edgell* [1990] Ch 359 (CA); *R v Chief Constable for the North Wales Police, ex p AB* [1999] QB 396 (CA); *Woolgar v Chief Constable of Sussex Police* [1999] 3 All ER 604 (CA).

[121] [2004] UKHL 47; [2005] 1 AC 593 [17].

have has the effect of hiding the *special* value of a free media and of undermining the justification for special privileges for the media. Section 4 of the Defamation Act 2013 (UK) which replaces the *Reynolds* responsible journalism defence,[122] now directs the court to make allowance for editorial judgment as it considers appropriate. The need to give some weight to editorial judgment was emphasised by Lord Hoffmann in *Campbell v MGN Ltd.*[123]

Some people would prefer the expression 'matter of public importance' to the expression 'matter of public interest' as the relevant factor to be balanced against the claimant's privacy interests. This is to emphasise the point that, surprisingly, still needs to be made, that 'public interest' is a legal term rather than a broad description of the seemingly vast range of matters about which the prurient members of the public are interested or curious. Lady Hale in *Campbell v MGN Ltd* usefully set out a hierarchy of matters of public interest that may support the right to freedom of expression:[124]

> What was the nature of the freedom of expression which was being asserted on the other side? There are undoubtedly different types of speech, just as there are different types of private information, some of which are more deserving of protection in a democratic society than others. Top of the list is political speech. The free exchange of information and ideas on matters relevant to the organisation of the economic, social and political life of the country is crucial to any democracy. Without this, it can scarcely be called a democracy at all. This includes revealing information about public figures, especially those in elective office, which would otherwise be private but is relevant to their participation in public life. Intellectual and educational speech and expression are also important in a democracy, not least because they enable the development of individuals' potential to play a full part in society and in our democratic life. Artistic speech and expression is important for similar reasons, in fostering both individual originality and creativity and the free-thinking and dynamic society we so much value. No doubt there are other kinds of speech and expression for which similar claims can be made.

Freedom of expression, important as it is, is not however the only matter of public interest that has to be weighed in the mix. Given the very different contexts in which breach of privacy claims may be made in the digital era—judicial and other governmental investigative proceedings, online media delivery, social media, electronic health records, electronic banking and trade and commerce—there is these days a case for arguing that there are a number of matters of public interest which the law must recognise as *relevant* at least, but not necessarily as weightier than that, to whether an invasion of privacy may be justified:

- the efficient and cost-effective delivery of government services;
- the promotion of open justice;
- the enhancement of national security and civilian safety;
- the prevention and detection of fraudulent activity;
- the protection of vulnerable persons; and
- the capacity for individuals to engage in digital commercial and social communications.

[122] See Warby (n 94).
[123] Above n 4, [59], [63], and [77].
[124] ibid [148].

It may be that 'public interest' is much too broad a rubric for these issues and that greater and more appropriate protection for privacy would be achieved if the law framed them in narrower terms and made them the subject of more precise defences. For example, in today's digital era, in which technology allows widespread covert surveillance and interception of communications, many would argue that 'national security' as a justification for an invasion of privacy should arguably require precise lawful authority rather than be considered merely as a broad balancing factor, leaving it to the judgment of an individual judge as to whether the balance justifies the defendant's behaviour in the particular case. A precise defence may sometimes be to the advantage of defendants who can clearly bring themselves within it, in that no 'balancing' need be argued. A disclosure of the private information of a vulnerable person by emergency services in the course of a rescue, for example, may be better seen as falling within the doctrine or defence of necessity, which justifies intentional torts to prevent a greater evil but only in emergency situations rather than as a solution to long-term problems.

6. CONCLUSION

The legal protection of privacy has developed extraordinarily quickly over the last 10 years. There can be few areas of law where the changes of the law have been made so rapidly by case law alone and where a cause of action has become so well-established and so well-used in such a short space of time. It is as though there has been a bursting of a dam of stored-up complaints, grievances, and issues waiting for a chance to be aired and determined by the courts. Some key legal issues related to the protection of privacy are still being resolved, as the most recent cases show. Tugendhat J has noted that judges, in our adversarial systems, cannot develop the law unless the parties, or others who may be affected, present the court with claims, defences, arguments and evidence to give them the opportunity to do so:[125]

> English law develops in two ways. First, it is made by Parliament. The Prevention from Harassment Act 1998 and the Human Rights Act 1997 are two privacy statutes referred to in this judgment. Second it is developed by case law, as judges apply the statute to particular cases. At the second stage it is essential that the parties to litigation put their evidence and submissions before the court. It is by weighing up arguments and counter arguments that judges are best able to interpret the law. The circumstances of injunctions applied for out of hours on the telephone are not favourable to a considered development of the law. That is one reason why judges order cases to come back before the court for full consideration on the evidence. That happened on 4 March. But there was no argument then because NGN chose not to argue its case. And other media organisation notified of the injunction chose not to argue the case in court. To the extent that media defendants choose not to submit evidence and argument to the courts, judges will find it difficult to develop the law of privacy to meet the needs of society.

In a law that is just over 10 years old, there are many arguments still to come. Much attention has been paid to the interests underlying the protection of privacy and

[125] *Goodwin v News Group Newspapers Ltd* (n 16) [145].

those that compete with it. More attention is needed on the appropriate place of the cause of action in the classification of obligations, on the essential ingredients of the action and on the defences that may legitimately be raised. Commentators must to a certain extent rely on the energy, resources, and will of interested parties to submit these issues to the attention of the courts, unless legislators step into the field as they have done with defamation law in the United Kingdom. Privacy protection does not have the long history that defamation law has had, and may not have as chilling an effect on freedom of speech as defamation has had (without the benefits of the broad public interest defence only recently legislated), but already privacy protection has raised a difficult issue of classification that needs to be settled so that other issues may more easily be settled in their turn.

16

Some Recurring Issues in Relation to Limitation of Actions

ANDREW BURROWS*

THE LAW OF limitation of actions is neglected in law schools at least in this jurisdiction. It is seen as too practical and technical, and possibly even too dull, for consideration on law degree courses by academics and students. Matters are not helped by the fact that most of limitation law rests on statute, rather than on the common law, and, as we all know, students do not like statutes. Yet the truth is that the law of limitation raises many fascinating questions, involving a mix of case law and statutory interpretation, which often require a wide-ranging knowledge and understanding of the civil law. Indeed, much like the conflict of laws, one's understanding of causes of action and remedies is often put most sharply to the test when it comes to applying the law on limitation. Such is their practical complexity and importance, that it is common for cases on the law of limitation to reach the appellate courts.[1] Their number far exceeds those on, for example, the law of unjust enrichment.

In focusing on the defence of limitation in the English law of tort, this chapter considers a number of recurring problematic questions.

1. WHY DO WE NEED, AND DO WE NEED, A DEFENCE OF LIMITATION?

Before we move to more practical questions, we should first step back from the details of any particular system and think about the basic rationale of the defence. Why do we have a defence of limitation at all?[2]

The most obvious answer is that the limitation defence is there to protect defendants in two main senses. First, fairness to defendants indicates that, after a certain period of time, defendants should be free from the worry and uncertainty of having

* I would like to thank Andrew Dyson, James Goudkamp and Fred Wilmot-Smith for organising the excellent workshop at which a draft of this chapter was presented. I am also grateful to Fred and the participants for their helpful comments.

[1] This chapter was written prior to the decision of the Supreme Court in *Williams v Central Bank of Nigeria* [2014] UKSC 10; [2014] 2 WLR 355 which held that, applying s 21 of the Limitation Act 1980 (UK) (a notoriously difficult provision), there is a six-year limitation period for, eg, the equitable wrong of dishonest assistance.

[2] See Law Commission, *Limitation of Actions* (Law Com No 151, 1998) paras 1.22–1.38.

a legal action hanging over them. In Lady Hale's words, defendants should 'not be harassed with stale claims'.[3] To respect their autonomy to lead their lives as they would wish, defendants should be secure in the knowledge that they are free from litigation relating to particular conduct and are not going to have to find the assets (or maintain liability insurance) to satisfy claims against them dating back many years. Secondly, the deterioration in evidence over time—especially oral evidence—may mean that there is a difficulty in the defendant denying the claim. It may be that the defendant had a perfectly good riposte or defence but that there is now no good evidence that it can rely on to make out its case. In other words, part of the reason for the law of limitation is to ensure that the defendant has a fair civil trial.

Aside from the principal concern with protecting defendants, the law of limitation also has benefits for claimants and for the State. As regards the former, the law of limitations provides an incentive for claimants to act relatively quickly once they realise that they may have a claim and that, in turn, may mean that good evidence for the claimant is preserved and not lost. Moving swiftly may also keep down costs. And for the State, the more reliable the evidence, the more likely it is that its dispute resolution process will be non-arbitrary and fair thereby complying with the rule of law.

However, at least some of these 'policies' could be dealt with by considering the fairness of the trial (taking into account the quality of the evidence) on a case-by-case basis. Indeed, irrespective of the limitation defence, the courts have the power to strike out a claim for abuse of process under rule 3(4)(2)(b) of the Civil Procedure Rules.[4] It is clear, therefore, that the law of limitations acts as a somewhat blunt instrument (albeit that it has the merit of certainty) to achieve the goal of a fair trial. Moreover, one may question just how strong the policies are for protecting defendants against claims many years after particular conduct. If we know that the defendant had no possible defence, and the claimant can prove its case, why should the defendant escape liability simply because of the effluxion of time?

Imagine a world where there were no limitation periods for torts. Would that be so bad? After all, in English criminal law,[5] at least as regards more serious (that is, indictable) offences (for example, theft, burglary, assault occasioning actual bodily harm, rape, manslaughter, murder), there is no law of limitation as such albeit that a case may be thrown out as an abuse of process. This essentially depends, case by case, on the fairness of the trial and on whether under Article 6 of the European Convention on Human Rights (ECHR) it is being held 'within a reasonable time'. This in turn will depend, in particular, on the quality of the evidence.

[3] *AB v Ministry of Defence* [2012] UKSC 9; [2013] 1 AC 78 [164].

[4] By this rule, 'The Court may strike out a statement of case if it appears to the court - ... (b) that the statement of case is an abuse of the court's process or is otherwise likely to obstruct the just disposal of the proceedings'.

[5] Contrast the criminal law in many other jurisdictions where there are limitation periods. Eg, under the German Criminal Code, s 78 the limitation periods are tied to the seriousness of the offence as determined by the maximum prison sentence. So limitation periods are 30 years for life-sentence offences (certain murders are excluded); 20 years for offences with a maximum of 10 years+; 10 years for offences with a maximum of five to 10 years; five years for offences with a maximum of one to five years; three years in all other cases. There are some exceptions, dealing with people who have been residing abroad and cases where the victim is under 18.

However, Lord Sumption, dissenting in the recent equal pay case of *Abdulla v Birmingham City Council*,[6] put the case for there being limitation periods very strongly. The question in that case was whether the six-month limitation period for equal pay claims before an employment tribunal could be outflanked by bringing the claim in the ordinary courts within six years. The majority held that it could. Lord Sumption (with whom Lord Carnwath agreed) dissented. By way of introduction, he said the following on limitation periods:[7]

> [I]ssues of limitation are bedevilled by an unarticulated tendency to treat it as an unmeritorious procedural technicality. This is, I think, unjustified. Limitation in English law is generally procedural. But it is not a technicality, nor is it necessarily unmeritorious. It has been part of English statute law for nearly four centuries. It has generated analogous non-statutory principles in equity. Some form of limitation is a feature of almost all other systems of law. And it has been accepted in principle in the jurisprudence of both the Court of Justice of the European Union and the European Court of Human Rights. Limitation reflects a fundamental and all but universal legal policy that the litigation of stale claims is potentially a significant injustice. Delay impoverishes the evidence available to determine the claim, prolongs uncertainty, impedes the definitive settlement of the parties' mutual affairs and consumes scarce judicial resources in dealing with claims that should have been brought long ago or not at all.

Certainly, when working on the reform of the English law of limitations at the Law Commission in the 1990s, I do not recall anyone seriously suggesting that we do not need a law of limitations at all. I am certainly not suggesting that now. Nevertheless, standing back and considering the underlying reasons for the defence does indicate that the defence operates in a somewhat blunt manner; and this suggests to me, although Lord Sumption would no doubt disagree, that where, for example, the rules of limitation do allow discretion to the courts in deciding whether to allow a claim to proceed or not,[8] the courts ought to err on the side of allowing the claim to proceed provided time has not so diminished the quality of the evidence as to render the trial unfair.

It is a separate point that, *if* there is to be a limitation defence, it should be one that seeks to recognise the interests of claimants as well those of defendants and the State. In particular, in relation to latent injury and damage it has been perceived as unfair that a claimant may be out of time before it could reasonably have known that it had a claim. As the Law Commission expressed it, in seeking to articulate the policy interests that should underpin any proposals for reform of the limitation regime:[9]

> [A]ny limitation system must balance the interests of the defendant, the state and the plaintiff. ... [A]ny limitation system will involve some injustice either to the plaintiff who does not have sufficient time to bring a claim, or to the defendant, who is asked to defend a claim after several years of the plaintiff's inaction. Any limitation system must attempt to minimise this injustice, and reconcile, as far as possible, the conflicting interests involved.

[6] [2012] UKSC 47; [2012] ICR 1419.
[7] ibid [41].
[8] See the discussion of s 33 of the Limitation Act 1980 (UK) below at pp 323–24.
[9] Law Commission (n 2) para 1.38.

2. WHO HAS THE BURDEN OF PROVING LIMITATION?

Lord Sumption in the *Abdulla* case baldly said, 'Limitation is a defence'.[10] Similarly, James Goudkamp is clear that, in drawing his helpful distinction between denials and defences, limitation is a defence: 'It scarcely needs to be said that limitation bars are defences. It is axiomatic that the absence of a limitation bar is not part of any action in tort'.[11] This reflects the fact that, as far as I am aware, no one has ever suggested that limitation should instead be viewed as specifying an element of the cause of action.[12] Yet the English law is equally clear that the legal burden of proving limitation is on the claimant.[13] That is, it is for the claimant to prove that its claim falls within the limitation period not for the defendant to prove that the claim falls outside the limitation period. Admittedly it is for the defendant to plead limitation. So, as laid down in the relevant Practice Direction in the Civil Procedure Rules, 'The defendant must give details of the expiry of any relevant limitation period relied on'.[14] But once it has done so, the legal burden is on the claimant. What should one make of this?

One approach is to conclude that the burden of proof is not a conclusive indicator of whether the law in question is a defence or not. Rather the only practical consequence of the division between liability and defences is that it shows who has the burden of pleading the matter. Although unusual, one can sensibly divide up who has to plead limitation from who has the burden of proving limitation. Certainly it can be argued that the present approach has the merit of appearing to put the burden of proof on the party who is most able to discharge that burden although, if that is one's concern, one might be able to deal with it by merely shifting the evidential, and not the legal, burden of proof.

The alternative, and it is submitted preferable, approach is to say that the law has here taken a wrong turn. The very notion of a defence, and the drawing of a distinction between liability and defences, carries with it the practical consequence

[10] Above n 6 [42].

[11] J Goudkamp, *Tort Law Defences* (Oxford, Hart Publishing, 2013) 131.

[12] Some textbooks on tort (eg, WVH Rogers, *Winfield and Jolowicz on Tort*, 18th edn (London, Sweet and Maxwell, 2010)) chs 25 and 26 divide between defences and the discharge or extinction of liability and include limitation within the latter. But with rare exceptions (see s 3(2) of the Limitation Act 1980 (UK) dealing with extinction of title and the tort of conversion), limitation does not extinguish liability. If one thinks across to contracts, limitation belongs alongside factors rendering a contract unenforceable which plainly do not deny that there is a cause of action (so, eg, money paid under a time-barred debt cannot be recovered back in unjust enrichment because the money is owed) but instead stop the claimant enforcing the claim in the courts. Those factors are therefore defences. Contrast factors which make a contract void (and therefore deny the cause of action) rather than unenforceable.

[13] *Cartledge v E Jopling & Sons Ltd* [1963] AC 758 (HL) 784; *London Congregational Union Inc v Harriss and Harriss* [1988] 1 All ER 15 (CA); *Crocker v British Coal Corp* (1995) 29 BMLR 159 (QBD); *Arab Monetary Fund v Hashim* [1996] 1 Lloyd's Rep 589 (CA); *Lloyds Bank plc v Crosse & Crosse* [2001] EWCA Civ 366; [2001] PNLR 34 [41]; *Fiona Trust & Holding Corp v Privalov* [2010] EWHC 3199 (Comm) [135]. It has sometimes been suggested that the burden of proving constructive knowledge under s 14(3) of the Limitation Act 1980 (UK) is on the defendant (see *Driscoll-Varley v Parkside HA* [1991] 2 Med LR 346 (QBD); *Parry v Clwyd HA* [1997] PIQR P1 (QBD) P14 but even this limited reversal of the standard burden is contradicted by the third and fourth of the cases referred to in the first sentence of this footnote.

[14] Civil Procedure Rules 16 PD 13.1.

that the legal burden of proving a defence is on the defendant.[15] Certainly I am not aware of any other defence in civil law where the legal burden of proof is on the claimant.[16] Support for this may be derived from the closely linked equitable doctrine of laches where the burden of proof falls on the defendant.[17] There have also been cases in other jurisdictions which have challenged the orthodox position.[18] Moreover, it seems very odd to require the defendant to plead limitation without having any onus of proof.

3. IS THE PROLIFERATION OF DIFFERENT TORT LIMITATION REGIMES JUSTIFIED?

In English law, there are no less than six different regimes applicable to central tort claims even leaving to one side: first, special provisions for successive conversions (section 3 of the Limitation Act 1980 (UK)); secondly, particular statutory causes of action, for example, under the Merchant Shipping Act 1995 (UK) or the Human Rights Act 1998 (UK); and thirdly, complications if the remedy sought is not compensatory damages but an injunction or a restitutionary remedy.[19] The six regimes, all contained in the Limitation Act 1980 (UK), are as follows:

(i) By the most general provision, the limitation period is six years from when the cause of action in tort accrued (ie the date of the tort).[20]

(ii) For torts causing personal injury or death, the period is three years from the accrual of the cause of action or discoverability (ie date of knowledge), whichever is the later,[21] but with a discretion under section 33 of the Limitation Act 1980 (UK) to disapply the limitation period.

(iii) For other damage or loss (ie property damage or pure economic loss) in the tort of negligence, the period is six years from the accrual of the cause of action or three years from discoverability, whichever is the later, subject to a long-stop limitation period of 15 years running from the date of the breach of duty.[22]

(iv) For defamation and malicious falsehood, the period is one year from the accrual of the cause of action[23] but with a discretion under section 32A of the Limitation Act 1980 (UK) to disapply the limitation period.

[15] Goudkamp (n 11) takes this view at 138–39 without mentioning that the defence of limitation is inconsistent with it: cf at 4, where he rejects defining a defence by reference to the burden of proof precisely because the limitation defence does not fit that definition.

[16] It is clear, eg, that in contrast to criminal law where the legal burden of disproving self-defence is on the prosecution, the burden of proving self-defence in civil law is on the defendant: see *Ashley v Chief Constable of Sussex Police* [2008] UKHL 25; [2008] 1 AC 962.

[17] For the doctrine of laches, see below at pp 325–29. That the burden of proof in relation to laches is on the defendant is indicated by *Lindsay Petroleum Co v Hurd* (1874) LR 5 PC 221, 241.

[18] Eg, *Pullen v Gutteridge, Haskins & Davey Pty Ltd* [1993] 1 VR 27 (SC); noted and supported by N Mullany, 'Australian Limitation Law—Relieving the Burden' (1993) 109 *LQR* 215.

[19] For discussion of those complications, see below at pp 324–29.

[20] Limitation Act 1980 (UK) s 2.

[21] ibid s 11.

[22] ibid ss 14A and 14B.

[23] ibid s 4A.

(v) For actions under the Consumer Protection Act 1987 (UK), the period is three years from the accrual of the cause of action or discoverability, whichever is the later, subject to a long-stop limitation period of 10 years running from when the defendant supplied the defective product to another.[24]

(vi) For actions founded on fraud (most obviously, the tort of deceit) the period, by reason of section 32(1)(a) of the Limitation Act 1980 (UK), is six years from discoverability.

It is hard to see any good reason for there being so many different regimes. They render the law needlessly complex and lay traps for the unwary. It is a shameful indictment of the operation of statutes within our legal system that Parliament has created such a mess. The Law Commission[25] recently tried to improve the position—not merely for torts but across all the law on limitations—but to no avail. The scheme devised by the Law Commission would have unified the system to some degree around what was labelled a 'core regime'. Under that core regime, applicable to all causes of action, there would have been a limitation period of three years running from the date of discoverability subject to a long-stop of 10 years from the date of the breach of the duty. In the Law Commission's view, exceptions to that core regime had to be carefully justified but included, for example, damages for personal injury and death. A detailed Bill was drafted and was all but agreed within the different ministries. Then at the eleventh hour in September 2007 a point on the Equal Pay Act 1970 (UK) was raised which I and my successor as the Law Commissioner in charge of the project, Professor Hugh Beale, were able to advise on and solve within a few weeks of being asked. Unfortunately by then the momentum for the Bill to be given Parliamentary time in the next session had been lost. Two years later, the Government announced that it would not be taking forward the Limitation Bill for reasons that were not disclosed to Hugh or me or, as far as I am aware, to anyone else in the Law Commission. There appears to be no prospect of it being resurrected. Such are the frustrations of being involved with law reform, at least in this jurisdiction.

4. WHEN DOES THE CAUSE OF ACTION ACCRUE IN THE TORT OF NEGLIGENCE IN RELATION TO PURE ECONOMIC LOSS?

A long-standing difficult issue—which although arising in the context of the statutory provisions on limitation is purely a question of common law—is the date at which a cause of action in the tort of negligence accrues. It is clear law in England that the cause of action accrues at the time when the claimant suffers the injury or damage irrespective of whether the claimant knows or reasonably could know anything about it.[26] Hence the issue is often portrayed as the problem of *latent* injury or damage.

[24] ibid s 11A.

[25] Law Commission, *Limitation of Actions* (Law Com No 270, 2001).

[26] The leading cases are *Cartledge v E Jopling & Sons Ltd* (n 13) (personal injury); and *Pirelli General Cable Works Ltd v Oscar Faber and Partners* [1983] 2 AC 1 (HL) (damage to property).

In the context of personal injury the practical problems consequent on time running before the claimant could reasonably know that he or she had a cause of action have been effectively removed by statutory reform (now contained in section 11 of the Limitation Act 1980 (UK)) which, as an alternative to time running from the date of the accrual of the cause of action, allows the claimant the same limitation period of three years running from discoverability. The courts in any event have a statutory discretion to disapply that limitation period under section 33 of the Limitation Act 1980 (UK). In the context of personal injury, the precise date at which the cause of action accrued is therefore no longer of major importance.

As regards property damage and pure economic loss, the relevant statutory reform of the Limitation Act 1980 (UK) (inserting sections 14A and 14B) by the Latent Damage Act 1986 (UK), has similarly reduced the difficulties caused by latent damage or loss. However, there is no discretion to disapply the limitation period and the relevant statutory provisions retain a six-year period running from accrual of the cause of action—as an alternative to a period of three years from discoverability—and this may mean that the date at which the cause of action accrues is still of practical importance. This will be so where the claimant argues that, although falling outside the three years from discoverability, it has brought the claim within six years from accrual.

So when is it that a cause of action accrues in the tort of negligence for property damage or pure economic loss? The answer for property damage is easy. The cause of action accrues at the date when the property is damaged.[27] For pure economic loss the answer is less clear-cut. To say that the cause of action accrues when the claimant suffers the loss, irrespective of knowledge of the loss, raises the further difficult question as to when precisely that is. A number of cases, dealing with the negligence of professional advisers, such as solicitors and accountants, have explored this. Although some of these cases pre-date the Latent Damage Act 1986 (UK) and might not be decided in the same way if the provisions of the Act were to be applied, they remain valid authorities on accrual.

In *Midland Bank Trust Co Ltd v Hett, Stubbs and Kemp*[28] the defendant solicitor had negligently failed to register in the claimant's favour an option to purchase a farm. That option should have been registered in March 1961. The farm was sold, defeating the option, in August 1967. The claimant brought an action in contract and tort against the defendant in 1972. As regards the tort claim it was held that the cause of action accrued in August 1967 so that the claim fell within the six-year limitation period and was not time-barred. One might strongly argue, however, that the loss occurred in March 1961 when the solicitor first failed to register the option albeit that that was before the claimant knew anything about that loss and even though the loss was at that stage contingent in the sense that, had the owner of the farm decided never to sell it, the claimant would never have been able to exercise that option.

The leading case for many years was *Forster v Outred*[29] which is not easy to reconcile with *Midland Bank*. Here the claimant was a mother who, in February 1973,

[27] *Pirelli General Cable Works Ltd v Oscar Faber and Partners* (ibid).
[28] [1977] Ch 384 (Ch).
[29] [1982] 1 WLR 86 (CA).

had charged her home as security for her son's liabilities. Her solicitor, the defendant, had failed properly to advise her as to the dangers of that transaction. She was called upon to pay off her son's debts so that the charge was enforced against her in January 1975. Her claim in negligence against the defendant solicitor was commenced in March 1980. It was held by the Court of Appeal that that action was time-barred, by the six-year limitation period, because the cause of action accrued in February 1973 and not January 1975. That was so even though at the time the charge was created in February 1973 the claimant's liability was contingent in the sense that the charge might never be enforced against her. There appears to be a clash with the *Midland Bank* case although one can perhaps reconcile the two by saying that in *Forster* the claimant suffered an immediate loss when the charge was created, because the value of the claimant's property was immediately diminished by that charge irrespective of whether it was later enforced, whereas in the *Midland Bank* case the failure to register the option did not diminish the value of the claimant's existing property.

The House of Lords had to grapple with this issue for the first time in *Law Society v Sephton & Co.*[30] A corrupt solicitor misappropriated funds from a client account. As a consequence, the Law Society paid out compensation to the client from the solicitors' compensation fund. The claim by the client against the Law Society for compensation from the fund was made in July 1996. In May 2002, the Law Society brought a claim in the tort of negligence against the auditors of the corrupt solicitor's accounts. It was held by the House of Lords that that claim was within the limitation period of six years because the cause of action accrued when the client made its claim for compensation against the Law Society. Prior to then, there was no cause of action because the liability was merely contingent. In Lord Hoffmann's words: 'A contingent liability is not as such damage until the contingency occurs. The existence of a contingent liability may depress the value of other property, as in *Forster v Outred* ... But standing alone, as in this case, the contingency is not damage'.[31]

So, according to the House of Lords, one has to distinguish between a pure contingency which does not constitute damage/loss and a contingency which devalues the claimant's property which does constitute damage/loss.

What exactly constitutes a pure contingency was further explored in *Axa Insurance Ltd v Akther & Darby.*[32] After-the-event legal insurance was provided by the claimant insurers. That insurance covered failed legal claims provided the defendant panel solicitors had vetted the claims in advance as having a 50 per cent chance of success or had notified the insurers, for the purposes of withdrawing cover, if the chance of the claim succeeding fell below 50 per cent. The claimants had to pay out on a large number of failed claims and they alleged negligence against the panel solicitors both as regards vetting and failing to notify. The negligence proceedings were commenced in June 2008. The insurance policies had been issued in reliance on the vetting prior to June 2002 and the alleged failure to notify, and hence the continuation of the policies, also occurred before June 2002.

[30] [2006] UKHL 22; [2006] 2 AC 543.
[31] ibid [30].
[32] [2009] EWCA Civ 1166; [2010] 1 WLR 1662.

The majority of the Court of Appeal (Arden and Longmore LJ, Lloyd LJ dissenting) decided that, at the point of issuing an insurance policy, or continuing the policy, the insurers had more than a purely contingent liability. There was damage/loss to the insurers at that point because they had issued or continued policies that were disadvantageous. As that issuing or continuation of disadvantageous policies occurred prior to June 2002, the claims were statute-barred.

In contrast, Lloyd LJ considered that the insurer's loss did not occur until the claim being insured against was lost so that there was an actual liability to pay under the after-the-event insurance policy. Prior to then the liability was purely contingent so that the claims in the tort of negligence were within the six-year limitation period and not statute-barred.

It is clear from this disagreement in the Court of Appeal that the concept of a purely contingent liability is open to more than one reasonable interpretation. The judgments in the *Axa* case are long and difficult. While it is easy to say that a diminution of the claimant's property (as in *Forster v Outred*) falls on the other side of the line from a purely contingent liability, the central question is whether one must also include as being on the other side of that line disadvantageous transactions entered into by the claimant as a result of the defendant's negligence even though that disadvantage might never eventuate. There was no such transaction in *Law Society v Sephton & Co* but there was in *Axa Insurance Ltd v Akther & Darby*.

In deciding whether the majority or minority was correct, the earlier House of Lords decision in *Nykredit Mortgage Bank plc v Edward Erdman Group Ltd (No 2)*[33] is helpful, albeit that it concerned the accrual of the cause of action for the purposes of deciding the date from when interest should be awarded rather than the running of a limitation period. This followed the notorious *SAAMCO* case[34] which dealt with the correct measure of damages where, in the context of a fall in property prices, financial institutions had taken inadequate security for loans made as a result of negligently high valuations of properties by the defendant valuers. *Nykredit* followed on *SAAMCO* with the question of when interest on the damages should start to run which depended in turn on the date when the cause of action accrued. Their Lordships decided that the cause of action accrued as soon as the disadvantageous transaction (the loan and security) was entered into. This was so even though there was a cap on the loss that could be recovered and even though one might argue that the loss was contingent in the sense that the lender might never default. Although both the majority and Lloyd LJ in *AXA* drew on the analysis in *Nykredit* to support their different positions, it would appear that the decision supports the majority view that entering into a disadvantageous transaction as a result of the negligence constitutes relevant damage or loss and is not purely contingent.

In this difficult terrain it is also important to step back and to make two general points both of which suggest that the notion of a pure contingency should be narrowly interpreted with the consequence that the cause of action should tend to be viewed as arising earlier rather than later.

[33] [1997] 1 WLR 1627 (HL).

[34] *South Australia Asset Management Corp v York Montague Ltd* [1997] AC 191 (HL).

The first is that the problem of latent damage has been dealt with by statutory reform (the Latent Damages Act 1986 (UK) inserting sections 14A and 14B into the Limitation Act 1980 (UK)) that introduces an alternative discoverability starting point. In deciding when the cause of action accrues, there is therefore no need to take account of when a claimant would realise that it has suffered the particular loss or when the claimant would realise that it has a claim worth pursuing. On the contrary, it would undermine the reform if one elided the question whether the claimant would reasonably think it worthwhile bringing a claim with the question of when the cause of action accrues because the statute assumes that one has an accrued cause of action prior to the point at which it is reasonable to launch proceedings.

The second is that there is a close link between the measure of damages and the accrual of the cause of action. Relevant loss from a single cause of action can mount up over the course of time. Viewing the claim in retrospect allows one to see the point in time at which the loss started in a way that one cannot do if one approaches the question by looking at accrual through the eyes of the claimant in the position it was in at the time of the accrual. Nevertheless, provided one is willing to accept that at least in the context of claims for economic loss one can have damages for loss of a chance,[35] one can say that in most cases[36]—even those involving contingent liability—the claimant would have a valid claim for loss of a chance damages if one were to put oneself into his or her position at the time of accrual. In other words, unless the contingency is too speculative, the claimant would have an action for damages. There must therefore at that point be an accrued cause of action.

It is submitted therefore that the majority in *AXA* was correct; that the purely contingent liability in *Law Society v Sephton* should be viewed as a rarity because in most cases a contingent liability will be linked with other relevant loss which includes that a transaction is disadvantageous; and that *Midland Bank v Hett Stubbs and Kemp* was wrongly decided because from the first moment that the option was not registered the claimant's assets were rendered less valuable than they ought to have been so that one was not dealing with a purely contingent liability.

5. DIFFICULTIES IN APPLYING THE 'DISCOVERABILITY' APPROACH

The last section has shown that, irrespective of the fundamental objection that starting time running from the accrual of a cause of action is unfair to the claimant who does not, and could not reasonably know, of that cause of action, the concept of the accrual of the cause of action can raise very difficult questions. However, it should not be thought that the alternative discoverability (ie, a date of knowledge) starting point has no problems. A general, often overlooked, point is that, applying a discoverability approach, the claimant will still need to have an accrued cause of action so that the issues discussed in the last section cannot be eliminated altogether

[35] This was accepted in, eg, *Spring v Guardian Assurance Co* [1995] 2 AC 296 (HL). For personal injury the position is more complex: see, eg, *Gregg v Scott* [2005] UKHL 2; [2005] 2 AC 176; *Barker v Corus (UK) Plc* [2006] UKHL 20; [2006] 2 AC 572.

[36] Loss of a chance damages will not be awarded if the lost chance is too speculative: see AS Burrows, *Remedies for Torts and Breach of Contract*, 3rd edn (Oxford, Oxford University Press, 2004) 62.

albeit that their importance (and the precise need to fix when the cause of action accrued) will be diminished in importance. More specifically, new difficulties may arise—and certainly have arisen in England—when one tries to define the date of knowledge. Looking at the English position, some of these appear to be difficulties that any discoverability regime must face. Others stem from the particular approach taken in the English statutory provisions. These are contained in sections 14 (for personal injury) and 14A (for latent damage other than personal injury) of the Limitation Act 1980 (UK).[37]

Standing back from the detail, four difficulties can be isolated in the present English approach to discoverability.

First, how objective is the assessment of the claimant's knowledge? Constructive, as well as actual, knowledge (ie, what the claimant ought reasonably to know as well as what he or she does know) is rightly included[38] but, as in other areas of the law where the objective/subjective issue arises,[39] there has been difficulty in pinpointing exactly how objective the test is. The House of Lords in *Adams v Bracknell Forest BC*[40] resolved a conflict in the cases by favouring a highly objective interpretation that takes into account the situation the particular claimant is in but treats as irrelevant the personal characteristics of the claimant, such as intelligence, shyness, embarrassment or a reluctance to make a fuss.

Secondly, how firmly does the claimant need to know? What is the degree of certainty required before the claimant has knowledge? It has been indicated that suspicion is rarely enough but a firm belief may be.[41] The Supreme Court in *AB v Ministry of Defence*[42] has approved the test, first formulated by Lord Donaldson in *Halford v Brookes*,[43] that the belief must be held 'with sufficient confidence to justify embarking on the preliminaries to the issue of a [claim form], such as submitting a claim to the proposed defendant, taking legal and other advice and collecting evidence'.

Thirdly, and closely linked to the second difficulty, what does the claimant need to know? What degree of detail of the facts constituting the cause of action is required for the claimant to have knowledge? Certainly, factual causation which, leaving aside torts actionable per se, is an element of the cause of action is spelt out as one of the facts that must be known in order for there to be knowledge. So section 14(1), as regards personal injury, and section 14A(8)(a), as regards other damage, requires that the claimant has knowledge, actual or constructive, that the injury or damage 'was attributable in whole or in part to the act or omission which is alleged to constitute' the breach of duty. Linked to this is that, by reason of section 14(1) and 14A(9), ignorance of the law as to whether there has been a breach of duty is irrelevant although the House of Lords has recognised that, in the context of omissions,

[37] Section 14A of the Limitation Act 1980 (UK) was inserted by the Latent Damage Act 1986 (UK).

[38] Section 14(3) and 14A(10) of the Limitation Act 1980 (UK).

[39] Eg, the issue of 'enrichment' in the law of unjust enrichment: see, eg, *Benedetti v Sawiris* [2013] UKSC 50; [2013] 3 WLR 351.

[40] [2004] UKHL 29; [2005] 1 AC 76.

[41] See, eg, *Nash v Eli Lilley* [1993] 1 WLR 782 (CA).

[42] Above n 3 [12] (Lord Wilson). See also Lord Nicholls in *Haward v Fawcetts* [2006] UKHL 9; [2006] 1 WLR 682 [9].

[43] [1991] 1 WLR 428 (CA) 443.

it is difficult to approach the question of causation unless one posits that the claimant has knowledge that the defendant owed a duty.[44] In *Haward v Fawcetts*[45] it was held by the House of Lords that a claim against an accountant for negligent advice (or failure to advise) leading to loss-making investments in 1994 and 1995 was statute-barred. Applying section 14A(8)(a), the claimant had the relevant knowledge more than three years before commencing proceedings in December 2001. Their Lordships recognised that knowledge that the defendant had given 'flawed' advice was necessary under section 14A(8)(a) but that the courts could safely look for knowledge that factually 'something had gone wrong' without contravening the provision that ignorance of the law regarding breach of duty is irrelevant. In *AB v Ministry of Defence*[46] the Supreme Court (by a majority of four to three) established that a claimant must be regarded as having the requisite knowledge of attributability once he has issued proceedings. The majority therefore held that claims for injury or death, allegedly caused to ex-servicemen by radiation exposure during nuclear testing in the 1950s, were time-barred. The majority reasoned that it was incorrect to think that the weak case of the claimants was not time-barred because better evidence as to attributability might yet emerge. In the words of Lord Wilson JSC, 'it is a legal impossibility for a claimant to lack knowledge of attributability for the purpose of section 14(1) at a time after the date of the issue of his claim. By that date he must in law have had knowledge of it'.[47]

A fourth difficulty relates to the requirement—beyond knowledge of the cause of action (against an identified defendant)—that the English statute has added, namely that the injury or damage must be 'significant' (or under section 14A(6) that the facts must be 'material'). What does this mean? Section 14(2) (and 14A(7)) go on to define an injury as significant (or the facts as being material) if the claimant would reasonably have considered (or, under section 14A(7) a reasonable person would have considered) the injury or damage 'sufficiently serious to justify his instituting proceedings for damages against a defendant who did not dispute liability and was able to satisfy a judgment'. The idea here is that time should not start to run against a claimant where the cause of action is so trivial that a reasonable person (and their Lordships in *Adams v Bracknell Forest BC*[48] stressed, as we have seen above, that the test is highly objective) would not think it worth commencing proceedings. Plainly, postponing the running of time until the claimant knows or ought to know that there is a cause of action that is more than trivial adds another layer of uncertainty to the law. However, once one has made the policy decision that, to be fair to the claimant, time should run from the date of knowledge and not from the date of accrual of the cause of action, it is entirely appropriate, in line with that policy, that time should run against the claimant only when it is apparent that the claim is more than trivial.

It can be seen from these four central difficulties that there are intriguing questions in applying a discoverability approach. Put another way, there are important

[44] *Haward v Fawcetts* (n 42) [15] (Lord Nicholls), [115] (Lord Mance).

[45] ibid.

[46] Above n 3.

[47] ibid [3].

[48] Above n 40.

choices to be made in how one implements a discoverability regime. It is clear, therefore, that, while moving away from accrual as the starting point solves some fundamental problems, it is far from being problem-free.

6. HOW DO THE COURTS APPLY THE DISCRETION IN SECTION 33 OF THE LIMITATION ACT 1980 (UK) TO DISAPPLY THE LIMITATION PERIOD?

Section 33 of the Limitation Act 1980 (UK) is a classic illustration of a statutory structured discretion. Section 33(1) lays down that if, having regard to the prejudice that the claimant and the defendant would respectively suffer from applying or disapplying the limitation period applicable to an action for personal injury, it appears to the court that it would be 'equitable' to allow the action to proceed, then the court may direct that the limitation period shall not apply. In shorthand, where, having regard to the balance of prejudice, a court considers it fair to do so, it should disapply the limitation period for personal injury. Section 33(3) requires the court in deciding that question to have regard to all the circumstances of the case and in particular to six factors which are listed at (a) to (f). These include, perhaps most importantly:

> (a) the length of, and the reasons for, the delay on the part of the plaintiff; [and]
> (b) the extent to which, having regard to the delay, the evidence adduced or likely to be adduced by the plaintiff or the defendant is or is likely to be less cogent than if the action had been brought within the [limitation period].

Perhaps not surprisingly with such a wide-ranging discretion, different courts have taken markedly different views in applying section 33. So, for example, the predominant view until recently was that the claimant had a heavy burden to discharge for the section 33 discretion to be exercised in her favour. Put another way, the discretion was seen as one that should be exercised only in exceptional circumstances with the prima facie position being that the limitation period applied. However, in an important recent case, *Sayers v Hunters*[49] the Court of Appeal has rejected the view that the burden on the claimant is a heavy one. Again in balancing the prejudice, it used to be assumed that the loss of the protection of the limitation period was included as relevant prejudice to the defendant. However in *Cain v Francis,*[50] the Court of Appeal decided that loss of the limitation defence does not in itself count as a relevant prejudice to the defendant. This was on the reasoning that a limitation defence should be seen as a windfall to a defendant who would otherwise be liable to pay damages. The relevant prejudice to the defendant should therefore be confined to asking whether the delay has disadvantaged the defendant in defending the claim. In the words of Smith LJ:[51]

> [T]he basic question to be asked is whether it is fair and just in all the circumstances to expect the defendant to meet his claim on the merits, notwithstanding the delay in commencement. The length of the delay will be important, not so much for itself as to the

[49] [2012] EWCA Civ 1715; [2013] 1 WLR 1695.
[50] [2008] EWCA Civ 1451; [2009] QB 754.
[51] ibid [73].

effect it has had. To what extent has the defendant been disadvantaged in his investigation of the claim and/or the assembly of evidence, in respect of the issues of both liability and quantum?

It is submitted that these recent moves favouring claimants in the exercise of the discretion under section 33 should be supported. As has been explained earlier,[52] the major underlying policy behind having a limitation defence is to protect a defendant against an unfair civil trial: provided a fair trial is possible, the courts should err on the side of allowing the claim to proceed.[53]

7. COMPLICATIONS WHERE THE REMEDY SOUGHT IS NOT COMPENSATORY DAMAGES

We have seen that, irrationally and confusingly, there are several different limitation regimes for actions in tort.[54] A further complication is that, although the Limitation Act 1980 (UK) essentially focuses on different causes of action, the remedy sought may make a difference. What has been said above has been essentially focusing on a standard claim for compensatory damages. What is the law on limitation if the claimant seeks a different remedy for the tort, for example, an injunction to prevent a tort (or equitable damages in lieu of an injunction) or a restitutionary remedy? Surprisingly, the answer is unclear and, as we shall now see, involves some highly technical analysis.

7.1 What is the Law on Limitation if the Claimant seeks an Injunction to Prevent a Tort (or Equitable Damages in Lieu of an Injunction)?

The prohibitory injunction is the primary remedy where the claimant is seeking to stop the continuation or commission of a tort. Is there a limitation period that applies where one seeks an injunction? One would have thought that, for such an important remedy, the answer would be obvious. Yet that is not so. At the heart of the matter is the interrelationship between the equitable doctrine of laches and one of the oddest provisions on the statute book namely section 36 of the Limitation Act 1980 (UK). If we limit ourselves to the wording relevant to torts, that section reads as follows:

[52] Above, at p 313.

[53] In *AB v Ministry of Defence* (n 3), the majority of the Supreme Court held that the claim was time-barred and went on to decide briefly that the Court of Appeal had been correct to refuse to exercise its s 33 discretion to disapply the limitation period. This was in particular because the claims had no real prospect of success. But this was an exceptional case where the merits of the case on causation had been meticulously examined by the Court of Appeal. Although in other less exceptional cases, the courts have regarded the strength of the claim as relevant under s 33 (see, eg, *Forbes v Wandsworth HA* [1997] QB 402 (CA) 417) the courts should be astute to avoid mini-trials, involving detailed considerations of the evidence. Indeed one might argue that the strength of the claim should not be assessed at all under s 33 because there is a more appropriate procedure for hopeless claims, namely striking out or (reverse) summary judgment.

[54] Above, at pp 315–16.

(1) The following time limits under this Act, that is to say—
  (a) the time limit under section 2 for actions founded on tort;
  (aa) the time limit under section 4A for actions for libel or slander, or for slander of title, slander of goods or other malicious falsehood;

...

shall not apply to any claim for ... for an injunction or for other equitable relief, except in so far as any such time limit may be applied by the court by analogy in like manner as the corresponding time limit under any enactment repealed by the Limitation Act 1939 was applied before 1st July 1940.

(2) Nothing in this Act shall affect any equitable jurisdiction to refuse relief on the ground of acquiescence or otherwise.

What is clear is that, *assuming that there is no statutory limitation period applicable by analogy*, the equitable doctrine of laches applies where an injunction is being sought. Indeed on one interpretation this may be what section 36(2) is declaring. In general terms,[55] the doctrine of laches applies where the delay by the claimant[56] in seeking an equitable remedy is such that it would be unjust to grant that remedy, especially where the delay has prejudiced the defendant or a third party although it would appear that prejudice is not a necessary element of the doctrine. While laches has often not been separated out from acquiescence, the essential difference is that acquiescence, unlike laches, requires a representation by the claimant, usually implied from its conduct, that it is giving up/waiving its rights which the defendant then relies on. Acquiescence is therefore a form of estoppel. In contrast, laches can be established by a delay, without any representation. It is noteworthy that laches (as well as acquiescence) requires the claimant to have sufficient knowledge of the facts relevant to the remedy before the delay deprives the claimant of the remedy.[57] In other words, the equitable doctrine, without any statutory intervention and in contrast to the common law, has long been applying a discoverability approach so that the claimant cannot lose the remedy before reasonably knowing of it.

If all that is relatively clear, there are two difficult questions. First, applying the exception in section 36(1), is there a statutory limitation period of six years that applies by analogy to a (final) injunction for a tort? Secondly, if there is such a statutory limitation period, does that preclude the operation of laches during that period?

One might say that an injunction for a tort is analogous to damages for a tort because both are remedies for torts. This would especially be the case where the injunction is being sought to prevent the continuation of a tort rather than 'quia timet'. However, there appears to be no case in which that analogy has been

[55] A classic formulation of the doctrine was given in *Lindsay Petroleum Co v Hurd* (n 17) 239–40 which was a rescission case.

[56] Inevitably, as regards *interim* injunctions, relatively short periods of delay will bar the remedy by reason of laches because an interim injunction stops the defendant's conduct prior to the claimant establishing at trial that a tort has been, or is about to be, committed.

[57] *Lindsay Petroleum Co v Hurd* (n 17).

drawn.[58] Although not concerning an injunction as such, the most detailed examination of the 'by analogy' argument in relation to a non-monetary remedy was in *P & O Nedlloyd BV v Arab Metals Co*.[59] The Court of Appeal there decided that the six-year limitation period applicable to damages for breach of contract did not apply by analogy to a claim for specific performance of a contract. This was because, first, one was a monetary remedy and the other was not; and, secondly, because, in contrast to common law damages, specific performance does not necessitate that there has been a breach of contract. The first of those reasons (although perhaps not the second) would indicate that the six-year period is most unlikely to be applied by analogy to an injunction for a tort. If that is correct then laches alone—and not a statutory limitation period—applies to a claim for an injunction to prevent a tort.

Even if there were a statutory limitation period of six years, there would still be a question as to whether the courts could apply laches within that period. It might be thought that section 36(2) means that the courts could still apply laches despite the statutory limitation period. However, in so far as the laches is concerned purely with delay, the more persuasive interpretation—which avoids undermining the purpose of a statutory limitation period—is that laches should not operate during that period. As regards the general approach to statutory limitation periods and laches (although no case has dealt with injunctions and torts), this appears to be the favoured view in the authorities;[60] and it was fully and clearly articulated in obiter dicta of the Court of Appeal in *P & O Nedlloyd BV v Arab Metals Co*.[61] Moore-Bick LJ precisely reasoned that, if one is talking about mere delay and not delay plus prejudice, and a statutory limitation period is applicable allowing a claim for the remedy to be brought within six years, it would directly contradict the statute to bar the remedy within those six years. On that interpretation, it is only where laches involves delay plus prejudice that laches could operate to bar the remedy within six years.

Does the position change at all if the claimant is seeking damages (ie equitable damages) for a tort in lieu of an injunction under what used to be Lord Cairns' Act and is now section 50 of the Senior Courts Act 1981 (UK)?[62] There is no authority on this. In this situation, there is a clear analogy with common law damages—both are monetary remedies—so that the case for applying a six-year period by analogy

[58] The 'by analogy' argument has succeeded where a monetary remedy (eg, equitable compensation) has been claimed for an equitable wrong, such as breach of fiduciary duty. See, eg, *Paragon Finance plc v DB Thakerar & Co* [1999] 1 All ER 400 (CA).

[59] [2006] EWCA Civ 1717; [2007] 1 WLR 2288.

[60] Certainly several cases have indicated that one cannot rely on laches within a statutory limitation period: see, eg, *Re Pauling's Settlement Trusts* [1962] 1 WLR 86 (Ch) 115 (Wilberforce J) approved in [1964] Ch 303 (CA) 353; *Cattley v Pollard* [2006] EWHC 3130 (Ch); [2007] Ch 353.

[61] Above n 59.

[62] Such damages may be awarded where a tort is anticipated whereas common law damages can only be awarded where the cause of action has accrued. Conversely it is of course not being suggested that laches ruling out equitable damages leaves the victim of the tort without any claim to common law damages. It is just that the victim cannot claim those damages until the tort has been committed. So, eg, if D trespasses on C's land, C's delay in seeking an injunction or damages lieu of an injunction my bar those remedies but C would still have the normal six-year limitation period, running from the date of the (continuing) trespass, to bring an action for (common law) damages for loss caused by the accrued tort.

under section 36(1) may be stronger than where an injunction is sought.[63] However, probably the more persuasive view is that, as the power to award damages rests on the power to grant an injunction, the same answer must be given where equitable damages are being sought as is given where an injunction is being sought so that the relevant limitation period is that which would apply had an injunction been sought.

7.2 What is the Law on Limitation if the Claimant Seeks Restitution for a Tort?

This is not the appropriate place in which to rehearse the arguments for and against the availability of gain-based remedies for torts. Let it simply be stated that the present English law accepts that, at least for proprietary torts, a claimant can choose a gain-based remedy rather than a compensatory remedy. That gain-based remedy may in some circumstances be common law (for example, an award of money had and received or common law damages calculated to strip some of the tortfeasor's gains) or equitable (for example, an account of profits or equitable damages in lieu of an injunction calculated to strip some of the tortfeasor's gains). What is the law on limitation applicable to such restitutionary remedies?

The answer is unclear. Assuming that the division between restitution for wrongs and restitution for unjust enrichment is accepted, we are here concerned with restitution for a tort. In so far as one is then talking about a common law remedy (whether money had and received or damages), it would appear that section 2 of the Limitation Act 1980 (UK) should normally apply so that there would be a limitation period of six years running from the date of the tort.

Unfortunately, *Chesworth v Farrar*,[64] which is the only case directly in point, is not easy to interpret and was decided before modern developments in, and understanding of, the law of restitution. The claimant brought an action for money had and received to recover the proceeds of sale of converted goods. The question at issue was whether this was 'a cause of action in tort' for the purposes of the old six-month time limit for tort actions against the deceased tortfeasor's estate (the remnant of the common law *actio personalis* rule for tort actions). Edmund Davies J held that it was not and that the action should rather be regarded as equivalent to a contractual action so that a six-year time limit applied. Yet in modern parlance he appeared to view the claim as one for restitution for the wrong—because he thought it essential that the claimant should establish the tort of conversion[65]—and not restitution for unjust enrichment.

Birks argued that, assuming this was restitution for the wrong, the decision must be incorrect because a bar expressed as applying to a tort—and the words of section 2 of the Limitation Act 1980 (UK) clearly refer to the cause of action not the

[63] But equitable damages are most likely to be sought where the tort is anticipated rather than accrued so that, in that respect, the analogy may still be regarded as weak.

[64] [1967] 1 QB 407 (QBD).

[65] The crucial passage from his judgment is ibid 417.

remedy—must bar restitution for a tort.[66] This is clearly correct as a matter of logic albeit that the decision might be defended on wider policy grounds as being concerned to evade the much criticised *actio personalis* rule. Today (after the abolition of any remnant of the *actio personalis* rule) there is no such policy reason for the courts to reject, in respect of restitution for a tort, the modern time limits (normally six years) laid down for torts. Certainly in relation to restitution for unjust enrichment (rather than restitution for wrongs) the courts have shown themselves to be only too anxious to force claims into the six-year statutory bar despite there being no clear wording in the 1980 Act applying to claims founded on unjust enrichment.[67] No such distortion is needed in respect of restitution for a tort. It would seem therefore that, applying section 2 of the Limitation Act 1980 (UK), a six-year time limit should normally apply to common law restitution for a tort; and by other sections of the 1980 Act special limitation periods should apply to restitution for certain torts (for example, defamation) just as they do to compensatory damages.

Under section 2, the six years runs from the accrual of the cause of action. When does the cause of action accrue for restitution for a tort? As the cause of action is the wrong (and not the wrongful enrichment), the cause of action for restitution for a tort accrues, as for compensation, at the date of the tort. Indeed it is worth stressing that it is the law on limitation that most clearly shows that the cause of action in respect of restitution for wrongs is the wrong and not the wrongful enrichment. Say, for example, a defendant publishes a book that contains libellous comments about the claimant. The royalties on the book are not paid to the defendant until one year after publication. *If* restitution were available for the tort of libel, the limitation period applicable to a claim for restitution for libel running under section 4A of the 1980 Act (UK)[68] from accrual of the cause of action would, as for compensatory damages, start on the publication of the book and not on the date that the defendant first receives royalties. In other words, the cause of action is the tort, the libel, not the wrongful *enrichment*. If this were not so—and if the cause of action were to accrue only on the date of the wrongful enrichment—the peculiar position would apparently be that a new cause of action would accrue each time gains were received from the wrong.

What if the restitutionary remedy sought for the tort is equitable rather than common law? The most obvious example of this is an account of profits which is a standard remedy for intellectual property torts. Section 23 of the Limitation Act 1980 (UK) specifically provides that for 'actions for an account' the relevant time limit is that 'applicable to the claim which is the basis of the duty to account'. Although there appears to be no case on this question (which is surprising given how commonplace an account of profits is as a remedy for the intellectual property torts) it would seem to follow that, as the basis of the duty to account is the tort, the time limits applicable to torts apply to the account of profits so that the usual

[66] P Birks, *An Introduction to the Law of Restitution*, rev edn (Oxford, Clarendon Press, 1989) 348–49. Dicta of Denning J at first instance in *Beaman v ARTS Ltd* [1948] 2 All ER 89 (KBD) are sometimes cited in support of this.

[67] See, eg, *Kleinwort Benson Ltd v Sandwell Borough Council* [1994] 4 All ER 890 (QBD) 942–43 (Hobhouse J).

[68] See at p 315, point (iv).

period, as laid down in section 2, is six years from the date of the tort. As an equitable remedy, one would also need to consider the doctrine of laches. Applying the approach articulated above,[69] the best interpretation is that it is only where laches involves delay plus prejudice that laches could operate to bar the remedy within the statutory period of six years.

Finally, as regards the law on limitation for equitable damages, what has been said above on this[70] applies equally whether those damages are assessed on a restitutionary or a compensatory basis. It would seem, therefore, that the relevant limitation period is that applying had an injunction been sought.

8. CONCLUSION

The defence to a tort of limitation raises many recurring and fascinating issues. Some are extremely technical but (at least for a doctrinal lawyer) intriguing none the less. Some require detailed and careful statutory interpretation, while others are pure matters of common law (for example, the date of accrual of the cause of action). Still others are of a fundamental kind: do we need a defence of limitation and what does it say about defences generally that the burden of proof of limitation is on the claimant? This chapter has sought to 'bring alive' some of these issues which, at least in England and Wales, have sadly been largely ignored by the legal academic community.

[69] See at p 326.
[70] See at pp 326–27.

Index of Authors

Index

www.ingramcontent.com/pod-product-compliance
Ingram Content Group UK Ltd.
Pitfield, Milton Keynes, MK11 3LW, UK
UKHW020132290926
15471UKWH00003B/446

9 781509 914166